Despite the lively tradition of scholarship on Dutch painti
enteenth century, scholars continue to grapple with the pr
the strikingly realistic characteristics of art from this period can be reconciled with its possible meanings. With the advent of new methodologies, these debates have gained momentum in the past decade. *Looking at Seventeenth-Century Dutch Art*, which includes classic essays as well as contributions especially written for this volume, provides a timely survey of the principal interpretative methods and debates, from their origins in the 1960s to current manifestations, while suggesting potential avenues of inquiry for the future. The book offers fascinating insights into the meaning of Dutch art in its original cultural context as well as into the world of scholarship that it has inspired.

Looking at Seventeenth-Century Dutch Art

Looking at Seventeenth-Century Dutch Art

REALISM RECONSIDERED

Wayne Franits
Syracuse University

CAMBRIDGE
UNIVERSITY PRESS

PUBLISHED BY THE PRESS SYNDICATE OF THE UNIVERSITY OF CAMBRIDGE
The Pitt Building, Trumpington Street, Cambridge CB2 1RP, United Kingdom

CAMBRIDGE UNIVERISTY PRESS
The Edinburgh Building, Cambridge CB2 2RU, United Kingdom
40 West 20th Street, New York, NY 10011-4211, USA
10 Stamford Road, Oakleigh, Melbourne 3166, Australia

First published 1997

Printed in the United States of America

Typeset in Janson

Library of Congress Cataloging-in-Publication Data

Franits, Wayne E.
Looking at seventeenth-century Dutch art : realism reconsidered /
Wayne Franits.
p. cm.
Includes bibliographical references and index.
ISBN 0-521-49609-8 (hardcover).
1. Painting, Dutch. 2. Painting, Modern – 17th–18th centuries –
Netherlands. 3. Realism in art – Netherlands. I. Title.
ND646.F7 1997
759.9492'09'032 – dc20 96-36607
CIP

A catalogue record for this book is available from the British Library.

ISBN 0 521 49609 8 hardback

REALISM

We are not so badly off if we can
Admire Dutch painting. For that means
We shrug off what we have been told
For a hundred, two hundred years. Though we lost
Much of our previous confidence. Now we agree
That those trees outside the window, which probably exist,
Only pretend to greenness and treeness
And that the language loses when it tries to cope
With clusters of molecules. And yet this here:
A jar, a tin plate, a half-peeled lemon,
Walnuts, a loaf of bread – last, and so strongly
It is hard not to believe in their lastingness.
And thus abstract art is brought to shame,
Even if we do not deserve any other.
Therefore I enter those landscapes
Under a cloudy sky from which a ray
Shoots out, and in the middle of dark plains
A spot of brightness glows. Or the shore
With huts, boats, and, on yellowish ice,
Tiny figures skating. All this
Is here eternally, just because once it was.
Splendor (certainly incomprehensible)
Touches a cracked wall, a refuse heap,
The floor of an inn, jerkins of the rustics,
A broom, and two fish bleeding on a board.
Rejoice! Give thanks! I raised my voice
To join them in their choral singing,
Amid their ruffles, collets, and silk skirts,
One of them already, who vanished long ago.
And our song soared up like smoke from a censer.

–*Czeslaw Milosz*

(*Translated, from the Polish, by the author and Robert Hass.**)

Contents

Illustrations

Acknowledgments

LIKE all books, this one owes a considerable debt to a substantial number of colleagues whose generous contributions ultimately made its completion possible. First and foremost, I must express my gratitude to Beatrice Rehl of Cambridge University Press who invited me to edit a book of essays for the Press on Dutch seventeenth-century art. My initial feelings of gratitude were promptly doubled when she graciously granted me the latitude to determine its subject. Once the book's subject had been established, I was most fortunate to receive positive responses from all of the authors whose essays I requested to reprint here. I wish to thank them as well as the editors who granted permission to reproduce studies that had previously appeared in the following publications: *Art History; Art in History, History in Art; Studies in Seventeenth-Century Dutch Culture*, Santa Monica, The Getty Center for the History of Art and the Humanities, 1991; *Holländische Genremalerei im 17. Jahrhundert; Symposium Berlin 1984 (Jahrbuch Preussischer Kulturbesitz*, Sonderband 4), Berlin, 1987; and *Simiolus, Netherlands Quarterly for the History of Art.* Moreover, I am grateful to those colleagues who accepted my invitation to contribute new essays of potentially demanding scope.

As *Looking at Seventeenth-Century Dutch Art* slowly began to materialize, other individuals and institutions stepped in to offer timely and invaluable assistance. Perhaps this was most evident when I confronted the formidable problem of how to pay for translations of a very lengthy essay in Dutch and a shorter one in German. With regard to the former, the erstwhile Interim Chair of Syracuse University's Department of Fine Arts, Alan Berger, interceded on my behalf to help arrange financial assistance from the Department as well as from the Office of the Dean of the College of Arts and Sciences (Robert J. Jensen) and the Office of the Vice-President for Research and Computing (Benjamin J. Ware). I should add that a translation of the Dutch essay would not have even been possible if the outstanding translating team of Katie Kist and Jennifer Kilian (Kist-Kilian Communications) had not generously offered a discount for their services. An initial translation of the German essay was ably completed by one of our former graduate students, Monica Antje Hahn-Koenig. (The appendix to this essay was translated by Barbara C. Goldstein.) Much-needed corrections to the final version of the translation were unselfishly provided by my colleague at Syracuse University, Gerlinde Ulm Sanford.

The daunting task of tracking down those photographs that the contributors to the volume had been unable to provide was greatly facilitated by the assistance of Christopher Brown, Susan Foister, Friso Lammertse, Walter Liedtke, and Lawrence W. Nichols. Herbert H. Westphalen III also provided some timely assistance in this regard. Other problems – namely, those of an editorial nature – were enthusiastically tackled by another one of our former graduate students, Lynda Shield. Lastly, I must thank my colleagues Victoria Beck, Laurinda Dixon, Gary Radke, and Beatrice Rehl for their critical readings of earlier drafts of the introduction.

I would be remiss to close without mentioning the support of my wife, Linnéa, and my son, Aidan Charles (b. July 18, 1996), who, in sickness and in health, has worked miracles in putting my life and academic career in perspective.

Contributors

ANN JENSEN ADAMS *Associate Professor of the History of Art, The University of California, Santa Barbara CA, USA*

SVETLANA ALPERS *Emeritus Professor of the History of Art, The University of California, Berkeley CA, USA*

CELESTE BRUSATI *Associate Professor of the History of Art, The University of Michigan, Ann Arbor MI, USA*

EDDY DE JONGH *Emeritus Professor of Iconology, Utrecht University, Utrecht, The Netherlands*

J. A. EMMENS *Formerly Professor of Iconology, Utrecht University, Utrecht, The Netherlands*

WAYNE FRANITS *Associate Professor of Fine Arts, Syracuse University, Syracuse NY, USA*

IVAN GASKELL *Margaret S. Winthrop Curator of Paintings, Fogg Art Museum, Harvard University Art Museums, Cambridge MA, USA*

LAWRENCE O. GOEDDE *Professor of Art History, University of Virginia, Charlottesville VA, USA*

PETER HECHT *Professor of Art History, Utrecht University, Utrecht, The Netherlands*

ELIZABETH ALICE HONIG *Assistant Professor of the History of Art, The University of California, Berkeley CA, USA*

ALISON McNEIL KETTERING *Professor of Art History, Carleton College, Northfield MN, USA*

WALTER LIEDTKE *Curator of European Paintings, The Metropolitan Museum of Art, New York NY, USA*

KONRAD RENGER *Chief Curator, Bayerische Staatsgemäldesammlungen, Munich, Germany*

HERMAN ROODENBURG *Research Fellow in Cultural History, P. J. Meertens Instituut (Royal Netherlands Academy of Science), Amsterdam, The Netherlands*

ERIC J. SLUIJTER *Associate Professor of Art History, Leiden University, Leiden, The Netherlands*

Looking at Seventeenth-Century Dutch Art

Introduction*

LOOKING *at Seventeenth-Century Dutch Art: Reconsidering Realism* consists of fourteen essays by prominent scholars that explore, through various approaches and perspectives, the significance of seventeenth-century Dutch art for its original audiences. From the outset, Dutch paintings have enjoyed enormous popularity. When compared to the large-scale, epic pictures produced in other European countries during the seventeenth century, the subject matter of Dutch art might appear to the student to be modest.[1] Nevertheless, its depictions of, among other subjects, housewives at work; fields, canals, and wooded landscapes; sitters posed soberly yet resolutely in portraits; frolicking peasants; and still lifes depicting the bountiful rewards of commerce all were eagerly sought at the time by collectors and connoisseurs, both at home and abroad. Nor would the passion for these pictures decline even as the Dutch Republic itself did during the course of the eighteenth century. Indeed, the high esteem in which Dutch art has been held has continued unabated to this present day.[2] The history of the general aesthetic appreciation of Dutch painting is as long as it is illustrious. Yet, in the not too distant past, the long-heralded realistic appearance of Dutch art paradoxically impeded a more comprehensive understanding of its meanings for seventeenth-century viewers.

It is well known, for example, that the verisimilitude of Dutch paintings led many nineteenth-century writers to believe that these works objectively represented the everyday world, that they provided unmediated, tangible access to contemporary life. This unfounded, pragmatic view flourished until well into the twentieth century. As Konrad Renger's essay demonstrates, it was only around the period of World War II that scholars slowly began to reassess time-honored perceptions of Dutch paintings. In their seemingly faithful rendition of the surrounding world, and in their painstaking attention to detail, Dutch paintings can rightly be called realistic. Nevertheless, their realism is merely plausible because they do not simply transcribe daily life. Renger's essay sheds critical light on the work of several earlier scholars who perceived that the verisimilitude of Dutch paintings, their presentation of a plausible reality that had for so long been esteemed, simultaneously served as a conduit for a multitude of ideas and associations.

These first, hesitant steps toward the interpretation of Dutch art – namely, the analysis of its potential meanings – proved decisive. A younger generation whose work would exert a profound impact soon followed. Many members of this group labored at the University of Utrecht, whose Institute of Art History would gain international recognition as a center for interpretive studies of Dutch painting. Among the most prominent was Jan Emmens, a gifted scholar (and poet) whose career ended tragically with his untimely death in 1971.

* I wish to thank Victoria Beck, Laurinda Dixon, Gary Radke, and Beatrice Rehl for their assistance in preparing this introduction.

An English version of one of Emmens's essays is reprinted in this volume. In it, Emmens provides a fascinating interpretation of an eighteenth-century copy of a now-lost triptych by Gerard Dou. Emmens argues that despite its seemingly realistic, "earth-bound" appearance, this triptych actually expresses abstruse intellectual notions about artistic training.[3]

Although Emmens and others made solid contributions to the interpretation of Dutch art, it is Eddy de Jongh who must be credited with securing its legitimacy as a viable and important endeavor within the field. His numerous essays illuminate the meanings of scores of Dutch paintings, and equally importantly, he was the first to address more substantial issues pertaining to methods of interpretation.[4] In this sense, De Jongh's work is deeply indebted to that of the eminent art historian Erwin Panofsky (d. 1968), specifically the latter's iconological method.[5] Panofsky argued that three interrelated strata of meaning or subject matter – the two terms are construed as equivalent – are present within a work of art: (1) primary or natural subject matter, consisting of motifs – that is, "pure forms" – apprehended as carriers of meaning (pre-iconographical description); (2) secondary or conventional subject matter – that is, combinations of motifs that can be identified as representing particular stories or concepts (iconography); and (3) intrinsic content, referring to the underlying contexts that inform the depiction of these particular stories and concepts (iconology proper, or as Panofsky himself defined it, "iconographical interpretation in a deeper sense").[6]

Panofsky's iconological method was constructed with reference to Italian Renaissance art. When confronted with the problem of detecting meaning in the boldly realistic, interpretively recalcitrant art of Northern Europe – as Panofsky was in several early studies and in his monumental *Early Netherlandish Painting* (1953) – he attached certain theoretical addenda to his method – hence the development of his well-known hypothesis of disguised symbolism.[7] For example, in his seminal study of 1934 on Jan van Eyck's celebrated *Arnolfini Portrait* (London, The National Gallery), Panofsky explained the complicated symbolic program of the painting, concluding that within the artist's visually striking pictures "medieval symbolism and modern realism perfectly reconciled that the former has become inherent in the latter. The symbolical significance is neither abolished nor does it contradict the naturalistic tendencies; it is so completely absorbed by reality, that reality itself gives rise to a flow of preternatural associations, the direction of which is secretly determined by the vital forces of medieval iconography."[8]

Inspired by Panofsky's hypothesis, De Jongh applied the principle of "disguised symbolism" (with some necessary modifications) to seventeenth-century Dutch art.[9] De Jongh maintains that Dutch paintings were intended to instruct and delight viewers: Their sheer visual beauty engages the beholder who is consequently stimulated to uncover their concealed meanings, ones principally didactic or moral in nature. He therefore contends that the frequently moralizing meanings of Dutch pictures are conveyed by symbolism that is not immediately apparent but lies hidden beneath their seemingly realistic surfaces.[10]

De Jongh adduces an impressive variety of seventeenth-century sources to support this hypothesis. For example, the authors of some of the most popular emblem books of the period repeatedly expounded upon the concept of concealed meanings.[11] Their explanations of how emblems communicate meaning become applicable to paintings on the basis of Horace's celebrated doctrine *ut pictura poesis* (as is painting, so is poetry), which established the close relationship between art and literature, or the "sister arts" as they were known in the seventeenth century.[12] Moreover, the contemporary art theorists Karel van Mander and Samuel van Hoogstraeten also discuss the hidden symbolism of paintings.[13] De Jongh further argues that the veiled symbols intrinsic to Dutch seventeenth-century paintings can be deciphered with the assistance of sources such as prints with inscriptions, popular literature, and emblems.[14]

De Jongh's research has been enormously influential, so much so that it was difficult to decide which one of his many publications to reprint for this volume.[15] In the end, his essay "Realism and

Seeming Realism in Seventeenth-Century Dutch Painting" (first published in Dutch in 1971 in the catalogue of the exhibition *Rembrandt en zijn tijd;* Rembrandt and His Time) clearly proved the most suitable candidate. Of all of De Jongh's manifold publications, this one provides the most exhaustive exposition of his methodology; indeed, it is the only one of his essays in which he attempts to apply his iconologically based interpretive method to nearly all of the diverse genres in which seventeenth-century Dutch artists worked: portraiture, still life, landscape, history painting, and genre painting. It is nearly impossible today to appreciate the original impact of this essay, accustomed as we have become to countless studies along similar lines. Perhaps it pays testimony to the influence of "Realism and Seeming Realism" that so many studies exist today that ultimately owe their inspiration to questions, issues, and insights advanced by De Jongh back in 1971 and even earlier.[16]

Despite the widely acknowledged contributions that De Jongh has made to the study of meaning in Dutch seventeenth-century painting, other art historians have begun, in recent years, to examine his iconological approach with a more critical eye. Interestingly enough, Panofsky's method, which strongly influenced De Jongh's, has simultaneously undergone extensive reassessment.[17] Many of these scholars find it difficult to reconcile the realistic look of Dutch art with its purported symbolic program – once again, its presentation of a plausible reality has become the focus of intense debate. First and foremost is the problem of how to detect veiled symbols in numerous, meticulously wrought Dutch paintings that so convincingly and seductively present a coherent impression of reality. In other words, if this symbolism was so well concealed, how could seventeenth-century viewers – let alone modern-day ones – recognize it?[18] In theory, and especially in practice, the presumed presence of hidden symbols is difficult to reconcile with the exquisitely crafted surfaces of Dutch paintings.

Still other aspects of the iconological method are problematic, thereby compromising its overall effectiveness and versatility. For example, the method is most suitable for analyzing history paintings and genre paintings since these possess a narrative component. This begs the question of how landscape and still-life painting, vast numbers of which were produced in the Dutch Republic, fit into the scheme. Panofsky himself was conscious of this potential problem. He argued that landscape, still-life, and genre painting – the latter now generally considered conducive to iconological interpretation – necessitate a direct transition between the first stratum of meaning, primary subject matter or motifs, and the last one, intrinsic content. The absence of the second stratum, secondary or conventional subject matter, in these works of art compelled Panofsky to alter his method, even though its roots in Italian art had already led him to categorize images other than history paintings as "exceptional phenomena, which mark the later, oversophisticated phases of a long development."[19]

In this respect, historians of Dutch art are continually confronted with the problem of utilizing a method developed primarily in relation to fifteenth- and sixteenth-century Italian history paintings for the study of Dutch seventeenth-century landscape and still-life paintings. Judging from the current state of scholarship on these genres, the results have been decidedly mixed.[20] One cannot help but wonder how this method can be so enthusiastically endorsed if its suitability for Dutch art is limited, as vast numbers of pictures resist its interpretive aims.

Although these shortcomings alone would be sufficient to cause us to question the suitability of the iconological method for interpreting Dutch paintings, another problem must still be considered, namely, its propensity to divorce form or style from content.[21] The iconological effort to interpret a work of art typically avoids analysis of the style in which it was produced in favor of investigating individual motifs whose aggregate reveals its meaning. In other words, to employ those well-known polemical descriptors, the question of "what" is represented is deemed far more important than that of "how the what" is represented. Within this approach, then, style rarely, if ever, seems to be pertinent. This is another reason why landscapes and still lifes seem so resistant to iconological inquiries and, moreover, why practitioners of this method are often forced to conclude awkwardly that a picture must be meaningless if it does not contain motifs conducive to explication.[22]

It is precisely these inherent shortcomings that have led to a growing dissatisfaction with the iconological method. Therefore, it should come as no surprise that the problem of form or style, or, phrased more generally, the realistic appearance of Dutch paintings, versus content, has become the subject of intense debate in recent years. Fundamental in this regard is Svetlana Alpers's stimulating and controversial book, *The Art of Describing* (1983), which almost single-handedly initiated the debate.[23] In her book and in her contribution to this volume, Alpers takes issue with the notion of seeming realism, with the theory that meaning in Dutch art lies hidden beneath the surface. Such a view is hopelessly entangled within interpretive strategies developed in relation to Italian – as opposed to Dutch – art. Employing Roland Barthes's concept of the "reality effect,"[24] Alpers calls attention to what she terms the "pictorial mode of Dutch art," its singular capacity to offer a compelling "perceptual model of knowledge of the world," which ties it to widespread "empirical interests in this age of observation." In essence, Dutch seventeenth-century paintings do not somehow try to capture reality itself but rather the manner in which reality is perceived, and in doing so, they afford intriguing parallels with scientific developments of this period. As Renger observes in the newly written postscript to his aforementioned essay, Alpers's book "struck the scene like a lightning bolt." With hindsight, among the many accomplishments of *The Art of Describing* was Alpers's success in redirecting our attention to the long-neglected visual appearance of Dutch painting and how this appearance itself (without recourse to concealed symbols) attests to concomitant cultural phenomena.

Eric Jan Sluijter has emerged as another outspoken critic of the iconological status quo. In a major article first published in Dutch in 1988 and reprinted in this volume, Sluijter decried the scholarly preoccupation with hidden meanings, sophisticated literary allusions, and didacticism in Dutch art.[25] Although Sluijter does not deny that such phenomena are occasionally present in paintings, his careful analysis of a number of theoretical works written between 1620 and 1670 compel him to conclude that in general, contemporaries did not consider signification pivotal to art. Dutch art theorists were rarely interested in it; to the contrary, they were far more frequently enthusiastic about the visual appeal and delight of paintings. In fact, their enthusiasm for the remarkable ability of Dutch art to imitate nature with great precision was shared by many contemporary collectors and connoisseurs.[26]

Peter Hecht also questioned the concepts of disguised symbolism and moralizing meanings in his important exhibition catalogue *De Hollandse fijnschilders* (The Dutch Fine Painters; a group of genre painters active during the second half of the seventeenth century).[27] This catalogue generated further controversy because Hecht strongly downplayed the interpretive possibilities of the paintings, arguing that contemporary viewers and patrons of art were likely more attentive to the virtuosic simulation of reality in paintings than to their capacity to elicit meanings. Premises such as these were hotly debated at a symposium organized by the Rijksmuseum in Amsterdam in December 1989 and in several articles and reviews about the catalogue and Dutch genre painting in general that appeared shortly thereafter.[28] Hecht's eloquent (and witty) response to his critics, first published in 1992, is reprinted here.[29]

The reaction to the iconological approach, which has increased in intensity in recent years, has not been purely one of criticism. For example, the work of Sluijter and Hecht does more than simply critique iconology; in effect, these scholars suggest some possible avenues of future inquiry thereby providing important modifications to the iconological approach. The same can be said for Ivan Gaskell's essay, "Tobacco, Social Deviance and Dutch Art," first published in 1987 and reprinted in this volume. In it, Gaskell persuasively argued that greater attention must be paid to the historical context in which images were initially created and had their meaning. His specific focus is the dialogue between social conventions and literary ones so often invoked by iconologists. In Gaskell's view, social conventions, retrievable by means of historical research, contribute to the formation of specific subjects in Dutch art, among them, representations of smokers and smoking. Early in the seventeenth century, tobacco was associated with socially deviant behavior, which likely explains the existence of many pictures that show members of the lower echelons of society smoking. Therefore, the plausible realities presented in Dutch paintings were involved in complicated interactions with the social and historical realities of the society that produced them. In the end, Gaskell's readings of the paintings display much greater subtleties than those of more customary interpretations that rely heavily upon developing specific, one-to-one correspondences between motifs in art and literature.

Readers of this book will also find a reprint of a fascinating essay by Alison McNeil Kettering on Gerard ter Borch's depictions of women. Kettering likewise expands upon the iconological approach by skillfully incorporating the postmodern insights of feminist criticism, film theory, and theories of reader/viewer reception and response. Concerns for style are accentuated in Ter Borch's pictures of women, a long-heralded hallmark being his splendid delineation of satin garments. In Ter Borch's adroit hands, shimmering satin becomes an agent of empathic projection for the viewer, allowing him or her to weave narratives of vicarious participation from the luminous imagery depicted on the canvas. Confronted with the startling and beautiful realism of these paintings, Kettering modifies a number of iconological premises, among them, the principle that art simply "reflects" the culture in which it is produced. In her view, art plays an active role in constructing ideologies – in the case of Ter Borch, those pertaining to acceptable social and sexual behavior among females. Moreover, whereas traditional iconology tends to establish fixed, almost immutable meanings for paintings exclusively from the perspective of the artist, Kettering shifts attention to the audience. She argues that contemporary responses to paintings were multivalent, contingent on any number of external factors including the gender, occupation, sensitivities, and values of particular viewers.

Looking at Seventeenth-Century Dutch Art: Reconsidering Realism also contains six new contributions (in addition to the essay by Alpers) that consider matters of realism and meaning in Dutch art from a variety of methodological perspectives. Walter Liedtke, for example, raises some fundamental issues concerning the importance of style in any interpretive endeavor. Liedtke is surely correct to consider style central to the evaluation of meaning in Dutch art since the study of the latter hinges in an essential way upon the former. For Liedtke, the consideration of style must not be discounted because of its connection to traditional connoisseurship, concerned with the attribution of paintings to specific artists: "Stylistic and iconographic schemes are complex parts of a larger picture; to ignore them is like studying a language without a basic comprehension of its grammar and vocabulary."

The conventional nature of style and subject matter in Dutch art is the subject of Lawrence O. Goedde's contribution, which concentrates on landscape painting. Despite the exceedingly large quantities of landscapes produced by seventeenth-century Dutch painters, only a limited number of subjects were depicted, ones that rely heavily upon the repetition of specific stylistic and thematic formulations. Therefore, the much-vaunted reality represented in landscapes is, like all Dutch paintings, primarily conventional. As Goedde perceptively observes, the seemingly straightforward, unmediated, and accurate rendering of places in landscape is pure fiction: "These pictures are constructs of the imagination shaped by artistic traditions and depending upon the manipulation of patterns of style and subject matter." Goedde ascribes great importance to conventions because they enable the researcher to investigate meaning in a manner that conveniently sidesteps the shortcomings of the iconological approach. Conventions of subject and style are themselves replete with significance. The sheer selectivity of landscape imagery, or more precisely, the conventions by which it is governed, bespeaks an intrinsic level of significance within the individual themes themselves – for not only artistic concerns, but more importantly, popular attitudes and ideas dictate the existence and production of conventional imagery.[30] Therefore, conventions were always socially and culturally determined; since artists worked for an implied audience, their paintings encode the expectations of that audience.[31] Thus, seventeenth-century viewers did not necessarily need access to specific texts in order to extract hidden meanings from landscapes, for the very representation itself was saturated with meaning.

Celeste Brusati makes comparable observations in her insightful essay on Dutch still-life painting in which she questions traditional readings. Once again, the realistic look of these paintings explains the widespread tendency to assess them purely in terms of the artist's ability to imitate accurately the objects set before him or her. In order to explain aspects of still life that do not square with this premise – namely, physically impossible combinations or arrangements of things – scholars often create artificial dichotomies between that which is said to be symbolic and that which is said to be realistic. To the contrary, Brusati maintains that meaning in still life is generated pictorially through the very act of representation, an act that reconstitutes the material world on canvas or panel for the beholder. Therefore, the realistic appearance of still lives is ultimately fictitious and consequently possesses the intrinsic capacity to signify, like landscape or genre paintings, in multivalent ways "to enhance the eye's reach and to stimulate visual modes of comprehension and reflection."

Nowhere are the fictions of realism engendered by Dutch art more deceptive than in portraiture. The confrontation with the bodies and particularly the physiognomies of the long-deceased exert such a powerful effect that viewers often temporarily suspend consciousness of pictorial devices and historical distance, imagining themselves in the presence of actual persons whose characters seem open to scrutiny. Ann Jensen Adams begins her essay on seventeenth-century Dutch portraiture by explaining how the ostensibly realistic qualities of portraits have often led to fundamentally ahistorical conclusions about the sitters' personalities. Moreover, these very same qualities – among them, the supposed ability of an artist to "express character" – have led to inadequate standards for the study of Dutch portraits.

Despite the existence of many illuminating iconological readings of portraits, Adams considers this method inadequate. Iconologists typically limit their investigations to motifs in portraits that potentially bear significance by passively reflecting external cultural values and truths. What remains unexplored are aspects of portraits that resist such analyses as well as the critical question of how these works of art actively participate in constructing cultural values and truths. For Adams, the three-quarter length portrait serves as a prime example of how Dutch seventeenth-century portraiture is embedded in larger cultural systems. Historians of Dutch art have customarily overlooked and at times even disparaged these works because the sitters' general absence of movement supposedly lacks meaning while simultaneously evidencing insufficient talent on the part of their creators. In contrast, Adams argues that the impassive face and body were richly encoded and can be associated with the neo-Stoic ideal of tranquillity, a highly desirable behavioral trait among the elite. Her contribution goes on to explore the active role that such portraits played in creating social cohesion for certain elite groups within a heterogeneous yet increasingly hierarchial society.

Notions of elite demeanor in seventeenth-century Dutch art and culture, particularly in relation to class and social standing, are central to Herman Roodenburg's essay. Drawing from such varied source materials as the diary of Constantijn Huygens and theoretical books on painting, Roodenburg's essay examines Dutch art from an historical-anthropological perspective. Historical anthropology studies the significance of rituals, ceremonies, and behaviors in past cultures.[32] By adopting the insights and approaches of this emerging field, Roodenburg investigates the importance of pose or stance in art as a communicator of meaning. Specifically, he demonstrates how the ideal of correct posture, associated as it was with the elite, informs Dutch paintings and prints in a manner that was directly accessible for contemporary viewers. Like Adams, Roodenburg believes that the seemingly banal aspects of art – aspects that are too often dismissed under the rubric of meaningless form – merit interpretation as they are potentially rich in cultural significance.

Adams and Roodenburg illuminate in their essays the signifying functions of posture in Dutch art, thereby expanding the parameters of what constitute valid sites of scholarly investigation. Elizabeth Alice Honig does much the same for the depiction of domestic interiors in her complex and absorbing contribution. In her view, paintings of domesticity pay persuasive testimony to the ways in which interiors were gendered in Dutch art – by both artists and beholders – in a society still actively engaged in demarcating male versus female roles in relation to private versus public spaces.[33] In this respect, the paintings do not simply "depict" domestic life as it was lived in the seventeenth century, nor do they necessarily admonish women to behave in socially and morally acceptable ways. Rather, Honig maintains that they provide "imagined solutions to problems of lived existence." In these pictures then, the concept of domestic virtue is positioned within the behavior of the female protagonists as well as in the very nature of the space that they inhabit. Honig's essay, along with those of Adams, Alpers, Brusati, Kettering, and Roodenburg, transcends more traditional modes of inquiry in order to address how the plausible realities of Dutch art actively produced – versus passively reflected – cultural mores and values.

Looking at Seventeenth-Century Dutch Art: Reconsidering Realism provides the student of Dutch seventeenth-century painting with thought-provoking examples of scholarly efforts to confront the enduring problem of reconciling the realistic aspects of this art with the manifold meanings that it must have elicited for contemporary audiences. In recent years, scholars have gradually shifted the focus of their investigations and expanded the methods by which to implement them and have consequently reached conclusions about realism and meaning that do not always concur with those of their esteemed predecessors. If anything, these changing, often contradictory perceptions, as well as the spirited debate that they inspire, bear witness to the continued vitality of the field and, ultimately, to the beauty and mystery of Dutch painting.

On the History of Research Concerning the Interpretation of Dutch Painting*

Konrad Renger

It is only in recent years that we have become aware that deeper meaning lies beneath the everyday world made visible in Dutch genre painting, and that the domestic scenes, the conversation pieces, the merry companies, and kitchen interiors are often only disguises for moral lessons. But this knowledge is actually offered for the first time to the German public with this exhibition in Brunswick. In 1976 the Rijksmuseum in Amsterdam had already dedicated an exhibition to this theme under the title *Tot lering en vermaak* (To Instruct and Delight).[1] The Utrecht professor Eddy de Jongh was an active participant in its conception and scholarly preparation. He also wrote the introduction for the Dutch exhibition catalogue, which appears at the beginning of this catalogue in German translation.The Amsterdam catalogue explains the images that were on view with the help of different sources, for example, contemporary emblem literature and prints. By 1967 De Jongh had already published a book, in connection with a Dutch radio program, in which the findings of research into the meanings of pictures were disclosed for the first time to a wider public.[2] Although interpretation was not the focus of the exhibition *Rembrandt and His Time* organized in Brussels (Palace of Fine Arts) in 1971, it was addressed by De Jongh in a catalogue essay.[3]

The groundwork for today's increasingly important branch of art history, which deals with the content of pictures (iconography) and their meaning (iconology), was laid almost ninety years ago when Aby Warburg turned to an approach to art other than the customary aesthetic or stylistic one. He received a doctorate in 1892 in Strassburg with a thesis on Botticelli's *Birth of Venus* and *Primavera*,[4] in which he was able – with the aid of contemporary literature – to explain these works, beyond the recognizable mythological elements, as evidence of certain notions about antiquity. For Warburg and the scholarly community that he had formed in the Hamburg Library, the afterlife of antiquity in literature and the visual arts was of central interest. The chief aim of the Warburg circle, however, was not directed toward Dutch art but rather toward Italian or at best early Netherlandish art.

The best-known representative of this group, Erwin Panofsky (d. 1968), provided an important contribution to seventeenth-century Dutch art with his comprehensive essay on Rembrandt's *Danae* in the Hermitage in St. Petersburg.[5] Panofsky completely supported his interpretation of the painting with the image tradition or "type history of the Danae myth," as he called it, in which he drew more upon antique than contemporary literature. Yet Panofsky's essay was not the first contribution to the interpretation of Dutch painting. The previous gen-

* Editor's note: Konrad Renger's essay originally appeared under the title "Zur Forschungsgeschichte der Bilddeutung in der holländischen Malerei," in Exhib. cat. Brunswick, *Die Sprache der Bilder; Realität und Bedeutung in der niederländischen Malerei des 17. Jahrhunderts*, pp. 34 – 8, Herzog Anton Ulrich-Museum, 1978. It was translated by Monica Anke Hahn-Koenig and Wayne Franits. Several additional endnotes were added by Wayne Franits. The postscript was translated by Barbara C. Goldstein.

eration of F. Schmidt-Degener and Carl Neumann had already made a start by referring to the influence of contemporary literature on Rembrandt's work.[6] These general references were defined more precisely with regard to a group of Rembrandt paintings in 1920 by Hans Kauffmann, who was of Panofsky's generation. In his essay, "Rembrandt und die Humanisten vom Muiderkring" (Rembrandt and the Humanists of the Muiderkring – the literary circle of Muider castle),[7] he determined that Rembrandt had incorporated very specific poems of that Amsterdam circle of scholars and poets to which Jacob Cats (who is cited often in this exhibition catalogue) belonged. With this contribution the Warburg method of image interpretation from contemporary sources was first employed consistently for Dutch art.

The aforementioned investigations, however, concerned themselves only with history paintings, that is, representations from the biblical, mythological, or literary realms. Dutch genre painting continued to be considered superficially as a transcription of everyday life without deeper meaning. Hans Kauffmann supplied the decisive push into the exploration of this realm in 1930 with his review of Wilhelm Valentiner's edition of the works of genre painter Pieter de Hooch.[8] Here, he contradicted for the first time the general opinion that "the people and their existence [are] taken from reality . . . [and] that Dutch genre painting represents – on the whole – a complete portrait of the land and its people" (p. 802). Even if this way of considering Dutch painting held true for many cases, the question, according to Kauffmann, still remained one of where the boundaries lay for its stock of motifs. He named the traditional representation of the "Five Senses" as one of the most important sources to which the subjects of the seventeenth century are oriented, that is, to the allegorical engravings and paintings of the sixteenth century.[9]

The paintings of the seventeenth century show "the fall from the ideal world into the realm of experience and life. . . . The once ideal beings were individualized, made common . . . the deallegorization or the veiling of allegory in paintings of social gatherings began" (p. 803). Kauffmann would not, of course, like to see a representation of the Five Senses in each of these pictures, not "every picture is to receive its meaning from these requisites . . . in many cases it also remains at best doubtful whether the master placed these references in the foreground consciously" (pp. 804 ff.). Kauffmann first developed these fundamental ideas for Pieter de Hooch and then extended them in 1943 to all Dutch painting, to Ter Borch and Steen and also to Rembrandt.[10]

In the meantime, with a similar method but another theme, Hermann Rudolph had determined in 1938 that the paintings of gold- and pearl-weighers by De Hooch and Vermeer were not merely representations of everyday life but that the *vanitas* (vanity) tradition survived in them. Thus these pictures, as do still lifes, contain references to the transitory nature of earthly goods.[11] From this tradition Rudolph interpreted not only genre painting – that is, scenes of domestic and social life – but also still lifes as allegories of transitoriness. In his fundamental studies of 1947 and 1955, Ingvar Bergström expanded upon Rudolph's essay about Netherlandish still life by establishing various meanings.[12] In 1970 the Museum "de Lakenhal" in Leiden mounted an exhibition on one aspect of this pictorial type: the *vanitas* still life.[13]

For another genre of painting, landscape, it was not until quite recently that W. Wiegand established content in the work of Jacob van Ruisdael that went beyond the immediately visible.[14] This work as well as the iconological interpretation of Ruisdael's *Windmill at Wijk bij Duurstede* (Fig. 81) (Amsterdam, Rijksmuseum), published by Hans Kauffmann in 1977,[15] are the first attempts in this direction.

But let us return to genre painting after this brief discussion and jump ahead in time. In the same year as Rudolph's 1938 work, a dissertation appeared by Sturla Gudlaugsson, which had originated under the auspices of Wilhelm Pinder at the Friedrich-Wilhelms-Universität in Berlin. This work called attention to a further significant aspect: the theater.[16] Gudlaugsson observed its influence alongside poetry and prose in the work of most of the great painters of the seventeenth century. He presented these ideas in his important book of 1945, *De komedianten bij Jan Steen en zijn tijdgenooten* (The

Comedians in the Work of Jan Steen and His Contemporaries),[17] in which he determined that the wittily contrived figures of Jan Steen were fixed types in the repertory of the theater.

With these essays the territory from which Dutch painting is interpreted has largely been made accessible. *Emblemata*, toward which attention today has been intensified (perhaps a little one-sidedly), were also drawn into iconology, although they were not generally the object of the research. First of all, however, a brief explanation of the "emblem" is in order. The word is from the Greek and originally denoted the inlay of mosaics and craft work. Since the sixteenth century, this term has been applied to the associations of literary formulations with visual motifs. Under a title (*motto* or *lemma*) appears a picture (*pictura* or *icon*), to which a longer text (*epigramm*, *explicatio*, or commentary) is attached. None of the three parts is comprehensible by itself; only together do they yield a meaning.

The sources for emblems are, on the one hand, late medieval heraldic mottos; sovereigns would have a symbol next to their coats of arms with an explanatory inscription (a well-known late example is the motto of Charles V: two pillars symbolizing the ends of the earth, with the text *plus ultra*, "further onward"). On the other hand, the sources go back to research into hieroglyphics conducted during the Italian Renaissance. The Florentine humanists of the late fifteenth century did not know that the Egyptian script was composed of characters. Rather, they read the symbols as a picture puzzle, a rebus (from which our modern newspaper pastime also derives). The fantastic "translations" and attempts at interpretation exercised their influence, for instance, on so famous and widespread undertakings as the wood carvings of Kaiser Maximillian's victory carriage and triumphal arch, on which Dürer, among others, worked.

The *Emblematum liber* (Emblem Book) of the Milanese humanist Andrea Alciati (1492–1550), which appeared first in Augsburg in 1531, was also based on these humanistic and philological endeavors. Over the next hundred years, this very first emblem book was expanded, reprinted, and commented upon. Successive emblem books in the manner of Alciati's were written in every European country, first mostly in Latin, soon after in all European languages. In the Netherlands the emblemata followed a unique development. Here the visual language of the icon, otherwise considerably condensed, was expanded into detailed scenes that almost became genre pictures in and unto themselves: for example, a book of 1618 by Jacob Cats and, above all, one of 1624 by Johan de Brune, up to and including Adriaan Spinniker's *Leerzaame zinnebeelden* (Instructive Emblems of Virtue), which appeared in 1714.[18]

The systematic investigation of *emblemata* began in the second half of the nineteenth century. In the 1870s Henry Green published several studies of Alciato.[19] The history and bibliography of Netherlandish emblemata, published by A. G. C. de Vries in 1899,[20] followed Green's fundamental essays. In 1939 the first edition of Mario Praz's *Studies in Seventeenth-Century Imagery* appeared, which was followed by a comprehensive bibliography in 1947.[21] These essays originate less from an art-historical standpoint than from one of literary history. The most important work of more recent times in this regard is Albrecht Schöne's *Emblematik und Drama im Zeitalter des Barocks* (Emblematics and Drama in the Age of the Baroque) of 1964, in which the manifold interrelationship between literature and *emblemata* is demonstrated.[22]

The first investigations of this subject to which art historians contributed were the fundamental works on hieroglyphics by Karl Gielow (1915) and Ludwig Volkmann (1923), in which emblems themselves, however, were barely mentioned.[23] Only in 1942, in the Albrecht-Ludwigs-Universität (Freiburg im Breisgau) dissertation of E. F. von Monroy, *Embleme und Emblembücher in den Niederländen 1560–1630* (Emblems and Emblem Books in the Netherlands 1560–1630), did emblems become the central topic.[24] Monroy follows chiefly the development of the emblems' visual form of representation and does not examine quite so closely the possibility of drawing upon them to interpret contemporary paintings.

After the occasional references to *emblemata* in the aforementioned early works, the immediate application of emblems to image interpretation came oddly enough not in writings about Dutch painting but rather in Rubens research, as in the studies by Hans Gerhard Evers and Hans Kauffmann.[25] Kauffmann's essay on the interpretation of marriage pictures was extended in 1961 by De Jongh and P. J. Vinken to a similar subject by Frans Hals, thereby employing emblems for the first time in the interpretation of a Dutch picture.[26] Two years later, Seymour Slive developed an iconological interpretation of another important Hals work, the *Malle Babbe* (Berlin, Gemäldegalerie), admittedly not based on *emblemata* but rather on other contemporary sources.[27] In 1967 De Jongh explained a large number of genre paintings for the most part on the basis of *emblemata* in his aforementioned *Zinne- en minnebeelden in de schilderkunst van de zeventiende eeuw* (Emblems of Virtue and Love in Seventeenth-Century Painting). The comparisons are extraordinarily convincing; the illustrations almost speak for themselves.

Not coincidentally, these investigations came out of the Utrecht Art Historical Institute, where William Heckscher worked for some years, laying important groundwork for iconological research with the library and indices. Heckscher had written the article "Emblem" in 1959 in the *Reallexikon der deutschen Kunstgeschichte* (Encyclopedia of German Art History), which would later appear in an expanded edition by Karl-August Wirth.[28] With this extensive contribution, emblem literature finally became accessible to more general scholarship outside the narrow realm of specialized research. *Emblemata*, the handbook of the art of the emblem by Arthur Henkel and Albrecht Schöne, is the only other work of comparable impact.[29] Here the most important emblem books are included, reproduced, and translated and made completely accessible through indices.

The comprehensiveness with which the emblemata have been explored bespeaks the fondness that exists for them in modern research, which can somewhat overestimate their influence on the visual arts. The frequent lack of verification of their research value for the image in question is methodologically dubious. Moreover, there is often the danger that instead of interpreting a picture, a new rebus may result from too many individually quoted emblems.

In examining emblems today, the pictorial traditions in which older investigations were so interested are too often ignored. Ingvar Bergström provided an important contribution to meaning through pictorial tradition with his essay of 1966 about Rembrandt's *Self-portrait with Saskia* (Dresden, Gemäldegalerie), in which he was able to infer moralizing allusions to the prodigal son from the pictorial tradition of the sixteenth century.[30] In a lecture at the Herzog Anton Ulrich-Museum in Brunswick in 1971, Jan Emmens pointed out the moral-religious meaning of market and kitchen images of the sixteenth century, which as forerunners of seventeenth-century still lifes are not without consequence.[31] Pictorial traditions were also traced via the development of the work of individual artists. Particularly notable are the monograph on Willem Buytewech by Egbert Haverkamp-Begemann (1959), the book on Ter Borch by Sturla Gudlaugsson (1960), and Seymour Slive's work on Frans Hals (1970–74).[32] They interpret their respective subjects through various sources: history, literature, *emblemata*, and pictorial precedents.

The artists also process their prototypes in completely distinct ways. In the art of Jan Steen, it is immediately evident that he intended the same moralizing statement as the model he used – an emblem or an etching of the sixteenth century. In contrast, an artist such as Ter Borch concealed the suggestion much more in the representation of everyday activities. One asks oneself whether he intended to reproach vanity and transitoriness, in his *Girl Before a Mirror* (Amsterdam, Rijksmuseum), with the same moralistic severity as his precursors, on whom he doubtlessly depends. It was just this elegant reservation, this ambivalence between deeper meaning and more superficial depictions of the everyday, that Gudlaugsson established as a characteristic of Ter Borch's work. Just by considering these artists with contrasting methods of painting, unsubtle Steen and discreet Ter Borch, it becomes evident not only that care must be taken in the selection of sources – the literature of the rhetoricians did not have nearly as much meaning for Ter Borch as it did for Steen – but also that one must differentiate between the interpretations themselves. The moralizing allusions of the images, their "moralizing sermons," are meant with varying degrees of severity; besides artistic individuality, differences arise as well from generation or local traditions.

Even in the work of a single artist, there are differences in the intent and clarity of the message. For example, in his early work, Vermeer executed his unsubtle genre paintings completely in the manner of his generational contemporaries in Delft; his later works are almost anachronistic allegories, furnished with uncommon symbols and attributes. Robert Keyszelitz described such differences in his 1956 Munich dissertation *Der "clavis interpretandi" in der holländischen Malerei des 17. Jahrhunderts* (The "*clavis interpretandi*" – keys to interpretation – in Dutch Painting of the Seventeenth Century). Here he attempted to bring these differences into a theoretical system, whose application to research has remained controversial.

As concealed meanings are increasingly discovered, the duality between painted reality and the hidden contents of the picture are now being discussed, which De Jongh addresses in his introduction to this catalogue. Does the painter intend a representation of the everyday world around him or a primarily allegorical, moralizing message? Older and above all, German – research, which still did not suspect deeper meanings in these pictures, had been preoccupied primarily with the definition of the term "genre."[33] It was stipulated that the term "genre" implied that no deeper ideas may be hidden in the images of the everyday. This title means nothing more than "type" or "manner" and was not applied to representations of everyday life in the seventeenth century. Since the era of the eminent historian Jacob Burckhardt (the mid to late nineteenth century), it was believed that Denis Diderot used the term for the first time in reference to these images. Wolfgang Stechow determined, however, that the term appears for the first time not in Diderot's *Essais sur la Peinture* (Essays on Painting), published in 1795, but rather in 1791, in the *Considérations* (Considerations) by Quatremèrre de Quincy.[34]

Yet in his "Netherlandish Genre Painting (1874)," Jacob Burckhardt already questioned the usefulness of attempting to define the term "genre" and applied it also to history paintings and portraits (a sacrilege, really).[35] Meanwhile, in the wake of the writings of Kauffmann and Rudolph, who ascertained deeper meanings in the ostensibly "pure" genre paintings, the earlier attempts at definition were fortunately forgotten, and the term "genre" was applied simply as a category in order to distinguish scenes of daily life from landscapes or still lifes.

Recently, a further fundamental debate has indeed begun about the aforementioned duality between reality and allegory. Seymour Slive contributed the first essay in 1962, in which he summarized the previous findings of image interpretation and determined that the duality of reality and allegorical meaning belongs to the very nature of Dutch painting.[36] In 1968, starting not from iconographic but formal considerations, Uwe Schneede posed the question of "Dutch Realism" using the example of Metsu.[37] Metsu, like other genre painters, used certain props or figure studies in different pictures, always in new combinations.

All discussions about reality – as the concomitant discussion debate in literary criticism likewise shows – suffer from insufficient definition. Every use of the word is based on a different understanding. Generally one proceeds from the nineteenth-century conception of reality formulated through literature and literary scholarship, which refers to the representation of the visible. Whether this concept applies also to the seventeenth century is questionable. At that time, one had, for instance, very different conceptions of sketching from nature (*naer het leven*, from the living model, as it was called in one case), as the work of E. K. J. Reznicek and Hessel Miedema has shown.[38]

De Jongh chose for these contrasts the exaggerated formulation, "Realism and Seeming Realism." Seeming realism would formally imitate reality (even a picture composed in a studio?) and would at the same time be a realized abstraction; it expresses much less about Dutch life than it does the mentality of the people.[39] But the definition of the term does not necessarily lead to an understanding of the images; perhaps more important is the question of what the contemporary viewer saw in them, what he perceived as reality. Did he not also see allegories even in nature, as did the emblematist Nicolaus Taurellus (cited by Albrecht Schöne) in 1602? Taurellus saw two ears of corn, one full and bent, one empty and erect; from this he derived an allegory of imagined learnedness and weighty knowledge.[40] The conception of morality is part of reality, in everyday life as in the visual representation of the commonplace.

POSTSCRIPT (1995)

Not until after the Brunswick exhibition, *Die Sprache der Bilder* (The Language of Pictures), in whose catalogue this essay appeared in 1978, has a broad theoretical discussion been undertaken about iconology, or more specifically, about the interpretation of genre painting. In some cases this discussion has been conducted with all the bitterness of a religious struggle like that of the Council of Nicea. Svetlana Alpers's book, *The Art of Describing*, published in 1983, struck the scene like a lightning bolt.[41] For Alpers, the accurate observation and exact reproduction of nature are characteristic of Dutch art. These Dutch notions of vision and representation differ fundamentally from those exemplifying the visual culture of Renaissance Italy, and Alpers develops a critical terminology that illuminates the ways in which the former were embodied in paint. This book constitutes a fundamental confrontation with the pictorial interpretation promulgated by more recent Dutch art-historical theory. Herein, emblems are replaced by maps, mirrors, and the microscope. The inherent danger of this at times fascinating book is that hypotheses rapidly metamorphose into declarations of fact. In the end Alpers stands in complete opposition to extant emblem research. She perceives in the paintings more the work of a skilled hand addressing an attentive eye than the work of a learned mind.

In the meantime, De Jongh himself has warned of fanatical exegetes and careless emblematic interpretation. Moderate yet substantial criticism of this method was also expressed by former collaborators who worked on the 1976 exhibition *Tot lering en vermaak* (On Instruction and Amusement). In 1990 Jan Baptist Bedaux published a collection of essays under the title *The Reality of Symbols*.[42] These essays, which originally appeared in 1986 and 1987, dealt with both Panofsky's concept of "disguised symbolism" and De Jongh's method of pictorial interpretation. Bedaux utilizes De Jongh's sources but enriches his own interpretations with more general and readily intelligible meanings.

In his catalogue, *De hollandse fijnschilders* (The Dutch Fine Painters), Peter Hecht maintains a moderate position, which he achieves by taking pictorial execution just as seriously as content.[43] Hecht acknowledges the possible existence in the seventeenth century of an aesthetic view of painting that did not differ from that of the nineteenth century. An altogether new approach was introduced by Hans-Joachim Raupp in 1983, based on the placement of genre painting within the categorical hierarchy and standards of seventeenth-century literature on art theory.[44] With this approach Raupp applies poetic and rhetorical terminology from antiquity as well as from contemporary literature. Raupp's formulation of the problem reveals new possibilities of interpretation and achieves a moderate balance between *docere* and *delectare* (instruction and amusement).

A detailed account of various historic, national, social, and iconographic/iconological aspects of Dutch art is presented in the series of collected essays, *De Gouden Eeuw in perspectief* (The Golden Age in Perspective), in which an article by De Jongh offers an overview of specifically Dutch research on iconology.[45]

A Seventeenth-Century Theory of Art

NATURE AND PRACTICE*

J. A. Emmens

GERARD Dou is no longer looked upon as a major artist. Yet for a long time he ranked as the equal of his teacher Rembrandt, some eighteenth-century critics even considering him the better of the two. However this may be, since the end of the seventeenth century Rembrandt and Dou were regarded as the leading representatives of the two traditional types of painting distinguished long ago by Horace. Dou was the model for the smooth and "neat" technique and Rembrandt for the rough and "free." The free style was judged by Karel van Mander in 1604 to be the more difficult and dangerous, and he accordingly advised his pupils to start by employing the smooth technique.[1] This opinion was reversed, however, in 1641 by Dou's less well-known fellow citizen in Leiden, Philips Angel, who praised the "curious looseness" in the refined style of "the never sufficiently lauded Gerrit Dou," and added a warning: "Whoever works in this way [that is, painting smoothly] will be more ridiculed than praised. So, let artists who do not and cannot attain such finish work at mastering a loose, lively, and fluent brush-technique, rather than suffocate in stiff nastiness."[2]

To judge by the following couplet with its light-hearted comparison, which later in the classical period was to be taken quite seriously, it appears that the Dutch poet Jan Vos, writing in the 1650s, was an admirer of the free technique:

> I love this painting, for it's loosely made: but you
> Who made it (this I hate), oh, you're a loose one too.[3]

Even Samuel van Hoogstraeten, a moderate classicist, was as late as 1678 a firm supporter of a "bold stroke" and a "lively brush," as opposed to the "stiff smoothness" of someone like Gerard van Honthorst, whose work was rated much higher by true classicists as Joachim von Sandrart and Arnold Houbraken.[4] And when Wybrandt de Geest in 1702 described the two styles in his version of the passage from Van Mander referred to above, he cannot help adding that the then generally less approved free style, which nevertheless was apparently still held in high esteem, was the style of Rembrandt.[5] It is not surprising that Houbraken, himself a painter in the smooth style, should refer in his *De groote schouburgh der Nederlantsche konstschilders en schilderessen* (The Great Theatre of Dutch Men and Women Painters, 1718) to the "noble" Dou because of his smooth way of painting.[6] "Noble" had once been Rembrandt's epithet, bestowed upon him by the poet Joost van

* Editor's note: Jan Emmens's essay originally appeared in *Delta; A Review of Arts, Life, and Thought in The Netherlands* (Summer 1969), pp. 30–40. This was, in turn, an abridged English version without footnotes of an article that had been published in Dutch several years before: "Natuur, onderwijzing en oefening; bij een drieluik van Gerrit Dou," in *Album discipulorum aangeboden aan Professor Dr J. G. van Gelder*, pp. 125–36, Utrecht 1963. Wayne Franits translated the original footnotes and added them to the abridged English version reproduced here.

den Vondel in 1658.[7] The smooth manner, even if it retained a certain looseness, was the style of the painters with a classical bent, and as the way people live and the art they like are much the same thing according to classical – and not only classical – ideas, the "loose" technique was the sure sign for the classicists of "loose" or licentious painters, who obeyed the rules of neither life nor art. So Rembrandt's fate was often that he was valued only as a rough diamond, while Dou was noted as the representative of true or classical culture.

It is, therefore, all the more remarkable that Houbraken addresses to "noble" Dou the same reproach as he does to Rembrandt, who in his eyes was much less noble. Dou also suffered, according to Houbraken, from the evil which, in his view, had been brought into the world by Caravaggio, although Van Mander, echoing the Italian Giorgio Vasari, had already blamed Albrecht Dürer for it – that he followed nature and forgot all about beauty. "It is a pity that this man's common sense did not lead him to grander conceptions and that he did not apply his brush to depict more dignified and more praiseworthy objects. But it is useless to complain or hope. His work is what it is and no changes in it can be made, for he and all his contemporaries are in their dark graves and are no more of this world. We can guess at two possible causes for his unremitting recording of insignificant objects. First, that he had accustomed himself to such a detailed rendering of life that he could not or would not attempt anything outside it (following Michelangelo da Caravaggio's example). He was incapable of attempting historical themes, for those who do must sometimes rely on ideas of their own. Second, that his genius was unable to reach those heights, and so (as far as his choice of subjects is concerned) remained imprisoned on lower levels."[8]

In so far as this means that Dou made much less use of books with examples from Antiquity than Houbraken exhorted others to do, there is perhaps little to disagree with in the above complaint. After all, the number of Dutch books on Antiquity was considerably smaller in Dou's time than in Houbraken's some sixty years later. But in so far as it means that Dou's canvases must be considered solely as realistic genre paintings, as we have been accustomed to think of them (thanks to Houbraken), we may wonder if Houbraken was not responsible for an error of judgement that totally misinterprets Dou's intentions.[9]

It is with some hesitation that I call upon the Fleming Cornelis de Bie (1627–1711) as chief witness, for this author sometimes proved to write with great facility about painters whose work he can scarcely have known. Among the countless poems of praise written by De Bie in the prevailing jargon of the time, his eulogy on Dou is remarkable for a few lines which are more than mere clichés. He says Dou's paintings must be seen as "agreeable works . . . Which scatter all the darkness of our understanding / And bear our spirits higher than the stars."[10] At first sight this is unexpected praise. But De Bie's work appeared in 1661, half a century before the *Groote schouburgh*, while Dou was still alive. This is sufficient reason, I think, to attach more credence to his words than to those of Houbraken, who was De Bie's successor as a writer on the history of art in the Netherlands and one with many more readers.

The painting that moved Houbraken to criticize Dou's down-to-earth imagination was the famous triptych known as *The Lying-In Room*, which was the jewel of the renowned Braamcamp collection. Purchased in 1771 for Catherine of Russia, it was lost in a shipwreck in the Baltic with many other paintings acquired from the collection. Although it has never been possible, therefore, to admire it in the Hermitage, an impression can be had from the copy made by Willem Joseph Laquy for Gerrit Braamcamp between 1763 and 1771 (Fig. 1). Houbraken's description of the original can be checked against this copy, which is one of the few triptychs representing secular subjects to have been preserved.[11]

Of the centre panel, Houbraken says: "Here two rooms are depicted. In the foremost, where a beautifully painted tapestry hangs as a curtain, a woman is suckling a child. Nearby is a cradle and other basketry, a table with a rug bearing a graceful silver and gilt jug, a brass chandelier, and other still-life objects. The second room is a barber's shop where,

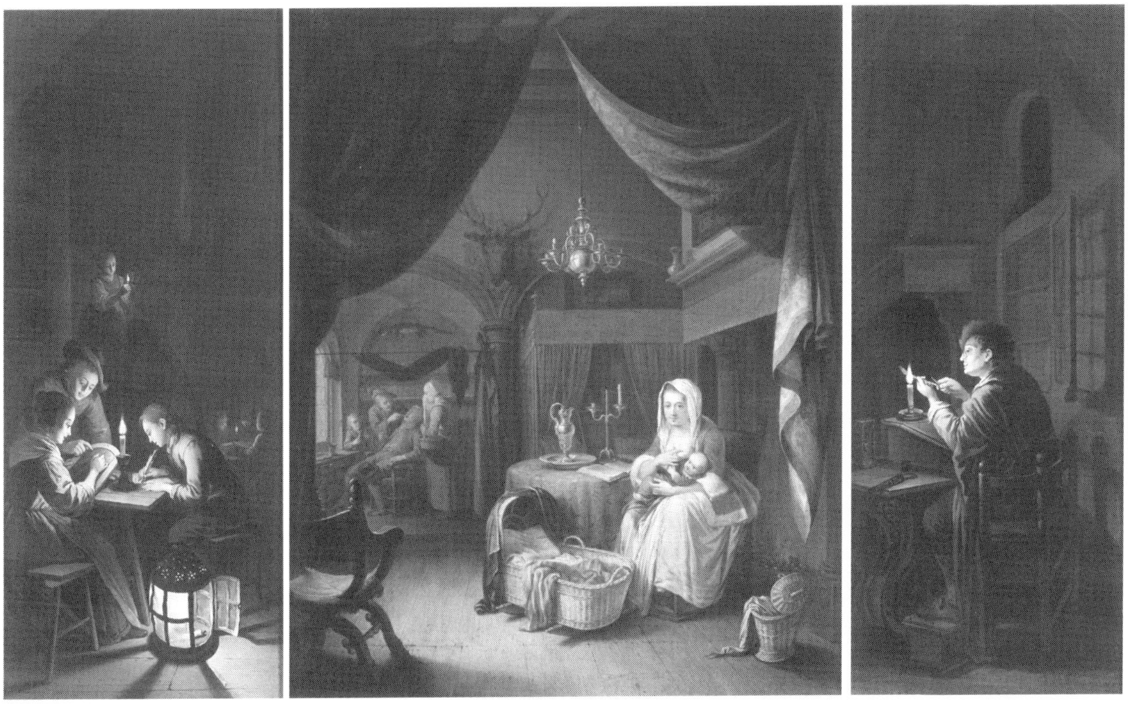

Figure 1. Willem Laquy, *Triptych: Allegory of Art Training,* copy after a now lost triptych by Gerard Dou (center: oil on canvas, 83 × 70 cm; wings, oil on canvas, each 80 × 36 cm). Amsterdam, Rijksmuseum. Photo: Rijksmuseum-Stichting.

among other scenes, a peasant is having his throat examined, while an old woman stands by weeping. The two side panels reveal on the one side a study, in which an old man is trimming a pen by candlelight. On the other side is a school for writing and arithmetic with children sitting at desks, artfully illuminated by candles and a lantern. Everything is painted according to nature, cleverly, richly, and as minutely as is possible to conceive. The outside of the panels which enclose this artistic scene is skilfully adorned with images of the liberal arts, in grisaille by Coxie." Then follows the above-quoted tirade on Dou's imagination.[12]

Had Houbraken not been such a fervent supporter of the classical advantages and so prejudiced against pre-classical Dutch art, the "images of the liberal arts" (which, incidentally, were not copied by Laquy), might have given him some inkling of the particular idea which lay at the basis of Dou's composition. It was a concept quite familiar not only to the seventeenth-century world of art but also to Houbraken himself, as may be seen from the biography of the painter Michiel van Musscher. In this Houbraken, referring to Aristotle's observation, says: "Three things are needed to achieve learning: nature, teaching, and practice; but all will be fruitless unless practice follows nature and teaching."[13]

As I see it, Dou's triptych is an illustration of this Aristotelian proposition. When the triptych was closed, one saw the liberal arts, perhaps emblematically in the form of instruments. When it was opened one saw the three things necessary to master these arts to the full: Nature, centre (*The Lying-In Room*); Teaching, left (*The Evening School*); and Practice, right (*The Pen-Cutter*). I shall try to explain this idea in more detail.

Aristotle's thesis that natural skill, teaching, and practice were essential for a good education was widely known since the Renaissance. It was to be found in the most important educational writings of Antiquity. As *Natura*, *Ars* or *Disciplina*, and *Exercitatio*, the triad was familiar from Cicero's and Quintilian's systems of education for Roman orators – which is the reason why the three principles are referred to or expounded during the seventeenth century by the Dutch poet Theodore van Rodenburgh and by such writers as Franciscus Junius and Van Hoogstraeten. I shall have more to say on this aspect of the application of Aristotle's principles presently.[14]

A classical work dealing with education intended to produce a man of all-round virtue was Plutarch's much-read and often translated treatise *The Education or Bringing Up of Children*. From this source, for example, Erasmus borrowed his three conceptions of *Natura*, *Ratio* (or *Doctrina*), and *Usus* (or *Exercitatio*) – variants which are clarified in the quotation below. Plutarch's *Golden Book*, as the work was called in the Netherlands, was very popular in the seventeenth century. At least three different Dutch translations appeared, one of them being twice reprinted. Plutarch writes: "We must now speak of education. As a general statement, the same assertion may be made in regard to moral excellence that we are in the habit of making in regard to the arts and sciences, namely, that there must be a concurrence of three things in order to produce a perfectly right action, and these are: nature, reason, and habit. By reason I mean the act of learning, and by habit constant practice. The first beginnings come from nature, advancement from learning, the practical use from all combined. . . ."[15] If Dou was not familiar with the triad, and further totally ignorant of ancient sources, he could have brushed up his knowledge by reading a translation of Plutarch's *Golden Book*.

Let us now return to Dou's painting of this theme, the triptych *The Lying-In Room*. This title, obviously inspired by the central panel, is curious, to put it mildly. The scene in the left background is in any case quite irrelevant to it. It may be remarked in passing that we do not have to agree with Houbraken that it shows a peasant having his throat inspected. It is far more likely to represent the "surgeon's shop" which often recurs in Dou's work and is intended quite seriously, and the scene is described as such in the auction catalogue of the Braamcamp collection. The scene in the right foreground does not justify the usual title either. In the Netherlands of the time mothers were recommended to breast-feed their babies, thus the woman in the foreground to all appearances is not the wet-nurse but the child's mother, who, dressed in all her finery as she is, could hardly be called a woman in childbed. In addition, the baby is of comparatively advanced age, to judge by his or her steady gaze levelled at the spectator. The emphasis in the painting is, therefore, certainly not on the birth but on the suckling of the child, or rather, on the way in which the child is to be fed.[16]

At first sight these two scenes have little in common with the "naked woman with her breast full of milk, holding a vulture on her hand," who, according to Cesare Ripa, represents Nature. Ripa's further description, however, clarifies much: "Nature, as Aristotle defines it in his second *Physics*, is the principle . . . by means of which change all corruptible things are produced. It is depicted as a naked woman, who shows this principle in its two forms, the active or real and the passive or suffering. The active or real is represented by means of breasts full of milk, for the form or figure is what feeds and sustains all created things, as Woman feeds and sustains her children with her breasts. The vulture, greedy for prey, serves the second principle, called matter or material, which, moving and changing because of the desires of its figure or form, destroys in time all corruptible things."[17]

We see here the dualistic conception of nature put forward by Aristotle. Now it seems to me that while Ripa puts this Aristotelian conception of nature's dual function as an allegorical personification in true Italian style, Dou has done it in the Dutch way, as we know it from illustrations in Dutch emblem books by means of two *genre*-paintings. Active or real nature is painted as a woman about to nurse her child, as a domestic descendant of the Mother Nature of Antiquity, who is also the archetype of Ripa's personification. Passive or suffering nature – perhaps following Aristotle's own use of the image of physician and patient to explain his ideas – is shown as a sufferer or patient whose throat is being examined by a doctor.[18] I should like briefly to draw attention to a number of objects in the room which must have had emblematic meanings connected with the underlying purpose of the picture. To what extent the washing bowl and the mirror on the table represent respectively the active and the contemplative life, I am not sure. But it is certain that the deer's head on the spigot between the two arches marking the division between foreground and background signifies the long life which everyone will wish the child in the foreground, at least if that life is going to be well spent.[19]

How this life could be well spent is shown in the two side panels. On the left panel, which Houbraken mistakenly took to be the right-hand panel, we see education that trains reason through the medium of art, in this case the arts of reading and writing, which introduced and formed part of the first of the liberal arts, grammar or the art of letters. In depicting this idea Dou was able to make use of the traditional representation of grammar as a teacher surrounded by his pupils, a tradition from which most of the seventeenth-century paintings of schools usually derive.[20] Dou's panel is different from most in that he shows a so-called evening school, a subject providing him with the opportunity (which he often took) for the "very sensuous" painting of "lamps and burning candles," which Van Hoogstraeten and many after him were to admire so much in his work.

However, I raise the question – without being able to answer it – whether this work and other paintings do in fact show an evening school or a school which began very early in the morning. In any case the lamp and candles surely represent the light of understanding which is handed on from the teacher to his pupil – a process perhaps illustrated by the girl in the background.[21] The man cutting a pen in the right-hand panel represents practice. Ripa gives two versions of "Practice," conforming to the two ideas of *Studium* and *Exercitatio* current in Latin and Italian. Although the idea intended in the Aristotelian triad is usually translated as *Exercitatio*, and the three ideas are accordingly discussed by Ripa under the heading *Esercitio*, Dou's painting tallies more with Ripa's *Studio*, or practice in the arts: a pale young man, an open book in his left hand, a pen in his right hand, seated near a lamp and a cock. Here, too, we see the characteristic difference between Italian and Dutch allegory: those elements of Italian personification not encountered in everyday life are omitted in the Dutch painting. Dou shows us a middle-aged man seated near an hour-glass (symbolic of time which must be used well), cutting his pen by candlelight (guided by reason trained by education).[22]

The significance of this interpretation calls for some further discussion. The pen-cutter was one of the popular, though now forgotten, themes of seventeenth-century genre painting. While this figure occurs occasionally before 1600, in the seventeenth century it was painted not only by Dou but also by Adriaen Brouwer, Salomon de Koninck, Jan Lievens, Gabriel Metsu, Jan Steen, Rembrandt, and others. The specific occupation, pen-cutting, points to the great importance attached to the art of writing and at the same time to the emblematic meaning that could be read into this activity. *Nil penna, sed usus* – not the pen but its use is of value – runs a saying which is not out of place here, and which was frequently illustrated by an ostrich, exemplifying an owner of useless quills. *Senze taglio non vaglio* – uncut I am useless – says another proverb, referring to the pen itself and alluding in general to the fruitful results that adversity often brings and in particular to the training of reason, which in Vondel's words is worthless if it is "unsharpened."[23]

Vondel used this phrase in his translation of Horace's treatment of the problem whether versification (which may be learnt) or natural ability should have priority in the development of a poet. This a problem closely linked to the Aristotelian triad; it goes more fully into the relationship between the first two principles, in which the second – art which can be mastered – appears to implicate the third, practice. It seems to me to be typical of the popularity of the current representation of "practice in the arts" as a pen-cutter that Vondel translated Horace's words *rude ingenium* as "unsharpened reason."[24]

With Horace's comments on the first two of Aristotle's three principles we have entered the realm of poetics, and also that of art theory, for in the seventeenth century this was closely related to the Horatian theory of poetry. We have already established that Dutch art theorists took the triad from Latin rhetoric. The influence of Horace appears, however, to have preceded that of Quintilian. In Van Mander's writings the triad has not yet made its appearance, although he pays a great deal of attention to the same problem as Horace, that of the relationship between natural talent and art that can be acquired, and on the other hand repeatedly refers to the virtues of practice. Writings on poetics from the same period show that the triad as such was already known, as is clear from *Poetens borstweringh* (Poet's Rampart) by Van Mander's contemporary Van Rodenburgh.[25] In 1637 Junius seems to have been the first to introduce the three principles into Dutch art theory, and to give them equal weight.[26] The Swedish art historian Allan Ellenius has recently explained that (under the influence of Quintilian) the plan of Junius' second book was inspired by the triad, *Natura-Ars-Exercitatio*.[27] Following Junius, Van Hoogstraeten wrote in 1678 a comprehensive study of Nature, Learning, and Exercise, discussing the relationship between Nature and Learning on the basis of Horace's ideas, while comparing the connection between learning and exercise to that between theory and practice.[28]

This identification of theory with study and practice with exercise appears to be characteristic of classicism. The distinction between classicist and earlier theories is, after all, not only a shifting of the accent from natural talent to acquired skill – a change perhaps corresponding to the increasing influence exerted by poetics – but primarily the growing tendency to theorize about art, rather than to continue to regard it as in the past as a craft, the practice of which could be learnt. Only if art has been studied along the lines of correct theory are practical exercises of any use, proclaimed the classicists. Hence their criticism of exercise – merely considered as practice – unless accompanied by a conception of art schooled by theory. Revealing examples of this type of criticism occur in biographies of Rembrandt written by the classicists.[29]

While we tend today to think that "practice makes perfect" is a typically classicist saying, it must actually have been much more typical of the early seventeenth century. Rembrandt, in any case, was convinced of the truth of this maxim. In fact he suggested the theme of the pen-cutter, personifying "practice in the arts," to Dou, his pupil in his Leiden studio. Rembrandt's father was asked to sit as model in this traditional pose, thus impressing upon the pupil that art was not to be mastered on the basis of natural talent alone but had to be acquired above all by continuous practice. Even though the painting (of which two versions are known) did not turn out to be Dou's masterpiece, it is valuable as evidence of the theory of art which Rembrandt propounded to his young pupil.[30]

Realism and Seeming Realism in Seventeenth-Century Dutch Painting*

Eddy de Jongh

The originally Hegelian notion that artists express the *spirit* of their time (the controversial *Zeitgeist*), or even herald that of the future is closely connected to the realistic-impressionistic one that artists depict the daily *life* of their own time and milieu.[1] These two concepts have prevailed until this day, primarily in a hybrid form. Moreover, their accuracy is thought to be verified by the abundant proof provided predominantly by seventeenth-century Dutch paintings.[2] After all, this art is still most frequently characterized by the term "realism."

Pausing to consider this much discussed term, however, it should be remembered that in the seventeenth century instances of actual realism coincided with others more appropriately described as expressing a "seeming realism," and that this phenomenon is based on a mentality which can be partly reconstructed. For the purpose of this article, realism is defined as meaning the "reflection of reality." Seeming realism, on the other hand, refers to representations which, although they imitate reality in terms of form, simultaneously convey a realized abstraction.[3] While this recent insight somewhat dilutes the concepts just mentioned, assuming that art is somehow related to the culture from which it springs, we can say that the so-called realism of seventeenth-century Dutch art is perhaps more characteristic of the mentality (the *spirit* or *geist* – to use this term once again, though without any Hegelian implications) than of the *life* of the time as it was enacted on the street or in the sitting room, so to speak.

It is not my intention here to reconstruct a historical mentality via the art of the period, but rather the reverse; namely, to determine the original intentions of artists via the seventeenth-century mentality. This is a world of ideas about which contemporary literature and other written documents inform us far better than do paintings. Incidentally, I will not attempt to provide an exhaustive definition of the seventeenth-century mentality (that is, varying, yet closely intertwined mentalities) but will focus instead on several aspects – all inherited from preceding centuries, but all obviously having evolved – which played a role in this mentality.

Truly pervasive in the period under question is the tendency to moralize, which often boils down to the encouragement of virtue, or an allusion to the transience of life and the finality of death.[4] Moralization was also manifested in works of art, under many guises and with varying degrees of overt or covert emphasis; the casual blend of moralization and libertinism is often quite surprising. The marked preference for disguising, veiling, allegory, and ambiguity, in short for all that is enigmatic, is a second important feature of the mentality of the period, which is highly consistent with the

* Editor's note: Eddy de Jongh's essay originally appeared under the title, "Realisme en schijnrealisme in de Hollandse schilderkunst van de zeventiende eeuw," in Exhib. cat. Brussels, *Rembrandt en zijn tijd*, pp. 143–94, Paleis voor Schone Kunsten, 1971. It was translated for this volume by Kist Kilian Communications.

associative way of thinking typical of contemporary literature.[5]

Initially the *rederijkers* (rhetoricians) played an important role in this development, both with their *landjuwelen* (festive competitions between groups of rhetoricians), or lavishly designed public spectacles, and their blazons, which were frequently embellished with extremely sophisticated rebuses.[6] A comparable playful element is found in the many riddle books which enjoyed great popularity at the time. For example, children were frequently inculcated with biblical knowledge by means of "spiritual riddles."[7] Thus, it should come as no surprise that emblem literature – that branch of literature in which metaphorical thinking received its most pregnant expression – could attain such heights in the Netherlands in the seventeenth century.[8] One of its ablest practitioners was Jacob Cats, arguably the most widely read writer of his time. His *Sinne- en minnebeelden* (Emblems of Virtue and Love) of 1618, and later, the *Spiegel vanden ouden ende nieuwen tijdt* (Mirror of the Ancient and Modern Times) of 1632 each went through numerous reprints.[9]

A characteristic feature of *Sinne- en minnebeelden* is the multivalent explanation given for each emblem, a practice based on a longstanding tradition. Every picture receives an amorous, a social, and a religious explanation.[10] In his foreword, Cats asks the reader "not to misinterpret the fact that we have used the same images and comparisons to represent both human ideas and divine deliberations, all without the least distinction and sometimes even with contradictory modifications, something we might judge as blowing hot and cold." Next he appeals to the Bible, in which "it is not unusual to find that one and the same thing is alternately considered good and bad in the Parables."[11]

Strictly speaking, we know of no parallels for such "hot and cold" extremes in painting. However, many pictures lend themselves to more than just a single interpretation: Not infrequently, seventeenth-century painters deliberately devised vague representations for the benefit of the public's imagination, or made them deliberately ambiguous by means of a method which "technically" deviated little from that of Cats.[12] Countless paintings, particularly genre scenes, had to be "read" in a manner comparable to studying riddles and rebuses. The mentality, or spirit, of the makers of such paintings could not possibly have differed much from that of the compilers of riddle and rebus books.

In prints, whose inscriptions frequently left little to the imagination, we know that a lute player and his sweetheart, for example, could sometimes symbolize the sanguine temperament, and at others the element Earth, or the sense of Hearing, or the Age of Twenty.[13] A seventeenth-century person, familiar with this type of print, could "read" all these meanings with equal justification into painted representations of a lute player and a woman.

One should bear in mind though that the seventeenth-century viewer, like ourselves, also ascribed meanings to paintings which were probably never intended by their makers. In fact, a given artist may not have meant to represent anything more than meets the eye. It is difficult for us to imagine that in spite of the propensity for moralizing, not all paintings were infused with hidden meaning. The fact that people in the seventeenth century could variously interpret the subject of a painting is described by the Jesuit priest Adriaan Poirters, whose popularity in the Southern Netherlands was equal to that of Cats in the Northern Netherlands.[14] Poirters discusses a composition of a dog with a skull under its paws. With regard to its meaning, he states that "various opinions exist," which he then proceeds to summarize.

In the foreword of *Spiegel vanden ouden ende nieuwen tijdt* (Mirror of Ancient and Modern Times), Cats returns to the phenomenon of polyinterpretability, this time with regard to proverbs that are "entirely malleable and open to interpretations for all manner of things." Moreover, he makes a plea for the principle of disguise:

> That they [that is, maxims and proverbs] are particularly attractive, thanks to a certain agreeable obscurity, and while they appear to be one thing, in reality they contain another, of which the reader, having in due time seized the exact meaning and intention, experiences wondrous pleasure in his soul; not unlike one, who, after some searching, finds a beautiful

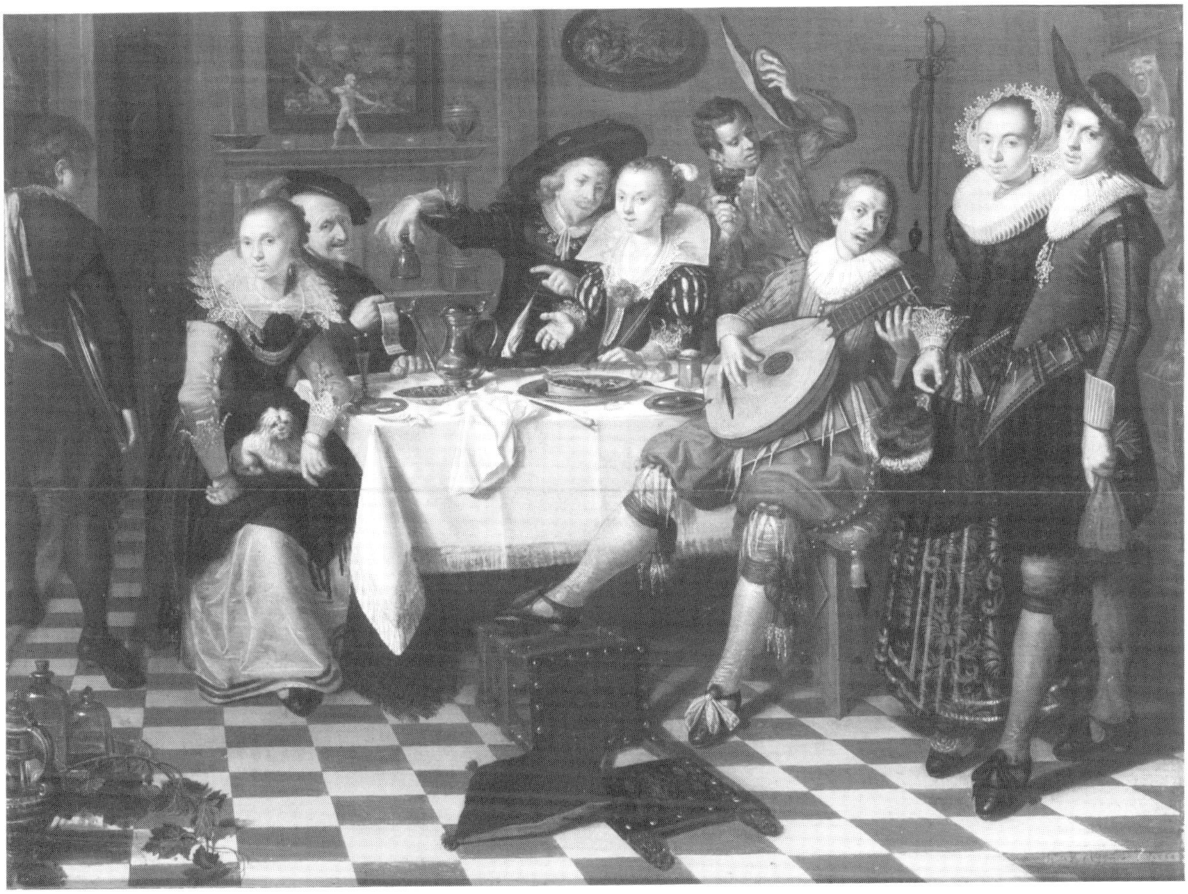

Figure 2. Isack Elyas, *Merry Company* (oil on panel, 47 × 63 cm). Amsterdam, Rijksmuseum. Photo: Rijksmuseum-Stichting.

bunch of grapes under thick leaves. *Experience teaches us that many things gain by not being completely seen, but somewhat veiled and concealed* [italics mine].[15]

Cats was not alone in recommending that subject matter be veiled; other authors of emblem and device books posited similar assertions. Some used the fact that Christ had spoken in parables as an argument in favor of disguise. Others reasoned from an "aristocratic" standpoint, namely that emblems should serve to stimulate thought, but that not "just anyone" – Roemer Visscher literally refers to "every Tom, Dick, and Harry" – should be able to understand them "at first sight."[16]

The perceptions of writers on art were entirely in keeping with those of the emblematists. The painter and theoretician Samuel van Hoogstraeten, for example, was particularly clear in this matter. In his 1678 *Inleyding tot de hooge schoole der schilderkonst* (Introduction to the Lofty School of Painting), he devotes a chapter to "byvoegsels door zinnebeelden en poetische uitvindingen" (additions by means of emblems and poetical inventions) that begins as follows: "Although the art of painting is great in and of itself, Pliny says, nonetheless, the profound discoveries and secret reasons that can sometimes be found are its particular glory; certainly here the profound intelligence of the master manifests itself: . . . it is thus . . . the splendor of the paintings, that they are cloaked in one or another instructive significance." Further on, Van Hoogstraeten offers the following advice in rhyme:

Of the many ways in which to ornament a
solitary piece,

The best is certainly to embellish it
With accessories that explain something
covertly:
An emblem formed from collected images.[17]

GENRE

A good example of "bywerk dat bedektlijk iets verklaert" (accessories that explain something covertly), and for that matter seeming realism and ultimately moralizing, is a *Merry Company* of 1620 (Fig. 2) by the virtually unknown Haarlem painter Isack Elyas.[18] As a "demonstration," I will discuss this painting in some depth. Elyas admonishes the spirited figures in this work by means of a traditional seventeenth-century device: the painting-within-the-painting. Visible on the wall behind the group are two small pictures. The one at the left depicts the Deluge and the oval one at the right a battle scene; images with nothing merry about them. The Deluge alludes to the downfall of man, while in my opinion the battle must be interpreted as the visualization of certain biblical texts which were repeatedly quoted and paraphrased by sixteenth and seventeenth-century Catholic and Protestant authors alike. For instance, in his *Christeliicken waerseggher* (Christian Truth-Teller) of 1602–3, the Antwerp Jesuit Johannes David wrote in connection with the book of Job: "*Militia est vita hominis super terram:*" Man's life on earth / is a struggle. This world is the battlefield / where the struggle takes place and the blows fall: our life / is a time of fighting / and contending for the crown: followed by the time for coronation / of those who fought well.[19] Similarly, the Calvinist Johan de Brune, invoking Saint Augustine, formulated this thought (one related to the Last Judgement) in his *Emblemata* of 1624 as follows: "This earth is like a battlefield, where we are tested against our enemies. Eternal rest is the proffered prize of constant unrest. In this battle we have no other weapon but faith reinforced by love."[20]

Prior to Elyas, Dirck Barendsz. had included a similar warning in a composition which also depicted a company dining, *Mankind Awaiting the Last Judgement*, the final outcome of which can be seen in the right background (Fig. 3).[21] And following Elyas, the battle motif recurs with the same meaning in, among others, a painting by an unknown Delft School artist (London, The National Gallery; circa 1655) of a woman rejecting the advances of a man offering her a filled glass.[22] In a work attributed to Hendrick van der Burch, the concept of life as a battle is portrayed somewhat differently (Fig. 4). An image of the Last Judgement hangs on the wall, while the battle itself is embodied by the principal figure, who has exchanged his elegant clothing for a soldier's uniform complete with gun.[23]

However, much more can be said about Elyas's work. A striking feature of the composition is that the couple at the right does not partake in the meal, but rather stand and look out of the picture plane toward the viewer. There are other scenes in which a man and a woman, perhaps bride and bridegroom, are relegated to the outer edges of the composition, also on the fringe of some group activity. In these works we must reckon with an allegorical charge. The scenes depicted around these couples may function as moral mirrors. Jan Miense Molenaer, for example, confronted such a pair with a ball game which, as various emblems instruct us, is a metaphor for amorous potential, and – in another painting – with a number of figures who, together, symbolize *Temperantia* (Moderation) as the key to a harmonious marriage.[24] Likewise, the "realistic" group next to the couple in Elyas's work also proves to be an allegory. An allegory, moreover, which is typically Dutch in nature, a seventeenth-century bourgeois interpretation of the more sublime manifestations that enjoyed greater popularity elsewhere, for instance in Flanders. While abstract allegorical concepts were almost always cloaked in the form of fantastic personifications, in Holland they generally appeared as "normal" people in everyday garb.[25] The diners in Elyas's painting represent an allegory of the Five Senses, and in the seventeenth century would have been understood as symbolizing an entire range of sinful possibilities. These options are presented to the standing couple as "hidden persuaders," while at the same time the images of the Deluge and the battle scene make painfully clear the fate awaiting sinners.

Though indispensable, the senses were perceived as being rather treacherous possessions.[26]

After all, they were the gateway to the mind and soul. With reference to Aristotle, the Dordrecht municipal physician Johan van Beverwijck formulated this concept in his widely read *Schat der gesontheyt* (Treasure of Health), as follows: "There is nothing present in the soul, which has not been filtered through the senses."[27] Should the senses be used improperly, the soul was irrevocably poisoned. Ever since Plato, the senses have aroused philosophical suspicion. They were considered misleading and unreliable, beliefs which moreover accorded with the tenets of Christianity which had always staunchly associated the senses with sin. The intense preoccupation with the senses in the sixteenth and seventeenth centuries, and particularly the emphasis given to their unreliability, appears characteristic of the prevailing mentality.[28] In this respect, Elyas, who incorporated the senses in a "sinful" context, is a representative "spokesman" of his time.

The mutual hierarchy of the senses has been central to numerous discussions.[29] In Platonic circles, for instance, a distinction was made between superior senses (Sight and Hearing) and inferior ones (Smell, Taste, Touch). On the other hand, this hierarchy was also subject to different views. Influenced by the evolving sciences (especially physics), a philosophical appreciation for the senses grew as the seventeenth century progressed; as a consequence of a more innovative concept of the world, people began to adopt a more open-minded attitude toward nature.

Representations of the senses gained steadily in popularity from the sixteenth century on and, in fact, underwent a remarkable development. Initially they were personified exclusively by static, allegorical female figures. Later they were illustrated by animated figures, or by couples whose identity can be deduced from their attributes and actions.[30] In the iconography of the Five Senses, painters followed the example set by the graphic artists, sometimes even to the point of making five small, separate images. Generally, however, as in Elyas's painting, we find the senses united in a single composition, and eventually becoming so camouflaged as to lose their identity. Undoubtedly, at times artists may have wanted to be deliberately vague in this respect. There is some justification for assuming that the Five Senses are present in Jan Steen's *Epiphany* (Kassel, Staatliche Kunstsammlungen);[31] similarly, Frans Hals's *The Merry Toper* (Amsterdam, Rijksmuseum), holding a glass in his hand, could exemplify the sense of taste, though admittedly there is nothing in the image to specifically substantiate this supposition. Men holding glasses sometimes represented wine merchants, and sometimes even functioned as personifications of *Gula*, the sin of gluttony.[32]

The great attention devoted to the senses in the seventeenth century can, in part, be explained by the simple fact that they formed a fixed series complete in itself. A preference had existed since the Middle Ages for anything that could somehow be united in a series, a phenomenon which – once again under the influence of science – received new impetus during the Renaissance. In addition to the senses, there was a scientific, literary, and artistic interest in the elements, the temperaments, the eras of human history, the seasons, times of the day, and the ages of man – "educational series" which continued to inspire often rather clever moralizations.[33] Correlations were made between several of these series which, for example, led to Youth being associated with Spring, the element Air and the Sanguine temperament. Following another system, the Sanguine temperament was coupled with the astrological sign Sagittarius,[34] and it is this associative strategy that Elyas alludes to with the statue of an archer placed on the cabinet behind the predominantly sanguine company in his painting of 1620.

As was the case with the Five Senses, in the sixteenth century all of these series were still represented as straightforward allegories. Later, however, they became shrouded in "realism," until finally they emerged individually from their serial context. Of these series, the Five Senses retained some shred of their original identity the longest. In any case, when looking at independent seventeenth-century genre scenes and landscapes, it is useful to remember that the categories to which they belong stem at least partially from the inherent "prefabrication" of these edifying series.

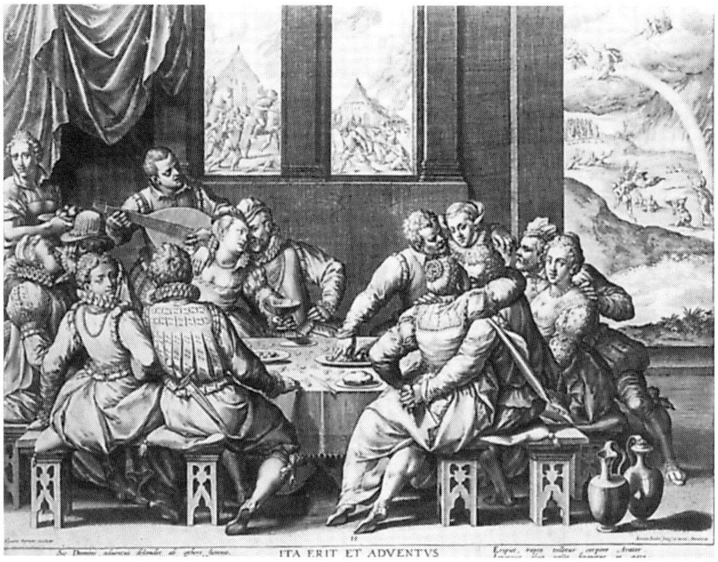

Figure 3. Johan Sadeler after Dirck Barendsz., *Mankind Awaiting the Last Judgement* (engraving). Amsterdam, Rijksprentenkabinet. Photo: Rijksmuseum-Stichting.

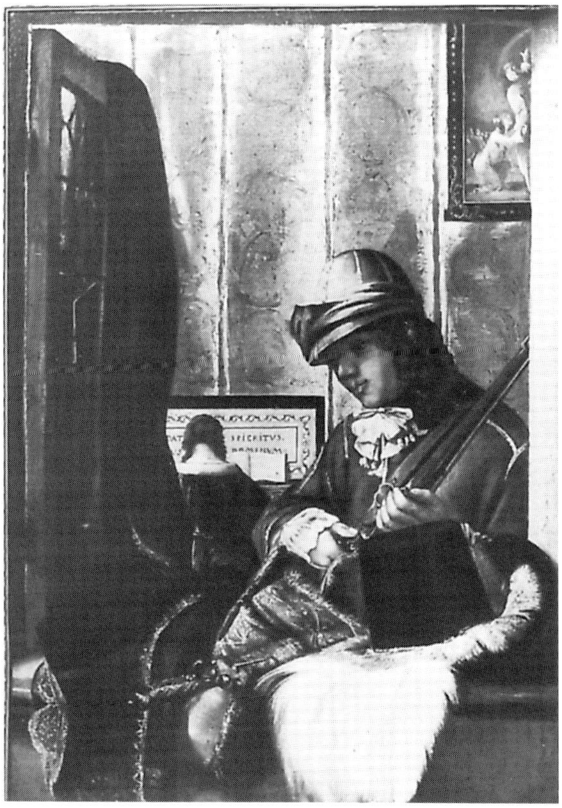

Figure 4. Hendrick van der Burch (attributed to), *The Soldier* (oil on canvas, 112 × 70 cm). Present location unknown.

LANDSCAPE

Naturally, genre scenes were better suited than landscapes for conveying a particular “message”: I am not referring here to landscapes with more or less pronounced biblical or other kinds of subject matter. It might even be suggested that seventeenth-century Dutch landscapes, more than any other artistic genre, reflect a certain “art for art's sake" sensibility, a concept that would only be formulated two centuries later. However, when addressing the essential question of whether landscapes and seascapes were painted purely for their own sake, we must always consider the fact that seventeenth-century thinking – the literature alone provides a wealth of evidence for this – was permeated with both the notion of the transience of nature and of nature as divine revelation.[35] Constantijn Huygens's statement “The goodness of God is to be seen in every dune's top,” from which we can infer that for this poet a landscape was not merely a scenic view, is surely representative of the beliefs held by many of his contemporaries. The star witness in this matter is, of course, Jacob Cats. For him, the most diverse natural phenomena served as a point of departure for drawing valuable

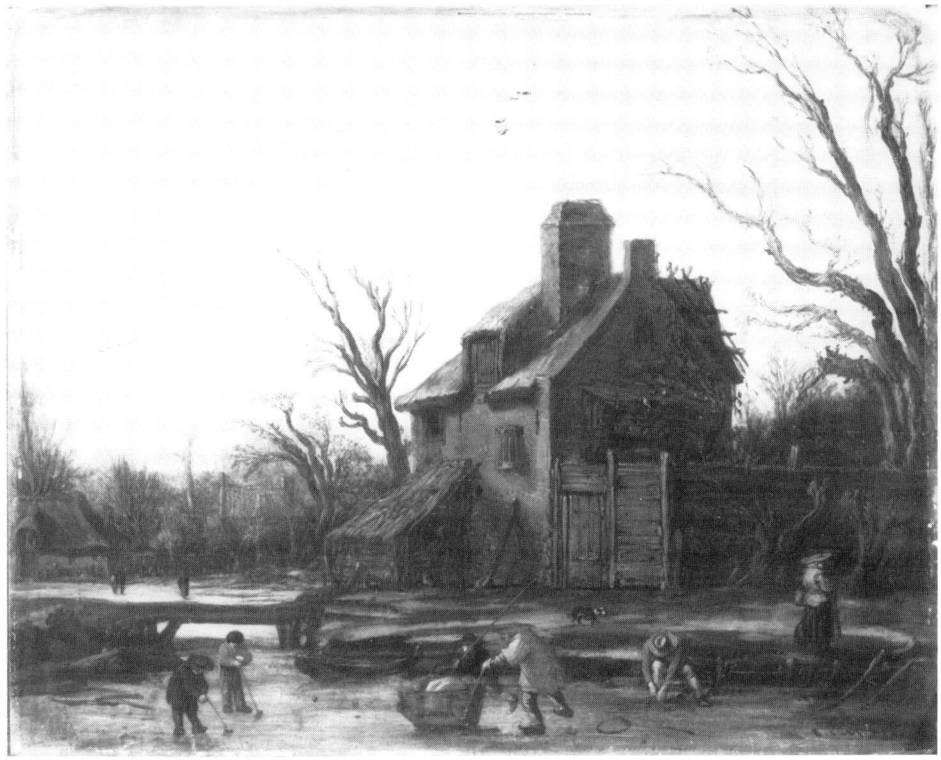

Figure 5. Esaias van de Velde, *Winter Landscape*, 1624 (oil on panel, 26 × 32 cm). The Hague, Mauritshuis. Photo: A. Dingjan, The Hague.

lessons. And at his country estate *Sorghvliet*, Cats could not take a single step without elevated thoughts on the miracle of creation welling up within him.[36]

It would be wrong to suppose that when devising their landscapes and seascapes, painters were unaware of contemporary concepts, such as the transience of nature or "the goodness of God" expressed in their work. A concrete example of this is Esaias van de Velde's *Winter Landscape* of 1624 (Fig. 5). While conceived as an independent work of art, it could just as easily have been part of a seasonal pairing of Summer and Winter, as Esaias indeed painted on occasion, or of a series of the four seasons, known from countless prints and from painted versions by Adriaen van de Venne and others. The passage of the seasons, the waxing and waning of nature, could be seen as a parallel to the course of man's life from the cradle to the grave. We cannot wholly exclude the idea that Esaias may have been inspired by such a thought when painting this *Winter*, even though as far as we know the work is not part of a series. For other painters, too, including Aert van der Neer and Lieve Verschuier, who depicted pendant paintings of *Morning* and *Evening* at the end of the 1640s and around 1670 respectively, conveying a certain moralizing message did not seem to be out of the question.[37] In these instances, however, it is equally possible that we are dealing with a process of sublimation, one inherent in the evolution of all series during the seventeenth century. Hence, the form remains while the allegorical or moralizing contents evaporate.

Turning to the "moralizing" landscape, it seems to fit the definition of seeming realism formulated above, namely that while the form is taken from reality, it is also a realized abstraction. In turn, the form of a painted landscape is also based on seeming realism, albeit of an entirely different order. Seventeenth-century landscape painters, both those working in their own country and the Italianates,

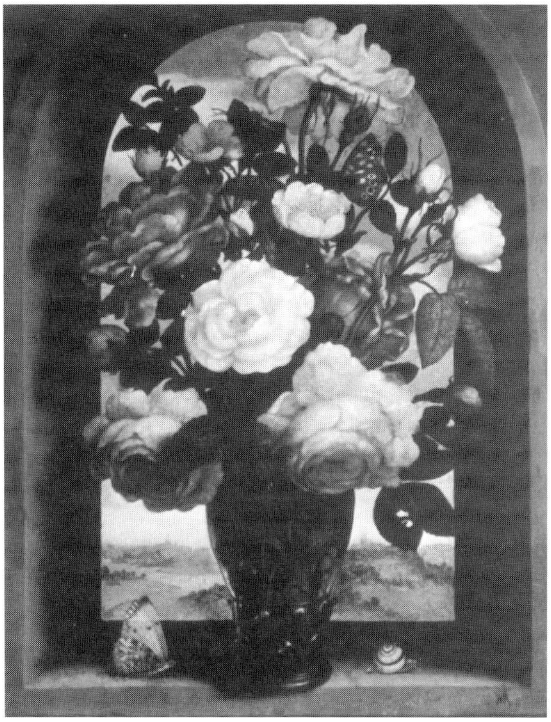

Figure 6. Ambrosius Bosschaert, *Vase with Flowers in a Niche* (oil on copper, 27.5 × 23 cm). Present location unknown. Photo: D. Broda, Syracuse.

manipulated nature with great ease, usually for compositional purposes and without any ulterior motives. Accordingly, a single landscape might combine all kinds of topographical motifs which in reality do not belong together, for example church spires appropriated from various towns. Hercules Seghers even went so far as to situate the houses in Amsterdam's Noorderstraat, which he looked out on from his studio, at the foot of a gigantic cliff (Rotterdam, Museum Boymans-van Beuningen).

Artists venturing into the countryside recorded parts of it by means of relatively accurate sketches (drawing out of doors was common, whereas painting in the open air was exceptional). These sketches served as a point of departure for paintings. While landscape painters sometimes closely followed their sketches, without introducing creative recombinations or changes and thus producing a "faithfully rendered" painting, they more usually relied on their imagination when composing the final work.[38]

This artistic practice concurs with Karel van Mander's emphatic injunction to work "*uyt den gheest*" (from the imagination), as voiced in his *Schilder-boeck* (Book on Painting) of 1604.[39] What is so characteristic is that the results almost always make a natural impression: They are nonexistent landscapes that nevertheless could have existed. Perhaps Seghers, who created the imaginative reconstruction mentioned above, should be counted among the exceptions. On the other hand, there is something so forthright about his depiction that one hardly notices the improbability of the combined motifs. Generally speaking, the seventeenth-century landscape painter working "from the imagination" is entirely credible, just as much so as his colleague, the genre painter, who embellishes his images with naturalistically garbed symbolism.

STILL LIFE

Equally believable is the flower painter who composes the most unlikely bouquets, intimating that all the blooms are fresh and in season, or at least were picked at the same time.[40] The symbolism of the flower still life is akin to that of genre painting, and as such can be called "seemingly realistic," while its form or pictorial expression is actually closer to that of landscape. The very realistic-looking bouquets frequently include flowers that bloom in different seasons and therefore – like the various elements in landscapes – do not strictly speaking belong together. In this genre too, artists seldom painted "from life," but rather after nature once removed: Numerous flower painters consistently used sketches and model books as their point of departure.[41] Consequently, science and art experienced a progressive reciprocal interaction. The herbals and anthologies that appeared with increasing regularity from the mid-sixteenth century (first in Latin, later also in the vernacular) and attested to the development of botany, attracted such unexpected users as painters and engravers from 1600 on. Sometimes these books were specially made for the artists, as was an Antwerp antholo-

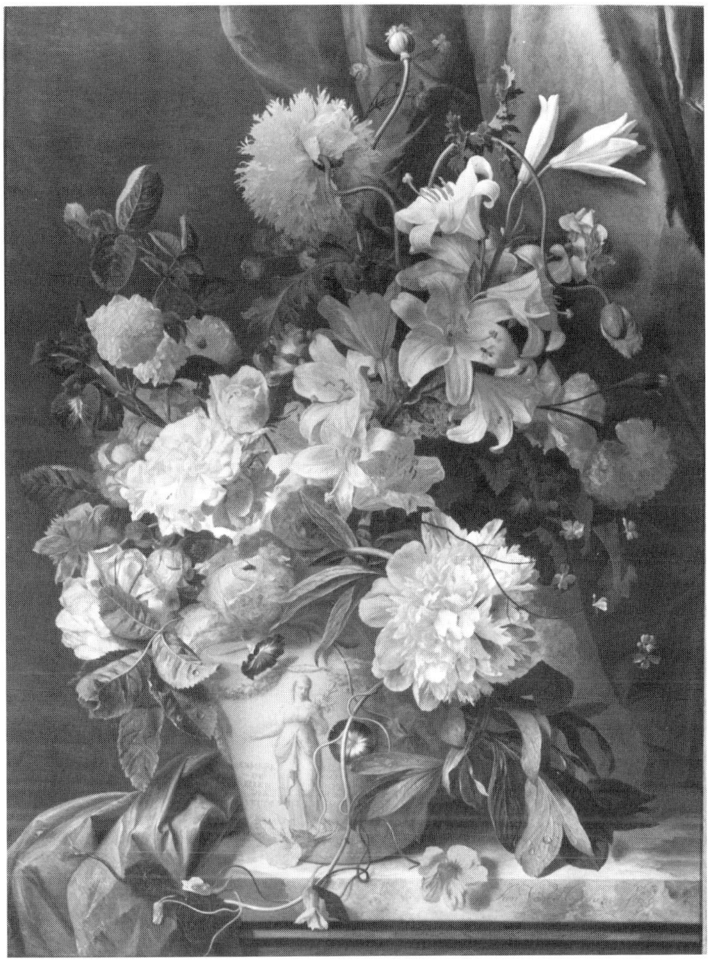

Figure 7. Jan van Huysum, *Flower Still Life* (oil on canvas, 80.5 × 62 cm). Amsterdam, Rijksmuseum (on loan from the city of Amsterdam). Photo: Rijksmuseum Stichting.

gy with illustrations by Adriaen Collaert, "pictoribus, sculptoribus . . . mire utilis et necessarius" (for painters and sculptors . . . wonderfully useful and necessary).[42] The work of Ambrosius Bosschaert, for example, can be considered as an artistic extension of scientific naturalism, for instance in his painting of a flower still life in an open niche (Fig. 6). The incredible precision lavished on every detail is particularly noteworthy.[43]

The incorporation of symbolism in painted flower still lifes was rarely so overt as in the work of Jan van Huysum, who at the beginning of the eighteenth century perpetuated seventeenth-century iconography in his painting of an opulent and varied bouquet (with two kinds of lilies) set in a terracotta vase (Fig. 7). A female figure is depicted on the vase and part of a verse from Matthew 6 can be deciphered: "Consider the lilies of the field; even Solomon in all his glory was not arrayed like one of these." The meaning of these words, underscored by their biblical context, is highly reminiscent of Huygens's pious verse cited above, "The goodness of God is to be seen in every dune's top." Huygens's sentiment is typical of much seventeenth-century thinking, and also conveys the more general idea of nature as divine revelation.

Despite the impression given by this work by Van Huysum, symbolism in seventeenth-century flower pieces is usually cloaked in a realistic disguise, and is in principle no different than that in genre painting. The principal focus is on the awareness of transience.[44] What inscriptions on prints say about flowers is unequivocal in this respect (Fig. 8). In paintings, the (biblical) consideration that flowers, like people, wither – "man's life is like that of a flower" – is usually implicit.[45] This general tendency is often underscored by associations that are embodied in various details, such as a snail and two butterflies included in the work by Bosschaert. Presumably, the snail refers to man's "*aerdtsche ghesintheyt*" (temporal nature) to use Van Mander's words, while the butterfly is an age-old symbol of the soul.[46]

The concept of transience also often informs other types of still lifes. The most obvious of these is the *vanitas* still life, examples of which are the late work by Adriaen Coorte (Rotterdam, Museum Boymans-van Beuningen) and an imposing specimen by David Bailly included here (Fig. 9).[47] It is always difficult to determine the extent to which the *vanitas* concept is applicable to other still lifes lacking such overt attributes as a skull, burnt-out candle or fragile bubbles. If we take literally the text from Ecclesiastes which Bailly included in the lower right corner of his composition: *Vanitas Vanitatum et omnia Vanitas* (Vanity of vanities, all is vanity), then by extension Abraham van Beyeren's sumptuous still life (Toledo, Toledo Museum of Art) should also be viewed in this light. However, the question remains whether Van Beyeren himself maintained such a rigid point of view.

This does not mean, however, that we should expect nothing in the way of moralizing from Van Beyeren. Contemporaries will probably have immediately understood his reason for situating an open pocket-watch amidst the opulent display. It is the artist's way of exhorting those feasting their eyes on these sumptuous delicacies to exercise restraint and moderation. Watches were one of the traditional symbols of moderation.[48] In the Dutch translation of Cesare Ripa's *Iconologia*, a popular manual of allegories, we read that the timepiece is painted "to demonstrate the duty of moderation: which consists of men bridling and curbing the impulses of the heart."[49] Van Beyeren's watch is analogous to the paintings in the background of

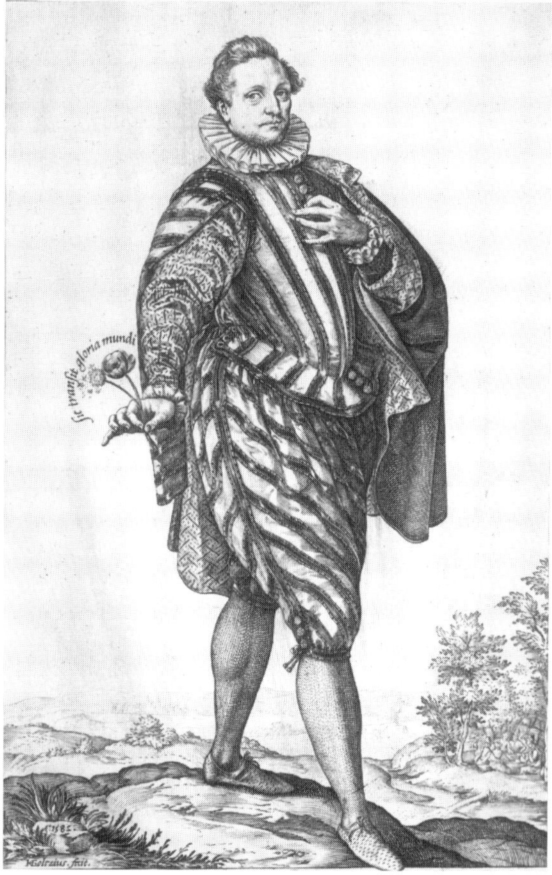

Figure 8. Hendrick Goltzius, *Sic transit gloria mundi* (engraving). Amsterdam, Rijksprentenkabinet. Photo: Rijksmuseum-Stichting.

Elyas's *Merry Company* which, as we have seen, also contain a warning. In its entirety, Van Beyeren's still life is once again a typical example of seeming realism: forms derived from reality, serving to concretize an abstract idea.

PORTRAITURE

An artistic genre in which seeming realism had but a slight chance of prospering was portraiture. After all, the possibility for artistic creativity in this category was fairly limited. Historically, patrons have always stated their demands. The seventeenth-century patron wishing a faithful likeness "from life" expected a high degree of realism from the painter; the one wanting to be idealized, obliged the painter

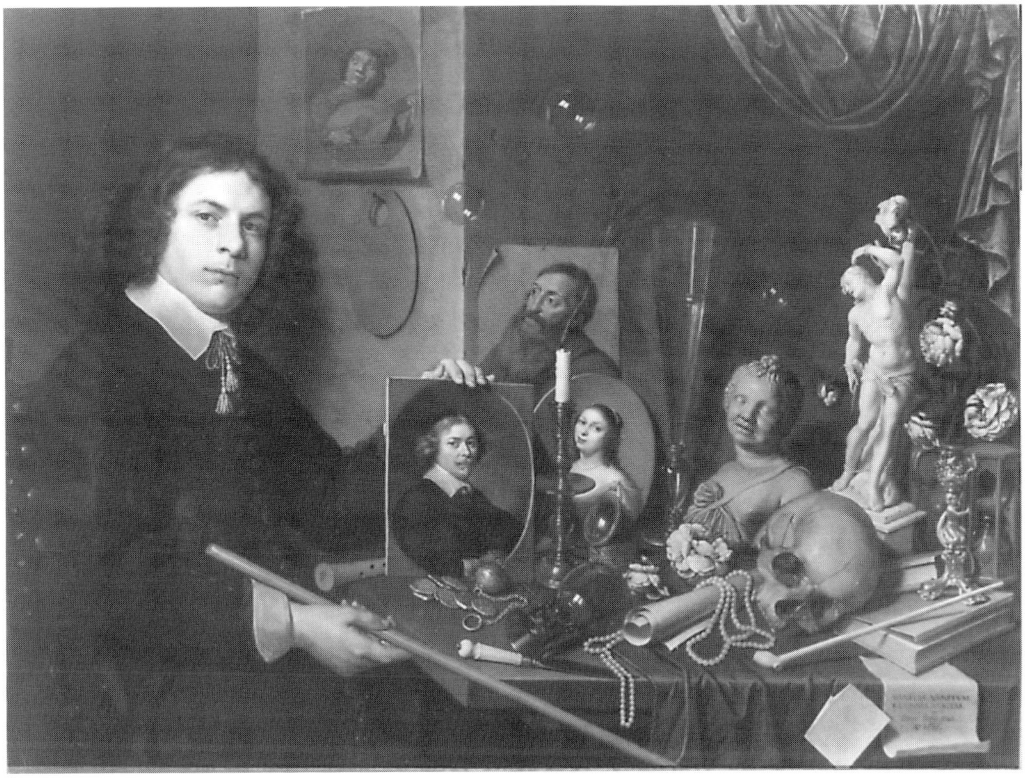

Figure 9. David Bailly, *Vanity Still Life with a Portrait of a Young Painter,* 1651 (oil on panel, 89.5 × 122 cm). Leiden, Stedelijk Museum "De Lakenhal." Photo: museum.

merely to embellish – seemingly, indeed – yet this directive did not encourage artistic creativity, or painting "from the imagination." With great relish, Arnold Houbraken relates how Nicolaes Maes incurred the displeasure of a particular patron:

> A certain Madam (whose name I prefer not to mention), who was by far not the most beautiful [creature] had her portrait painted by him, which he did, faithfully rendering all those pockmarks and wrinkles. Standing up and looking as offended as she might, she said to him: "The Devil, Maes, what for a monstrous *tronie* [face] of me have you painted! I do not wish it to be made like this, the dogs will bark at it if it is carried through the street." Maes, who immediately realized what he had to do, said: "Madam, it is not yet finished," and asked her to sit again: he took a fine fur paintbrush and removed all the pockmarks, painted her cheeks rosy and said, "Madam, it is finished, please have a look at it now." After having looked at it, she said: "Yes, this is the way it should be." She was satisfied that it did not resemble her.[50]

In general, we must assume that seventeenth-century patrons also provided instructions concerning, or even specifically stipulated, possible "bywerck dat bedektlijk iets verklaert" (accessories that explain something covertly). The watches (or clocks), for example, in various still lifes by Van Beyeren, are also encountered in portraits of magistrates as a symbol of their "moderate," that is, judicious administration, and were undoubtedly added at the sitter's behest (Fig. 10).[51] Similarly, the floral symbolism in Frans Hals's portrait of the Massa-Van der Laen couple, and in Bartholomeus

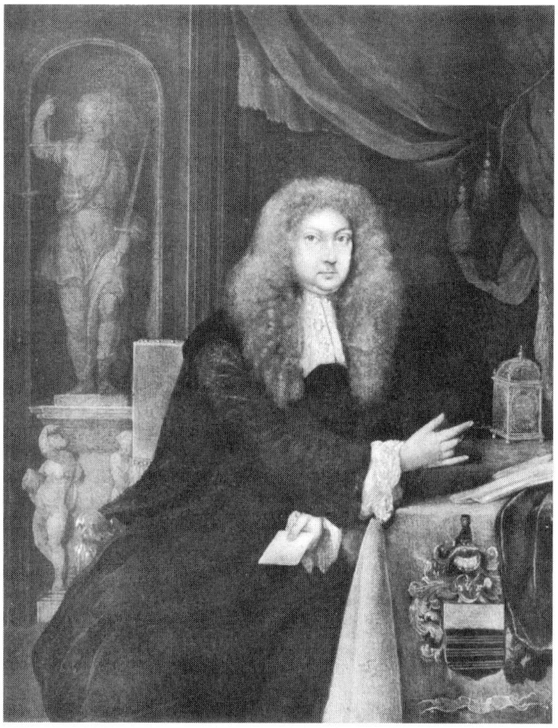

Figure 10. Eglon van der Neer, *Portrait of a Magistrate.* Present location unknown.

van der Helst's portrait of Abraham del Court and his wife (Fig. 11), was most likely included at the request of the sitters.[52] Touching a rose bush, as Del Court's wife does, was a metaphor for love's joys and sorrows, as can be deduced from an illustration in Otto van Veen's *Amorum emblemata* (Emblems of Love; Fig. 12).

The restrictions usually inherent in portrait commissions were responsible for the low esteem in which this genre was held by seventeenth-century artists. At least, this is what we read in the theoretical treatises of the time. Accordingly, portraiture was practised purely for the money and rarely for acclaim, although Gerard de Lairesse does not lose sight of the fact that the artist "in this way [namely, portrait painting] sooner than with the others [artistic genres] would procure a gold medal, hanging on a chain of the same."[53] Portrait painters were "privileged to paint the likeness of the Supreme Prince and in this way amass great riches." However, De Lairesse begins his explanation of "Afbeeldsels of Counterfeitsels" (Portraits or Likenesses) very sceptically: "As concerns this matter [portraiture], it has often seemed strange to me how someone can give up his freedom to become a slave, deviating from the perfection of this noble art to subjugate himself to the imperfections of nature."

This conviction, prevalent around 1700, had already been formulated a century earlier by Karel van Mander, who in his biography of Michiel van Miereveldt calls "imitating from life . . . a side road of the arts."[54] Elsewhere Van Mander indicates that Abraham Bloemaert and his friend Cornelis Cornelisz. van Haarlem, among others, shared his opinion. In this context, he wrote of Bloemaert that "He has no time for making portraits so that his spirit will not be hampered by it." And with regard to Cornelis, we learn that he paints "portraits which

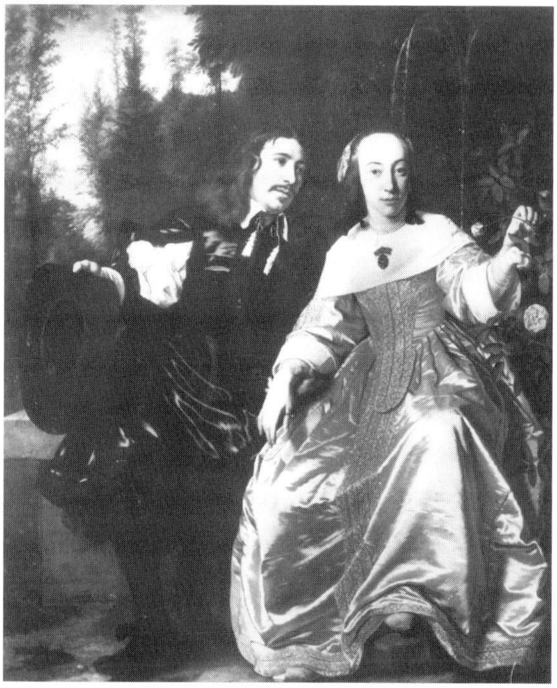

Figure 11. Bartholomeus van der Helst, *Portrait of Abraham del Court and Maria de Keerssegieter,* 1654 (oil on canvas, 172 × 146.5 cm). Rotterdam, Museum Boymans-van Beuningen. Photo: copyright Frequin-Photos, The Hague.

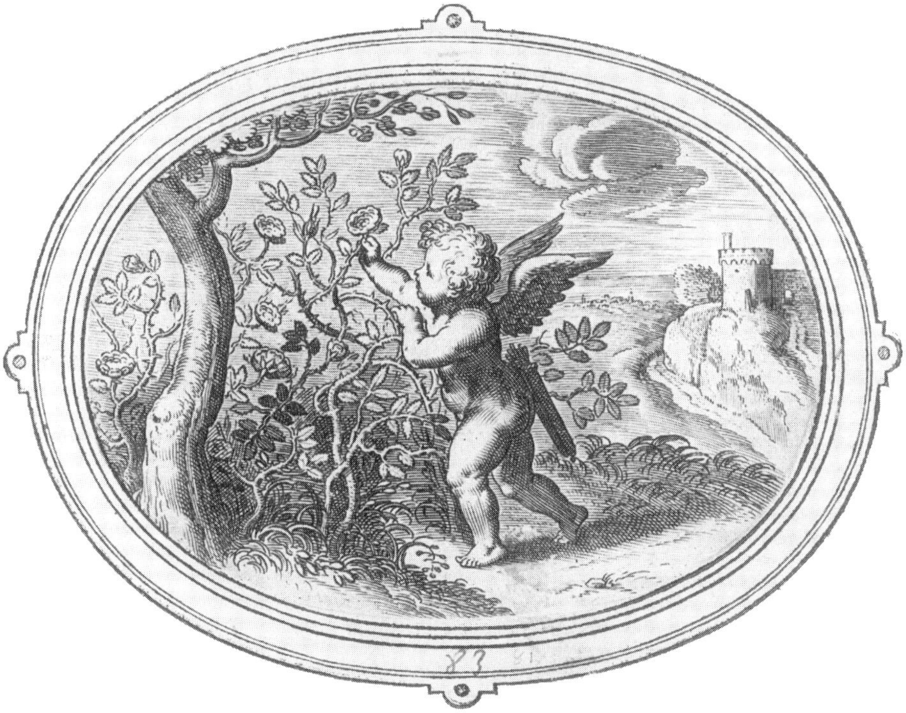

Figure 12. Emblem from Otto van Veen, *Amorum Emblemata*, Antwerp, 1608. Utrecht, UniversiteitsBibliotheek Utrecht. Photo: courtesy UniversiteitsBibliotheek Utrecht.

he does well rather than willingly because he cannot dedicate his talent to such a specialised subject."[55]

Samuel van Hoogstraeten, who ranks the various artistic genres hierarchically, also subscribed to this low opinion of portraiture.[56] Prior to the aforementioned anecdote of the pockmarked lady, Houbraken describes a visit Maes apparently made to Jacob Jordaens in Antwerp during which the two artists derided the art of portrait painting. Upon learning that Maes was a portraitist (Maes admitted this "in a faint voice"), Jordaens blurted out: "*Brother, I pity you, are you one of those martyrs* [italics mine] who reflects on the unpleasant reprimands of your patrons and your slavish submission to their every whim; such painters must often be consoled."[57]

The disparaging view of portraitists that emerges in the contemporary art literature is curiously at odds with the sublime likenesses produced in the pursuit of this art. Should artists such as Rembrandt van Rijn, Hals, Johannes Verspronck, Gerard Ter Borch, and Van der Helst, or even less important ones such as Paulus Bor, have experienced any aversion to their task as they sat before their easel and faced their sitters, no trace whatsoever of this can be detected in their work.

In Hoogstraeten's hierarchy, history painting ranks at the top, while portraiture trails somewhere at the bottom. This relationship approximates that put forth by other Dutch theoreticians of the time as well. The seventeenth century also witnessed the emergence of another type of portraiture, a curious hybrid of portraiture and history painting which has been dubbed "*portrait historié*" (historiated portrait).[58] Individuals, sometimes accompanied by their entire family, had themselves depicted in the guise of biblical, mythological, pastoral, "literary," or actual historical figures. This hybrid category had a special value, for fused with the history piece, the portrait thus acquired a higher status. Greater challenges inherent in the genre tested the artist's creativity, while the sitters were transported out of their mundane existence to more exalted realms.

These portraits sometimes also contain a moralizing aspect. Accordingly, a subject such as the Finding of Moses was used as an image of charity and considered a suitable theme for regentesses of an orphanage to "act out." Dutch ladies also gladly assumed the role of Diana, thus adopting a reference to the proverbial chastity of the goddess. Military figures identified with the heroic David, other men with the virtuous Hercules.[59]

Rembrandt, too, painted various historicizing portraits. Aside from himself, however, they feature only people from his immediate surroundings, for example his mother, Saskia, Hendrickje, and Titus, portrayed as classical or biblical figures.[60] Rembrandt depicted himself as the Prodigal Son in the company of Saskia. In addition to relating the message of the biblical parable, he may also have intended to convey the persistent notion that everyone is in essence a prodigal son.

At the beginning of the 1630s, Rembrandt showed himself as the executioner's assistant at the foot of the cross, a conceit based on the idea that Christ's wounds bleed ceaselessly because man continues to sin.[61] At the end of his life, Rembrandt identified personally with the Apostle Paul. He may have been acting with similar intent when he depicted his son Titus in a monk's habit (Amsterdam, Rijksmuseum). The subject of this portrait has traditionally been identified as Saint Francis, with Titus serving as the model; however it could equally be a representation of Titus in the role of Francis, with a tacit reference to and sympathy for the words and deeds of this saint.

"PROFIT" AND "HONOR"

That the term "history painting" encompassed a broad range of meanings can be deduced solely from the diversity of subject matter within the *portrait historié* genre. In addition to representations of actual and alleged historic events, history painting also included biblical, mythological, and allegorical scenes. Rembrandt was a history painter *par excellence;*[62] Johannes Vermeer a practitioner only in his two allegorical paintings; while Hals was "merely" a portraitist. It should be pointed out that in Holland not every artist was ambitious of becoming a history painter. In fact, countless masters never took a step in that direction, instead concentrating exclusively on the less highly ranked specializations.

Specialization is a striking feature of seventeenth-century Dutch art and only a handful of artists – with Rembrandt again leading the way – tested their skills in several different areas. Selecting a specialization would have involved not only a particular talent for a given genre, but also economic factors. Artists in Holland worked for a large and primarily free market, only rarely receiving commissions from major patrons.[63] Unlike their colleagues in Flanders, Dutch artists could expect very little in the way of patronage from the church and the aristocracy.[64] They depended instead on town councils and wealthy individuals, the latter of whom probably ordered mostly portraits. With respect to the free market, still lifes, landscapes, seascapes and genre pieces were frequently literally sold at the (annual) market and also at *kermissen* (fairs), sometimes at sites specially established by the guild, and of course through art dealers and in the painter's own studio.[65] If we are to believe the scant seventeenth-century reports, Dutch homes – even those of farmers and humble burghers – were filled with paintings.[66] An English traveller, Peter Mundy, related this phenomenon in 1640 as follows:

> As For the art off Painting and the affection off the people to Pictures, I thincke none other goe beeyond them, there having bin in this Country Many excellent Men in thatt Facullty, some att presentt, as Rimbrantt, etts, All in generall striving to adorne their houses, especially the outer or street roome, with costly peeces, Butchers and bakers not much inferiour in their shoppes, which are Fairely sett Forth, yea many tymes blacksmithes, Coblers etts., will have some picture or other by their Forge and in their stalle. Such is the genrall Notion, enclination and delight that these Countrie Native(s) have to Painting.[67]

Specialization generated routine, which led to high production and thus – with a patently acquisitive public – to significant sales. Many painters worked with assistants and apprentices in an assembly line fashion, producing endless variations of a number of more or less fixed subjects. In his verse, Jeremias de Decker optimistically noted that: "O, Lady Painting . . . more (it seems) devoted to honor than profit, / You will not have been of meagre benefit to your followers."[68] Still, it would be wrong to conclude that painting was a lucrative occupation: In general, the economic position of a large number of painters was anything but favorable.[69]

Whether the profession of painting garnered esteem – the "honor" mentioned by De Decker – is another matter. From a sociological aspect we are poorly informed on this point. While some seventeenth-century art theoreticians did, indeed, comment positively on the contemporary regard for painters, once again some reservation is justified.[70] As a case in point, Rembrandt, a miller's son, strove to improve his standing – something that was considered respectable in his own time – and largely succeeded in achieving his objective. His success, however, was not solely based on his artistic skills. His climb up the social ladder was greatly facilitated by his marriage to a burgomaster's daughter, the fact that he lived in an elegant house and, moreover, that he had assembled an encyclopedic collection of art and curiosities – an elitist hobby at the time.[71] This encyclopedic collection, which has been erroneously discredited and perceived as a jumble of old odds and ends, served in Rembrandt's day as evidence of *curiositas*, or universal interest. Someone preoccupied with amassing such a collection was considered a "gentleman-virtuoso," that is, a financially independent man of standing deeply immersed in the arts and sciences.

Incidentally, Rembrandt's Flemish counterpart, Peter Paul Rubens, conducted his life on an even more extravagant scale. This distinguished "gentleman among painters" was a courtier, scholar and diplomat. These credentials notwithstanding, he was deemed unsuitable for an ambassadorship in London because it was considered unacceptable for someone who earned his living by working with his hands to assume the position of Minister of the King.[72] Writing to his friend Peiresc, Rubens explained his reason for not choosing a noble woman for his second wife, as so many had suggested he do, but instead one "who would not blush when I pick up my paint brushes."[73] At the very least, we can conclude from these two examples that certain (social) restrictions applied to even the most prominent seventeenth-century artists in the Netherlands. Rembrandt won esteem, albeit only partly through his artistic achievements, and the highly respected Rubens was ultimately prevented from attaining an even higher social level precisely because he was a painter.

While these summary notes on Rembrandt and Rubens give us some insight into the status and the social appreciation of artists, two paintings by Hendrick Goltzius reveal how the artist himself attempted to determine, enhance and defend his position in society while also more generally advancing the status of the profession. I will discuss these depictions of *Minerva* and *Mercury* here in detail because they illustrate concerns that *mutatis mutandis* played a role throughout the entire seventeenth century (Figs. 13 and 14).[74]

In these works painted in Haarlem in 1611, Goltzius represented the ancient gods as protectors of the arts: Minerva embodies the scholarly, theoretical aspect, and Mercury the actual practice of painting. The helmeted and otherwise nude Minerva holds a lance in her right hand and leans on the Medusa shield with her left arm. On the ground lie several books that, like the goddess's standard attribute – the owl – allude to her wisdom. Juxtaposed with this is King Midas with the ears of an ass, standing behind her, who since antiquity had served as *the* symbol of stupidity and ignorance. In this instance, at least this is how I interpret it, Goltzius portrayed a contemporary person in the guise of Midas – as a negative *portrait historié* if you will. The vista at the left affords a glimpse of part of the Colosseum, a reminder of Goltzius's visit to Rome twenty years earlier, but more specifically a reference to Van Mander's credo that a good painter should study the remains of antiquity in Italy.[75] Ruins, possibly remnants of the Forum Romanum, also fill the background of Minerva's pendant.

Mercury as the patron of painters was already a somewhat old-fashioned figure in Goltzius's time.

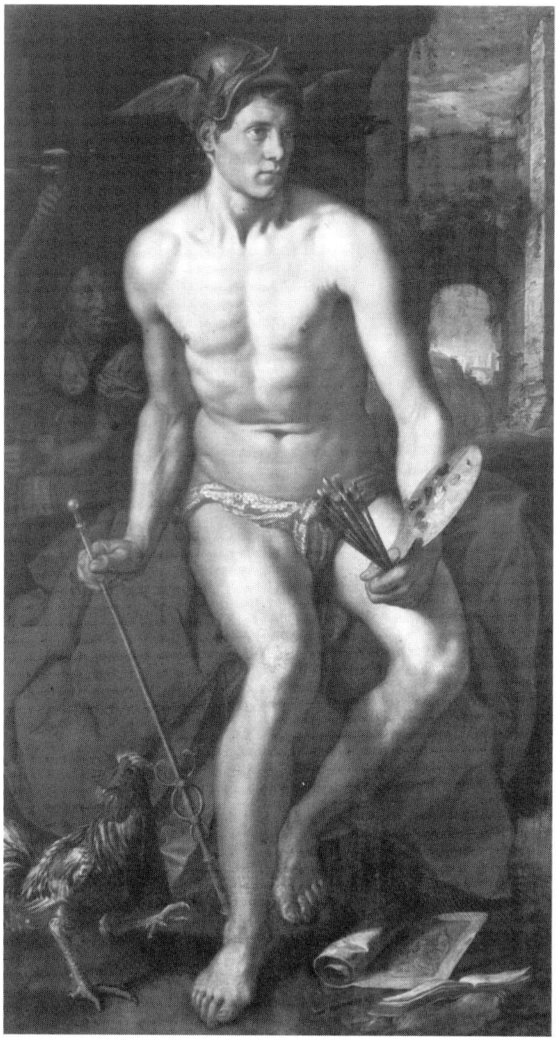

Figure 13. Hendrick Goltzius, *Mercury*, 1611 (oil on canvas, 214 × 120 cm). The Hague, Mauritshuis, on loan to Haarlem, Frans HalsMuseum. Photo: A. Dingjan, The Hague.

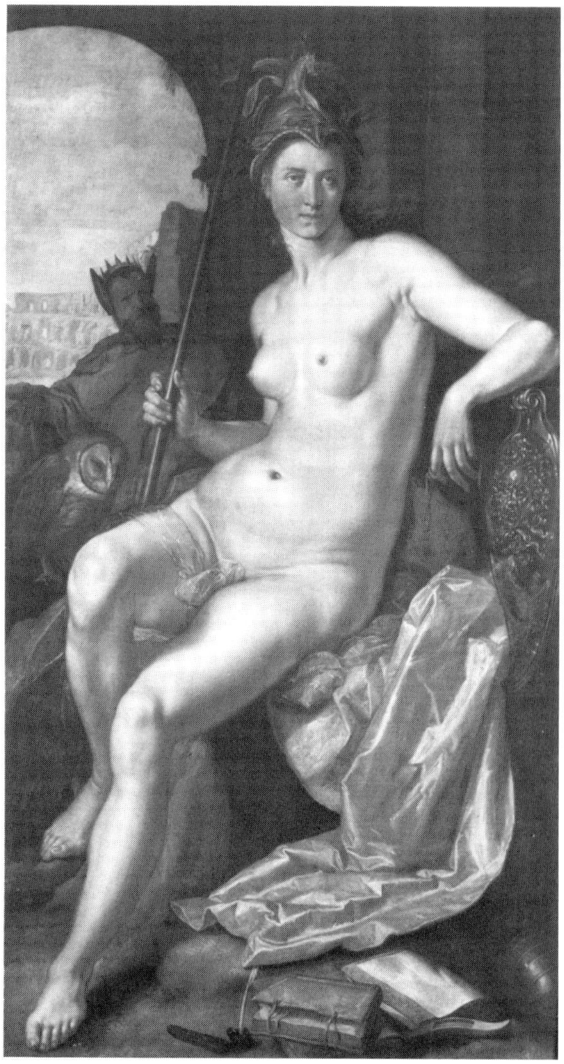

Figure 14. Hendrick Goltzius, *Minerva* (oil on canvas, 214 × 120 cm). The Hague, Mauritshuis, on loan to Haarlem, Frans HalsMuseum. Photo: A. Dingjan, The Hague.

He was a medieval invention derived from the astrological relationship drawn between painters, sculptors, and architects on the one hand, and Mercury on the other. Artists were expected to work under this astrological sign and accordingly were sometimes called the "children of Mercury."[76] Goltzius appears to have taken the facial features of the young god from a living model, as he did for Midas. Virtually nude save for a loincloth and a winged and wreathed helmet, Mercury holds a palette and several brushes in his left hand and the traditional caduceus, simultaneously serving as maulstick, in his right. The latter attribute in particular stresses Mercury's role here as the personification of painting. According to Goltzius's friend Van Mander, the equally animated rooster in the left foreground indicates that Mercury was also the "God of Commerce / profit / and of almost all the arts / where People are

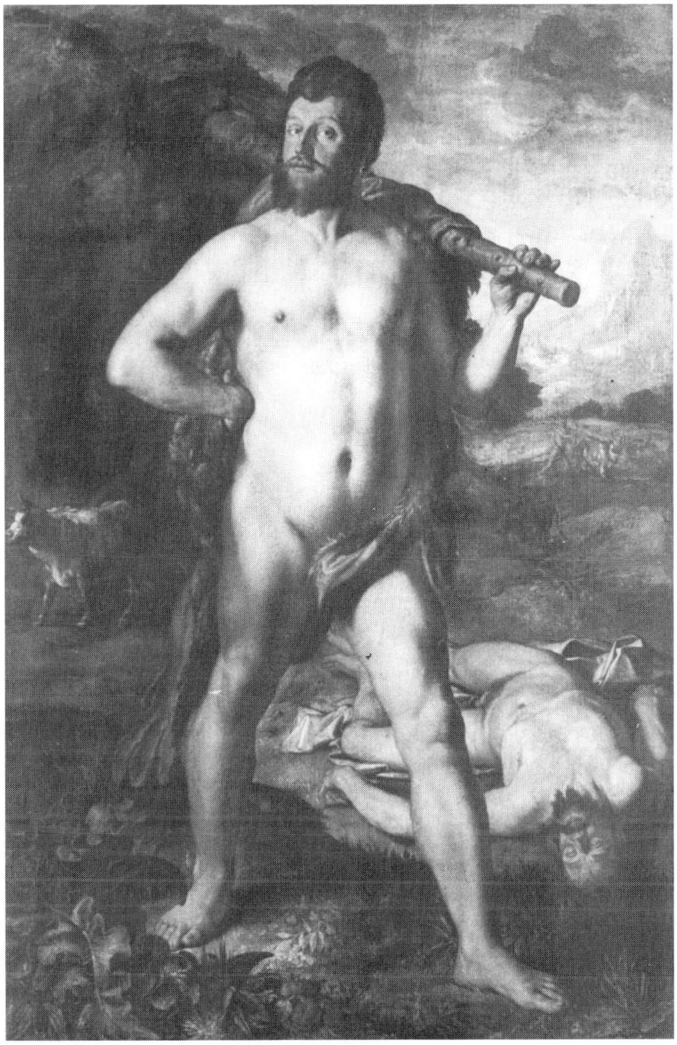

Figure 15. Hendrick Goltzius, *Hercules and Cacus,* 1613 (oil on canvas, 207 × 142.5 cm). The Hague, Mauritshuis, on loan to Haarlem, Frans HalsMuseum. Photo: A. Dingjan, The Hague.

diligent and alert / like the Rooster / which is considered the symbol of vigilance."[77] Behind Mercury stands an old woman sticking out an exceptionally long tongue and holding a magpie and a rattle. She personifies Slander as well as Envy or Jealousy, and as such is the traditional obstacle of painting.[78] A square, an open book and a partially rolled-up drawing lie at Mercury's feet.

Jealousy is also featured in this drawing. Its subject, to the extent that it is visible, is the *Calumny of Apelles,* a classical theme that regained currency in the fifteenth century and is discussed at length by Van Mander in his biography of this "Prince of Painters."[79] While at the court of King Ptolemy, the legendary Greek painter Apelles incited the jealousy of the painter Antiphilus who accused him of treason. Enraged, the king threatened Apelles with death. Fortunately, his innocence was proven; as compensation he was given a hundred gold talents and Antiphilus became his slave. Not satisfied, Apelles avenged himself by painting a complicated allegory, the *Calumnia,* or false accusation, in which both the king and Antiphilus are cast in sinister roles. "Thus Apelles," Van Mander wrote, "very ingeniously made known his adventure. And this work was greatly appreciated for the innocence, the virtue and the art of the master as well as for the truly beautiful invention *which can serve as an exam-*

ple of a happy outcome to those who are still subject to the people's false slander [italics mine]."[80] Van Mander thus advised painters who fell prey to gossip to defend themselves by painting this classical subject. Samuel van Hoogstraeten would later speak of "satirical paintings" and "painters' exercises in revenge."[81]

We cannot entirely exclude the possibility that the *Minerva* and *Mercury* were painted on commission. Yet even if this were the case, the patron at the very least must have had a personal interest in the status of painting as well as in Goltzius's view on the matter. That the artist wished to express himself programmatically, if not polemically, is beyond doubt. The "bijwerck" (accessory) speaks for itself; in this respect the *Calumny of Apelles*, recommended by Van Mander for "modern" use, is decisive. Moreover, Goltzius supplemented the two pendants in 1613 with a painting of *Hercules and Cacus*, a subject, as I will attempt to demonstrate, he used to bolster the "statement" he had made two years earlier (Fig. 15).

Given that Hercules's features, like those of Mercury, are markedly individualistic, we are again most likely dealing with a *portrait historié*. However, Goltzius's primary interest here is not portraiture, but patronage of the arts, which had been offered by artists not only to real gods, but also to deified heroes such as Hercules.[82] Hercules protected the arts particularly in his capacity as *Virtus*, the personification of Virtue. His slain opponent, Cacus – the monstrous thief of his cattle – functions as an emblem of Evil, who has met his sad demise at the hands of Virtue. For a more detailed "instructive explanation of Cacus," Goltzius could once again turn to his friend Van Mander, who metaphorically compares the cattle thief to the "false and misleading intimation / or lie / which thievishly and surreptitiously steals the obedient herd of virtue." Concluding the moral, Van Mander solemnly states: "His [Cacus'] injustice having become known, it cannot uphold itself in the presence of his disgrace, and the false, evil-fostering thoughts / vanish like the owls of the night."[83]

Various seventeenth- and eighteenth-century representations are known in which ancient gods and heroes – especially Minerva and Saturn, but also Hercules and occasionally Mercury – actively battle the enemies of art, usually Envy and Ignorance. The origins of these works are generally related to disputes between "academic" painters and guild members, or between artists and lesser craftsmen.[84]

Given this tradition, it is possible that Goltzius's representations, whether or not they were commissioned, were connected to a conflict taking place at the time within the extremely discriminatory St. Luke's Guild of Haarlem.[85] The ignorant King Midas, the old hag representing Malicious Gossip, and Cacus personifying "false, evil-fostering thoughts," may allude to adversaries, for example the craftsmen belonging to the "lower echelons" of the guild, whom such eminent and learned artists as Van Mander, Cornelis Cornelisz, and Goltzius may well have disdained. In the Haarlem guild, the painters wielded the proverbial sceptre, and the measures they introduced in 1590 and 1631 are clear proof of the separation they were so anxious to maintain between their own profession and the tin workers, slaters and plumbers, as well as book printers and gold and silver smiths who were members of the guild as well – professions, incidentally, that were also under the "protection" of Mercury in the Middle Ages.[86] However, it is more likely that with his gods and later Hercules, Goltzius, on behalf of his profession, a possible patron, and even himself, was addressing "art haters" in general. Famous as an engraver, he was not exceptionally successful as a painter, and we know, moreover, that he had enemies and critics towards the end of his life.[87] "Art haters" included those who had insufficient regard for art and even scorned it, as well as those who contested the status of its makers, who since the Renaissance had struggled valiantly to defend their position. Werner van den Valckert makes explicit reference to this in the motto "Cunst heeft haters" (Art has haters), which he included in a drawing of 1618 depicting a satyr roughly grabbing a nude woman, the personification of painting.[88] These words could just as easily be applied to Goltzius's painting of *Mercury*. In the foreword to his *Gulden cabinet* (Golden Cabinet; 1661), the artist's biographer Cornelis de Bie touches on the same points: "I know quite well, gracious READER, that many ... will eschew praising the ART OF PAINTING, because many people are the enemy of this art and are not pleased to hear someone speak its praise, even envying it because of an innate sense of pride, I shall console myself by thinking of the Latin proverb: *Ars nullum habet inimicum nisi ignorantem*, according to which only the ignorant are the enemies of Art."[89] This proverb – and we now enter the field of literature – was used by the Amsterdam poet Jan Harmensz. Krul in 1634 as a caption for a book illustration within the context of a controversy with other literati.[90] While the exact subject of this engraving is not particularly relevant here, it is useful to note that both Minerva and Mercury are among the cast of characters and, moreover, that Minerva is being trampled by a man riding a donkey ("An Enemy of Art").

Krul's polemical style mirrors that of Theodore Rodenburgh whom he greatly admired, and who in 1619 published the *Eglentiers poëtens borst-weringh* (The Eglentier [=Eglantine: an Amsterdam rhetoricians' group] Poets' Rampart), an elaborate defense of poetry against the "zuffighe Poëten-verachters" (sulking despisers of Poets). Rodenburgh drew inspiration from, and even largely copied Sir Philip Sidney's *Defence of Poesy* (1595), probably the most famous in a long series of defenses written in Europe from the fifteenth century on.[91]

Rodenburgh and Krul were by no means the only individuals in the Netherlands in the seventeenth century to defend themselves against critics advancing both moral and aesthetic objections to poetry.[92] It is worth noting here that the arguments made by the champions of poetry are virtually identical to those of the defenders of painting. Not coincidentally, Cornelis de Bie, in advocating the cause of the visual arts, employed the same disdainful adage as the poet-polemicist Jan Krul.

If we translate Goltzius's *Minerva* into words, as this very "literary" artist invites us to do, we draw the same conclusion: Ignorance is an enemy of art. For Goltzius, however, ignorance is not the only enemy, as the Latin proverb cited above implies. The two other paintings demonstrate that mali-

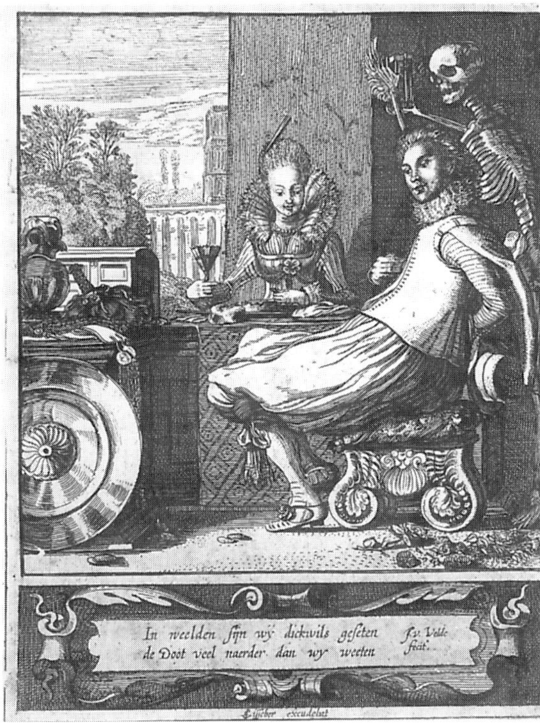

Figure 16. Jan van de Velde, *Death Surprising a Man and a Woman* (engraving). Amsterdam, Rijksprentenkabinet. Photo: Rijksmuseum-Stichting.

cious gossip and lies (the "duysterlievende valsche meeningen") are no less malevolent than ignorance. Regardless of whom Goltzius specifically opposed, we can say that he has left us an image in the guise of Minerva, Mercury and Hercules, of a "painters' rampart," to paraphrase Rodenburgh, from the beginning of the seventeenth century.

This lengthy digression on Goltzius should not create the impression that every seventeenth-century painting prompts similarly far-reaching considerations. I mentioned earlier that this is not the case, and in this respect it could be added that the "specific gravity" of the meaning of a representation differs from painting to painting. Since the nineteenth century, particularly under the influence of the doctrine of art for art's sake and Impressionism, a certain distrust of so-called literary art and, indeed, an even greater distrust of any analysis of it have arisen in certain circles based on the fallacious insight that interpretation spoils beauty.

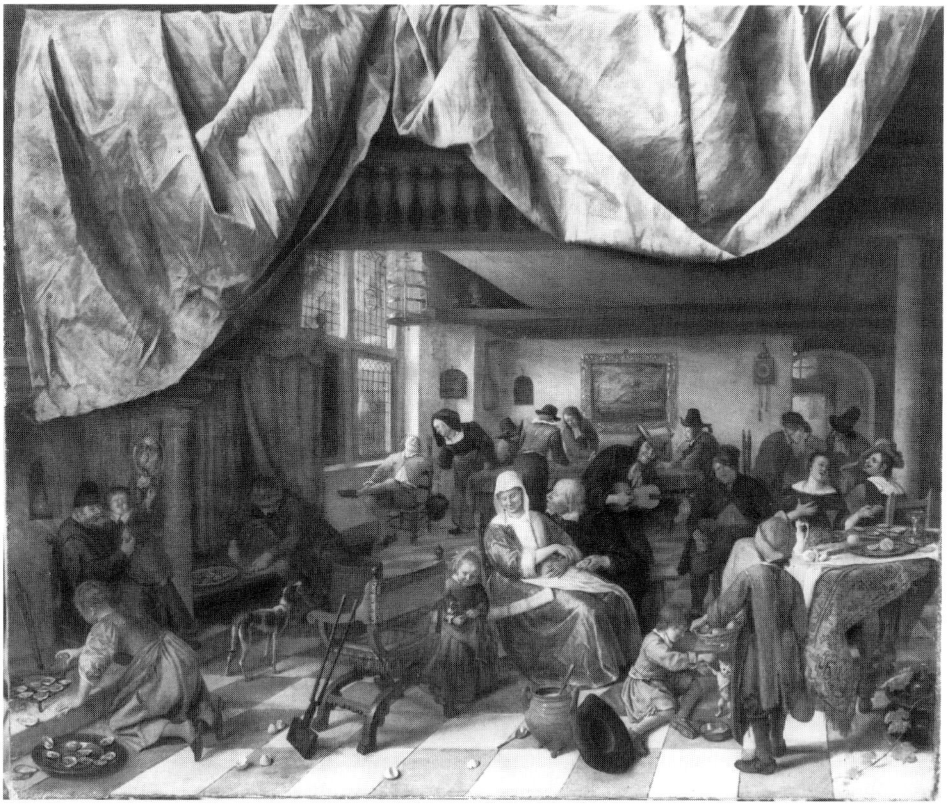

Figure 17. Jan Steen, *The So-Called Brewery of Jan Steen* (oil on canvas, 68.2 × 82 cm). The Hague, Mauritshuis. Photo: A. Dingjan, The Hague.

It should be clear that I do not share this distrust. On the other hand, I am not suggesting that "literary" components – to keep using this term – might somehow serve to elevate the artistic quality of a painting. Nor do they decrease the quality: There is absolutely no direct relationship between quality and meaning. We can say, however, that a beautifully executed painting with impressive subject matter provides two levels of *ogenlust* (visual pleasure): It not only satisfies the viewer aesthetically but also intellectually.

The rather fuzzy and difficult to define term "quality" need not be discussed further here given that it is sufficiently addressed by the exhibition. The criterion informing the selection of works for *Rembrandt en zijn tijd* (Rembrandt and His Time) was quality, a typically twentieth-century point of departure. Not that quality was unappreciated in the seventeenth century – in fact it was highly regarded – but, once again, such factors as moralization, disguise and symbolism played an equally important role. It seemed useful to analyze and expose precisely these aspects by means of a "historical" approach, thus complementing the aesthetic premise on which the exhibition was founded. In the second part of this article, I will discuss a selection of paintings with intriguing features, the significance of which will not be readily apparent to most people.

II

As mentioned earlier, notions of love and death permeate seventeenth-century iconography. In this part of the article I will address these two themes to the exclusion of others, both for the sake of clarity, but especially because love and transience played

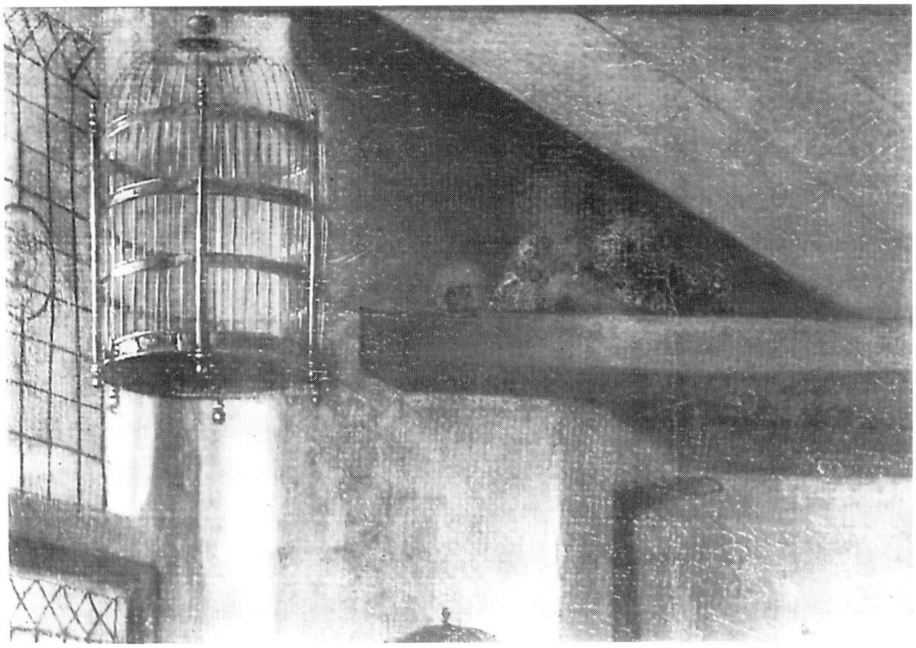

Figure 17a. Detail of Figure 17.

such a dominant role in the art of this period. These, like all other themes in the seventeenth century, were integrated into works of art in a variety of ways: as the central focus, as subsidiary themes, or by means of a casual allusion, to mention just three possibilities on a descending scale of importance. Love and death – sometimes only vague allusions to love and death – could, moreover, be combined in one image. Given the underlying moralism (both in literature and in art), it is probably more accurate to say that love, eroticism, and ultimately life in general fell under death's shadow.

A print by Jan van de Velde illustrates this point: A young man and a girl surrounded by a wealth of worldly goods are surprised by Death while enjoying a meal in the open air (Fig. 16). Embroidering on a centuries-old tradition, the inscription to this scene warns that: "We are oft-times seated amidst luxury / with Death far closer than we know." This theme is the subject of numerous seventeenth-century drawings and prints. In paintings of the time, however, explicit personifications of Death are rare (although they can be found in works by Leonaert Bramer, among others). Painters wishing to include Death generally did so in a more subtle and indirect fashion. They preferred to keep up the appearance of realism, eschewing nonexistent phenomena such as walking skeletons. Human skulls, on the other hand, were sanctioned and were frequently included in sixteenth-century portraits and seventeenth-century still lifes, though only occasionally in seventeenth-century portraits and genre scenes.[93] Jan Steen ingeniously incorporated this attribute in his so-called *Brewery* from the end of the 1660s (Fig. 17). A skull is placed next to a boy lying in the loft of the house, blowing soap bubbles as he looks down at merrymakers intent on pursuing more worldly concerns (Fig. 17a).[94] Like many before him, Steen gave pictorial form to the standard expression *homo bulla* (man is as [fragile] as a soap bubble).[95] A serious warning indeed! As the reader will remember, Isack Elyas had the same idea in mind when he included the two small paintings behind his merry company.

Love (or *minne*, as this type of frivolousness would have been referred to in the seventeenth century)[96] is represented in Steen's lively scene by the matchmaker conducting her business in the left background, the woman holding an oyster and singing accompanied by the lute player at the right,[97] and by the old man offering an oyster to the woman seated next to him in the middle. It should be noted that, as both Cats and Van Beverwijck point out, oysters were considered an aphrodisiac at the time.

In his *Houwelyck* (Marriage) Cats denounces the use of "minne-kruyden," or love herbs, as being "moes van Bever-geyl . . . door kitsigh netel-zaet geroert in Spaensche pap, door artisocke-mergh, en siltigh oester-sap . . ." (beaver scent [that is, "castor oil"] . . . combined with fiery nettle seed in a potage of Spanish fly, with artichoke flesh and briny oyster juice . . .). Van Beverijck reports that oysters "appetijt verwecken, en lust om te eten, en by te slapen, 't welck alle beyde de lustighe en delicate luyden wel aenstaet" (whet the appetite, and the desire to eat and to have intercourse, both of which appeal greatly to lusty and delicate people). And Ripa mentions that Pliny associated the oyster with Touch, generally deemed the most ignoble of the senses, which in turn was linked to the libido.[98] In Jan Steen's *Brewery*, entire platters of oysters are being prepared for consumption.[99] In some of his other works as well (and in paintings by Metsu and the Van Mieris family), this delicacy must be understood as a reference to eroticism.

The bubble blower who mocks the vanity of human endeavors appears in various guises in the seventeenth century. Another typical example of seeming realism is the motif of children playing with or blowing up the bladder of a cow or pig. Generally, it is incorporated into scenes of people butchering a freshly slaughtered animal. This subject had been part of the standard artistic repertoire in the Northern and Southern Netherlands since the sixteenth century.[100] Isack van Ostade is one of the artists who depicted this subject on numerous occasions. For example, his 1645 composition set in a stable shows a group of children with a bladder standing in front of a peasant and his wife at work, and at the left, a disemboweled pig stretched on a rack (Fig. 18).

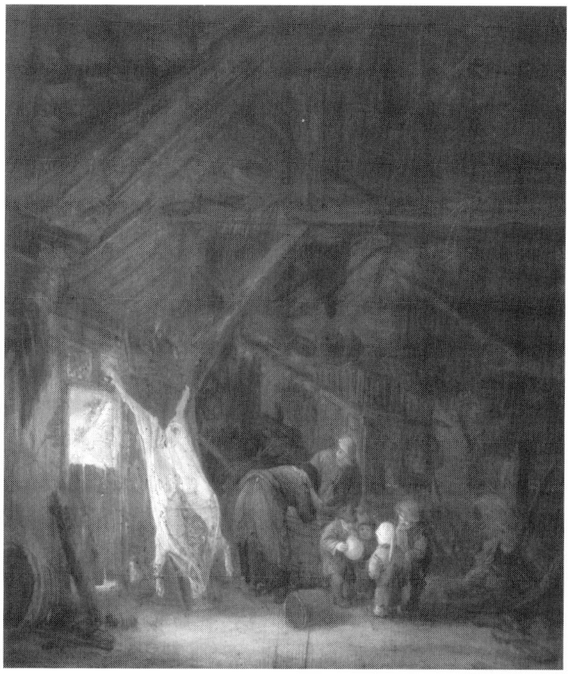

Figure 18. Isack van Ostade, *The Slaughtered Pig*, 1645 (oil on panel, 57 × 31 cm). Lille, Musée des Beaux-Arts de Lille. Photo: museum.

There can be no doubt that the significance of a child with a cow's or pig's bladder is equivalent to *homo bulla*, the boy with water or soap bubbles.[101] On this topic, popular writers such as Cats and Jan Luiken ("Wat is de Waereld, die het ziet? Een Blaas vol wind en anders niet:" What is the world that we behold? No more than a bladder full of wind) provide clear information both in image and word.[102] While scenes of slaughtered animals thus acquire a hint of *vanitas* through the presence of the child with the "bladder full of wind," in and of itself the slaughtered creature, which is always the focus of these compositions (and emphasized by the lighting), was an image of death in general. This symbolism recurs, though in a far more explicitly eschatological form, in a verse accompanying an illustration of November (the slaughtering month), in the *Groote comptoir almanach* (Large Office Almanach) of 1667 (Fig. 19).[103] Given that almanacs were the epitome of popular reading and were sold by street vendors, they are a "statistically" very useful source.[104] The verse in question reads as follows:

> Thee who for thy pleasure
> Ox and swine and calf doth slaughter;
> Ponder how on the day of reckoning
> You will face God's judgment.[105]

The primitive woodcut contains the same key elements as Isack van Ostade's painting: a slaughtered pig, a boy blowing up a bladder, and people – in this case women – butchering the meat. In my opinion, Van Ostade's picture must be seen as embodying the same *memento mori* connotations as the woodcut. This also applies to other representations of slaughtered animals, including the two famous versions by Rembrandt.[106] In essence, the "message" contained in these works is identical to the moralizing meaning expressed in other artistic genres, for example *vanitas* still lifes.

Esaias van de Velde's *Outdoor Party* of 1614 (Fig. 20) contains a potential reference to transience in the form of the small bone lying next to several playing cards in the middle foreground. Should this be the case – and at this juncture I am assuming it is – the tenor of this representation coincides with that of the aforementioned print by Esaias's cousin, Jan van de Velde (Fig. 16). Perpetuating a centuries-old tradition, the accompanying inscription warns us that: "We are oft-times seated amidst luxury / with Death far closer than we know." However, this sort of *Outdoor Party* (Esaias painted a series of them) is also closely allied to other subjects. Its roots lie in sixteenth-century iconography, specifically in themes such as *The Banquet of the Gods*, *Mankind Awaiting the Last Judgement* and, above all, *The Feast of the Prodigal Son*, which was as popular in the first half of the seventeenth century as it had been in the sixteenth century.[107] That the behavior of Esaias's merry company is not beyond reproach is indicated by the playing cards, about which contemporary literature rarely had anything good to say. Furthermore, the representation is "tainted" by the matchmaker in the left corner who is attempting to win the favor of one of the dinner guests, as well as the woman standing in the center of the composition flaunting a feather fan.

In a context like this, a feather headdress frequently implies reprehensible behavior. Peacock feathers were commonly used to indicate pride, while feathers in general alluded to transience and eroticism. For example, in the first half of the sixteenth century, Cornelis Anthonisz. of Amsterdam placed a large black feather in the hand of his personification of Unchastity, something Frans van Mieris the Elder would also do later in his representation of a coquettish girl with a black veil and a daring *décolletage* (Basel, Öffentliche Kunstsammlung), perhaps with the same intention (leaving aside here the degree of sublimation).[108] Finally, in Cats we encounter a lady as extravagantly outfitted as the one in Esaias's *Outdoor Party*, also holding a feather fan (with more feathers adorning her head),

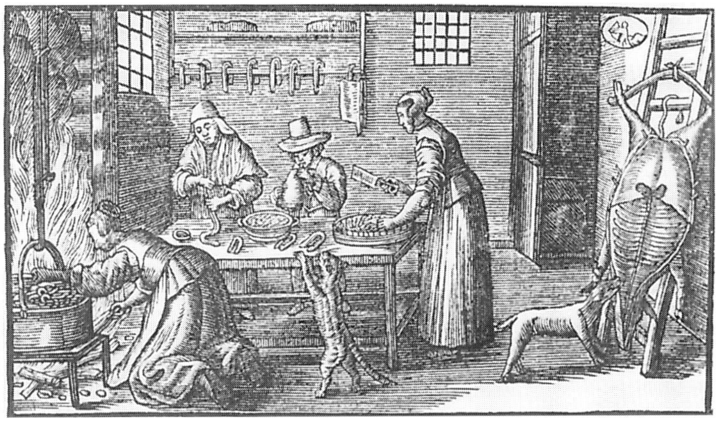

Figure 19. Illustration from Anon., *Groote comptoir almanach*, Amsterdam and Hoorn 1667. Amsterdam, UniversiteitsBibliotheek Amsterdam. Photo: courtesy Universiteits-Bibliotheek Amsterdam.

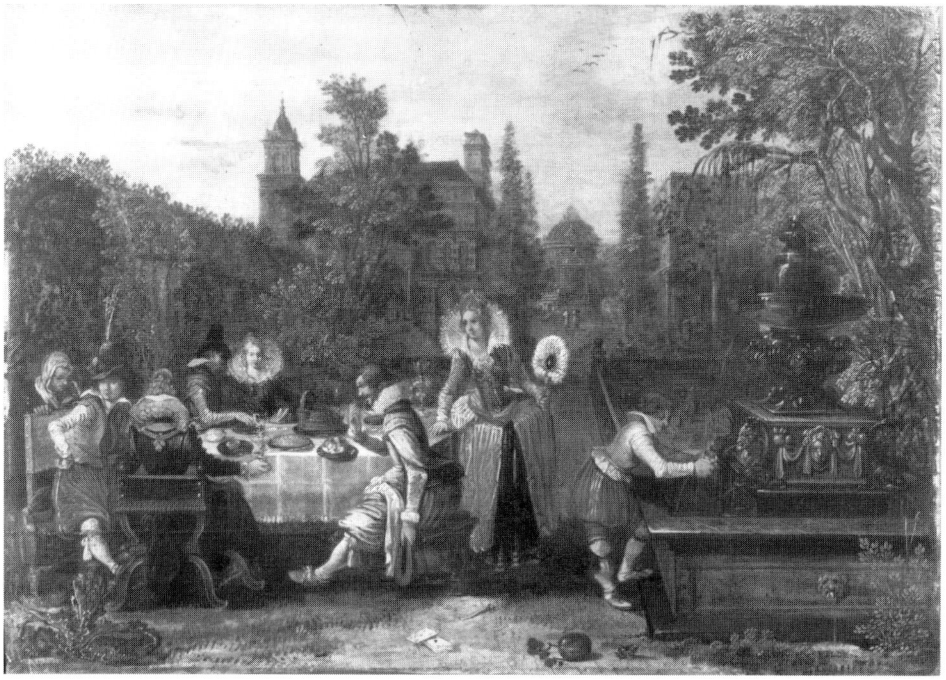

Figure 20. Esaias van de Velde, *Outdoor Party*, 1614 (oil on panel, 28.5 × 40 cm). The Hague, Mauritshuis. Photo: A. Dingjan, The Hague.

and accompanied by a disgusting pig! Cats makes clear that we need entertain no illusions about her, and the motto accompanying the picture apprises us that "When lewd women are beautiful / That's called jewels on a swine." In the verses that follow he describes in detail just what kind of "a silly woman, slattern, a true slut" this "lady" in fact is.[109]

This analysis of the *Brewery* by Jan Steen, the *Slaughtered Pig* by Van Ostade and the *Outdoor Party* by Esaias van de Velde has revealed that regardless of how unlikely this may seem initially, these paintings are permeated with a certain Christian morality. Naturally, one need not look for such moralization in every work of art. In many instances, the moral is literally tucked away in the dimmest corner, as in Steen's loft; and sometimes it is doubtful whether any moralizing per se has even been incorporated. However, a genre painting without any ostensible layers of meaning should not be excluded from discussion.

We should also remember that "mute poetry" as a synonym for a painting was not an entirely unfounded cliché.[110] In the seventeenth century, people were seldom at a loss to come up with an anecdote or joke, even if it was nothing more or less than a clever allusion or paraphrasing of the subject at hand. However, it is precisely the *bijwerk*, that minimal addition, which makes us, who are so much better at verbalizing than "empathizing," fail to notice certain essential parts of the puzzle.

Fortunately, Jan Steen did not make matters too difficult for following generations. The meaning of his *Doctor's Visit* (Fig. 21) is presented as a riddle, as it were, by means of the piece of paper on the floor of the room in which the scene transpires: "Hyr baet geen medisijn, waar het is soete pijn" (No medicine can cure her, as it is a sweet pain). In other words, the girl lying in bed is lovesick, that is, pregnant. Other details also allude to this state of affairs, including the statue of Cupid above the door and the painting of an amorous (mythological?) couple on the wall. Steen painted numerous variations of this theme, always including the doctor garbed in what was then considered clownish, old-fashioned clothing; a stat-

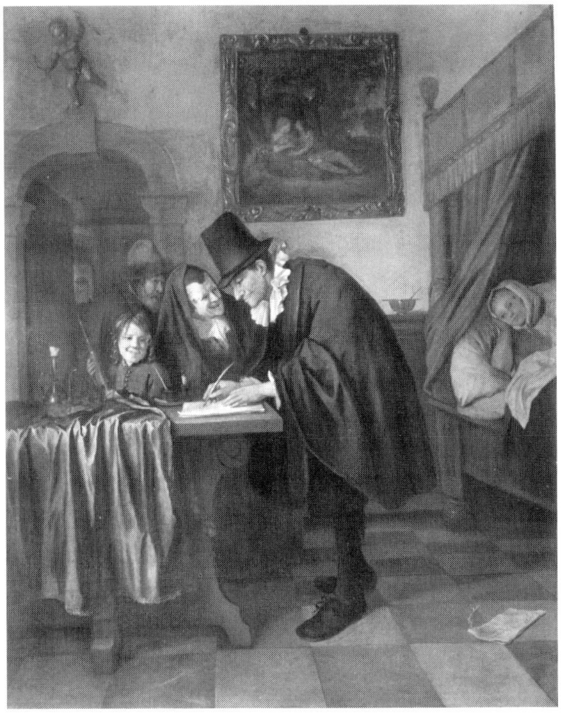

Figure 21. Jan Steen, *The Doctor's Visit* (oil on panel, 61 × 49.5 cm). Rotterdam, Stichting Willem van der Vorm, Museum Boymans-Van Beuningen. Photo: copyright Frequin-Photos, The Hague.

ue of Cupid; as well as the aforementioned painting; and other meaningful elements.[111] No matter how charged these references may seem, Steen always creates the impression of having captured reality with photographic fidelity. In contrast, it is noteworthy that in Gesina ter Borch's drawn version of a lovesick girl (Fig. 22), Cupid is cast as a living figure (as was Death in other representations).[112] This is something which, to my knowledge, Steen never did. However, in one of his paintings he did assign the role of Cupid to a small boy playing with arrows on the floor of the room where the lovesick girl is being examined by the doctor.[113]

Erotic jokes and allusions are standard features of Steen's work, whether or not he counteracts them with an admonitory detail, such as the bubble blower in the *Brewery*. In this regard, Steen was certainly no exception. These witticisms, which were later – in so far as they were still understood – dismissed by more demure generations as coarse and scabrous, should be seen in the context of the seventeenth-century mentality, one that was far from modest. While the Dutch in the seventeenth century were certainly God-fearing and moralizing, they were anything but Victorian in character. The vocabulary of the time was generally uninhibited. The freedom of language, expression and tone can be assessed not only from the countless farces, comedies and "vulgar" love poems, but ample evidence of this tendency is also found in works by the pious Joost van den Vondel and by the courtier and moralizer Huygens.[114]

To return to Steen, it is clear that his contemporaries enjoyed his paintings and were in no way put off by them. The ambiguities in the painting known as *The Red Stocking* will undoubtedly have been more evident to the average seventeenth-century viewer than they are to the unsuspecting museum visitor today (Fig. 23). A key to the "secondary" meaning of this work is once again provided by sev-

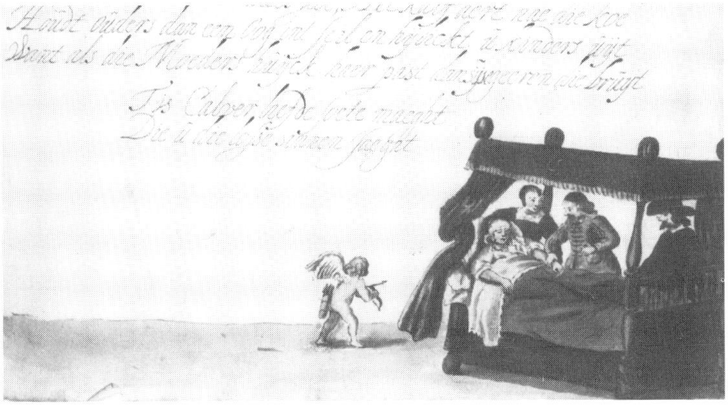

Figure 22. Gesina ter Borch, *The Sick Maiden* (watercolor from her Poetry Album). Amsterdam, Rijksprentenkabinet. Photo: Rijksmuseum-Stichting.

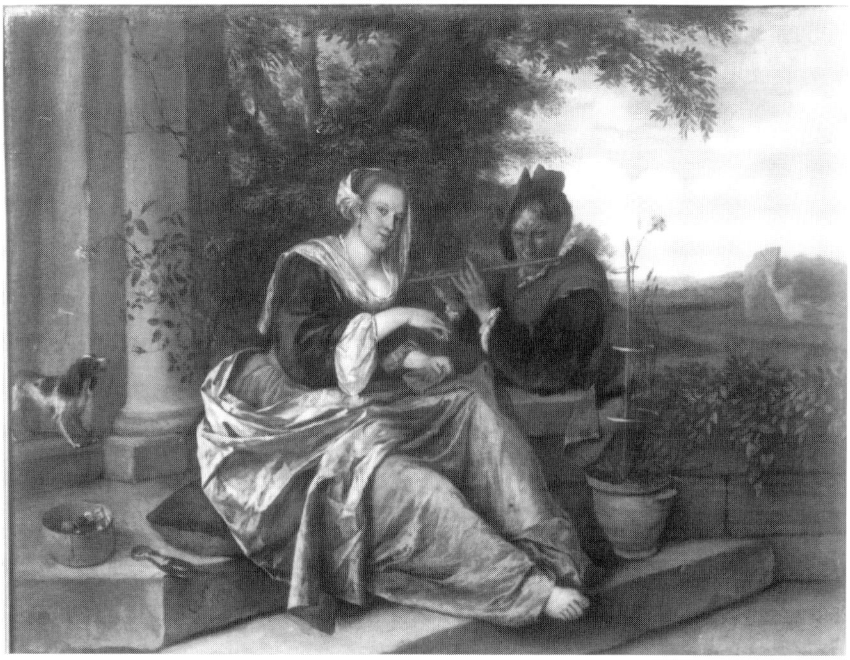

Figure 23. Jan Steen, *The Red Stocking.* Private collection, The Netherlands.

enteenth-century vernacular. The word *kous* (stocking) was a common term for the female genitals, as well as being an ignominious appellation for women in general. In this sense the word was routinely employed by authors of farces, among them Gerrit van Santen, Willem Dircksz. Hooft and Matthijs Tengnagel. "Kaart, kous en kan maakt menig arm man" (Cards, stockings, and pitchers are the downfall of many a poor man) was a popular expression, which in turn spawned numerous interpretations in the visual arts.[115] Jan Steen twice depicted a girl sitting on a bed, pulling on her stocking.[116] Any uncertainty concerning the erotic implications in these two works is eliminated when they are compared to a painting attributed to Adriaen van de Venne in the museum in Warsaw (Fig. 24).[117] Just as in Steen's paintings, a girl is seated on the edge of a bed, pulling a stocking onto her upraised leg. Here, however, she is joined by a jester who, popping out from behind her bed, demonstratively points to her stocking. With this gesture he is actually showing the viewer (as in a rebus) exactly which detail should be emphasized to grasp the essence of the picture. Incidentally, the answer to the visual riddle is given in the upper left corner of the composition: "Geckie met de kous" (The Fool and the Stocking). It is clear that "Geckie" refers to the jester and that "kous" not only signifies the stocking but logically also the other person, the woman seated on the bed dressing herself.

With her red stockings, Steen's girl appears to have the same scruples as the one in the painting attributed to Van de Venne, and is fittingly accompanied by a man playing music while she tends to her mending. Here too, we are dealing with a kind of "Geckie met de kous," even though we are faced with a satyr-like figure instead of a real jester. If (as described in contemporary interpretations of physiognomy) a satyr-like countenance alludes to lust, then the fact that this figure also plays a flute leaves absolutely nothing to the imagination.[118] The phallic symbolism of the flute has parallels in other paintings by Steen, as well as in works by Van Mieris and an engraving by Bartholomeus Dolendo (circa 1571 to circa 1629) after Lucas van Leyden (Fig. 25).[119] This print of a flautist is accompanied

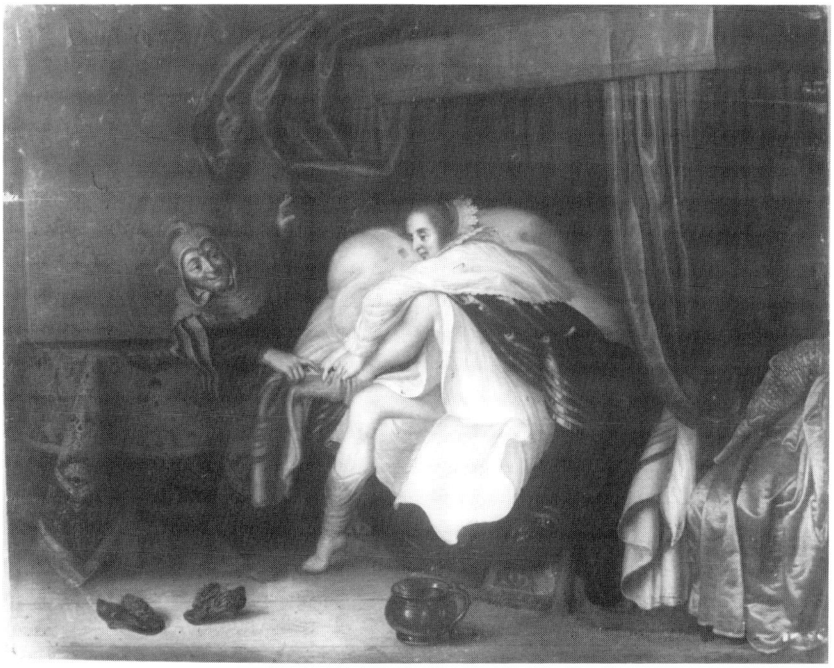

Figure 24. Adriaen van de Venne, *The Fool and the Stocking* (oil on panel, 54 × 75 cm). Warsaw, Museum Narodowe. Photo: museum.

by a verse in which "to play the flute" (fluiten) is used in the sense "to copulate" and the word *luit* (lute) means woman: "Oh, joyful flautist / quench my desire. Play your flute upon the lute / that I may feel your fire."

However, we should not conclude on the basis of this that every flute and every lute in seventeenth-century art had erotic connotations.[120] The context and the interrelationship of the various elements always determine the meaning of a representation in its totality. In Steen's *Red Stocking*, diverse details reinforce one another, and together clarify the content of the painting.[121] Such is not the case, for instance, in Judith Leyster's *Flute Player* (Stockholm, Nationalmuseum). Attempting to explain this painting by drawing parallels with Dolendo's print would be absurd and, moreover, an example of irresponsible scholarship. Judith Leyster's painting lacks, at least for us, any specific clues that might allow for some kind of interpretation, although an allusion to or reminiscence of the sense of Hearing may well have crossed the painter's mind.

Having found ourselves with Steen in the second half of the seventeenth century, let us now go back somewhat in time, to the 1620s, and consider a work by Gerrit van Honthorst. Eroticism, ultimately derived from Italian sources and more elegant in nature, also plays a role in Van Honthorst's *A Soldier and a Maiden* (Fig. 26). This painting is a splendid example of the Dutch contribution to Caravaggism, the style introduced by Caravaggio and his followers in Italy.[122] Characteristic of this school of painting are the refined chiaroscuro, the clothing, and the theatrical appearance of the individuals portrayed, as well as the fact that they are shown half-length. The man drapes his left arm around the girl's shoulders and fondles her right breast with his right hand, while she lights a candle with a glowing ember held by tongs. With pursed lips, she blows the coals to keep the flame alive. At least this is what we see on the "outside." Apprehending this scene on a metaphorical level, as the artist ultimately wants us to do, it appears to combine the sense of Touch and *min*, that frivolous type of love discussed above. The soldier's libidinous gesture should be understood as a visual metaphor for this "inferior" sense, and the girl's activity as "fanning the fire of love." After all, in the words of Jan Harmensz. Krul, "Love (as you know) is likened to fire."[123]

Emblems provide a series of variations on this theme with figures alternately outfitted with fire tongs, a torch, or a piece of burning wood.[124] In the work of Cats and Krul, gentlemen play with the dangerous fire; in Otto van Veen and Daniel Heinius, it is Cupid who does so; and in De Brune, the girl holds the tongs.[125] An indefatigable and relentless moralizer, De Brune immediately broaches the subject of death in his motto and epigram, telling "jongelien" (youth) that "ghy nu heet van bloede, Haest stijf en kout van leen, tot asschen zult vergaen" (hot-blooded as you may be now, soon your limbs will be stiff and cold, and [eventually] you will turn to ash). The amorous poem under Cats's emblem (Fig. 27) is less somber; the first four lines are as follows:

> Firewood and Love are two separate matters,
> But are alike in how one should touch them,
> Because whether one hastens to the Fire or
> Love,
> handling them requires a certain skill.

Heinsius calls *min* a "*wreeden brandt*" (evil fire), and Van Veen compares the restless lover, among other things, to a flame that cannot be extinguished. The work of these and other emblematists also includes Cupid fanning the fire with a bellows or even blowing on it himself, as the girl in Van Honthorst's painting does.[126]

We encounter the same amorous symbolism in various details in *The Love Letter* by Johannes Vermeer (Fig. 28). The letter to which this painting owes its name has just been handed by a maidservant to a young woman, who interrupts her lute-playing to inspect it. Behind her hangs a painting of a ship at sea. I believe that the key to interpreting this painting is the combination of the letter, lute, and ship – significant elements that clarify and reinforce each other's meaning and that of the picture as a whole.

Vermeer was not the first to employ the combination of a letter and a marine painting: Dirck Hals, Pieter Codde[127] and Gabriel Metsu had done so earlier, each with their own variation on the theme. In Metsu's scene (Fig. 29) the central figure is occupied in reading the letter while a maidservant draws aside the curtain protecting a painting (a common feature in the seventeenth century) hanging on the back wall. Her gesture serves to emphasize the connection between the letter and the wave-tossed ship on the high sea. However, those believing the sender of the letter to be the lady's seaborne lover would be mistaken. Metsu produced a surprising pendant to this painting which shows a man writing a letter in a domestic interior, rather than a man at sea as one might expect. The "signal," the marine painting to which the maidservant suggestively draws our attention, evidently may not be interpreted literally.

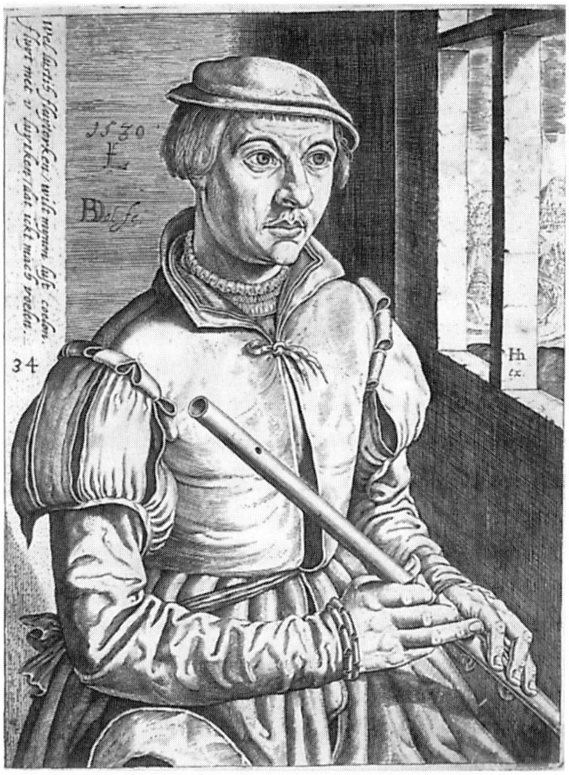

Figure 25. Bartholomeus Dolendo after Lucas van Leyden, *The Flutist* (engraving). Amsterdam, Rijksprentenkabinet. Photo: Rijksmuseum-Stichting.

Given seventeenth-century figurative language, however, we can conclusively decode Metsu's pen-

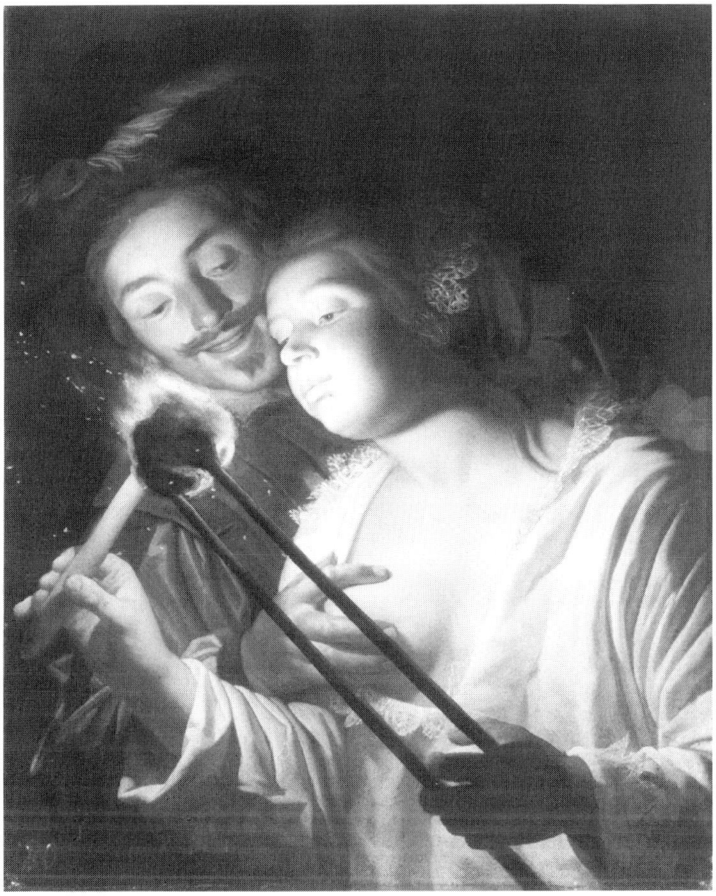

Figure 26. Gerrit van Honthorst, *A Soldier and a Maiden* (oil on canvas, 82.6 × 66 cm). Brunswick, Herzog Anton Ulrich-Museum. Photo: B. P. Keiser, Brunswick.

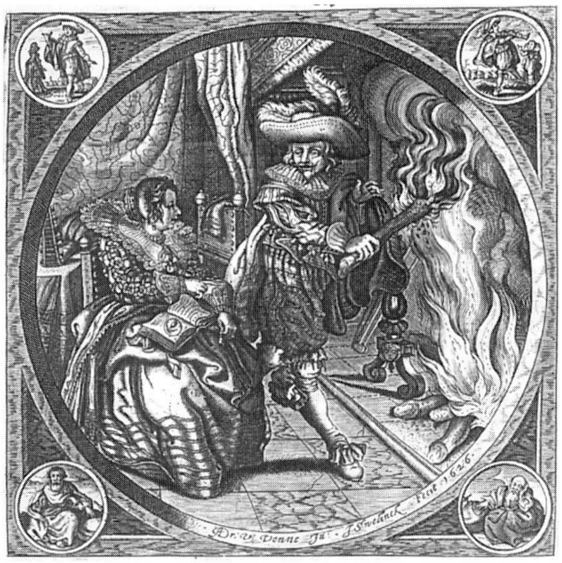

Figure 27. Emblem from Jacob Cats, *Proteus ofte minnebeelden verandert in sinnebeelden*, Rotterdam, 1627. Amsterdam, Rijksprentenkabinet. Photo: Rijksmuseum-Stichting.

dants by means of metaphorical interpretation. Support is found, for example, in a poem by Krul in which he compares the sea with love and the ship with the lover.[128] The poem accompanies an emblem of a sailboat (Fig. 30) bearing the motto "Though far away, you are never out of my heart." There is no reason to assume that in combining a letter and a seascape Vermeer intended anything essentially different than Metsu. His ship, too, provides the "key" to the contents of the letter. That the epistle in question is a love letter is evidenced, moreover, by the lute (actually a hybrid of a lute and a cittern) resting in the woman's lap.[129]

Captions on prints alone supply abundant information with respect to the lute as an erotic symbol.[130] In the verse in Bartholomeus Dolendo's engraving cited above, the lute was identified with women. Elsewhere, the lute figures as an image of

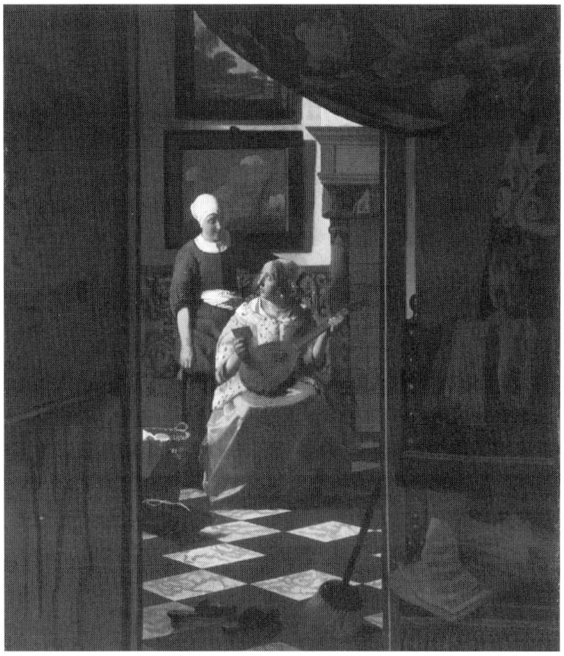

Figure 28. Johannes Vermeer, *The Love Letter* (oil on canvas, 44 × 38.5 cm). Amsterdam, Rijksmuseum. Photo: Rijksmuseum-Stichting.

the female genitals – thus it is understandable that prostitutes in paintings are often shown with a lute. This instrument also appears as an attribute of Lust or Unchastity.[131] On the other hand, Harmony, the concordance of spirits, can also bear a lute. In Vermeer's painting, this instrument would seem to function as a general amorous symbol in more or less "neutral" terms, echoing Jacob Westerbaen's poetic incitement to "Learn to play the Lute, learn to play the Harpsichord / For the strings have the power to steal someone's heart."[132]

A letter as the central motif of a painting figures more than once in Vermeer's *oeuvre*. In this, he was not alone. In fact, from the mid-seventeenth century on, letters being delivered, read, or – somewhat later – written became part of the standard artistic repertoire.[133] It is not entirely clear whether the popularity of letters – love letters – in painting coincided with the increase of epistolary activity in daily life which took place during the first half of the seventeenth century. One should assume that this was, indeed, the case. After all, the emergence of a particular theme was almost always somehow connected to reality, a reality that painters imitated and, if they desired, infused with symbolism so that it could be read metaphorically.

In the course of the seventeenth century, the art of letter writing in Holland was greatly influenced by French practice. An extensive series of *manuels épistolaires* appeared in France, some of which went through dozens of reprintings. This included *Le secrétaire à la mode* by Jean Puget de la Serre, which was also published by Elzevier in Amsterdam in 1662.[134] More important for our purpose is that as of 1651, Dutch adaptations of these manuals appeared under the title *Fatsoenlicke zend-brief-schryver* (Fashionable Missive Writer).[135] Over

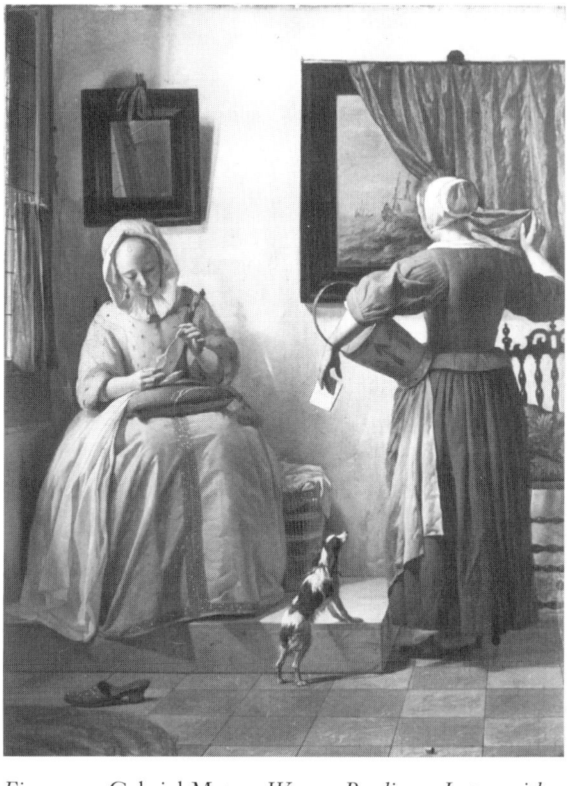

Figure 29. Gabriel Metsu, *Woman Reading a Letter with a Servant* (oil on panel, 32 × 20 cm). Dublin, The National Gallery of Ireland. Photo: museum.

thirty pages of this volume are devoted to "Verscheyden minne-brieven, op allerley begevingen en gevallen" (Various Love Letters for All Kinds of Quandaries and Situations).

The most popular of these manuals was the collection of model letters compiled by Daniël Mostart, municipal secretary of Amsterdam, and published by Dirck Pietersz. Pers, the translator of Ripa's *Iconologia*. One of the sections in Mostart's *Nederduytse secretaris oft zendbriefschryver* (Dutch Secretary or Missive Writer) is devoted to "bezoekbrieven" (calling letters). Love-smitten, but not particularly talented, letter writers could select an appropriate model from this category to inspire their epistolary endeavors.[136] The book was reprinted by Pers in 1637, and more elaborate versions appeared in 1643 and 1649. From 1656 on, it was also reprinted by other publishers. The astonishing number of editions attests to its wide dissemination.[137] We must assume that the great demand for these fashionable manuals came especially from what we would now call the Dutch middle and upper classes. And, it is precisely these social milieus that are portrayed in paintings of ladies reading and writing letters by Metsu, Ter Borch, Vermeer, and others.

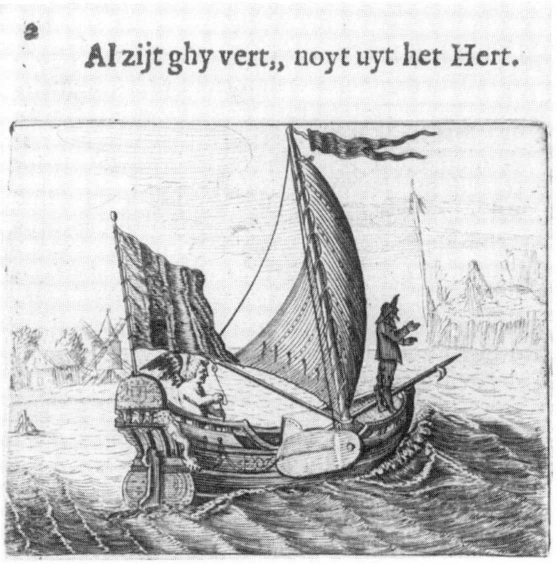

Figure 30. Emblem from Jan Harmensz. Krul, *Minnebeelden*, Amsterdam, 1640.

At the time that Vermeer produced *The Love Letter*, Gerard Dou also painted a lady with a servant, albeit in a totally different setting. Dou's composition of 1667 shows a *Young Woman at Her Toilet* (Fig. 31), whose hair is being arranged by a maidservant. In principle, our analysis of this work could include the two paintings hanging on the wall in the background. Unfortunately, the panel has suffered to such an extent in this area that the subject of these representations is virtually unidentifiable. Only in the painting at the right can a woman seated at a table be distinguished. In spite of this, in my opinion the main scene affords sufficient information to allow an interpretation of its subject.

A woman having her hair dressed by a maidservant while looking in a mirror was a favorite subject in the seventeenth century. Furthermore, it is an example of what we have termed seeming realism: an imitation of reality which is at the same time a realized abstraction. The symbolism of mirrors is exceptionally diverse and, not surprisingly, this object had both negative and positive connotations.[138] The mirror could indicate wisdom, self-knowledge, and the Virgin's chastity; but also such largely overlapping (negative) concepts as the deception of appearances, impurity, worldliness, transience, pride, and, naturally, the sense of Sight, the symbolism of which sometimes differs little from that of pride.

Naturally, we cannot precisely ascertain which variant or variants Gerard Dou (who seldom refrained from moralizing) wished to accentuate. In any case, Dou's painting is remarkably similar to a representation of *Sight* by the French engraver Abraham Bosse, whose work was so influential in the Netherlands. Less striking, but no less relevant, is its connection with certain *vanitas* representations, such as those produced by Jacob de Gheyn and Jan Miense Molenaer (Fig. 32). In Molenaer's painting various facets – *vanitas*, worldliness and impurity – are subtly intertwined. Although Dou expresses the concept less clearly, I feel there is sufficient justification to acknowledge both *vanitas* and *voluptas* elements in his *Young Woman at Her Toilet*.

While the mirror in Dou's representation surely stands for transience, the open parrot cage hanging directly above the "vain" woman is, in this instance, a sign of lost virginity. At least this is how the motif was perceived by Cats. In his *Sinne- en minnebeelden* (Emblems of Love and Virtue), a girl lets a bird escape from a *doos* (box), a metaphor for her lost "honor."[139]

As I have demonstrated elsewhere, the central figure in the aforementioned painting by Molenaer is so-called Dame World, the embodiment of all vain desires and earthly temptations, which originated in the Middle Ages.[140] The map of the world on the wall serves as a two-dimensional substitute for the globe, the standard attribute adorning the head of the more traditional Dame World. Molenaer's representation of Dame World is already partially dissociated from allegorical imagery and has partially assumed the "reality" of genre painting. A subsequent stage in the development of Dame World is found in Jacob Ochtervelt's *Lady with Servant and Dog* (Fig. 33), which is devoid of any unrealistic detail (for example, the skull lying at the feet of the woman in Molenaer's version), and in which Dame World has become a worldly woman. However, she remains closely allied to the world map behind her: In a two-dimensional sense one of the hemispheres still rests on her head, like the globe in the traditional allegorical version of Dame World. A final stage of evolution is attained in Nicolas Maes's *Luistervink*, or *The Eavesdropper*, where the attribute leads a life of its own (Fig. 34). It now hangs "independently" on the wall, yet continues to symbolize in a general way the same concerns as Dame World, from which it is derived.[141] In short, one can say that the world map, a portion of which Maes included at the right of his composition, expresses the "worldly" life, earthly temptations. While it would be incorrect to claim that every world map that appears in paintings implies "worldliness," in this case there is virtually no room for doubt, given the complementary meaning of a number of other details.

Although the story of the "eavesdropper" is not particularly evident,[142] the main figure on the stairs, the *luistervink*, clearly draws our attention to the maidservant and her lover, who are so engrossed in each other's company that they do not notice the cat snatching a piece of meat from a dish in the kitchen. That this couple represents the "worldly" life is not only indicated by the map, but also by the thieving cat, a motif Maes more than once included in erotic scenes.[143] While the cat itself is an image of *voluptas*,[144] the act of snatching a piece of meat underscores the metaphor and is an explicit visualization of carnal lust, something of which the Southern Netherlandish social critic Adriaan Poirters was also aware. Urging parents to keep a sharp eye on their daughters during "their vulnerable youth," Poirters employed the following metaphor: "More than once has [it] been espied, that creeping cats have stolen meat from the pot."[145]

While several details in Maes's *Luistervink* lend themselves to elucidation, the essence of the painting as a whole nevertheless continues to elude us. This is certainly not an isolated case. Much of what we think we can unravel has to do with fragments only, rather than the heart of the matter. On the other hand, sometimes I have the feeling that my suggestions are indeed on target. The accessibility of seventeenth-century paintings varies: Works by Steen are generally easier to decode than ones by Metsu; Metsu is usually more comprehensible than Dou; and Dou, in turn, provides greater access than Vermeer. The assumption that certain works were intended to be more or less ambiguous does not help us much. Just where the symbolism stops and the "empty" form remains can never be precisely indicated. Some artists working at the end of the seventeenth century appear to be completely "aliterate," while others active approximately fifty years later prove to be fully proficient in traditional metaphorical language.

In the course of time, the original meanings of seventeenth-century paintings were often forgotten or not recognized, particularly in the nineteenth century when bourgeois mentality had lost all affinity with the rather different one of the Golden Age. In the first half of the nineteenth century, seventeenth-century art was predominantly used (by Potgieter and others) to explain (Dutch) national

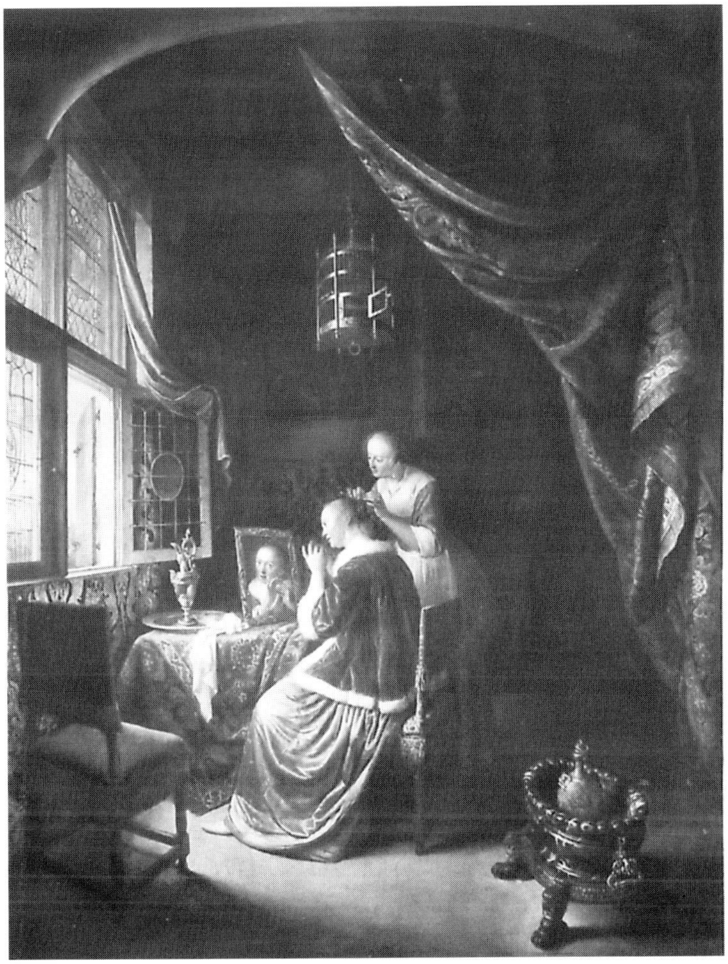

Figure 31. Gerard Dou, *Young Woman at Her Toilet*, 1667 (oil on panel, 75.5 × 58 cm). Rotterdam, Museum Boymans-van Beuningen. Photo: copyright Frequin-Photos, The Hague.

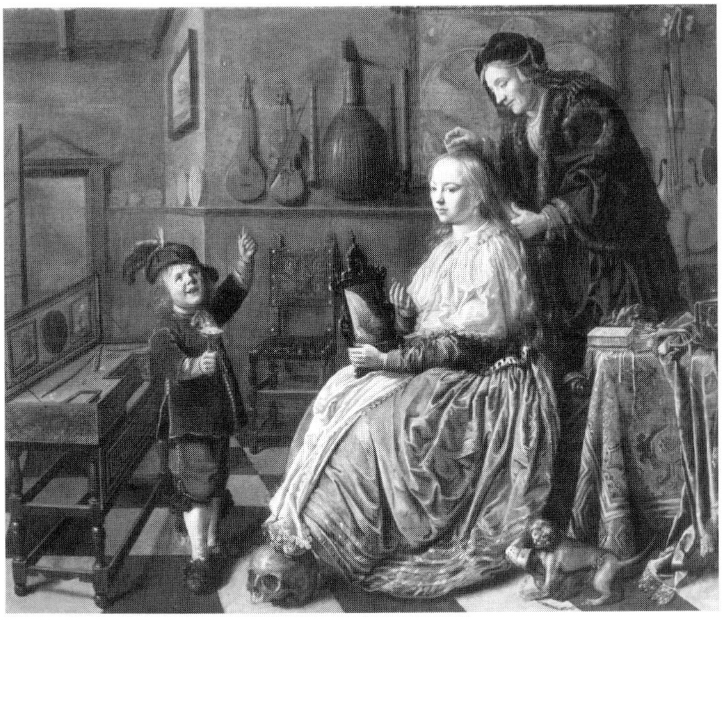

Figure 32. Jan Miense Molenaer, *Woman at Her Toilet (Lady World)*, 1633 (102 × 127 cm). Toledo, The Toledo Museum of Art. Photo: museum.

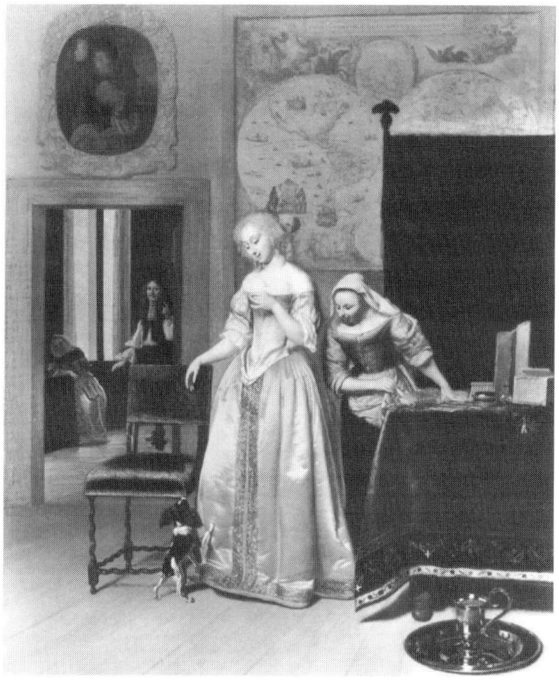

Figure 33. Jacob Ochtervelt, *Lady with Servant and Dog* (oil on canvas, 68.9 × 58.1 cm). Pittsburgh, The Carnegie Museum of Art, Henry Lee Mason Memorial Fund, 54.1. Photo: museum.

history; in contrast, later in the nineteenth century and under the influence of Impressionism, artistic interest was more aesthetically determined, and focused more on the form of works of art than their content.

The present century witnessed a new transition as interest in artistic subject matter gradually revived. The imaginative universe of the Italian Renaissance particularly began to draw attention on all fronts. That of seventeenth-century Dutch art has only really been studied since the end of the 1930s. Freud and Jung's psychological theories, as well as the emergence of certain "literary" movements, primarily Surrealism, in the visual arts, may well have stimulated iconographical interest in our time. However, we should bear in mind that while similarities between twentieth-century symbolism, whether Freudian or Surrealist, and seventeenth-century symbolism, do indeed exist, the differences are even greater.

The abiding task of art-historical scholarship is to channel free association properly through historical discipline. Several attempts to do so have been ven-

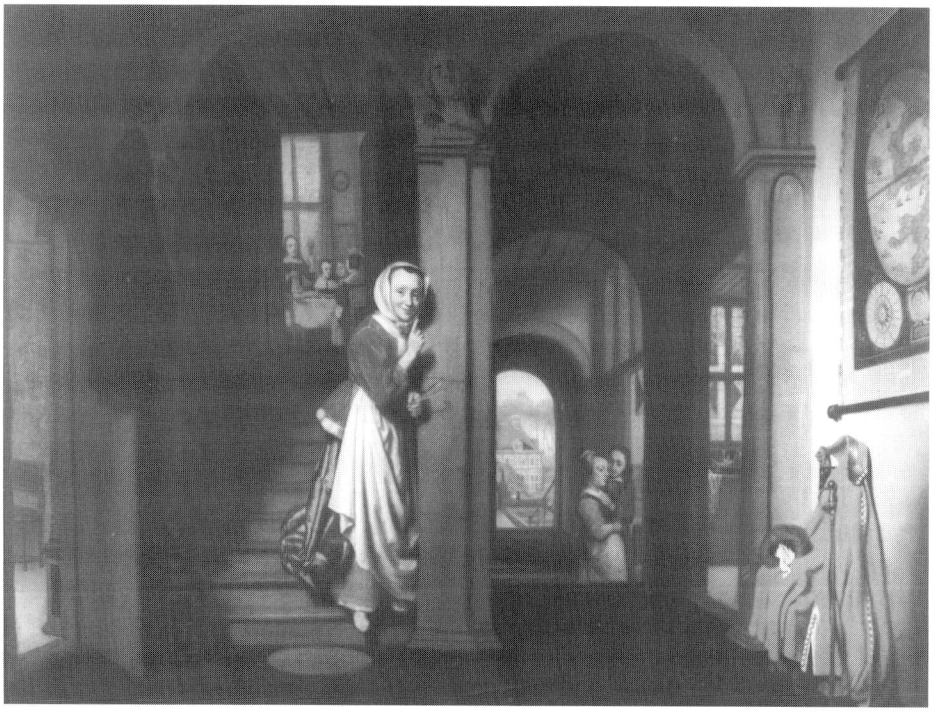

Figure 34. Nicolas Maes, *The Eavesdropper,* 1657 (oil on canvas, 92.5 × 122 cm). The Hague, Rijksdienst Beeldende Kunst, on loan to Dordrecht, Dordrechts Museum. Photo: museum.

tured in this article. What art historians as self-appointed exegetes are still lacking, however, are adequate controls. After all, nothing guarantees that they have indeed – to cite Cats once again – discovered the "beautiful bunch of grapes" hidden under the thick foliage. Because of this, too, the interpretations forwarded here should be considered "truths" only for the time being.

POSTSCRIPT: A QUARTER OF A CENTURY LATER

"Realism and Seeming Realism," an investigation into the "meaning(s)" of seventeenth-century Dutch paintings, was written twenty-five years ago. The answer to the question whether it is an oddity in this volume, or a piece of work with useful insights, is left to the reader's discretion. Although I should have preferred purging some of my initial assertions, would that not amount to tampering, I believe that – even after all these years – it should not be relegated to the wastepaper basket. Incidentally, I am aware that I benefit from the relatively long "shelf life" of art historical research. In this respect, art history is better off than, for example, the natural sciences or medicine, fields in which most publications are more rapidly superseded.

Having said this, I do not wish to suggest that "Realism and Seeming Realism" has endured the test of time unscathed. The past decades have witnessed intense debate concerning the understanding and interpretation of seventeenth-century Dutch paintings. In that process my work inevitably came under fire: The term "seeming realism" immediately precipitated unease and elicited criticism. However, I did keep one step ahead of my reviewers, if only in a note, by covering myself with respect to the watertightness of the term.

Both the aforementioned debate and the subsequent (re)evaluation of my standpoint stimulated me to reconsider certain issues in more relative terms, including the tendency to moralize in the seventeenth century. Naturally, there is no single seventeenth-century type of individual or seventeenth-century mentality. I noted at the time that we were actually dealing with diverse yet closely intertwined mentalities.

The prevalence of moralization in seventeenth-century painting still seems to me irrefutable. In fact, it has even been posited that every image of this period grew out of ethical considerations. However, this all-encompassing view says very little. Alongside paintings with moralizing allusions there are many in which not a single trace can be detected, at least not by our far from innocent eyes. I formulated this point in 1971, albeit somewhat more casually. Upon further deliberation, it seemed prudent to distinguish a third category, and to assume that much pseudo-moralizing was visually expressed in this period as well.

As my article makes clear, morality (or edification) was frequently conveyed by means of symbolic embellishment. Symbolism is a versatile phenomenon, since symbols can also function as vehicles for the immoral, for every imaginable vice. With respect to the use of symbolism, I should like to reiterate here a corrective that I introduced in later publications: In addition to the substantial number of painters who drew from the rich arsenal of symbolism, there were also many (in 1620, 1650, or 1690) who, for whatever reason, did not or only to a limited extent.

In a certain sense, symbolism is a form of veiling or disguising. These terms, which I occasionally used, also raised objections. Some critics maintain that virtually no veiling exists in seventeenth-century Dutch painting. This, it seems to me, is a matter of definition and choice of words. The stocking in Adriaen van de Venne's painting in Warsaw (Fig. 24), for instance, represents itself while simultaneously alluding to the sexuality of the woman to whom it belongs. It covertly expresses the scene's ultimate meaning. In the art of the past, the nature of veiling was not intended to be impenetrable. A well-conceived veiling was such that with some mental gymnastics, the viewer was able to discern and disclose that which was disguised.

This principle is almost always embedded in the details of a work of art. The main point I was trying to make in 1971 and which I still champion, is that objects, particularly in genre paintings, are often multivalent; while serving as the actual objects that we see, they simultaneously symbolize something else, usually an abstract concept. I am in no way suggesting here that simply "adding up" the decoded symbolic details provides *the* meaning of a work of art. The visual components, form, color, brushwork and composition are by definition also signifiers, only they cannot be deciphered in the same way.

In this respect, it may be useful to mention Samuel van Hoogstraeten's advice to augment the significance of a painting with "accessories that explain something covertly," a practice which, I maintain, was widespread in the seventeenth century. For assuming that this also applies to genre painting, I have been charged with misinterpretation. While not denying that Van Hoogstraeten was discussing history painting, the fact that "his" principle was common currency is evidenced by numerous publications of the time in which no distinction is made with respect to medium or subject. No genre painter familiar with this passage will have thought that it was solely limited to the most elevated category of art and was thus unsuitable for the lesser ranked genres. Moreover, it is debatable whether genre painters even needed the instruction of a theoretician, since the incorporation of significant "accessories" was embedded in a long tradition and must have been standard studio practice.

The validity of my interpretations of various paintings in "Realism and Seeming Realism" has not been seriously challenged in the course of the past twenty-five years. Only Goltzius' triad (Figs. 13, 14, and 15) has been subjected to several thorough analyses resulting in more refined or different interpretations. Each of the five categories that I treated in succinct sections – genre, landscape, still life, portrait, and history painting – have subsequently been extensively explored in a vast number of publications by myself and others. Regardless of what this body of work may have produced, one thing is certain, it has fortunately yielded no *communis opinio.* As long as the philosopher's stone remains tantalizingly out of reach, the debate will no doubt continue.

Picturing Dutch Culture*

Svetlana Alpers

It has been a pervasive and limiting assumption of the study of art history that meaning takes the form of "iconicity," that the sense that pictures make is located in the meaning of the people or objects represented. In the study of the predominantly secular and nonnarrative Dutch art of the seventeenth century, this has been coupled with the assumption (one with ancient precedent) that such meaning or sense is a message, instructionally intended: You may delight in the people and objects in pictures but are meant to attend to the moral instruction that they offer. The model for such pictures has been located in emblem books. It was a major accomplishment of the work of Eddy de Jongh to discover the relationship between certain motifs in Dutch painting and the images accompanied by texts in the popular emblem books. Images so conceived lend themselves to words; they originate with texts in mind.[1]

The "reality effect" peculiar to much Dutch painting has persuaded many viewers that the art registers how things are or how they were. Art historians have argued that things are not what they seem to the eye – they are devised with meanings in or (if hidden) out of view. But the notion that therefore Dutch pictures are only apparently real (because they have hidden meanings) or selectively or subjectively real (because the painted world is creatively chosen and one person's view) is misleading. For, along with the appeal to moral meanings, it effectively suggests that we can bracket, or bypass the pictorial mode itself – the reality effect – so basic to these pictures. Painters make paintings, not meanings. It is to the mode – the reality effect – that I turned my attention. And it was with reference to this pictorial mode that I tried to ground Dutch painting in its culture.[2]

It was while looking at Johannes Vermeer's *Art of Painting* (Fig. 35) that I began to consider another manner of interpretation. The wall map depicted by Vermeer does not signify a longing for a lost political unity, nor is it a sign of the vanity of worldly concerns; it is a piece of painting. Vermeer painted a map and incidentally signed his name on it as its maker. This painted map first drew my attention to the link between painting and mapping at the time. The map–painting relationship can be described as a matter of *format:* the absence of a positioned viewer as if the world came first before the viewer, the absence of a prior frame; a formidable sense of surface on which words along with objects can be inscribed. It can also be described as a matter of *function:* Maps as pictures and picture-like maps were both engaged in gaining knowledge of the world. I had the good luck to find a painting by Jan Christaensz. Micker where Amsterdam was laid out on the surface like a map but with unseen clouds casting shadows on it (Fig. 36). It provides what might be called the missing link that demon-

* Editor's note: Svetlana Alpers's essay is a revised and expanded version of one that originally appeared in: *The Low Countries. Arts and Society in Flanders and The Netherlands; A Yearbook* 1 (1993–4): 158–65.

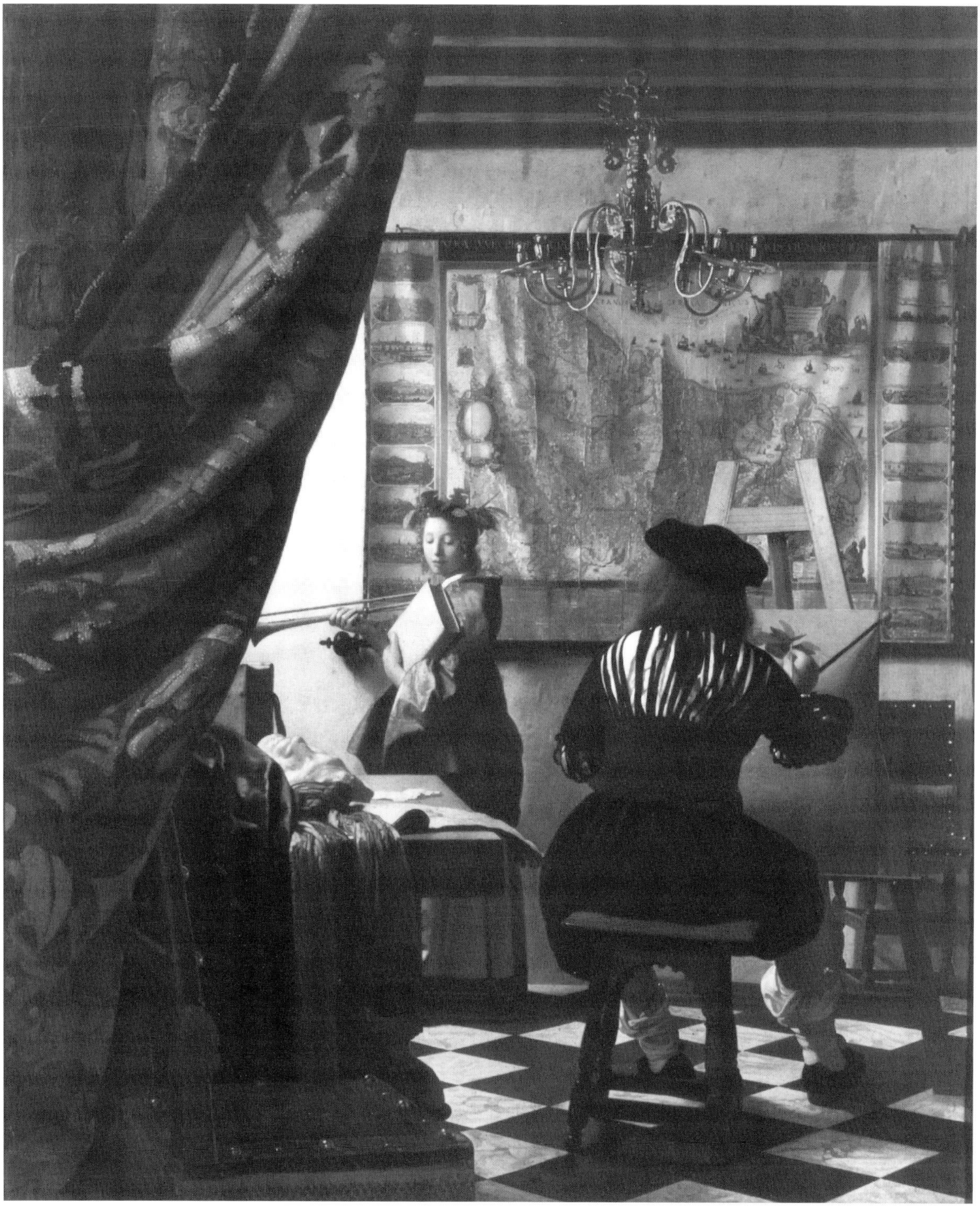

Figure 35. Johannes Vermeer, *The Art of Painting* (oil on canvas, 120 × 100 cm). Vienna, Kunsthistorisches Museum. Photo: museum.

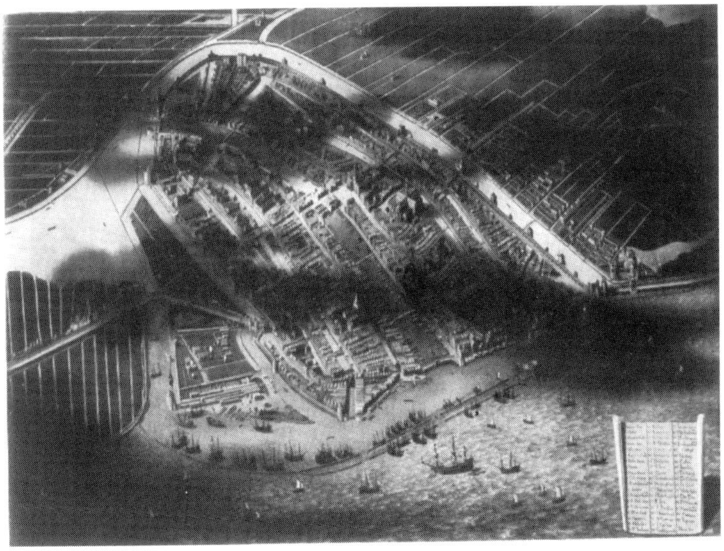

Figure 36. Jan Christaensz. Micker, *View of Amsterdam* (oil on paper, 100 × 137 cm). Amsterdam Historical Museum, Amsterdam.

strates the close relationship at the time between painting and mapping.

Dutch paintings were like maps, but they were also like mirrors. When Johannes Kepler, in his study of the mechanism of the eye, defines *to see* as *to make a picture*, he provides a model for the particular relationship between finding and making, between nature and art, that characterizes much painting in northern Europe. The operation of the eye is, so he proposed, like a camera obscura – and this illustration of its operation is a good analogy to a picture like Vermeer's *View of Delft*. Like so many Dutch pictures, this is produced in an age of observation – the sky is scanned, land surveyed, flora and fauna observed and described. Instead of a direct confrontation with nature, we find a trust to devices, to intermediaries that represent nature to us. The major example of such a device is, of course, the lens. Painting can be described as another such intermediary.

If we take the pictorial mode – the reality effect – not as hiding moral instruction, but as offering a perceptual model of knowledge of the world, then pictures are related to the empirical interests of this age of observation. The picture takes its place beside the many other devices – the eye, the microscopic lens – which squeeze and press nature so that we can experience (or experiment, in the seventeenth-century use of the word) her. The attentive eye and crafty hand of the painter are here related to the eye and hand of the experimenter. Painting itself is like an experiment.

Readers outside the field of art history have been receptive to this analysis. The definition of a mapping impulse brought landscape painting to the attention of geographers and offered new confirmation of their already expanding and problematizing notion of maps as conventional representations. The definition of Dutch painting as sharing a perceptual view of knowledge and an interest in craft with seventeenth-century experimental science has made links with current studies in the history and sociology of science. There historians are also concerned with the conventional and crafted nature of natural knowledge at the time.

But the academic specialists studying Dutch art remained upset and unconvinced. Indeed, it appeared to them that I was not even looking at the same objects that they were. Why? I think it is largely a matter of certain professional habits.

Art historians who study Dutch art have made two objections – one basic and one less so. The basic one involves a misunderstanding or simple nonattention to the place of the word *art* in the title *The Art of Describing*. The book is not about describing but about the *art* of describing. Artifice, one might say, is assumed from the beginning. The phrase "the art of describing" does not claim that pictures picture the world as it is but rather the world as it is seen, microscoped, mapped, crafted, in short as it is represented. The argument is that pictures are an attempt to make sense (by which I mean produce understanding) rather than meaning out of the world.

The second objection had been the worry about the subtitle: *The Art of Describing: Dutch Art in the Seventeenth Century*. The distinction I drew between two modes – descriptive and narrative, northern and southern, Netherlandish and Italian – was of course noted in the past. There is a famous remark attributed to Michelangelo that described northern art in its particularity as an art appealing to women. The distinction was for me at least partly a heuristic device, a way to get away from what I see as the dominance of an Italian or Albertian model of the picture in European writing on painting. I anticipated that exceptions could be found and indeed built them into my account. I defined a mode of painting that can be generally, but is not uniquely, attached to the pictorial tradition of a specific part of Europe. One could say that within each pictorial tradition, northern and Italian, the other is possible: Caravaggio, for example, is Italian by tradition but descriptive in mode.

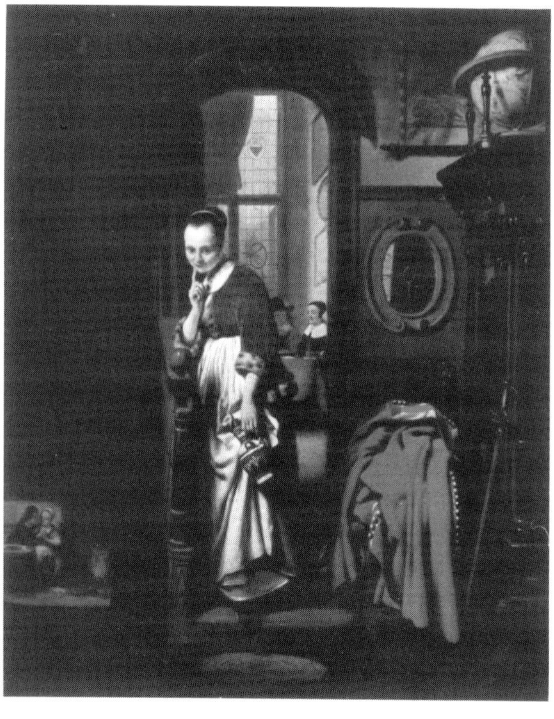

Figure 37. Nicolaes Maes, *The Eavesdropper*, 1657 (oil on canvas, 83.9 × 69.9 cm). London, The Wallace Collection. Photo: The Wallace Collection.

What I had not anticipated was the denial by Dutch art historians that there is such a thing as Dutch art! Or maybe, to be fair, that there is *one* such thing as Dutch art. Surely to deny the fact that there is something called Dutch painting is rather like denying that there was an Elizabethan theater or a Russian novel. From Chardin and Hogarth to Manet, Cézanne, Picasso, and Braque, a secular, domestically oriented, realist mode of painting with roots in the Netherlands is a feature of the European tradition of painting.[3]

But Dutchness is not only a matter of painting. It is notable that in the seventeenth century, when travelers and policy makers from abroad repeatedly marvel at the economic miracle of the Netherlands and comment on what seemed to them striking about the society, the native people lacked chauvinism. So many cultural norms were under construction in Dutch seventeenth-century life, and I would argue, in Dutch seventeenth-century painting: our bourgeois way of living, sense of individuality, and ways of organizing society from banking to the bourse, notions of punishment, civic charity, and most particularly the household and the family. But I am struck by the manner in which Dutch historians, many of them working in the manner of the French *Annales* historians, are wary of making claims specific to their culture. They want their findings about Dutch history not to be Dutch-specific but to corroborate general truths. French historians also, of course, seek general truths in their account of details, but the difference is that *Annales* historians in France think that it was in France that general social truths were manifest!

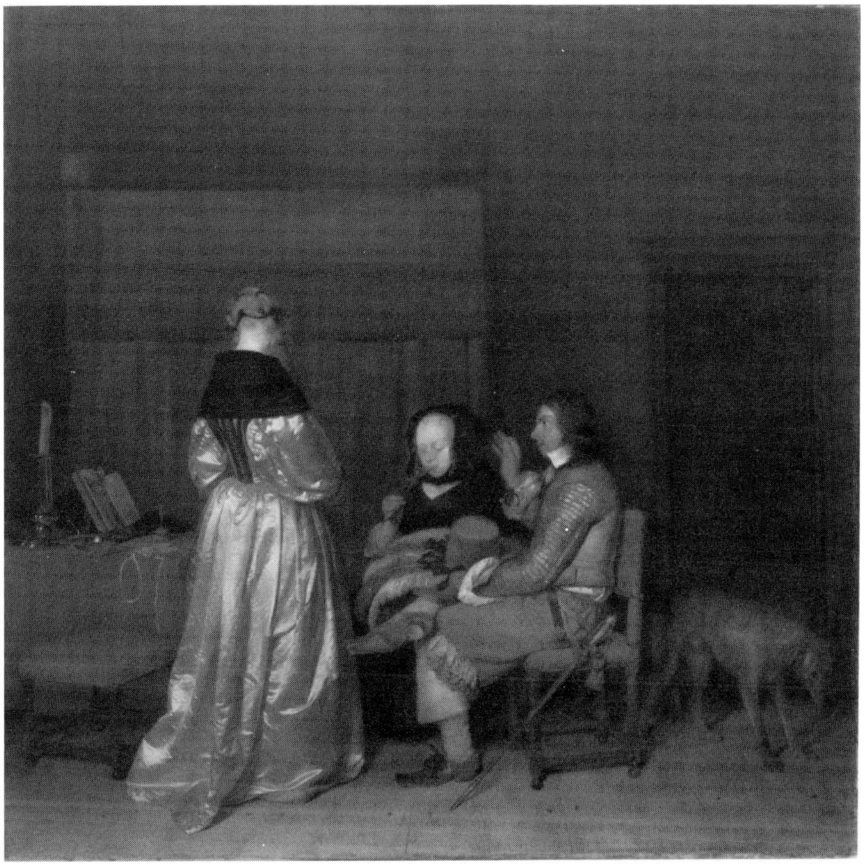

Figure 38. Gerard ter Borch, *The Paternal Admonition* (oil on canvas, 71 × 73 cm). Amsterdam, Rijksmuseum. Photo: Rijksmuseum-Stichting.

I wonder if the practice of tolerance does not have some bearing on the absence of chauvinism. In the seventeenth century, the northern Netherlands was a land that gave asylum to many immigrants. It was famously tolerant, but the price for toleration was conformity, or the fiction of it. A kind of low-keyed conformity covered or protected difference – city from city, province from province, person from person – and allowed nothing to stand out, not even, as it were, a common culture. In this kind of situation, to claim something as distinctively Dutch was perhaps to threaten the delicate fabric woven out of different people. A general distinctiveness is divisive if a society is trying to be inclusive. This old suspicion of national pride was given new life during World War II.

In my study of Dutch art, I situated the interest in the art in attention to a pictorial mode. The circumstances were registered as constraints, or conditions, on the enterprise of creating knowledge of the world. Effectively, I defined the place that the practice of painting took up or made for itself within a particular epistemological or economic system.[4] It is, then, production rather than consumption that was my primary interest. This distinguishes my work from those circumstantial studies – mostly of the modern period where the evidence is so rich – that take reception as their major evidence and concern.

I would like now to turn to the home, to the territory of household and family that is the subject of so much Dutch so-called genre painting. These images have been the site of the most insistent emblematic readings. They have been read as showing how not to behave or, in more recent accounts and with attention to different cases, how in fact one ought to behave. What, if not illustration or moral example in particular about the life of women, can the impetus to make such pictures have been? Why did painters so obsessively paint the household?

In his fascinating study of Dutch society and culture, *The Embarrassment of Riches*, Simon Schama has described Dutch culture as a consensus reached between opposites, a coexistence achieved between competing value systems. But on evidence of the pictures, it looks as if Dutch culture was less settled than Schama implies. I also think that rather than reflecting a culture, as Schama seems to think, painting often is constructing it in subtle ways.[5]

Nicolaes Maes and Gerard ter Borch – two of the most ambitious painters of the home – seem to me not to be warning or recommending this or that, nor, in the newest post– and anti–De Jongh art historical account, simply making skillful paintings.[6] Rather, they are examining, through representing, tensions in the system of social behavior. There are indeed some pictures that seem to illustrate the system proposed in the *Houwelyck* (Marriage) of 1625 of Jacob Cats that divides lives of women into six ages: *maeght* (girl), *vrijster* (maid), *bruyt* (bride), *vrouwe* (wife), *moeder* (mother), and *weduwe* (widow). Cats was a political figure and a popular, didactic poet whose works, so they say, stood on the shelf next to the Bible and served as a kind of Bible of Dutch manners. Ter Borch's painting of a *Woman Spinning* (Rotterdam, Museum Boymans-van Beuningen) is related to an emblem illustrating the behavior of the virtuous housewife. And although moralizers have tried to take it over (calling the woman a miser, a miseress, or an image of sloth), a drowsy *Housekeeper* by Maes (St. Louis, The Saint Louis Art Museum) is veridical in its depiction of a woman handling accounts. It was a task for which Dutch women were particularly praised. To judge from their size, the books are mercantile rather than domestic in nature.[7]

There are a number of paintings by artists such as Willem Buytewech or Esaias van de Velde that represent young couples enjoying themselves in a garden as *vrysters*, or betrothing maids and youths. It is the world of flirtation and courting that we sometimes find illustrated in the engraved frontispieces of song books intended for such occasions. This is the stage in a woman's life preparatory, as it were, to marriage. But how did a woman transform herself from the necessarily flirtatious, erotically engaged courting girl into the worker in and manager of a household? or, to use Cats's terms, from *vryster* to *vrouwe?* And how was the transformation viewed? I am not making up these questions. They seem to me to be posed by a number of ambiguous, intentionally puzzling, mid-century paintings by Maes and Ter Borch (Figs. 44 and 45).

Maes represents the problem in terms of the relationship between mistress/housewife and maid: As mistress is to maid, so *vrouwe* is to *vryster*. He investigates this doubled or split persona of a woman in a series of distinctive paintings featuring divided domestic interiors with the housewife situated between the flirtatious maid down in the kitchen and the refined guests above. The narrow, tall Dutch house is offered as a setting parcelled out – as indeed was then happening to Dutch houses – for different roles. In one painting by Maes (London, The National Gallery), we see the kitchen beneath, the main room above, and the housewife in-between on the staircase. The mistress of the house directs our attention to the maid asleep on the job, perhaps neglecting the guests visible upstairs. A not too subtle erotic note (referring to the dreams of the maid?) is added by a rapacious cat. But a moralistic account about the censuring of duty neglected for thoughts of love is undermined by the sense that the mistress is concerned with someone very much like herself. The maid is her double, as it were. It is as if, under the pressure of her situation, this wife was split into two persons: house manager but also still lovelorn maiden. The appearance of the housewife – her youth, cheerful, careless demeanor, jug in hand – relates her to the appearance of the maid. Her gesture and glance at the viewer seem to indicate that she, the maid, also is me, the mistress.[8]

In another painting by Maes, the maid, once again with cat, is in the kitchen making love, and a couple sit decorously at table upstairs (Fig. 37). The markedly young housewife on her way, in place of the maid, to refill the wine pitcher is between two scenes and part of neither. Beside her are a map, a globe, and the discarded outer jacket and sword of an unseen man. But which man and where? upstairs or down? Indeed, her attitude (finger raised, and amused face turned out of the picture toward the viewer) seems less a warning than a kind of amused invitation to collude with the kitchen goings-on. The pictorial handling does not warn or recommend, does not blame or praise, but instead registers the tensions in the social order of things.

What Maes does by doubling, Ter Borch does by what I shall call "overlapping." While Maes concentrates on the running of a household and how or if the woman of the house has left flirtation behind, Ter Borch, in an impressive group of pictures, concentrates on courtship. A woman's conflicting roles are posed as a question of identity: *vryster*-whore. The erotic and the domestic aspects are represented in one and the same woman, and his pictures take a certain delight in the uncertainty that results. What kind of negotiation is going on in his famously puzzling painting known as *The Paternal Admonition* (Fig. 38)?

Unlike the Maes house, Ter Borch's generalized, darkened, boxlike settings (spaces in which beds still persist in the public rooms) give us no clue to the answer. An elegantly dressed young woman, light gleaming off her expensive white silk dress, face hidden from the viewer, neck exposed, stands beside the seated figures of an older woman sipping wine and a man, legs dashingly crossed, sword at his side, his hand raised in a gesture. (The mixture of clarity and uncertainty suggested by describing from behind was a specialty of Ter Borch before he found his theme. He began his career by depicting a splendid horseman seen from the back.)

It is Goethe's staging of a *tableau vivant* (in his novel *Die Wahlverwandtschaften*) based on an engraving after Ter Borch's painting that put the problem of the subject in play. Goethe took the painting to depict a father admonishing his daughter. But Goethe was made to seem a bit of a fool with the discovery of painted traces of something, perhaps a coin, in the man's upheld hand. Could it be the picture of a young man negotiating to pay a whore? If the hand originally held a coin, we would have the negotiation for a prostitute. If, however, the hand had once held a portrait medallion rather than a coin, as in a painting by Caspar Netscher (Budapest), then it could represent a proposal of marriage. Whichever the case, Goethe's emphasis on the appearance of propriety was not mistaken. And marital arrangements, in this respect not unlike arrangements with whores, were also concerned with money and sex. Women, after all, brought dowries to marriage and, in the Netherlands at least, could maintain control over their share in the marital economy. In his painting, Ter Borch appears to delight in the suggestion that if the woman in the house might be represented as behaving like the woman in the brothel, so the reverse might also be true.

Money, then, seems to have entered Ter Borch's picture not simply as part of the domestic economy, as in the Maes *Housekeeper*, but also as part of the alternative economy of prostitution. This economy was taken as a subject by Dutch painters as, for example, by Dirck van Baburen in his so-called *Procuress* (hanging on the wall in Fig. 39) depicting a man, coin in hand, with two women – a pimp and a whore. The link between women and money had become a feature in painting in mid-sixteenth-century Antwerp. Money and its proper use were a matter of concern in this great center of banking. Writers on the subject distinguished illicit gain from usury with approved profit, meaning that which was earned from investment in land or good partnerships, of which marriage was a prime example. Painters treated the behavior of women as a vehicle for distinguishing between economic virtue and economic vice. If the household economy, the economy in the Aristotelian sense, with which women were properly concerned, was a model for the proper use of money, prostitution represented its obverse. For example, there is one painting by Quentin Metsys that represents a man with his wife testing the balance of their scales and another one that represents a foolish old man being robbed by the accomplice of a young whore.

Though doubt may always remain about what is represented in the painting by Ter Borch, there is

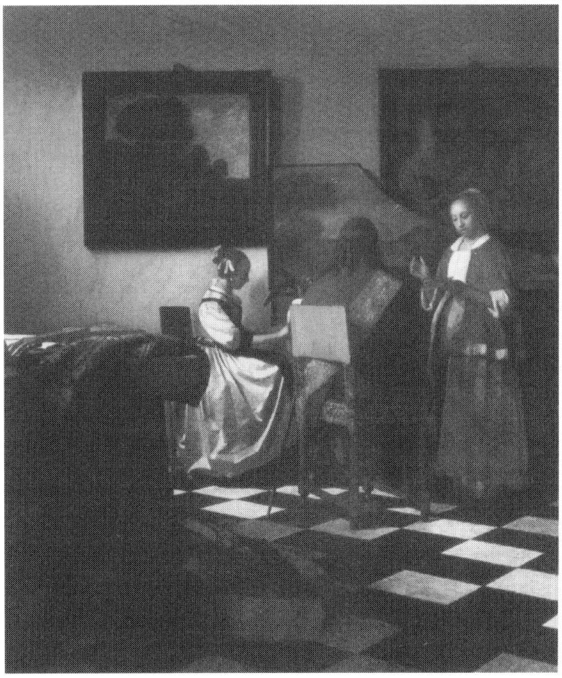

Figure 39. Johannes Vermeer, *The Concert* (oil on canvas, 69 × 63 cm). Boston, Isabella Stewart Gardner Museum.

no doubt that the rituals of courting and whoring were represented by Dutch artists as overlapping each other. The overlap was not only a matter for art. In an interesting book about the Amsterdam bordellos published in 1681, a male visitor who is being shown around by the devil mistakes the whores for wives. Seeing a man with an elegantly dressed woman wearing a gold ring, he asks his guide why a man would take his wife to such a place. That's not his wife, he is told, that is a whore.[9] Simon Schama has suggested that there was a balance struck between the good home and the bad – the musicos or brothels as the negative alternative to the orderly household. But Ter Borch shows that the problem was that the difference was not clear. Until this day, prostitutes in Amsterdam display themselves through the windows, or at the doors, of domestic interiors. For Amsterdam to construct bordellos on the model of the domestic house is not a demonstration of balance but a testimony to the continuing uncertainty about whether there is any difference between the two. It was a problem for women as well as for men.[10]

The kinship between home and whoredom was played out and commented on in paintings in a dazzling number of ways. Ter Borch's younger associate, Johannes Vermeer, juxtaposed a domestic courting scene (once again, a man between two women) with the Van Baburen *Procuress* on the wall (Fig. 39). (The Van Baburen was owned by Vermeer's mother-in-law, in whose house Vermeer lived.) A further comment on the relationship was offered by Samuel van Hoogstraeten in an unusual picture known as *The Slippers* (Paris, Musée du Louvre). A Ter Borch woman is introduced into a household that reminds us of Maes – broom, empty pattens, and keys in the door represent the domestic world, which is, however, conspicuously emptied of people. The woman viewed from behind depicted in a painting within the painting hanging on the far wall represents the attractions of the courtship world seen from within the home – and also gives an indication of the presence that Ter Borch's courtship paintings would have had hanging in a house.

There is no need to argue the centrality of the household/family to Dutch social and political organization, but this would not necessarily have made it a central subject for painting. It is worth inquiring why it should have become such. An important and generally overlooked element is the identification of the painter with the family. Painting was celebrated in a familial context. Parents, wife, and children all take their place beside the artist: The so-called Frankfurt Master decorates his 1496 self-portrait with his wife with emblems of the painter's guild and chamber of rhetoric; Jacob Jordaens celebrates his entry into the painter's guild by making a portrait of himself with his family; Gerrit Dou, a committed self-portraitist, on one occasion depicts himself holding a painting of his parents; and Adriaen van der Werff depicts his wife with child as his muse even when sending a painting off to a court patron. There is a practical basis for this. Family members often served the artist as models. But more importantly, the family provided the artist's ambience: A room in the house was the painter's working space.

Well into the seventeenth century, the painter's identification with the family was confirmed by others. In the first illustrated schoolbook, the 1658 *Orbis Pictus* of Johann Comenius, it is not the tailor or shoemaker (who like most other men at the time worked out of the home) but the painter and his family that is made to stand for *the* family. The numbered list of objects opens with the father – artist, who begets children and, having gone through their upbringing, ends with the work of the father (the palette is labeled *laborando*) as the means to support them.

Comenius does not acknowledge it, but there were problems for the artist working at home amongst his family. There is a 1577 drawing by Marcus Geeraerts that shows how impossible it was for the poor artist to get any work done at all while distracted with the demands of wife and children. Historically, European artists had deserted the house for the court. And the court artist, as we see him, for example, in an engraving by Abraham Bosse, looked down on the vulgarity of the householder. But most Dutch artists did not have the choice.[11]

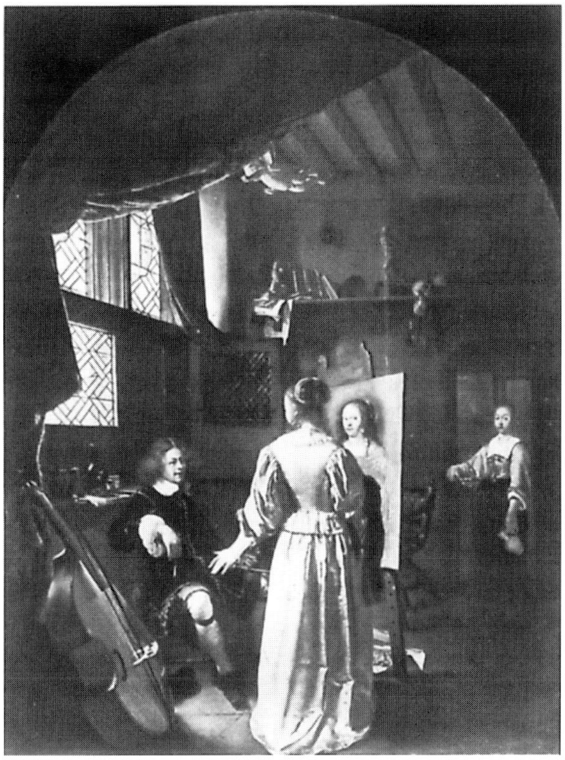

Figure 40. Frans van Mieris the Elder, *The Studio* (oil on canvas, 60 × 46 cm). Formerly Dresden, Gemäldegalerie Alte Meister; presumably destroyed.

It was in the middle of the seventeenth century that some Dutch painters registered the house as their workplace by accounting for their own place in it. This acknowledgment of the house as the painter's workplace produced diverse pictorial results. Frans van Mieris the Elder, in a painting (formerly in Dresden, Gemäldegalerie) distantly related to Vermeer's *Art of Painting*, represented himself in the midst of the social activity of the household: A maid is coming in the door, the model/sitter poses for us as much as for him, and he too poses for us (Fig. 40). The painter represents himself engaged in a public activity. By contrast, a painting of the interior of a house by Pieter Janssens Elinga (Frankfurt, Städelsches Kunstinstitut) shows the mistress reading, the maid sweeping, and most extraordinary notations of direct light, reflected light, and shadow. Light, of course, is represented in paintings of Dutch house interiors by Pieter de Hooch, and with a similar diminished attention to figures. But there is an intensity, an obsessiveness even about Elinga's attention to the effects of light in this house. Perhaps he represents it as a light box because he is marking it and hence observing it as his workplace. Through the door in the far room, the painter lets us catch sight of his back, legs, and perhaps an arm raised to work at an unseen easel. We are permitted a glimpse of Vermeer in his house, too, secreted in an even more complex way in the reflected leg of the easel in the mirror of the so-called *Music-Lesson* (London, Collection of Her Majesty the Queen). In the *Art of Painting*, he appears to celebrate the painter's place in the home as his studio. This is Van Mieris with a difference: Though in the home, the painter's room is not subject to the comings and goings depicted by Van Mieris (though Vermeer, we must remember, fathered at least eleven children and lived in a troubled household.) And what Vermeer attends to in the doorless room that is his studio is not the Elinga's play of light but the woman in view in the light. The painter paints with a single woman in view. Beneath the trappings assembled to make her into the *Art of Painting* (the title goes back to an inventory drawn up by Vermeer's wife), the painter has fashioned a woman in the home into his model.

Whereas Rembrandt as a painter deserted the home to construct a studio apart and brought the world, including Hendrickje Stoffels, his common-law wife, in to perform, Vermeer set up his easel at home and turned the women into privileged models. The difference between Rembrandt and Vermeer paintings of women with letters is not only a question of narrative – Rembrandt's *Bathsheba* versus a household scene – but also the assumption of different work sites.

Vermeer's achievement as a painter has been linked to the series, made toward the end of his short career, of distinctive representations of solitary women in the household. The women are upright, impressive, self-possessed, and separated from children and from men. What is interesting about them is less what they do (mostly traditional domestic and pictorial activities such as making lace, reading letters, and cooking) than how they are represented. Indeed, the so-called *Young Woman with a Water Jug* does nothing but pose in the home (Fig. 41).

In these paintings, Vermeer effectively removes the representation of women from the tensions, as we have seen them, that concerned other artists. (In Vermeer's paintings, mistresses and maids collude with each other openly and frankly rather than focusing the problem of identity, as we saw in Maes.) There is a difference between using family members as one's models and taking the woman in the home as *the* model. While Ter Borch offers us the virtue of a woman spinning, Vermeer offers us the virtue of the woman posing in the home.

Vermeer's pictures have been plumbed for their psychological depth. The nuance with which the absent male painter attends, past the barrier of chair or table and rug, to the self-absorbed woman in view has been remarked on. It has been said that Vermeer overcame his inhibitions to celebrate women and let them simply be. That is to treat them as objects of his generous feeling. But there is another aspect to this: The basis of Vermeer's attention to these women rests on the way he represents the house as his studio and the women in the house as his models.

To paint women in this way took a certain daring. This is registered not only in the extraordinary nuance of Vermeer's invention and execution, which has often been remarked on, but also in their scale. When looking at reproductions, one tends to forget that these pictures are astonishingly small – at forty-centimeters high, the *Young Woman with a Water Jug* is no bigger than Vermeer's life-sized head of the *Woman with the Pearl Earring* (The Hague, Mauritshuis). A condition of the extraordinary presence of these painted women is the reduction in scale from Vermeer's earliest genre paintings. Another condition was the market. We know from recent research that one patron in Delft bought the greater part of Vermeer's small production of paintings. Unlike Rembrandt, Vermeer, it seems, could paint without having to intervene in the marketplace. Vermeer with his single patron was, then, rather in the position of Velázquez and the Spanish king, but his workplace was the household instead of the court. Like Spain, the town of Delft was economically depressed in just these years. So for each painter, there was an element of retreating to a safe harbor mixed with the success of finding patronage.

It was argued in the Netherlands at the time that woman's place should be in the home. Jacob Cats wrote that the husband must be on the street to practice his trade while the wife must stay at home to be in the kitchen. But here, as elsewhere in his writings, Cats appears to have been prescriptive rather than descriptive. Though there is evidence that the Dutch household was conspicuously small compared to those in other places at the time and the servants few, it was not only lived in but also

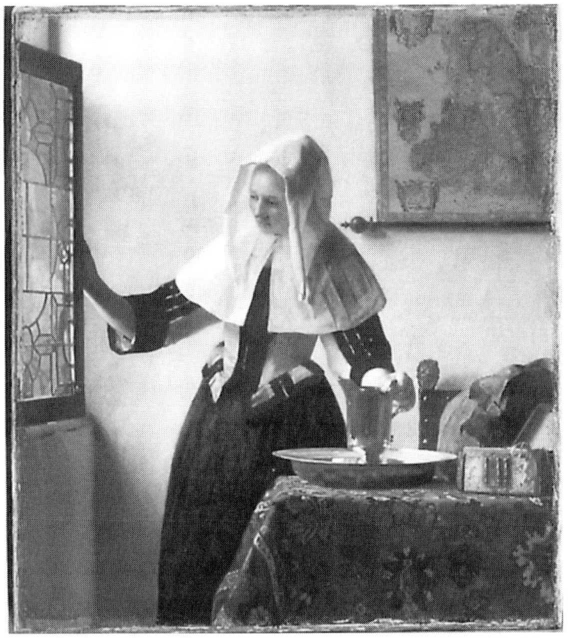

Figure 41. Johannes Vermeer, *Young Woman with a Water Jug* (oil on canvas, 45.7 × 40.5 cm). New York, The Metropolitan Museum of Art, Gift of Henry G. Marquand, 1889. Photo: museum.

worked in by men as well as women. It had not yet become the female domain it was to become in the nineteenth century. Vermeer, then, is not registering the social fact of domesticity but is producing it in his pictures. This is one reason that they appear to us to be not only pictorial performances of great skill but also socially valid. Vermeer's pictures of these women are enabled by the relationship he establishes between his practice as a painter and social practice. There is an element of entrapment about the situation – the condition of female idealization is domesticity. But the artist in the home-studio is also trapped. As so often occurs in European painting (one could, a bit outrageously perhaps, compare Vermeer to Picasso in this), the artist's power is not in his use of but in his identification with the situation of the women in the studio who are his models.

The proof of this is revealed in the small *Lace-Maker* in the Louvre. The isolated worker, bending over strands of colored paint and lit unexpectedly, like the painter, from her left side, is akin to Vermeer (Fig. 42).

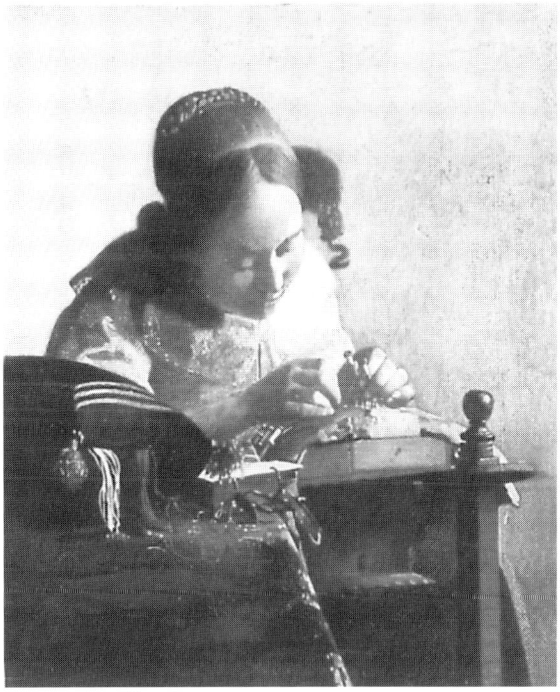

Figure 42. Johannes Vermeer, *The Lace-Maker* (oil on canvas, 24 × 21 cm). Paris, Musée du Louvre.

Tobacco, Social Deviance, and Dutch Art in the Seventeenth Century*

Ivan Gaskell

In the exploration of iconography one can easily lose sight of the historical context in which images were initially created and had their meaning. Considerable attention is now paid to literary conventions as well as to pictorial traditions in order to elucidate the processes whereby visual meaning is generated; yet the role of social convention, discoverable by means of historical rather than art historical research, often gets short shrift from the art historian. This paper represents an attempt to discover some of the means by which social conventions contributed to the development of an iconography – that of tobacco – and suggests that such an approach can reveal lines of enquiry regarding pictorial association which might otherwise not be so accessible. The association of tobacco with the imagery of both the Five Senses and vanitas allegories is well known; yet its place in the pictorial – and literary – language of festive comedy is less familiar. The latter is the subject of this paper.

The use of tobacco has quite a long history: some four hundred years in Europe. Smoking, to which use tobacco is most popularly put, has quite different social connotations today from what it had in Holland three hundred years ago in 1684; and in 1634 the connotations would have been different again. Social conventions surrounding tobacco are forever changing, yet conventions always exist. For instance, many would be surprised if someone were to light a cigarette here in the hall while I am speaking. To do so would be to contravene one of the conventions of the academic symposium in the 1980s and furthermore, it is against the rules of the museum. But let us look at another discussion group: the synod of the Dutch Reformed Church of South Holland in the 1630s. Its members met each year to transact the ecclesiastical business of the province, different towns acting as hosts in successive years. This involved the dispensing and enjoyment of a certain amount of municipal hospitality. But in 1630 at Schoonhoven the delegates apparently trespassed beyond the bounds of propriety. The following year, when they assembled at Schiedam, a complaint was brought that the members of the synod had consumed, to their great disgrace, a hundred guilders' worth of tobacco at the public's expense. The fact that such alleged behaviour was thought scandalous and could not be ignored is suggested by the fact that the burgomaster of Schoonhoven attested to this disgrace. The members of the synod rebutted the charge, claiming that they had always eaten at their own expense, not at that of their brothers, let alone the public. This declaration of innocence was accepted by the 1631 synod and nothing further is heard of the affair.[1] We can infer that the burgomaster and his fellow citizens resented the cost of entertaining the synod which must have been high-

* Editor's note: This article, based on a lecture delivered by the author in June 1984, was originally published in *Holländische Genremalerei im 17. Jahrhundert; Symposium Berlin 1984* (*Jahrbuch Preussischer Kulturbesitz*, Sonderband 4), ed. H. Bock and T. W. Gaehtgens, pp. 117–37, Berlin, 1987.

er than they had anticipated. In seeking redress they chose to attack the members' consumption of tobacco, while the synod members defended not their smoking, but their eating habits. This suggests that not only was the use of tobacco the weak spot in the synod's defence, but also that the use of tobacco by the elders and ministers may well have genuinely shocked some of the righteous citizens of Schoonhoven. Why should this have been the case? There was, of course, no clear precedent or pronouncement in the Bible to the authority of which the Dutch Calvinist ministers or their critics could appeal, for tobacco was a novelty. Lay scholars were similarly on their own. Classical precedent, to which they usually appealed, was of no avail, for tobacco had been unknown to antiquity. So the popular writer was thrown back upon the generalizing response such as is to be found in Roemer Visscher's emblem book, *Sinne-poppen*, in which we find the emblem of a man smoking a pipe with the motto "Often something new, seldom anything good" (Fig. 43): in other words, an expression of a general distrust of novelties.[2]

In tobacco we have a phenomenon which was new towards the end of the sixteenth century: one of a number of consequences of the discovery of the New World which could not be accounted for by anything in the experience of the Old. By examining the impact of this previously unknown substance upon a sophisticated, changing society it may be possible to discover something of the character of conformity and deviance within that society. In particular I want to explore how the recreational use of tobacco came to be associated with social deviance and how later, in the course of the seventeenth century, it became respectable. Of course this exposition has entailed begging several questions, such as what is to be understood by conformity, respectability and deviance in the seventeenth century Dutch context. Working definitions may emerge in the course of the paper.

At the time of the synods of Schoonhoven and Schiedam the use of tobacco was a matter of public concern. The first book on the subject to be published in the United Provinces appeared in 1622: *Tabacologia* by Johann Neander.[3] Much of his information is derived from earlier botanical, herbalist and apothecary writers. His text epitomizes the framework within which tobacco was discussed in educated circles at this time. Essentially a contrast is drawn between the medicinal use to which apothecaries' preparations from the plant were put and the recreational use of smoking it in pipes. Neander advocated its value as an apothecary preparation and gave instructions for growing it in the herb garden and for preparing it. He recommended its use, in combination with other apothecaries' drugs, as a treatment for most diseases. In seeing tobacco as something of a herbal panacea, Neander was far from isolated. On the other hand, he was opposed to smoking it for pleasure. Interestingly, however, in view of the early seventeenth century scholar's reflex mental reaction to consult classical precedent, Neander points out that the use of smoke (though not, of course, tobacco smoke) was medically supported by the authority of Aristotle, Galen and Hippocrates. This almost desperate search for guidance from antiquity is recurrent in early discussions of tobacco. So here we have the three questions most commonly discussed in the early seventeenth century regarding tobacco: is tobacco of use as a herbal preparation, can smoking it be sanctioned on medical grounds and is smoking for pleasure permissible? The third – concerning the social use of tobacco – would appear to have most to do with social deviance and consequently the aspect of iconography which it is the purpose of this paper to explore, yet it is important to place this in the context of medical discussion.

In view of its novelty there could be no classically derived orthodoxy regarding tobacco from which medical commentators could deviate. Theorists had virtually nothing upon which to base their opinions. As a result the door was open for the kind of speculation which elevated tobacco to panacea status. Neander's enthusiasm for it has been remarked upon. The most widely read Dutch medical writer of the century was Johann van Beverwyck and in his *Schat der gesontheydt*, first published in 1636, he claimed that tobacco was a prophylactic against plague.[4] This notion was subsequently taken up by Isbrand de Diemerbroeck in his treatise on the disease published eight years later.[5] In 1636 the plague had been epidemic in Holland and such claims for the power of tobacco and its smoke may have given rise to hopes provoked by desperation. This notion soon achieved the status of a popular medical belief and was discussed as such by James Primrose in his widely published work on popular medical ideas which first appeared in London in 1638 and the following year in Amsterdam.[6] While refuting the idea that tobacco had an antidotary quality against the plague, Primrose nonetheless acknowledged the possibility that the drying effect of the smoke might cleanse the body and make it less susceptible to receiving the poison of the disease. The medical mythology of the plant continued to expand. In spite of the fraudulent use which must have been made of tobacco and its preparations by unlicensed or vagrant practitioners, the place of tobacco in polite medical circles was so volatile – by turns ignored and treated as a panacea – that questions of deviance in terms of the medical profession and its imitators are impossible to pin down.

The herbal use of tobacco effectively helped to sanction the medical use of tobacco smoke. Anthony Chute, whose book on tobacco was published in a Dutch translation in 1623, argued that smoking tobacco in pipes, as well as using it in apothecary preparations, could have a beneficial medicinal effect.[7] This in turn provided a justification for recreational smoking as well as for smoking as a form of medical treatment in specific circumstances, for instance, as a plague prophylactic, as has been mentioned. The use of such a general medical justification for smoking for pleasure meant that medical theorists were in a cleft stick. If smoking was good for you, yet socially undesirable for reasons to be discussed below, how could it be properly condemned? The anxiety underlies contemporaneous discussions of tobacco by medical writers. They found it difficult to justify their ideal that its use should be controlled by medical practitioners.

Why was smoking for pleasure distrusted? Firstly it was a question of the observed effects and secondly of who did it. Its supposed narcotic, or stupefactory, effect was noted by the eminent Flemish botanist, Rembert Dodoens, in 1574. He noted that

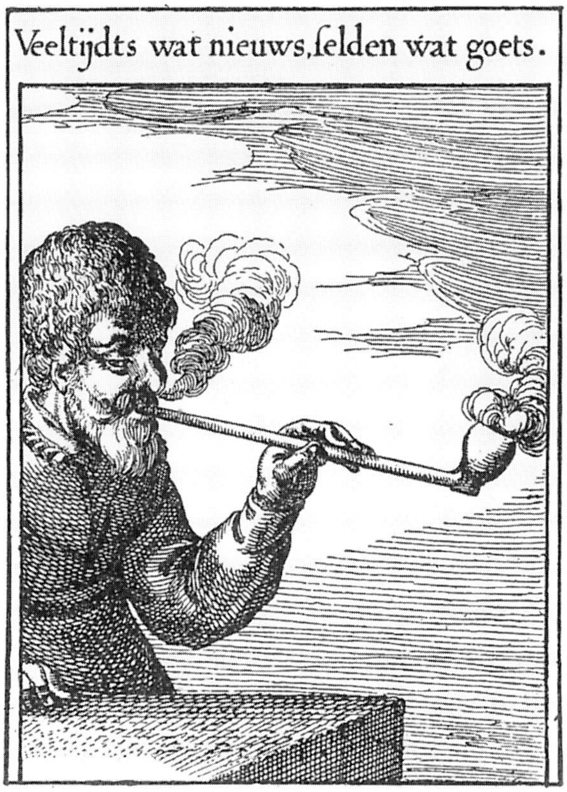

Figure 43. Emblem from Roemer Visscher, *Sinne-poppen*, Amsterdam 1614.

"Peruvian henbane", as he called it, induced a condition like drunkenness.[8] This affinity of effect caused it to be treated like alcohol. Indeed, the very vocabulary and syntax of smoking was determined by this similarity. Tobacco was said to be sipped, or drunk, and the contemporaneous chronicler of the Dutch revolt, Emmanuel van Meteren, described its use, the growth of tobacco inns and the similarity with alcohol of its effects.[9] It was introduced into the Netherlands through the western sea ports by ships' crews during the 1580s and local regulations soon treated it on the same terms as alcohol. Its use by sailors, a distrusted sub-cultural group whose members had their own distinctive dress, slang and even gait, and tobacco's reputation for inducing a form of drunkenness led to its becoming associated inextricably not only with wealthy rakes, but predominantly with the lowest social groups. Smoking gave them some compensation for hardship and an air of bravado. The soldiery was another such group with a bad reputation amongst the

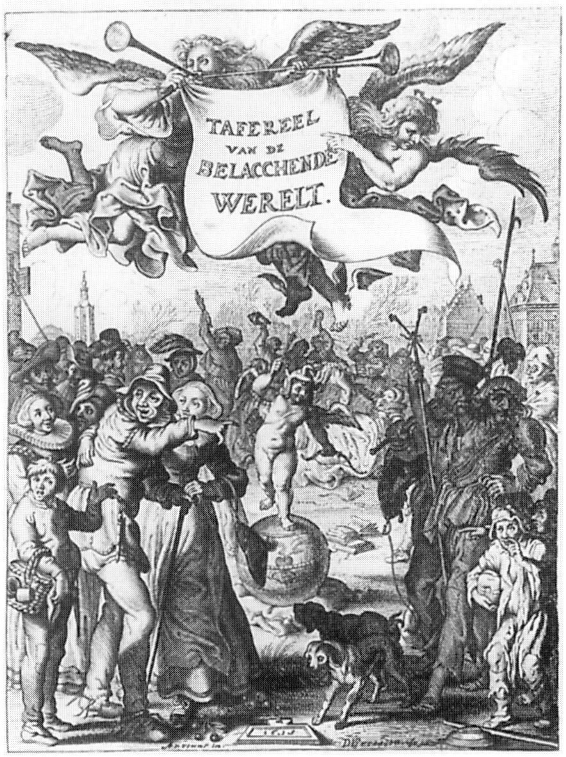

Figure 44. Frontispiece from Adriaen van de Venne, *Tafereel van de belacchende werelt*, The Hague, 1635. London, The Warburg Institute, University of London. Photo: The Warburg Institute.

respectable citizens which quickly developed a taste for tobacco. The Englishman, Thomas Raymond, when serving as a common soldier in Prince Frederik-Hendrik's army in 1633, used tobacco for the first time. He wrote, "I had not yet come to know the virtue of tobacco, but in this hard march was wished to take some. I tryed but could by no means like it, for it made me sick and ill all daye".[10] Because of its effect, smoking became a badge of manliness which inevitably appealed to soldiers. Sutlers soon took to supplying tobacco as well as drink. "Every morneing", wrote Raymond, "there went fellowes about crying 'Brandie, wyn, toback'."[11] Furthermore, English soldiers appear to have been responsible for introducing the craft of pipe making in Gouda and possibly Amsterdam during the early years of the century.[12] To the socially suspect groups – from the point of view of the urban middle class – of sailors and soldiers can be added the lowest rural classes as abusers of tobacco. The inebriation and stupefaction of boors in low taverns became an oft-repeated theme in the art of low life painters such as Adriaen Brouwer and later the Ostade brothers and David Teniers II.

Although the use of tobacco for pleasure was far from confined to these low social groups, the fact

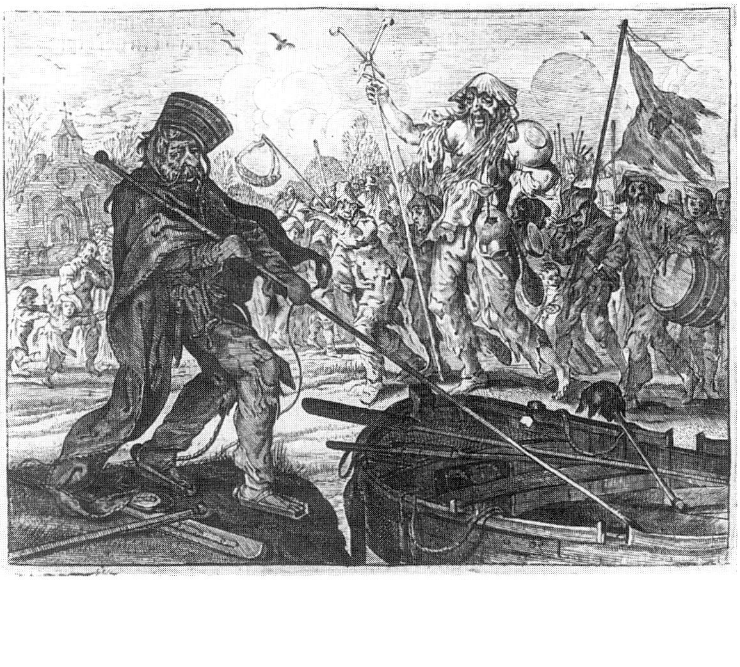

Figure 45. Illustration from Adriaen van de Venne, *Tafereel van de belacchende werelt*, The Hague, 1635. London, The Warburg Institute, University of London. Photo: The Warburg Institute.

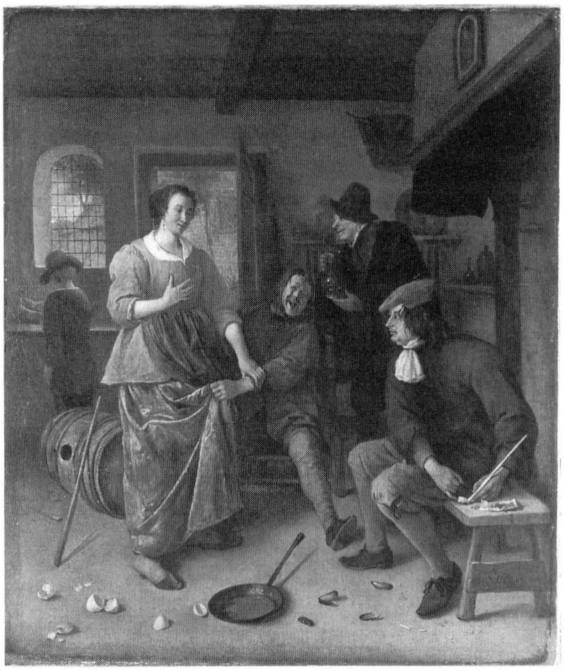

Figure 46. Jan Steen, *Interior of an Inn* (oil on canvas, 43.3 × 38.1 cm). London, The National Gallery. Reproduced by courtesy of the Trustees, The National Gallery.

that these groups had adopted the substance for their own distinct, sub-cultural use prompted anxieties regarding propriety on the part of those sections of society which might be termed respectable. This concern underlies much of the medical discussion of the plant when smoking is being considered. For example, the chapter, "Of the right use of Tabacco" from James Primrose's medical treatise of 1651, is largely concerned with its use for pleasure, though he never openly states this. Since it has a violent purgative effect, he wrote, it should only be smoked in moderation in which case it cheers the brain by its heat. He undermines its recreational use by stating that it should not be taken with drink as this counteracts the smoke's drying effect and fills the head with vapours.[13] Other medical writers who were more forthright in their attempts to discredit the use of tobacco for pleasure recount horror stories. Johann Neander reported a case of a smoker who had lost his sense of smell through smoking tobacco.[14] On dissection, the brain of another young smoker was found to have been covered with black soot.[15] The report evidently played upon a major fear about tobacco: that its intoxicating effect might be the result of the smoke acting directly upon the brain and doing permanent damage. Primrose devoted a chapter to the subject in which he refuted this notion, arguing that the smoke does not rise to the brain, for as much is expelled as is inhaled. Furthermore, he argued that dizziness and intoxication are caused by the overheating of humours, rather than by the smoke as such. Nonetheless, the notion persisted that smokers were progressively incapacitating themselves and that such behaviour, though it might fit the lower classes (whose members were in any case progressively incapacitated by the nature of their labours and deprivations), certainly should not affect the respectable element of society for whom physical integrity was an unspoken ideal.

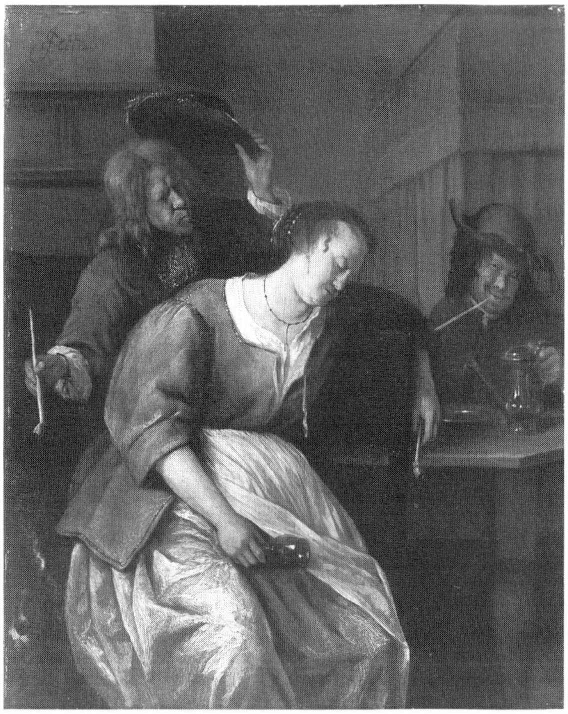

Figure 47. Jan Steen, *A Man Blowing Smoke at an Inebriated Woman* (oil on panel, 50.2 × 24.8 cm). London, The National Gallery. Reproduced by courtesy of the Trustees, The National Gallery.

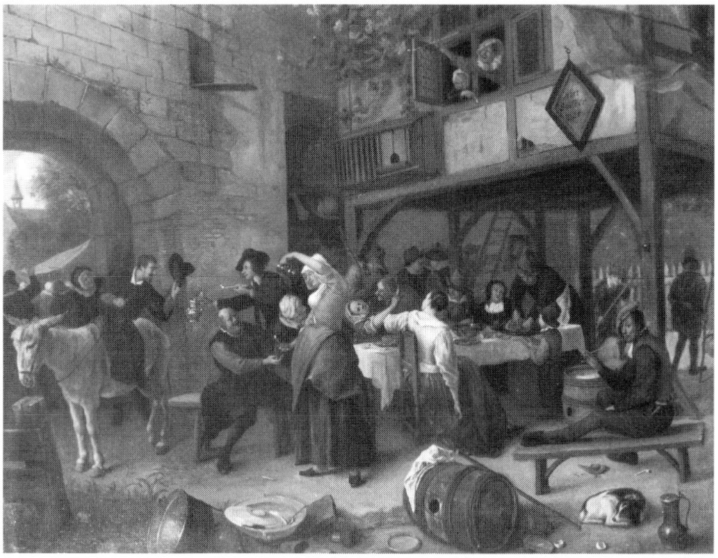

Figure 48. Jan Steen, *Rhetoricians' Feast* (oil on canvas on panel, 65 × 84 cm). Present location unknown.

Actual contemporaneous practice, its observation by the middle classes and the accompanying beliefs led to the association of tobacco smoking with low life; and to these must be added the development of literary and artistic conventions which did so much both to promulgate and to reflect middle class reactions. Tobacco was used for pleasure most conspicuously by social groups from which members of the urban middle class were anxious to dissociate themselves. The appropriate treatment of the lower orders in literature and art was conventionally comic. Tobacco soon became a subject of comedy. Arguments both for and against the use of tobacco for pleasure were couched in comic terms. The writer and artist Adriaen van de Venne wrote two short, comic stories, published together in 1634, on the theme of tobacco smoking. In the first, a praise of one of the country's most important products, peat, a farmer is seen smoking on a peat boat which leads to comic attempts to extinguish what is thought to be a fire threatening the cargo. In the second, a blacksmith and his assistant discover a herb which they plan to turn into tobacco. Smoking is praised by the assistant, for it clarifies poor eyesight, expels lice and drives away wives.[16] The comic justifications rely on medical and social assumptions. The property of expelling lice helps to tie its benefits to a certain social class, while driving away wives alludes to the question of domestic pollution. The houseproud character of the middle class urban housewife has been remarked upon many times. Relentless cleansing and ordering of her domestic realm of an almost ritualistic nature was frequently commented upon by foreign visitors in the seventeenth century. The contention that smoking tobacco is good for the eyes illustrates the manner in which medical discussion of the substance could be deployed in the context of comedy. The same justification is used by Lubbert, the central character in another book by Adriaen van de Venne, *Tafereel van de belacchende werelt*, published in 1635. Lubbert is a simple rustic whose experiences at the great annual fair of The Hague form the substance of the comedy. He defends tobacco smoking when confronted with two apes, one with a pipe, dancing in a rope dancer's tent.[17] Smoking, made fun of with the popular device of animal satire, is presented as a festive activity: festivity, comedy and low life being conventional partners in the literature and art of the day.

While Adriaen van de Venne set a discussion of smoking during a kermis, Pieter Schrijver also used the conventions of festive comedy in his light satire against smoking, this time of carnival. He called his pamphlet, published in 1630, *Saturnalia, or a Poetical Shrovetide Play,* appealing to a popular genre which went back to the time of Hans Sachs and beyond. Under this carnival mask he stated the argument with which we are now familiar: the only legitimate use of tobacco was medical. Smoking for pleasure was time wasting and dirty.[18] Schrijver's appeal to the forms of festive comedy is significant, for it helped to define the social connotations of tobacco for the Dutch.

Smoking became an indispensable property of the burlesque. When, at the beginning of his burlesque description of the city of Amsterdam, Pierre le Jolle invokes a modern muse, the muse of Pantagruel, the muse of the burlesque, he describes her exhaling the tobacco smoke from her pipe through her nose.[19] A pipe and tobacco smoke had become the attributes of the personification of topsy-turvydom. Under her auspices the world was turned upside down. The poem, published in Amsterdam in 1666, is dedicated to "the most vilanous, most filthy, most ugly, most ungracious, most ignorant gentlemen, the scavengers and dredgers of the canals of that city". The climax of the poem is the familiar setting for the festive comedy of inversion, the kermis, when, as Le Jolle writes, those whose occupations are the vilest mix freely with everyone. And now, at last, the question of social deviance comes to the fore.

Festive occasions, in literature and art and perhaps in fact, saw the temporary dissolution of hierarchies; hierarchies of class, caste and age. During the kermis the dredgers of the canals mixed freely with the prosperous merchants and regent oligarchs – in theory, at least. Those who were otherwise rigorously excluded from the life of the urban community entered the town and mingled with its members. Amongst these, the most prominent were the vagrant poor. These were the most conspicuous social deviants of the Republic in the eyes of the settled population. Former sailors and soldiers, carters and bargees, refugees from the devastation of war or failed harvests, convicted criminals: these were the people who had broken the bonds with a settled community. Such bonds were all-important in the seventeenth-century Netherlands, for they defined social and political existence in a country of fierce parochial sentiment and claims of sovereignty. The most common form of criminal punishment in serious cases was judicial exile from town or province: the outcasts suffered complete social death, for beyond the confines of his immediate polity he was deemed not to exist. These vagrant outcasts had no claim upon the famous charitable institutions of the Dutch towns, for these were exclusively parochial in their responsibilities. The most they could expect would be three nights' lodging in a casual ward followed by expulsion. But they were the stock characters of the kermis and as such the reality of their condition was overlaid by the images of literary and artistic convention. Adriaen van de Venne describes a band of vagrants at the kermis of The Hague and introduces material familiar from the literature of roguery: a cant vocabulary and a list and description of forty-two different categories of beggar, such as those who claim to be former Turkish prisoners, repentant prostitutes, fake lepers and many others.[20] This list is given by their leader who is named Oud Roembout. He appears in two etched illustrations to the book, both after Van de Venne's own designs, one of which is the title page (Figs. 44, 45). He is a swaggering fellow, clad in rags. A bowl and a basket are employed as makeshift epaulettes and his bonnet is a sagging cabbage leaf. From his waist hangs an assortment of pots and pans and a broken jug. His long staff, which he holds prominently like a wand of office in both prints and in a related grisaille painting, is topped by a pair of crossed tobacco pipes. In the painted version a similar pair dangle from his waist.[21] Instruments of smoking constitute the standard of this mock-heroic leader of the band of vagrant beggars in burlesque disguise who inhabit the festive comic, topsy-turvy world of the kermis.

If we trace the imagery of topsy-turvydom in Dutch art we find tobacco to be a key element in scenes of comic disorder. This can be done most conveniently in the work of one artist: the great painter of comic themes of the seventeenth century, Jan Steen. Pipe smoking is regularly depicted in Steen's paintings, but pictorial emphasis is only placed upon it in certain circumstances, the vast majority of which reflect its burlesque and licentious associations. Two settings associated with topsy-turvydom, in that domestic order is permanently reversed, were the tavern and the brothel. Steen made use of smoking motifs in both contexts, usually to evoke sexual licence. In several tavern scenes Steen included a figure of a man stuffing the bowl of his pipe with a finger to underline the sexual suggestion of tavern flirtations (Fig. 46).[22] Another motif Steen used to evoke the comedy of sex was that of a pipe leaning against an earthenware bowl, or chamberpot on the floor of rooms in taverns or brothels in which couples are involved in sexual encounters.[23] Tobacco was also included amongst the stimulants by means of which clients at brothels or taverns of assignation were befuddled and robbed, a comic theme treated several times by Steen.[24] Literary allusions also make the role of tobacco clear in the context of the brothel as a means of comic degradation. Early in its history smoking had become an almost exclusively male activity, associated as it was with the masculinity of sailors' and soldiers' society. Women who smoked were therefore seen as perverse and degraded. This provided a comic theme of inversion for Jan Steen who painted several works in which women smoking, or being offered a pipe by a grinning man, are depicted (Fig. 47).[25] The ugliest prostitutes in the lowest brothels described by the author of a late seventeenth century book on prostitution in Amsterdam are characterized by their short tobacco pipes.[26]

One of Steen's most explicit images of the festive role of tobacco smoking is a *Rhetoricians' Feast*, last recorded on the London art market in 1979 (Fig. 48).[27] Rhetoricians were guilds of amateur actors and poets which performed during fairs and held their own festivals, the heyday of which was in the sixteenth century. During the decline of the rhetoricians' guilds in the seventeenth century they developed a reputation for promoting good fellowship and the festive indulgence and topsy-turvydom associated with the kermis. In this painting a rhetoricians' feast is in progress beneath the headquarters of the chamber, a building beneath which a stage could be erected. Some of the members are eating and drinking while others are smoking. The pleasures are made plain by the verses which are inscribed on the floor beam: "When everyone has eaten and drunk heartily, don't forget the friendly pipes." Two laughing figures lean out of a window, one smoking, the other holding his pipe in the air, while below a youth offers a flagon and a pipe to a man with a donkey. Through the arch of the gateway the kermis stalls and crowds can be seen, making the festive setting of the scene quite clear. Steen used the accoutrements of drink and tobacco in other scenes depicting rhetoricians: crossed pipes could even be their emblem.[28]

Given this comic association of tobacco with festive disorder we should not be surprised that almost the only domestic scenes by Steen in which smoking plays a part are those which illustrate proverbs of topsy-turvydom. One of the proverbs which Steen illustrated several times encapsulates the notion that children will inevitably imitate their elders thus ensuring that the follies of the world are perpetuated: "as the old sing, so the young pipe" (soo de ouden songen, soo pijpen de jongen). Steen makes visual puns on the word "pijpen" – to pipe, or the plural of the noun, pipe. In one version, in the Mauritshuis, The Hague, children play recorders while adults smoke tobacco pipes; whilst in another in the same museum a man holds a pipe to a boy's willing lips.[29] In the version in the Rijksmuseum, Amsterdam, three children have actually got hold of pipes by themselves.[30]

This motif is also to be found in Steen's most stylized image of domestic topsy-turvydom: a picture in which a selection of proverbs of reversal and foolish behaviour are brought together to form a coherent scene of domestic disorder.[31] The boy on the left blows pipe smoke into his sleeping mother's face. In a similar scene in the Wellington Museum, London, the head of the household philanders with a young woman in the centre of the composition while smoking a pipe.[32] Above the heads of the participants in both these scenes, and in several other similar ones, hangs a basket containing instruments of retribution which is to serve as a warning against the follies depicted: the beggar's clapper and crutch and the birch of judicial whippings can be seen clearly.[33] The implication is clear: such behaviour leads inevitably to punishment, poverty and beggary. Those who persist will join Oud Roem-bout's band of roving beggars and will suffer the stigma of irreversible social deviance. In his pictures Steen makes the role of tobacco clear in this form of conventional proverb wisdom and festive comedy, as does Adriaen van de Venne in his description of Oud Roem-bout's band. Among those most likely to follow Oud Roem-bout's staff with its crossed tobacco pipes are, wrote Van de Venne, tobacco sippers who lose their money and waste their days.[34]

Although we are in search of social nuances which are very difficult to pin down, it should now be evident that tobacco smoking was not an entirely respectable pastime in the 1630s and beyond. It was associated most strongly with social groups which were either viewed askance by the dominant middle classes, or, like vagrant beggars, seen as outright deviants. Smoking was not, of course, confined to these groups, but when a number of ministers indulged together, as at Schoonhoven in 1630, more than a few eyebrows were raised. Conventions were to grow up, however, which were to make the recreational use of tobacco acceptable to the respectable burghers. The main reason for this appears to have been economic: in short, the commercial capitalist profit motive complemented by the fiscal needs of the Republic.

Dutch merchant vessels sailing to and from the Americas captured a valuable share of the Spanish and, more particularly, the English carrying and direct import trade in tobacco in the years following the 1609 truce. By 1620 Amsterdam and Rotterdam were the two principal continental ports of entry for tobacco. This in turn stimulated the growth of a tobacco processing industry which involved curing, spinning and cutting on a large scale. The two latter processes when developed on a commercial scale allowed the retail sale of tobacco to be undertaken by non-specialists, especially in inns; whereas previously apothecaries experienced in preparing and cutting herbs had dominated the domestic retail trade. The major part of the commercially processed tobacco was exported to other parts of Europe, most notably to the Baltic. This new commerce attracted taxation and Johannes Neander claimed in 1632 that the States-General was in receipt of some fl. 30,000 a year from tobacco imports.[35]

The Amsterdam merchants in particular were not content with an import, processing and export procedure. The desire to influence the price of overseas leaf on the Amsterdam market in their favour led Amsterdam merchants to encourage and to sponsor the domestic cultivation of the crop. This development is in marked contrast to the stifling in England of domestic tobacco cultivation in order to protect the interests of the Virginia Company and it highlights commercial differences between the two countries. Tobacco was grown on a significant scale in the province of Utrecht from about 1615 onwards, the region near Amersfoort becoming the centre of the cultivation. The initiative was taken by Amsterdam tobacco merchants and businessmen who formed agreements with local Amersfoort interests and specialist growers, sometimes from England, and provided the risk capital. This led to the development of a new pattern of agriculture in the provinces of Utrecht, Gelderland and Overijssel.[36] These inland provinces soon derived considerable fiscal income from taxes on the new crop, in Utrecht from 1628 and Gelderland in 1647.[37] The domestic leaf was mixed with the more expensive American product and the resulting mixture was used to undercut Spanish and English competition in European markets.

Parallel to the growth of a significant tobacco industry was the growth of the manufacture of the most important accessory, the pipe. Pipe making appears to have been begun by English soldiers before and during the Twelve Year Truce in the early years of the century. The town of Gouda became and remained the main centre of pipe manufacture. It was begun there in 1617 by English mercenaries.[38] Pipe making entailed the development of a service trade, for the best pipe clay came from England. This had further administrative ramifications, both nationally and locally, for the States-General derived an income from the periodic sale of the monopoly right to import and sell the material, while the municipality of Gouda appointed a clay measurer in about 1635 to oversee and regulate trading.[39]

With so many powerful commercial and governmental interests becoming involved in every aspect of the tobacco industry and with ever increasing capital investments and revenues at stake, especially from the mid-1630s onwards, it is understandable that the image of tobacco using had to be improved so that any social stigma attached to it should be lost. In the first place the end product itself appears to have been improved so that nausea and stupefaction were no longer the almost invariable consequences of smoking a pipe. Pipe stems were lengthened so that the smoke was cooled and lost some of its acrid quality during its journey from bowl to mouth. Length of stem and degree of finish and polish became an important index of respectability. Recent excavations of rubbish tips in Amsterdam reveal that in prosperous burgher areas well-finished, burnished pipes with maker's marks on the heel predominate, whilst in sailors' districts the finds are mainly of unburnished, unmarked or roughly marked short pipes.[40] By the 1660s the use of a long-stemmed, finely polished and heel-marked pipe was regarded as respectable by many burghers, whilst the short-stemmed, unpolished pipe remained the emblem of the lower classes and the socially deviant. This convention can be seen operating in conjunction with those described above in an account of Amsterdam brothels of 1681. In one such establishment the minders dressed like sailors and smoked short-stemmed pipes in order to suggest a taste and capacity for ruthless violence.[41]

Although by the 1660s commercial encouragement and familiarity had made tobacco generally acceptable, the ruling burghers nonetheless formulated codes of propriety governing its use. Its association with manliness effectively made smoking a male preserve and it was best done away from the scene of domestic orderliness, in the tea and coffee houses which were introduced during this decade. For those who still distrusted or disliked smoking, snuff was introduced, the taking of which was untainted by long established associations. As a symbol of their appropriation of tobacco for recreational purposes, the burghers dictated the ways in which it might be used. On no account was it to be mixed with work. On 15 December 1668, the regents of Gouda passed an order on the misuse of tobacco. It noted that workmen, members of guilds and even children were seen in the streets, or even at work, with pipes. It ordered that no-one was to smoke at work, except during specific rest periods, under penalty of a fine of fl. 3.[42] Work and recreation should on no account be confused, the order implied, and labour was certainly not to be polluted.

We have moved from attempts to limit tobacco to medical uses near the beginning of the century to attempts to limit it to use during periods of rest fifty years later. Its early association with deviant social behaviour and outcast groups still survived in the conventions of art and literature which themselves were involved in a complex interplay with historical social realities. As tobacco grew from being a small scale amusement for fringe groups into big business, so its social image improved and the nature of deviance in relationship to it was redefined. The vagrant hordes of Oud Roem-bout might still haunt the imagination of the respectable burgher, but the fact of wielding a tobacco pipe had lost its power to shock. The vagrant deviants had been disarmed by the power of Amsterdam capital on the one hand and the burlesque muse on the other, expelling smoke from her nose.

Didactic and Disguised Meanings?

SEVERAL SEVENTEENTH-CENTURY TEXTS ON PAINTING AND THE ICONOLOGICAL APPROACH TO DUTCH PAINTINGS OF THIS PERIOD*

Eric J. Sluijter

Judging from numerous recent publications, the debate concerning the nature of seventeenth-century Dutch painting – especially genre painting – is still raging. In recent years countless investigations have focused on the meaning and function of this art within its historical context.[1] Little agreement has been reached, however, regarding the goals pursued by Dutch painters and the perception of their works by contemporary audiences. In a recent summary Jan Bialostocki listed three possible answers: In 1876 Eugène Fromentin asserted that the painter had no other motivation than a purely artistic need to depict reality; a hundred years later iconologists, of whom E. de Jongh may be considered the most important, have suggested that the intention of these artists was *"tot lering en vermaak"* (to instruct and delight); Svetlana Alpers has offered another solution, suggesting that the aim of Dutch painters was to increase the visual knowledge of reality.[2]

The iconological method of explaining seventeenth-century Dutch genre painting – which has been enthusiastically employed since the 1960s, particularly by Dutch art historians – has been the most successful. Its results have significantly enriched our knowledge of Dutch genre art. Generally speaking, this method, which has also been somewhat imprecisely typified as "emblematic interpretation,"[3] attempts "to decipher layers of meaning and literary allusions hidden in paintings and to relate the significance of genre painting to the classical concept of *docere et delectare* (to teach and delight)."[4] As a result, a non-narrative art, which for the most part appears to be devoid of any relationship to textual references, has nevertheless been joined to texts. This has led to such far-reaching conclusions as the following: "The joyful, often coarse domestic and tavern scenes have been convincingly established as instructive lessons, warning against sin, recalling death, challenging the viewer to lead a God-fearing life."[5]

These new insights have been translated into literature intended for a broad, nonspecialized public – educational brochures, exhibition wall texts, newspaper articles, and a recent survey of Dutch art. Such materials lead one to believe that a general consensus exists concerning seventeenth-century audiences' perception of this art.[6] Furthermore, in contrast to what Josua Bruyn believed in 1981,[7] guides leading tours in Dutch museums extensively, and almost exclusively, inform visitors about the hidden meanings, disguised symbols, and moralizing messages contained in genre pieces, still lifes,

* Editor's note: This article is reprinted, with some minor revisions, from *Art in History, History in Art; Studies in Seventeenth-Century Dutch Culture*, ed. D. Freedberg and J. de Vries, pp. 175–207, Santa Monica 1991. (Book © 1991 by The Getty Center for the History of Art and the Humanities. All rights reserved. Published 1991. Printed in the United States of America.) In that volume, it was published for the first time in English, having been translated by Kist Kilian Communications; originally appeared under the title "Belering en verhulling? Enkele 17de-eeuwse teksten over de schilderkunst en de iconologische benadering van Noordnederlandse schilderijen uit deze periode," *De Zeventiende Eeuw* 4 (1988), pp. 3–28.

and even landscapes. Viewers are told what a painting "really means." Its "message," disguised by the painting's realistic appearance, usually contains an easily formulated warning and an edifying lesson.[8]

One must ask, however, whether a number of notions that have become familiar due to the success of iconological investigations (e.g., ideas regarding didactic function and the disguising of meaning) are fully justified and whether arguments in their favor are sufficiently valid. It is not my intention to analyze or elaborate on the criticisms that have been leveled at the iconological method as applied to Dutch art.[9] I merely want to take this opportunity to question several notions that have taken hold in wider circles. I will do so by using the same type of material that iconologists have so often employed to defend their arguments, namely, seventeenth-century texts. It should be emphatically stated that the important insights and results yielded by this iconological research are by no means to be dismissed; on the contrary, it is precisely these results that allow one to question whether the frameworks in which they have been placed are adequate or whether they require revision.

One of the well-known obstacles for the iconologist attempting to comprehend the aims and aspirations of the seventeenth-century Dutch painter, as well as the attitude of the artist's public, is the scarcity of contemporary literature shedding light on the matter. Given the period on which I wish to concentrate, circa 1620–1670 (qualitatively and especially quantitatively, the period of Dutch painting's greatest development), the only substantial text about painting is Philips Angel's little treatise *Lof der schilder-konst* (In Praise of Painting), published in 1642. This was the text of a lecture given to the community of painters in Leiden on Saint Luke's Day in 1641.[10] One might expect that this speech by an average painter, which was presented to an audience consisting primarily of landscape, still life, and genre painters[11] and was intended to underscore the dignity of their shared profession, would have played an important role in attempting to trace the ideas of seventeenth-century Dutch artists. It has not yet, however, been sufficiently considered within the framework of art literature.[12] A closer look at Angel's treatise may help us to grasp some of the concepts considered significant enough at the time to be formulated for that group of painters.

First, however, I would like to consider briefly Jacob Cats's account (cited by Angel) of the painter and the poet who fought for the hand of Rhodope. It serves as a useful point of departure since it reveals much about the image of the painter and the art of painting.[13] The passage, which is taken from "De beschryving van de op-komste van Rhodopis" (Description of the Rise of Rhodope) – the most extensive story in Cats's *Trou-ringh* (Wedding Ring) of 1637 – relates how a poet and a painter, together with a military officer, a counselor, a merchant, and an embroiderer, vie for the hand of the lovely Rhodope. In order to impress her, each suitor gives a detailed description of the dignity of his profession.

S. F. Witstein has demonstrated that the seventeenth-century reader of Cats's story would indeed have recognized in the poet's plea the contemporary image of "the poet" and that his role as philosopher of morals would have been entirely familiar.[14] In contrast to the other suitors, the poet presents himself as engaged with higher matters; he determines ethical principles and provides instruction regarding virtues and passions. This description is in agreement with the intellectual and moral duties traditionally identified with the art of poetry. The Horatian dictum "*Omne tulit punctum qui miscuit utile dulci*" (He who unites the useful with the pleasant is praised) is central to this ideology.[15] Furthermore, the poet gives a sample of his emblematic faculties when he perceives a "*diep geheym*" (profound secret) in the conduct of a flea that jumps onto him from Rhodope. Finally, he assures her that her name will live forever should she marry him.[16]

In contrast, the painter mentions no high intentions or lofty principles in describing his art,[17] although his narrative begins with the traditional comparison between painters and poets. The painter creates mute poetry, while the poet makes paintings that speak; both art forms serve "*de weerelt tot vermaecken*" (to amuse the world) and ease the mind. It should be noted that even in this account of shared intentions, the painter does not broach the loftier goals stressed by the poet. The painter believes that his art ranks higher than poetry for the following reason: the poet, he says mockingly, earns praise, laurels, and eternal fame with his mind and its "*hooghe vlucht*" (lofty concerns), but he can neither make a living nor support a wife and children. The painter, on the other hand, can earn money with his art.

> The worthy art of painting deserves the highest praise,
> Since, besides the pleasure it brings, it produces gain.
> I earn a lot of money, I paint great works,
> And also I know how to portray monarchs in print.
> With this I conduct trade, free and with great profit,
> And that is useful for home and family.[18]

The painter relates that he has recently been paid handsomely by a monarch who also presented him with a gold chain. In contrast, his friend the poet received only a laurel wreath and a coat of arms from the same monarch for a poem "*enckel geest en van een hooghe toon*" (full of noble spirit and lofty thoughts). The painter is thus led to remark:

> But why dwell any longer on this? I can invent things
> that can entertain you, princes, and all other people,
> And which in addition give me profit.[19]

A little later the painter also compares himself with the merchant and assures Rhodope: "Soo ghy een Coopman lieft, Ick kan oock handel drijven, En kan noch door de Konst mijn saecken beter stijven."[20] (Should you love a merchant, well, I can also conduct trade, And can swell my purse through art.) Furthermore, the painter claims to be a better tradesman than the merchant because he produces his own merchandise. His art will never desert him, while a merchant would go bankrupt if, for example, his merchandise were to be lost in a shipwreck.

As an alternative to the poet's promise that he can make Rhodope's name eternal, the painter claims that he can capture "*dit aerdich Beelt van uwe jonghe daghen*" (the beautiful image of your youth) and preserve it for succeeding generations, so that for a thousand years all will be able to admire her. Thus, through his art she will live eternally. The warrior's suit is parried by the argument that the painter can depict everything; he can even show Rhodope battles, if she wishes to experience them without risk. Should she find the counselor attractive because he frequently works in courtly circles, she must bear in mind that princes have honored painters for aeons.[21]

Cats starkly contrasts the painter with the poet in various ways. The painter derives his dignity not from the pursuit of lofty goals but from the production of superior merchandise, which brings him profit, and from the appreciation, largely financial in nature, that powerful patrons bestow on him.[22] The aim of his art is to delight and "*vernoegen*" (entertain), to represent what people wish to see, and, finally, to fix transient physical beauty, thus vanquishing time.[23]

Cats's description of the painter as a respected craftsman who produces superior products must have been entirely acceptable to someone such as Angel, even though Cats, the poet, undoubtedly meant this characterization, unfavorable from the standpoint of the liberal arts, to be derisive. Angel repeats this characterization in extenso when lauding the dignity of his profession, and he ranks the painter above the poet. After devoting more than three of the fifty-eight pages of his treatise to quoting Cats, Angel concludes: "Siet daer, door een Poët selfs de Schilder-Konst boven de Poësy ghestelt!" (See there, a poet himself has placed the art of painting above poetry!)

Furthermore, Angel gives no indication that the lofty, didactic aims of poetry are equally applicable to painting; he makes no mention of teaching and edification, deeper wisdom, or other intellectual pretensions. In this respect, the idea of *ut pictura poesis* (like painting, like poetry) seems to play no role for Angel. He appears equally unconcerned that existing humanistic art theory was predominantly based on the rules of poetics and rhetoric, although he gratefully makes use of Karel van Mander when it suits him. Angel must also have been aware of Franciscus Junius's *De schilder konst der oude (The Painting of the Ancients)*, which had just been published in Dutch;[24] however, he seems to have been interested in the foreword by Jan de Brune the Younger as opposed to the book itself. The pragmatic painter Angel culled from existing theoretical vocabulary about painting only those aspects that suited his needs at the moment.

When Angel wants to demonstrate the dignity and the venerability of his profession, he plunders Van Mander for names and biographies of painters from antiquity.[25] Characteristically, he concludes this section with the story of Zeuxis and Parrhasius as exemplifying the highest rank of painting reached in antiquity. Zeuxis could imitate nature so perfectly that even birds were deceived by the grapes that he painted on his panel. Nevertheless, Parrhasius surpassed Zeuxis because his imitation of nature could fool even a reasoning being, including a painter; Parrhasius painted a cloth over his painting which Zeuxis tried to pull aside.[26] When Angel discusses the high esteem that people in power have accorded painters throughout history, he again uses examples drawn primarily from Van Mander. It is apparent, however, that Angel considers the painter's status and recognition to be predominantly linked to the financial rewards that he continually and emphatically notes. He sets the conclusion of this section within the ramparts of Leiden with a discussion of the successful Leiden painter Gerrit Dou, who received five hundred *gulden* annually from a connoisseur who wished to have first choice among the paintings produced by the artist. According to Angel, this establishes how "*geacht en ghe-eert*" (respected and honored) painters are.[27]

Next, Angel addresses the traditional comparison between painting and sculpture (basing his arguments mainly on Jan de Brune's preface to Junius's work); this is followed by the comparison between painting and poetry – which has been discussed above – in order to show that painting deserves more praise than the other two arts. Angel's most important argument for ranking painting above sculpture is based on the fact that the former can imitate all that is visible in nature. To help convey this point, he enumerates subjects that can be rendered in painting but not in sculpture, including insects such as flies and spiders; the physical appearance of different kinds of metal; and intangible natural phenomena such as rain, lightning, clouds, mist, dawn, dusk, night, and reflections. Painting's capacity to capture "*schijn sonder sijn*" (semblance without being) satisfies his most important criterion.[28]

When Angel finally discusses in detail the requirements that the artist must meet and the qualities that he must possess to be worthy of the title of painter, he divides the various components of this art into specific categories. A few of these can, with some effort, be traced to such traditional theoretical notions as *iudicium*, *ingenium*, *disegno*, and *decorum*. Angel's characteristically simplified descriptions of these concepts, however, have little to do with the more learned connotations used in humanistic art theory.[29] His first requirement, "*recht oordeel*" (right judgment), only consists of a warning that one should not borrow indiscriminately from the compositions of others. Next, he advises a "*ghewisse Teycken-hant*" (steady hand for drawing): one should make no mistakes in draftsmanship. He gives the drawing of a "*tronie*" (head) as an example and points out that one eye is often not aligned properly with the other, the ears are too small, the nose too short or too long, etc.[30] "*Vloeyende ende eyghentlijcke by een voeghende gheest*" (capacity for combining things in a fluid and natural manner) refers to the painter's ability to imagine many different subjects and compose them according to their nature in order to produce an "*aenghenamen bevallijcken luyster*" (pleasantly attractive splendor). Furthermore, what has been represented must be completely comprehensible to the observer.[31] "*Kennisse van Hystorien*" (knowledge of history) means that in order to portray correctly "*Goddelicke, Poëtische en Heydensche Historien*" (religious, poetic, and mythological histories), an artist must carefully read the stories to be represented and accurately render the information that they contain. The concept of "*hooge na-gedachten*" (lofty reflections) or "*verre en eyghentlicke nagedachten*" (profound and natural reflections) means that what has been read must be thoroughly considered, so that everything depicted is consistent with what is described in the narrative – even aspects not specifically related in it. Once again, the observer must be able to discern clearly what is taking place.[32] Angel says nothing about expressing the deeper meanings contained in these stories, nor does he emphasize the expression of emotions as a means of appealing to the viewer's feelings.

Angel constantly stresses the need to imitate visible things precisely, so that they appear "almost real." Light and shadow must be distributed in such a way that even objects that seem virtually inimitable with brush and paint *"seer eyghentlijck schijnen"* (appear like the thing itself). Furthermore, the *"waerneminghe van d'eyghen natuyrlicke dinghen"* (observation of the actual natural things) ensures that the artist carefully observes optical effects and reproduces them faithfully.[33] Given that *"wy nabootsers van 't leven sijn"* (we are imitators of life), Angel states that no effort should be spared if it means that one *"de natuerlicke dingen daer mede nader by komt"* (comes nearer to natural things). In support of this, he cites examples of specific features that painters should closely observe: *"Bataelje-Schilders"* (battle painters) and *"History-schilders"* (history painters) should study the effect of a wheel turning; *"Zee-Schilders"* (marine painters), the smoke trailing from a cannon shot; *"Landschap-schilders"* (landscape painters), the reflections in water; and the painters of the *"Corteguarden"* (guardrooms), the effect of a fuse glowing as it is swung around.[34]

Angel speaks of anatomy in terms of the precise observation of limbs and muscles and their movement without mentioning correct proportions or ideal beauty.[35] He also mentions the careful rendering of texture – a seemingly typical requirement at this time – distinguishing among fabrics such as velvet, wool, and satin.[36] Most noteworthy in this discussion of working carefully after nature is a passage concerning the relationship between *"natuyrlicke na-bootsinge"* (imitation of nature) and *"handelinghe"* (manner of painting). In this passage Angel maintains that a painting by the best master should be recognizable not by any particular manner of painting but rather *"uyt de ongewoone overeenkominge die het met het leven heeft"* (by the exceptional resemblance it bears to life). He states that the highest praise one can receive is that "men noyt te voren van sulcke na-by-kominghe nae 't leven gehoort en had" (one had never before heard of such close renderings after life).[37] As a final point, Angel advises *"netticheyt"* (neatness, i.e., a careful, smooth, and finely detailed manner of painting) that must, however, be coupled with a certain *"lossicheyt"* (looseness) to prevent lapsing into a *"stijve nette onaerdigheyt"* (stiff [and] tidy unpleasantness); the *"noyt ghenoegh ghepresen"* (never sufficiently praised) Gerrit Dou is cited here as an example. Should this prove too much for the painter, he continues, it would be better to apply a *"los, wacker, soetvloeyend Penceel"* (loose, lively, smoothly flowing brush), or the artist's results will be greeted by ridicule rather than praise.[38] Finally, of course, pleasant behavior, virtue, and diligence – the latter is particularly emphasized – are necessary to attain the highest honor and fame.[39]

In discussing these requirements, Angel's constant emphasis on the need to appeal to the observer's eye is indeed remarkable. The *"aerdigh-vercierende Rijckelijckheydt"* (abundance that pleasantly embellishes, i.e., the representation of a variety of subjects in a painting) is particularly necessary because of the

> rousing affection this kindles in the art lover's mind . . . so that they [the paintings] delight the eyes of art lovers and fill them with desire; and through this the painter will sell his paintings all the better.

Furthermore, rendering texture skillfully is *"op 't aengenaemste voor yders ooge"* (the most appealing to everyone's eyes).[40] Through the *"schijn eyghentlijcke krachte (soo noem ick het)"* (appearance-simulating power [as I phrase it]), which is achieved through a proper distribution of light and shadow, one will *"het ghesichte der Konst-beminders overweldighen en in nemen"* (overwhelm the sight of art lovers and captivate them).[41] The meticulous observation and rendering of optical effects must "niet min behaeghlijck, als natuerlijck zijn in de ghemoederen der Konst-beminders, en oock een meerder begheerlust tot de Kunst verwecken" (be no less pleasant than natural in the minds of art lovers and must also arouse more desire for art), while a true-to-life palette of colors "onse Konst in 't ooghe van de Kunst-beminnende Liefhebbers en wel-ghevallen doet hebben" (makes our art appealing in the eyes of art lovers).[42] Angel's dedication of his "*Schilders Konsts-Lof-spraeck*" (encomium to painting) to Johan Overbeeck is meant to express his gratitude for having been given the opportunity to see the latter's art collection, where he was able "*te versadighen de lust van mijn nieuwsgierighe ooghen*" (to slake the desire of my inquisitive eyes) on the "*menichte van die uytnemende aerdigheden*" (multitude of excellent niceties).[43] Once again, not a word is spared for painting's edifying function. On the contrary, its appeal and delight to the eye are emphasized at length.

Finally, there is no conscious hierarchy to be discerned for the various genres in Angel's treatise.[44] As mentioned earlier, when he wants to clarify an aspect in his discussion of the requirements that a good painter must fulfill, he presents a "*tronie*" (head) as an example in his passage on drawing. Elsewhere, he cites with equal ease the work of painters of battlefields, history pieces, seascapes, landscapes, and guardroom scenes.[45] Angel apparently considered these various subjects to be specialties, which they were at the time. He does require that painters of history pieces carefully read narrative texts in order to faithfully represent them in a clear, correct, and suitable manner; he then discusses representations of various biblical and mythological subjects extensively. Yet he does not view the painting of history pieces as the painter's highest goal.[46] His admiration for Dou, who at the time painted primarily interior scenes and *tronies*, is no less than that he expresses for Rembrandt or Jan Lievens. It is these three painters – not coincidentally all from Leiden – who receive his greatest praise.[47]

Although Angel's treatise, like any other seventeenth-century treatise, does not give much information about a painter's choice of subject matter and content, I have reviewed both Cats and Angel at some length in an attempt to delineate what would have been the important points of discussion for a Leiden painter around 1641, when the status of the painter and his art were at stake. (It should be noted in passing that Angel undoubtedly saw himself as being fairly learned and was, most likely, above average in this regard.) In the first place, emphasis was placed on painting as a distinguished and respectable craft, not on the painter's intellectual aspirations.[48] Angel's audience probably included painters such as Dou, David Bailly (portraits and still lifes), Pieter van Steenwijck (still lifes), Pieter Dubordieu (portraits), Quiryn van Slingelandt, Louys Elsevier, and Maerten Frans van der Hulst (landscapes), Jan van de Stoffe (battle scenes), Cornelis Stooter (seascapes), Johannes van Staveren, Abraham de Pape, and Adriaen van Gaesbeeck (genre painters and followers of Dou), all of whom presumably listened with approval.

Angel only broaches literary aspects of content when discussing the clear rendering of a narrative text.[49] Indeed, no mention is made of a "noble, didactic purpose of the art of painting."[50] Furthermore, despite the fact that Van Mander was an important source, links with humanistic art theory can only be detected with some effort. As mentioned earlier, Angel had no interest in Junius except for De Brune's preface and the names of a few classical painters and writers on art, which he borrowed from the text.[51]

In fact, it is difficult to find anything in texts on the art of painting from this period that would indicate that didacticism was an important aim.[52] We cannot assume that the lack of writing on this subject resulted from the fact that it was considered self evident. This is highly implausible if only because literary-theoretical discourses and innumerable prefaces to literary works reiterated time and time again the Horatian ideology *utile dulci* (uniting the useful with the pleasant), the edifying function, the deeper wisdom packaged in an amusing form. Assuming that the notion of *ut pictura poesis* was deeply rooted, it would be natural to address these issues, especially if one wanted to say something about the dignity of an art that, more than literature, can give rise to substantial misunderstandings about such moralizing intent. Moreover, this art could be censured by critics as being "*schoubaer oogh fenijn*" (venom for the eyes)[53] precisely because of its amusing, appealing, and sensual appearance.

The fact that these issues were not addressed should, at the very least, give us cause for thought.

Art historians have put forward analogical arguments defending the principles of didacticism and disguise as points of departure for the interpretation of seventeenth-century Dutch paintings (particularly genre paintings), frequently considering these principles as the essence of the meaning of these paintings.[54] These arguments originate from a stretching of *ut pictura poesis*, which has led to an oversimplified equation of the functions and aims of poetry and painting. The passages cited as examples of "*belering en verhulling*" (didacticism and disguise) are taken from Roemer Visscher's preface to *Sinnepoppen*, Cats's prefaces to *Proteus* and *Spiegel vanden ouden en nieuwen tijdt*, Bredero's preface to *Geestig liedboeksken*, etc.[55] Thus, commonplaces taken from emblem literature in particular have been projected onto painting, despite their entirely different nature, context, function, tradition, and pictorial themes.[56] As stated above, one searches in vain in texts about painting for clichés concerning the hard outer shell and the sweet kernel within, edification through amusement, and the display of vices as a warning and an exhortation to virtue. These notions are, however, endlessly repeated in emblem books and innumerable prefaces to other types of literature, including songbooks, comedies, and adaptations of mythological material.

When, occasionally, arguments are drawn from texts that are directly related to painting, they prove inadequate. The often cited poem by Samuel van Hoogstraeten about "*bywerk dat bedektelijk iets verklaert*" (accessories that explain something covertly), for example, has been used to justify the idea of deep, hidden meanings secreted within genre painting.[57] However, Van Hoogstraeten's words are specifically directed at historical scenes with single figures (personifications, for example) in which the "accessories" (such as particular attributes) unobtrusively make clear that which is actually represented. This passage explains nothing about genre paintings; moreover, Van Hoogstraeten does not speak about hidden meanings but rather about clarifying the representation in order for "*de toezienders haer beeld te doen kennen*" (the observers to comprehend the image).[58]

Adriaen van de Venne's verses about "*sinnecunst*" (emblematic art) in his *Zeeusche mey-clacht: Ofte schyn-kycker* form another case in point.[59] In my view, these verses exclusively concern images accompanied by texts, such as emblems, and not painting in general. The first half of the poem speaks of painting as a source of joy. It captures beauty, arouses desire, and entices the eyes; it can record and visualize all that exists. A number of the significant aspects of painting frequently encountered in texts are treated in this section of the poem. Van de Venne, who was also a poet and an illustrator of emblem literature, then proceeds to discuss the sister arts of painting and poetry, noting that the latter can express "*hooghe en diepe dinghen*" (high and deep things). He demonstrates how the two arts can be combined and how their different characteristics complement each other. This leads Van de Venne to "*sinne-cunst*" – almost certainly meaning the combination of image and text – which he finds so admirable because the mind is "*soo sin-rijck meegedeelt*" (so significantly informed) by it.[60] Van de Venne does say that, among other things, painting can represent virtue and vice as well as human flaws, but this is the closest he comes to a didactic approach.[61]

Karel van Mander wrote his *Schilder-boeck* within the context of a literary-humanistic circle; it was written at a time when painting in general and the art market were on the verge of entirely new developments: history painting still dominated, specialization in the various genres had yet to develop, and the production and collecting of paintings had by no means attained the quantitative leaps that were to become noticeable several decades later. Surprisingly, Van Mander's text does not explicitly mention a didactic function or deeper meaning of painting in either the *Grondt* (a pretentious poetic work that makes extensive use of intellectual metaphors and exempla) or the *Levens*.[62] When Van Mander mentions paintings in the *Levens*, he says remarkably little about their subject matter and nothing about their content or literary aspects. He is almost exclusively interested in outward appearance.[63] The common assertion that Van Mander saw didacticism as the most important function of painting is not convincing.[64] Considering that seventeenth-century authors, as stated above, found it important to elaborate continually on this function in their discussions of poetry, emblem literature, etc. (Van Mander makes extensive use of such ideas elsewhere, for example, in his introduction to *Wtlegghingh op den metamorphosis* [Explanation of the Metamorphoses]),[65] it seems all the more remarkable that he does not address it.

It is impossible to sustain the idea that the didactic goal of painting is repeatedly underscored in the aforementioned literature.[66] Equally untenable is the assertion that in this art literature the aspect of people gaping at the physical appearance of paintings while remaining unaware of their hidden meaning was lamented.[67] In short, based on these sources, one has to ask whether such didactic principles had an important place in the minds of the majority of Dutch painters of this time and whether their audiences considered moralizing an important function of the paintings. By no means do I wish to argue that didactic-moralizing intentions are never present in paintings but rather that it appears incorrect to use such notions as the basis for interpretation.

A continually recurring notion encountered in texts pertaining to the art of painting or to individual paintings is that a painting imitating nature possesses the power to render everything, to capture beauty, to entice and seduce the eye, to arrest earthly transience, and thereby to "conquer" nature.[68] Furthermore, the fascination with imitation is often manifest, as is the play with appearance and being and the "deception" of the eye.[69] This is expressed in many variations, and it should come as no surprise that extremely successful painters such as Gerrit Dou and Frans van Mieris were frequently compared to Zeuxis and Parrhasius.[70]

Van Hoogstraeten summarized such ideas wonderfully in the beginning of his chapter "Van het oogmerk der schilderkonst; watze is, en te weeg brengt" (On the Aim of the Art of Painting: What It Is and What It Brings About): "De Schilderkonst is een wetenschap, om alle ideen, ofte denkbeelden, die de gansche zichtbaere natuer kan geven, te verbeelden: en met omtrek en verwe het oog te bedriegen" (Painting is a science that can represent all the ideas or concepts offered by all of visible nature and which deceives the eye with contours and paint). After again referring to Parrhasius and Zeuxis, Van Hoogstraeten continues with the frequently quoted statement: "Want een volmaekte Schildery is als een spiegel van de Natuer, die de dingen, die niet en zijn, doet schijnen te zijn, en op een geoorlofde vermakelijke en prijslijke wijze bedriegt" (Because a perfect painting is like a mirror of nature, making things which do not exist appear to exist, and which deceives in an acceptably amusing and honorable manner).[71] He goes on to mention the fact that poets made a connection between the origin of painting and Narcissus and, without actually saying so,[72] evokes associations with vain and transient beauty (which Narcissus could not preserve, but which painting can); these associations are also implied by the mirror metaphor. This may serve as a nice description for a great deal of Dutch painting of this period: the rendering of pleasant and amusing images, which, like a reflection, appear deceptively real. "As if [looking] in a mirror," the viewer is confronted by the associations evoked by what is reflected (with all the connotations of self-knowledge, beauty, vanity, and transience related to the mirror metaphor).[73] Didactic lessons as such are not obviously implied but are not excluded. In my opinion, however, we can discount the idea that meanings were intentionally hidden or disguised.

It should be pointed out that the often-cited qualities of semblance and "deception" of the eye could also be perceived as dubious, and they are frequently mentioned in the context of negative opinions about painting. Both the positive and negative views of the enticement of the eye through appealing and deceptive appearances are recurring topoi. These were all the more powerful because it was written time and again that the eye, and thus the sense of sight, aroused sensual feelings and lust.[74] Naturally, these are often old topoi derived from classical texts, but the way in which they are continually repeated seems no less significant. Following the footsteps of Johannes Evertsz. Geesteranus, Dirk Rafaëlsz. Camphuysen, himself once a painter, even goes so far as to denounce the art of painting as being a *"verleydt-Ster van 't gezicht dat sich verstaart op 't sterffelijck"* (seductress of sight, spellbound by all that is transient). His opinions, though extreme and formulated from an orthodox religious standpoint, are revealing in their vehemence. He even says that paintings have no use or purpose and contain nothing worth learning, but are merely: "Een vleyend'd oog bedroch, 't welck naackt t'aenschouwen geeft, Hoe dat hy is in 't hart die 't maeckt en die het heeft" (A seductive deceit of the eye, that shows us openly what the real disposition is of those who make and possess them).[75] Shortly before, Camphuysen had stated:

> What the eyes behold gives the senses sweet satisfaction
> And the illusive image will reign over the mind.
> In this way (while the eyes are deceived,
> And the heart is astonished by the beautiful lies of painting)
> One wants to do and to have
> Everything which one beholds in a painting.
> Thus desire is fed by painting,
> And vice is generated by these foolish contrivings of the painter's brain.[76]

Not surprisingly, seemingly contradictory impulses can be detected in a society wherein a certain segment showed an incredible avidity for paintings. (Who today has between 100 and 250 paintings in his or her house? In the second and third quarter of the seventeenth century, a substantial number of Leiden inventories, for example, can be found with such high numbers.) Yet the same society also displayed an ambivalent attitude toward the image and the sense of sight; hence, it is understandable that preoccupations with pleasure, seduction, earthly beauty, and transience are so often inseparably linked in paintings and directly expressed in both subject and style. In this regard, the innumerable genre pieces in which love, youth, virtue, and vice play an important role – usually with a young woman as the focus – come to mind. Also evoked are the almost always idyllic, amorous mythological and pastoral scenes, as well as many still lifes and landscapes. A certain "moral" is definitely present, and moralizations are often readily accessible for application within specific contexts. However, this does not mean that such paintings were generally intended as warnings or didactic-moralizing messages disguised by a realistic *mom-aensicht* (mask). It seems more likely that thoughts and attitudes about nature and human endeavors were visualized and represented in paintings in an immediately recognizable way. Associations were given direction through selective choice of subject matter, motifs, and related conventions for the representation of daily life. The subjects and motifs depicted in non-narrative paintings transmitted meaning to the viewer through adaptation to or deviation from pictorial conventions; through stereotypes recognizable to the public for whom they were intended; and through the visualization of simple, accessible metaphors.[77] The viewer or buyer could make these connotations more specific by interpreting them in terms of his own intellectual, social, and religious background.[78]

Few seventeenth-century viewers would have expected to be edified by the visually appealing images of vice, pleasurable pastimes, and amorous or erotically tinged scenes that were so frequently found in Dutch paintings of the time. That moralizations – which might be formulated to justify such paintings – could be seen as merely verbal additions with no essential bearing on the representation was stated by Camphuysen as follows:

> Yet it still has its use [you say]. One can explain [the image].
> One can reveal all of life, name and deed in word,
> But [oh!] what explanation and what praise can safely withstand,
> The things displayed which by their very nature shame the mind?[79]

Perhaps the somewhat titillating tension between sensual pleasure and "dangerous" seduction was one of the factors determining the appeal of many subjects.[80]

The iconological method was initially developed for interpreting fifteenth- and sixteenth-century art, which was often closely related to textual sources; this art frequently originated within the context of programmatic commissions and was intended for a specific place. Such a method has been applied with insufficient adaptation to an art that, to a large degree, lacks these specific aspects. As has been shown, its use has been justified by placing great emphasis on the idea of *ut pictura poesis*, which stems from humanistic art theory, and by transferring literary principles to the art of painting, supported with arguments primarily drawn from emblem literature.

Furthermore, one gets the impression that the goal of iconography, namely bringing to the surface and "deciphering" significant elements no longer obvious to the modern observer, has been confused with the existence of disguised or hidden meanings.[81] It also seems that the means used for this type of deciphering – specifically with regard to emblems – are equated with the painter's own sources, and this has frequently given rise to overly specific interpretations.[82] In addition, interpretations involving such a use of emblematic and literary-theoretical sources have often projected an extremely unlikely intellectual load and erudition onto the painter, his paintings, and his public.[83]

The limitations that this approach can place on interpretation also result from the separation between form and content and, related to this, the curious distinction between meaning and meaninglessness.[84] Searching for *the* meaning – usually in fairly isolated interpretations that do not consider an entire thematic group with its conventions and deviations – has only aggravated the problem. In my opinion, because of the separation between form and content, late medieval and sixteenth-century concepts have been all too easily transferred to the seventeenth century without taking into account the tremendous changes that occurred in the outward appearance of paintings and the context in which they functioned.[85] In so doing, the radical seventeenth-century developments in form and subject matter, the production and trade of paintings, and the differentiation of the art-purchasing public, which filled its houses with numerous paintings, have been underestimated. These factors must have had far-reaching consequences for the way in which the seventeenth-century consumer perceived paintings.

People at the time were aware that something special was happening with their "own" art, produced by the "*Verciersels van ons Vaderlandt*" (embellishments of our fatherland).[86] In 1629 Constantijn Huygens wrote that his Dutch compatriots had progressed further than anyone in their ability to render all sorts of shapes and poses of people and animals and the appearances of trees, rivers, mountains, and other elements of the landscape.[87] In 1678 Van Hoogstraeten, in the course of admonishing rulers of the republic to buy more art to present as gifts abroad, stated that "de Schilderkonst in onzen staet, als in een nieuw Grieken, in 't best van haer bloeijen is" (the art of painting in our own land, as in a new Greece, is at the height of her glory). He continued to say that therefore the art of painting, "den Vaderlande eygen, als een onkostelijke mijne, parelvisserye, en edelsteente groeve, dagelijx veel rijke juweelen van kabinetstukken kan uitleveren"[88] (as befits our fatherland, like an invaluable quarry, a pearl fishery, or mine of precious stones, can daily produce many rich jewels of cabinet painting).

The loving attention with which such paintings were produced and with which the visible was rendered is not merely a modern projection. Not only the paintings themselves make this apparent but also the following lines by Van Hoogstraeten. As the primary requirement of the painter, he cites: "Dat hy niet alleen schijne de konst te beminnen, maer dat hy in der daet, in de aerdicheden der bevallijke natuur uit te beelden, verlieft is"[89] (That he not only appears to adore art, but that he in fact is in love with representing the pleasantries of beautiful nature). Numerous questions concerning the reasons for the great profusion as well as the strict selectivity of those lovingly rendered "*aerdicheden der bevallijke natuur*" (pleasantries of beautiful nature), the associations they aroused, as well as the relationship between style, choice of subject matter and the public, have not as yet been satisfactorily answered. While the iconological approach has indicated many fruitful directions, its limitations should be kept in mind.

Dutch Seventeenth-Century Genre Painting

A REASSESSMENT OF SOME CURRENT HYPOTHESES*

Peter Hecht

ALTHOUGH I was flattered by the invitation, I am not sure whether it was a good idea to address an audience interested in *Main Trends in Cultural History* with a talk as limited as mine. Compared to my colleague Alpers's aim to come to grips with the Dutchness of Dutch art and its so-called picturing culture, I must admit that my concerns are of a far more modest nature, and that indeed I have grave doubts as to the possibilities of handling such all-embracing questions successfully at all. The debate I have become involved in with my book on the *Fijnschilders*, too, is much less of a global affair than the pandemonium that accompanied Svetlana Alpers's *Art of Describing*, but then we do share the honor of having both been severely reviewed by Josua Bruyn.[1]

And if I read him correctly, the cause for Bruyn's concern may even have been the same in both cases, for no matter how different our work, it is revisionist to a certain degree, and it has called into question some of the more or less generally accepted hypotheses about the nature of Dutch seventeenth-century art, more specifically about the nature of that conceptual morass called genre painting. Having myself been trained in the school of Emmens and De Jongh, it has taken some time for me to realize how many important and characteristic seventeenth-century Dutch pictures cannot in any way be understood if one were to go by the basic assumptions developed by these two scholars and perhaps most forcefully put forward in the introduction to De Jongh's 1976 Rijksmuseum catalogue, *Tot lering en vermaak*. It may seem naive, but it was only in the course of my work on the *Hollandse fijnschilders*, while trying to select paintings that would not necessarily exemplify some iconographical problem, but rather bring out the best and the most typical in the art of masters like Gerard Dou and Frans van Mieris, that I came to observe that the choice of subject matter in the *oeuvres* of these genre painters so frequently accords with what I thought I recognized as their artistic aims and possibilities, that it became tempting indeed to try and understand the *what* of their pictures by having another look at the *how*. To me, the results of this little exercise were something of a revelation, and I was delighted to find that seventeenth-century Dutch art literature, which is so alarmingly silent about the supposed hidden meaning and didactic quality of these paintings, does comment quite regularly on those very features which to my mind make up the essence of their pictorial wit and thus account for the fame they once enjoyed. By pointing this out in the introduction to my catalogue, and by toying with the possibilities

* This is the text of a lecture that was delivered on 20 June 1991 as part of an Amsterdam University graduate program on *Main Trends in Cultural History*. It is the intention of the organizers to publish a volume with all twelve papers presented on that occasion, which included one other art-historical contribution, namely, Svetlana Alpers's "Painting Culture: Some Dutch Examples." I would like to thank Guido Jansen and Michael Hoyle for their careful reading of my manuscript – and for their patience, I might add. [Editor's note: Peter Hecht's essay was originally published in *Simiolus* 21 (1992), pp. 85–95. It was previously reprinted in *Main Trends in Cultural History*, ed. W. Melching and W. Velema, pp. 150–63, Amsterdam, 1994.]

that such an observation offers in my discussion of some of the individual paintings on display, I seem to have wreaked far more havoc than I ever intended, and if anything, this seems to have caused the debate on symbol and meaning in Dutch genre painting to flare up once again. The ensuing situation is a rather muddled one, with Eric Jan Sluijter trying to show that my observations are simply the other side of De Jongh's controversial views, whereas Reindert Falkenburg is trying to make it clear that Sluijter and I nevertheless have quite a lot in common and should in fact be seen as part of one and the same movement, a movement which Hessel Miedema has in the meantime dubbed the "neo-sensitive." Jan Bedaux in turn has been tugging at yet another corner of the carpet in the introduction to his recent dissertation, and Josua Bruyn has made it clear that as far as he is concerned, all this heretical clamor is most unwelcome.[2]

Our problem, of course, begins with the irrefutable observation that Dutch genre painting can rarely, if ever, be considered to faithfully, let alone photographically, render slices of daily life, as they were once so innocently called. Dou's 1652 *Kitchen-Maid* (Fig. 49) no doubt contains all sorts of information relevant to the history of Dutch seventeenth-century culture, but the picture does not portray anything like a real cook in the window of a contemporary kitchen. The fantasized stone niche with its sculpted relief parallel to the picture plane does, however, provide the artist with an opportunity to emphasize that the panel on which he did his painting is flat – a pictorial confession which is then very cleverly used to demonstrate how well he can handle his problems of perspective and make his composition recede convincingly in space. Similarly, the combination of this kitchen-maid with fish, flesh and fowl does not seem to be a realistic one, referring to some forgotten recipe, but rather one that was arranged to more or less plausibly show off an indeed incredible technique in portraying feathers and scales and fur, such virtuosity being one of the great ideals of modern painting in 1652, expressly praised by Dou's Leiden contemporary Philips Angel in his 1642 *Lof der schilder-konst.* In fact, Angel did so in a traditional *paragone*, a comparison of the relative merits of painting and sculpture, and given that context it seems no coincidence to me that Dou should insist on showing how real and lifelike he can do his cabbage and his carrot leaves – as against the poor sculptor, whose pseudo-antique ornamental greens on the window-frame look awfully stiff and stony.[3]

Now even if a picture like this one can be analyzed in terms of the artistic achievement I think it represents, this does not necessarily preclude its motif having carried some additional meaning or some set of associations of its own. Sluijter, for instance, is convinced that paintings of this type had an evident sexual innuendo, because kitchen-maids had something of a reputation in seventeenth-century Holland, and so did fish and flesh and fowl. But then my problem is, just what should we think of the same ingredients in Dou's slightly later *Young Mother* (Fig. 50), a picture of a so-called *Kitchen* which carries evident overtones of domesticity and virtue, if one need specify its mood at all? For here they are, the hare, the cock and the fish, or should I say the fur, the feathers and the scales, again in combination with a cabbage and with carrots, with wicker baskets, shiny copper, and the type of broom that according to tradition took Dou days on end to paint. Also, and that is yet another piece of artifice which must have delighted the painter's audience at the time, the direct and indirect daylight in this picture is complemented by the light of a fire in the background, as if to underline that there was indeed very nearly nothing on God's earth that Dou's virtuoso brush could not successfully imitate.[4]

Apart from all the art and artfulness that went into this picture, though, I think we cannot help but notice that this lovingly rendered encyclopedia of details does not add up to a plausible, that is pseudo-photographic, image of a seventeenth-century Dutch interior, be it of a hall or a kitchen. Of course not, says my critic Bruyn, because the faithful reproduction of the visible world was not what a seventeenth-century painter would have been after to begin with. His art was essentially symbolic, and thus it is only to be expected that Dou's interiors, too, should raise the question of their meaning. I

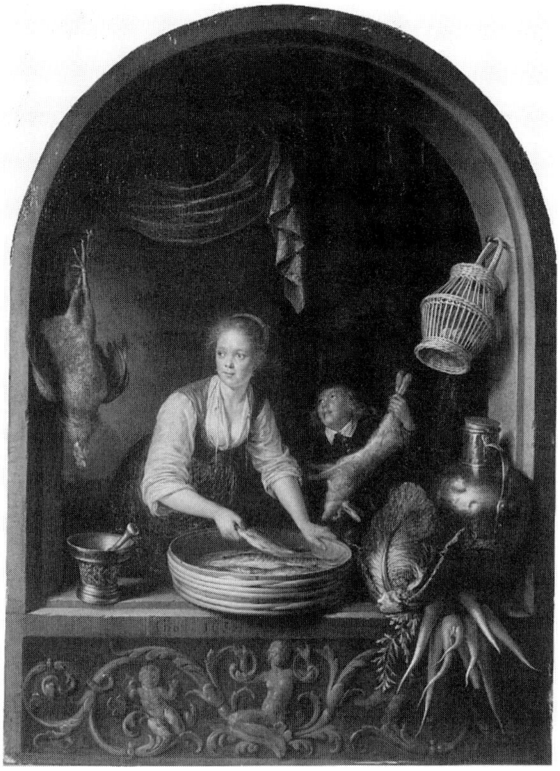

Figure 49. Gerard Dou, *Kitchen-Maid,* 1652 (oil on panel, 33 × 23.8 cm). Karlsruhe, Staatliche Kunsthalle. Photo: museum.

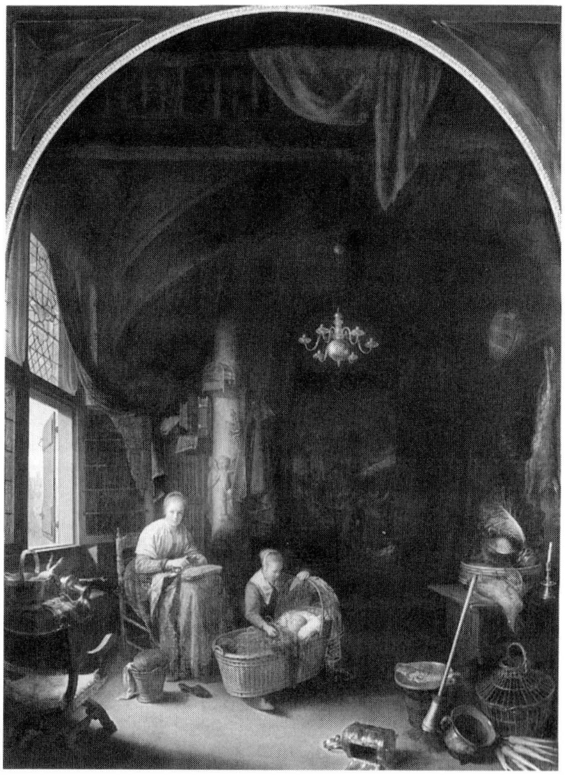

Figure 50. Gerard Dou, *The Young Mother,* 1658 (oil on panel, 73.5 × 55.5 cm). The Hague, Mauritshuis. Photo: A. Dingjan, The Hague.

find this line of reasoning very hard to understand, and what is worse, I have not been able to find the slightest bit of evidence that Dou's contemporaries would have ever looked at his pictures in such a contrived way. In the inventory of King Charles II, who received the *Young Mother* as part of the so-called Dutch gift in 1660, the picture is simply described as "Dow. A Dutch woman at worke her childe in ye cradle, her maid by with fowle & severall other things," and when John Evelyn came to see the picture in Whitehall later that year he only spoke of his delight about this "drolerie, or rather a Dutch kitchin, painted by Dowe so finely as hardly to be at all distinguish'd from enamail." The earliest Dutch sources do not speak otherwise about Dou's art and subject matter, his Leiden contemporary Traudenius encouraging us to relish the lifelike imitation of edibles in such a *Hollandsche boerekeucken* too. It is "game for our eyes," he says, comparing the artist's achievement with that of classical Parrhasius, the master whose painted curtain had even deceived the experienced eyes of Zeuxis. At the beginning of the eighteenth century, however, the initial praise for such well-nigh absolute mimetic skill started to cool down a bit. Classicist critics felt that Dou had more or less wasted his talents on painting such meaningless trifles, and the history painter Houbraken, especially, went to some length to explain how regrettable it was that a man of such pictorial genius should have had so little to say.[5]

To me it seems significant that a seventeenth-century connoisseur like Evelyn should speak of a "drolerie" in connection with Dou's work, and I find it important to know that the poet Traudenius, who is even likely to have been acquainted with the master, should refer to these pictures in terms of imitation only. Also, I think good note should be taken of the fact that Houbraken and his like were later to complain about the futile and meaningless character of Dou's art, but those who subscribe to the theory of a hidden meaning and symbolic content in his pictures dismiss such information out of hand. They say it is only to be expected that the earliest sources and documents should not speak about the true nature of these paintings, because that is not what the authors of such texts were concerned with at the time. The testimony of Houbraken's generation is also considered to be useless, for when he and his colleagues finally picked up their pens all the so-called hidden meaning in the work of Dou and others had already been forgotten. If true, this really must have been quite a culture shock. Dou's paintings, after all, were among the most famous and highly prized on the market in those days, and I for one find it impossible to believe that their iconography had become a complete riddle within some 35 years of the artist's death.[6]

Now leaving aside the sources and the present-day disagreement about the relevance of what they have to say, we are still stuck with the problem of the unlikely interior in Dou's *Young Mother* and the impossible setting of his *Kitchen-Maid*. To us, these paintings are only "realistic" in an ambiguous way, and as soon as we think that they were nonetheless meant to look as real as can be, it is tempting to suppose that Dou's contemporaries, too, must have been quick to feel somewhat uneasy about their many obvious improbabilities. Studying the development of Dou's most important pupil, Frans van Mieris, I became convinced that this was probably indeed the case, for almost every step the younger painter took can quite plausibly be explained as part of a consistent search for a greater degree of naturalness and probability than his teacher had ever achieved. This, amongst other things, made Van Mieris reject the sample-card formula of Dou's abundant staffage, and led him to experiment with more complicated forms of perspective as well.

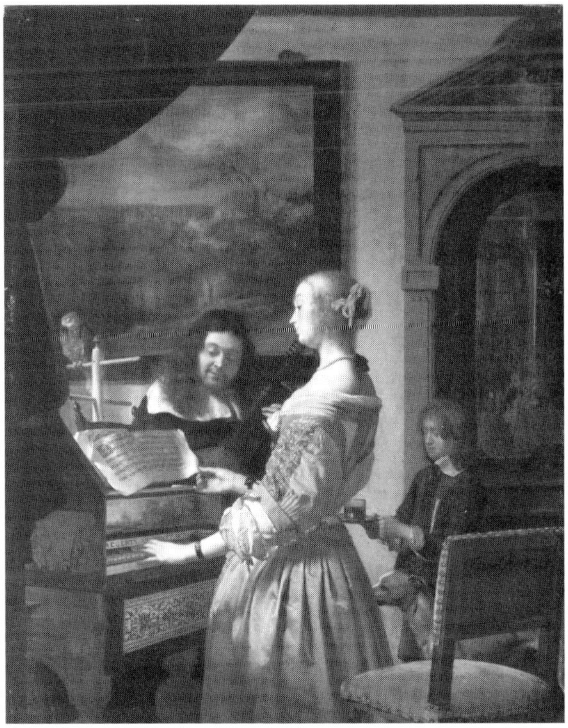

Figure 51. Frans van Mieris the Elder, *The Duet*, 1658 (oil on panel, 31.5 × 24.6 cm). Schwerin, Staatliches Museum. Photo: museum.

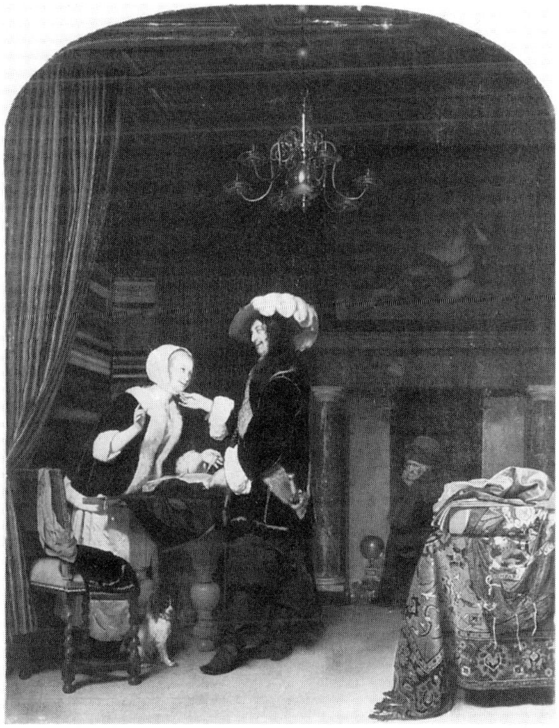

Figure 52. Frans van Mieris the Elder, *The Cloth Shop*, 1660 (oil on panel, 54.5 × 42.7 cm). Vienna, Kunsthistorisches Museum. Photo: museum.

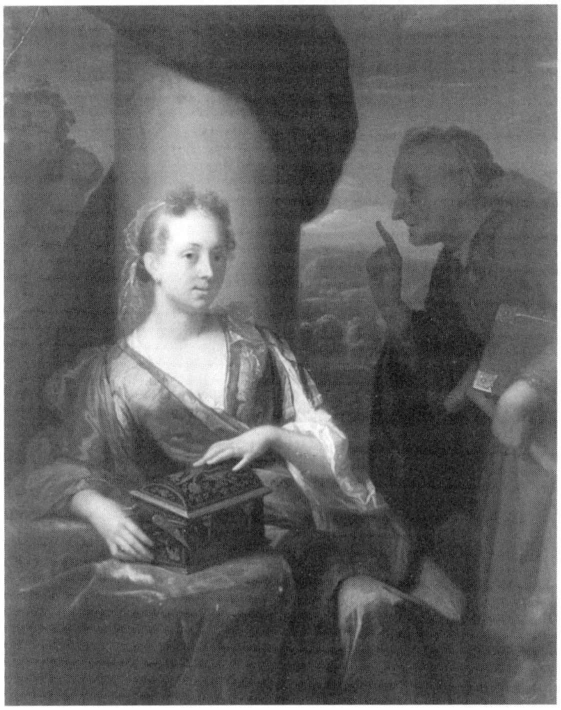

Figure 53. Godfried Schalcken, *The Useless Lesson* (oil on panel, 35 × 28.5 cm). The Hague, Mauritshuis. Photo: A. Dingjan, The Hague.

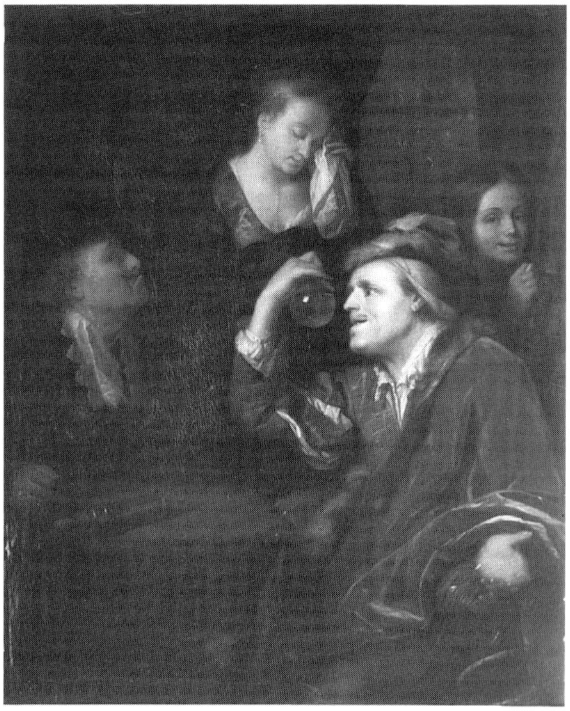

Figure 54. Godfried Schalcken, *The Doctor's Visit* (oil on panel, 35 × 28.5 cm). The Hague, Mauritshuis. Photo: A. Dingjan, The Hague.

Dou's box-with-one-side-open or niche-with-an-overlap was exchanged for the type of close-up that Vermeer was to capitalize on soon after. In this respect, Van Mieris's 1658 *Duet* (Fig. 51), painted when the artist was only 23, is little short of a revolution, for it is not only as perfect in its material imitation as the very best work of Dou, but it is also completely sound in terms of the plausibility of the image we are shown. Here we are truly given the impression of being witness to a man and a beautiful young woman about to perform some music with each other, he presumably tuning his instrument to the pitch she offers, while she is listening to his efforts and perhaps deciding what to play. To me, this outstanding picture is indeed no more than a convincing portrayal of a man and a woman in a wealthy home, getting ready to perform some music, and I fail to see what else it might have been about. In saying so, and in pointing to a contemporary print which reproduces Van Mieris's picture with a caption saying little else, namely that it is nice to make some music at home and thus forget about the troubles of the outside world, I seem to have rather overstepped the mark in the eyes of some of my older colleagues, for here I suggested that we perhaps encounter a notion of art which does not essentially differ from what was later to become known as *"l'art pour l'art"* – a concept whereby a picture's subject is essentially no more than the vehicle for its form. This does not exclude the possibility, I added in a footnote at the time, that some seventeenth-century art-lovers may have had so much poetry in their heads that they could not see a painting like Van Mieris's *Duet* without being reminded of the age-old metaphors about harmony in music and in love. The picture itself though, does not seem to prescribe such a reading, and nor have I found an early comment to endorse

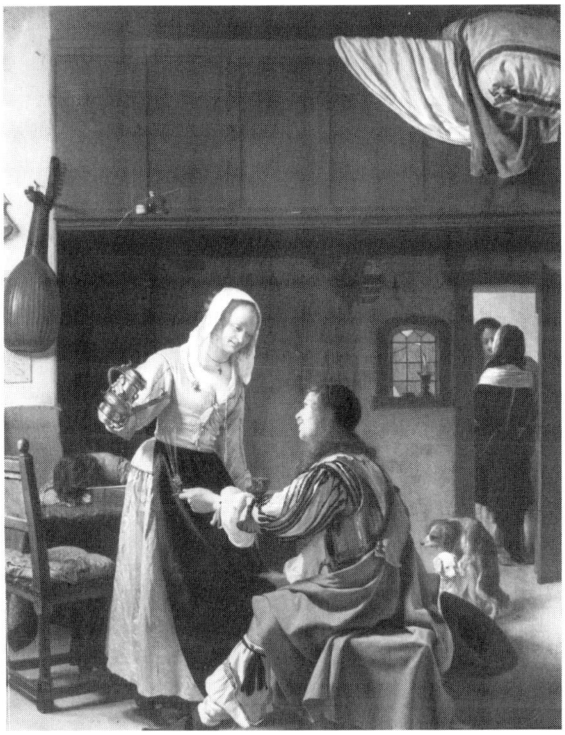

Figure 55. Frans van Mieris the Elder, *Inn Scene,* 165(9?) (oil on panel, 43 × 33 cm). The Hague, Mauritshuis. Photo: A. Dingjan, The Hague.

it, for whatever our scant sources are worth. To De Jongh and Bruyn, however, the possibility of a seventeenth-century painter going about picking a subject which suits his artistic rather than some other purpose, is absolutely out of the question, or so I have since been made to understand.[7]

Yet I think that even a picture with an unmistakable little story, like Van Mieris's 1660 *Cloth Shop* (Fig. 52), might very well owe its witty iconography to considerations of an artistic nature in the first place, its unusual setting providing a well-nigh perfect opportunity for the painter to show off his unrivalled technique in rendering different kinds of fabric. As we know, the *Cloth Shop* was commissioned by Archduke Leopold of Austria, and it seems only appropriate that Van Mieris should have wanted to impress his noble patron with the rendering of a subject that would allow him to make the best of his most prized skill. This is not, of course, to deny that the *Cloth Shop* is also a picture in which an officer is making a pass at a girl, flirtatiously comparing the softness of her chin to the softness of the silk she has brought out to sell. And if we want to go on comparing, as the Latin pun on the painting suggests we should, we might as well note the amusing difference between the young and rakish cavalier and the unhappy old grump in the background, who is evidently going to be the loser of the day. To read a moral into this picture however, to sermonize this "drolerie," and to make it refer to original sin by identifying the painting with the *Mourning of Abel* above the fireplace as the unmistakable key to Van Mieris's more profound intentions – that, I feel, is taking things a bit too far. Van Mieris was surely trying to be funny here, and again, in case we do not trust our modern eyes, the earliest records of the picture will not have it otherwise. Von Sandrart, who must have seen the *Cloth Shop* in Vienna when it had only just arrived, later remembered especially how well the silk and wool and ribbons had been done, and Houbraken, who is likely to have received his information on this painting from Van Mieris's youngest son, explains to his readers that the cavalier only feigns an interest in the girl's merchandise, while in the meantime leering at the pretty wench herself.[8]

If I were now to be asked whether I intend to take issue with each and every attempt to arrive at a more specifically meaningful, let alone moralistic reading of Dutch seventeenth-century genre painting, I would decidedly say no. At the same time, however, I would like to make it clear that I no longer believe that every detail in such a picture which is perhaps implausible to us should be considered pregnant with some hidden or at least forgotten meaning, let alone that even completely plausible genre scenes somehow should be tinkered with until they, too, seem to reveal a meaningful intent. I guess nobody can ever have missed the allegorical and moralistic import of a painting like Hendrick Pot's Haarlem *Vanitas*, with an old hag showing a skull to a young and pretty lady, and it is always reassuring to see that most of Jan Steen's painted proverbs and moralities retained their original meaning until well into the nineteenth century.[9] Steen's so-called *Large Inn*

(Fig. 17), too, was still correctly described and understood in Steengracht's 1829 Mauritshuis album, the author making sure to point out that the little boy, placed next to the skull in the attic, is blowing his bubbles to indicate the vanity and nullity of the carousing going on below (Fig. 17a).[10] The well-known theme of the bird in the coffer, which will escape as easily as a girl's virginity if circumstances allow, was still recognized and classified with its emblematic sense as late as 1881, when the compiler of the catalogue of the Van der Hoop collection quite correctly referred to the 21st emblem of Cats's *Zinne- en minnebeelden* as the most likely source for the iconography of an ungainly picture of this type by Frans van Mieris. Steengracht, too, was in no doubt as to the original meaning of Schalcken's popular pendants in the Mauritshuis (Figs. 53, 54), calling the first one by its old title of *The Useless Lesson*, and explaining that the little boy's gesture in the *Doctor's Visit* was meant to indicate precisely what had caused the young girl's malady.[11] Whether Cats's moral rigor applies to naughty pictures such as these – pictures which we might not even want to designate as genre, given their evident literary source – I would be very hesitant to say, but looking for proverbial wisdom or a moral lesson in Van Mieris's *Inn Scene*, strikes me as decidedly absurd (Fig. 55). This, again, is one of those amusing pictures which make sin look beautiful indeed, and, much as in Van Mieris's *Cloth Shop*, there is little hidden as far as its meaning or message is concerned. The two doggies, about which an amazing amount of art-historical ink has been spilled, only serve to elucidate the rest of the scene, as a 1783 comment already pointed out, and I don't think many of those who visit the Mauritshuis nowadays would fail to make a similar observation. The idea that this picture was perhaps meant to be

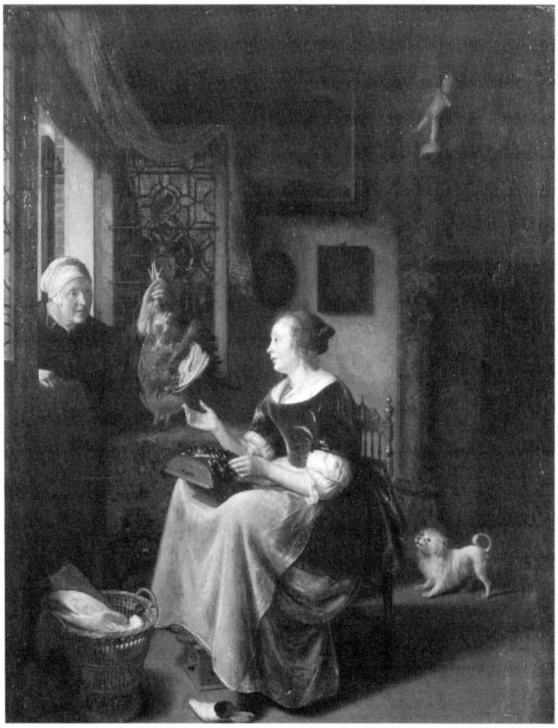

Figure 56. Pieter van Slingelandt, *The Lace-Maker Disturbed*, 167(2?) (oil on panel, 35.5 × 28 cm). Dresden, Gemäldegalerie Alte Meister. Photo: Sächsische Landesbibliothek, Abteilung Deutsche Fotothek, Dresden.

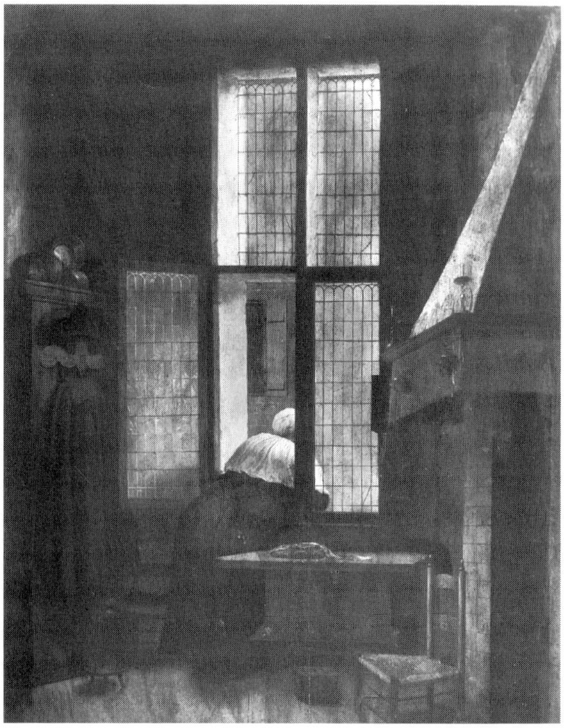

Figure 57. Jacob Vrel, *Woman at a Window*, 1654 (oil on panel, 66 × 47.5 cm). Vienna, Kunsthistorisches Museum. Photo: museum.

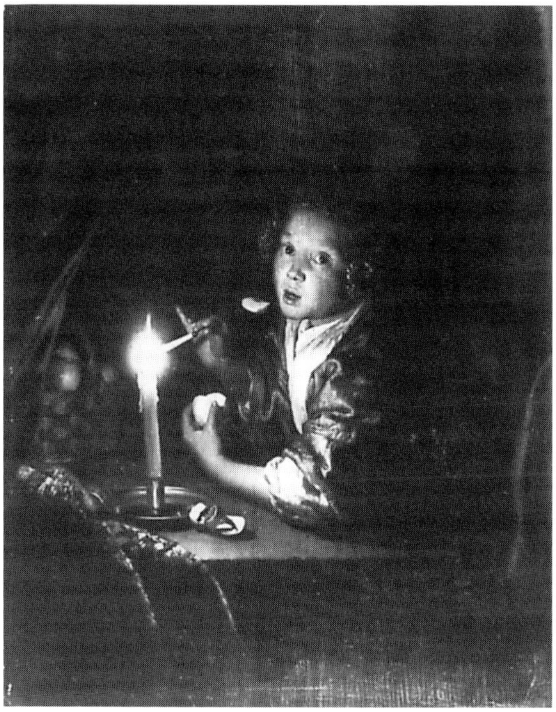

Figure 58. Godfried Schalcken, *Girl Eating an Apple* (oil on panel, 32.3 × 24.8 cm). Schwerin, Staatliches Museum. Photo: museum.

read as an emblem of impudence, as was proposed by an art historian who thought that the extinguished candle in the windowsill must refer to an old Dutch saying about shame leaving the house when the lights are out, seems almost too silly to refute. Even in the seventeenth century, I am sure, candles were not lit when the sun was shining, so we might as well take the candle and the candlestick at face value, or, if we really cannot do without a symbol, we might ask Dr Freud for a little comment on their shape.[12]

This may seem risible, but having arrived at the banalities we might as well go on and take a look at a picture by Van Slingelandt (Fig. 56), which I think has a meaning as hidden as they come. Here, the innocent art-lover may indeed have to look twice before he recognizes what the painter wanted him to see, although the artist's intentions were not at all high-flown and it takes no humanistic training to understand his rather timeless pun. As soon as we voice what the old crone might be saying to the diligent young girl – something like: "Hey honey, don't you want a cock?" – the painter's joke is more than clear. This is not a hidden meaning, but a *dou-*

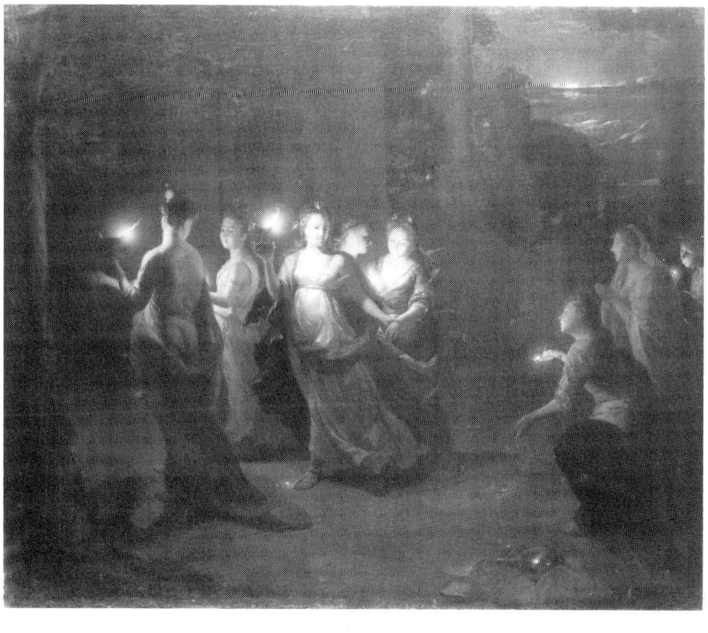

Figure 59. Godfried Schalcken, *The Wise and Foolish Virgins*, 1700 (oil on canvas, 94 × 114 cm). Munich, Alte Pinakothek. Photo: Bayerische Staatsgemäldesammlungen, Munich.

ble entendre where we might expect it, namely in the ever-ambiguous field of sex, and it is good to see that even an insipid critic like Charles Blanc still recognized this cock for all it was worth in 1860, thus once again giving the lie to that most curious early eighteenth-century loss of memory which is supposed to have stripped Dutch genre painting of any meaning it may originally have had.[13]

These are a few pictures which all somehow raise the question of their so-called meaning, albeit in very different ways. A great many Dutch genre paintings of the period do nothing of the kind, however, and I think we would look in vain for any specific message or even nameable association in, say, Vrel's *Woman at a Window* (Fig. 57), to take but a random example of a painting which to my mind does no more than exploit its motif pictorially. This is indeed "a little piece . . . in which . . . a woman is looking out of the window," to quote the 1659 inventory of the Archduke Leopold's collection, and I have no reason to presume that the artist would have seen it otherwise.[14] Perhaps my opponents will object to a picture by the somewhat marginal and idiosyncratic Vrel being used to illustrate a general characteristic of Dutch art, so I had better present a more mainstream example of such *genre pur* as well. For here, too, in Schalcken's *Girl Eating an Apple* (Fig. 58), I think we have a picture which simply cannot be supposed to raise a question regarding the referential meaning of its subject. The theme of a *Girl Eating an Apple* is as natural as the motif of a *Woman at a Window*, or of a man and a woman making music, to mention Van Mieris's *Duet* yet again. In the case of Vrel and Schalcken, though, there is not even the possible context of a traditional poetic metaphor to go by if one were obliged to aim for an interpretation. In fact, to put it rather harshly, there is nothing at all which I think could make such harmless images fit into that straitjacket of a symbolic reading that Bruyn and others believe to have been the daily costume of seventeenth-century Dutch art.[15]

In a recent paper De Jongh has made it clear that as far as he is concerned there is something badly amiss with "those young art historians who cannot think of anything better to do than shove Dutch seventeenth-century art in the direction of art for art's sake," somewhat disappointedly adding that even Ernst Gombrich has recently made a slide in that direction.[16] But then, is it really so unlikely that form would have been more important than subject matter to the seventeenth-century collectors who bought pictures like Van Mieris's *Duet* or Schalcken's *Girl Eating an Apple?* And what can Schalcken's picture possibly be about, if *not* about a cute little girl doing something perfectly natural in the subtle candle-lit setting which was this master's personal specialty? Schalcken's concern was more often than not to paint such candlelight scenes, and as far as I can see he did not necessarily do so for symbolic reasons. When he was asked to make a *Self-Portrait* for Cosimo de Medici in 1694, he suggested that he might perhaps best portray himself by candlelight, this special effect being something like his artistic trademark and the reason for his fame.[17] He even chose his biblical subjects to accord with his personal painterly skill, so I think it should not surprise us to find him doing a nocturnal *Denial of St Peter*, or a picture of the parable of the *Wise and Foolish Virgins* (Fig. 59), a theme which required at least as many different lights as the famous multi-candle *Evening School* by his teacher Gerard Dou. Come to think of it, it was terribly clever of Schalcken to decide to illustrate this story, because it provided him with an opportunity to handle the artistically impressive problem of the many different lights in a history rather than a genre painting, thus improving on his master's intellectually more meager repertoire. Nevertheless, no matter what the Classicist pretensions about the importance of a story for a serious work of art, the self-awareness of the painter seems to have been so strong that even the what of a biblical subject was subordinated to the how of his artistic ambition, and I find it hard to believe that the original collectors of such pictures would have felt this differently, that they would not have been collecting their art "for art's sake," so to speak.[18]

Having dealt with these pictures, it might be useful to summarize what I hope my examples have already revealed by implication, namely that I cannot but reject the idea that all Dutch seventeenth-century art was meant to be read symbolically, and that I fail to see why its presumed meaning should have been hidden to serve this aesthetic or didactic purpose which contemporary sources never speak about. Also, I feel one cannot help but wonder *why* the true nature of Dutch art should never have been mentioned in the appropriate literature of the time, and I am honestly at a loss to understand how all the relevant lore of that impressive pictorial culture could have been collectively forgotten before the seventeenth century was over. Personally I think that a lot of the work that has been based on these assumptions should therefore be most critically reviewed, the earliest documentation and the pictures themselves being brought back into the witness stand as soon as possible. Such revisionist investigations may seem little more than drudgery to those whose aim it is to study cultural history at large. But then, it may be worth the trouble to try and discover to what extent Dutch seventeenth-century painting was conceived of to convey symbolic meanings, and to what extent it only meant to celebrate the ever-increasing possibilities of its miraculously lifelike art. One might even *have* to find this out, so as to avoid creating an all too unrealistic picture of Dutch civilization in the past.

Ter Borch's Ladies in Satin*

Alison McNeil Kettering

Gerard ter Borch (1617–81) is well known as a genre painter whose descriptive brilliance creates both dazzling surface effects and delicate nuances of character. Among the most familiar and provocative of his works is a group that feature ladies dressed in shimmering light-colored satin. Gerard produced these ambitious paintings between about 1652 and 1662, at the height of his career: *The Paternal Admonition*, Berlin (Fig. 60); *The Fiancée*, Paris (Fig. 61); *The Suitor's Visit*, Washington (Fig. 62); *The Lady at her Toilet*, Detroit (Fig. 63); *Curiosity*, New York; *The Letter*, Buckingham Palace (Fig. 64); and *The Introduction*, Polesden Lacey (Fig. 65).[1]

In Ter Borch's time, these pictures would have been designated by subject and grouped under such general rubrics as *gezelschapjes* (companies), *conversaties* (conversations), or *juffertjes* (young ladies). Here, however, I will refer to them by the titles their present-day owners use, in some cases anecdotal titles introduced in the eighteenth and nineteenth centuries. Anecdotal titles – even more than most titles – are interpretive rather than strictly descriptive. While useful for purposes of identification, their application to works so ambiguous as these by Ter Borch has proved, at best, to be reductive, and at worst, to be misleading.

Scholarly interpretations of these works over the years have been diverse and contradictory, principally because of the paintings' reserve, their subtlety, their refusal to give away their meanings easily or lightly. Gerard's paintings have been understood as domestic narratives, as didactic allegories, as enigmatic tableaux whose ambiguities were intentional, as virtuoso depictions of costly attire. In each case the questions asked, the assumptions held, and the models employed, have differed.

The approaches just cited ignore some of the most important ways in which Ter Borch's pictures communicated. The present study will ask how these works conveyed prevailing ideals of social and sexual behaviour, and helped to construct those ideals. It will examine the extent to which their narrative and pictorial structure conformed to, or departed from, the conventions of Dutch genre painting, especially conventions relating to gender. It will discuss the contemporary literature of love, looking there for parallel structures and sentiments that may illuminate our understanding of pictorial treatments of similar themes.

THE INTERPRETIVE ISSUES

The Paternal Admonition (Fig. 60) is the best example of the interpretive problem in Ter Borch's oeuvre. The image first received a title in 1765, when

* A version of the present article was first given at the Historians of Netherlandish Art conference in Cleveland, Ohio, in October 1989. Among the many people who responded with helpful suggestions to this and later versions of the paper, I wish to single out for thanks: Hans Luijten, Eric Jan Sluijter, Lauren Soth, Joanna Woodall. [Editor's note: Alison Kettering's essay was originally published in *Art History* 16 (1993), pp. 95–124.]

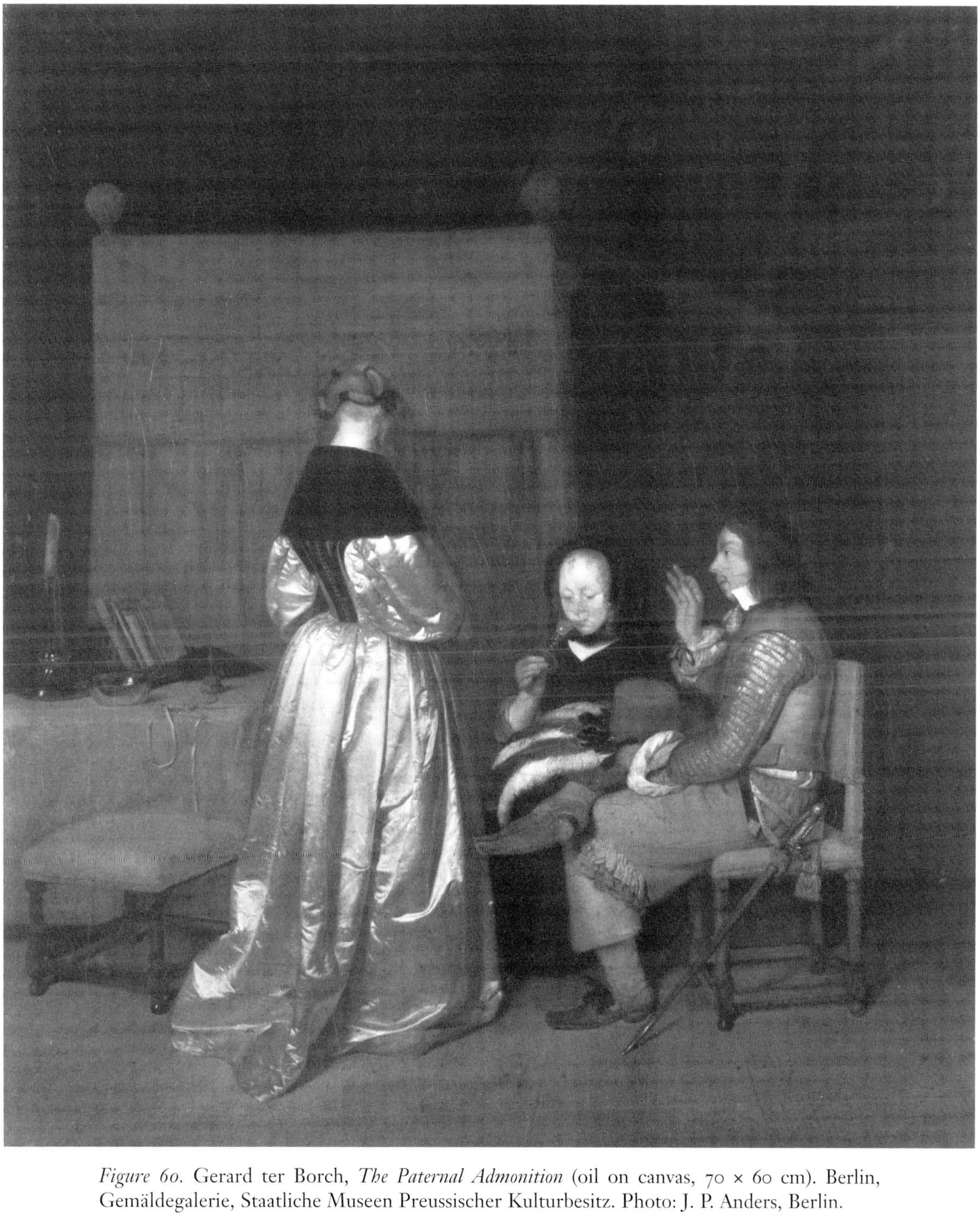

Figure 60. Gerard ter Borch, *The Paternal Admonition* (oil on canvas, 70 × 60 cm). Berlin, Gemäldegalerie, Staatliche Museen Preussischer Kulturbesitz. Photo: J. P. Anders, Berlin.

the German engraver J.G. Wille inscribed 'Instruction Paternelle' on his print after the Berlin version of the painting.[2] He underscored his verbal interpretation with one slight visual change, altering the features of the officer just enough to make plausible his role as a well-bred family man. Goethe accepted Wille's basic notion of the scene in his novel *Wahlverwantschaften* of 1809.[3] There he appropriately described the man in the print as a 'noble knightly-looking father' and the lady as a 'striking figure in a folding drapery of white satin', who responds to her father's gentle admonition by 'collecting herself' into an image of dignity, while her mother averts her eyes in embarrassed silence. The image was familiar and uncomplicated, illustrating a specific instance of ordinary behaviour.

By the mid-twentieth century, art historians reacted quite differently to the Berlin canvas, and to many of the other Ter Borch paintings as well. Using an iconological approach, a number of them reinterpreted *The Paternal Admonition* as a didactic allegory of Vanity and Luxury, bearing a cautionary message. They pointed as evidence to the red-draped bed, the dressing table, the mirror, the candle,[4] and especially to the man's upraised hand, which they assumed originally to have contained a coin.[5] They argued that *The Paternal Admonition* was intended not as a family tableau, but as a scene of high-class prostitution: the officer was a client, the woman in the middle a procuress, the standing figure a courtesan. For them this was a mid-century *bordeeltje*, a variant of earlier seventeenth-century examples which likewise warned against the very behaviour they depicted.[6]

To be sure, many of these critics were bothered by the presentation of such venal pleasures in so elegantly formal and decorous a manner. Some have called specific attention to this paradox, arguing that the perceived ambiguities were quite intentional. Sutton has suggested that Ter Borch deliberately made his representations vague and obscure in order to sustain viewers' interest.[7] A decade earlier Guépin drew attention to audience reaction, arguing that Ter Borch's viewers might well have read a variety of meanings in the works.[8]

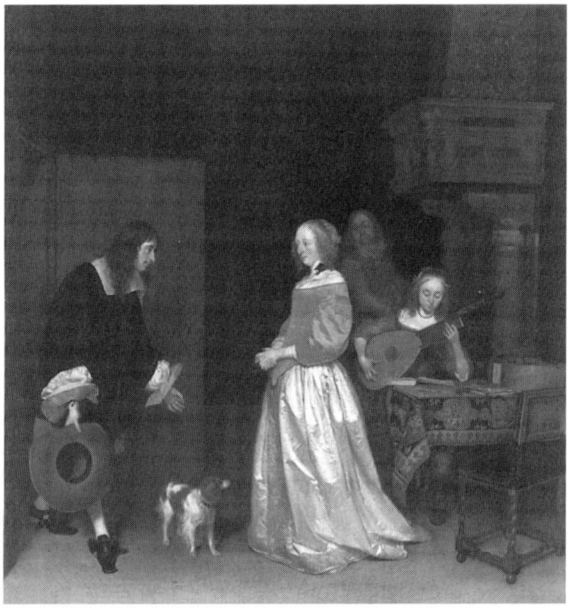

Figure 62. Gerard ter Borch, *The Suitor's Visit* (oil on canvas, 80 × 75.5 cm). Washington D.C., National Gallery of Art, Andrew W. Mellon Collection. Photo: museum.

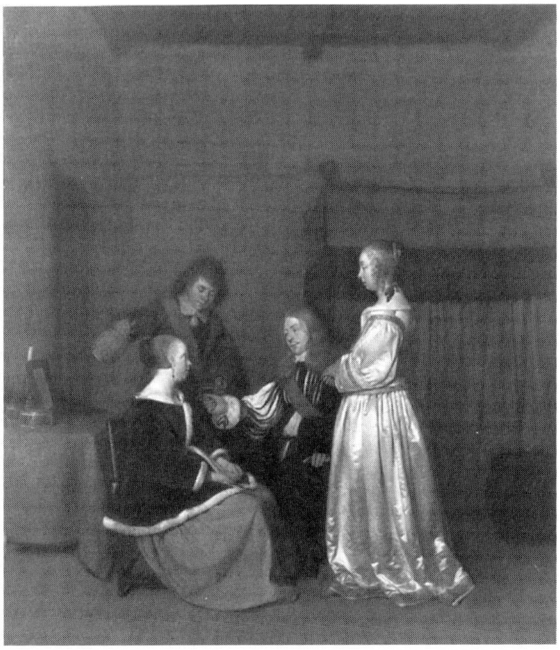

Figure 61. Gerard ter Borch, *The Fiancée* (oil on canvas, 91 × 71 cm). Paris, Petit Palais, Collection Dutuit. Photo: Musées de la Ville de Paris, Paris.

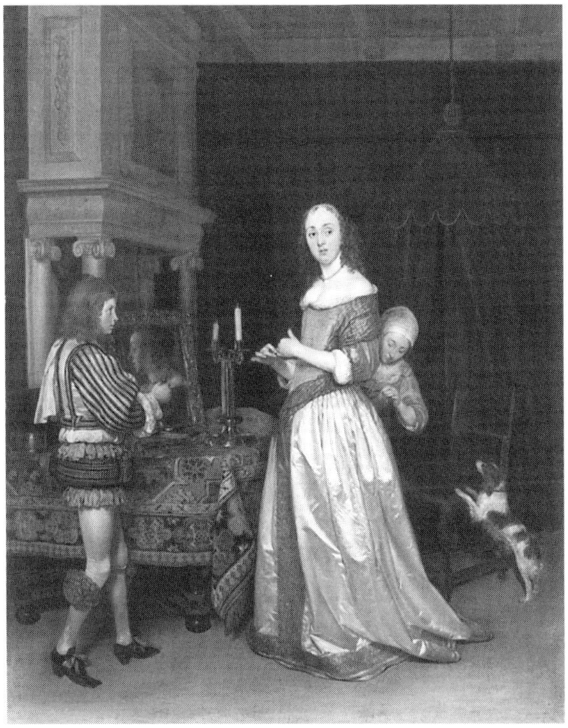

Figure 63. Gerard ter Borch, *The Lady at Her Toilet* (oil on canvas, 71 × 58 cm). Detroit, The Detroit Institute of Arts. Photo: museum.

Other art historians have shifted attention from these ambiguities to the way Ter Borch's description of surfaces functioned in the visual culture of the period. Stone-Ferrier, for one, has interpreted the Ter Borch paintings not as moral lessons but as virtuoso demonstrations of surface effects. The viewer enjoys the works for their brilliantly crafted displays of satin and admires the artist for his technical skill.[9]

I join the present-day historians who concern themselves with how the paintings were received. But in contrast with earlier twentieth-century writers, I am actually sympathetic to Goethe's manner of reading the works. Our differences are a matter of focus and of basic historical assumptions. I will assert that at the centre of the value system that Ter Borch shared with his audience lay various notions of woman – how they should look, how they should behave, and particularly how they should interact with men. I share with feminists, film historians and

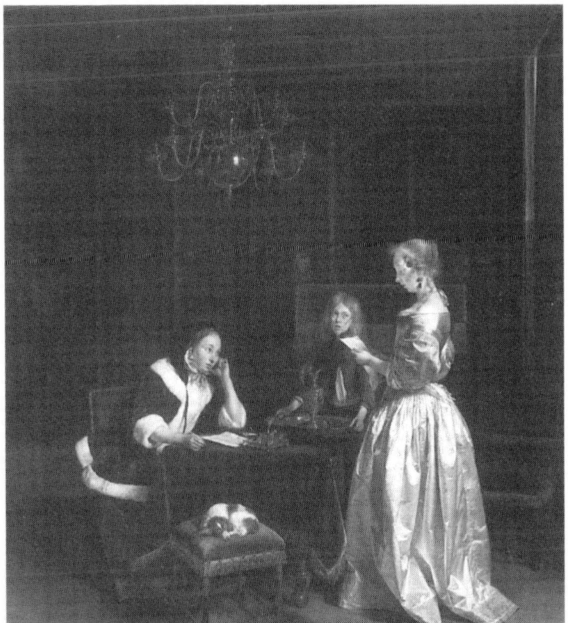

Figure 64. Gerard ter Borch, *The Letter* (oil on canvas, 79.5 × 68 cm). London, Collection of Her Majesty the Queen. Copyright reserved; reproduced by permission of the Lord Chamberlain's Office.

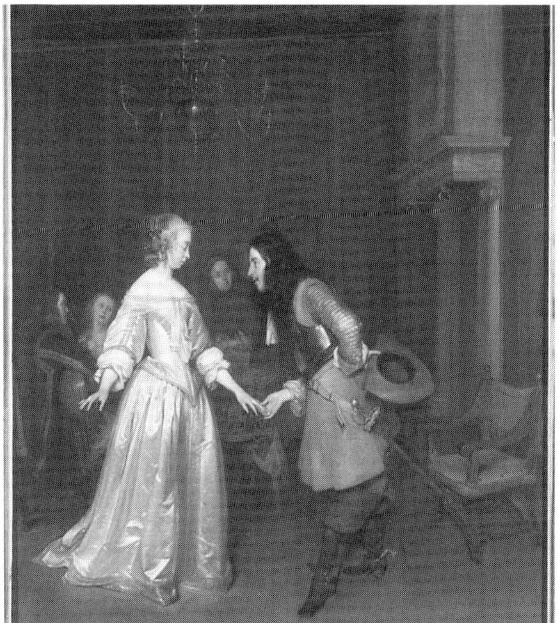

Figure 65. Gerard ter Borch, *The Introduction* (oil on canvas, 76 × 68 cm). Surrey, Polesden Lacey House, The National Trust.

literary critics a concern with the gaze and with gender-differentiated response. This last is a thorny subject, insofar as historical proof for a specifically male or specifically female way of viewing is hard to muster. But the issue is well worth considering, since by doing so we may enrich our understanding of these 'ambiguous' works, whilst sacrificing none of their complexity.

THE LADY

First, more on the paintings. All of them feature young men and women of marriageable age from what appears to be high-born society. This was a society accustomed to well-appointed settings complete with fancy-dress pages. The actors are few in number. The subtlety of the narration and the believability of the characters encourage an empathetic response. The viewer's interest is further engaged by the refinement of surface description for which Ter Borch received such acclaim.

One figure invariably attracts the greatest attention: a single woman clad in light-coloured satin. More often than not she is standing, with an erect, graceful posture. A strong light from an unknown source concentrates directly on her form, so as to create a compact silhouette against the dark background.

The strength and appeal of this image become all the more striking when compared with traditional high-life and garden-of-love pictures.[10] In the representations of elegant companies produced a decade or two earlier by Pieter Codde and Antonie Palamedesz., for example, the women's dark, broad, blocky forms are interspersed with the figures of the men along the broad horizontal axes of the panels. The flashes of white at their collars and cuffs serve to unravel the forms and intertwine them with the company.[11] Notice the contrast with the Ter Borch works, in which the special pictorial force of the lady dominates the image. Here is a discrete, contained figure. Her erect posture is reinforced by the upright format of the canvas and the verticality of the furnishings. Her body is shown in precisely defined profile, or three-quarter, or backview positions, allowing the lady to take on the posed look of a costume print figure.[12] The elegance of her presentation also brings to mind Van Dyckian full-length portraiture.[13] Like Van Dyck's graceful sitters, Ter Borch's ladies are ceremonial figures, whether displayed in the semi-public setting of the company picture or in the seemingly private one of the toilet or letter scene. Moreover, Ter Borch's handling of paint – crystal clear articulation of the satin close to the picture plane, successively more generalization further back in space – 'foregrounds' the lady quite literally. She becomes the most tangible element in the picture, yet one endowed with an uncanny, luminous presence.

The characteristic "Ter Borch lady" began to emerge in a variety of sub-genres around 1650, soon after the artist's return home from his travels. She appears first in the toilet scenes and pastorals for which his sister Gesina began serving as model.[14] In *The Shepherdess* (*c.* 1652, Anholt) and the related *Two Shepherdesses* (*c.* 1652, private collection), for example, the lady appears full-length in a frontal pose, which shows off her white satin bodice and skirt to brilliant effect.[15] That same general attire is worn several years later by the figures in the *Paternal Admonition* (*c.* 1654, Fig. 60), the *Lady at Her Toilet* (*c.* 1655, Dresden, Gesina as model[16]), and *The Fiancée* (*c.* 1655, Fig. 61). The dress even appears in several of Gerard's paintings of the 1660s, including the *c.* 1662 *Introduction* (Fig. 65; with Gesina again as model), though by this time its skirts have turned more flouncy, the sleeves are fuller, the bodice is tighter, and the modest collar present in the *Paternal Admonition* has been removed.

Elements of the light-coloured basic gown did correspond to modish attire of the period, as evidenced by various inventories, letters and diary entries.[17] But contemporary portraits of adult women only occasionally feature light satin, and then primarily to convey such associations as chastity,[18] arcadian innocence,[19] ephemerality,[20] the newly wedded state,[21] or aristocratic status.[22]

Married women from the middle and regent classes preferred to see themselves portrayed more soberly in black bodices and overskirts, a dress code signalling their good standing in society.[23] Certain-

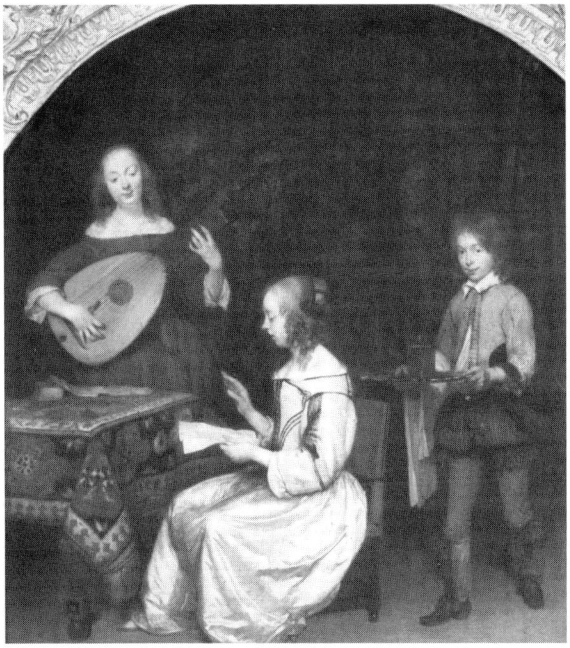

Figure 66. Gerard ter Borch, *The Concert* (oil on panel, 47 × 43 cm). Paris, Musée du Louvre. Photo: Réunion des musées nationaux, Paris.

ly that is how the women dress in all of Ter Borch's own portraits (Fig. 67). Bright satin is confined to the underskirt, and the lines of the entire ensemble are restrained. In his genre paintings, as Anne Hollander has observed, the artist "has created figures in an ideal clothed shape which could only have been momentarily achieved by living people, plump Dutch girls whose stays would have wrinkled under the pressure of actuality."[24] To put it succinctly, the smooth, unbroken, bell-shaped expanses of satin in these genre scenes were designed to function at a level different from ordinary life. In Ter Borch's hands the dress became a semi-fiction, with an important role to play in constructing identity.

THE SATIN

Viewers, critics and historians have responded so enthusiastically to the satin over time that we might conclude that the beauty of the fabric elevates it to the main object of the beholder's attention.[25] The otherwise terse descriptions of the eighteenth- and nineteenth-century inventories, for example, often insist on the satin as a *sine qua non* of Ter Borch's renderings of women.[26] That Ter Borch's was a new, "*moderne*" method of painting satin, Houbraken noted in a reference to Ter Borch in his "Life of Adriaen van der Werff."[27] "Modern" was evidently meant to describe Gerard's juxtaposition of warm and cool tones to convey the complicated reflecting surfaces of the fabric.

Using the twentieth-century perspectives of psychoanalysis and anthropology, we can go a step further and argue that in Ter Borch's pictures the satin's immediacy, its visual intensity, enlivened it beyond the status of fabric to the status of fetish. An encounter with the satin involved the viewer in a projection in which the gown became a surrogate for the woman's body. One can observe as well that the gown's shiny surfaces – like those of the objects in *pronk* (sumptuous) still-lifes – endowed it with a symbolic commercial value as an image of costly fabrication.[28]

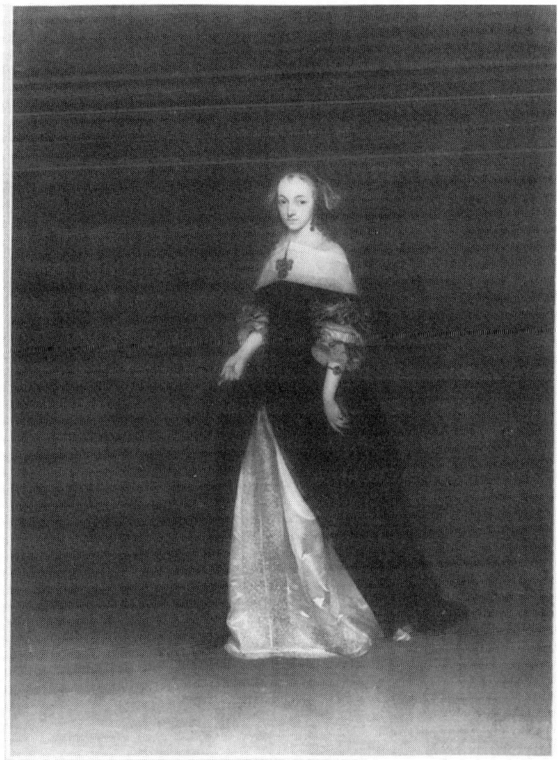

Figure 67. Gerard ter Borch, *Portrait of Catrina Luenink*, 1663 (oil on canvas, 80 × 59 cm). St. Petersburg, Hermitage.

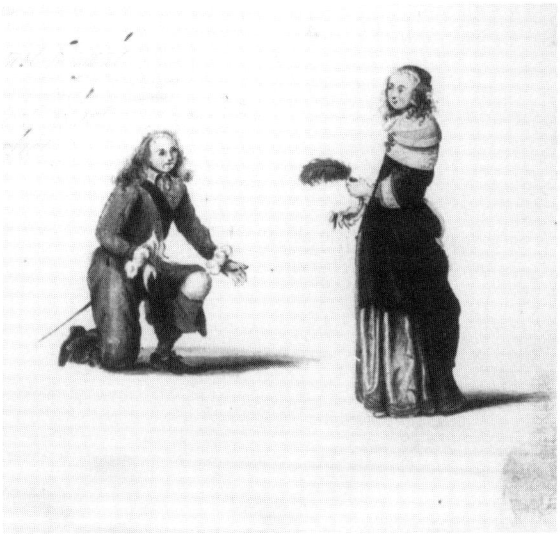

Figure 68. Gesina ter Borch, *Gentleman Kneeling Before a Lady* (watercolor from her Poetry Album). Amsterdam, Rijksprentenkabinet. Photo: Rijksmuseum-Stichting.

Because such representations as these were so labour-intensive, and therefore relatively expensive to produce and to purchase, the "commercial value" added by the satin was literal as well as figurative. As Van de Wetering has argued in his discussion of the rendering of satin in the context of studio practice, the artist aiming to produce the optical effects for which Ter Borch gained such fame found it crucial to place this fabric (more than any other material) directly before his eyes as he worked. The purchaser was thus assured of a hand-crafted object of the most supreme technical refinement.[29]

With these considerations in mind, we can examine more closely the values that the wearer of this gown, the Ter Borch lady, embodied. How did her place in the pictorial world of Ter Borch correspond with the expectations of his audience? What social and literary associations contributed both to the making of the image and to viewer response?

PETRARCHISM

Our search for answers takes us to Gesina ter Borch, Gerard's younger half-sister and his favourite model. Gesina modelled for the ladies in many of the paintings discussed above. She was also an amateur watercolourist. During the very period in which she posed for Gerard's paintings, she was herself collecting and illustrating love poems for three different albums. Though the private work of an amateur, these give us modest but unusual access

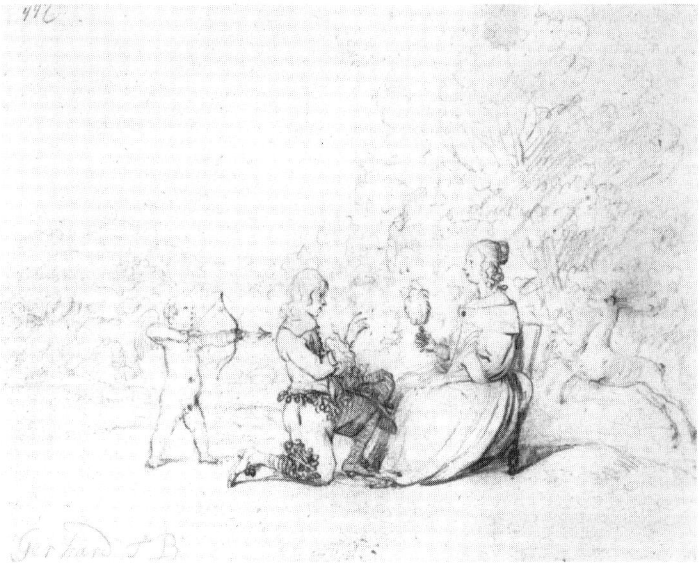

Figure 69. Gerard ter Borch, *Gentleman Kneeling Before a Lady, Attended by Cupid and a Stag* (pencil on paper, 15.3 × 19.9 cm). Amsterdam, Rijksprentenkabinet. Photo: Rijksmuseum-Stichting.

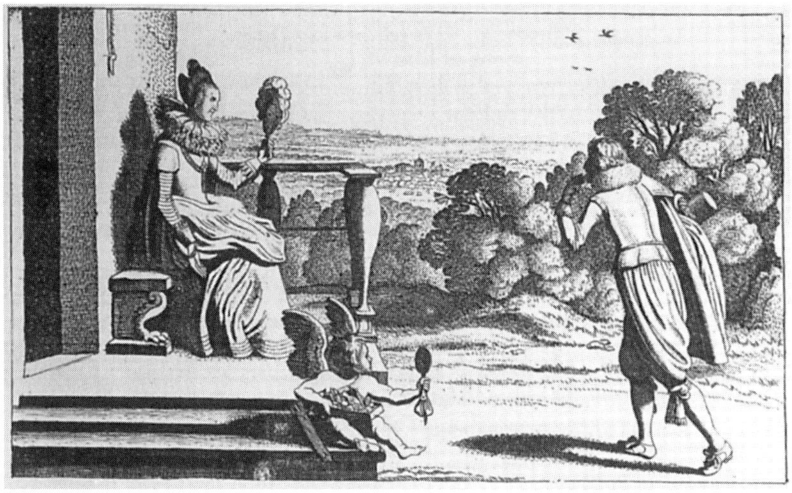

Figure 70. Illustration from Jan Jansz. Starter, *Friesche lust-hof*, Amsterdam, 1621.

to the creative world she shared with her brother, as well as to the assumptions of one significant beholder of his paintings.[30] Though Gesina never did marry, around 1660 she developed a friendship with an Amsterdam merchant and amateur poet, Henrik Jordis, which almost certainly included courtship. The albums reveal that love was much on her mind during this period of her life. Two-thirds of the album entries are devoted to amorous songs, and the majority of these are saturated with Petrarchan diction and content.[31]

Originating in the fourteenth-century lyrics of Petrarch, the conventions of Petrarchism entail a fixed system of gender relations. The man is always the victim, the martyr, driven by the arrows of love; the woman is the hard-hearted bewitcher, the sweet enemy.[32] Unreachable in her beauty and superiority, she is powerful in the ways she can wound. He, in turn, suffers slavishly, effusively, declining into a melancholy that only death can cure. As consolation he celebrates her beauty, recounting her physical traits – ruby mouth, rosy cheeks, ivory skin, golden hair, eyes like stars – in an endlessly repeated catalogue of parts.

By the seventeenth century, Petrarchan rhetoric had become the accepted language of love throughout Europe. Dutch songbooks and emblem books (such as Hooft's *Emblemata Amatoria* of 1611) have been described as 'vehicles of Petrarchism', firmly embedded within the European literature of love.[33] Among the Dutch who worked with Petrarchan conventions we find four of the best poets of the age: P. C. Hooft, Daniel Heinsius, G. A. Bredero and Jan Starter.

Gesina ter Borch's albums are filled with the efforts of less accomplished poets (though Starter does appear), along with the often anonymous writers anthologized in the printed songbooks.[34] Their language is more straightforward, their meanings more transparent, their themes closer to home: jealousy, unreciprocated affection, unequal economic and social status, gullibility, deceit, faithlessness. But many of the conventional Petrarchan conceits are present, not to mention the hyperbolic expressions, antitheses and oxymora typical of Petrarchan rhetoric.

In illustrating these poems, Gesina kept her renderings simple. Just to the side of the texts she isolated figures of gentlemen and ladies dressed in the attire of polite society, and less often, shepherds and shepherdesses in the dress of the pastoral pleasance. Next to one song, the cold-hearted beauty buries her hands in her skirts, refusing the ball the suitor has vainly tried to toss her (fol. 19). Next to another, 'Galathea' presents her back to the viewer as she wills the waves of the sea to quench her admirer's fire (fol. 45). Another young woman turns decisively away while her distraught suitor plunges a dagger into his breast (fol. 71). Upon occasion, the hard-hearted lady does face her admirer, especially when the suitor bows deeply before her (fols. 29 and 60, Fig. 68), or devotedly leans to tie her shoes (fol. 54), or reaches out to touch her hand (fol. 97). The suitor tying the lady's shoes illustrates a typical poem, by Jan Harmensz. Krul, in which the speaker addresses his Rosamonde. Her breath cools his burning desire to touch her lips; if he can only kiss those lips he will "suck the sweet nectar" of love.[35]

Gesina's amateurish album illustrations, *qua* illustrations, belong to an identifiable artistic tradition, one that was quite separate from Dutch painting.[36] Nevertheless, a case can be made that her brother created his pictures with Petrarchan poems in mind. Perhaps Gesina's watercolours and the printed illustrations that gave them inspiration also indirectly influenced Gerard. Certainly we find numerous formal and thematic parallels between his paintings and her illustrations. The nature of the artist–model relationship also suggests that Gerard and Gesina spent hours in conversation, or at least in each other's presence.[37] Furthermore, several of Gerard's drawings from the mid-1650s seem to have been made directly for Gesina.[38]

One of them, a delicately finished courtship scene (Fig. 69), takes place not in a domestic setting, but in an imaginary garden of love, with a gentleman-suitor kneeling before a lady (compare Gesina's Poetry Album illustration, Fig. 68). The pair is framed by a cupid and a hart – Heinsius's emblem for the doomed Petrarchan lover.[39] The combination of this figural motif and the two obvious symbols of love puts the image squarely within the context of contemporary emblem and songbook illustrations. See, for example, Starter's *Friesche lusthof*, with illustrations by Jan van de Velde (Fig. 70). These are sources of which Ter Borch otherwise makes little direct use. Simultaneously, the drawing adheres to the old pictorial tradition of gardens of love, a genre that had never died out in Netherlandish art as a setting for amorous relationships.[40] Although the lady in Gerard's drawing is seated rather than standing, her suitor adopts a position sufficiently submissive to convey the central Petrarchan conceit. Whatever the siblings' personal and artistic relationship, this drawing provides a tantalizing link between the work of Gerard and Gesina.[41]

Artistic intention is less my interest here than viewer response. To be sure, little is known about specific purchasers of Ter Borch's genre paintings beyond what can be extrapolated from a few inventory references. From these we can assume that the paintings quickly made their way to the western cities where Ter Borch had long nurtured contacts. The detailed knowledge of Gerard's inventions that many Holland genre painters showed in their own art further suggests that his works could be seen in Amsterdam, The Hague and Delft.[42] Two known owners may well be representative: Petronella de la Court, the wife of a prosperous Amsterdam brewer, who owned a depiction of a trumpeter by Ter Borch, and the well-to-do Delft printer Jacob Dissius, son-in-law of Pieter Claesz. van Ruijven (Vermeer's *maecenas*), who counted three Ter Borch pictures in his collection.[43] Another indication of the nature of the market for Ter Borch's pictures is his use of Johannes de Renialme, an important Amsterdam art dealer oriented toward a wealthy clientele.[44] The public for Ter Borch's "high-life" pictures was likely composed of the families of prosperous merchants and manufacturers, administrative officials, regents and various professional men, a class to which the artist's own family belonged.[45] It was a public prosperous enough, too, to purchase "non-essential" literature, like songbooks and poetry anthologies.[46]

The Ter Borch family's literary taste is well established, and while we cannot with certainty specify the taste of Gerard's entire audience, the Petrarchan framework for the subject of love was so pervasive in seventeenth-century Dutch culture that we may assume every literate viewer would have been familiar with it. The attitudes, values and images found in the poetry surely comprised a significant portion of the original viewers' frame of reference.

THE SOCIAL CONTEXT

Few of Ter Borch's contemporaries would have been likely to confuse Petrarchan rhetoric with reality. The pretty conceit of cruel mistresses dominating despondent admirers stood too patently at odds with the gender norms of this patriarchal society.

In the seventeenth century women were generally considered weak, fragile, flighty and in need of careful guarding, first by their parents, and later by their spouses. They were encouraged to develop virtues attractive to appropriate male partners – meekness, patience, silence – and above all to maintain their chastity. Because marriage was indissoluble, the choice of a partner was all-important. The pair should belong to the same class, age group and religion. Young women were encouraged, for a whole constellation of social, economic and even medical reasons, to wait until their early twenties to marry. That meant some years of adulthood in the parental household and a long period of mature courtship.[47] All overt initiative in the courtship continued to be taken by the male, of course: The young man began it with small talk, then asked the woman's father or guardian for *access* and eventually made a formal proposal of marriage. The two families involved still channelled the choice of partners, however, monitored their meetings, and had the final say about their mating.[48] The wealthier the pair, the more actively involved was the family. Starter, illustrating the Dutch domestication of Petrarchan conventions, makes parental control vividly apparent in one of the poems from his *Friesche lusthof*, where the suitor's misery is caused not only by his ladylove's coolness but also by her parents' rejection of their budding relationship.[49]

Though the paintings I have been considering are clearly imaginative constructions, not documentaries, they do echo important aspects of the realities of contemporary courtship. The scenes represent supervised meetings where the opposite sexes appear in company, or show women alone attended by harmless pages. The dress and manners of the courting figures suggest that they belong to the same class: They appear to be close in age to one another.[50] The women are models of restraint, passivity and self-control. Notice, by contrast, the quicker pace and expansive postures of the men portrayed in their presence.

We may question whether young Dutch women in actuality behaved with such restraint. Foreign visitors commented on the playfulness and flirtatiousness of the young women they encountered.[51] Other sources noted the relatively liberal rights enjoyed by women of all ages in the Netherlands.[52] But the many conduct books written at the time leave no doubt about the *ideal* of feminine passivity. Jacob Cats, the author whom the Dutch middle class knew best, wrote eloquently on the subject. Young women, Cats urged in his 1618 *Maechden-plicht*, should not "speak lest they should appear to desire a husband, which in maids is not seemly . . . [I]t is . . . in the nature of women to be silent."[53] Rather than enticing suitors with a laugh, the lady should act "bitter as gall" and keep the suitor hanging.[54] The conduct books are equally explicit in their directions for women about the social correctness, not to mention the moral soundness, of upright postures and slow, measured movement.[55]

Clearly in this widely disseminated prescriptive literature there is more than a hint of Petrarch. Here poetic conventions and social ideals begin to coincide. In relations with the opposite sex, whatever the context, woman was to resist "servitude to Venus" and maintain a decorous reserve, all the while her suitor attempted to bring her over to love.[56]

PROBLEMATIC BEAUTY

Ter Borch's satin-clad figures thus conformed both to a principal ideal of feminine behaviour and to the comportment of the ideal Petrarchan lady. But in the eyes of some contemporary viewers these figures could not overcome one damning flaw: They were beautiful.

Moralists among seventeenth-century Dutch writers, whether religious or secular, were highly suspicious of beauty no less than of pleasure. They warned against visual splendour, noting its deleterious effects. Time and again Jacob Cats and Johan de Brune associated personal beauty with vanity, self-indulgence, transience and deceit.[57] In line with such thinking, the engraver Hendrik Bary published a print after Ter Borch (his lost painting of a young woman in a black beret) complete with an inscription associating beauty with ephemerality.[58] And the indictment went further, implicating beauty among the principal seductions toward sexual transgression.

This view of physical beauty was so widely promulgated, particularly in the first half of the seventeenth century, that we cannot doubt its presence in the minds of most of Ter Borch's audience. We can, however, seriously question whether that presence was a controlling one – whether the moralists' suspicions played anything like a dominant role in the general viewer's response to Gerard's lovely ladies.

No Dutch writer produced a treatise on female beauty comparable to those by sixteenth-century Italians, but a number of Dutchmen did engage in the Renaissance debate about the nature of women. The popular physician – author Johan van Beverwijck wrote the best known of the Dutch apologies for women, his 1639 *Van de wtnementheyt des vrouwelicken Geslachts* (On the Excellence of the Female Sex).[59]

In the tradition of Erasmus and Vives, Van Beverwijck devotes considerable attention to woman's intellectual capacities and moral education. Nevertheless, he concerns himself first with the excellence of her physical attributes, and in the process argues the relationship of her exterior qualities to the nobility of her soul. Citing a range of Platonic and Neo-Platonic writers – including, predictably enough, Petrarch and Ficino – Van Beverwijck explains and justifies this encomium to woman's physical appearance. For him, as well as for these forerunners, the enjoyment of feminine beauty must be chaste and its contemplation distanced, but beauty itself he understood to be an unmixed good.

As Van Beverwijck recognized, this celebration of beauty as an inspirational force had been directly incorporated into Petrarchan poetry. It was there that the seventeenth-century reader – and viewer – would have found the greatest encouragement for construing beauty in positive terms.

Petrarchan poets took pains to show the object of the lover's worship as fully worthy of his devotion. The beloved was, in fact, portrayed as perfection personified, and her virtue was made manifest in her physical beauty.[60] A glance at the work of any number of Dutch poets will reveal this pairing of physical and spiritual perfections to be conventional to the Petrarchan mode. P. C. Hooft is only the best example among many. In several of his poems, the beauty of the beloved's body, her golden hair, white skin, and blushing cheeks direct the lover's thoughts toward the beauty of her soul. "*Min*" becomes "*Eer*"; the amorous is transformed into the noble and chaste.[61]

If, as I contend, Petrarchism provided a context for the Ter Borch ladies' bearing and behaviour, it seems reasonable to suggest that Petrarchism also provided a compelling "excuse" for their "dangerous" beauty. Indeed, insofar as the seventeenth-century viewer's response was shaped by Petrarchan conceits, he or she would have been disinclined to see this beauty as anything other than exemplary.

Certainly Ter Borch encourages the Petrarchan, rather than the moralist, response. Even in his *Lady at Her Toilet* (Fig. 63) – where the model's features most closely conform to the contemporary ideal of loveliness, and where the lavish setting and splendid page heighten the intimation of beauty on parade – the aloof, stately, distanced bearing of the central figure undercuts any possible fantasies about her sexual attainability.[62] Her outward-turning pose does not so much seduce as draw the viewer into her self-absorbed, pensive state of mind.

And this is the extreme case. In the other works under discussion, we need hardly argue the precedence given to a chaste (and therefore, in seventeenth-century terms, positive) valuation of beauty. Typically the lady's body is described minimally, apart from her face. Only a limited expanse of rounded flesh appears above her neckline. Below falls the shimmering satin gown. The satin, not the physical figure of the woman, becomes the primary material expression of her beauty. The gorgeous fabric obscures – and substitutes for – the female body, rendering the form more chaste, less troubling. The viewer's potential desire for her body is immediately displaced to something more safely possessible.

In analogous ways, the Petrarchan poets fetishized the beloved's veil, or her brooch, or her eyes, mouth, or neck. By asking one laudable part to carry the significance of the whole, they neutralized any latent sexual threat implicit in a discussion of her entire person.[63]

PETRARCHAN READINGS

I have suggested that not only Gesina ter Borch, but others of her class and experience, would have been prepared to see images of relations between the sexes in light of Petrarchan *topoi*. How might this large group of viewers have read Gerard's paintings? Their imaginations enriched by poetic images of gallantry, refusal, importunings and hesitations, they could have interpreted *The Paternal Admonition* (Fig. 60) as a courtship narrative in domestic surroundings. For them it could represent a visit from an officer; the begowned beauty is the marriageable daughter; the woman at the back acts as chaperone; the parents who encouraged the meeting are discreetly absent. The daughter may have just finished her preparatory ablutions, but now that the encounter is under way, she turns from the suitor with an air of aloofness. Whilst compelling the full force of his attention, she herself looks elsewhere. She seems deliberately oblivious to his upraised hand; might it contain a ring or some other token of love, or might it be raised in a purely rhetorical gesture?[64] She is oblivious as well to the foot that dares to invade her space, and his perhaps-too-casually crossed legs. What he sees is a vision of loveliness in a modest black collar and a shimmering white gown, but only the profile of her face. Her expression is likely as enigmatic to him as it is invisible to the viewer.

In *The Suitor's Visit* (Fig. 62), painted several years later, the meeting has only just begun. The gentleman bows deferentially from the doorway. The lady, a moment before, had been playing the instrument on the table, accompanying her lute-playing friend and the gentleman behind (is he an officer as well?).[65] She now faces her suitor directly. With hands clasped, she stands a measured distance away, acknowledging his tentative address with dignified poise.[66]

In *The Introduction* (Fig. 65) of *c.* 1662 the suitor – an officer wearing spurs and ceremonial breastplate – has gained full admittance to the salon. (Now the door is not even visible.) He approaches with a bow of greeting, ever so slightly obsequious but for the arm held akimbo, a gesture of assertion typical of military figures in art.[67] Although the lady allows him to come close enough to touch her fingertips, she maintains a cool reserve, expressed by her erect posture, delicately arched hands and averted gaze. Her reserve is encouraged by the chaperone hovering behind them, whose watchfulness seems all the more necessary because of the man's military profession.

The suitor in *The Fiancée* (Fig. 61) is more desirable, and the company appropriately cosier. His recent arrival is suggested by his upraised glass, which the page is just beginning to fill. For once the suitor devotes his attention to the chaperone.[68] But the object of his visit stands just behind him, close enough to feel the brush of his clothes, yet pictorially distanced by her gesture, posture and gleaming white silhouette. Might the chest placed by the bed contain her trousseau?

In *The Concert* (Fig. 66) the suitor stands just outside the picture, in the viewer's space. The page has taken his large black hat under one arm and proceeds now to bring him a man-sized glass of beer, whilst welcoming him to the table with a knowing glance. In *The Letter* (Fig. 64), in *Curiosity*, and in *The Lady at Her Toilet* (Fig. 63) the suitor is entirely absent. But in all three pictures his presence is felt symbolically, through a letter, a handkerchief and a ring. These instruments of courtship succeed in bringing an image of the gentleman vividly into the lady's mind.[69] Conscious of his imagined gaze, she shapes herself into a suitable icon: a tall luminous form that conveys the superiority of the poetic beauty.

My rhetorically expansive readings, while hypothetical, rest on the assumption that Dutch beholders viewed these paintings empathetically. This response is what Goedde has termed "participatorial viewing."[70] Goedde relates such viewing to the literary tradition of *ekphrasis:* detailed, evocative description of visual phenomena. Noting "the highly rhetorical character of all descriptions of works of art in the seventeenth century," he reminds us that Dutch writers "entered empathetically into every detail of the pictures, imagining situations, emotions, locations, and weather . . . ."[71]

Dutch genre painting was particularly amenable to an emphatic response. In his *Groot schilderboek*, the late seventeenth-century theorist–painter Gerard de Lairesse drew parallels between the passions elicited by genre pictures and those engaged by history painting. He described *gezelschapjes* – in chambers, garden houses and salons, with a few ladies sipping tea and gentlemen drinking wine – as little dramas, involving the passions of "entreating and refusing." By offering extended readings of such works, he showed the degree to which any scene involving human interaction, however subtle, could yield an elaborate narrative.[72]

Applying De Lairesse's way of viewing to Ter Borch's paintings, one can argue that the limited number of figures, their psychological engagement with one another, and the presence of a compelling heroine, moved beholders to identify with the situations depicted and to create similarly expansive narratives out of these still images. In this regard, Ter Borch's pictures contrasted with earlier high-society scenes by Codde and Palamedesz., whose stereotyped crowds discouraged such projection. The subtlety and open-endedness of the narrative action in Ter Borch's works would have allowed viewers to construct not just one story line but a variety of them, and in some cases merely the fragment of a story.

De Lairesse's seventeenth-century discussion of genre scenes is as rare as it is valuable. Late twentieth-century literary theorists have written at length and with conviction of the related notion of readers actively constructing the meanings of texts. As many art historians and film critics presently assert, the viewer has always been active in similar ways – the eye was and is a "performing agent."[73]

VIEWING AS A MAN

It has been argued thus far that many viewers' emotional and intellectual responses to the art were framed by their engagement with certain poetic conceits and cultural assumptions. But what the argument has omitted is a consideration of how viewers' genders may also have shaped their looking. Imaginative reconstruction of male and female viewing positions is, of course, an interpretative strategy with implications for understanding all art.[74] As Showalter states, the hypothesis of gendered reading changes our understanding of a work, "awakening us to the significance of its sexual codes." At the very least it serves as a rhetorical device to bring out the range of possible response.[75]

Unfortunately, any gender-inflected enumeration of likely viewer reactions runs the risk of reductiveness and stereotyping, especially insofar as the experiences of men and women overlap at many levels. Nevertheless, late twentieth-century psychology gives evidence that women construct social reality differently from men.[76] Feminist literary critics and film theorists have long postulated a continuity between the differing actual experiences of men and women and the way each gender reads and perceives. To oversimplify, when the image contains a woman the male viewer psychologically possesses what he sees, the female identifies with the object of his gaze.[77]

What follows is an attempt to develop historically plausible gendered readings – viewings – that draw on these twentieth-century critical perspectives. First, some male responses.

The narrative descriptions of the works sketched above often implicitly assume a male viewer. In many cases Ter Borch's pictorial structure seems to imply a conjunction between suitor and viewer. When the page in *The Concert* (Fig. 66), for example, pointedly acknowledges the viewer, the conjunction is direct. More often it is indirect, the suitor acting as a generalized stand-in for the male beholder.

A male viewer could have approached his encounter with these pictorial ladies from a variety of perspectives – social, ideological, psychological, literary. One possible position could be taken by what we shall call the economic man, someone who responded to the Ter Borch ladies' splendour in terms of their material worth. Stone-Ferrier argues that he could have responded with patriotic pride to the ladies' satin as a product of the Dutch textile industry, and with individual pride to its capacity to suggest wealth.[78] In Van der Helst's 1654 portrait of *Abraham del Court and Maria Keerssegieter* (Fig. 11), for instance, the display of the bride's white satin dress may well have been encouraged by her husband's occupation as a cloth merchant.[79] By extension, the hypothetical male viewer of Ter Borch's pictures could see all the sumptuous objects in the painting, and not just the satin, as instruments of consumption, and could indeed view the woman portrayed as an attractive commodity.[80]

Alternatively, a man could understand the Ter Borch ladies more abstractly, as secular Virgins – inspiring in their perfection, their virtue, their chastity, their otherness – especially so if Petrarchan literary *topoi* played prominently in his imagination. White or light-coloured satin for him would have functioned allegorically, connoting the most positive of virtues. (In the *Iconologia*, Ripa specified those virtues as purity and righteousness; in the colour charts that Gesina included in her albums, white again signifies purity.[81]) These gleaming, pristine surfaces discouraged imagined touching, touch being the most physical, and therefore the most potentially inflaming of the senses.[82] In any event, this tendency to see woman as the elevated "other" is a function of cultural attitudes alive since the Middle Ages, and assuredly present in seventeenth-century Holland.[83]

On the opposite side of the coin, a man – perhaps even the same man as the above – could view these female beauties voyeuristically. This would have entailed converting the Petrarchan Virgin into an Eve, a figure more to be desired than adored. For the voyeur, *Curiosity* and *The Letter* (Fig. 64), in particular, could be read as private, dark and inviting.[84] But all the works present an attractive lady for his appraising gaze, her person no less than her gown a pretty object for his visual possession. Though these pictures offer, I would argue, only the most minimal encouragement for such a response, it is possible that some male viewers would have failed to distinguish the differences between, say, Moreelse's 1627 *Young Woman with a Mirror* (Cambridge, Fitzwilliam), a figure displayed for sexual enjoyment, and Ter Borch's *Lady at Her Toilet* (Fig. 63), seeing the latter simply as a sophisticated version of the former.[85]

In related fashion, a man with a moralizing cast of mind (or a guilty conscience) could judge these ladies as vain and egotistical, see their society as socially pretentious, and read the narratives as cautionary tales about temptation and seduction. From this perspective the gorgeous attire itself would signal narcissistic display, and the lady's preening in it, unseemly exhibitionism. Such a viewer would be unlikely to perceive the significant contrast between Ter Borch's obvious representation of a bordello, *The Gallant Military Man* (Louvre, *c.* 1654, Fig. 71) and *The Paternal Admonition* (Fig. 60), insisting, simply, that both be categorized as *bordeeltjes*, stock representations of erotic themes.[86]

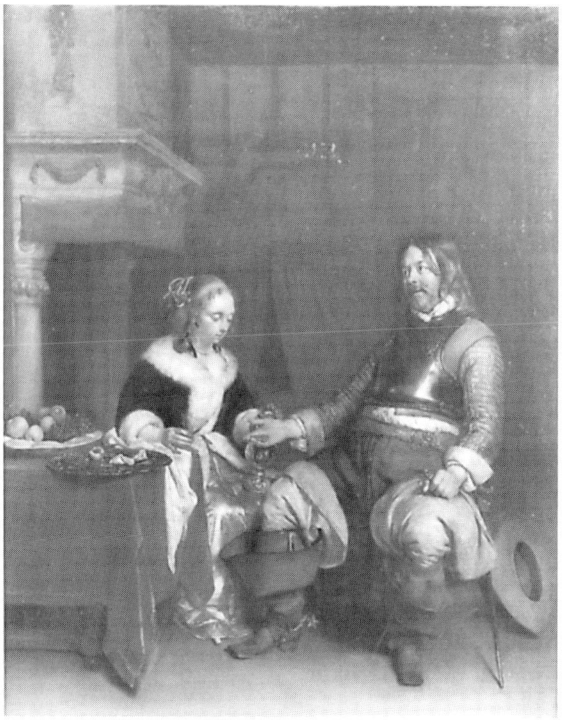

Figure 71. Gerard ter Borch, *The Gallant Military Man* (oil on canvas, 67 × 55 cm). Paris, Musée du Louvre. Photo: Réunion des musées nationaux, Paris.

VIEWING AS A WOMAN

Female viewers, of course, could respond in virtually all of the above ways. Living within a patriarchal culture, women traditionally have adopted the male perspective. Co-opted, they have imaginatively participated in experiences that oppose or even exclude their own.[87] As a consequence, they, too, could have seen these works in economic terms, or as idealizations, or as emblems of *luxuria*, or as cautionary images.[88]

Developmental psychologists have discovered that one particularly strong characteristic of female, as opposed to male, development is the need to identify with other human beings as a means of finding connections outside the self. This identification extends, I would argue, to persons represented in works of art. A modern female viewer could take on a male response – seeing, for example, a pictured woman as a spectacle for the male viewer's pleasure; but she is at least as likely to identify with the woman portrayed, imagining the pictured woman's experience, and comparing her own appearance and behaviour to those depicted.[89]

In the seventeenth century as well, a female viewer of Ter Borch's pictures would have found it natural to identify personally with the elegant ladies who formed the focus of his paintings. At the most basic level, she could have enjoyed the imagined pleasure of posing center-stage, admired and perceived as beautiful. Equally immediate would have been her identification with the depicted lady's delight in wearing such a shimmering gown. By imaginatively projecting herself into this pictorial context, a woman transported herself into a milieu of leisure and beauty.

By the middle of the century, moralists' attacks on luxurious attire had begun to dwindle, as the increasing materialism – and concomitant shift in taste – within this wealthy society convinced all but the most diehard to keep silent.[90] The prosperous Dutch recognized the power of fine clothing to suggest rank and status. Certainly ample documentary evidence indicates their responsiveness to the latest styles. Moreover, readers of the *vryerijboeken* – Dutch versions of Ovid's *De Arte Amandi*, intended for a broad public – would have been alert to the role that an attractive appearance played in courtship.[91] Ter Borch's idealization of actual clothing could only have enhanced the vicarious pleasure for the female beholder.

Identification of a more intimate sort was encouraged by Ter Borch's very special treatment of the woman *in* the gown.[92] For Gesina and the other family members whom Gerard used as models, gazing at his paintings would have meant self-recognition – the small eyes, fine hair and receding chins they inherited from their mother were all preserved. Though few female viewers in the western cities where the paintings presumably sold would have known the models' identities, for them the portrait-like, unstereotyped face above the costume would have given the Ter Borch lady a three-dimensional, sympathetic presence largely unavailable in most contemporary genre works.[93] As Betterton has argued, female viewers are able to achieve a more comfortable relationship to a pictorial image of their gender when the gap between the idealization of the woman and her reality is narrowed.[94]

Gerard's pictorial woman not only seems real, she seems possessed of an inner life. Her facial expressions and body language convey an individual, private experience at the depicted public moment. Her striking poise and self-possession suggest a living personality – rather than a mannequin – with a personal history that precedes the image and will continue after it. Surely nothing went further to invite the female viewer into the painting than this psychologically nuanced presentation of one of her gender.

As I have indicated above, insofar as the seventeenth-century viewer carried Petrarchan ideas and ideals in her head, an identification with the pictured woman as "a beauty," and thereby with beauty itself, would have been perceived as positive. Her satin dress, by drawing the imagined admirer's eye toward its own beautiful surfaces and curves – and away from hers – served to confirm the moral soundness of the role. Far from calling her virtue into question, this association with beauty would have affirmed it.

But identification with the Ter Borch lady would have entailed more than simply donning her pretty dress and taking on her attractive persona. It would have required the female viewer to participate in the pictorial narrative.

Certainly the social context for the scene, the courtship rituals, would have been familiar to her. It is less certain, however, that the specific props in these particular vignettes would have seemed so familiar. Ter Borch does not document the typical mating game in the typical drawing room. Instead, he presents his limited *dramatis personae* within a very judicious arrangement of elegant objects. The concision of their presentation combines with the innate quality of the things depicted to heighten the atmosphere. Similarly, the small number of actors aids in their individuation, and serves to heighten the drama.

What drama? The seventeenth-century female would have been drawn into constructing her own interpretation. The amorous ambience presumably defined the direction of her responses. But because Ter Borch left each situation so open-ended, only her own experience and personality could flesh out, as it were, the particulars of the narrative. Her own thoughts, inevitably, became those of the satin-clad lady.

Identification with the lady's imagined mental state invited a wide range of responses. Identification with her *behavior* considerably narrowed the range. She was visibly reserved, passive, decorous, controlled; still she remained the centre of attention. Suitors, pages and viewers approached her, not she them. She was, in short, the proper Dutch woman described in the conduct books and simultaneously the ideal Petrarchan beauty.

In this respect, the act of identifying with the lady in satin aided the seventeenth-century female viewer's compliance with the patriarchal social agenda. The apparent gender reversal in all Petrarchan imagery – that is, the celebration of female dominance and male submissiveness – actually served to affirm the traditional hierarchy of gender. For the woman's supposed power lay in her ability to be still; her strength was proportional to her restraint. Thus the illusion of feminine power offered by both the poems and the paintings encouraged women toward the very behavior that was most prized in this male-dominated society.

THE INFORMED VIEWER

What has remained unacknowledged thus far is the probability that a viewer of either gender would have come to any single work with a wealth of other, prior images already in mind.

Though relatively few seventeenth-century viewers could properly be called "connoisseurs" or "critics," a good many would have been what I shall term "informed viewers," who approached these works with some knowledge of their place among the artistic products of their time.[95] An informed viewer might readily have been able to distinguish among genres, for example, or to identify certain artistic conventions.

Such a sophisticated beholder could not have seen any of the paintings under discussion without reference to the traditions out of which they emerged: merry companies, high-life interiors, toilet scenes and bordellos. At the same time, he or she could not have ignored the ways in which these paintings deviated from, undercut or conflated the conventions common to those traditions.

The satin-clad ladies of Ter Borch presented this informed viewer with a host of disjunctions and contradictions. How was he or she to understand the uneasy overlap in a single painting of hints of virtue and hints of vice? of overtones of Petrarchan purity and overtones of sex for cash? In contrast to the moralist, who had only to identify the broad iconographical category to which a given work belonged in order to judge it, the informed viewer would have realized that these works could not, in fact, be reduced to mere exemplars of familiar types.

With this in mind, let us return briefly to *The Paternal Admonition*, and specifically to the first version of the painting in the Rijksmuseum (Fig. 38). Here the greater width of the canvas allows space for a dog to hang around the officer's chair. This mangy, slinking hound, poor relation to the groomed spaniels in Figs. 62–4, strikes a disquieting note. In the Berlin version (Fig. 60), probably produced later in the same year, the dog has been eliminated. The verticality of the picture – the format favoured by Ter Borch from this time forward – directs the formal and narrative focus to the left. The balance shifts to the lady, with all the associations (many of them Petrarchan) that her posture, glance and brilliant attire evoke. But though upstaged, and unaccompanied by the dog, the not-entirely-Petrarchan officer remains, with his worryingly careless pose and ambiguous gesture.

In similar fashion, *The Introduction* (Fig. 65) and *The Suitor's Visit* (Fig. 62) carry vestiges of the sexual relaxation and easy pleasure found in traditional merry companies. Yet here the decorous and polite have demonstrably gained the upper hand

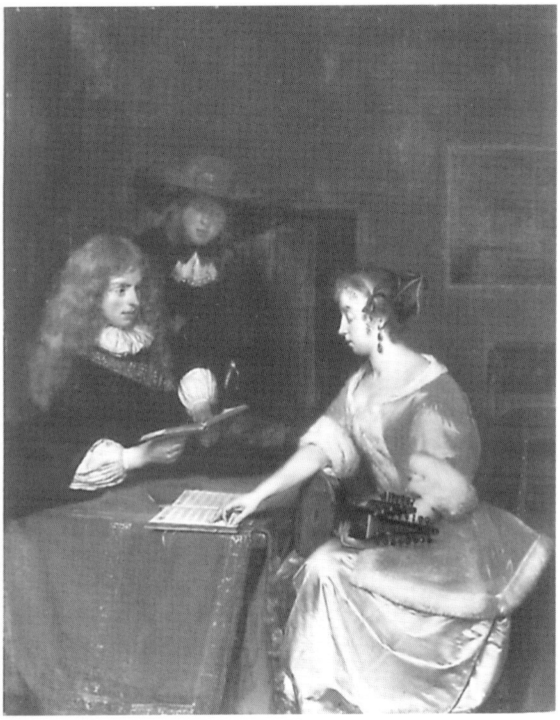

Figure 72. Gerard ter Borch, *The Music Party* (oil on panel, 58.1 × 47.6 cm). Cincinnati, Cincinnati Art Museum, bequest of Mary M. Emery. Photo: museum.

over the loose and unsavoury. The same can be said of *The Lady at Her Toilet* (Fig. 63). It differs from the censorious toilet scenes of earlier artists by virtue of the sympathetic handling of the lady: her modesty, noble bearing and self-possession. Her admirer is a boy, rather than a man, further reducing the sexual charge. In a poignant visual sub-plot, her profile in the mirror acknowledges his rapt devotion. But in the main pictorial narrative, she distances herself both from him and from the viewer, compelling both, perhaps, to recast their initial response.

In confronting the above works, the informed viewer would have been forced to reconcile competing sets of values and associations, and to determine for him- or herself the extent to which the positive force of the satin-clad lady, along with other alterations of convention, transformed the image into something beyond the typical and the expected.

It should be noted in this regard that Ter Borch's reputation as a virtuoso painter of satin rested on his entire *oeuvre* of genre works, of which I have discussed only a significant portion. Not all of the scenes in which satin-clad figures appear invite a Petrarchan reading. *The Gallant Military Man* (Louvre, 1662–3, Fig. 71), and *The Glass of Lemonade* (Hermitage, *c.* 1663–4), both represent more frankly sexual encounters, and thus more closely approximate conventional bordello scenes.[96] In such contexts, the "pure white" satin appears to reflect low-class mimicry of high-class taste and style.[97] Ter Borch manages to compromise the beauty of the satin pictorially as well as socially. In both works the fabric's flow is halted, either bent into angular shapes or partially covered by a jacket whose soft fur trim complements the soft flesh that it frames. Subject and treatment combine to send the informed viewer a unified signal – these women are no ladies.

In Ter Borch's later works with musical themes, the situations described and the specifics of their rendering again seem designed to create an atmosphere of eroticism. In *The Music Party* (*c.* 1675, Fig. 72), for example, the lady not only is outnumbered by the gentlemen present, but she also shows her inclination toward love by actively involving herself in music-making. She undercuts the modesty of her downward glance by extending her arm and bending her body forward, offering up a décolletage sensually fringed by a border of fur. The informed seventeenth-century viewer would presumably have perceived at once what we must infer with more effort: this is no aloof Petrarchan beauty, withholding both her consent and her person from suitor and viewer, but a willing participant in the game of love, subtly playing to her admirers' desire.

OPEN END

For the seventeenth-century viewer, male or female, informed or otherwise, the messages to be found in Ter Borch's bordello scenes and later musical companies should have been relatively clear. In contrast, the messages to be found in the works I have called Petrarchan would have been decidedly *mixed.* Like most works produced in that fecund artistic milieu, they would have been owned and viewed by middle-class persons of varying occupations, sensitivities and ages, capable of responding in multiple and sometimes contradictory ways. But the "Petrarchan" works would *in themselves* have elicited widely varying interpretations. More than most contemporary genre scenes, they encouraged serious rather than casual viewing, and invited the viewer actively to construct their meanings.

Here I have tried to suggest several likely contexts for contemporary responses: courtship patterns, attitudes toward beauty, ideas about satin, ideals of conduct, gender differences, pictorial conventions and, above all, poetic notions about relations between the sexes. Clearly these contexts would not have been mutually exclusive.

It is this complexity of seventeenth-century response that I wish to affirm. Standing before these works, the original viewers could see icons of beauty *and* images of conspicuous consumption, could discern elements of social reality *and* elements of pictorial convention, could respond to Petrarchan romance *and* to technical display. The contexts for viewing were plural. The visual signals were plural. And assuredly the responses were no less plural than they are today.

Style in Dutch Art

Walter Liedtke

The appreciation of style in Dutch art is impeded for some viewers by the diversity and particularity of its subject matter, and by the seemingly straightforward description one follows, line for line and from object to object, in a typical landscape, still life, portrait, genre scene, and so on. "Such life-like representations of cabbages, turnips, cauliflowers, and peas," Nathanial Hawthorne observed at the Art Treasures Exhibition in Manchester in 1857 (he was describing a painting not by Pontormo but by Gerard Dou). After a fortnight's effort, Hawthorne claimed to have made "some progress as a connoisseur, and [to] have got so far as to be able to distinguish the broader differences of style as, for example, between Rubens and Rembrandt."[1]

Hawthorne might have advanced more quickly had he studied the Bellinis, Carraccis, and Correggios (which he never mentioned), and less so if he had stuck with painters of turnips and peas. Critics are routinely tongue-tied when it comes to describing naturalistic pictures as art.[2] Even today, "when it comes to talking about Dutch 'realism' stock phrases like 'extreme precision of execution' and 'apparently faithful reflection of reality' are used repeatedly; art historians appear to know that Dutch art is not realistic, but to be unable to say why not."[3]

The reason for this is essentially that scholars of the "visual culture" have become inattentive to and therefore inarticulate about style.[4] Many of our current interests do not require concentration upon the formal aspects of Dutch painting, which is encouraged (as Hawthorne discovered) by viewing actual objects, and discouraged by academic discussion of polemical issues such as whether this "craft of representation" can be savored in the same manner as that in which we admire murals by Raphael.[5]

General discussions of Dutch art usually focus on a select group of artists, the same ones who were covered by Thoré-Bürger (1858 – 60), Taine (1868), James (1872), Fromentin (1876), Bode (1883), and Valentiner (1914).[6] This is only natural; the reader, at the words "typical landscape" in the first sentence of this essay, more likely had a mental image of a scene by Jan van Goyen or Jacob van Ruisdael than of a composition by Joachim Wtewael (Fig. 73), Abraham Bloemaert (Fig. 74), or Roelant Savery. In describing a landscape by one of the latter artists, most writers, even those who strongly favor one of the other approaches to Dutch art represented in this volume, would find it appropriate to mention stylistic currents and influences that originated outside the Northern Netherlands. The analysis would inevitably repeat phrases familiar from somewhat dated texts, but it would also cite cosmopolitan artists and ideas that influenced many Dutch painters – for example, those active in Utrecht during the first half of the seventeenth century.

When Rubens visited Utrecht in 1627, he met the German painter and future art critic Joachim von Sandrart at Gerard van Honthorst's house. Rubens expressed a desire to visit Bloemaert, Cornelis van Poelenburgh, "and others."[7] At the time,

Bloemaert was sixty-three and the most respected master in Utrecht; thirty-five years earlier, the city's historian, Aernout van Buchell, predicted that "the judgment of time will give still greater fame" to Bloemaert and Wtewael.[8] Poelenburgh had just returned from Rubens's beloved Italy and had sold a *Banquet of the Gods* (now in Dessau, Schloss Georgium) to the city fathers for presentation to the Stadholder's wife.[9]

Since Rubens ordered two pictures from Poelenburgh, it might be permissible to imagine for a moment that he had asked to meet that artist, Bloemaert, "and others" who might have fine landscape paintings for sale. Van Honthorst (had he not been indisposed) and his pupil Von Sandrart would likely have taken the Fleming to the two painters he named and also to Savery and Wtewael, but others, such as Joost Cornelisz. Droochsloot and Adam Willaerts, would probably have been passed over on the grounds of quality and style.

The painters that Rubens visited in Utrecht and their immediate associates comprised the most influential school of painting in the Netherlands during the 1620s. Their figural compositions of that decade, which were based in part upon Italian models, employed patterns that were shared with artists in France and Flanders, and that were adopted, largely from Utrecht, by painters active in Leiden, Delft, The Hague, Amsterdam, Haarlem, and Leeuwarden.[10] Of course, Utrecht's importance for Dutch art in general went well beyond its role in transmitting Caravaggesque and other early Baroque conventions. For example, Savery was a pioneer of still-life and animal painting as well as a landscapist,[11] and Poelenburgh was the first of several Utrecht artists who specialized in Italianate scenes. Bloemaert's influence on landscape and genre painting as well as on religious and mythological pictures was decisive in the city where he taught successive generations of artists and remained active until his death in 1651 (the Vaduz picture, Fig. 74, is dated 1645).[12] Every category of his work was more widely known through engravings. Even Wtewael, who is now regarded as the most modish of Mannerists and therefore, in the view of some scholars, as hardly Dutch, painted large altarpieces that were made for communities of worshippers, not circles of aesthetes.[13] The known collectors of his small and exquisite paintings on panel and copper were not foreign princes or even Dutch princes but members of the upper middle class.[14]

Rubens would have recognized that in a composition like that of *The Golden Age* (one of nearly countless Dutch illustrations of Ovidian episodes),[15] Wtewael had moved beyond the "Sprangerism" of the 1590s, if not so far beyond as the point to which Goltzius and his Haarlem colleagues had progressed in their paintings of about 1600 – 10. The landscape, the still lifes of fruit and shells, and the animals (Fig. 73a) – which are as naturalistic as any painted at about this time – recall works by Jan Brueghel the Elder and his circle in Antwerp, while the figures are strongly modelled, realistically proportioned, and arranged with such clarity that one might describe the picture as a Dutch equivalent of Annibale Carracci's *Triumph of Bacchus and Ariadne* on the ceiling of the Farnese Gallery (1597–1600).[16] In schematic surveys Wtewael has been useful as an example of what seventeenth-century Dutch artists abandoned after 1600, but in the actual art world of Utrecht (where he remained from 1592 onward), he was, like Hendrick Goltzius, Cornelisz van Haarlem, Bloemaert, and others, a contributor to the foundation of a new Netherlandish style.

None of these artists is discussed in books on the "Philosophie de l'art dans les Pays-Bas" (Philosophy of Art in the Low Countries; to employ Taine's title of 1868); most of them are not even mentioned in the latest essay along these lines, Alper's *The Art of Describing*, despite its subtitle, *Dutch Art in the Seventeenth Century*.[17] More relevant to the present topic would be a rereading of Gombrich's *Art and Illusion* and reference to recent books such as those by Crary, Kaufmann, Kemp, and Summers;[18] these studies help one to understand that any Dutch, Flemish, Italian, French or whatever kind of painting, drawing, or print, even the most naturalistic of them, makes use of pictorial and other conventions that, consciously or unconsciously, reflect the artist's cultural background, training, and personality. In other words, all Dutch art has style.[19]

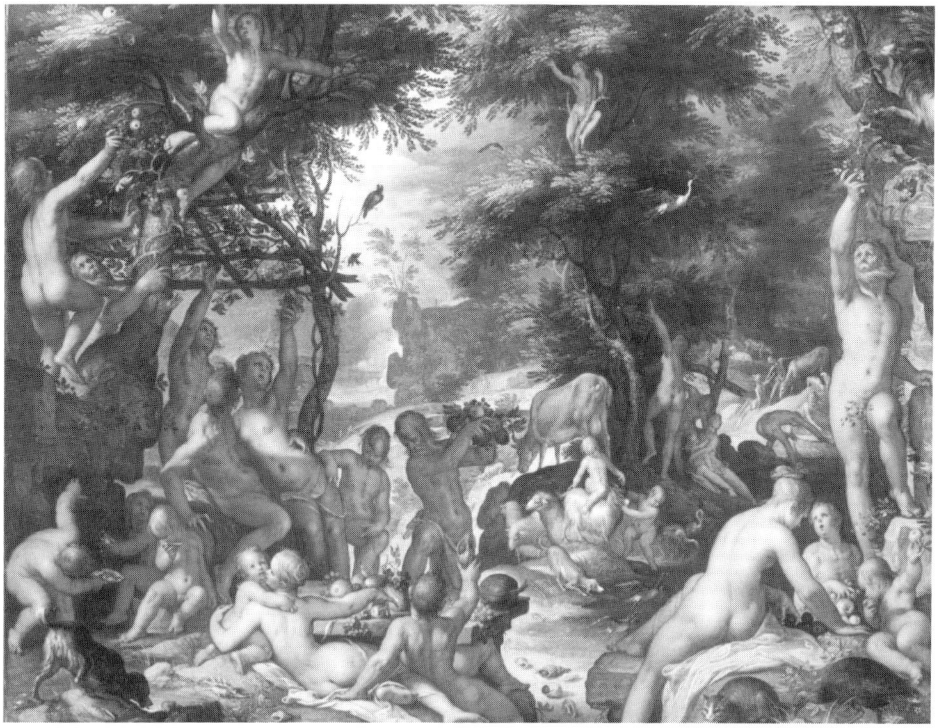

Figure 73. Joachim Wtewael, *The Golden Age*, 1605 (oil on copper, 21 × 30.5 cm). New York, The Metropolitan Museum of Art. Photo: museum.

Samuel van Hoogstraeten revealed an awareness of this fact throughout his eclectic *oeuvre* (see Fig. 79) and in many pages of his *Inleyding tot de hooge schoole der schilder-konst* (Introduction to the Lofty School of Painting; 1678). In various passages he comments explicitly on the relationship between art and observation, maintaining for example that young painters should "become accustomed to imitating things from life even as they appear so that in time, when they have acquired an understanding of things, they will have the discrimination to select the most beautiful."[20] Thus, the picture of, for example, an actual site (such as Jacob van Ruisdael's views of the castle at Bentheim) could be said to resemble an essay on an historical period: Certain aspects of the subject will be suppressed, others will be arbitrarily enhanced, and in general the actual evidence will be represented from a particular point of view and in a manner distinctive of the author and in accordance with the fashions of her or his time.[21]

The importance of aesthetic factors will be conceded even by scholars who have focused narrowly on the "empirical" interests of Dutch artists[22] – for example, painters who seem to have employed the camera obscura;[23] who attempted in other ways to approximate visual experience (for example, Carel Fabritius in the *View in Delft;* London, The National Gallery);[24] who served the interests of various scientific fields (from botany to zoology);[25] or who otherwise have inspired art historians to read about contemporary figures such as Francis Bacon, Cornelius Drebbel, Johannes Kepler, Athanasius Kircher, and so on.[26] Students who approach this material objectively will note parallel interests in some examples of Dutch art, in contemporary science, and in other modes of observation. They will also gain renewed respect for the role of received ideas, the importance of training and tradition, and the prevalence of shared conventions.[27] Stylistic and iconographic schemes are complex parts of a larger

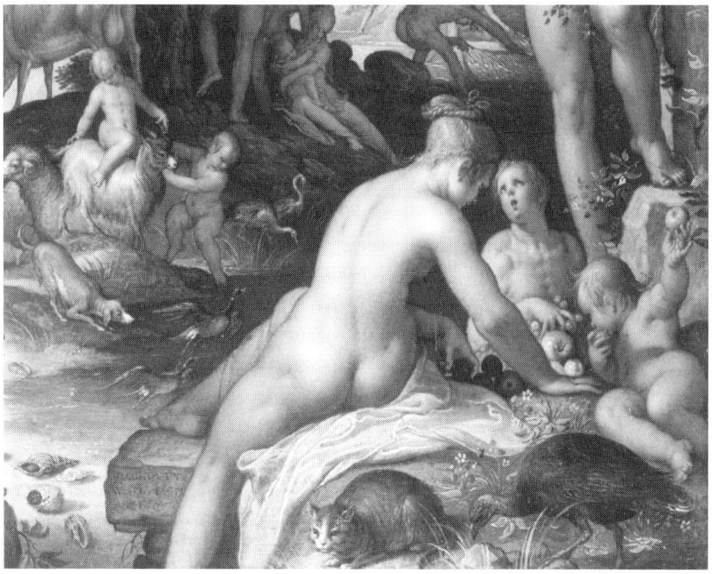

Figure 73a. Detail of Figure 73.

picture; to ignore them is like studying a language without a basic comprehension of its grammar and vocabulary.[28] This is essentially what observers of "the 'reality effect' peculiar to much Dutch painting" have done.[29] Like intellectual tourists, their Baedekers replaced by Barthes, they discover the typical and bring home descriptions dating from pre-Gombrichian times.[30]

Any Dutch landscape of the kind one may describe as naturalistic (or "realistic," as the word is often employed) bears upon this argument. As is well known, landscape paintings and many land-

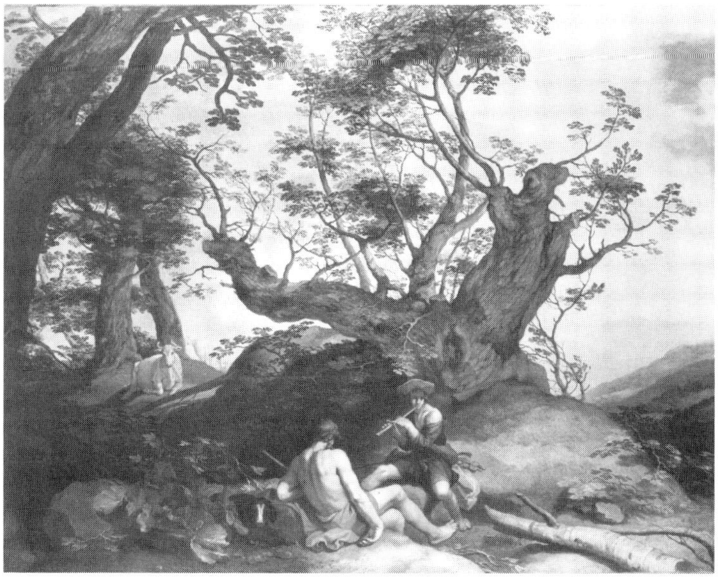

Figure 74. Abraham Bloemaert, *Mercury and Argus,* 1645 (oil on canvas, 79 × 104 cm). Vaduz, Collection of the Reigning Prince of Liechtenstein.

scape drawings were produced in the studio; they may have been based upon or informed by sketches made out of doors, but their compositions and many motifs were adopted from artistic sources, such as the painter's earlier inventions or works by other artists. Two of "the leading members of the group of artists who brought pictorial realism in Dutch landscape to a climax,"[31] Van Goyen and Salomon van Ruysdael, painted river views in the 1630s that "are sometimes difficult to separate;"[32] it is probably relevant that Van Goyen, a resident of The Hague, was fined by the Haarlem guild in August 1634 for painting pictures in the local art dealer and painter Isaack van Ruysdael's house (he was Salomon's brother).[33] The great majority of the hundreds of known sketches by Van Goyen are ideas for compositions, not records of actual sites (as are the leaves of his Bredius sketchbook).[34] Van Ruysdael depended even more exclusively on studio sources, to judge from his recycling of motifs and entire compositions, and the fact that only a few drawings by him are known.

Recent surveys of Baroque art, much less the early efforts of Wölfflin and Riegl, do little to clarify Dutch developments of this kind.[35] Indeed, there is not much resemblance between that literature and classic studies of Dutch art such as Stechow's survey of landscape, which deals with specialized questions of style on almost every page. At the same time, Stechow constantly offers insights of broader interest; for example, when the young Van Ruisdael had difficulty composing pictures that conveyed his admiration of majestic trees, he fell "back upon a careful study of Cornelis Vroom's achievements. . . . Some works of 1646 are as closely related and as deeply indebted to Vroom as work of genius can ever be to work of talent."[36] The remark recalls the closing lines of Stechow's introduction: "The synthesis of new discoveries in nature and the exigencies of tradition and craft which characterize Dutch landscape painting of this era has never been better formulated than by Samuel van Hoogstraeten's term '*keurlijke natuurlijkheid*' (selective naturalness), with which he credited the art of 'that great Raphael of marine painting,' Jan Porcellis. 'Selective naturalness'!"[37] This subjective approach to reality and many other kinds of personal experience (Savery, Jan Lievens, Esaias van de Velde, and other artists are mentioned informatively on the same page) are shown by Stechow to make for far more complex stylistic developments than those that have been described (often too simplistically) for artists of other countries who worked for the church and state or within academic or large studio systems. Alpers makes the same point differently: "It is, finally, hard to trace stylistic development, as we are trained to call it, in the work of Dutch artists."[38] We may be grateful that authors such as Stechow, Ingvar Bergström, Hans Jantzen, Jakob Rosenberg, Seymour Slive, and many younger scholars have performed the task so well.[39]

Their methods, as Haverkamp-Begemann observes,[40] remain valid for the study of Dutch art, including such naturalistic pictures as a Haarlem (?) artist's view of a rugged road with travelers (Fig. 75). The small panel was sold at auction in 1989 as from the "Dutch School, c. 1700,"[41] but its description of brilliant daylight and meteorological events such as a bracing wind and the small rain shower in the right background are pictorial conventions (whether or not they were based upon firsthand experience) that make such a late dating implausible. The freshness of observation and compositional devices such as the off-center massing of trees, and the use of a forked path in combination with the diagonally ascending white clouds to structure the entire design on an unobtrusive X-pattern, strongly recall features of Jacob van Ruisdael's earliest works (about 1645–8).[42] The artist here, however, differs from Van Ruisdael and his relatives (for example, his father Isaack, mentioned earlier), and from minor figures such as Gerrit van Hees, in that he imparts a flowing rhythm to almost everything, from the roller-coaster road to the jaunty traveler and hounds. This quality is distinctive, although it may have been inspired partly by some earlier example, such as the aqueous patterns found in a few of Goltzius's landscape prints.[43]

The picture was ascribed to the painter and early Haarlem printmaker Pieter Molijn (1595–1661) by a dealer after he had brought it to New York and visited the Dutch galleries of the Metropolitan

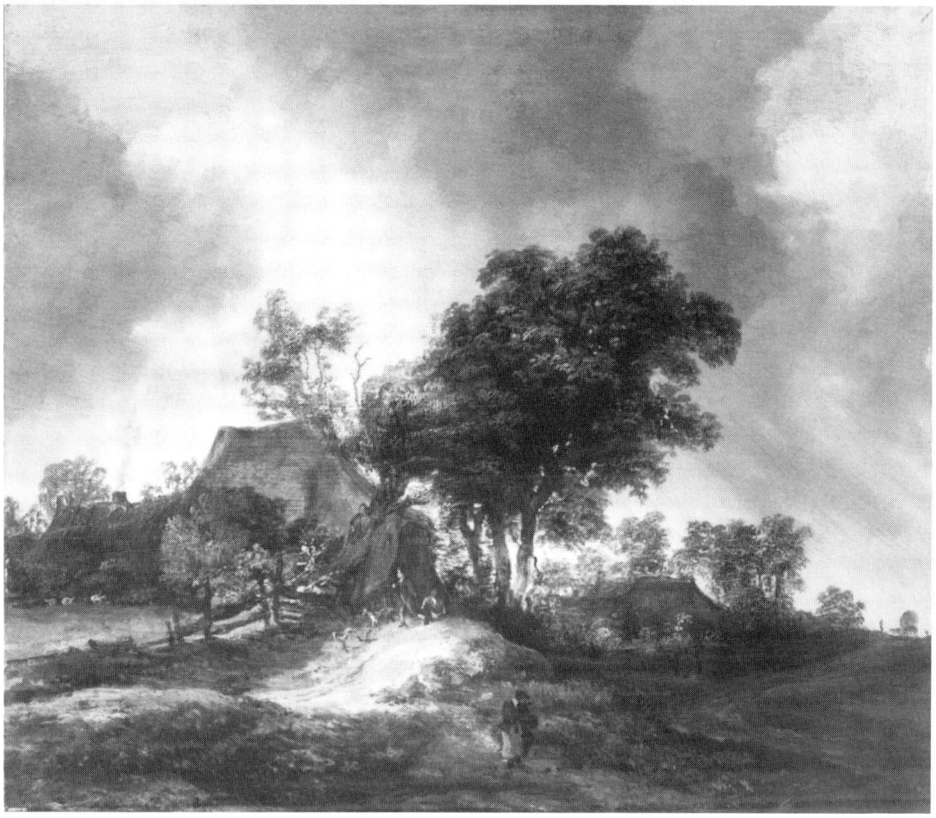

Figure 75. Haarlem Artist, *A Rugged Road by a Farmhouse* (oil on panel, 30.5 × 36.5 cm). Private collection.

Museum of Art.[44] Molijn's *Landscape with a Cottage* of 1629 in that collection is not very similar in composition, but the gentleman noticed immediately that it had the same sense of rhythm and touch. Removal of the imported panel's frame revealed the authentic inscription "P Molyn 1650" in the original paint layer. The artist's late work is not well published, but numerous drawings and paintings resembling this one are known.[45]

Some readers might dismiss this story as one about connoisseurship, the discrimination of individual hands, which they would consider incidental to the study of Dutch culture as a whole. For scholars of Dutch art, however, placing a painting or a drawing in the right social context and identifying the artist are often aspects of the same approach. To compare the products of this society with oriental carpets or "the Scythians' gold," as one writer has,[46] is to ignore the importance of authorship, of distinctive personal styles, in the view of seventeenth-century Dutch artists (many of whom, like Vermeer, routinely appraised and authenticated works), critics, collectors, dealers, and tax agents.[47] Prices, reputations, and careers rose and fell accordingly, which is essentially why so many Dutch pictures are signed (and why one artist, probably in emulation of Raphael, started using his first name, Rembrandt, instead of "RHL").

In his diary of about 1630, Constantijn Huygens (as is well known) compares the manners of Rembrandt and Lievens, wishes they would visit Italy, and hopes they will do "what I wanted of Rubens, to compile an inventory of their works," and to describe their methods, "indicating how and why (for the admiration and benefit of later generations) they had designed, composed, and worked out each

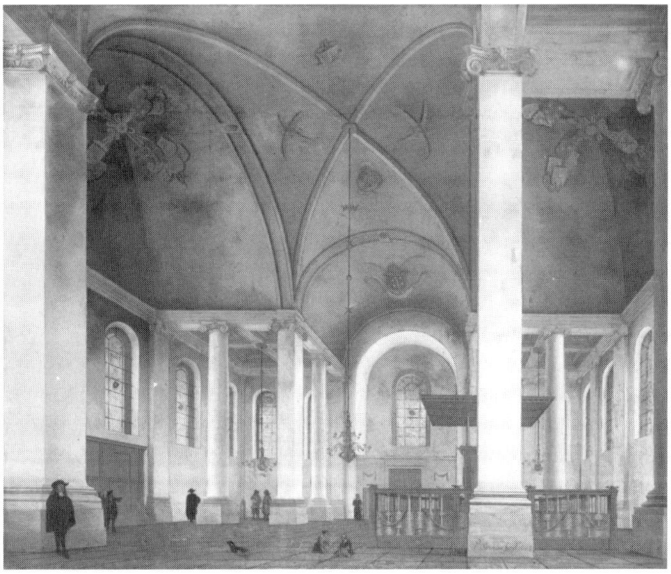

Figure 76. Pieter Saenredam, *Interior of the New Church, Haarlem, View to the North*, 1653 (oil on panel, 86 × 103 cm). Budapest, Szépmüvészeti Múzeum. Photo: museum.

painting."[48] This was a sensible suggestion, given that Lievens at about the age of twelve (according to Jan Orlers in 1641) "copied two outstanding pieces by the excellent master Cornelis Ketel of Haarlem" and that the copies were "sold as originals from the estate of Mr. Boudewijns,"[49] and that Heyman Dullaert (or so Houbraken had heard) was the actual author of a painting sold as a Rembrandt in Amsterdam.[50] What is significant about these stories, which conform to a topos employed by Vasari (on Raphael) and by Van Mander (on Goltzius, whose *Circumcision* was passed off as a previously unknown engraving by Dürer), is that the "consummate skill [which] astounded numerous connoisseurs" (as Orlers wrote of Lievens) was not an art of describing or a matter of craftsmanship but a display of artistic ability, of such remarkable facility that the individual could just as well practice in the style of another master rather than his own – Lievens, according to Orlers, "usually [invented] his own compositions and ideas to boot."[51]

Of course, imitation was not always admired. Houbraken complains that Gerbrand van den Eeckhout "stuck with the same way of painting [Rembrandt's] to the end of his life,"[52] and recalls that Govert Flinck "gave up this way of painting with great effort and difficulty; since before the death of Rembrandt true connoisseurs opened the world's eyes to the influence of the Italian manner, and the bright style came back into fashion."[53] Nicolaes Maes, by contrast, "soon departed from that manner of painting, the more so when he devoted himself to producing portraits, and realized that young ladies in particular found white more pleasing than brown."[54]

There are, it is true, numerous unattributed Dutch paintings that on stylistic grounds may be assigned only to a particular province or town and to a certain period (for example, South Holland, c. 1630).[55] This does not mean that the historian of Dutch art should venture forth like Margaret Mead in Samoa. To recognize a picture as, for example, a Haarlem work of about 1650 or as a painting by Molijn is to draw distinctions that mattered to members of the artist's society (who knew, better than we do, that there were important cultural differences between Haarlem in 1650, Utrecht in 1630, and so on), and which allow historians to pursue whatever other approaches to Dutch art they find illuminating.

Few artists raise questions about realism and style so precisely as does Pieter Saenredam. Despite her impatience with the notion of stylistic innova-

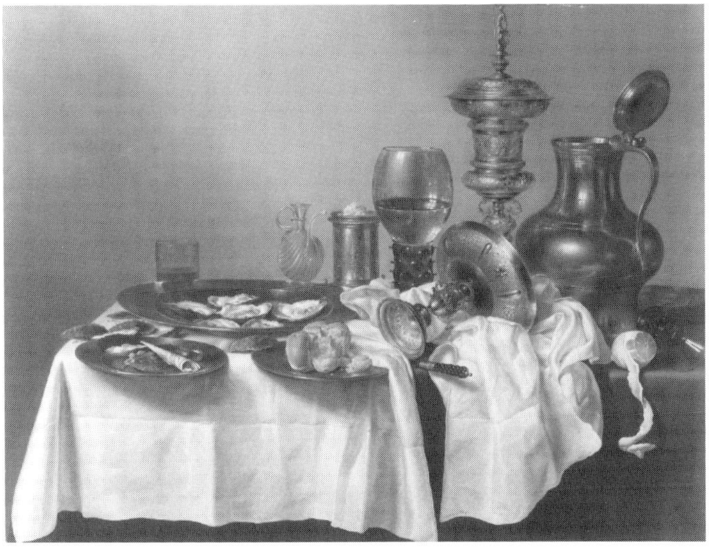

Figure 77. Willem Claesz. Heda, *Still Life with Guild Cup, Tazza, Pewter Tankard, and Oysters,* 1635 (oil on panel, 88 × 113 cm). Amsterdam, Rijksmuseum. Photo: P. Cuming Associates, Ltd., London.

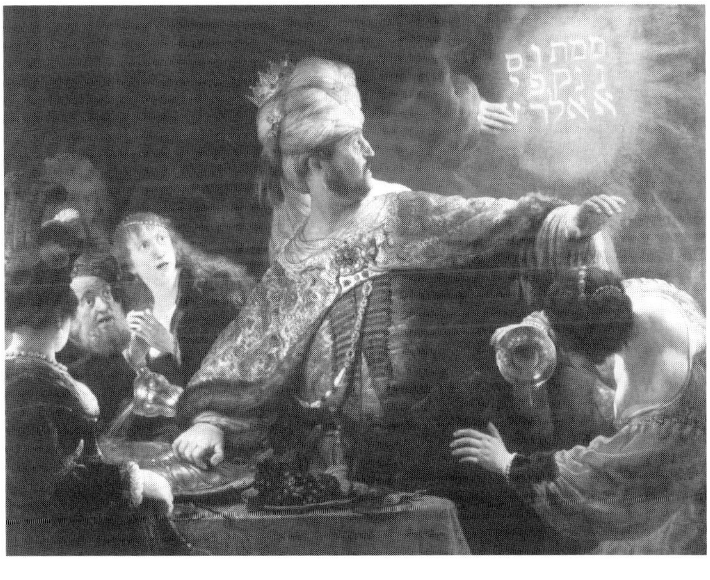

Figure 78. Rembrandt, *Belshazzar's Feast* (oil on canvas, 167 × 209 cm). London, The National Gallery. Reproduced by courtesy of the Trustees, The National Gallery.

tion, especially of the Mannerist or Classicist kind (two currents in Haarlem that influenced Saenredam), Alpers admires the architectural painter's "striking idiosyncrasies," which she describes with the old chestnut about "Mondrian *in nuce.*" In the end, however, Saenredam's exquisitely designed panels (see Fig. 76) are interpreted as "represented seeing," or as "views of architecture viewed."[56] Whatever one calls them, these portraits of actual churches are more conspicuously stylized than almost any other artist's work in the genre. Even more telling about the nature of Dutch art, although more difficult to appreciate without comparing the actual site, is that in his drawings of the New Church in Haarlem, Saenredam anticipated the arbitrary arrangements of his painted compositions as he was carefully recording the details of Jacob van Campen's design.[57] This was not "represented seeing" but (like most of Van Goyen's drawings) a foreseeing of representations in the artist's own style as he recorded motifs "from life." Saenredam's selection and cropping of often unexpected views in the interiors of large churches such as St. Bavo's are (like the way he colored his drawings) more obvious examples of his aesthetic approach.

Of course, there is much more to Saenredam's work than that he had (as Van Hoogstraeten recommended) "the discrimination to select the most beautiful." He himself would have associated the New Church with his colleague Van Campen, with the profession and a contemporary style of architecture, with a religion, a neighborhood and members of the congregation, and with the virtues of their home town.[58] One may pursue these subjects and appreciate at the same time that Dutch artists discovered the beautiful in their own surroundings, which of course required describing their subjects selectively in some artistic way.[59] This response to the wonderful works of God and man has little to do with "the mapping impulse in Dutch art,"[60] as is evident immediately when one considers still lifes – many of them (see Fig. 77) represent and were themselves rare and costly objects – or almost any subject other than topographical views,[61] and when one recalls that an essential function of most Dutch paintings was to decorate private homes.[62]

So many questions of style, expression, and social context are passed over when one reduces Dutch art to Hawthorne's turnip, Alpers's radish,[63] or van Mander's "side road or byway" of working "from life."[64] The alternative is not Wölfflinian pigeonholes; no modern scholar would describe Rembrandt's history paintings of the mid-1630s (see Fig. 78) as "Baroque" works in the same vein as contemporary pictures by Rubens or Guercino, although the Fleming influenced Rembrandt in these years,[65] and the Italian was asked to use his "early vigorous manner" in a pendant to Rembrandt's *Aristotle* (Fig. 80).[66] But whatever the shortcomings of art-historical terminology, it remains true that Rembrandt, Lievens, Flinck, Jacob Backer, and other Rembrandt associates adopted a Dutch version (for it came mostly through Utrecht) of an international style and that there was a cosmopolitan market for this sometimes bombastic imagery. Whether one may associate this development with Amsterdam's new prominence on the world stage or in national affairs is a question for another time.

The subject of regional and local styles is no less problematic than that of national schools. However, our inability to generalize about societies and historical circumstances on the basis of fragmentary visual evidence is no excuse for stylistic illiteracy. The predominance of quiet compositions with finely modulated shapes and tonal values (see Figs. 76, 77) in the *oeuvres* of many Haarlem painters of the 1630s (including portraits by Frans Hals and by Johannes Verspronk) is one of many signs that their community differed from Rembrandt's Amsterdam and Bernini's Rome. Of course, a few painters worked in a similar manner in other cities (Van Goyen in The Hague, Jan den Uyl in Amsterdam), and some qualities, such as precise description, cannot be considered unique to any Dutch place or period, or for that matter to the Netherlands. Nonetheless, the still lifes of Abraham van Beyeren and Willem Kalf seem a city and a generation apart from those of Willem Claesz Heda and Pieter Claesz; like Amsterdam portraits of the 1650s and 1660s, they convey an impression of grandeur and velvety luxury.

Diversities of style reflect those of society; this is why "Dutch historians . . . are wary of making claims specific to their culture."[67] Alpers forged ahead by calling for a study of Dutch pictures "through a consideration of their place, role, and presence in the broader culture," from which she excluded the cities of Utrecht and Middelburg, the court at The Hague, almost any kind of Dutch history painting, the entire Rembrandt school, Dutch artists active in other countries, and most of what was produced during the first and last quarters of the seventeenth century. But the greatest loss was an account of artists as individuals.[68] Famous figures of other countries stand for the concept, but no nation compares to the Netherlands in this regard. A drawing of a nude figure, which for most Dutch draftsmen was as much a *naer het leven* (from life) subject as a radish or a bug, will be immediately recognized as a work by Goltzius, Bloemaert, Backer, Rembrandt,

Jacques de Gheyn, or one of many other artists. Their eyes may have been comparable to the camera obscura, but their heads were filled with ideas.[69]

The point is illustrated by Van Hoogstraeten's well-known passage about the personal styles of Van Goyen, Porcellis, and François Knibbergen. In a contest lasting one day, Knibbergen rapidly rendered forms in a landscape like "letters flow from the pen." Van Goyen brushed out broad areas of light and shadow, from which he gradually conjured motifs, so that "one saw a completed painting before one could properly make out what there was in front of him."[70] Porcellis sat and thought, and then began to work slowly; by evening his landscape had *keurlijker natuerlijkheit* (more selective naturalness) and was accordingly "judged by the connoisseurs to be finer than the other two."[71]

The story is about artistic invention and experience. "At first it appeared as though [Porcellis] were purposely wasting time, or did not know how to begin; but this was because he was forming the whole design of his work in his imagination before he put his brush into the paint."[72] Porcellis was a past master of naturalistic description, but he also had "the discrimination to select the most beautiful."[73] This was also Van Hoogstraeten's message in his introductory pages: "When I once pestered my master, Rembrandt, with too many 'whys' and 'wherefores,' he answered me very well. 'First learn to use what you already know in your work and the secrets about which you ask will be discovered soon enough'."[74]

As a teacher Van Hoogstraeten adopted Rembrandt's method of assigning biblical subjects to students, so that they would learn to visualize narratives effectively.[75] When a pupil such as Arent de Gelder (who studied with Van Hoogstraeten in the early 1660s) turned in an unsatisfactory composition, he was required to read the relevant passage from the Bible to his colleagues in the studio. Each of them could thus form "the whole design . . . in his imagination" and see for himself how the first effort might have been improved.

Scholars have participated in such a critique by debating the subject of a Rembrandtesque canvas in St. Petersburg (Hermitage; Fig. 79). In each analysis of the image, it is simply assumed to be the master's example and therefore a compelling representation of some biblical episode. However, the painting's style (whether it is by Rembrandt or by a follower) strongly suggests a date of about 1648–52, which in turn raises the question of its authorship.[76] It does not require expertise in the area of Rembrandt connoisseurship to see that the picture fails to approach the standards of execution and expression that are set by works like the *Aristotle* (Fig. 80). Iconographers have had trouble puzzling out the subject of the Hermitage painting because its author did too. In my view, the canvas is considerably more interesting as an example of Rembrandt's teaching or influence (and, incidentally, as an early work by Van Hoogstraeten) than it ever was as a supposedly mature picture by Rembrandt.

Another essay on style in Dutch art might review different categories, such as personal styles (with subdivisions such as early and late); local, regional, and national trends; Flemish fashions and Italianate manners; painterly, tonal, and *fijnschilder* styles; and the influences of various masters, such as Spranger, Elsheimer, Caravaggio, Lastman, Rembrandt, Titian, and Van Dyck. The sheer complexity of stylistic conventions in Dutch art does not allow for a concise overview, which would unavoidably resemble the outlines of our discipline's *maîtres d'autrefois*.[77] Dutch artists did not study in institutions comparable to the French *Académie*, which would have made it easier for us to discuss them in terms of *Rubenistes* and *Poussinistes*, or of nineteenth-century notions such as the academical and the non-academical.[78] On the contrary, minor masters (like Knibbergen and Van Goyen's many other followers) tended to depend on a restricted range of locally available models,[79] whereas more gifted painters such as Rembrandt and Vermeer willfully reviewed numerous stylistic and other alternatives in their early years and then formed personal styles that cannot be described simply in terms of artistic influences.[80] Attending to these questions occasionally leads one beyond issues germane to the "broader culture" of the Netherlands, but is that really, for

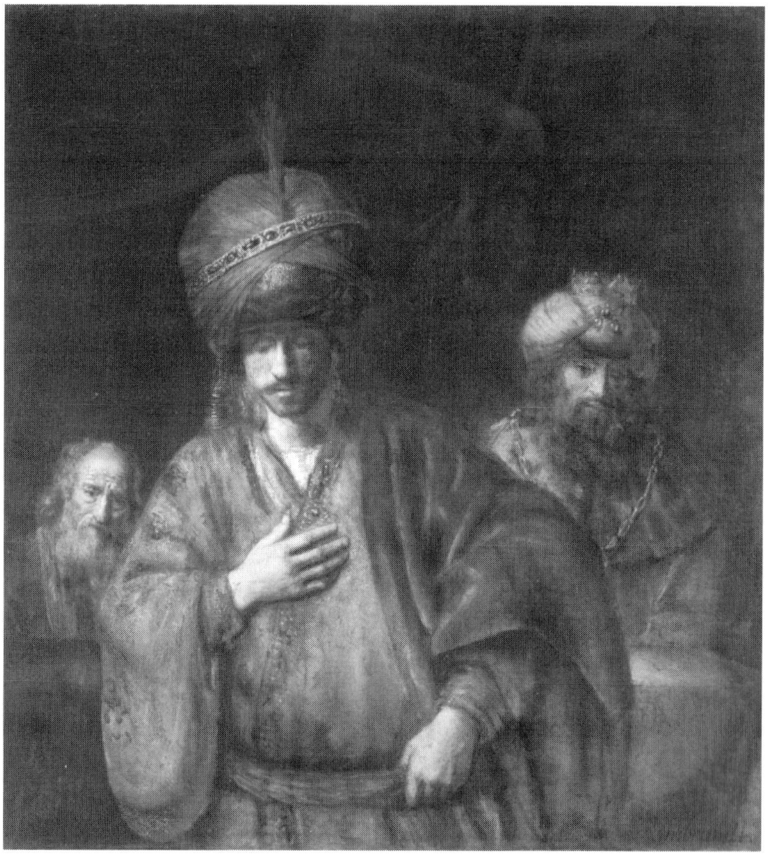

Figure 79. Samuel van Hoogstraeten (attributed to), *Haman Recognizing His Fate* (oil on canvas, 127 × 116 cm). St. Petersburg, The Hermitage.

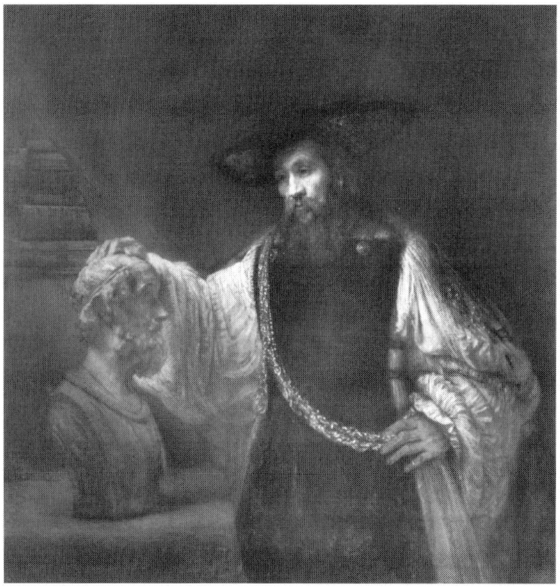

Figure 80. Rembrandt, *Aristotle with a Bust of Homer*, 1653 (oil on canvas, 143.5 × 136.5 cm). New York, The Metropolitan Museum of Art. Photo: museum.

every student, the Holy Grail? There may be some viewers of Dutch pictures who are mainly concerned with European traditions, with psychology or perception, with forms of expression or of art.

Such a viewer might wonder why two paintings, one by Rembrandt and one by Vermeer (Figs. 80, 41), depict single figures in similar poses, each somewhat more than three-quarter length (the *Aristotle* was cut at the bottom), with a table in the foreground, a wall plane (one defined by a curtain) closing the intimate view, and some element in the background echoing the table's horizontal line. The viewer might press on further (perhaps too far) to observe that in both pictures the figure's hands and the objects they touch are highlighted, while shadows play over the faces, enhancing the suggestion of thoughtfulness. That the two paintings have this expressive quality in common explains to some extent why the artists chose analogous arrangements, although Rembrandt's more theatrical treatment of light and shadow underscores the protagonist's dilemma (the choice between material and spiritual values), while Vermeer's quiet discourse of rectangular elements and nearly primary colors suits his subject of domestic harmony (material life ordered by the spiritual).

This is "visual culture" of a different kind than that meant by Michael Baxandall;[81] the two artists made intuitive judgments (Rembrandt's "secrets") that they themselves would have found difficult to explain. It is true that many Dutch pictures feature poses and devices similar to those seen here, so that an historian might be inclined to speak of a period style or classical tendency (which has little to do, in my opinion, with French art). At the same time, Vermeer's work may be placed within a regional context more restricted than that of Rembrandt's circle in Amsterdam. The stylistic conventions of genre painting as practiced in North Holland and Utrecht meant little to Vermeer in this mature composition, which may be seen as a very personal work within the South Holland tradition of domestic scenes produced in The Hague, Rotterdam, and Delft.[82] A related tradition of architectural painting flourished in the same cities and often has been connected with Vermeer.[83] However, one need not be familiar with these developments to appreciate the role of style in the paintings under discussion. One may simply imagine the subject of Rembrandt's *Aristotle* done in the style of Vermeer's painting, or vice versa. Despite the "reality effect," style matters greatly in pictures like these.[84]

Less eloquent testimony to the importance of aesthetic decisions is found in the comments of contemporary critics and diarists. Samuel Pepys, an educated man with a layman's understanding, admired realistic effects and refined workmanship but wrote little about style in the modern sense.[85] Even the critics quoted earlier, such as Van Hoogstraeten and Houbraken, did not employ anything like our terminology (mercifully enough) and rarely wrote what went without saying for their intended readers. But Van Hoogstraeten and his colleagues described the styles of living and earlier masters and general trends about which they had strong views (Flinck escaped the shadow of Rembrandt when he discovered "the Italian manner, and the bright style").[86] Although not an art critic or theorist, Constantijn Huygens incisively compared the styles of Rembrandt and Lievens ("the latter excels in grandeur of invention and in bold designs and forms").[87] For Orlers (1641), Lievens's original inventions and his imitations of a very different artist's style were consistent signs of virtuosity.[88] Philips Angel, by contrast, argued that an artist should not follow another master's manner ("*handelinge*"),[89] but he endorses that of Dou (who started a local tradition, according to Orlers, and to Simon van Leeuwen, writing in 1672).[90]

Nathaniel Hawthorne and later writers on Dou's style of description might have benefited from reading Willem Goeree's analysis of *houding* in pictures.[91] In a recent article on the concept, Paul Taylor notes that the modern art historian's "language would have seemed strange to a Golden Age art theorist, for whom 'incomparable realism' *was* a 'formal quality'."[92] Van Hoogstraeten and Gerard de Lairesse wrote chapters on *houding*, which means essentially the harmonious handling of color and chiaroscuro in order to create a convincing sense of space.[93]

These writers and highly skilled painters like Dou and Van Goyen would not have comprehended the arbitrary division of "description" and "style" that has surfaced recently in the wake of modern art theory, formalist criticism, and analyses along similar lines in art historical texts. The fact that Netherlandish artists had a special talent for naturalistic representation (as Vasari, Van Mander, and almost all the early commentators observed) likewise has taken on layers of significance – national, political, ethical, class, academic – which date mostly from the nineteenth and twentieth centuries.[94] For a painter and theorist such as Van Hoogstraeten, "imitating things from life even as they appear" was a foundation course from which artists with "discrimination" (for example, Raphael, or "that Raphael of marine painting," Jan Porcellis) would graduate.[95] Of course, there were also occasions upon which experienced Dutch draftsmen and, less frequently, painters would make reliable description their essential goal, as in some (certainly not all) scientific, technological, topographical, archaeological, and other kinds of illustrations.[96] And a few Dutch artists even demonstrated an exceptional interest in particular visual problems, the way things might look to the eye before reason intervenes.[97] In general, however, Dutch artists worked with buyers in mind, in a market that valued paintings subjectively.[98] For them, the "broader culture" was in good part a matter of taste and style.

Naturalism as Convention

SUBJECT, STYLE, AND ARTISTIC SELF-CONSCIOUSNESS IN DUTCH LANDSCAPE*

Lawrence O. Goedde

I

In recent decades the study of Dutch landscape has been transformed as scholars have reconsidered the meanings and functions of these pictures. The interpretations they have proposed, however, are in many respects contradictory. These range from readings that insist on a specific religious symbolism for each detail in a picture,[1] to the view that some landscapes are documents or commemorations of historical events and economic developments in the seventeenth-century Netherlands,[2] to the view that landscapes are best understood by analogy to the neutral, value-free, descriptive character of the New Science.[3] The older view that Dutch landscapes present nothing more than a faithful report of the Dutch countryside remains in eclipse, but there is an increasing recognition that the naturalism of this art has to be addressed in any consideration of the meaning of the pictures.[4] This development is accompanied by a growing – and healthy – caution about the iconological method, and especially the use of emblems, in interpreting landscapes.[5] In general, the fundamental issue remains how meaning was perceived in these images in the seventeenth century and how we may recover that significance in a way that has historical validity. What method or methods of analysis offer the possibility of looking at the images with something like the values and expectations of contemporaries?

Such questions raise complex issues that go to the heart of the larger debate on the interpretation of Dutch art, questions to which there is no single answer, just as there is no one method that will answer for all Dutch imagery.[6] But one feature of Dutch landscapes that relates directly to the issue of how they were perceived in their time has only begun to be exploited, that is, their conventionality.[7] It has become ever more clear that Dutch art even of the types considered most realistic is far from comprehensive and objective in its rendering of the world. Although many such images are plausible recreations of contemporary reality, they are in essence fictions, because some people, things, places, and incidents get into the art, and some do not.[8] Moreover, what is included and excluded is surprisingly consistent, surprising especially in view of the enormous number of pictures produced in the Dutch Republic.[9] My own study of images of storms at sea and shipwrecks in Netherlandish art demonstrates the extent of this conventionality.[10] Examining hundreds of pictures revealed that the vast majority conform to just six major types, two of which are uncommon. Each type possesses a distinctive range of incident, setting, and weather and a characteristic treatment of composition and light, giving each type a consistent range of expression and meaning. The great majority of Netherlandish storm scenes do not illustrate identifiable events, but even those that do depict real incidents at sea render history in terms of the conventional types.

* I would like to thank Mary McKinley, Stacey Sell, and Paul Barolsky for their comments on this essay.

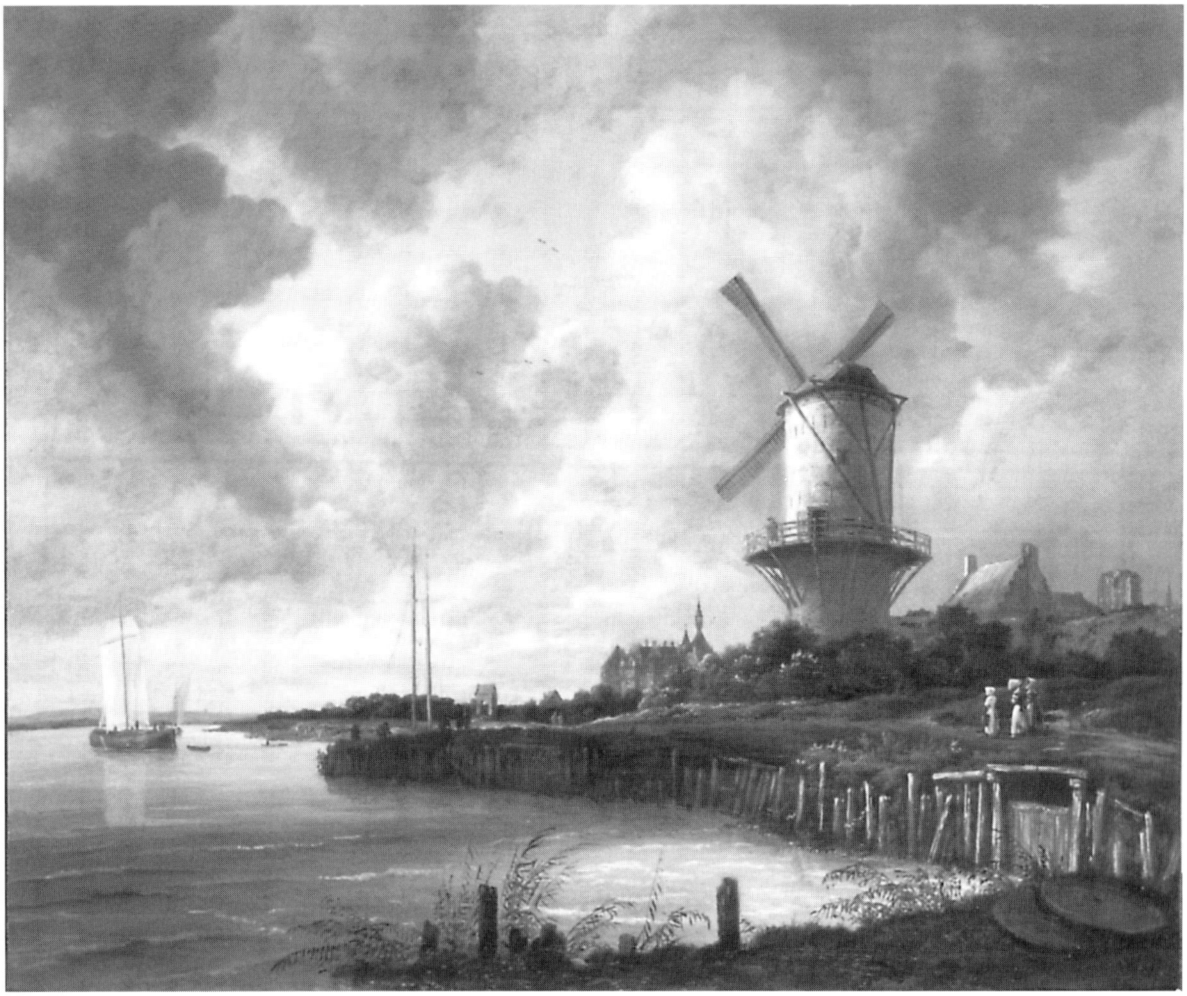

Figure 81. Jacob van Ruisdael, *Windmill at Wijk bij Duurstede* (oil on canvas, 83 × 101 cm). Amsterdam, Rijksmuseum. Photo: Rijksmuseum-Stichting.

The conventionality of Dutch art has much to do with the production of paintings for the market rather than to commission, since adherence to accepted formats, subjects, and styles would allow artists to make images with some confidence that they would find a buyer.[11] Innovations of subject and style in market circumstances would tend to emerge as incremental modifications of existing types in response to current events, changes in fashion and taste, and other artists' work, and only occasionally as radical departures from accepted patterns. The market is not, however, the sole or determining factor in the conventional character of Dutch art, for the whole Renaissance and Baroque tradition is type-bound, as are most artistic traditions.[12] The prevalence of conventionality reflects the fact that in any human culture the totally unfamiliar can scarcely signify or communicate. Moreover, the culture of the seventeenth-century Netherlands displayed a pronounced proclivity to seek in an experience or historical event the typical and general, that which fits an existing pattern of meaning.[13] A well-known example of this tendency is the relative rarity of images of contemporary history. Current and recent events were rendered, instead, in the guise of classical or biblical history.

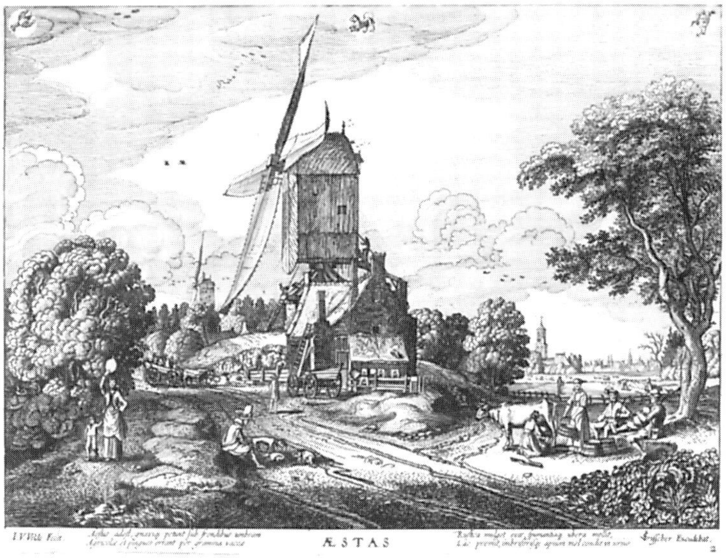

Figure 82. Jan van de Velde, *Aestas* (Summer), 1617 (etching). Amsterdam, Rijksprentenkabinet. Photo: Rijksmuseum-Stichting.

The revolt of the Netherlands against Spain, for instance, was depicted in terms of the revolt against Rome by the ancient inhabitants of the Netherlands, the Batavians, these putative ancestors of the Dutch serving to validate the contemporary world by reference to past prototypes.[14]

Understood as means of communication, conventions in Dutch art and the principles governing their selective treatment of experience are evidence of a primary level at which the pictures carried meaning.[15] Patterns of selective representation are inherently interpretive, and they allow us to perceive a significance that is immediately available in the structure of choices, assumptions, and concerns implicit in a pattern of convention and shared by artist and viewer alike. Ostensibly realistic pictures begin to look different when considered in terms of an artist's manipulation of the conventions particular to a subject. In the case of Jacob van Ruisdael's famous *Windmill at Wijk bij Duurstede* of about 1670 (Fig. 81), the painter depicts a real place but follows the conventional pattern in Netherlandish art in which artists render the windmill most often from a low viewpoint so as to emphasize its natural physical prominence.[16] As in Jan van de Velde's *Aestas* (Summer), an etching of 1617 (Fig. 82), the mill usually towers above the horizon, dominating the visual field, and it is often lit dramatically as it faces dark clouds or the setting sun or a distant horizon, further enhancing its nearly figural role in the composition.[17] The consistent treatment of the theme through time by a number of artists working in different styles argues against these resemblances being simply a matter of a shared pictorial source. Indeed, the degree of consistency from picture to picture strongly suggests that the subject was associated with a fairly specific formal and compositional treatment and that certain aspects of real mills were expected to appear in pictures and certain others were not.

In considering the meaning of Van Ruisdael's *Mill* and as a principle of interpretation in general, what is *not* represented is highly significant, for it makes the character of what is selected clearer. This is especially important in view of the realism used to depict the world, a realism so persuasive that for the most part we are unaware of how restricted its vision of reality is. In the case of the windmill, its ordinary work-a-day role in Dutch economic life is by no means fully documented in Dutch art. The omnipresent mills on city walls and the more specialized windmills used for, among other things, sawing wood, weaving, and draining polderland are rarely depicted in painting or the graphic arts except in images whose purpose is explicitly informational or commemorative.[18] The conventional treatment of the mill, on the contrary, seems designed to appeal to the imagination even when, as here, the locale is identifiable: In Dutch art the mill is rendered as an object of sympathetic identification, familiar and human in origin and purpose and associated, as we see in the text, to Jan van de Velde's etching, with the abundance of the earth reaped by human industry.[19] But the mill is far from prosaic, for it is also imposing and even heroic in its place between earth and sky.

The imaginative appeal of windmills, like other motifs in Dutch landscape, does not necessarily mean that either artist or beholder was conscious of the conventions or of the content. Even when followed formulaically, however, conventions like the elevated position and dramatic lighting of the mill communicate meaning and can be analyzed for evidence of what contemporaries expected to see – or not to see – and what they found significant and worthy of representation out of all the multiple possibilities of existence. In discussing film, Umberto Eco refers to what he calls a "smart audience," one able to recognize and appreciate conformity to and deviations from the typical and expected.[20] Most films are conceived and experienced with knowledge of and in reference to the formulas typical of a genre or subject; and viewers are expected to know and recognize – whether consciously or not – both the formulas and the departures from them. The study of the conventions of Dutch landscape provides exactly this kind of context, this awareness of what is usually included and excluded in treating a subject, that we need for interpreting Dutch landscape; indeed, it is the context in which we must weigh and test the meanings derived from social, economic, historical, and iconographic scholarship. When an artist's work, moreover, shows signs of a purposeful selection from and modification of conventional patterns, the analysis of convention becomes still more significant, for then it serves as a means of recognizing both distinctive interpretations of subject matter and style and the self-consciousness about image-making implicit in such choices.

Seen in the context of convention, it is evident that Van Ruisdael's *Mill* resembles other Dutch landscapes with mills in not being a *veduta*, for it treats topographical information in a selective way. Like other landscapes with mills, it does not depict details that would link it with a literary text[21] or that would identify it as an illustration of an historical event. And like other pictures of the subject (including Jan van de Velde's etching with its explicit reference to the cycle of the seasons and the signs of the zodiac), it emphasizes the heroic presence of the mill in the context of the cosmic forces of weather and light so as to intimate that the industry and prosperity that the mill represents is achieved in a larger context of divine order and purpose.[22] To suggest that the picture is exclusively or even primarily a document of economic reality is to omit the visual context that Van Ruisdael and other artists are at pains to provide for their mills.[23] Nonetheless, like other mill scenes, Van Ruisdael's painting is also not an explicitly emblemlike exegesis of the mill as a moral or spiritual metaphor, for the protagonist, the mill, is neither isolated as in an emblem icon nor located within the web of reinforcing symbolic details typical of a moralized landscape. Rather, Van Ruisdael's picture resembles other landscapes with mills in that he integrates the mill into a highly charged yet plausible human and natural context. But Van Ruisdael also reworks the theme so as to enhance its dramatized grandeur and to call attention by its visually compelling formal qualities to the place of the mill in a world of human and natural movement.[24]

The persuasive naturalism of pictures like Van Ruisdael's *Mill* has made them peculiarly resistant to iconological interpretation. This quality led Eddy de Jongh to view landscapes as unsuited to the iconological analysis that he has applied to portraiture and genre painting.[25] Indeed, attempts to read in Dutch landscapes specific moralizing meanings based mainly on emblematic sources have failed to persuade partly because of a tendency to interpret the paintings detail by detail, an approach contrary to their formal and dramatic unity, and partly because any given motif or feature of a picture could be interpreted in multiple and contradictory ways in the contemporary emblem literature.[26] Such studies have lacked persuasive methods both for dealing with the plethora of possible meanings available for any single motif and for relating such emblem-derived meanings to the dramatized naturalism of the picture as a whole. Dutch landscapes, moreover, characteristically lack the kind of semantic structure of reinforcing symbols derived from literary sources or identifiable narrative incident that serves to guide interpretation in typical allegorical and narrative images of the Renaissance and Baroque periods. In view of this, the analysis of patterns of selective representation becomes even more valuable for interpreting Dutch landscape, for such patterns permit us to see that naturalism itself, the appearance of being a straightforward, unmediated, accurate rendering of the appearances of real places, is a fiction: These pictures are constructs of the imagination shaped by artistic traditions and dependent upon the manipulation of patterns of style and subject matter. The illusion of spontaneity and directness of representation is the result of artistry and, in its most vivid forms, of self-aware, calculated artifice.

The heightened naturalism of Van Ruisdael's picture invites a wide range of responses, from simple pleasure in the scene, to more somber reflections on the struggle of human life in a world of turmoil and change, to more positive thoughts on the providential order of the universe. In emblematic sources we also encounter interpretations of windmills as signs and lessons of, among other things, humanity's role as harnessers and orderers of the elemental forces of nature, human ingenuity and enterprise as foundations of national prosperity, the need for a morally forthright response to conflicts in a world of change and uncertainty, and the necessity of openness to grace. All of these are meanings that have been suggested for this picture.[27] The image does not, however, require a single religious, moral, or historical interpretation, for its recasting of conventions guides and encourages meditation but does not provide a structure of obviously symbolic details that specifies an exact content or a precise metaphor. Indeed, the dramatic naturalism of the image would seem to leave it deliberately open to a wide range of responses, while at the same time inviting those responses.

A number of motifs and qualities of formal structure in Dutch landscapes encourage the viewer's reflective encounter with the images. These features are likewise conventional in Dutch landscape, but they are also capable of becoming, in the hands of some artists, vivid means of enhancing both the impression of truth to nature and the viewer's engagement with the scene. Among the most notable of these themes and devices is the prominence of roads, paths, rivers, and streams, populated by travelers on foot, or in carriages and wagons, or in boats and ferries, or on horseback (Fig. 82).[28] Some travelers rest by the road, and carriages stop at country inns, but the implication of a continuing journey is clear. Obvious objects of our empathy, such figures and their modes of conveyance invite our imaginative penetration into the depths of the fictive spaces of Dutch pictures. These figures not only move through the landscape, but they are frequently contrived so as to lead us from figure to figure by moving in a particular direction or looking at or pointing to the distance where another figure carries our attention further into the depths of a fictive but plausible world. In addition to the imaginative pull exerted by the figures, the paths into depth form a structure of diagonals that is at once spatial and dynamic, drawing us psychologically into the image.

The role of these conventional travelers in enlisting the viewer's imaginative engagement in the fictive spaces of landscape is essential to recent studies of meaning in landscape by Reindert Falkenburg and Catherine Levesque.[29] Though focusing upon landscapes dating a century apart – Falkenburg deals with the landscapes of Joachim Patinir in the early sixteenth century, and Levesque with series of landscape prints made in the 1610s and 1620s – their studies closely complement each other in that both emphasize travelers and roads as means of stimulating the viewer's participation in a meditative process of associative memory. Both argue that this viewer involvement proceeds through an allusive appeal to memory and imagination analogous to the kinds of descriptions found in texts.[30] Although they have quite different texts in mind appropriate to the different images they discuss – Falkenburg deals with devotional texts of the late fifteenth and early sixteenth century, and Levesque with historical and geographical texts of the sixteenth and seventeenth century dealing with specific places – both are persuasive in arguing that like the texts they analyze, landscapes possess formal structures and motifs that encourage and guide a viewer's imaginative engagement but remain open to considerable variation of personal response in the construction of meaning. Enhancing this effect in Levesque's view is the tendency in the seventeenth century to structure knowledge and memory in spatial terms, moving from detail to detail, concept to concept, in terms of three-dimensional metaphors of order.

Even a superficial scrutiny of Dutch landscapes reveals many comparable conventional motifs, including a number involving human beings in the world. Formerly dismissed as mere staffage, the figural presence in landscape offers a crucial opening for interpretation since these conventional motifs, however numerous, follow a fairly circumscribed set of standard patterns: All human life and behavior are not found in these landscapes. These typical subjects are, in some cases at least, analogous to literary themes and promise one of the best approaches to bridging the vexing gap between literary and visual landscape.[31] The possibilities of this kind of motif-analysis can be seen in Wayne Franits's discussion of the motif of the Hunting Party at Rest in Dutch landscapes.[32] Franits argues that the motif of flirtatious, elegantly dressed young people at leisure in these scenes is a visual counterpart to the highly conventionalized metaphor of love and courtship as a hunt, familiar especially in Petrarchan love literature (Fig. 83). Seen this way, such a motif is best interpreted not in terms of symbolism or emblematic significance, as though it were a pictogram slotted into an additive, diagrammatic structure. Instead, such motifs should be seen as alluding to real social values and customs while resonating with corresponding motifs in literature. The connotations of such themes are amplified within the evocative context of a specific picture that may well have no exact textual analogue.

A recognition of the conventionalized treatment of the contemporary world in Dutch landscapes is also central to Ann Jensen Adams's recent study in which she uses the *absence* of particular motifs from Dutch landscapes as a basis for interpreting pictures.[33] In discussing the dunes with country roads typical of the monochrome or tonal landscape, for example, Adams observes that the rise of the monochrome landscape (Fig. 84), with its accurate rendering of the local countryside of the west of Holland, exactly coincides with the tremendous drainage projects that between 1612 and 1650 increased the usable land in the northern part of the province of Holland by one-third. Yet the drainage projects themselves and the newly recovered polderland are strikingly rare in the monochrome landscape paintings contemporary with them and are scarcely to be found in any later Dutch landscape style. Adams explains what seems a "commercial disavowal" in this and other subjects and the simultaneous emphasis upon identifiably Dutch features in the landscapes as the result not of a desire to hide commerce but of an impulse to dramatize and give an historical dimension to sites and human activities that are part of a traditional Dutch identity. As plausible fictions rather than documents of the Dutch countryside or of the latest developments in the Dutch rural economy, their purpose in her view is to locate a traditional identity for the newly invented Dutch Republic.[34]

Adams's thesis notably avoids the assumption of naive historicism that contemporaneous historical developments must be directly mirrored in Dutch painting. Her thesis, however, remains only partly persuasive in that it demands a more ample examination of what, in fact, is selected for depiction and a more developed consideration of what Dutch artists omitted from their paintings. Dutch artists ignored not only positive developments in the Dutch countryside but negative ones as well. Dutch achievements in draining large areas are well known, but it is less widely appreciated that due to extensive digging and dredging for peat, the primary fuel of the Dutch Republic, the Dutch eventually lost to the water as much land as they gained in the seventeenth century.[35] The Haarlemmermeer actually increased in size in the seventeenth century, and extensive marshlands were created that

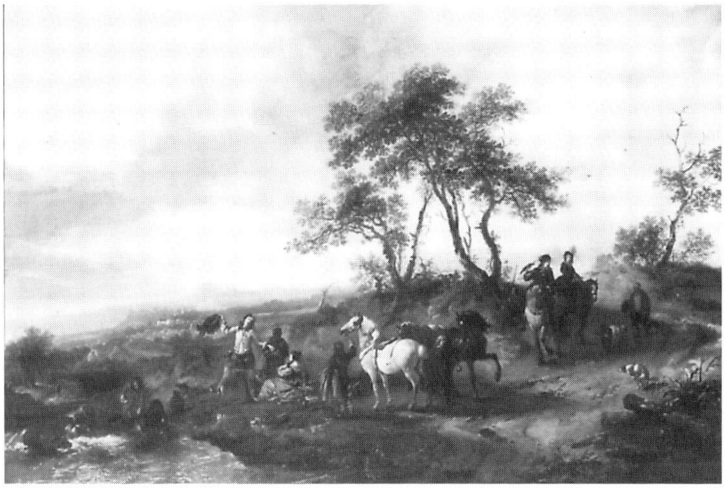

Figure 83. Philips Wouvermans, *Halt of a Hunting Party* (oil on canvas, 55.6 × 82.9 cm). London, Dulwich College Picture Gallery. Reproduced by permission of the Governors of Dulwich Picture Gallery.

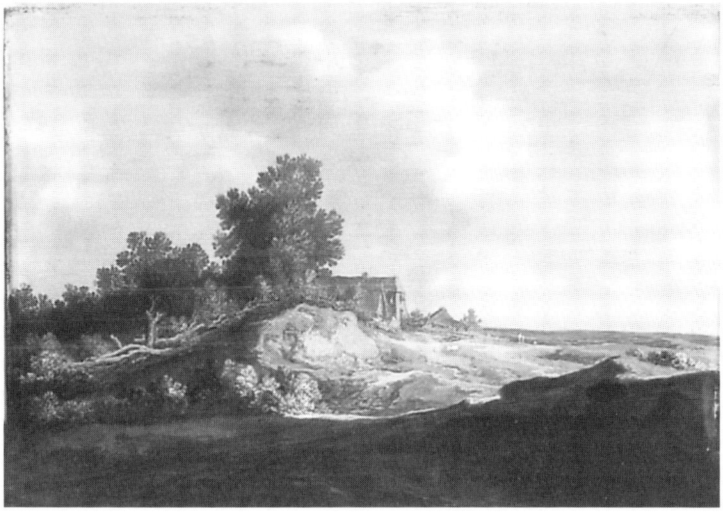

Figure 84. Pieter Molijn, *Landscape with Cottage*, 1629 (oil on canvas, 30.5 × 36.2 cm). New York, The Metropolitan Museum of Art. Photo: museum.

endure to the present day. If Dutch landscape artists ignored the productive enterprises of capitalism, they also ignored destructive and literally erosive behavior also driven by the prosperity of the cities.

Another issue in considering the relation of conventional motifs in Dutch landscape to contemporary history is the recurrence of motifs in the works of Dutch artists of different generations working in decidedly different styles, a phenomenon that would suggest that the meanings of such motifs may not be at all times as closely bound to specific historical circumstances as Adams proposes. The avoidance of polder landscapes, for instance, is not limited to tonalism. Such scenes are exceedingly rare in the landscapes of the generation of Jacob van Ruisdael and Meindert Hobbema; and in the 1640s, Rembrandt, too, passed up the chance to draw such new lands on his walks in the vicinity of Amsterdam when he made sketches of the countryside, which can sometimes be identified with a fair degree of precision.[36] Boudewijn Bakker has observed that although Rembrandt produced highly accurate renderings of contemporary farmhouses of identifiable types, he did not favor new farms in the new polderlands but instead frequently chose old, decaying structures.[37] This preference for old farmhouses that seem to be subsiding into the soil or are surrounded and covered by vegetation, as though nature were absorbing and protecting human structures, is also a prominent feature of the monochrome dunescapes.

The pronounced Dutch taste for the depiction of the old, the timeworn, the weathered, and the broken may be attributable to the fictitious historical identity that Adams proposes Dutch landscape provided for the people of a new country. But these themes and the apparent spontaneity of the style often used to record them were also identified by the Dutch themselves as "*schilderachtig*," a term whose meaning is intimately bound up with the conventions of Dutch realism. *Schilderachtig*, now translated as picturesque, means more literally painterlike or painterly.[38] When first encountered in the writings of Karel van Mander in 1604, this word usually refers to behavior suitable to a painter, though significantly in one instance Van Mander pronounces an old man's face *schilderachtig*.[39] By the middle of the seventeenth century, the word was apparently in use to describe both images that demonstrated an artist's ability – which is how Samuel van Hoogstraeten in 1678 uses it in reference to Rembrandt's *Nightwatch*[40] – and to describe subjects regarded as suitable for or like a painting. This latter usage is exceptionally revealing because it indicates that the conventions of subject and style used to create the plausible fictions of Dutch realism were sought and found in the experience of life itself. Already in 1647, Constantijn Huygens, in his poem *Oogentroost* (Consolation for the Eye), disparages the fashion for describing real views in nature as *schilderachtig*, which he criticizes as implying that God's creation imitates our puny paintings.[41] Unfortunately, he does not discuss the qualities that made landscapes *schilderachtig*. Our clearest sense of what this term came to mean during the second half of the seventeenth century is provided by a text by Jan de Bisschop of 1669 and in much greater detail by Gerard de Lairesse's *Groot Schilderboeck* (Great Book on Painting) of 1707.[42] Adopting the criteria of normative classicism, both authors criticize what they see as the commonplace – in their view erroneous – notion of *schilderachtig* subjects. These include rough, wild mountains; broken, blasted trees; ruins; broken down cottages; storms and rainshowers – as well as beggars, peasants, the deformed, and the elderly. These are, of course, familiar subjects in Dutch landscape, genre, and history.

The subjects that De Bisschop and De Lairesse identify as erroneously *schilderachtig* are exactly those excluded by the increasingly rigid and specifically Cartesian norms of decorum in subject matter found in the classicizing art theory of the last half of the seventeenth century.[43] These prohibited subjects involve the destructive effects of time, aging, and weathering; they are subjects, like ruins and storms, that involve process and change beyond human control; they are subjects involving chance, anathema to classicists;[44] and they are subjects involving marginal and outcast types like beggars and cripples. In sum, these are subjects that cast doubt on the ultimate authority of reason in life and the world and, by extension, in the making of art. Constantijn Huygens commented about 1630 on "the pleasure of ruins however grey or formless they may be," which would appear to document the taste and interest implied by the many ruins in Dutch landscapes of both the Italianate and native varieties.[45] In his use of the word "formless," Huygens indicates that the appeal of *schilderachtig* subjects lay exactly in qualities that, being outside the prescriptive rules of classical form, permitted a freer play of the imagination and invention, what the Italians term "*fantasia*" and the Dutch "*geest*."[46]

The use of the term *schilderachtig* to judge and categorize real views in nature distinctly resembles the search for picturesque, Salvatoran, and Claudian vistas in the real landscape of eighteenth-century England.[47] In the seventeenth-century Netherlands as well, it seems that pictorial conventions shaped not just the appreciation of landscape paintings but the ways people looked at, understood, and valued the natural world.[48]

II

The very act of distinguishing a landscape or other subject as *schilderachtig* implies the viewer's recognition, however unconsciously, of both artistic conventions and the values attached to those conventions. Such a judgment requires an awareness at some level of the selective treatment of reality found in the art – certain views are *schilderachtig*, and others are not – and it indicates some degree of consciousness that this selectivity permits certain kinds of imaginative responses to both images and lived experience. This self-consciousness about the artifice of Dutch landscape is not restricted to the later seventeenth century, however, but can also be found in early realistic landscapes. Indeed, the celebrated realism of Dutch art in general and of landscape in particular arises from self-conscious artistry and a self-aware manipulation of style conventions. This is evident in the earliest manifestations of the new naturalism in Dutch landscape, most notably in three small landscape drawings by Hendrick Goltzius dating from around 1603.[49] As exemplified here by the drawing in Paris (Fondation Custodia; Fig. 85), these drawings are apparently direct records of the Dutch countryside in the vicinity of Haarlem, in clear contrast to the artifice of subject and style typical of most earlier and contemporary landscapes. In contrast to the traditional world–landscape type, familiar from prints after Pieter Bruegel the Elder (Fig. 86), Goltzius drastically lowered the standard high horizon, and he focused narrowly on the local scene rather than surveying like Bruegel a vast, composite, and largely invented vista.[50] In contrast to the newer forest landscape type, as in pictures by Gillis van Coninxloo roughly contemporary with the drawing (Fig. 87), Goltzius eliminated the formulaic wing structures and diagonal avenues into depth typical of the forest type in favor of compositions that give the initial impression of an unplanned or even random recording of the artist's visual experience.[51] The Goltzius drawings have been recognized as the immediate forerunners of the landscape print series of the 1610s and 1620s and the monochrome landscape paintings of the 1620s and 1630s, works characterized by their modest subject matter and their apparently artless view of the domestic landscape.[52]

The role of Goltzius's drawings in the rise of realistic Dutch landscape is well established and familiar, and his sources of inspiration are also well known. However, if we view Goltzius's drawings somewhat differently, from the perspective of conventions of style and subject, it becomes apparent that his use of past art in fashioning these works means that their naturalism results from neither a naive copying of appearances nor a passively absorbed influence from the past; they are, instead, works involving Goltzius's sophisticated selection from and manipulation of past styles and subjects.[53] Considered this way, these drawings are only apparently spontaneous and unstylized, for they involve an artist's self-conscious reworking of a specific set of conventions of representation chosen from the wider range of conventions available at the time.[54] These conventions involve not only style but the treatment of subject and the handling of medium: What seems artless is, in fact, the consequence of artistic choice.

It is, however, this apparent lack of artifice that makes the dune drawings so striking and apparently anomalous in the context of Goltzius's virtuoso late Mannerist work. The overt artfulness of Goltzius's figures, like those in his pen drawing, *Venus Freezes without Ceres and Bacchus* of 1593 (Fig. 88), with their stylishly elongated proportions, tapering extremities, and gracefully convoluted poses, has little in common with these landscape drawings.[55] In contrast they seem plain and unstylized; their compositions have only the most subtle structures of receding diagonals and lack vertical framing elements at the sides, suggesting an unmediated and accurate record of the ordinary visible world. Goltzius's handling of the pen enhances this impression: His short strokes, dashes, and stippling, while rendering the effect of light and atmosphere, little resemble the virtuosity with which he frequently uses the pen to mimic the brilliant, ornamental effects of modelling typical of his engravings, drawings in which the pen imitates the swelling and tapering of engraved lines. Instead of such artful and witty mimicry, evincing a self-consciousness about style, the plain technique in the landscape drawings reinforces the impression of ordinary visual experience simply and directly recorded.

This impression of unstudied spontaneity, however, belies Goltzius's dependence on earlier art for

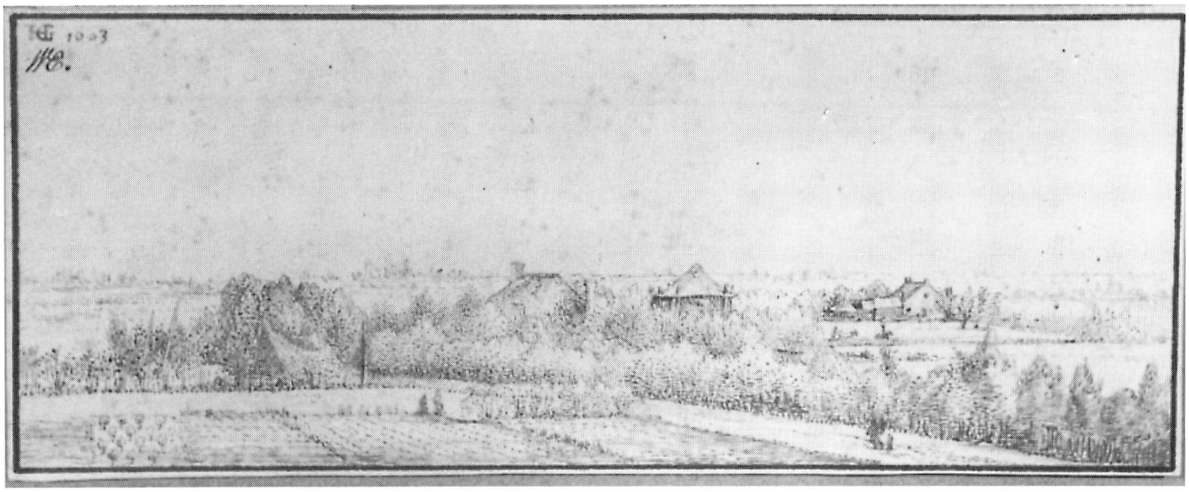

Figure 85. Hendrick Goltzius, *Extensive Landscape near Haarlem*, 1603 (brown pen and wash on paper, 7.9 × 19.9 cm). Paris, Fondation Custodia. Photo: M. Lemare, Paris.

features of both subject and style. It is well known that drawings by Pieter Bruegel the Elder and his followers are the source of Goltzius's vocabulary of dots and dashes for rendering light and atmosphere – it is an unusual technique whose roots lie far back in the fifteenth century and is immediately recognizable (Fig. 89).[56] Bruegel's work also served as a model for the modest subject and the unobtrusive compositional structure. Goltzius seems to have been aware as well of drawings by, and prints after, an anonymous Netherlandish artist known to us as the Master of the Small Landscapes.[57] A comparison with one of the engravings (Fig. 90) from the series, the *Small Landscapes of Brabant and Campine*, reveals Goltzius's adaptation of the Master's simple receding diagonals and absence of framing wing structures, thereby creating the sense of a direct encounter with a real countryside in which the world opens at your feet, leading you straight to an ordinary village. These prints date

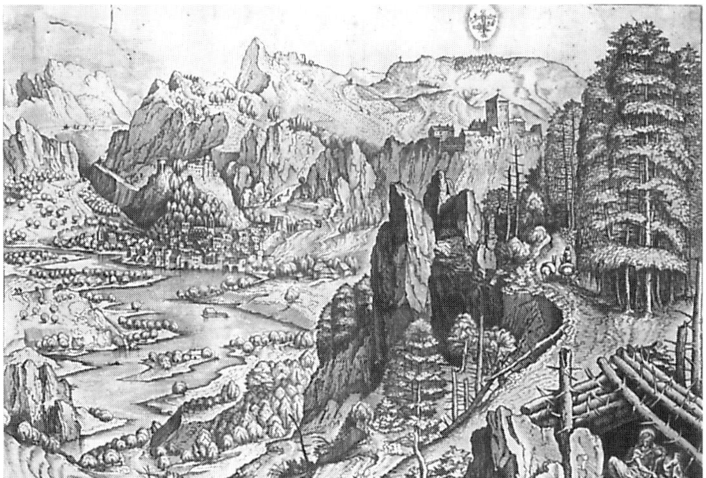

Figure 86. Hieronymous Cock after Pieter Bruegel the Elder, *Penitent Magdalen* (engraving). Washington D.C., National Gallery of Art, Rosenwald Collection. Photo: museum.

from 1559 and 1561, and were republished in 1601 in Antwerp by Theodor Galle. In the early seventeenth century, they were strongly associated with Pieter Bruegel the Elder and were even published under his name in 1612 in Amsterdam.[58] It seems likely that Goltzius, in working from the Master's drawings and related prints, thought he was imitating Bruegel's style.[59]

Goltzius was not the only artist of the time looking to these seemingly unremarkable images as models. Jacques de Gheyn the Younger, a brilliant draughtsman a bit younger than Goltzius, and Claes Jansz. Visscher, one of the most important figures in the development of the new Dutch landscape, adapted the compositions and graphic vocabulary of the Master of the Small Landscapes to convey the feeling of a direct encounter with the realities of the Dutch countryside.[60]

That the apparently unstudied, freely sketched, and realistic images made by Goltzius, De Gheyn, and Visscher depend so thoroughly on past art is revealing for a number of reasons. One is that if their naturalism is seen as a manipulation of already existing conventions, their drawings and prints are not at all anomalous with the art of late Mannerists like Goltzius and De Gheyn. Indeed, the works of both show a decided interest in imitating a variety of conventional landscape types and styles. Both produced landscape drawings of the world landscape type,[61] and Goltzius also produced Venetian pastoral landscapes, a distinct type, in his chiaroscuro woodcuts of about 1600. In them not only the shepherds but the lush twisting trees, hills, and clouds and the very medium of woodcut itself derive from the woodcuts of Titian and his followers.[62]

This consciousness of style is, in fact, one of the most distinctive features of Goltzius's art. His ability to imitate past styles and, even more, to create new works in them was celebrated by Karel van Mander, who saw in Goltzius's abilities to create a new "Dürer" or a new "Lucas van Leyden" (*The Adoration of the Magi* of 1594) or a new "Federico Barocci" evidence of Goltzius's universal mastery of art.[63] This attitude toward style also underlies Goltzius's ambition to invent a new medium, the *penwerk* or pen painting.[64] What we see in the dune landscape drawings is, then, consistent with Goltzius's concern to identify himself as a universal master, able to create freely in a wide variety of styles. In spite of their modest appearance and seeming realism, these drawings result from a sophisticated awareness and manipulation of style.

That naturalism should result from a purposeful selection of one set of conventions out of a number that were available suggests the possibility that what is involved in such a choice is the adaptation

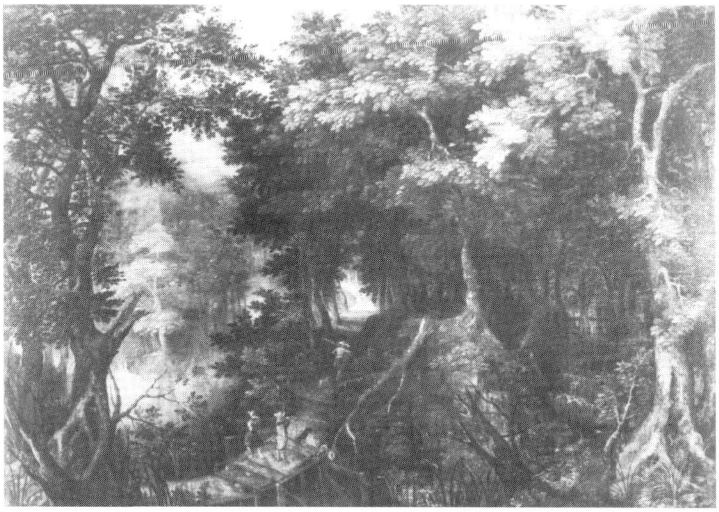

Figure 87. Gillis van Coninxloo, *Hunters in a Landscape*, 1605 (oil on panel, 58.5 × 83.5 cm). Speyer, Historisches Museum der Pfalz.

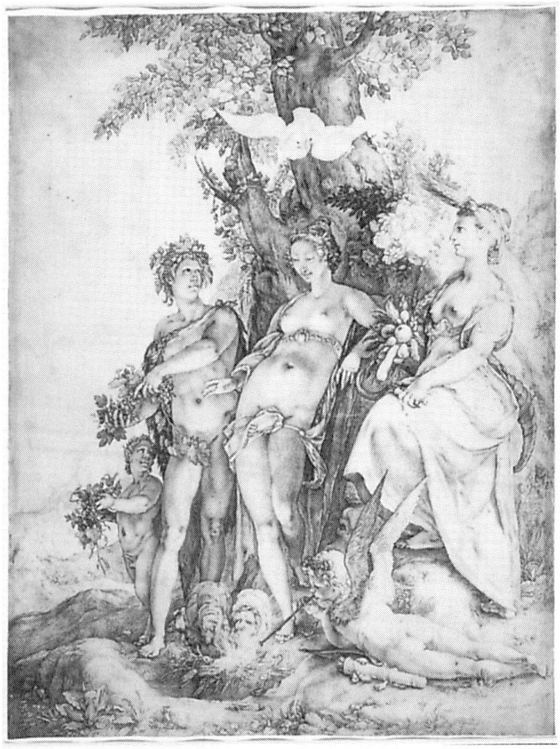

Figure 88. Hendrick Goltzius, *Venus Freezes without Ceres and Bacchus*, 1593 (brown pen on parchment, 63 × 49.5 cm). London, British Museum. Reproduced by courtesy of the Trustees, British Museum.

of the concept in literary rhetoric of different styles being suited to different classes of subject matter, the *genera dicendi* of classical poetics.[65] For both Goltzius and De Gheyn, the choice of more naturalistic conventions seems to have been associated with their specific subject matter, the farms, fields, woods, and dunes of the real Holland countryside. But a more suggestive parallel to or analogue with this artless style is another of the most important types of literary rhetoric of the late sixteenth and seventeenth centuries, Attic or Senecan rhetoric.[66] Such writing is distinguished from Ciceronian prose by its apparent lack of calculated structure, so that the reader has the impression that the writer is transcribing directly a train of thought as it develops, a style familiar in the writings of, among others, Michel de Montaigne, Francis Bacon, and Thomas Brown. Such authors contrive an effect of artless informality through a variety of formal devices strikingly analogous to those of both early drawn and printed landscapes and tonal landscapes: a tendency to abbreviation in phrasing, an ordering that seems spontaneous rather than logically calculated, the use of asymmetry in phrasing and diction, the omission of clear syntactic connectors, and a seemingly random variation in sentence length. Such nonrhetorical rhetoric would seem to offer a model for or parallel to the paradoxical artfully artless style of Dutch realistic landscapes, which fully exemplify the art of being natural central to the writing of Montaigne and other authors of the time.

An awareness of representational conventions consequently makes us aware that the celebrated realism of Dutch landscape – and perhaps of Dutch art more generally – that is, what is taken to be its documentary, descriptive relationship to the visible world of the contemporary Netherlands, is the result of self-consciousness about style and expression. Such a view runs counter to two distinct tendencies in assessing the nature of this realism. One is a pronounced proclivity to view the new naturalism of Dutch art as naive and unsophisticated because of its deviation from the principles of Italian art theory, in which the representation of edifying human action is the highest goal of art.[67] The naturalism of Dutch art in this view is a sort of "default" style, what an artist falls back on or turns to automatically if he does not know any better, or in this context, what a craftsman or artisan produces for an undiscriminating audience unfamiliar with classical art and theory. The assumption in this conception is that naturalism is ordinary and inevitable; but as E. H. Gombrich observes, naturalistic styles are rare in human history and have arisen only in exceptional circumstances of history and culture, and not as an automatic or reflexive pattern in human image making.[68] There is little reason to assume that the radical naturalism of early Dutch landscape is a spontaneous manifestation of ignorance, especially considering the sophisticated mannerism that immediately preceded it.

The second tendency is to see the artless and unmediated directness of Dutch art as a distinctively Northern inclination to describe the appearances of things. In this view Northern art is best under-

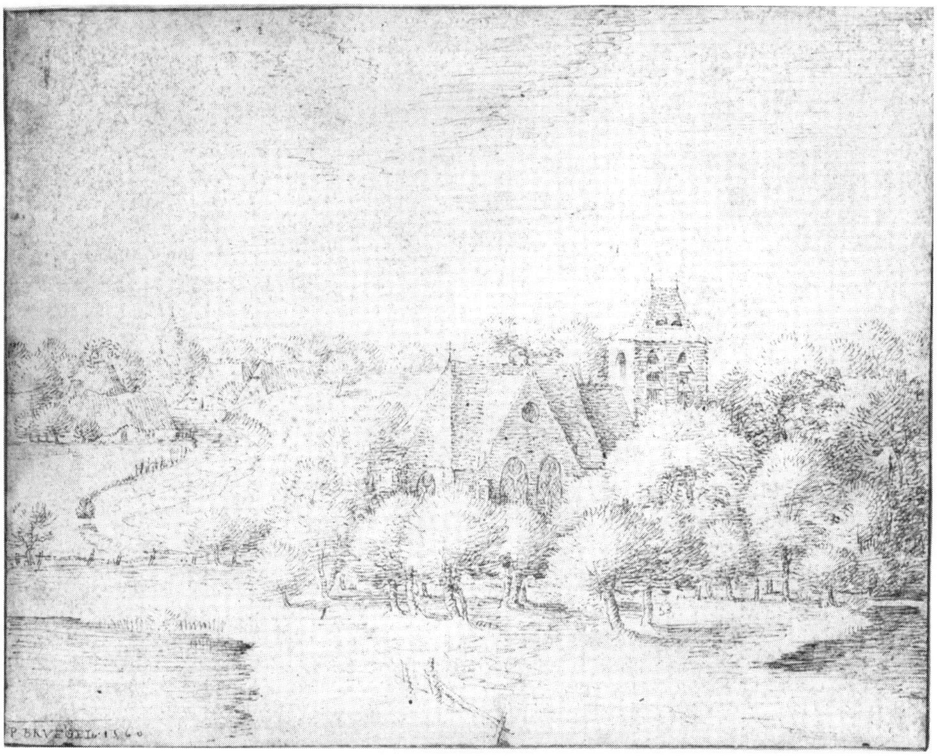

Figure 89. Pieter Bruegel the Elder, *Village,* 1560 (brown pen on paper, 14.2 × 19 cm). Berlin, Staatliche Museen, Kupferstichkabinett.

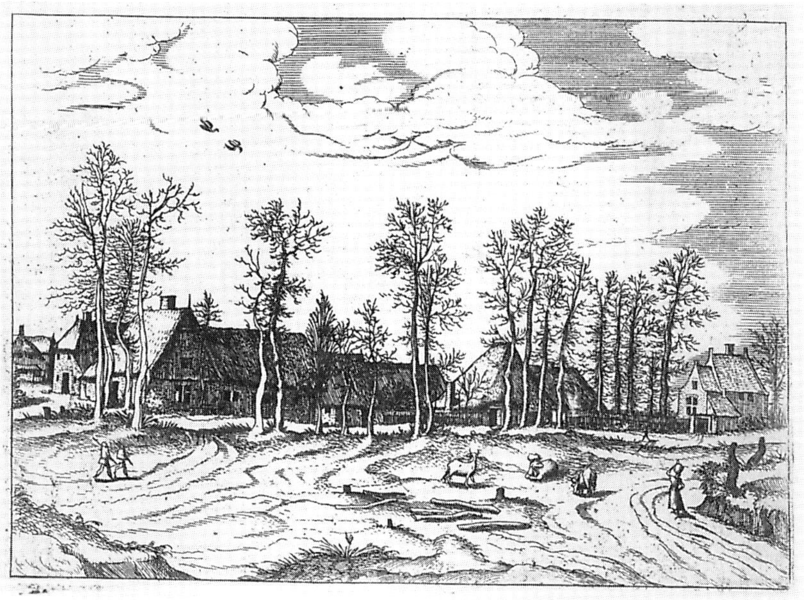

Figure 90. Jan or Lucas Duetecum (attributed to) after Master of the Small Landscapes, *View of a Village* (engraving from the series *Multifarium casularum ruriumque lineamenta curiose ad vivum expressa*), 1559. Washington D.C., National Gallery of Art, Rosenwald Collection. Photo: museum.

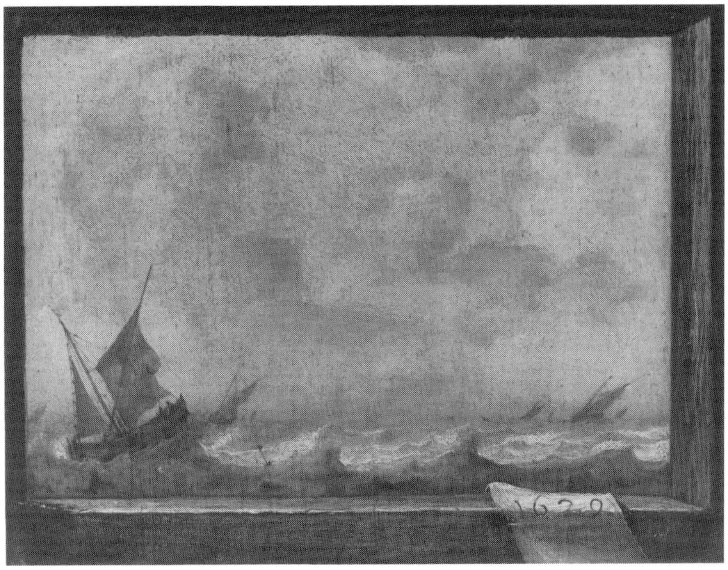

Figure 91. Jan Porcellis, *Single-Masters in a Rough Sea*, 1629 (oil on panel, 18.5 × 24 cm). Munich, Alte Pinakothek. Photo: Bayerische Staatsgemäldesammlungen, Munich.

stood as analogous to the New Science, a thesis championed most famously by Svetlana Alpers.[69] It is a thesis open to criticism on a number of counts, but in our context, this view likewise proves limited because in particular it seriously underestimates the degree to which Dutch realistic images are dependent on conventions of representation that differ decisively from those of scientific, informational, or descriptive images, that is, the images that the early scientists themselves either made or selected to illustrate their discoveries. The latter are typically neutral, diagrammatic, and schematic, and not at all characterized by the contrived informality and apparent spontaneity of realistic landscapes, which strongly suggest a purpose and taste altogether different from scientific imagery.[70] There are, in fact, a number of features of Dutch landscapes themselves that indicate sophistication of purpose and taste on the part of both artists and buyers of art.

Until more work is undertaken on ownership and provenance, it will be difficult to reach conclusions about who owned realistic landscapes and why. It is also still difficult to draw conclusions concerning the culture and taste of patrons who owned such pictures.[71] But in the specific case of the new monochrome style, the landscapes and seascapes themselves provide strong evidence for a sophisticated audience in that they are often images of the most exquisite subtlety of composition and color, clearly made for a group of viewers willing to look at pictures lacking in more obvious rhetorical brilliance and histrionic effect. *Single-Masters in a Rough Sea* by Jan Porcellis of 1629 (Fig. 91), like the *Landscape with Cottage* by Pieter Molijn (Fig. 84), exemplifies a tendency in the later 1620s and '30s toward compositional structures in which balance is achieved so unobtrusively that at first glance the pictures seem nearly random.[72] In Porcellis's painting, the vessels, which are the main objects of attention, are located at the edges, and their implied motion appears on the verge of taking them out of the pictorial field. The effect of chance is furthered by a fluent play of light that seemingly at random picks out some elements and relegates others to shadow. Again an art without art, pictures like Porcellis's are carefully composed to appear to be uncomposed, and in them we find, as in Goltzius's landscape drawings, a careful manipulation of theme and visual form in this effort to convey an accurate and completely unpremeditated view of the real world – and this in spite of such obvious artifice as the reduction in hue typical of tonalism to greys, blues, olive-greens, browns, and ochre, and the very painterly texture of the paint.[73] Indeed, the tension between illusion and the texture of paint is particularly acute in the Porcellis, in which the *trompe-l'oeil* frame and the thick impasto of the illusory piece of paper are played against each other in a way that can only be purposefully paradoxical.[74]

The broad paint texture of monochrome painting, which is very much at odds with Netherlandish traditions of fine painting, can also be seen as a sign of sophistication. Painterly techniques were associated in the seventeenth century with the exercise of the imagination, creativity, and artistic virtuosity, ideas deriving from the Italian Renaissance tradition and known to Netherlandish artists.[75] There must have been an appreciation for the painterly techniques of Rubens and Van Dyck, since their works were in such demand; some collectors and patrons even sought to acquire their oil sketches.[76] Rembrandt seems to have self-consciously set about drawing and later painting in a broad, sketchy manner that is unusual in Dutch art and has its closest parallels in Italian and especially Venetian practices. In his style and technique, Rembrandt in effect identified himself as a virtuoso artist in the manner of Rubens and the Italian masters.[77] It is unclear to what extent the painterly technique of the tonal style was linked to these notions, though an anecdote of a painting competition between three landscape painters including Jan van Goyen and Porcellis implies that speed and brevity of execution in this style were associated with creativity and virtuosity.[78] Thinking about the painterly technique of monochrome painting in such terms, however, is apparently contrary to the recent socioeconomic thesis proposed by J. M. Montias that this technical innovation is market driven: Painting this way, you can paint faster and sell more pictures more cheaply.[79] This may well be true, but close examination of tonal landscapes and seascapes also suggests that such breadth and brevity of application appealed then for the same reason it appeals now, which is its virtuosity. Nothing about its complex layering of numerous small brushstrokes suggests a lack of attention or mechanical or slovenly execution. On the contrary, technical examination reveals selective, calculated choices of materials and painting techniques to achieve specific visual effects. These effects include limited tonality, abbreviated handling of paint, and transparency of paint layers (involving the addition of ground glass in some pictures by Jan van Goyen), and in panels, the visibility of the wood grain.[80] Even if a response to market forces, the appearance of such a style presupposes a market open to this subtlety of color, this apparent absence or informality of composition, and this virtuosity of execution, in other words, a market characterized by sophistication of taste.[81]

From its first appearance in the drawings of Goltzius, the naturalistic Dutch landscape is notable for its verisimilitude, but this quality is, from the beginning, the result of artists choosing and reshaping conventions of representation in ways that reveal not a naive duplication of appearances but a purposeful, self-aware artistry. Many factors of history and culture unquestionably encouraged and affected the development of this landscape art, and we are only beginning to understand its relationship to the developing culture of the Dutch Republic in a period involving the reinvention of a cultural identity and an extraordinary openness to innovation. But arriving at a satisfying assessment of how this art came into being and what it meant will elude us if we insist on its descriptive character alone or attend only to its cultural context and ignore its artistry. Indeed, it is an awareness of both its descriptive accuracy and its artfulness that allows us to see this art as a manifestation of the characteristic seventeenth-century taste for paradox. In Dutch realism we find perfectly encapsulated the paradoxical nature of a mimetic art: The illusion of reality, the appearance of unmediated, natural experience, can only be achieved by the exercise of self-conscious artistry, however unobtrusive.

Natural Artifice and Material Values in Dutch Still Life*

Celeste Brusati

JEWEL-LIKE flower pieces, sumptuously laid tables, modest meals, austere scholarly mementoes of mortality, bizarre assemblages of rarities and superbly crafted collectibles, and the entire panoply of sights seen through the lens of Dutch still life have suggested a variety of cultural preoccupations to lay viewers and scholars alike. Long admired for its consummate craftsmanship and seductive visual appeal, still-life painting epitomizes the descriptive and illusionistic artistry for which Netherlandish artists were justly famed. It has also been interpreted as a sensitive register of many of the ethical, mercantile, and aesthetic values that have come to characterize Dutch culture in the seventeenth century, from the sheer visual delight in painting's pleasurable illusions, to its celebration of craft as productive of knowledge and value, to an obsessive awareness of the transience of life on earth and the expression of deep-seated anxieties about the unprecedented affluence of Dutch society.

Sound arguments can be made for still life's engagement with all of these issues, but however one interprets this art, there can be little dispute about the premium it places on representational skill and inventiveness. Even a casual look at the genre reveals how assiduous its makers were in devising a repertoire of pictorial artifices calculated to stimulate and gratify even the most voracious appetite for visual consumables. I am thinking of the curl of a paper or the lemon peel dangling over the edge of a table (Fig. 92), the inlaid handle of a knife projecting illusionistically just forward of the picture surface, the butterfly delicately poised on a picture's feigned stone frame, the richly colored ribbon and key suspended from a pocket watch set precariously on a marble ledge, and similar repeated motifs that insistently draw our attention to the liminal zone where our perceptions and the cunningly wrought pictorial illusions of still life meet (cf. Figs. 97 and 98). At the very least, these representational stratagems perform a double function, on the one hand creating compelling pictorial fictions, and on the other, inviting the viewer to reflect on the artifice by which those illusions are produced.

Until quite recently, art historians have treated the look and visual appeal of still life primarily in the context of realism rather than as a product of descriptive or illusionistic artifice. Virtuosic details such as those already mentioned tended to be discussed, with good reason, as evidence of the artist's skill in imitating nature or describing appearances. One scholar put this view of still life succinctly in the following comment: "The realism of these paintings derives from the careful grouping of objects, from the play of light, but above all from the refined painting techniques used to convey the texture of the materials represented. Through the choice of support, whether copper, panel, or canvas, and through the care with which rich impastos and subtle glazes were applied, these artists made every effort to simulate the character of the objects

* I am grateful to Jennifer Robertson and Thomas Willette for their thoughtful readings and comments on this essay.

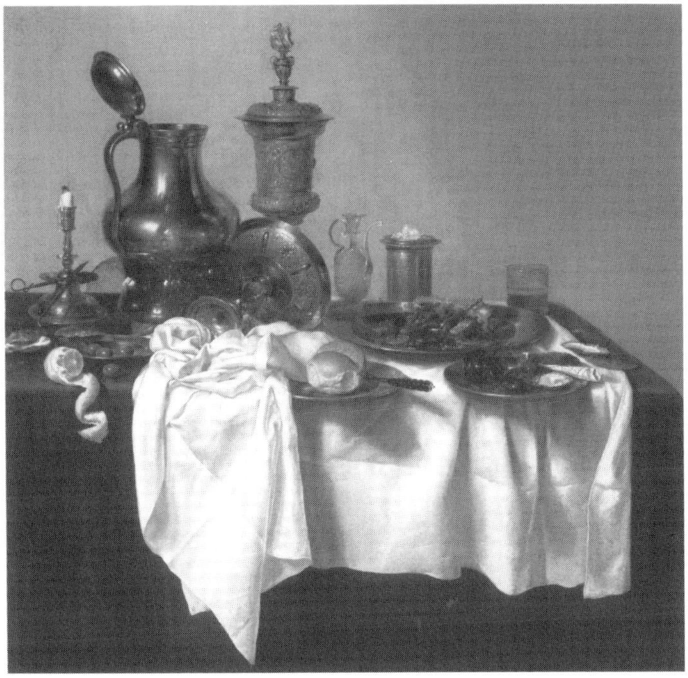

Figure 92. Willem Heda, *Monochrome Breakfast Piece,* 1635 (oil on canvas, 106.7 × 111.1 cm). Washington, D.C., National Gallery of Art. Photo: museum.

before them."[1] This realist view of still life, which articulates the aims and achievements of the genre in terms of the artist's manipulation of materials in the service of accurate imitation, is implicit in much of the literature on the subject. Frequently encountered features of still life that do not fit easily into this paradigm, such as physically impossible arrangements or combinations of objects, tend to be perceived either as symbolic (because not strictly realistic) or as simply inaccurate. Commentaries on Dutch flower pieces, to take a typical example, routinely point out that though individual blooms have been faithfully recorded, the naturalism of the painted bouquets of such artists as Jan Brueghel or Ambrosius Bosschaert is belied by their complex arrangements of flowers that bloom in different seasons and could not have been painted from a single "real-life" bouquet. Although the realist view acknowledges the artifice of these pictures, the artifice is treated as being at odds with, rather than productive of, their naturalism.

In other words, what realist interpretations of still life generally fail to acknowledge is that, contrary to the fictions the paintings purvey, still lifes do not record as much as they *remake* the material world for particular kinds of visual consumption. In this essay I argue that the persuasive power of these pictures lies precisely in the capacity of the still-life painter's artistry both to exploit and naturalize this representational transformation. Typically, artists draw attention to this naturalizing artifice by emphasizing particularizing details such as the tiny veins delicately enumerated on the petal of a flower, the complex play of light as it passes through and reflects off of glass and metalware, or the telling highlight that reveals the differentiated textures of lemon peel, grape skin, nutshell, engraved silver, or plush velvet. These highly formulaic elements all conspire to give these pictures the appearance of having been carefully observed and faithfully recorded. It is through such means that Dutch still lifes invite us to believe the fictive truth of their "eyewitness" testimony and to imagine that it is natural to contemplate the world stilled, objectified, and assembled in the ways that still life presents it to us.

Understanding Dutch still-life painting involves at some level coming to terms with the nature of this pictorial remaking and its effects. How and to what purposes do still-life pictures transform the visible? What is more, how do they shape their beholders' perceptions and ways of making sense of the world? In what follows I explore briefly some ways in which Dutch still-life paintings both naturalize their own representational artifice and call attention to its character and value. My aim in this exploration is twofold: first, to indicate some of the ways in which the self-reflexive aspects of still-life pictures can illuminate seventeenth-century notions of picture making and aesthetic values central to what is thought of as Dutch realism, and second, to suggest how particular representational practices bear on the ways that still lifes generate meaning.

Before embarking on this investigation, it may be useful to say a few words about how others have gone about interpreting Dutch still lifes. As indicated earlier, interpretive discussions of Dutch painting have tended for the most part to bracket realism and look for meaning in the subject matter of still life, leaving both representational ingenuity and its visual effects outside of the interpretive sphere. Most scholars have approached the objects in Dutch still life iconologically, that is, as examples of the "disguised symbolism" that Erwin Panofsky attributed to the naturalistic details of fifteenth- and sixteenth-century Netherlandish religious painting.[2] Citing the authority of the well-known adage, "Nihil est in rebus inane: Dat is: Daer is niet ledighs of ydels in de dinghen" (There is nothing empty or meaningless in things), widely circulated in the seventeenth century, influential studies by Ingvar Bergström and Eddy de Jongh argued that the objects in still-life paintings should likewise be seen as essentially symbolic or metaphorical and imbued with hidden meanings.[3] De Jongh went on to claim that the realism of still-life painting is only seeming realism (*schijnrealisme*) and acts as a veil for the allegorical or metaphorical significance of the objects depicted; thus, De Jongh reinforced the assumption implicit in much of the interpretive scholarship that meaning is by definition symbolic and that "realism" is not meaningful in and of itself. The iconologic interpretations that his work has spawned have focused almost exclusively on deciphering the symbolic and metaphorical meanings encoded in the fruits, flowers, books, documents, and other artifacts depicted in still life. Looking for what De Jongh has termed the "tone-setting elements" in the still life, interpreters generally designate one or more symbolically laden objects to serve as the key to the meaning of the picture.[4] Thus, in the case of a monochrome meal or *pronk* (sumptuous) still life (Fig. 92), the presence of a broken glass or a pocket watch serves to determine the reading of the entire picture as a reminder of the transience of material wealth and life itself. This method has predisposed many scholars to interpret the frequent appearance of stock motifs such as timepieces, skulls, extinguished candles, flowers in bloom, soap bubbles, and other ephemera as evidence that many, if not most, still lifes were intended as admonitions to be moderate, to be wary of the vanity of earthly pursuits and pleasures, and to be mindful of mortality.[5]

In more recent scholarship and critical writing on Dutch still life, the interpretive focus of attention has shifted somewhat toward analyses of the cultural and particularly the material-cultural significance of the genre. A variety of circumstances, including the European voyages of discovery, the expansion of European commercial and colonial empires, the growth of capitalism and the emergent culture of collecting, and the development of the empirical sciences, have been brought to bear on the subject matter of still life.[6] Although still centered largely on the meaning of objects in the pictures, contextual approaches have sought meanings more broadly in the social and economic significance of depicted artifacts and have linked the still-life repertoire of exotica, horticultural rarities, *naturalia*, comestibles, textiles, finely wrought metal and glassware, books, instruments, and so forth to relevant historical circumstances, social practices, and cultural values. Approaching still life with such issues in mind has certainly broadened our understanding of the multiple cultural contexts and practices within which still-life objects circulated, and it has alerted us to a range of meanings that are not primarily symbolic but derive instead from the cultural life of material things themselves. Interpretive consideration of the status of these objects as *pic-*

tured artifacts has played a relatively minor role in these analyses.

By contrast, representational practices and their meanings have come to the fore in the work of semioticians and cultural critics who have approached the issue of realism not as a function of accurate observation and recording but as a product of artistic conventions or signs that signify reality selectively, and therefore in culturally meaningful ways.[7] In these studies the interpretive project encompasses not only exploring the significance of specific objects (to a greater or lesser degree) but also the analysis of how objects are transformed and how meanings are generated in and through the process of representation. Instead of taking the pursuits of realism for granted, these analyses presuppose that both making and viewing are inextricably part of the process of meaning production and that these dynamics are of crucial interpretive interest.

The suggestive analysis of Dutch painting offered by French semiologist Roland Barthes in his essay, "The World As Object," has served as a stimulus for some of the most interesting commentaries on Dutch still life to date.[8] Barthes approached Dutch painting much as a cultural anthropologist might, looking at Dutch pictorial production as a semantic space or field of signs and practices in which artists and viewers represented and made sense of themselves and their society. Although he avoided analyzing particular images, he made several acute observations of general importance concerning the conventions through which still-life objects are represented. Two of these observations are worth mentioning here. First, he noted the simple fact that the objects in still-life pictures are never displayed alone but always in significant relationships to other objects. Second, he observed that objects depicted in still life are manipulated and displayed in ways that make their uses and attributes conspicuous aspects of their appearance. He saw in Dutch still life a predilection for the display of objects caught between functions to reveal their utilized aspect rather than their principal form. Thus, watches are opened to make their mechanical workings visible; glasses are broken, filled with colored liquid, or illuminated to reveal their brittle translucency; lemons are shown peeled to reveal many facets of their appearance, tactile properties, structure, and qualities suggestive of their taste.

Barthes's insights have been taken up in various ways by cultural theorists including Hal Foster and Norman Bryson, both of whom developed Barthes's interest in the gaze.[9] The *gaze*, as these writers use the term, refers to the ways in which still-life pictures manage the visual field and the perception of objects represented in it. They are especially concerned with the pictorial artifices of rendering and presentation that make visible in the depicted objects a dimension of value capable of justifying their representation. Both writers have sought explicitly to theorize Dutch still life with reference to cultural discourses of our own time.

By contrast, Svetlana Alpers has taken what might be called Barthian critical perceptions as an impetus for investigating the particular representational claims and artifice of Dutch still life in seventeenth-century terms. In *The Art of Describing*, Alpers linked the representational artifice of still life to the techniques of early modern scientific inquiry, and specifically to Baconian experimental artistry.[10] She paid particular attention to Bacon's belief that the best means of making the nature of things comprehensible to the attentive observer was through ingenious contrivances called experiments that manipulated nature to make its properties perceivable to the investigator. Focusing on the crucial role played by technical artifice as the means of grasping nature within the Baconian project, Alpers made a compelling case for understanding still life as a type of pictorial experiment that displays a comparable sort of ingenuity in its representational craft. Her argument is of special interest to the present discussion for two reasons: First, it treats the descriptive specificity of Dutch still life as a matter of purposeful contrivance rather than accurate transcription; and second, it places emphasis on the production of experience as a goal of this artistry.

It is with this double focus on the productive artifice of still life in mind that I will look more closely at some of the ways in which still-life painters made claims about their artistry part of the beholder's visual experience of their work. The celebration of artifice, as evident both in the ingenious productions of nature and in those of human fabrication, is a central concern of many of the earliest surviving still-life easel paintings, which depict flowers, shells, coins, and other collectibles. The fascination with such artifice is likewise evident in the passion for encyclopedic collecting that pervaded the courts of Europe and later filtered down to the wealthy bourgeoise in the course of the seventeenth century. The art of Jan Brueghel, the son of Pieter Bruegel the Elder, has a special place in this history, for he not only supplied these collections or *kunstkamers* (special rooms in which such collections were displayed) with minutely detailed pictures of flowers and other *naturalia* (Fig. 93); he was also instrumental in developing a new type of image set within the space of the *kunstkamer*. The splendid *Kunstkamer Visited by the Archduke Albert and Archduchess Isabella* (Fig. 94), which he painted in collaboration with Adriaen van Stalbemt, is one such work. This and other richly self-reflexive pictures of this type not only give an idea of the range of artifacts encompassed in the collection; they also present the activity of collecting, as well as the collections themselves, as attributes of the universal interests and intellectual curiosity of the collectors who amassed them. Typically, these collections privileged objects that were thought to exemplify such curiosity in their inventive refashioning of *naturalia* into novel artifacts. Jeremias Ritter's *Snail Nautilus Shell* (Fig. 95), which uses the goldsmith's art to turn a nautilus shell into a representation of a snail shell, is representative in this regard. Curiosities such as these displayed a kind of double artistry, evident both in the technical virtuosity of the metal work and the ingenious transformation of a shell exemplary of nature's artistry into a human artifact that represents yet another of nature's creations, in this case a snail conveniently enlarged and harnessed for transportation by its diminutive human passenger.

Brueghel's art is particularly instructive for its sustained engagement with such representational craft and its valorization. Nature, as it is represented both in Brueghel's painted collections and in his

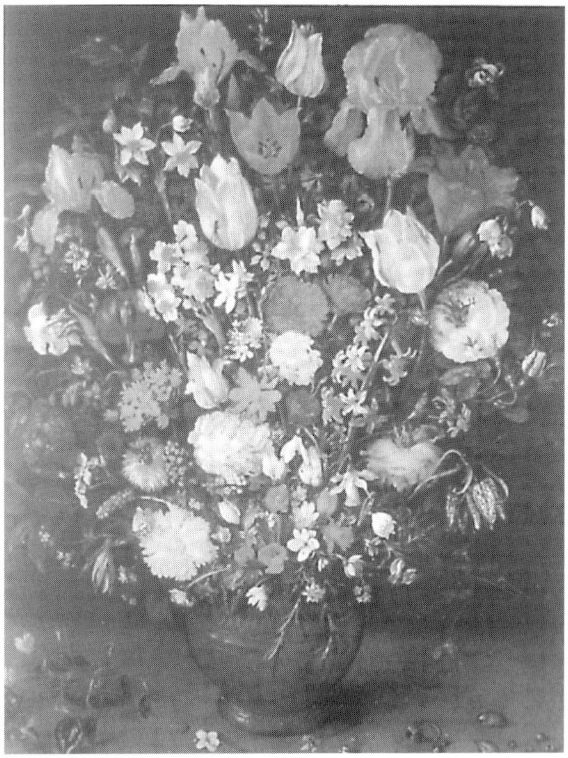

Figure 93. Jan Brueghel, *Flowers in a Clay Vase*. Vienna, Kunsthistorisches Museum. Photo: museum.

floral still lifes, is never simply imitated but is always shown conspicuously subjected to the transforming operations of artifice, manipulated or made over in some way for display and consumption. Brueghel's flower pictures generally feature a wealth of rare blooms liberally inhabited by tiny insects whose scale and subtlety invite sustained close viewing both of the diminutive creatures and their floral hosts. Most of the blooms in these bouquets are cultivated specimens of great value that offered exquisite but fleeting pleasure, since they withered soon after reaching their full splendor. Thus, far from being mere realistic depictions of humble objects, these pictures were themselves expensive and highly sought after collectibles, much like the flowers, coins, gems, and other valuables depicted in them. As recent studies of flower painting suggest, bouquets of striated tulips, fritillary, and similar cultivars may well have existed *only* as painted artifacts. Given the extreme costliness of these flowers, it seems unlikely that many purchasers would have

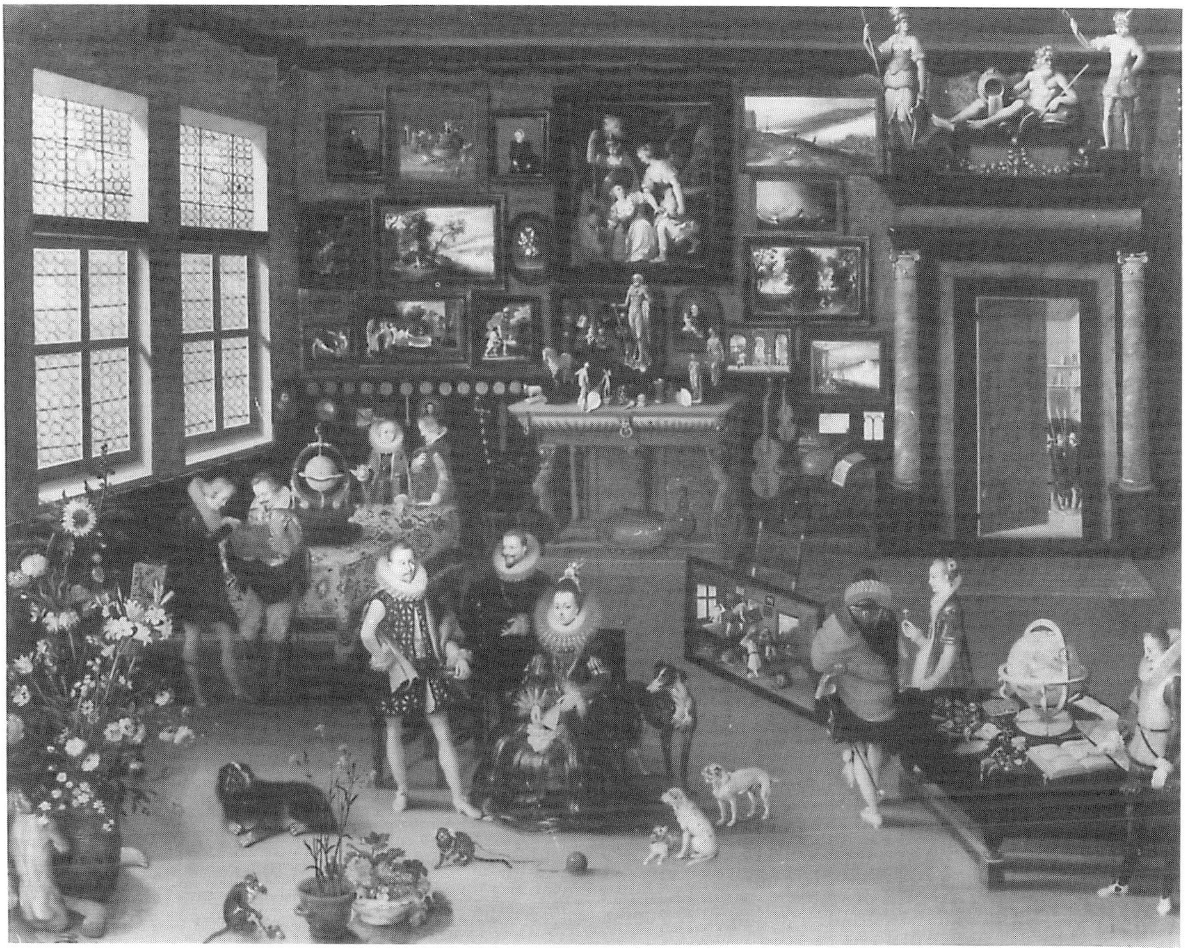

Figure 94. Jan Brueghel and Adriaen van Stalbemt, *Kunstkamer Visited by the Archduke Albert and Archduchess Isabella* (oil on panel, 94 × 123.3 cm). Baltimore, Walters Art Gallery. Photo: museum.

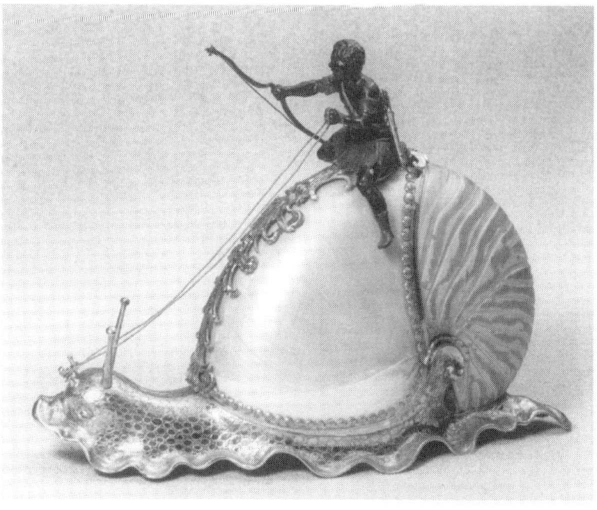

Figure 95. Jeremias Ritter, *Snail Nautilus Shell* (nautilus shell, enamel, and silver gilt). Hartford, Wadsworth Atheneum. Photo: museum.

been inclined to shorten the brief period of their blossom by cutting them for display in full bloom as they appear in still life.[11] Brueghel's flower paintings remade and preserved these horticultural marvels for extended enjoyment and contemplation in artificially constituted bouquets.

It should also be noted that the owners of Brueghel's pictures included such eminent patrons as Rudolf II, whose imperial *kunstkamer* was one of the most extensive collections of its time, and Cardinal Federico Borromeo, who assembled a collection of pictures intended to exemplify the ways that diverse styles and kinds of paintings could stimulate contemplative devotion.[12] Borromeo wrote of the particular pleasure he took in these painted bouquets, which allowed him to savor and keep his flowers in view long after their season had passed. He explicitly praised Brueghel's artistry for its capacity to preserve these wondrous displays of divine and human artifice and make them available to the eye for aesthetic and devotional contemplation. For his part Brueghel devoted considerable artistic energy not only to preserving these blooms but also to making visible in his pictures the value of his representational craft by likening it to the artistry of nature itself. His precise but loose brushwork, which makes tiny threads of paint seem to duplicate the veins in the flower petals, begs the viewer to compare his pictorial artifice to nature's own. In the profusion of colors and pattern, and the plethora of tiny insects enmeshed in these bouquets, Brueghel's brush seems to vie with nature as a propagator of species. The "natural" artifice of the painter does not only imitate or rival nature's productivity; in representing primarily cultivated blooms, it trumps the artistry of nature and that of the horticulturalist at once.

Occasionally Brueghel devised pictorial glosses on the value of his artistry, as in those cases when he placed jewels and coins alongside the vases of flowers so as to suggest a comparison between them. Brueghel revealed his pictorial witticism verbally in a letter of 1606, in which he wrote to Borromeo:

> Under the flowers I have placed a jewel with minted coins and rarities from the sea. Your excellency must judge for yourself if the flowers do not surpass gold and jewels.[13]

Borromeo, in his turn, confirmed Brueghel's artistry while displaying his own wit and munificence when, in 1625, he described a magnificent flower bouquet in his *Museaum* as a:

> battle of the flowers, whose merit Brueghel himself – who made them – indicated with a most graceful invention. He painted at the bottom of the vase a diamond, which makes us understand that which we would have thought just the same, namely: the work is as valuable as a gem, and we paid for it as such.[14]

Borromeo's words are revealing, for they speak clearly to the issue of the monetary and aesthetic value that Brueghel's representational prowess added to the exotic blooms and insect specimens he crafted in paint. Equally telling is his admiration for the pictorial analogy that Brueghel drew between his artistry and the processes of minting, gem cutting, and even collecting itself as practices that add value to what is already rare and precious in nature. By praising the coins and gems as a graceful invention, Borromeo makes clear that he attributes Brueghel's inventiveness in part to representational ingenuity.

I have dwelt at some length on Brueghel's bouquets because they offer such explicit and well-documented commentary on their own artistry. These commentaries suggest the extent to which this artistry could be valued in terms at once aesthetic, economic, and religious by seventeenth-century audiences. They can also serve as reminders that modern interpretations that are focused too exclusively on symbolic meanings are simply too reductive to account for the multifaceted significance of such images. Brueghel's bouquets are of further interest because they exemplify several types of descriptive artifice characteristic of Dutch still-life painting generally. First, the painted bouquets are additive assemblages of separately observed elements. Like topographic descriptions assembled in the studio, they are composites of motifs designed to be pieced together visually in the process of sustained attentive viewing. Second, the flower pictures operate as a type of collection, bringing artifacts from different times and places into view simultaneously within a single pictorial space. Third, their component elements are purposefully crafted and displayed to maximize the visibility of their attributes. If we think about them in this way, the impossible and "inaccurate" aspects of these pictures are not failures of realism but rather descriptive artifices designed to enhance the eye's reach and to stimulate visual modes of comprehension and reflection.

What sorts of reflection do still-life pictures invite? The answers offered most frequently in the literature on Dutch art focus on ethical considerations prompted by the metaphorical association of flowers and other ephemera with the brevity of life, the vanity of worldly pleasures and possessions, and similar moral admonitions. Yet as the commentary on Brueghel's flower bouquets suggests, such pictures could and did elicit contemplation of the nature and value of representational artistry as well. Brueghel's younger contemporary, Clara Peeters, elegantly thematized the value produced in and by the painter's representational artifice in her well-known *Still Life with Gold Goblets and Collectibles* of 1612 (Fig. 96). Like Brueghel, Peeters focuses our attention on a selection of collectibles on a table or ledge, but in her arrangement and recrafting of them in paint, she reveals not only the imitative but also the transformative power of her artistry. Her picture features a mixed bouquet of cultivated blooms and wildflowers in a German stoneware vase and a group of three shells from Asia and the Caribbean between which is an arrangement of exquisitely crafted objects – two elaborately worked, gilt silver double cups set diagonally opposite each other on either side of a Chinese celadon bowl. Peeters purposefully displays these objects so as to frame visual comparisons between artifacts produced by nature and those of human devising. The flowing patterns of stems, leaves, and petals in the bouquet are replayed in the floral designs embossed on the stoneware jug and engraved on the foremost gilt goblet; the thinness and texture of the porcelain bowl are played off of similar qualities of the shells alongside it. The celadon bowl contains a gold chain, part of which spills onto the table in a pattern that loosely echoes the small trail of overlapping gold coins and their neatly stacked counterparts placed alongside the foremost gold goblet. The linked display of the gold goblets, gold chain, and gold coins invites our visual consideration of how different transformations wrought by craft (that is, in the processes of gilding, forging, and minting) give or add value to this precious and intrinsically valuable natural product. In the gold goblet at the right, Peeters visualizes even more explicitly the transformative power of her own representational artistry (Fig. 96a). Like the other gold objects, it reveals how her art transforms base pigments into golden surrogates. Moreover, her virtuosic rendering of the goblet's mirroring globular surfaces transforms the artist herself into an array of tiny reflected images, which are presented as the ultimate testimony to her imitative skill. Through these diminutive reflections of herself at work, palette in hand, Peeters duplicates the mirrorlike artifice of the picture as a whole and sustains its fiction of being an exact reflection of what was placed before her skilled hand and eye.

It is important to recognize here that Peeters's self-images were not simply the product of her exact transcription of the reflections she observed while looking at the goblet. Reflected images of artists mirrored in the worlds they paint are abundant in Dutch still life, and during Peeters's lifetime, this motif became a well-established conceit through which Dutch artists pictorially claimed and identified with their representational artistry.[15] Peeters's self-inscription, with its dazzling play of attenuated reflections carefully positioned on the goblet's convex bubbles to appear precisely as they would from the artist's vantage point, is a pictorial *tour de force*. It would have been admired by at least some of her contemporaries as a display of skill in the art of reflection (*reflexy-const*), a category of pictorial expertise fundamental to Karel van Mander's influential account in the *Schilder-boeck* (Book on Painting) of the nature and achievements of Netherlandish painting.[16] Under this rubric, Van Mander distinguished a variety of descriptive prop-

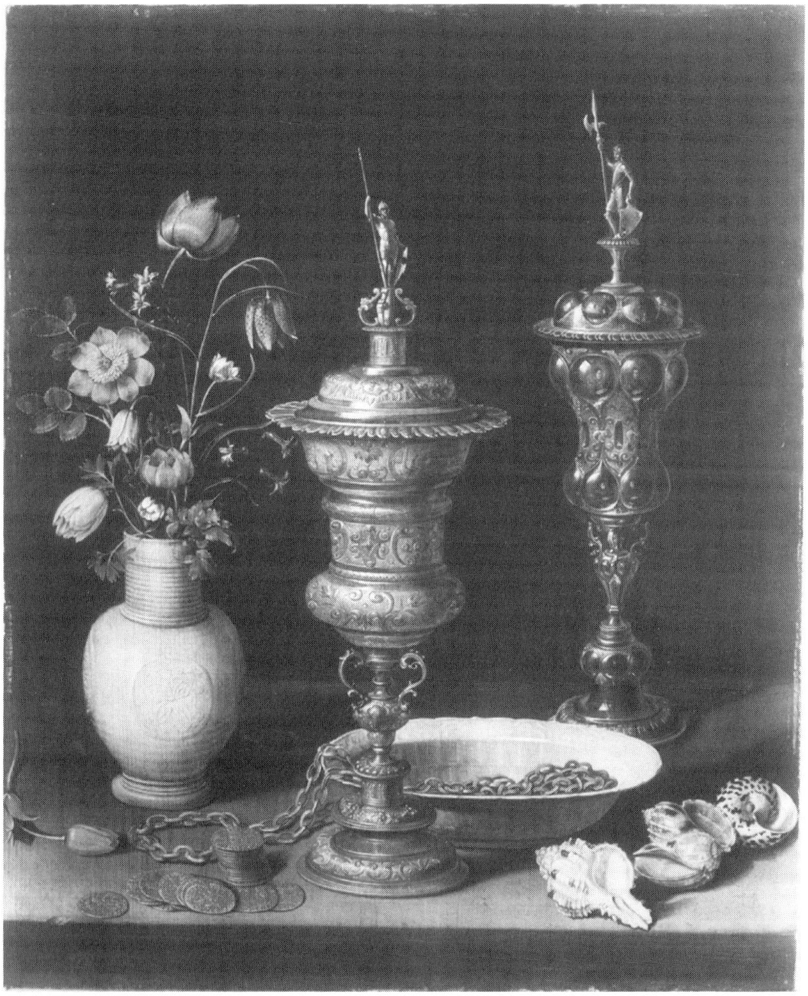

Figure 96. Clara Peeters, *Still Life with Gold Goblets and Collectibles*, 1612 (oil on panel, 59.5 × 49 cm). Karlsruhe, Staatliche Kunsthalle. Photo: museum.

erties of natural light in action, ranging from the sheen or luster (*glans*) produced by light hitting smooth, polished surfaces, to the reflection (*reflectie*) or action of colored light, which tints surfaces, to the mirroring (*spiegelen*) by which light turns reflective surfaces into fully defined mirrors of their surroundings. Most significantly, however, Van Mander used *reflexy-const* to link these imaging processes found in nature to the painter's descriptive skill in rendering the many kinds and degrees of refracted light. The force of the term is thus both critical in its articulation of a category of pictorial expertise and ideological in its identification of pictorial artistry with nature's own image-making capacities. When Peeters and her colleagues demonstrated their mastery of *reflexy-const* in registering these properties of reflected light, they were also implicitly locating the value of their representational artistry in the operations by which nature pictures and imitates itself.

Mastering the "natural" artifice of the *reflexy-const* enables the still-life painter to produce compelling descriptive effects. The artist does this, as Melion has astutely pointed out, by pictorially

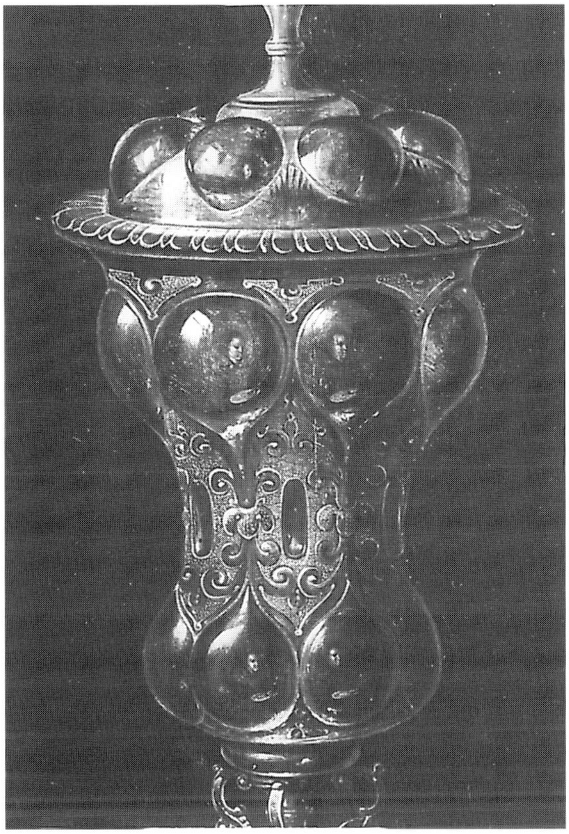

Figure 96a. Detail of Figure 96.

transforming objects into light-reflecting surfaces.[17] Pieter Claesz, Willem Heda, and other painters of the so-called monochrome breakfast pieces and laid tables routinely depicted glass and metalware ingeniously arranged and illuminated by directed light, which effectively transformed these objects into privileged sites for display of *reflexy-const* (Fig. 92). Through this artifice the constrasting textures of oysters and lemons are thus not only differentiated but also mirrored in polished pewter plates, whose sheen is rendered by the action of light glancing over their surfaces. Light focused on partly filled wine glasses projects upon them the reflected images of unseen windows and shines through their translucent contents to generate colored reflexes of reflected light, which in turn stain walls and tablecloths with the red and golden colors of the liquids they contain.

The range of these effects is multiplied and redoubled in the so-called *pronk* or sumptuous still lifes of the mid-seventeenth century, with their lavish displays of valuables and exotic foodstuffs. In works such as Jan de Heem's *Still Life with Lobster* (Fig. 97), the skillful display of *reflexy-const* transforms both edibles and finely wrought metal and glassware into similarly constituted visual consumables. Not only the silver tazza and elegant glassware but also grapes, plums, peaches, currants, and a shining lobster are pictorially remade into reflective surfaces whose qualities of sheen, opacity, translucence, and texture visually stimulate all the senses by suggesting the various tactile, gustatory, and olfactory pleasures they offer.

Through the play of light differentially registered on these surfaces, the *reflexy-const* also serves to mobilize the beholder's gaze and facilitate the eye's movement through the image. Barthes interpreted this artifice as a symptom of Dutch still life's capitalist ordering of the material world, and he suggested that it be understood as an effort to "lubricate man's gaze amid his domain, to facilitate his daily business among objects whose riddle is dissolved and which are no longer anything but easy surfaces."[18] Barthes read the optical veneer of similarity given to objects through the techniques of *reflexy-const* as a means of signifying their shared status as commodities in an economic system based on equivalence. Whether or not we accept the pertinence of this interpretation, with its obvious relevance to the *pronk* still life and similar displays of expensive or desirable commodities, Barthes's reading accounts only partially for the range of semantic uses that artists made of this representational strategy.

Simon Luttichuys's ambitious *Still Life with Attributes of the Pictorial Arts* of 1646 (Fig. 98) provides an excellent example of the ways in which the strategies of surface description also facilitated the optical production of meaning in still life.[19] In this work Luttichuys has ingeniously utilized the *reflexy-const* to orchestrate a splendid visual commentary on the capacity of the pictorial arts to still and encompass the complexity of life in representation. Luttichuys's picture is set in a corner of a room that we are to see as the painter's studio. It is

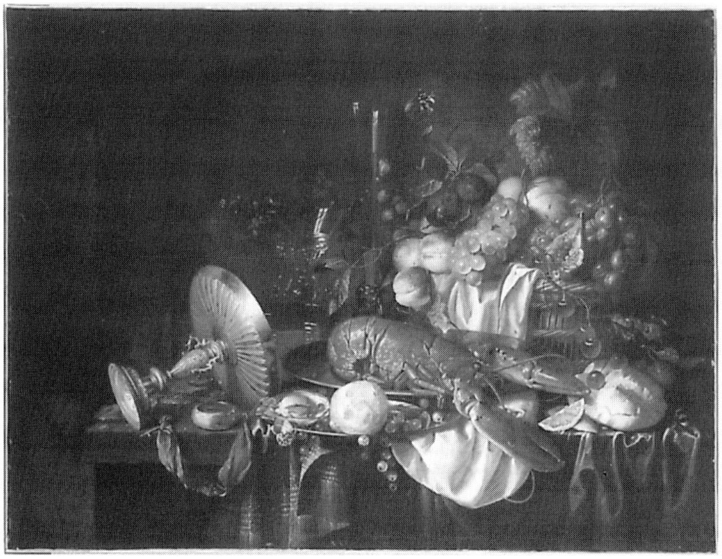

Figure 97. Jan de Heem, *Still Life with Lobster* (oil on canvas, 63.5 × 84.5 cm). Toledo, Toledo Museum of Art. Photo: museum.

designated as such through a device that exemplifies the skillful exercise of the *reflexy-const*, namely, the spherical mirror whose shining surface captures the familiar reflected image of the artist at his easel putatively painting the picture at which we are looking. Like the globular self-reflections on Clara Peeters's gold goblet, Luttichuys's self-reflexive mirror simultaneously reveals the specular power of the painter's art and the picture's *claim* to be a true, eye-witnessed account of the painter's observations.

But Luttichuys's spherical mirror does more than this. Hovering between its own shadow image on the wall and the celestial globe on the table below it, the mirroring sphere visually activates a play of formal correspondences that invite the beholder to see and draw comparisons not only among these three orbs but also between the reflecting sphere and the array of representational artifacts displayed on the table below it. The mimetic artistry demonstrated in the orb is set off against a virtual catalogue of pictorial representations arrayed on the table below it, ranging from the sculpted portrait busts and the engraved portrait of Rubens from Van Dyck's *Iconography*, to a richly figured celestial globe, a hand-colored map with pictorial vignettes, an illustrated herbal, a painting of a tempest, a figure drawing, and a character study. Viewed as a group, the assembled artifacts on the table demonstrate the encyclopedic grasp of the representational arts and thus pictorially reiterate the comprehensive mimetic claims of the mirroring sphere whose reflecting surface reveals an all-encompassing if distorted image of the room in which it hangs. Luttichuys thus deploys the *reflexy-const* not only to display descriptive skill but also to encourage the beholder to see and articulate potentially significant visual relationships among the depicted objects.

Luttichuys's picture further invites the viewer to make visual connections between elements of his still life through a variety of pictorial witticisms and artifices of display. For example, a circle of directed gazes formed by the sculpted portraits serves to lead the eye ultimately to the image of the painter's reflection in the glass, the picture's central conceit. Similarly, suggestive superimpositions of texts and pictures – of unique and repeatable images, of descriptive, allegorical, heraldic and narrative imagery – visually articulate a carefully differentiated range of pictorial representations. Luttichuys may also be visualizing familiar ideas through pictorially paired motifs. In this case the laurel-

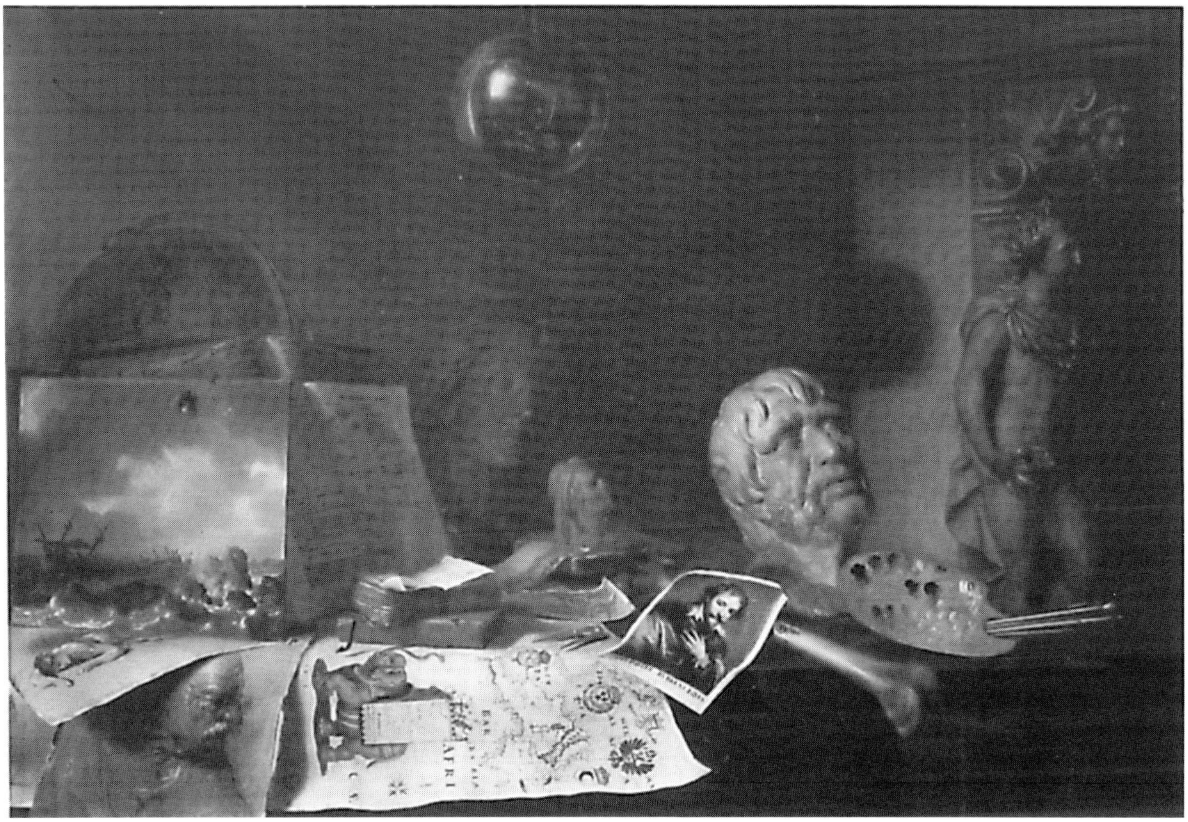

Figure 98. Simon Luttichuys, *Still Life with Attributes of the Pictorial Arts*, 1646 (oil on panel, 46 × 67 cm). Private Collection, USA.

crowned sculpted figure of Apollo supporting the mantle and the portrait of Rubens, whose fame is celebrated in a commemorative print placed atop a thighbone, may be compared in order to suggest the kinship of painting and poetry as sources of fame. The superimposition of the artist's portrait over a signifier of mortality, in turn, might also be read as a version of the adage that art is lasting and life short (*ars longa, vita brevis*). This same idea is reinforced by way of a visual analogy drawn by the artist between these objects and the similarly disposed palette and brushes resting on the bust of Seneca alongside them.

In suggesting that the disposition of objects in Luttichuys's still life invites interpretation in this way, I am implicitly taking issue with the strictly symbolic readings of this picture, which view it as a highly redundant illustration of the vanity and ephemerality of the arts and sciences. To support one such reading, the glass sphere has been seen as a pictorial translation of the expression, "homo bulla," the notion that human life is as fragile as a bubble.[20] Following in this vein, the thighbone has been interpreted as a reminder of mortality, the tempest picture as an image of portending death and destruction, the drawings of the naked youth and old man as illustrating the inescapability of death, the commemorative Rubens portrait as a reminder of the mortality of the artist, the bust of Seneca as a reference to his writings on the brevity of life, the plants in the illustrated herbal as an allusion to the biblical analogy of human life to that of a flower, and the fly deceptively casting its shadow on the painting as a symbol of decay.

Although the objects depicted in Luttichuys's picture may symbolically evoke such associations the thighbone a figure of art prevailing over death, it is also possible to interpret the proximity of the commemorative image to human remains as a reminder of the mortality of the artist. Both ideas were certainly current in the seventeenth century, and neither is implausible. The ambiguity of the image is not simply a matter of our inability to retrieve the "correct" original meaning or the artist's intention but is rather a function of the ways in which still-life pictures are capable of producing meanings.

Even a cursory view shows that Luttichuys's painted commentary on the pictorial arts owes at least as much to his ingenious representational strategies as to the objects he represents. Not only has he assembled a collection of objects that together reflect the range of media, genres, and diverse functions of pictorial images; Luttichuys also demonstrates the eye-fooling power of the

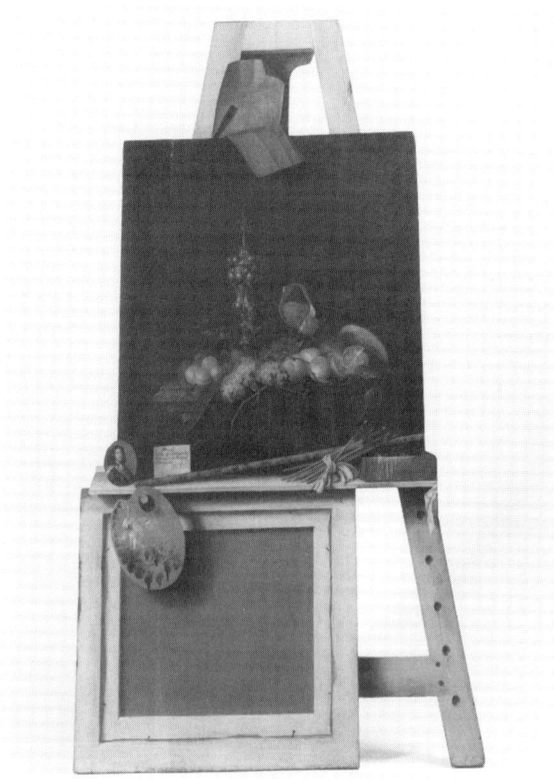

Figure 99. Cornelis Gysbrechts, *Trompe-l'oeil Easel*, Copenhagen, Statens Museum for Konst.

individually, reading the painting as an allegory in this way does not account for the formal relations between objects that modify these associations and produce others. Any interpretation that restricts itself to assigning symbolic meanings to single objects taken individually preempts consideration of those meanings that are generated *pictorially*, that is, through particular strategies of representation and display that propose conceptual and formal relationships among depicted objects. Not only is it necessary to take such strategies into account; it is crucial to recognize that the meanings they generate are inherently unstable. For even though still-life pictures may suggest connections through purposefully displayed objects, they cannot specify definitively the nature of those linkages. Thus, although I may see in Rubens's portrait covering

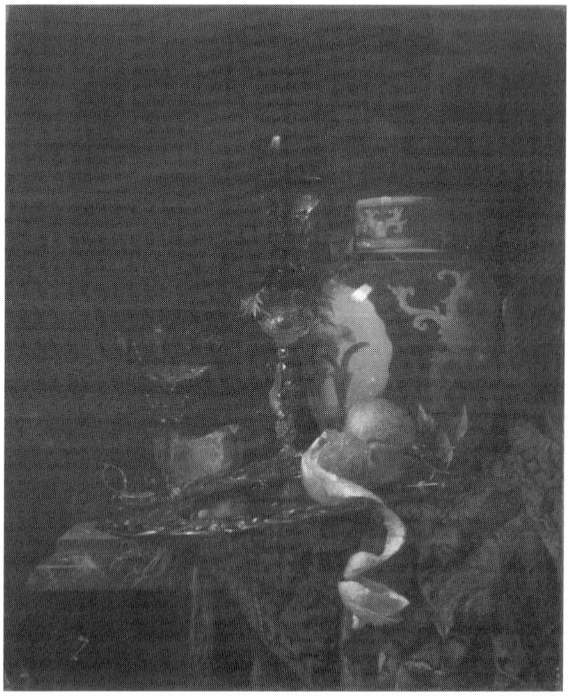

Figure 100. Willem Kalf, *Still Life with Ginger Jar*, 1669 (oil on canvas, 77 × 65.5 cm). Indianapolis, Indianapolis Museum of Art. Photo: museum.

painter's art in their representation.[21] He does this most strikingly in the curious passage at the lower left where a grisaille sketch, a nude figure drawing, and an oil painting are superimposed upon a brightly colored map displaying the coats of arms of Spain, France, the Netherlands, Germany, and the Ottoman Empire imprinted upon Europe, along with an elephant adorned with a cartouche carrying spear-bearing Africans across a landmass inscribed as "*Barbaria Africae*" (Barbary States of Africa). The interleaved images call our attention not only to the power of representation and the representation of power but also to the varieties of pictorial artifacts encompassed by his art, and to the virtual space before the table where the painter's illusions and our own perceptions meet. Luttichuys has wittily inserted the drawing of a prostrate male figure between two representations of the sea, one cartographic and one pictorial, so that the nude seems to be washed ashore by the painted tempest onto the dry ground of the drawing. The corner of this depicted drawing, which casts its shadow on the sketch below it, appears to project forward of the picture plane and thus explicitly challenges the viewer to determine where the world of the artist's making begins and ends. That challenge is repeated and redoubled in the *trompe-l'oeil* fly, which Luttichuys has painted cunningly so that its cast shadow appears in the cloudy sky of the tempest picture. Once again the artist calls attention to the threshold of his painted illusion, but this time by way of a visually irresolvable puzzle. Does the counterfeit fly cast its image on the surface of the still life or the seascape depicted within it?[22] Luttichuys's visual conundrum demonstrates his representational prowess by confounding the beholder's ability to discern the outer limits of the pictorial fiction.

In later seventeenth century still-life painting, the value of the painter's artistry became increasingly associated with its capacity to deceive the eye of the beholder through pictorial counterfeits and images that blurred the threshold between the perceived and the represented world. Painters who demonstrated their illusionistic prowess in such works utilized illusionistic artifice not only to celebrate but also to question painting's representational claims. On the one hand, artists such as Samuel van Hoogstraeten and Cornelis Gysbrechts asserted the power of their eye-fooling artistry to bring them princely recognition and social status in self-referential *trompe-l'oeil* performances (Fig. 99).[23] On the other hand, there were others such as Willem Kalf (Fig. 100) who stressed the fragility and tenuousness of their painted illusions.[24] One might say that Kalf took the *reflexy-const* to its optical limit in his pictures of the 1650s and 1660s. These shadowy, sparkling images transform very expensive luxury objects into reflective surfaces so selectively illuminated that their subtle contours vanish into obscurity even as the eye tries to trace them. In these glittering illusions of evanescent treasures, it is Kalf's representational artifice itself that induces beholders to experience these painted surrogates as elusively intangible and in so doing to reflect upon the moral implications of their attachments to them. Once again meaning is not simply a question of symbolic associations, but it results from the sense that the viewer makes not only of the objects Kalf paints but also the way he has painted them.

Later seventeenth-century still-life painting has often been characterized as less imbued with symbolic and emblematic meanings than works produced earlier in the century. Thinking about still-life's meanings as generated in and through the artist's representational craft leads to a different formulation. Whereas early seventeenth-century still-life painters such as Brueghel and Peeters took pains to establish the value of their artistry by asserting its similarity to forms of natural artifice, by Kalf's time it was the beguiling power and inescapable fragility of painting's optical illusions that captured the attention of painters and their audiences. Judging from the pictures still extant, what remained constant throughout the century was the energy with which Dutch still-life painters continued to find inventive ways of eliciting pleasurable and reflective viewing through their ingenious displays of natural artifice and consummate pictorial craft.

The Three-Quarter Length Life-Sized Portrait in Seventeenth-Century Holland

THE CULTURAL FUNCTIONS OF *TRANQUILLITAS**

Ann Jensen Adams

IN seventeenth-century Holland, portraits were everywhere, from finely wrought miniatures enclosed in filigreed lockets and informal sketches in *alba amicora* to imposing life-sized figures of political officials dominating town halls and castles of the nobility; from the genealogical portrait galleries lining the halls of Honselaersdijk, a residence of Frederik Henry, Prince of Orange, to the meeting rooms of such civic institutions as the Amsterdam Kloveniersdoelen displaying Rembrandt van Rijn's *Nightwatch;* from the family portrait collections of Pieter de la Court or Michael de Ruyter, through the interiors of the front rooms of brothels lined with portraits of the women available to clients; to such portrait prints as Rembrandt's etching of the Reformed preacher Jan Cornelisz. Sylvius, all providing to a broad audience images that served as a model of a life well lived for the viewer to admire and imitate. These images of family members, public leaders, and esteemed historic figures fulfilled a wide range of personal, social, and political functions.

Until recently, studies of sixteenth- and seventeenth-century Dutch portraits have been caught in the topos of the portrait itself – that of faithfully recording an individual's physiognomy – which left these cultural functions unexplored. That Dutch paintings do not merely illustrate the world in which the artist lived and worked is fairly well established for most genres of Netherlandish art. Nonetheless, inherited notions of the "realism" of the genre of portraiture have proved tenaciously resistant to reexamination and has generated two empiricist approaches to the portrait: one reflectionist, and the other expressionist. These were the premises on which Pope-Hennessy based his pioneering study of (mostly Italian) Renaissance portraiture published in 1966 whose opening sentence reads, "Portrait painting is empirical." A similar sentiment underlies Jakob Rosenberg's description, in his monograph on Rembrandt (initially published in 1948), of the portraits by most Dutch painters who "satisfied the primary demands of [Dutch] burghers for a good likeness and realistic rendering of costume."[1]

While describing portraiture as transcriptive, both Pope-Hennessy and Rosenberg attribute to the genre the capacity to reveal the human psyche, the depths of the human soul. Pope-Hennessy devotes a chapter to "The Motions of the Mind," while Rosenberg claims for Rembrandt the ability "to express his [man's] inner life, his spiritual existence . . . [his] portraits strongly reflect Rembrandt's susceptibility to the spiritual side of man and show both his breadth and profundity in the interpretation of human character."[2] Both authors imply that the artist probes their subject's character through a keen attention to empirical detail and

* I am grateful to Wayne Franits for his generous comments on an earlier draft, and to Abigail Solomon-Godeau for thoughtful conversation about the theoretical armature of this essay and her close reading of the text. Moreover, I would like to thank Rainer Mack for his help with the translation of the Latin titles that appear in the text.

conveys it through an expressive handling of paint and the effects of light and shadow.

At the same time, both authors acknowledge that in spite of transcribing reality, a portrait may idealize the features of its subject almost beyond belief. Rosenberg notes that "when Sophie of Hanover met Henrietta Maria of England, whom she had known only from Anthony van Dyck's portraits, she was amazed at the queen's crooked and ill-proportioned figure and her ugly, protruding teeth."[3] Pope-Hennessy admires the art produced by idealization, such as the "new poetry and depth" of Titian's portrait of Philip II (whose Hapsburg jaw is softened by shadow), and the elaboration of fine detail in the mannered portraits of Bronzino. Yet he simultaneously accuses the patron of responsibility for any deviance from likeness by the artist who otherwise would have been more honest: "It is important to remember," he writes, "that the determinant in many ruler portraits was the sitter's self-conceit."[4]

Such an empirical approach to portraiture makes possible a-historical conclusions about a sitter's character from the author's interpretation of their face. Projection in the study of portraiture has been a fundamental and longstanding problem, frequently illustrated through a comparison of dramatically variant readings by different authors. For example, the sitters in Frans Hals's *Regents of the Old Men's Alms House* (Fig. 101) and *Regentesses of the Old Men's Alms House* (Haarlem, Frans Hals Museum; c. 1664) were praised by a poet at the end of the eighteenth century as "gods toward humanity" and "wise and beneficent almoners." They were viewed subsequently in a highly negative light from the mid-1870s when J. de Vries described the third figure from the right as portrayed in a drunken stupor, and Eugene Fromentin attributed Hals's free paint handling to a "painter [that] is three-quarters dead." These regents were finally rehabilitated in 1963 by P. J. Vinken and Eddy de Jongh, who plausibly proposed that the countenance of the seemingly drunken regent was due to Hals's faithful transcription of his partial facial paralysis.[5] Both reflectionist and expressionist approaches credit portraiture with providing direct access to the once living subject and artist.

The assumption of portraits' transparency to their sitters' physiognomies follows seventeenth-century Dutch theorists who describe portraits as transcriptions of an objective reality, as unmediated visual analogues for actual persons. It lies behind Karel van Mander's disparagement of portraiture in these oft-quoted lines from his life of the portraitist Michiel van Miereveldt, "painter of Delft," who

> from among other talents with which Nature abundantly endowed him, chose portrait painting. . . . [In] our Netherlands there is this deficiency or unfortunate situation, especially in these present times, that there is little work to be had that requires composition so as to give the youngsters and painters the opportunity to become excellent at histories, figures and nudes through practice. For it is mostly portraits that they get the opportunity to paint; so that most of them, because of the allure of profit, or for their survival, usually take this side-road of art (that is: portrait painting) and set off without having time or inclination to seek out or follow the road of history and figures that leads to the highest perfection.[6]

Van Mander grudgingly admitted, however, that because it depicted the noble subject of the human body, it should be accorded at least some respect: "One can also make something worthwhile from a portrait: that a face, after all the most important part of the human body, contains quite enough so as to be able to disclose and reveal the quality and efficacy of art."[7] At the end of the century, Samuel van Hoogstraeten disdained "the portrait makers, who can render reasonably good likeness, and properly imitate eyes, noses and mouths, I wouldn't even place beyond, or above the first level [of painting]."[8]

Although the empirical approach represented by the work of Pope-Hennessy and Rosenberg could result in interpretations based on viewers' subjective responses, the work of these authors was instrumental in focusing attention on, and providing a new appreciation for, early modern portraiture as a genre. Their books were followed by a large number of important studies of aspects of the single-figure Dutch portrait, each of which differently frames its subject. In 1967 A. Wassenburgh surveyed the seventeenth-century portraits produced in the northern province of Friesland from the perspective of attribution and style.[9] R. E. O. Ekkart's publications of early portrait collections and his essays identifying little known artists have given new life to portraits that had languished as attributions to anonymous artists or incorrectly in the margins of the *oeuvres* of better known masters.[10] Important archival discoveries by I. H. van Eeghen and S. A. C. Dudok van Heel in notarized documents and inventories, especially when combined with inscriptions and coats of arms on portraits themselves, have allowed scholars to identify an increasing number of sitters and provide new information about the lives of artists and their patrons. Many of their findings have been published over the past twenty-five years in the Dutch journal *Amstelodamum* and continue to be fundamental for the study of portraiture from nearly all perspectives and methodological approaches. Truus van Bueren has written a physical history of the *Portraits of the Commanders from the Convent of Saint John in Haarlem*, painted in two stages – in 1562 and after 1580 (Haarlem, Frans Hals Museum). This, together with archival investigations of the circumstances of the two periods in which it was painted, furnishes insight into the changing political function of the image.[11] Her work provides a model for the kind of investigations that might be undertaken for portraits of later periods as well. Finally, two recent collections of essays on the Netherlandish portrait consider individual artists, works, and themes from a variety of points of view.[12]

While these methods materially describe and situate the portrait with regard to individuals – the artist, sitter, collector, and patron – the approach to Dutch painting most widely practiced today has been the iconological investigation of the image itself. Among other things, iconology attempts to circumvent the psychological projection behind interpretations made by the assumption that character can be read by the twentieth-century viewer directly from the body and particularly the face.[13] As originally described by Erwin Panofsky in the 1930s, iconology investigates an image through three steps. First, the "primary or natural subject matter" of the image is described on the basis of "empirical observation." Second, the "secondary or conventional meanings" of "symbols" are identified through "iconographical analysis" with recourse to literary (and as practiced today, more broadly cultural) sources. Finally, an "iconological interpretation" is made by specifying the larger cultural systems that may, often unconsciously, have directed the interpretation of the work in its time.[14] As practiced, however, iconology all too often collapses back into iconography. Michael Ann Holly and others have pointed out that studies rarely investigate the larger cultural "assumptions" and "habits of mind" that Panofsky outlines in his third step and that he argues inform the "meaning" of a work.[15]

The leading proponent of this approach to Dutch art, Eddy de Jongh, devoted his earliest investigations to seventeenth-century Dutch portraits.[16] These were followed by a series of detailed iconological[-graphical] studies of themes presented in portraiture by him and several other scholars including P. J. J. van Thiel and Jan Baptist Bedaux published over the last thirty years in the journals *Oud Holland* and *Simiolus*.[17] De Jongh has recently returned to the genre in a masterful study of Dutch marriage portraits that has become a landmark in the field.[18] H. Perry Chapman's recent monograph on Rembrandt's self-portraits employs the basic tenets of this method to investigate the multiple identities that Rembrandt explored through paintings that took himself as their model.[19] Finally, sociologist Erving Goffman describes how our experience of, and communication with others in daily life is mediated through visual codes represented through the body.[20] Citing this work, David Smith has undertaken a number of studies of body comportment, performed in life and reproduced in portraiture, that presented to the viewer communally acknowledged traits of character.[21]

Iconological [-graphical] investigations of Dutch art, and those that follow its paradigm by linking an element in a work with an object or idea in the culture, assume that at least some elements in a portrait are symbols for traits or ideas that otherwise remain hidden. Iconology is thus also an empirical search for an identifiable meaning, one that exists not in the body nor in the sitter's character but in the realm of ideas. One of the attractions of this method is the apparent security of the interpretive link between the symbol in the image and its meaning. This security, however, is illusory. Art historians frequently accept at face value these cultural referents and do not subject them to the same rigorous analysis that they demand of their investigation of the visual images themselves. An iconographical "meaning" recognized by Panofsky's second step, as well as those systems that an iconological investigation might identify, must similarly be subject to interpretation. The investigation of these systems will never be complete, however, for each investigation establishes another system that must be elucidated. In addition, such investigations run the risk of being circular, for the components of a system that one selects to investigate are already implied by the conventions and signifiers that one seeks to illuminate.[22]

As De Jongh himself was the first to caution, within an iconological [-graphical] system, symbols themselves can bear multiple meanings.[23] The obvious problem of transferring a symbol from one context to another has been recently underscored by Jan Baptist Bedaux, who demonstrates that such methods frequently only identify pictorial homonyms.[24] The only solution offered to prevent the misinterpretations that De Jongh and others recognize are possible – indeed frequent – is to plead restraint.[25] "I may seem to resemble Satan rebuking sin," De Jongh writes, "but I have become increasingly concerned about the craze for interpretation that threatens to run more prudent iconology underfoot."[26] More recently he has articulated a "method" of restraint that limits investigation to only those elements "in semiological terms, with a high signal value."[27] This restricts investigations to facets of a work that appear to the art historian as odd, or apparently unmotivated. It excludes most visual aspects that are so "descriptive" that they do not call attention to themselves in the eyes of the twentieth-century viewer – precisely the kinds of elements that predominate in portraiture.

Whether viewed as transcriptive or explained by iconology, the portrait is assumed to refer to some external truth. Portraits themselves reinforce this assumption. As the subject of a painting, the represented body has a powerful effect as it creates an imaginative relationship between the subject and the viewer, mediated by the artist. Because we live in bodies ourselves, we believe that we bring a great deal of knowledge about the body to the portrait. This knowledge can overpower our consciousness of the processes through which meaning is produced, stimulating viewers to suspend their awareness of the devices of representation and believe they are in the presence of an actual person. Even when we remain aware of the artificiality of the representation, we respond almost involuntarily to representations of the human body as true, no matter how distorted or schematized they may be. Georg Simmel wrote that when looking at a portrait, the viewer is involved in "a kind of interaction: the bodily appearance, by virtue of its aesthetic unification, evokes the idea of a soul in the mind of the viewer, and this idea in turn works back upon the picture to give it additional unity, firmness, reciprocal justification of features."[28] This process is vividly demonstrated by the numerous examples of treatments of portraits throughout the centuries – from kissing them to damaging them – as if they were actual persons.[29]

As I have described them, then, each of these approaches has one thing in common: They view the portrait as the passive vehicle of a message – understood as the images's "meaning" – from the artist, perhaps in consultation with a patron, to the viewer. The problem raised by De Jongh of multiple "meanings" suggests, however, that we should reexamine the approach itself. The meaning of a portrait at any given moment, both as an object and as an image, does not inhere in the external referent of its symbols but is produced by the infinite number of systems of belief or knowledge – sometimes called discourses – that they help to produce.[30]

Portraits are not only a cultural product but also active participants in a cultural process.[31] In their

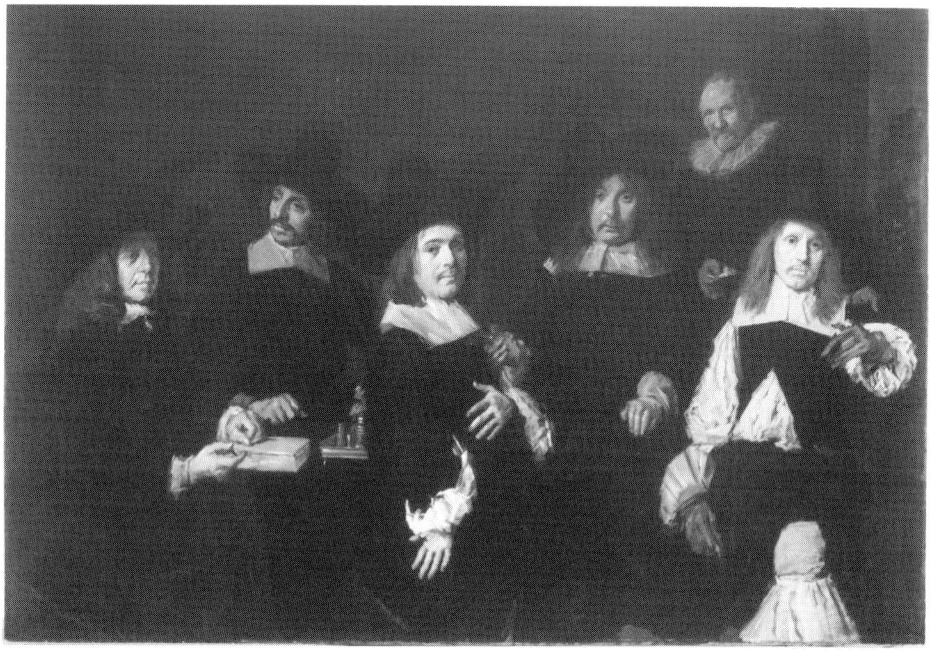

Figure 101. Frans Hals, *Regents of the Old Men's Alms House* (oil on canvas, 176.5 × 256 cm). Haarlem, Frans Hals Museum. Photo: museum.

material production, portraits potentially involve more individuals than any other painting genre: an artist, patron, sitter, and viewer (at the same time, the self-portrait can involve the fewest, the artist alone). In the imaginative "space" between the patron, artist, the portrait's human subject, and its assumed viewer, a portrait functions as an interpretive medium, organizing the experiences of their viewers. For each of these individuals, the portrait generates and structures ideas about experience in at least three areas: the sitter's perceived character and history, contemporary social structures and cultural issues, and the visual tradition. The portrait thus participates in setting the terms through which perceptions about the individuals it portrays are produced, the cultural discourses through which they are understood, and the devices and associations of the visual tradition. Each viewer of an image, at each viewing moment, brings a unique perspective to the image and unique experiences to the process of understanding. The effect of any experience of a portrait thus depends upon the relation of the viewer's position within each of the discourses generated by the experience, and their perceived power and relationship. This creates a distinctive system of associations out of which multiple "meanings" are produced. These meanings are thus always contextual, always contingent, and never completely recoverable.

Moreover, ideas, power relations, and values generated by, and circulating within, discourses are never fixed but are modified by use. Because artists, patrons, and viewers in all periods are experientially embedded within these discursive systems, they may appear "natural," making them difficult to detect or even partially recover. (Not only historical experiences but also contemporary approaches can become so naturalized. For example, the iconological approach to seventeenth-century Dutch painting, while occasionally questioned, has become so familiar that it remains the paradigm within which most other approaches are understood.) These systems can overlap and may contradict one another. The often unperceived slippage between systems can also hide their effects. We should seek, therefore, not to identify the messages embedded in a portrait by its artist and discovered by a viewer, but to investigate how portraits may participate in creating these larger systems of belief and knowledge and to identify at least some of those that are historically retrievable.[32]

While the matrix of experience and knowledge produced by these systems and their interactions is seamless, we can investigate them only by artificially selecting a limited number of conventions and signifiers within a work and the objects, ideas, and systems to which they may refer in the culture. Moreover, the linear conventions of exposition limit one to a single perspective at a time. One kind of approach investigates the experience of specific individuals – the artist, patron, or viewer (at any historical moment) – either by interpreting empirical records of viewing experiences or by hypothesizing a representative experience formulated through indirect evidence. Another approach – the one I take here – seeks to understand how conventions of signification are selected, valued, and structured to create meaning at any given time and to describe the larger discursive systems within which individual images are embedded. These two (of many) approaches are of course related, and they differ only in focus. The latter, for example, may reveal the range of discourses available at any historical moment – what Hans Robert Jauss has called the "horizon of expectations" at the moment of reception – and thus help illuminate why an individual artist and patron may select a particular constellation of conventions for any particular image.[33] Such a study must be judged by how exemplary appear the conventions of signification and discursive systems investigated, and the coherency of the description of how they may have been related by historical viewers.

I clarify this abstract description and hope to underscore the productivity of such an approach through an analysis of a portrait genre that has been usually viewed as lacking in "meaning." This is a genre that may be described, in De Jongh's terms, as having "low signal value:" the three-quarter length life-sized portraits produced in the Northern Netherlands in the late sixteenth and seventeenth centuries that represent their subjects as having a sober – even impassive – demeanor, a minimum of facial or bodily gestures, and few if any auxiliary objects. As a group, these portraits have been customarily disparaged in studies of Dutch art. They picture their subjects, sometimes with mildly idealized faces, with eyes gazing calmly toward the viewer, their gestures slight, and their bodies almost stiff. The vigor of sitters depicted in physical movement, such as Rembrandt's *Portrait of a Man Rising from His Chair* (Fig. 102) or his *Portrait of a Seated Man* (Vienna, Kunsthistorisches Museum) are often admired as conveying "character" and "emotion." In contrast, such icons of static sobriety as Nicolaes Eliasz. Pickenoy's *Portrait of Cornelis de Graeff and His Wife Geertruid Overlander* (Amsterdam, Vaderlandsche Fonds), Thomas de Keyser's *Portrait of Frans van Limborch* and *Portrait of Geertruyd Bisschop* (Figs. 103 and 104), and similar portraits by such artists as Ferdinand Bol,

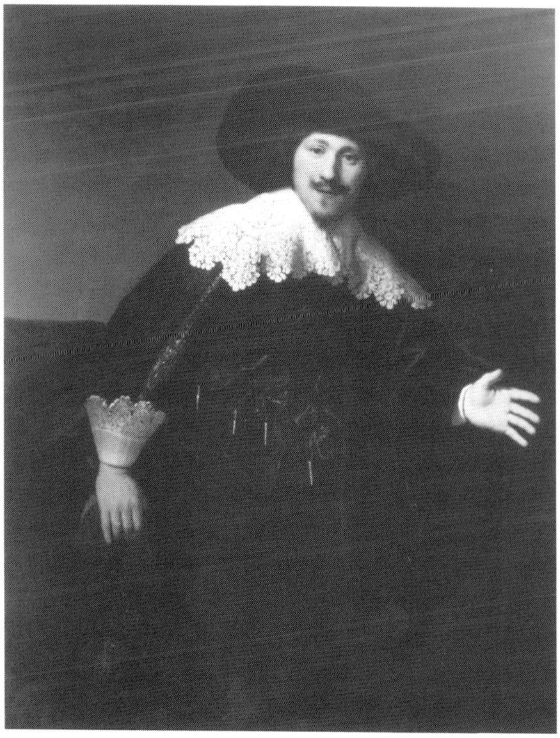

Figure 102. Rembrandt van Rijn, *Portrait of a Man Rising from His Chair*, 1633 (oil on canvas, 124.5 × 99.7 cm). Cincinnati, The Taft Museum. Photo: museum.

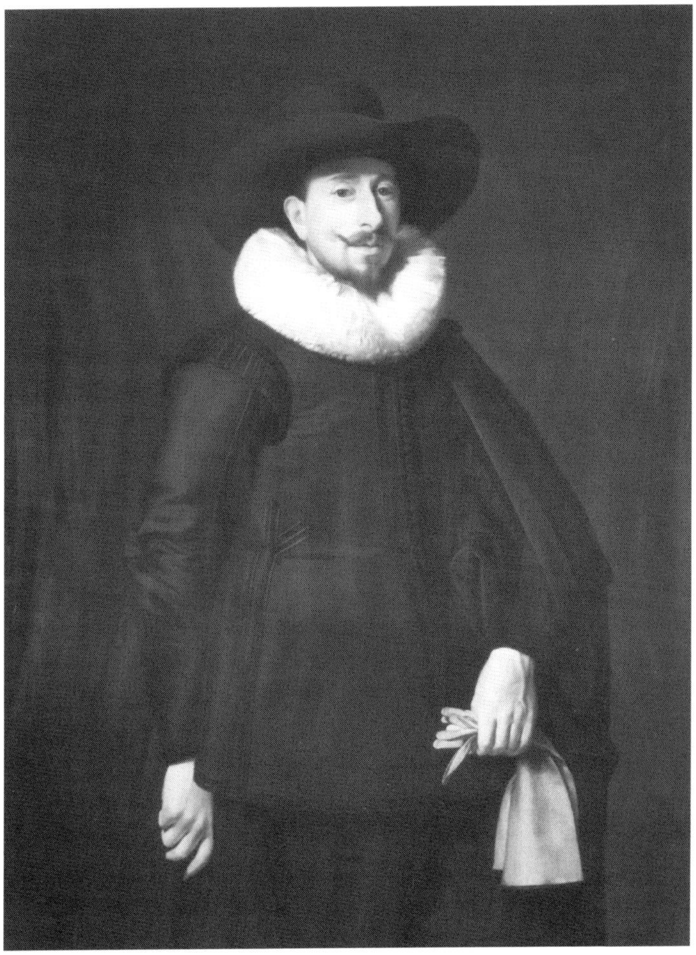

Figure 103. Thomas de Keyser, *Portrait of Frans van Limborch*, 1632 (oil on canvas, 117 × 87 cm). Hull, Ferens Art Gallery. Photo: museum.

Michiel van Miereveld, Johannes Verspronck, and Cornelis van der Voort, all have attracted little attention from students of Netherlandish painting.[34] Situated within a paradigm of stylistic evolution, they are characterized as *retardataire* and often considered only to highlight what is described as Rembrandt's unusual sensitivity to the psychology or character of his sitters. Situated within an iconological system, they appear to display no overtly symbolic elements.

Jacob Rosenberg, for example, writing in 1948, disparaged Thomas de Keyser's *Portrait of a Man* (Kassel, Staatliche Kunstsammlungen) and the *Portrait of Maria Swartenhout* by Nicholas Eliasz. Pickenoy (Amsterdam, Rijksmuseum), in comparison with Rembrandt's *Portrait of a Man* (Vienna, Kunsthistorisches Museum):

> Theirs [De Keyser's and Eliaszs.'s] was an unimaginative but fully descriptive style which combined the qualities of good photography with pronounced modelling and a moderate pictorial attraction . . . But how much greater is the coherence of design (in the portrait by Rembrandt) than in any of the portraits by Rembrandt's immediate forerunners, and how much more animated is his characterization![35]

Similarly, Albert Blankert compared two female portraits of this type by Bol with the pendant to the man so admired by Rosenberg, the *Portrait of a Woman* (Berlin, Staatliche Museen, Gemäldegalerie), which was at the time believed to be by Rembrandt:

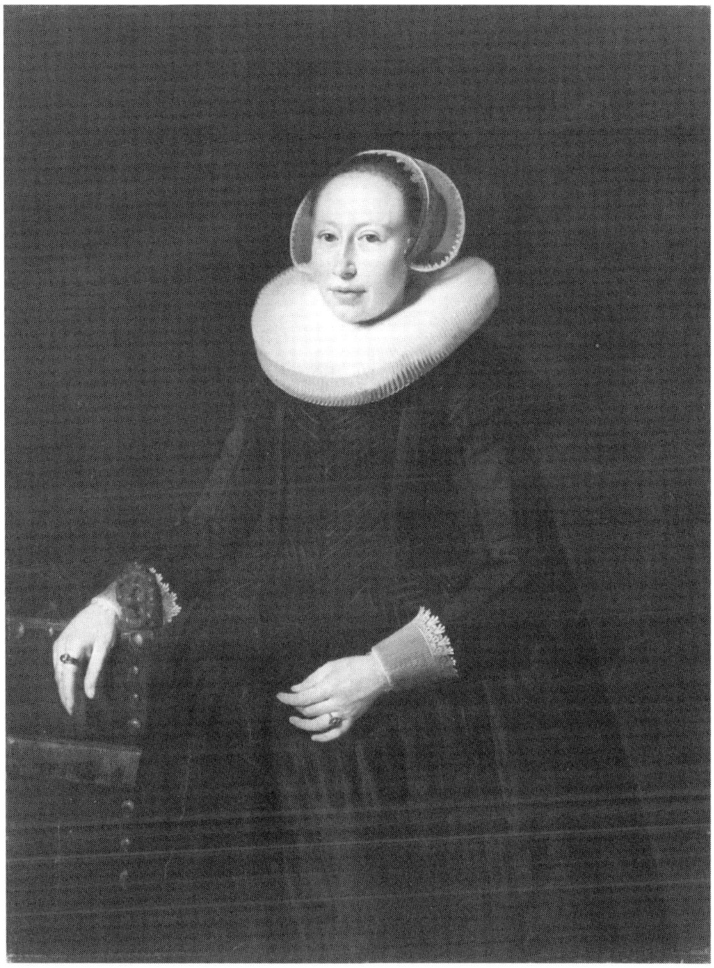

Figure 104. Thomas de Keyser, *Portrait of Geertruyd Bisschop* (oil on canvas, 118.4 × 89.6 cm). Brooklyn, Brooklyn Museum of Art. Photo: museum.

> In Bol's case this approach led to portraits in which the rendering of the individual personality is almost totally lacking – this can certainly not be said of Rembrandt's portraits . . . The relationship between external appearance and inner emotions, a problem Rembrandt posed time and again, was alien to Bol. This *Portrait of an Old Lady* in East Berlin is so stately, indeed almost hieratic, that even an association with icons is evoked. And the facial expression and attitude of the models in this and his other early portraits is so diffuse – so poly-interpretable, one might say – that one remembers them as images, not as living human beings.[36]

Such evaluations assume that these portraits' lack of "characterization," "personality," and "inner emotions" is due to the artist's lack of talent, rather than to his or her consciously choosing to depict a static figure or impassive facial expression that may in fact have articulated a meaningful expression of individuality.[37]

Such evaluations also assume that these artists unthinkingly adopted a generic formula, the motionless demeanor that, as has been noted by a number of scholars, became popular during the second half of the sixteenth century.[38] Long after more animated faces and gestures were created by seventeenth-century Dutch artists who are today most highly regarded for "animation and psychological insight," these static portraits continued to be produced by these same masters of some of the most prominent patrons and sitters of their time, and for among the highest prices paid for portraits.

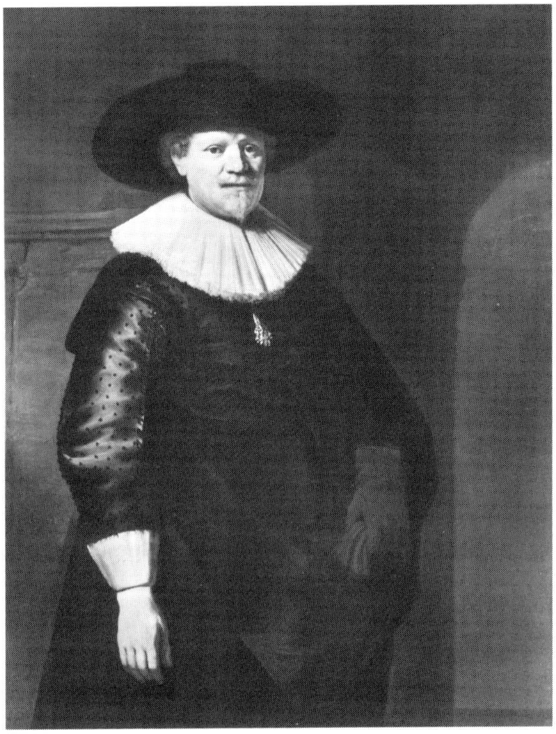

Figure 105. Rembrandt van Rijn, *Portrait of a Man*, 1633 (oil on canvas, 128.5 × 100.5 cm). Kassel, Staatliche Kunstsammlungen. Photo: museum.

Both Rembrandt and Frans Hals, for example, chose at times to portray sitters with little if any facial expression or bodily movement. Rembrandt's *Portrait of a Man* (sometimes identified as the Dutch poet Jan Harmensz. Krul) of 1633 (Fig. 105), and his *Portrait of Marten Soolmans* of 1634 (Paris, Private Collection) – of whose "bland" expressions Horst Gerson complained – should be classified among the type of Dutch portraits today considered expressionless.[39] Similarly, Frans Hals's portraits of Jacob Pietersz. Olycan and his wife Aletta Hanemans of 1625 (The Hague, Mauritshuis) depict their subjects with great dignity and as absolutely immobile.[40] Moreover, the subjects and patrons of many of these static portraits were members of the urban elite, who numbered among the most influential of society's citizens. Finally, this format was one of the most expensive produced in the Netherlands in the seventeenth century: Such portraits could cost as much as five hundred guilders each.[41]

Thus, long after mobile facial expressions and animated bodily demeanor had become part of the vocabulary of seventeenth-century Dutch portrait painting, wealthy members of the urban patriciate continued to commission portraits depicting themselves in this impassive demeanor, suggesting that such a bearing must have continued to articulate a desirable aspect of identity.[42] The standards by which we as twentieth-century viewers have come to judge Dutch portraits – movement of both the body and the face – and the methods through which we have come to investigate them – stylistic analysis or iconology based on emblems and texts – may thus be inadequate. We may assume that elite sitters did not commission costly portraits from skilled artists without some intended purpose. This purpose, however, has no meaning outside of the discourses that the image participated in producing.

In the two disparaging evaluations of three-quarter length life-sized portraits by De Keyser, Eliasz., and Bol cited previously, animation of the

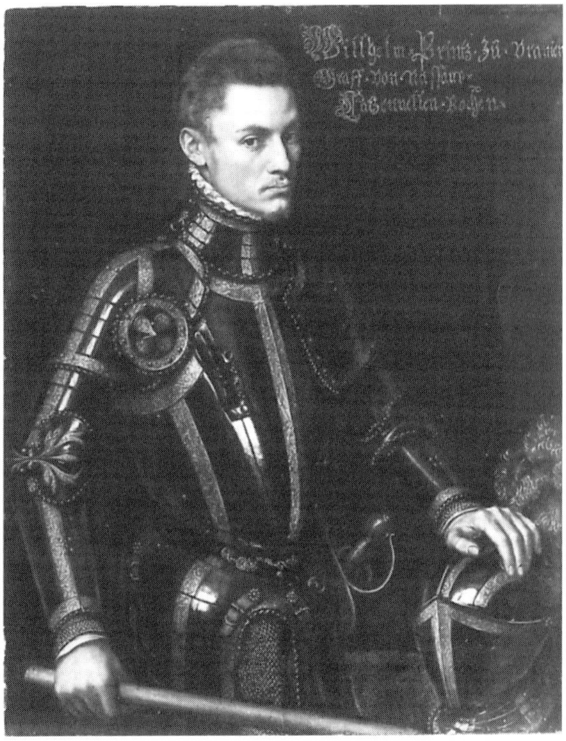

Figure 106. Antonio Moro, *Portrait of Willem of Nassau, Prince of Orange* (oil on panel, 105 × 81.5 cm). Kassel, Staatliche Kunstsammlungen. Photo: museum.

face and gestures by the body are interpreted by twentieth-century critics as psychologically revealing of their subjects, while the lack of movement is interpreted as displaying only the artist's inability to render the sitter's character or state of mind. Such statements are based on an idea of progress among artists who successively master skills of representation, an idea in which "realism" – here defined as "movement" – is an implicitly privileged term.[43] I believe, however, that the impassive face and body were as highly encoded as active ones. Specifically, for at least some Dutch sitters, the emotional calm and detachment conveyed by a tranquil face and impassive body displayed in portraits of the elite classes across Europe was associated with the neo-Stoic ideal of *tranquillitas* (tranquillity). What I shall argue, however, is that neither this impassive stance nor the neo-Stoic ideal to which it sometimes referred had fixed meanings. Rather, the associations and functions of this demeanor varied according to the discursive frame within which it was interpreted. Moreover, the mobility between these discourses, the potential for viewers to situate themselves simultaneously in more than one discursive frame, potentially exercised political effects.

The following argument develops as follows. First, as represented in portraits, this demeanor helped to define the visible signs of a psychological state described more abstractly in texts. Second, these portraits defined for their viewers the concept of *tranquillitas* as a private discourse of self-mastery available to all for the containment of their emotions. At the same time, they also engaged a second, public discourse of political theory: For a male elite, the ability to control one's emotions was a sign that one had the ability to govern others. As I will elaborate later, the visual realization of these two discourses contradicted one another, potentially producing a powerful political effect. Specifically, the private rhetoric of self-control in these Dutch portraits obscured the political power of its public counterpart. Finally, within this highly mobile, unstable, and heterogeneous society, these images imaginatively created, in sociological terms, a "status group" of individuals who affiliated themselves through the performance of this demeanor, at least in their portraits. This inclusive status group, apparently made up of citizens from a variety of backgrounds, helped to weave a social fabric at a time of great social instability and political uncertainty.

Throughout seventeenth-century Europe, men and women were conscious of the body as an eloquent vehicle for personal expression and an indicator of social distinction, a trope that had a long and distinguished history.[44] Signs for character were thought to be revealed not only by physiognomy (body shape and markings) but also through demeanor (posture and movements that could be performed). This was particularly true in court circles, where both informal and complex ritual marked social boundaries. In the Northern Netherlands, particularly during the first half of the seventeenth century, highly codified markers seem to have been less obvious than in the rest of Europe: Contemporary observers from both within the Republic and without commented that the Dutch did not designate class distinctions as obviously.[45] The hundreds of surviving Dutch portraits that do not appear to flatter the bodies of sitters, for example, suggest that idealized physiognomy was not a strong social marker. Attention to the more elaborate aspects of social behavior and demeanor may also have been less self-conscious, for fewer books of civility were published in the Northern Netherlands than elsewhere during this period.[46] We should not conclude from this, however, that dress and body demeanor were not a highly communicative means of expressing social affiliation and distinctions within the Republic; not all evidence for cultural experience must come from texts. As I elaborate later, the limited number of portrait formats and large numbers of sitters displaying similar demeanors suggest that demeanor, at least in portraiture, was highly communicative and may have played a role in social cohesion.

The three-quarter length format of these portraits was a variant of one that had been employed in the sixteenth century for members of the nobility across Europe: by Titian for the Venetian aristocracy, by Antonio Moro for Hapsburg monarchs and members of the nobility (Fig. 106), and by Peter Paul Rubens in Flanders.[47] Not only the format but also their impassive comportment was also performed by contemporary Spaniards. A Dutch traveler, François Aerssen van Sommelsdijck (1630–58), observed that in Spain "gravité naturelle ou affectée" (natural gravity or affectedness) was cherished at court, although he had found the same behavior "fort rogue et fort fière" (very haughty and very proud) among all Spaniards.[48] The *Groot ceremonie-boek der beschaafde zeeden* (Great Ceremonial Book of Civilized Manners), published in Amsterdam in 1735, directed that when walking, one's gait should be "fixed in the Spanish way, as if not daring to turn one's head."[49] Spanish "gravity" was ridiculed by Bredero in his *Spanish Brabanter*, and Aernout van Overbeke recorded a number of jokes on the subject.[50]

It is possible that the three-quarter length format of these seventeenth-century Dutch portraits of the urban elite linked their subjects with the prestige of the social and political power of their aristocratic predecessors and contemporaries across Europe. The format and demeanor also had a strong tradition in the Northern Netherlands in portraits of leading citizens (see, for example, Fig. 106).[51] In my opinion, therefore, the format – and certainly its cultural uses – must be understood within the cultural particularities of the Northern Netherlands. Herman Roodenburg has suggested that what little increase in attention to codes of conduct that began to circulate in the Northern Netherlands during the first half of the seventeenth century were inspired by Flemish immigrants bringing their culture north, rather than directly from the court in The Hague.[52] It seems quite possible that the renewed interest in this format may have also been initially prompted by the social needs of this group. The popular ridicule expressed by Bredero suggests that the demeanor was easily recognized in Dutch culture and associated with the Flemish. Such ridicule does not suggest that it was eschewed by native Dutch men and women, however. On the contrary, ridicule helps reinforce boundaries between acceptable and unacceptable versions of the same behavior within a widely understood paradigm.

One of the most powerful signs of character that could be conveyed by the body was this impassive demeanor, associated with *tranquillitas* of spirit. *Tranquillitas* was an emotional state that became a valued personal ideal in the wake of a sixteenth-century revival of imperial Roman Stoicism. While influential in humanist circles across Europe, the Northern Netherlands was an important center of this movement.[53] Two of its major proponents had lived and worked there; each published influential editions of Seneca's philosophical works. Desiderius Erasmus's edition first appeared in 1515 (corrected edition Basel 1529) and another by Justus Lipsius was printed in Antwerp in 1605.[54] Seventeenth-century Dutch culture was pervaded and deeply shaped by Stoic ideals being taught and discussed at the University of Leiden, where Lipsius had been a professor between 1579 and 1591. The single most influential book on the subject was Lipsius's own *De constantia libri duo alloquium praecipue continent in publicis malis* (Two Books on Constancy, Which Especially Contain Consolation in Times of Public Adversity), first published in Latin in Leiden and Antwerp in 1584. It immediately became an international best-seller, being printed forty-four times in the original Latin, fifteen times in French translation, and in several other European languages including a Dutch translation published the same year.[55] Lipsius followed this with two additional neo-Stoic treatises, his *Manuductionis ad stoicam philosophiam libri tres* and *Physiologia stoicorum libri tres* (Three Books [Concerning] the Natural Philosophy of the Stoics), published both in Antwerp and Paris in 1604.

Stoic philosophy defined four passions, each of which were believed to be produced by concerns about good and evil, in the present and the future. These are distress (the result of concern about evil in the present), fear (the result of concern about evil in the future), delight (the result of concern about good in the present), and lust or desire (the result of concern about good in the future).[56] These passions were generated by man himself as a response to external events. These unleashed passions plunged him into evil and misery. As Erasmus put it, "As the body cannot support pleasures unless it is in good health, so the mind is not capable of true happiness unless free from fear and the other emotions."[57]

Following ancient Stoics, Renaissance man also believed that although he cannot change the circumstances of his life, the turbulence of the world cannot engender these passions if, through reason, he responds to it with indifference. Such rational control produces Constancy, through which man may confront what Lipsius called "this very sea of calamities."[58] Lipsius elaborated: "By Constancy I mean the correct and immovable strength of a mind that is neither elated by externals nor depressed by change mishaps. I define and understand Strength to be a firmness implanted in the mind, not by Opinion, but by good judgment and correct Reason."[59] The highest possible state of man in his earthly life, then, according to Pierre Charron in a book published in Leiden in 1601, is "tranquillitie of the spirit. . . . This is that great and rich treasure, which . . . is the fruit of all our labors and studies, the crowne of wisdome."[60] Tranquillity, the product of rational self-control, was a proud achievement attesting to a state of highest ethical virtue.

The control of the passions was an ideal in wide circulation and, in theory at least, available to all men and women. A broad spectrum of society was exposed to its principles in one form or another. The fundamental tenants of neo-Stoicism run broadly through much of the philosophy, literature, and painting produced in the seventeenth-century Netherlands. René Descartes, who lived and wrote his most influential works in the Northern Netherlands, spelled out the neo-Stoicism behind his *Discours de la method* (Discourse on Method), published by Jean Maire in Leiden in 1637.[61] In a letter to Elizabeth of Bohemia of the summer of 1645, he wrote:

> Seneca should have taught us all the principal truths whose knowledge is necessary to facilitate the practice of virtue. . . . It seems to me that every man can make himself content without any external assistance, provided that he respects three conditions, which are related to the three roles of morality which I put in the *Discourse on Method*.[62]

Spinoza's *Ethica* (Ethics) of 1677 similarly describes the passions as responsible for all of man's misery.[63] Contemporary Dutch literature and drama also promoted these concepts in plays by a number of authors who knew and corresponded with Lipsius directly.[64] Other popular texts such as emblem books and the best-selling moralizing writings of Jacob Cats reinforced the ideal of moderation and self-control. Northern painters, too, demonstrated an interest in Seneca through representations of both the man, of Diogenes, and occasionally Hercules, the subject of one of his plays.[65] Restraint is, of course, one of the themes in Dutch painting most often identified in recent iconological studies. Perhaps the finest tribute to the pervasiveness of the philosophy throughout Europe are the satires and parodies that it spawned, including scenes in Jakob Bidermann's *Cenodoxus*.[66]

Neo-Stoic ideals did not remain in the abstract realm of philosophy, drama, and painting, for Dutch men and women attempted to apply them to daily life. Personal letters reveal the attempt to use Stoic models to weather personal tragedy, frequently expressing the frustration at its failure. At the death of the wife of P. C. Hooft, for example, Tesselschade Visscher wrote of how she was surprised at the depth of his grief: "How now, dear sir, could you who have acquired such a large store of steadfast wisdom, be made miserable by the necessary course of the world?" Hooft replied: "How can he, who has always picked up pins and nails to fix what he loved securely to his heart, when it is ripped from there, be left with anything but unbearable rifts?"[67]

The broad appeal of self-mastery as an idea – even when not specifically identified with the ancient philosophy – is not surprising in this period of great social, economic, and political change. While the Northern Netherlands was relatively free from the war raging across the rest of Europe, for example, the threat of resumed hostilities was never far away. The full title of Lipsius's popular *De constantia libri duo* provides an indication of why neo-Stoic philosophy appealed so strongly to contemporary men and women: "Two Books on Constancy, Which Especially Contain Consolation in Times of Public Adversity."

In contrast to its personal and subjective applications that were in theory available to all, the concept of *tranquillitas* simultaneously participated in a second, public, realm. As Gerhard Oestreich has convincingly argued, neo-Stoicism lay behind much of the political theory of the seventeenth century that originated at the University of Leiden.[68] It posited that men's passions were in need of control by reason, a control provided by state apparatuses. Thus, those who could exercise private self-control possessed the reason necessary to govern others. Seneca's phrase, "He is most powerful who has power over himself," was echoed throughout the literature in the sixteenth and seventeenth centuries. Rabelais, for example, asked, "How shall I be able to rule over others, than have not full power and command of myself?"[69] Philip Massinger asserted in 1624 that "he that would govern others, first should be / Master of himself."[70]

In contrast to the appeal of the philosophy as a discourse of private psychology, this political philosophy was potentially an elitist doctrine and was deployed as such in other parts of Europe. It was generally assumed that the male social elite – the most wealthy and politically powerful members of society – could achieve *tranquillitas* more readily than women and especially the lower classes. The latter, considered to be closer to animals in their inability to control their violent emotions, were believed to be more susceptible to their passions. A "regular and conscious feature of the Stoic prescription for human trouble [was] that it was available only to the few," writes Bouwsma, continuing:

> The aristocratic impulses in Renaissance society found support in the powerful analogy between the order of the universe, the order of the human personality, and the social order, which suggested that society too must consist of both a higher rational principle and a lower, duller and less reliable component to which the higher force, personified by an elite, was in the nature of things superior . . . One of the marks of the Stoic humanist was his constant, rather nervous concern to differentiate himself from the vulgar crowd and to reassure himself somewhat in the manner at times discerned in the Protestant elect, of his spiritual superiority.[71]

Throughout the rest of Europe, this ideal was attached to monarchs and aristocrats and a select group of humanists. In the Northern Netherlands, however, exactly who was included in the class of men and women who had the ability to control their passions with their reason, experience *tranquillitas*, and therefore govern others was not clear. Oestreich describes how widely pervasive neo-Stoic ideals were in Dutch public culture, and its impact on both economic and political life:

> Neostoicism also demanded self-discipline and the extension of the duties of the ruler and the moral education of the army, the officials, and indeed the whole people, to a life of work, frugality, dutifulness and obedience. The result was a general enhancement of social discipline in all spheres of life, and this enhancement produced, in its turn, a change in the ethos of the individual and his self-perception. This change was to play a crucial role in the later development of both modern industrialism and democracy, both of which presupposed a work ethic and the willingness of the individual to take responsibility.[72]

The broad demographic basis of these ideals was self-consciously articulated at the time. In the Latin oration that he delivered at the opening of the new Athenaeum Illustré (which became Amsterdam University in 1877) on January 8, 1632, Caspar Barlaeus described with pride how the study of philosophy placed the material aspects of life in perspective and fostered self-control among the population as a whole. He praises the "public chair for the study of philosophy and literature . . . [so that] men shall better learn to measure this wealth by its true value, *learning its use from the works of the philosophers.*" Barlaeus also admired the results of this study, continuing, "when I behold your city . . . I discover the versatility, the wisdom, of those I am studying, the respect for the laws, the obedience of the *residents, their composure, and first and foremost, their desire for order* [italics added].[73]

As I have suggested, this composure could be expressed on, and read from, the body. Balthasar Castiglione described models in currency in internal court circles when in his *Book of the Courtier* he praised "a quiet manner as an enviable mark of the grave and dignified man ruled by reason rather than appetite."[74] Across Europe, the ideal of *tranquillitas* remained in circulation well into the seventeenth century. Edward, Earl of Clarendon, similarly praised the "grave" demeanor of Thomas Howard, Earl of Arundel, as that of "the most considerable men all which drew the eyes of most, and the reverence of many, towards him, as the image and representative of the primitive nobility, and native gravity of the nobles, when they had been most venerable."[75]

As a representation of the body, a portrait could also display this ideal. William Heckscher has suggested that the impassive facial expression of Holbein the Younger's portrait of Erasmus of 1523 was a conscious expression of *tranquillitas*.[76] Erasmus's half-length portrait shows the humanist standing behind a desk, his hands on a book, and before an elaborate background that includes an ornamental pilaster and a curtain hanging from a rod pulled back to reveal a shelf piled with books and other objects. The portraits produced in the Northern Netherlands a century later show their subjects in knee-length, displaying few gestures, and standing in a relatively unarticulated space. I believe that such portraits mediated experience and helped to produce a series of frameworks within which individuals could understand themselves and their social relations. It is to these potential cultural functions that I now turn.

By displaying a recognizable demeanor, the sign for an internal state, these portraits provided a model of behavior for their viewers. Seventeenth-century discussions of both literary theory generally and education directly, emphasize that the most effective means of education and of moving men's emotions were through the provision of models of specific individuals in particular situations rather than ideal types or abstract explanations. In his well-known *Ars Poetica* (Art of Poetry), Horace described how this should be accomplished in poetry through empathy. "Not enough is it for poems to have beauty," he wrote, "they must have charm, and lead the hearer's soul where they will. As men's faces smile on those who smile, so they respond to those who weep."[77] In drama, Daniel Heinsius advocates characterization that uses models and examples, specifically actors who act out their emotions in particular situations rather than characters who declare their intentions and feelings.[78] The book of manners, Giovanni della Casa's popular *Galateo*, initially published in 1546, demonstrates several points by giving examples of a behavior enacted by real persons writing:

> The fact is that things are more easily said than done. Also, most men, and especially laymen and uneducated persons like me, are always readier with the senses than with the intellect; therefore, we learn better through specific examples than through general principles and syllogisms (which in the clearer vernacular tongue must mean the reasons) . . . to live by and illustrate in my habits the above-mentioned rules, making of them a visible example. . . . This is so because in matters dealing with manners and customs of men it is not enough to know the theory and the rule, it is also necessary, in order to put them into effect, to practice.[79]

Among the subjects considered by contemporary debates within literary and dramatic theory was that of how to curb the reader/viewer's passions, troublesome both to his or her spiritual comfort and to society's stability. Some argued that the emotions should be aroused in order that men and women may rationally examine them; others that this arousal itself purged them, habituated men and women to the experience of taming them.[80] The educated seventeenth-century viewer would have thus been trained by such conventions to respond more to demonstration than to the description of abstractions. And people on the street would have been familiar with the techniques of demonstration through sermons and popular plays.

While portraits ranked low in the hierarchy of genres because they pictured real men and women rather than abstract ideals, paradoxically it was their representation of distinct human beings that increased their rhetorical power. This was recognized at the time. The Dutch humanist and diplomat Constantijn Huygens, for example, confided to his diary in about 1630 that portraits

> perform a noble work, that more than any other is necessary for our human needs, that through them we in a true sense do not die; furthermore as descendants we can speak intimately with our most distant ancestors. This pleasure is so dear to me that nothing more agreeable can befall me than reading or hearing stories about someone's life and character – whether he be a good or bad man – (and this sort of history particularly attracts me) [which] is made easier by looking at his portrait.[81]

That images should actively move or psychically change their viewers was a value that was derived from the parallels drawn between painting and poetry. Joannes Vossius makes this clear in the last chapter of the first book of *De quatuor artibus popularibus, de philologia, et scientiis mathematics . . . libri tres* (Three Books Concerning the Four Popular Arts, Philology, and the Mathematical Sciences), published posthumously in Amsterdam in 1650, where he compares painting and rhetoric.[82] It was believed that viewing portraits could involuntarily move the viewer and empathetically produce the internal state – here self-control – that was represented.

Portraits such as those under discussion here were viewed in two contexts: Some three-quarter length life-sized portraits of the princes of Orange and their extended families hung in public places like town halls; others of leading citizens hung in guild chambers or other semipublic spaces; pair portraits, those that included women, hung in domestic spaces, including front halls where they would have been seen by family members and friends.[83] As a medium of communication, then, in general these portraits spoke to other members of the same classes from which they were commissioned.

The potential effects of these portraits took place through the interaction of discourses produced in two spheres. First, as I mentioned, *tranquillitas* was an attribute of character in the private sphere, produced above all by the relation of individuals with themselves. Portraits displaying this trait were often commissioned of a husband and wife (Figs. 103 and 104), underscoring the private nature of the exercise of restraint. These images do not overtly assert power relations. Standing to her husband's left, the viewer's right, the wife reflects her husband's demeanor. These respective positions are very often the only indication of an hierarchic relationship.[84] At most, the husband is a model for his wife; he does not dominate her. Moreover, many of these images show the man hatless – often holding his hat – in the viewer's presence. Their subjects thus do not even assert social rank over the viewer.

As Norbert Elias has observed, power during the seventeenth century was increasingly internalized, moving from agents of material, external, coercion to psychic, internal, discipline.[85] I would like to suggest that these portraits participated in this internalization of discipline, because in presenting a model for behavior, they help to create a standard. By picturing self-discipline they made concrete an abstract concept and an example of comportment for their viewers. The power of this model is generated by the social dynamics of normativity: Paradoxically, men and women achieve their "individuality" not by deviation from a standard but by approximating the ideal state as closely as possible. These portraits promoted personal values that must have helped to transform conceptions of the individual and attitudes toward their behavior in the world, helping to produce a disciplined self that fundamentally altered both Netherlandish society and its political structures.

At the same time, these images functioned in a second, related, sphere: that of social prestige and, for their male subjects, of political power. Simply as objects in their size and support (frequently expensive panel), and as images displaying costly silk and brocade garments, jewels, and lace, these portraits assert their sitters' social and economic status.[86] I have mentioned that elsewhere in Europe the format and demeanor was most frequently employed for male subjects, monarchs, and aristocrats, and thus engaged a political discourse of rulership. In the Northern Netherlands, this theme was engaged by some portraits in this format as, for example, the series of officer portraits painted by Jan Anthonisz. van Ravesteyn probably for Prince Maurits (The Hague, Mauritshuis). Because women in the Northern Netherlands were excluded from political positions, their appearance in these portraits in larger numbers (usually paired with their husband) emphasizes the ethical and thus social, rather than political, superiority of their class. (Indeed, Dutch men seem to have been relatively reluctant to advertise political power publicly: Members of governmental organizations rarely commissioned public group portraits.)

How any particular viewer related to these multiple referents in both the private and public realms would have depended upon their perceived relationship to these ethical, social, and political systems. Representing an ideal toward which all individuals could strive, these portraits could mirror their viewers' ideals and affirm a sense of self and ethical worth. At the same time, any viewer who knew that they would never hold political office, or attain the wealth or social standing of the individuals pictured, would probably also experience deference. While modelling themselves on such images might promise the viewer equal moral power with the sitter, they could never hope to attain equal social – much less political – rank.

The very instability of the referents of the format and pictured demeanor for a large number of viewers, however, contributed to its power. The precise social, economic, and political positions of many viewers in the Northern Netherlands at this time was unclear: Eminence in these areas was neither always congruent nor fixed. As Peter Burke has observed, the economic elite of major cities at this time were not always the same individuals as the political elite.[87] These indistinct boundaries were not only a quality of social life but were also a characteristic of this genre of portraiture, for they seem to have been commissioned by a relatively broad social spectrum of men and women. At the least they pictured individuals with different religious beliefs, different political affiliations, and different regional origins. Because the names of the subjects of so many of these sitters have been lost, the actual composition and extent of the group of men and women pictured in this format remain relatively unclear. Of those whose identities have come down to us, many were members of relatively wealthy and influential – although not always regent – families. It is possible that the names of so many other sitters have been lost over the centuries because at least some of them were not members of the economic and political elite.

For the broad segment of the population whose social and political positions were unclear or changing, these portraits could invoke these two apparently contradictory responses, mirroring and deference, simultaneously.[88] On the one hand, the viewer would have to acknowledge the legitimacy of the political power by any regent portrayed. At the same time, these portraits suggest that the viewer actually "ruled him or herself": Any authority claimed by pictured members of the regent class could be viewed as merely a material formality. Together, these two experiences could unconsciously co-opt the viewer into acquiescing to the legitimacy of the social and political power claimed by members of the regent class while reducing the apparent strength of that power. Specifically, if a viewer believed that they were ethical equals, the economic or political power possessed by another individual is less absolute.

What I am suggesting, then, is that this mobility of meaning between discourses in the public and private realms made these portraits a potentially effective vehicle of community cohesion and social control. The relatively limited number of portrait formats, compositions, and pictured demeanors – particularly before mid-century – appears to correspond with the limited number of codes of class distinction reported by contemporary observers.[89] It seems possible to me that these images may have helped to forge communalities among otherwise disparate social groups, creating what sociologists call a "status group" that was relatively inclusive. They may have created a cohesion among this larger group of individuals who, in this relatively mobile society, wished to see themselves as, and affiliate themselves with, an elite whose boundaries were very unclear. These portraits, therefore, had the potential to foster among this relatively mobile and heterogeneous group of individuals a class identity that papered-over difference and power. They imply that even if some of their subjects and viewers – particularly women and nonregents – do not actually exercise the economic or political power of others pictured in the format, nonetheless they possess shared interests. These portraits thus produce an imaginary cohesiveness among a heterogeneous group, securing a sense of commonly held concerns that could be marshalled to elide social contradictions. Circulating in pictorial form, this ethos discursively functioned to foster an emerging consensual society.

This process becomes more understandable in light of seventeenth-century demographics and events. First, Dutch society was relatively heterogeneous. It included a high percentage of immigrants from elsewhere in Europe – especially Flanders – and of men and women who moved from their place of birth within the country and frequently from rural to urban areas. This along with the possibility of some social mobility may have resulted in fewer codes generally recognized across class and regional boundaries. Second, although there are individual examples of self-conscious attempts to assert social status, at the same time there must have been a strong incentive to minimize certain kinds of social distinctions, particularly before the Peace of Münster.[90] Widely disparate social groups needed to work together against common enemies, from the Spanish empire on the one hand to internal divisions that threatened the viability of the Republic on the other. Indeed, social stratification became more apparent only after mid-century, paralled by the production of a larger number of portrait formats.

This discussion does not mean to suggest that all portraits in this format depict their sitters as self-conscious Stoics. In some cases portraits may have appeared stiff because the artist may in fact not have had the models or the skill to utilize a more complex pose. In other cases, once in circulation the format may have been selected for reasons of fashion. In the end, however, since "identity" can only be understood within a discursive system, control of that system is power. This control was exercised, of course, by those who could afford those portraits, which in turn helped to define the discursive systems that gave them status and power.

Portraits are potential sites of cultural contestation: embodiments of abstract terms, in constant flux, through which identity and power are defined. We will never completely recover how contemporaries experienced these portraits, nor the extent of the political and ethical discourses inscribed within them. Traditional art-historical studies frequently attempt to reduce an image to a single message. The multiple discourses that these portraits engaged, however – at times consciously and directly, at other times unconsciously and by implication – provided the source of their real power in lived experience.

How to Sit, Stand, and Walk

TOWARD A HISTORICAL ANTHROPOLOGY OF DUTCH PAINTINGS AND PRINTS*

Herman Roodenburg

I. AN UNWILLING LITTLE NECK

In 1632 Constantijn Huygens and his wife, Suzanne van Baerle, noticed much to their consternation that the head of their eldest son, Constantijn Jr., inclined a bit to the left. The boy, of whom we have a small portrait drawing (Haarlem, Teylers Museum) was then four years old. At first, the parents decided to refrain from interfering, though the mother had considered the possibility of bringing the child to a "famous peasant," possibly a bonesetter, in the village of De Rijp.[1] For the moment the parents turned to other, more "gentle" methods. They gave the boy a stiff collar, attached ribbons to his bonnet, and also steamed his little neck. It was only in 1637, when all these efforts had proved to be of no avail, that Huygens decided to have his son operated on by a physician from the city of Utrecht. It was probably not a very pleasant experience: the doctor made an incision two inches long in the poor boy's neck, separating (according to his own report) the many entangled sinews there and greasing the whole machinery with some oil.[2]

It is a weird and rather dismal story, but there is no reason to doubt its veracity; I have taken it from Huygens's own notes on the childhood and adolescence of his children. The charming little anecdotes contained in these entries and also the parents' feelings, their love and concern in seeing their children grow up, make these recollections among the most vivid and important documents within the history of Dutch family life. We learn, for example, about the illnesses of the children and the apprehension of their parents at such moments. We also learn about the first cautious steps of the children, the first words they uttered, their early presence of mind and their first lessons in reading, writing, Latin, mathematics, and music. Clearly, Huygens had ambitious plans for his children, especially for his sons, who received a broad, humanist training in preparation for professional careers in the highest circles of the Dutch Republic.[3]

Considering these high hopes, it comes as even more of a surprise that the parents exposed their eldest son to such a risky operation. Of course, in the years preceding the operation, they had tried other solutions. Moreover, feeling horrified about the potential incision, Huygens had asked the physician for a detailed description of the operation before he finally consented. But it remained a drastic intervention. Constantijn was away from his family for months and would even miss the birth of his little sister, Suzanne. Eventually, things took a very tragic turn when his mother contracted a fever in the childbed and died a few months later. In the

* I wish to thank Reindert Falkenburg, Wayne Franits, and Mark Meadow for their advice and assistance in preparing this essay. [Editor's note: Herman Roodenburg's essay is a revised and expanded version of his earlier article: "Over scheefhalzen en zwellende heupen; enige argumenten voor een historische antropologie van de zeventiende-eeuwse schilderkunst," *De Zeventiende Eeuw* 9 (1993), pp. 15–68. The present version was translated from the Dutch by the author and Wayne Franits.]

meantime, Constantijn's neck had definitely improved – the operation was a great success – but he would not see his mother again; the physician had deemed it better that he stay in Utrecht.

II. THE IMPORTANCE OF AN ELEGANT AND UPRIGHT POSTURE

Taking a closer look at the events, the seeming contradiction between the parents' plans for their children and the hazardous operation quickly disappears. Indeed, it seems quite likely that it was those very same ambitious plans – namely, the parents' wish to prepare their children for promising careers – that had caused them to become so alarmed about Constantijn's neck. During most of the early modern period in Europe, it was one of the most important requirements that well-mannered people keep their bodies and their heads erect. The elite had to know how to move, not only figuratively but also quite literally. Adopting an elegant and upright posture was therefore a central tenet within the prevailing codes of behavior.

Of course, the contemporary manners books deal with many more requirements than just that of an erect posture. For example, in his ground-breaking study on the "civilizing process," Norbert Elias strongly emphasized the rules governing the essential activities of life.[4] He discussed the more psychoanalytically significant prescriptions concerning urinating, defecating, and hiding one's nudity and also the lesser ones concerning blowing the nose, sneezing, coughing, and spitting – in short, all those activities that "we share with the animals," as the author of one of the most important manners books, the Frenchman Antoine de Courtin, explained.[5] But the manuals are far richer than Elias, with his strongly Freudian point of view, suggested. Generally speaking, they established codes of behavior, if only among the elite, for all sorts of relations in public.[6] In fact, the insights and explanations set forth in these treatises constitute an early, though already highly accomplished, example of the study of nonverbal communication. Thus, many of the manuals deal at length with phenomena such as posture, gesture, facial expression, and even paralingual phenomena (the pitch or intensity of the voice). Attention to such details, so readers were told, was a prerequisite for "conversing agreeably," for successfully moving in the upper walks of life. In order to explain the rules, the authors included all sorts of blunders and *faux pas*. We may rightly say that the manuals are teeming with all the larger and smaller social mistakes that for our own period were analyzed so carefully (and almost lovingly) by Erving Goffman.[7]

Erasmus's *De civilitate morum puerilium* (On Civility in Children) of 1530, one of the most influential manners books of all times, is a case in point. Elias discussed this little treatise at length, but Erasmus also cautioned his readers – a point not mentioned by Elias – that well-bred people should always keep their bodies upright. Of course, they should not exaggerate: "it is a sign of conceit to bend the body backwards." Instead, they should strive for a graceful and natural posture, a certain casualness that was also stressed by Baldassare Castiglione in his well-known *Cortegiano* (The Book of Courtier) of 1528.[8] "It is becoming," as Erasmus explained, "that the body is gently raised." Equally important was the way one carried one's head: "Let the neck hang nor to the left nor to the right side," a sure sign of "hypocrisy." And, since his book was written for a young boy, he even added a fatherly admonition: "Those who have become used to holding their heads to one side grow fixed in that habit, with the result that their efforts to alter it in later life are to no avail."[9]

We can trace the popularity of Erasmus's book not only in the numerous editions and translations that appeared all over Europe but also in its impact on manners books published later under the *ancien régime*. An interesting example is a booklet that was printed in Antwerp in 1546 and that, for the purpose of memorizing its contents, was written as a series of questions and answers. One of the questions that schoolboys had to answer was: "Who are used to bending the neck to the shoulders and to resting the head on them?" The answer was brief and to the point: "rude and lazy dreamers and those who fill their stomach so much that they desire only to dream."[10] Two centuries later, in the *Groot cere-*

monie-boeck der beschaafde zeeden (Great Ceremonial Book of Civilized Manners), published in 1735, the author still cautioned his readers that they should adopt the upright posture, thereby avoiding having their heads "constantly hanging to one side or the other."[11]

Unfortunately, it is still unclear when and, especially, to what degree the rules of *civilité* (civility) and *courtoisie* (politeness) were adopted in the Dutch Republic. It has been stressed that before the middle of the seventeenth century hardly any manuals on civility were translated into Dutch. Even Erasmus's little treatise, popular as it may have been in other European countries, was not widely read in the Northern Netherlands.[12] Judging from such data, one would almost say that the seventeenth-century Dutch, those *botmuilen* (literally "blunt mouths"), as they were disparagingly labeled by the Flemish, were hardly accustomed to any *civilité* or *courtoisie* and that their manners were still as "unfeigned" and "plain" as Erasmus described them jokingly in his *Praise of Folly* of 1509.[13]

But we should remind ourselves that the elite, the classes that were most interested in adopting the rules of civility, had a reasonable command of languages. Many of the regents and other wealthy citizens read French, had access to the French manuals on civility, and could thus disseminate the new rules among their families and acquaintances. Indeed, there were many oral and extralingual channels for learning social deportment. For example, in the course of the seventeenth century, it became more and more habitual for the sons of the elite to make the "Grand Tour." They traveled to France and Italy and could thus observe the rules of civility as they were practiced by French and Italian elites. At the same time, it became increasingly more common for the daughters of the Dutch upper classes to attend the so-called French schools. There they received a general cultural education (including learning French), but they were also instructed in the rules of *civilité* and *courtoisie*. In addition to these channels, education was provided by private instructors and dancing masters and, of course, by one's own parents.[14]

An early, and for us quite interesting, example is the education that Huygens received from his own father, Christiaan Huygens.[15] From 1578 to 1584, this extraordinary man had served at the court of William of Orange as one of his secretaries. It was there, so the son tells us, that he had observed the manners "deemed proper for young people of rank" and had apparently decided "to put this behaviour into practice at home with his children."[16] Part of the lessons consisted of teaching them the complexities of greeting and leave taking: "in the covering and baring of their heads, in offering their hands, grasping the knee, lowering the head and raising it for a candid look, and stretching the leg backwards." The father considered it of the utmost importance that his children be able to move in an easy and exemplary manner, even in the company of their superiors: "In meeting with people of higher rank we were not allowed to be more nervous than in meeting with people of equal rank, provided of course that the standards of civility and due respect were observed."[17]

III. THE USES OF CORSETS AND PHYSICAL EXERCISE

Before discussing other aspects of Huygens's education, let us first take a look at another source that may inform us about the significance of an upright posture. After all, it was not only the parents' consent but also the doctor's willingness to perform an operation that had subjected the little Constantijn to the knife. Indeed, doctors were quite interested in the carriage of the body, in the furthering of a good and healthy posture. As the French historian Georges Vigarello has argued, from the end of the sixteenth century on, the role of parents and physicians in overseeing children's growth, in molding, shaping, and straightening their bodies, was heavily emphasized.[18]

Vigarello based most of his observations on France, but we can easily confirm his findings with some data from the Dutch Republic. Quite telling is a letter written in 1733 by Count Willem Bentinck to his future wife, Charlotte von Aldenburg. Apparently, Charlotte, who was then seventeen or eighteen years old, had some problems with her spinal column. For a couple of years, she had worn a stiff leather corset that covered her body from the hips to the armpits. But the count was still dissatisfied with her ungraceful pose. He advised her "to carry herself upright, with her shoulders backwards." "When walking," so the count continued, "put your feet outwards, draw in your bottom, carry your head high and lofty, throw out your chest and let your arms hang loosely: that is how it should be." Not surprisingly, the marriage was unsuccessful.[19]

According to the doctors, the first months of life were already important, for it was then that the desired uprightness should be established, especially in swaddling the child. In 1636 the renowned Dutch physician Johan van Beverwijck observed that the children in his country were swaddled "from head to foot" because in this way the limbs were "best protected and kept straight."[20] Clearly, the straitjackets that the children of the elite had to wear until they were five or six years old served a similar purpose. In the middle of the eighteenth century, when opposition to such habits began, an opponent commented that most mothers put their children into straitjackets "because it is common practice and also, as they say, to keep them upright and to lend them a good posture."[21] The eighteenth-century physician Petrus Camper shared these criticisms. He challenged the general opinion that little children could only develop an erect posture with the help of such devices, objecting in particular to the stays that girls had to wear even beyond the age of five or six. "If the boys can grow upright without them, why not the girls," he wondered. It was an abuse that he had mostly observed in the towns, particularly "among the rich."[22]

Almost simultaneously with corsets for children, those for women had become popular as well. Unfortunately, our knowledge of the corsets' history is still as fragmentary as that of the children's stays, but it seems likely that the fashion originated at the French court and then spread to the courts and elites of other countries.[23] The French poet Henri Estienne spotted the new practices in 1579: "the ladies now use the whalebone corset," he wrote, and they do so "in order to keep straighter."[24] Corsets must have found their way from the French court and upper classes to the towns of Flanders, where the wealthy ladies were equally fond of them.[25] These same ladies may have introduced the new fashion in the Dutch Republic, particularly after the fall of Antwerp in 1585, when so many refugees, even from among the richest families, had fled to the north.[26]

Of course, a similarly erect posture was required of the sons of the elite, though most of them were freed from the corsets after the age of five or six. Instead, they were urged to exercise, to practice dancing, riding, or fencing, in order to develop the desired uprightness.[27] Looking at the Southern Netherlands, we encounter such views in a little known tract on the education of princes and nobles, written by Philips Marnix van St. Aldegonde. As it happens, Marnix and Christiaan Huygens were close acquaintances, a fact that makes the tract's contents even more interesting.[28] It was written around 1583, at the request of Jan van Nassau, the elder brother of William of Orange. Although the text was known to a restricted circle, it was only published in 1615, well after Marnix's death.[29] What strikes one directly is Marnix's emphasis on relieving mental exercise with physical exercise. Books are important, so the author tells us, but so is relaxation. Boys should exert their limbs and thereby develop an elegant gait and posture.[30] At the same time, they should avoid "rough lumpishness in manners and appearance," as well as the "shocking frivolity, which is currently often in fashion at the courts of monarchs and princes."[31]

It is not unlikely that Christiaan Huygens was one of those acquaintances who were allowed to read the manuscript, as he obviously shared his friend's ideas on the benefits of physical exercise. He provided his sons with lessons in fencing and horse riding and also attached great importance to dancing.[32] In 1610 he even decided to give the dancing lessons himself. Interestingly, when another friend, the Amsterdam minister Werner Helmichius, had reproached him for doing so, he had answered that he did not understand why the ministers made such a fuss about it. To him it was important that his children "from early on would get used to those things that create beauty in appearance and posture and make the gait elegant and unconstrained."[33] It is again his son who recorded this event. In another one of his recollections, he tells us that he loved skating with his friends, for example, when the meadows were under water. We are subtly informed that his skill attracted everyone's attention but also that he adopted "a graceful posture, because my father was also in this sort of relaxation very particular about this."[34]

Naturally, Constantijn Huygens conveyed these same attitudes to his children. We have no information on skating, but in 1644 he provided his eldest sons, Constantijn Jr. and Christiaan, with dancing lessons "in order that the body was put so much the better into good shape."[35] It is possible that some thirty years earlier, the period in which Huygens had received his own dancing lessons, the importance of dancing for developing good manners and a graceful posture (along with the very act of dancing itself) was still contested. But by the 1640s, when his own children learned to dance, most of the regent and other wealthy families must have shared Huygens's feelings. In 1643 the famous minister Gisbertus Voetius even complained that such arguments were repeatedly foisted upon him; so many parents had told him that the art of dancing would enhance their children's "*beleeftheyt der manieren*" (civility of manners).[36]

IV. THE ELEGANCE OF A SWELLING HIP

So far, using examples from various sources, I have tried to indicate that the carriage of the body was far from neutral within the Dutch Republic. In a wide range of sources – in manners books, in medical and educational writings, in memoirs, letters, and treatises on dancing – we have found statements suggesting that this deportment was extremely important to the regent and other wealthy families of the seventeenth and eighteenth centuries. As a result of the gradual strengthening of social hierarchy, the body was made increasingly subject to a growing discipline and formality of manners. Compared to the developments in the Southern Netherlands or in France and England, this process may have started relatively late. It also seems likely that due to the narrower range of social distinctions prevailing in the Dutch Republic, the rules of *civilité* and *courtoisie* were taken somewhat more lightly in comparison with those other countries. But it is beyond any doubt that the ruling classes, certainly those in the towns of Holland, were keen on distancing themselves in their public relations from those classes below them. They readily adopted the new rules of civility, including the formalization and stylization of their own bodies, their physical presentation of self.[37]

To the sources already mentioned, however, we might add another interesting type, namely, the contemporary painters' manuals, the so-called *schilderboeken*. In these treatises we often encounter observations that are quite close to the ideas we have thus far discussed. But they also help us to visualize the much-desired uprightness (and of course its opposite, a stooping and hunched over demeanor), either by providing helpful technical description or including illustrations.

In certain instances we even encounter remarks on a slanting neck that remind us immediately of the views expressed in the manuals on civility. We have seen how this posture was regarded by Erasmus as a sign of hypocrisy and how the author of the little manners book, published in 1546, considered it an attribute of a lazy character. The verdict passed by the authors of the *schilderboeken* was hardly less severe. In 1678 Samuel van Hoogstraeten concluded: "The head pushed backward over the neck points to haughtiness and pride, but falling headfirst to humility, and hanging sideways to faintheartedness."[38] Four years later his opinions were copied almost verbatim by Willem Goeree, who first stated as a general principle that "by moving our heads we reveal many states of our inner feelings." And again, in accordance with the prevailing psychology of the time, outward traits were interpreted as a direct and infallible guide to a person's inner nature. For example, a head "carried backwards and stiffly on the neck" revealed a "proud and haughty heart;" a head hanging headfirst pointed to a "humble, meek and dejected" nature, just as a head hanging sideways could only indicate an "unmanly faintheartedness." The adjective "unmanly" makes one suspect that all these observations, not only in the *schilderboeken* but also in the manners books and other sources, applied primarily to men. As a matter of fact, Goeree confirms this impression when he discusses the portrayal of women and explains that a slightly slanting neck can only enhance a woman's gracefulness and gentleness.[39] Indeed, we should always bear in mind – an aspect that was already touched upon by Castiglione[40] – that the rules of civility that applied to women were different from those applying to men, although this difference never served to neutralize the social distance between a well-bred lady and a woman from the lower classes. Of course, in using the term "unmanly," Goeree may also have alluded to effeminacy, at least in its seventeenth-century connotation of the shady skirt-chaser.[41] In discussing a head hanging to the left, he even speaks of an "adulterous and unchaste omen"; men like these would only have "scandalous things" in mind. The fact that Goeree dedicated his book to Constantijn Huygens Jr. imparts to these observations a curious twist. Obviously, he never knew of Constantijn's difficulties with his neck when he was a small boy.

For the moment it is hard to determine whether such specific readings, especially those of Goeree, were generally accepted. Perhaps they just remained the preoccupations of a few intellectuals who were versed in the classical writings on physiognomy and related subjects. But it is clear that Van Hoogstraeten and Goeree, as with the authors of the manners books, attached a negative meaning to a slanting neck. Apparently, they were well acquainted with the prevailing codes of civility and even felt that a painter, in depicting the human figure, should incorporate these codes. This becomes even more apparent where they discuss the whole carriage of the body, relating the human figure to social categories such as status, gender, and age.

A fine example can be found in Gerard de Lairesse's *Groot schilderboek* (Great Book on Painting), published in 1707. According to contemporary theory, the artist had to be well-versed in anatomy, physiognomy, and the principles of proportion in order to portray the human figure correctly. Another important requirement was the knowledge of *positur:* roughly, the techniques that are used to lend a standing figure a certain elegance, to embellish it with the suggestion of movement.[42] As De Lairesse explains, the body should always be rendered in such a way that its weight rests on one leg only as opposed to both legs. He writes: "It is certain that for the sake of standing well (*welstand*) all halting statues, be it man or woman, may only rest on one leg and carry the weight of the body, never on both legs simultaneously, by which then one hip will swell."[43]

De Lairesse was certainly not the first author to write on the theme of *welstand* or "the gracefulness in bending and turning."[44] Before him Karel van Mander, Samuel van Hoogstraeten, and Willem Goeree had touched upon the same subject and had equally emphasized the "swelling" or "swinging out" of the hip: the rules of classical *contrapposto* (the balanced pose of the body at rest) that had been more or less rediscovered by artists of the Italian Renaissance and subsequently encoded and developed in the writings of Leon Battista Alberti, Leonardo da Vinci, and Giovanni Paolo Lomazzo.[45] De Lairesse, however, takes a special position because he went into a full explanation of the social status of the figures to be depicted. For example, in discussing *contrapposto* he cautioned his readers that as a rule they should never render peasants in this way. Before him Van Mander had already made an exception for the portrayal of old age: If an old man or woman was depicted standing, he or she should hold on to something.[46] Goeree also pointed out that it would be risky for the old, sick, and weak to rest their weight on one hip only; if they did not need a cane, they would definitely need their two legs.[47] De Lairesse was less interested in the physical defects of the peasants than in their social defects, in their "boorishness" or lack of manners. He states first as a general rule that a painter should always portray his figures in accordance with their status, office, or dignity. He can express such differences by their "posture, nature, color and movement."[48] Peasants, for example, should have their feet planted firmly on the ground. De Lairesse

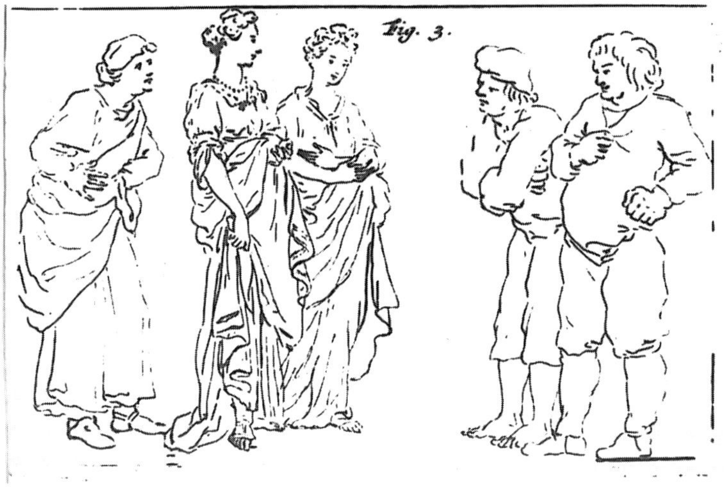

Figure 107. Illustration from Gerard de Lairesse, *Het groot schilderboek*, Amsterdam 1707.

obviously knew that peasants had a range of social distinctions and individual characteristics, that they hardly displayed the same gait and posture. Moreover, he goes on to explain that painters can exploit such differences, especially in introducing variety to the rendering of a crowd.

In order to clarify this point, De Lairesse included some illustrations depicting men and women of various social backgrounds. Employing one of these prints (Fig. 107), he tells us that a "rude peasant" not only stoops but that he also "rests and stands simultaneously on both legs, the toes being parallel to one another, the knees somewhat bent and the feet turned inwards." In the same print, he also showed a "better educated" peasant, a wholly different man: "The other one stands upright, resting his body most on one leg . . . the other leg slightly turned, a bit more to the front, and the stomach pointing slightly outwards; displaying a more graceful posture than the first one."[49] In other words, in depicting this second, more "cultured" peasant, one was actually allowed to apply the rules of *contrapposto:* The man might be given a more elegant and upright stance to distinguish him from the other men with his short and stocky posture. Still, his elegance should not be overdone. The painter had to take care "if some gracefulness had to be noticed, that it would be equally in the peasant manner."[50] This was especially important if some figures of higher rank were inserted among the peasants. As the author phrased it: "if one has to put an office holder (*amptman*) or fine citizen (*fraay borger*) among them," this man "ought to be known among them all by his well-bred gait and civil manners."[51]

Besides these rules concerning the handling of *contrapposto,* De Lairesse also established others regarding gesture and posture, including the different ways of sitting (sitting erect or hunching over) or holding a spoon, cup, or glass (using two or three fingers or using one's whole hand, etc.). Obviously, it would lead us too far afield to go into all of these details as well. But it should be evident that there were many correspondences between the instructions of the *schilderboeken* and the numerous rules of civility as they were encoded in the manners books. Historians and art historians have seldom written on this interesting connection, but the authors themselves were well aware of the analogies. Van Mander, for example, in discussing the portrayal of women, explicitly referred to Castiglione.[52] Lomazzo, in dealing with the unbecoming posture of crossing the legs, referred to a well-known manners book by Giovanni Della Casa published in 1558.[53] De Lairesse even pointed to the civility that one could observe in the streets and other public spaces. He urged his readers not to move within their own circles only. They should also mingle with the upper classes, with the *deftige gezelschappen* (fashionable society). Of course, not everybody had access to them, but then they could always use their eyes: in

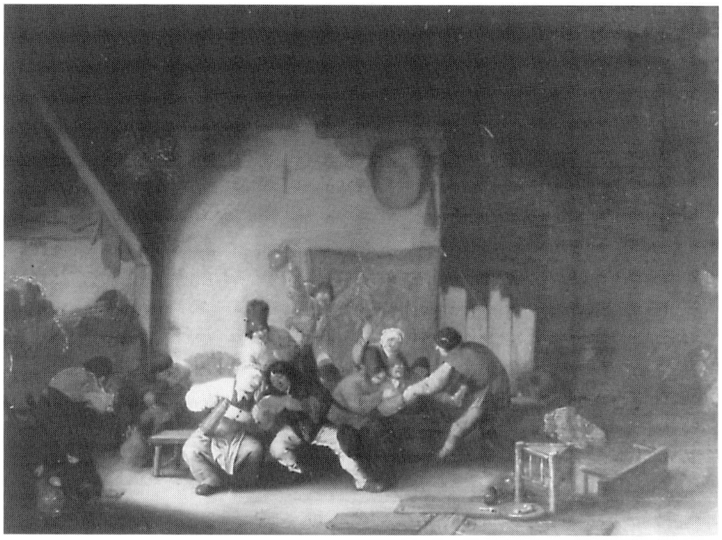

Figure 108. Adriaen van Ostade, *Festive Peasants*, 163? (oil on panel, 47.3 × 63.6 cm). The Hague, Mauritshuis. Photo: A. Dingjan, The Hague.

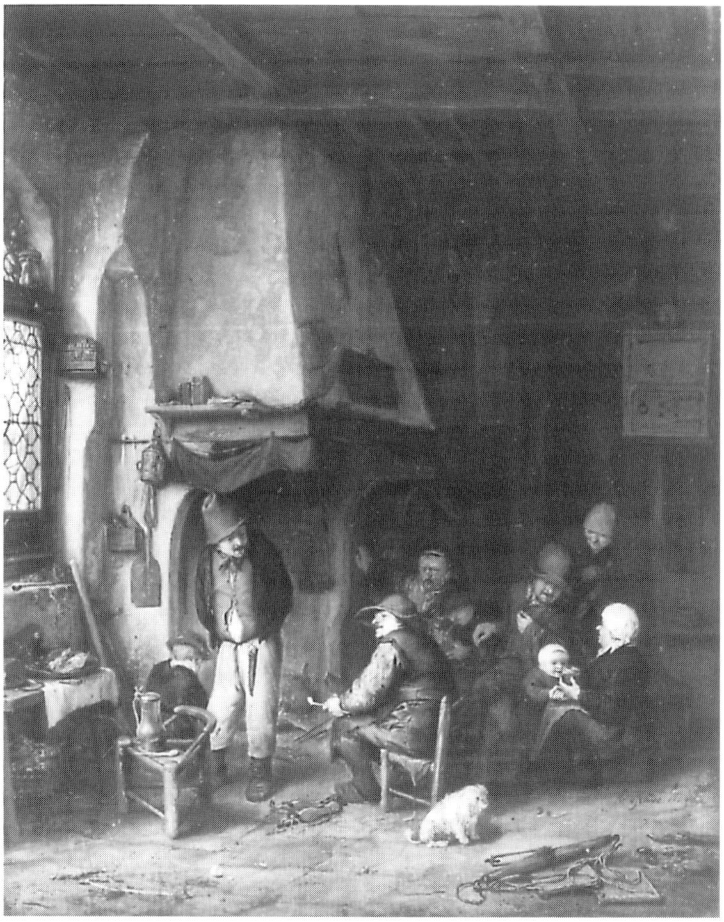

Figure 109. Adriaen van Ostade, *The Skaters: Peasants in an Interior*, 1650 (oil on panel, 44 × 35.5 cm). Amsterdam, Rijksmuseum. Photo: Rijksmuseum-Stichting.

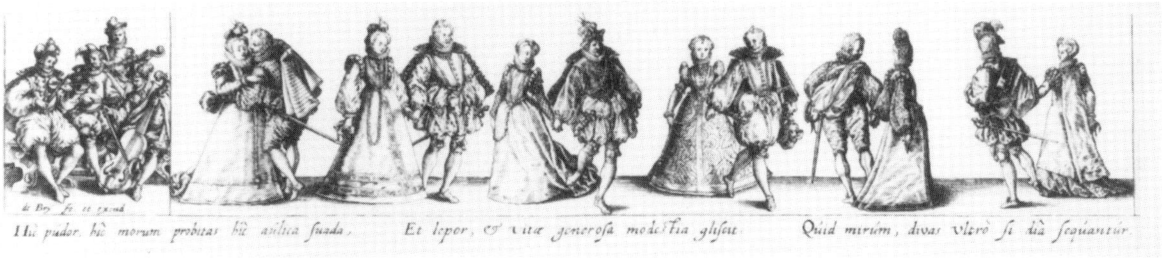

Figure 110. Jan Theodor de Bry (attributed to), A *Court Dance* (engraving). Amsterdam, Rijksprentenkabinet. Photo: Rijksmuseum-Stichting.

church, in the theater, or when promenading. On those occasions, they would have enough opportunity to see *fraaye lieden* (elegant people) and to watch their elegant manners. Before he himself was accepted in those circles, De Lairesse would always carry a notebook and when seeing, for example, a *fraaye juffer* (an elegant young lady), he would record why she appeared more graceful than others.[54]

It is rather surprising that the problem of how to visualize social distinctions was only raised in 1707, when De Lairesse's text was finally published. Indeed, for many decades painters such as Adriaen Brouwer, Adriaen van Ostade, and Jan Miense Molenaer had put on canvas what De Lairesse so much later was to put in writing. Obviously, as one of the most prominent adherents to French Classicism, he was hardly an admirer of their work. They depicted life "as it is presented to them," or, even worse, "one sees them imitate it even more unsightly than nature created it."[55] Clearly, Brouwer, Van Ostade, and Molenaer (Pieter van Laer is another one of De Lairesse's culprits) did not adhere to any *hoger trant* (higher style); they did not render life at its most elegant. But that does not alter the fact that by generally avoiding the use of *contrapposto* in their depictions of peasants, they had created a pictorial tradition or iconographic convention to which De Lairesse could refer in his discussions of posture and gesture.[56] After all, most of the figures depicted in their paintings are stocky and hunched over, even when sitting, and most of them twist their heads to all sides. Van Ostade's *Festive Peasants* is a case in point (Fig. 108); the manner in which they stoop looks ridiculous, especially given the height of the ceiling! But even when peasants were depicted standing, their postures were invariably not erect. The man in the front in Van Ostade's *Skaters* is a good example (Fig. 109). First, he keeps "both his hands at his arse," a gesture that was deemed "more boorish than respectful," according to Goeree.[57] Second, he has planted both his legs firmly on the ground. For him there is no graceful "swelling of the hip," no *contrapposto:* This is unmistakably De Lairesse's "crude" as opposed to his "better educated" peasant.

Of course, Brouwer and Van Ostade were not the first painters who made fun of the peasants. One of the best examples of the distinctions involved are two engravings attributed to Jan Theodor de Bry that date from the end of the sixteenth century (Figs. 110 and 111). The first one shows a city dance, the second a country or peasant dance. In the first the figures are almost static, elegantly upright, and almost fully vertical in posture. By contrast, the second shows a group of violently swirling figures, whose movement tends almost to be horizontal. We can even discern a couple of bare women's legs among the dancers. Almost the same comparison may be made with two later examples, *The Dancing Lesson* of 1627 by Pieter Codde (Fig. 112) and *The Dancing Peasants* (Fig. 113) painted around 1647 by Jan Steen. Such contrasts can be found in the work of other artists as well, among them Hans Bol, Jan van de Velde, and David Vinckboons. In some cases the elegant postures of the rich were even contrasted in a single scene with the stooping postures of dumb peasants.[58] An enlightening example is an anonymous engraving on the title page taken from one of the editions of *Bacchus wonder-wercken* (Bacchus's Miracles), written by Dirck Pietersz. Pers.[59]

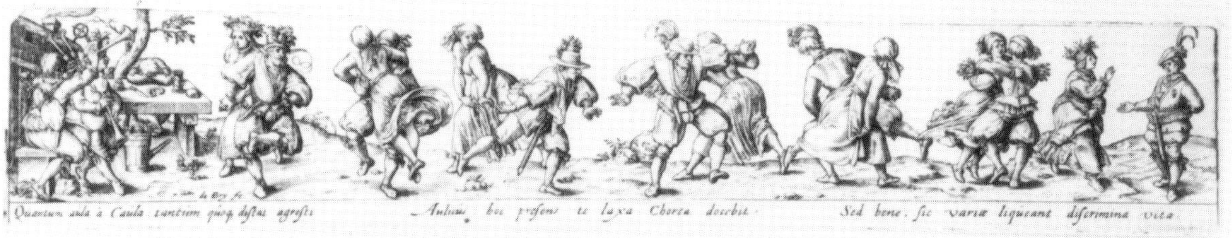

Figure 111. Jan Theodor de Bry (attributed to), *A Peasant Dance* (engraving). Amsterdam, Rijksprentenkabinet. Photo: Rijksmuseum-Stichting.

This print depicts both rich and poor crowded around the perpetually merry god of wine. To the left we see the rich, easily recognizable both by their fashionable clothing and their elegant, swerving hips. To the right we see the peasants and the poor. Their dress is simple or shabby, and they keep their feet planted firmly on the ground (Fig. 114).

As with all caricatures, these peasant scenes certainly contained a grain of truth. Farmwork was hard and strenuous, straining the body to the utmost. But when we compare this pictorial tradition with the ideals of elegance and uprightness as they were expressed in manners books, medical and educational writings, the *schilderboeken*, and other sources, we suspect rather that these scenes offer us no more than a caricature of lower-class life. Intentionally or unintentionally, they show us the exact opposite, a convincing and humorous mirror image of the elegant manners required, at least in public, among the Dutch upper classes.[60] To put it differently, the postures that we encounter in many seventeenth-century paintings were far from neutral, nor were their meanings very much concealed; to the contrary, they must have been directly accessible.

V. CONCLUSION

What I have wanted to make clear here with the help of a single example – the contemporary ideal of correct posture – is that the ostensibly more banal motifs in seventeenth-century Dutch paintings and prints are indeed capable of being interpreted.[61] It is by now axiomatic that in the iconological study of art, literary sources are primarily

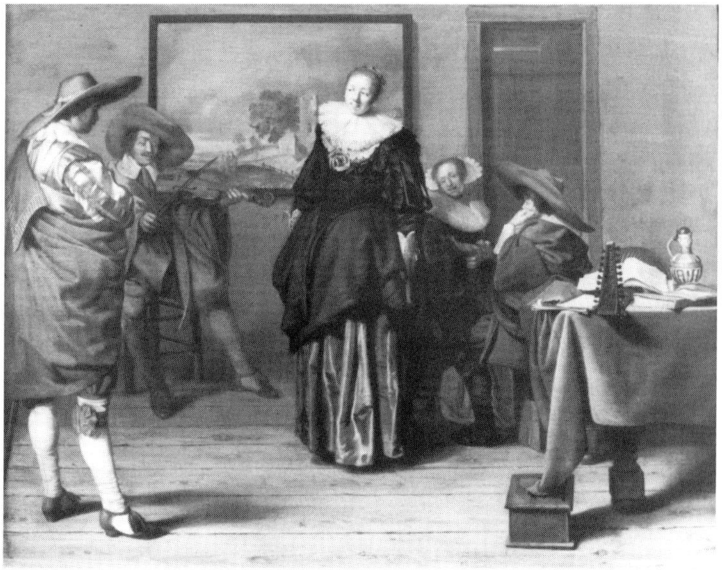

Figure 112. Pieter Codde, *The Dancing Lesson*, 1627 (oil on panel, 39.5 × 53 cm). Paris, Musée du Louvre. Photo: Réunion des musées nationaux, Paris.

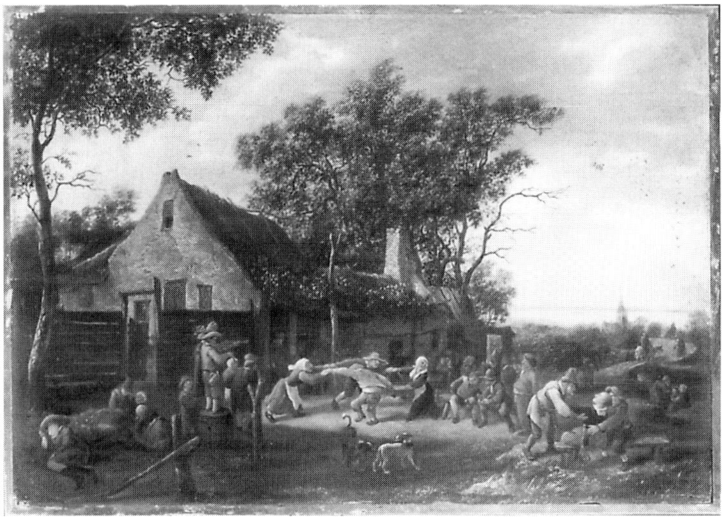

Figure 113. Jan Steen, *Dancing Peasants* (oil on panel, 40 × 58 cm). The Hague, Mauritshuis. Photo: A. Dingjan, The Hague.

invoked. As is the case with iconological investigations of Italian and French art of this period, art historians have been able to draw upon literary-humanistic material, in particular upon emblem books. This concern for "high" culture was of course in keeping with the principles of iconological interpretation, as established by Erwin Panofsky in the 1930s, although he himself saw no literary associations behind Dutch genre painting, landscapes, and still lives.[62]

Recent decades, however, have witnessed a gradual turn in scholarship in the field of history in which research has now been directed toward "low" or popular culture and, more recently, toward the role of signs and symbols within that culture. What is emphasized in this historical-anthropological or historical-ethnological approach is that even the most everyday, inconspicuous, and seemingly trivial actions and events can provide us with access to the culture in question. One can scarcely speak in this regard of a movement or school within the discipline of history itself. Nevertheless, historians who are interested in this approach for the most part have in common a predilection for qualitative research on a small scale in which social realities are approached as a "symbolic universe." From a theoretical standpoint, its diverse practitioners are influenced by the work of sociologists and anthropologists – among them, Erving Goffman – who have directly or indirectly built upon the work of Emile Durkheim.[63]

It seems to me that this historical-anthropological or historical-ethnological approach could be valuable, not so much as an alternative to more "traditional" iconology but above all as a broadening, an elaboration, or an enrichment of it.[64] From

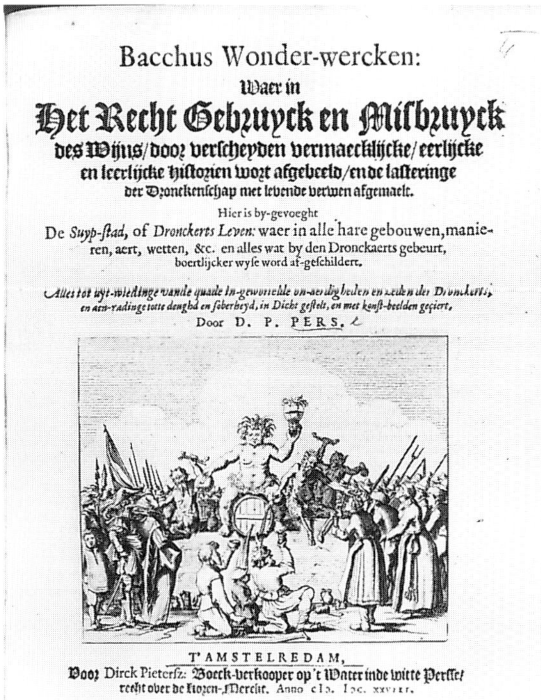

Bacchus Wonder-wercken:
Waer in
Het Recht Gebruyck en Misbruyck
des Wijns/door verscheyden vermaecklijcke/eerlijcke
en leerlijcke historien wort afgebeeld/en de lasteringe
der Dronckenschap met levende verwen afgemaelt.
Hier is by-gevoeght
De *Suyp-stad*, of *Dronckerts Leven:* waer in alle hare gebouwen, manieren, aert, wetten, &c. en alles wat by den Dronckaerts gebeurt, boertlijcker wyse word af-geschildert.
Alles tot uyt-wiedinge vande quade In-gewortelde on-aerdigheden en zeden der Dronckerts, en aen-radinge totte deughd en soberheyd, in Dicht gestelt, en met konst-beelden geciert,
Door D. P. PERS.

T'AMSTELREDAM,
Voor Dirck Pietersz: Boeck-verkooper op 't Water inde witte Persse/ recht over de Koren-Merckt. Anno cI ɔ. I ɔc. xxviii.

Figure 114. Title page from Dirck Pietersz. Pers, *Bacchus Wonder-wercken*, Amsterdam 1628. London, British Library. Photo: British Library Reproductions.

this point of view, the symbolic universe should not be limited to a series of specific motifs in seventeenth-century Dutch painting and the body of literary-humanistic thought to which they relate, but the content of this art should be more strongly linked than has hitherto been the case to the most casual, inconspicuous conduct in daily reality. After all, such simple postures as a bent or upright stance or a hanging of the head had specific connotations long before they were depicted by painters. It will not always be easy to recover such meanings. Clearly, information has to be gathered from very diverse sources.

Moreover, researchers, whether historians or art historians, must devote attention to such "technical" aspects of art as form, composition, coloring, and execution. We have already seen how a painter can distinguish between people he depicts by posture, disposition, and movement. But the handling of color was no less important as a carrier of meaning (as De Lairesse pointed out), just as the depiction of the elbow akimbo could have a significant function, to cite just a few examples.[65] In other words, attention to the codes of how to sit, stand, and walk can likewise contribute to a further exploration of the complicated connection between form and content.

The Space of Gender in Seventeenth-Century Dutch Painting*

Elizabeth Alice Honig

I. AN ALLEGORY OF PAINTING – I

In 1660 Gesina ter Borch, a young woman in the town of Zwolle, embarked upon a new project: a large Art Book or album, which she intended to fill with watercolor images of daily life as she observed, experienced, and imagined it in and around her home town. Since her adolescence she had been filling albums with calligraphy and illustrated popular romantic poems, but this was her most ambitious enterprise to date, and to inaugurate its beginning she, along with her close friend Henrik Jordis, devised an elaborate allegory to adorn its first full page: *The Triumph of Painting over Death* (Fig. 115). Over the following five pages, Jordis wrote out his long verse explanation of the allegory's intricate meaning.[1]

Jordis was evidently well acquainted with Cesare Ripa's *Iconologia* and based his ideas closely on that text: Mute Painting was to quell Time beneath her feet, and to be impervious to the assault of Death, her enterprise was assisted by Poetry (holding scroll and scepter) and History (writing in an open book). In Gesina's visualization, though, Ripa's aloof allegorical figures look like fashionable young ladies of Zwolle in fancy dress. Their costumes are elegant contemporary ones, modified to follow Ripa's iconographic dictates; their hair is frizzed into ringlets like those of Gesina herself in the oval self-portrait bust that she painted on the page following Jordis's poem. In the Allegory of Painting, such an oval self-portrait bust is borne into the room by two putti, one of whom crowns it with a laurel wreath, and they carry it downward along shafts of light – the radiance of inspiration.[2] This element of the allegory seems to have been Gesina's invention, for Jordis barely mentions it and does not explain it at all in his poem. Ostensibly, it is the self-portrait of Painting; but in the context of the album, it is difficult not to associate Pictura's fashionable, pert, proud visage in its oval frame with the fashionable, pert, proud face of Gesina. By this gesture Gesina neatly outdoes Ripa, for she is not merely the *practitioner* of painting – the art that triumphs over time and death – she *is*, herself, victorious and ingenious Painting.[3]

Furthermore, Gesina/Painting and her allies exercise their strength not in the arid space of allegory but in an actual place: the studio that is their home. Gesina has located her figures in a room that

* The ideas in this article developed out of three classes I have taught: "Rembrandt" and "Gender and Painting, 15th–17h Centuries" at Tufts University, and "The Boundaries of Domesticity in Early Modern Europe" at the Graduate Consortium for Women's Studies at Radcliffe College. My co-professors in the latter course, Erica Harth (Comparative Literature, Brandeis) and Anne McCants (History, MIT), stimulated and broadened my interdisciplinary approach to the study of Dutch painting. I also wish to thank the graduate students in those classes, particularly Paula Cuneo, Sarah Handwerger, and Timothy McElreavy. Other students – Suzanne Coleman, Alexis Guise, Palmore Hoyt, Antien Knaap, Melinda Linderer, and Timothy McElreavy – read earlier drafts of this essay and provided valuable comments and suggestions, as did my colleagues Margaret Carroll and Wayne Franits.

is spatially much like the domestic interiors shown later in the Art Book. At its left, by the implied window, a portion of the floor is slightly raised: the little platform on which Dutch housewives often sat to do their handiwork in the best light and above the drafty floor.[4] The other furnishings and decor of the room – draped table, framed painting – are also those of her pictured households. Gesina's proclamation of her personal artistic power may be signified through the arcane iconography of Ripa, but it is Ripa transmuted into that which is familiar, personal, and domestic.

Gesina ter Borch's allegory poses a paradox to the art historian. It speaks through the most standard, mainstream language of High Renaissance and High Art, and tells of genius, invention, and inspiration, yet it does so by means and within circumstances that have little to do with that tradition. Ripa's concretized abstractions were designed to articulate the ideals and aspirations of men, for whom Painting was the necessarily beautiful, seductive, and hence female Other, controlled and manipulated by a "genius" which was by definition male, and produced within the boundaries of public, masculine institutions.[5] Gesina ter Borch produces her art outside of such institutions, within a realm that is private and domestic. She is not a professional but an amateur – not, within the classic definition, an inspired inventor but the illustrator of popular poems and the recorder of the commonplace.

To understand the oddity of Gesina's work is, in part, a matter of locating the rather unusual place where issues of gender affect cultural production in the Dutch Republic. And determining that locus is very important, for it is not the same one where modernist art history, or feminist interventions into that art history, have generally situated gender issues.[6] Within that traditional narrative of post-medieval art, in which we pass from Michelangelo to the Mannerists, from Peter Paul Rubens to Jacques-Louis David to Eugène Delacroix, from Gustave Courbet to Édouard Manet to Picasso to contemporary painting and film, issues of gender are most often really "written on the body." It is a tale of passive female bodies – allegories, objects of desire, Others – and active male ones. It is a tale of penetrating male eyes and seen female forms, of a series of individual (male) artist–heroes carrying out their rivalries through exchanges, manipulations, and re-presentations of (female) objects. As a piece of diachronic historical anthropology, this is compelling; but it does not, I would argue, fit with the historical anthropology of the Dutch Republic and its art. For there, what we might term the "metaphors of the body" are primarily charted out onto space, and onto the organization of social relationships within that space.[7]

The primary concept I see as at stake here is that of "domesticity": a realm of experience set apart from that which is public, yet intimately connected to it, and one that has come to be defined as female, in opposition to the public, civic, and commercial spaces in which men operate. The Dutch home, it is often said, was conceptualized as the necessary obverse of the supposedly dangerous, capitalist world outside its boundaries, a haven of purity and privacy, obsessively cleansed and guarded by its housewives at the same time as it "protected" its own guardians from masculine contamination.[8] Historians, though, tend to portray this dichotomy far too neatly and absolutely. They are looking back from a post-Victorian perspective, and they see Dutch society as providing the predecessor of the rigid Victorian "feminine domestic sphere." But Holland was the *first* bourgeois capitalist society, and thus the first in which this new map of the public and private came to be drawn, together with its attendant rearrangement of expectations and experiences along the lines of gender.[9] Throughout our period, then, the boundaries of domesticity were contentious and troublesome ones, still fluid rather than fixed.

Artistic production both shaped and was shaped by these social border disputes. In certain ways we might say that painting was very much integrated into the sphere of the "domestic" while in other ways it played upon domesticity's border, and gained its own power from being able to mediate between spaces that were public and private, masculine and feminine. In the rest of this essay, I explore three ways in which the practice of painting intersected with the concept of domesticity: the

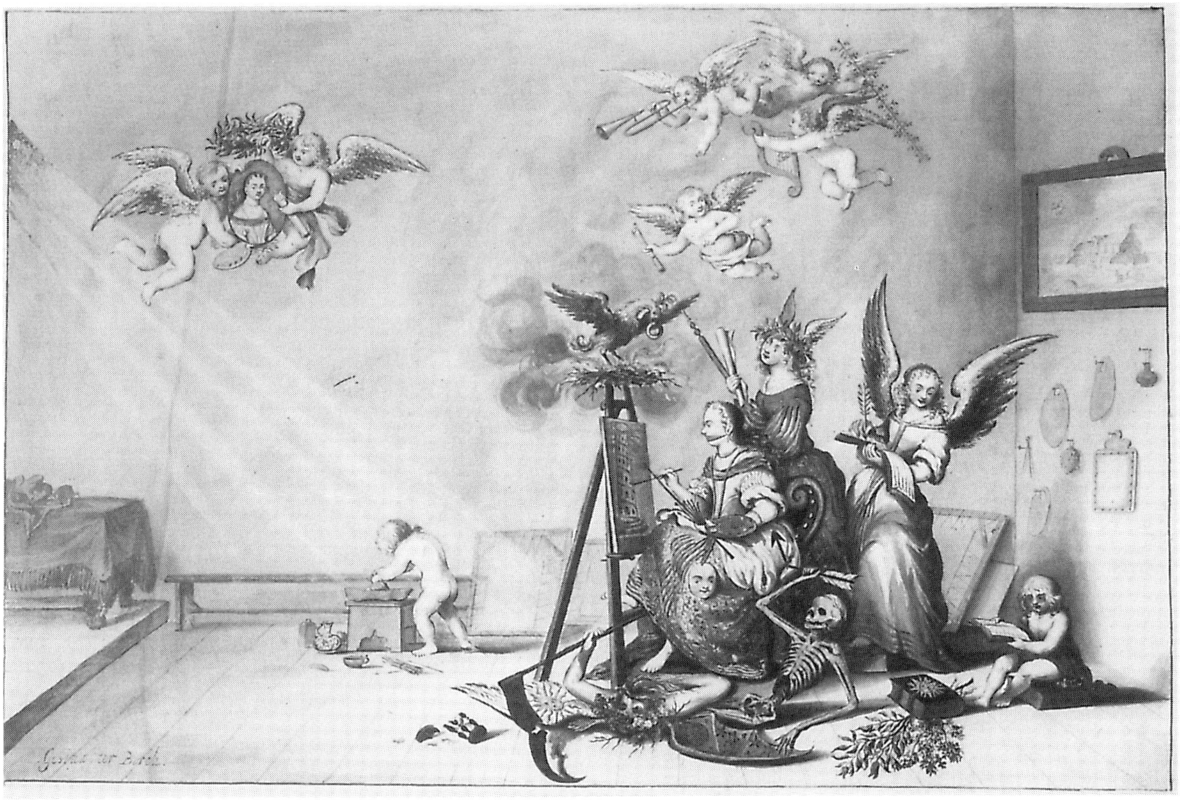

Figure 115. Gesina ter Borch, *The Triumph of Painting over Death*, 1660 (watercolor from *Family Scrapbook*). Amsterdam, Rijksprentenkabinet. Photo: Rijksmuseum-Stichting.

locus and manner of painting's production, the space of its consumption, and the content and treatment of its subject matter. Each of these issues provides a way of considering how issues of gender are implicated in seventeenth-century Dutch painting. And each of them, too, offers a way of understanding how Gesina ter Borch came to paint her own odd Allegory of Painting.

II. PRODUCTION: AT HOME IN THE STUDIO

The most obvious quality that sets Gesina ter Borch apart from the mainstream of seventeenth-century Dutch art is that she was an amateur rather than a professional painter. But just how unusual was this? Amateur art is notoriously ephemeral; neither collected nor culturally valued, it tends to disappear unless particular circumstances lead to its preservation.[10] Women's amateur art might be noticed and preserved if its maker was seen as "exceptional" because of a combination of social standing and intellectual achievement. Anna Maria van Schurman, "a remarkably learned lady," is one example: Besides producing numerous self-portraits in a variety of media, she even wrote a treatise arguing that [elite] women were particularly gifted in the fine arts.[11] Gesina ter Borch acted as her own family archivist, and in her scrapbooks she gathered not only her own works but those of her father, her brothers and sisters, and her female pupils.[12] All except one brother (Gerard) were amateurs, trained at home to observe, imitate, and invent, to express their perceptions of the world pictorially.[13]

It is likely that the Ter Borch family was not as peculiar as this accident of preservation makes them seem. Evidence of widespread amateur artistic ability is provided by *alba amicora*, a type of high-class autograph book particularly popular among university students.[14] On the pages of these books, friends of the owner wrote poetic, comical, or learned inscriptions, and often provided elaborate illustrations as well. Around 1600, a friend of the Leiden law student Johannes ab Amstel a Mijnden painted a comical scene in his album (Fig. 116). It shows an industrious student in his study interrupted by Cupid, who (according to the Latin poem below) urges him to stop wasting his time on work and instead to enter Venus's garden of love. This realm is represented by a secondary space at the right where nude Venus labors over a red-hot anvil, observed by a neatly clad bourgeois lady who is the hopeful recipient of the student's fiery ardor. Student albums were full of such basic humor about desirous women tempting upright men; here, though, my point is merely that even a law student had received sufficient artistic training to produce an image which, though it may appear naive to our eyes, is technically quite sophisticated.

Amateur art may exist in any society, and it has always been the primary arena of women's artistic production, from the lady watercolorist to the industrious needleworker.[15] But in Dutch society, amateur art existed not as an alternative to professional art but rather on a continuum with it. For what usually defines amateur art as amateur is not just that it is made for pleasure rather than for profit; it is that High Art – that which is not amateur – is produced within and for *public* institutions – within academies, for churches or palaces or (later) museums. Amateur art is thus that which remains within the private or domestic (feminine) sphere, made at home for an intimate circle of family and friends.

In Holland, though, professional painting too was practiced outside of any specifically "public" realm. Elite intellectual art academies never caught on there the way they had in other European centers.[16] Instead, the old guild system remained the predominant way in which artistic education, production, and distribution were organized; adapted to the demands of a competitive capitalist market society, it provided the security and protection that painters wanted.[17] Within this system painting, like any other craft, occurred in a realm loosely defined between the public and the private. The studio was closely tied to the home, if not actually a part of it; apprentices might lodge with the master and become integrated into the family – or they might be members of it already, as many painters came from artistic families. The woman of this domestic economic unit, the painter's wife, performed the traditional function of craftsmen's wives: helping to market the wares that her husband and his assistants produced. The most famous instance of this is Judith Leyster who, after her marriage to the painter Jan Miense Molenaer, largely gave up her own professional artistic career in order to manage his more successful enterprise.[18]

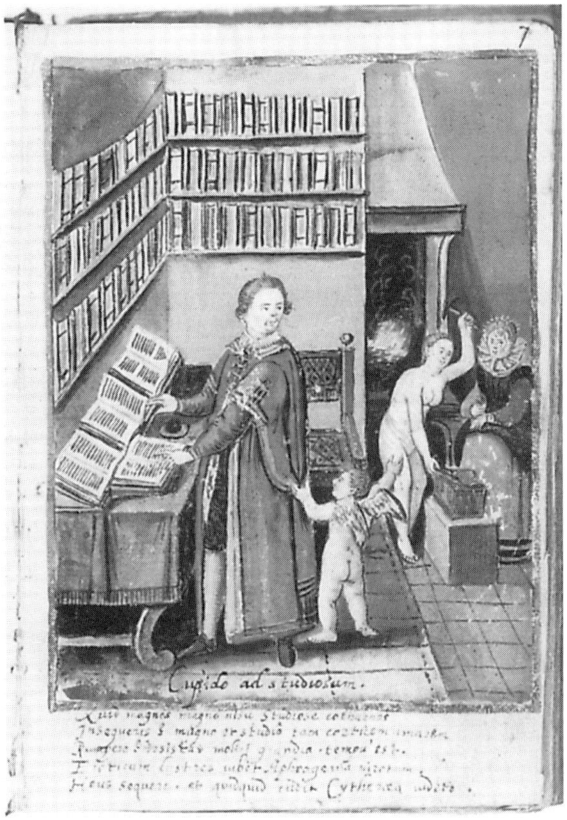

Figure 116. Anonymous, *Student Tempted by Cupid* from *Album Amicorum Johannes ab Amstel a Mijnden.* The Hague, Koninklijke Bibliotheek. Photo: Koninklijke Bibliotheek.

It has often been pointed out that Holland's painters considered their art as a craft and tried to "elevate" it to the status of a super-craft rather than to the supra-craft level of a liberal art – that they often eschewed claims to inspired genius or invention in favor of claims to masterful craftsmanly imitation.[19] This theoretical leveling of painting's ambitions went hand and hand with its social and spatial organization as a domesticated, nonpublic enterprise. Both theoretical and practical models combined to make the art of painting seem a practice in which a woman might feasibly engage. No masculine genius was required, only "a sincere hand and a faithful eye"; and its physical locus could also be seen as a woman's proper realm. This, perhaps, helps explain why women *did* paint in seventeenth-century Holland. Several dozen are known at least by name, and more remarkably, many seem not to have belonged to artistic families. By contrast, elsewhere in Europe, painting could evidently only be "domestic" enough for a woman if it was already the business of her father.[20]

The image of the European artist was generally of a figure operating within and receiving approbation from the public sphere. We hear little about the domestic life of Italian artists from Vasari, except insofar as they were hindered by any attention they paid to it. Some artists – those working in fresco, for instance – actually performed their main work within a public space; the studio activity that lay behind that performance, or behind any finished and presented work, was kept from the notice of the public. Not so in Holland, where artists were intensely aware of the studio as a *place* in which their art was

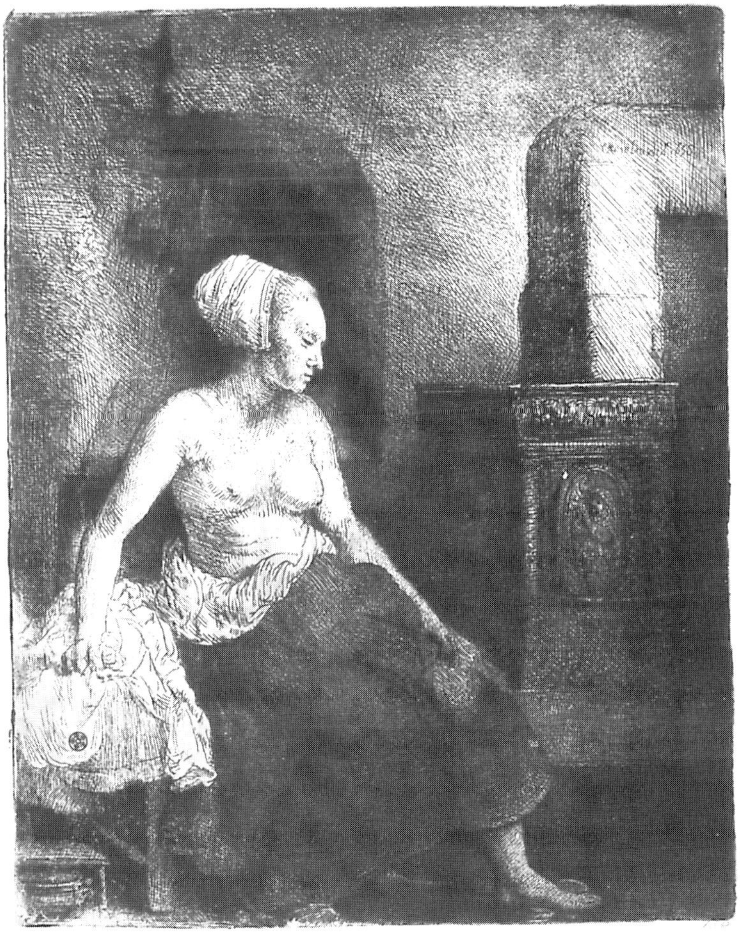

Figure 117. Rembrandt van Rijn, *Half-Dressed Woman by a Stove*, 1658 (etching). Amsterdam, Rijksprentenkabinet. Photo: Rijksmuseum-Stichting.

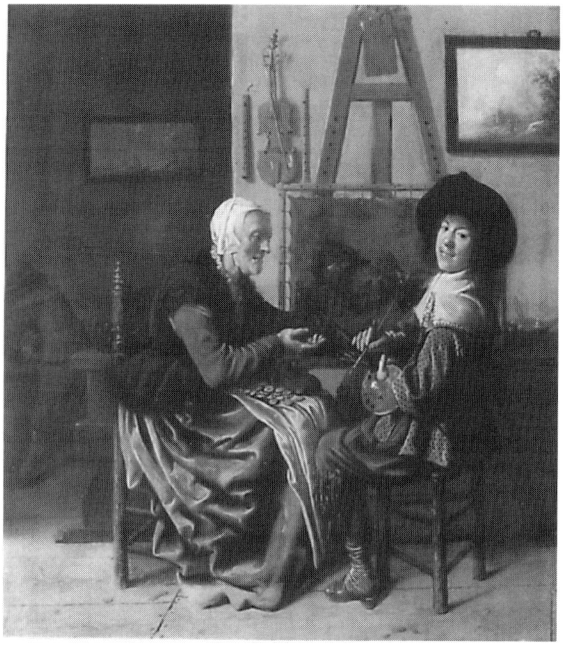

Figure 118. Jan Miense Molenaer, *Self-Portrait in the Studio with Rich Old Woman* (oil on panel, 40 × 36.5 cm). London, Collection Hans Raber. Photo: A. C. Cooper, London.

produced. Rembrandt van Rijn and his pupils produced dozens of drawings recording their work in this environment, whereas the equally large and active studios of Raphael or Rubens, for instance, produced none.[21] Moreover, Dutch artists seemed to go out of their way to draw public attention to the private, domestic locus of their production. A drawing of the studio may be dismissed as individual evidence of artistic self-consciousness, but a studio etching like Rembrandt's *Half-Dressed Woman by a Stove* is intended to enter the public sphere as a work of art (Fig. 117).

Rembrandt's image brings the viewer uncomfortably into a realm that is at once the studio and the home, a place provided with a simple stove to keep the woman – or the model – warm as she undresses.[22] I say "uncomfortably" because home is not the place in which the display or viewing of unclothed women was socially permissible. "Nudity" is the mode of the public sphere and is not so much a state of being as a way of presenting and beholding bodies as represented by Art.[23] But the "nakedness" of the unclothed individual is more an interior state than an exterior, viewable one; it is the mode of places so intensely private as to exclude the beholding eye.[24] To move representation of the body into that private space is to transgress an implicit boundary upon which a community of makers and beholders have long agreed; this is what Rembrandt does with his studio nudes. The long string of critics who decried these figures as hideous and ugly were not just responding to the physical qualities of bodies that often, as in the present case, were in no way unattractive.[25] Rather, what disturbs in Rembrandt's works – particularly in his graphic *oeuvre* – is the insistent presence of clues about the space of representation.[26] Rembrandt draws our attention to the fact of undress within the domestic studio and then pulls that which is private into the public eye by making saleable images of it. Exposing the place of artistic production, where naked bodies are transformed into nudes, he allows us an inappropriate view of the woman in a state of pre-aestheticized privacy. What Rembrandt manipulates here is not so much bodies themselves as the social organization of space surrounding their presentation and viewing.

Rembrandt's move here was only possible because he was addressing a public accustomed to – and evidently interested by – images of the studio as a familiar, homelike environment. Historians of Dutch art are so used to studio scenes that they sometimes forget how aberrant they are within the larger European context. From the neat interiors of Job Berckheyde or Frans van Mieris the Elder to the shabbier ones of Adriaen van Ostade, Dutch viewers were constantly provided with images of the space of painting, which corresponded closely to the domestic spaces depicted in these painters' other works.[27] The studio is generally a tidy room with a wooden floor, furnished with various regular household items (occasionally even a bed) as well as the painter's easel.

Jan Miense Molenaer, in one of his several studio paintings, shows just such a room (Fig. 118).[28] On its wall hang neatly framed paintings; They are not there as displays of *this* artist's work, as they are clearly by a different hand than the picture on the easel, but are simply household decoration. The painter, improbably at work dressed in the height of burgher fashion, has been engaged in executing a *vanitas* still life but is now interrupted by an elderly woman bringing a bag of coins. She grasps his arm with one hand and gestures toward the *vanitas* painting with the other as the artist turns to look at us with a complicitous grin.

A double play is going on here that involves a conjunction between social conventions about gender and social facts about women and art. The joke at which Molenaer is laughing is one of the oldest chestnuts in literature and art: the mismatched couple, and the notion that love cannot be bought. Every social expectation, voiced especially sternly in marriage manuals, dictated that people choose partners of their own age. The relentless comic imagery of the mismatched pair, with an older person attempting to "buy" the love of a younger one, served to render ludicrous the very idea that attraction could exist outside these prescribed limits.[29] Old age, it was said, should turn its thoughts to death, which is rapidly approaching, and not to the vain beauties of youth. But is this old woman really *not* thinking of death? She is, after all, gesturing toward a *vanitas* image, and the double play here comes from the fact that we do not really know whether her coins are intended to purchase the painting or its painter. Molenaer's joke would make no sense, or would at least be less complex, if it did not play upon a situation plausible in the Dutch art world: that women were, sometimes, the buyers of art.

III. CONSUMPTION: IS THE GAZE MALE?

In this section I wish to draw attention to what is perhaps an obvious point – that the consumption of Dutch painting, even more than its production, was located in the domestic sphere. Public art was a rarity in the Republic. The Reformed church would have none of it; the nobility were a minor force not much given to public patronage and display; and although civic bodies provided some commissions, these were primarily for portraits of their members.[30] Hence, the enormous output of the hundreds of active painters was made to be placed in buyers' homes.[31] Competition kept prices low, so works of art were distributed throughout a broad section of the population. Even the humblest artisan had a few simple paintings, while rich burgher houses were lavishly supplied with more elaborate ones.[32]

Domestic consumption affected every aspect of Dutch painting, from its size to its subject matter. "Genres" of painting – landscapes, flower pieces, still lifes, and, of course, domestic scenes – flourished here as nowhere else. All of these were precisely the sort of paintings that even a relatively unlettered woman could produce. No Dutch woman painter, to my knowledge, did history paintings, although in Holland even that most normatively public form of art was largely "consumed" or viewed privately.[33]

More importantly, however, the domestic locus of artistic consumption affected who viewed paintings, and how they viewed them. Art that is public appeals primarily to those who inhabit public spaces: men. They may be princes or prelates, businessmen or diplomats, connoisseurs or critics, but they are men. Of course, other European women did see public art – most obviously, they went to church, and elite women circulated at court. But the "public" beholder was defined as male; and hence, when we consider the gender of the gaze that a traditional European history painting constructs or presumes, we are usually safe in defining it as male, while the woman's look is the potentially subversive alternative, always seeing against the grain. This is simply not true of Dutch painting, an art made to be viewed within a sphere increasingly defined as "feminine." The anticipated beholder of this art must have been female at least as often as male, and the very act of beholding was a private, domestic one.

I believe, though, that the case could be put more strongly even than this. As I implied at the end of the previous section, women were not merely the chance beholders of art from within their private realm. They were also often its buyers in the public world of the art market.[34] Works of art were part of the household decor and were relatively inexpensive compared to such a major investment as a bed. And furnishing the home, creating the domestic environment, was the housewife's task. In a book entitled *De tien delicatessen des houwelicks* (The Ten Delights of Marriage [1678]), the anonymous author waxes rhapsodic about the joy of having a wife to decorate one's home, while in the accompanying illustration, the woman is shown at an art dealer's shop choosing what in fact appears to be a history painting to hang on her wall.[35] A parody of this book, advising men to remain bachelors, showed the wife out on a major shopping spree with a wheelbarrow piled high with such decorative items. Of course, there were men with a special interest in painting who wished to acquire an art collection that would reflect their cultivated taste, and who therefore bought the family's paintings themselves. But it seems safe to assume that many art purchases, especially less expensive ones, were made by women. Hence, paintings were made not just to be seen by women but to *appeal* to their ideals, their gazes, their tastes. They had to have qualities that a woman would wish to integrate into the domestic world that she controlled and inhabited.

This should mean that when looking at much of Dutch painting, the art historian would account primarily for a feminine gaze, and perhaps secondarily for a masculine (husband's) one, which viewed her choices. Unfortunately, that has not been the case.[36] When questions of the beholder's gender are raised at all, the argument has been that works of art – particularly domestic genre paintings – were "addressed" from a male society to a passive female subject. Pictures are seen either as offering "role models" for the housewife to follow or as admonitions that she *not* behave in certain proscribed ways.[37] Sometimes this was, no doubt, their authors' intention. But when we consider women's active role as purchasers of paintings, this general interpretive approach comes to imply that Dutch women were the victims of a sort of mass false consciousness, eagerly lapping up everything that was dictated to them by men regardless of their own interests or experiences. The questions that we should be asking instead might be, what was the female gaze? How was it socially constructed through feminine habits of viewing? What visual aspects of the world concerned women, and how did they then regard [men's] paintings, which in some sense represented their interests?

These are questions that would, I suspect, lead us to consider rather differently a wide range of Dutch artistic imagery.[38] Here, I can only suggest how they might be answered with regard to a single genre of painting: the domestic scene. Domesticity, "private" though it may have been, also had an important interface with the external, public world, and that interface was defined by vision and visibility. Consider the architecture of the Dutch urban burgher home, a single-family residence that provided, for its time, a quite unusual degree of family privacy – or, from a social point of view, a rather dangerous degree of secrecy. And yet, huge windows provided a clear view between the house's front rooms – the "public" rooms of privacy – and the street. The yards behind houses were part of the private realm and yet were outside; passageways sometimes connected them directly to the street, while back alleys gave more covert access.[39] The "boundaries of domesticity" were thus, in a very literal and physical sense, rather porous, allowing and indeed inviting at least visual penetration.[40]

At those borderlines of the domestic, before windows and in courtyards, women performed their daily tasks – sewing by the window's light, doing washing in the yard. And in paintings, women sit at windows, work in gardens, and stand at doorways (Fig. 119). Their lives are depicted not within the home but at its membrane with the public world. Domestic behavior becomes a performance, enacted within a space that is private yet geared to public viewing, an advertisement that, within *this* otherwise hidden household space, life proceeds according to agreed upon norms of propriety. Yet to be seen is also to see; for who were the intended beholders of correct female activity, if not other women? Only those who perform can truly judge other performers. "Community policing" was a crucial way in which social order was main-

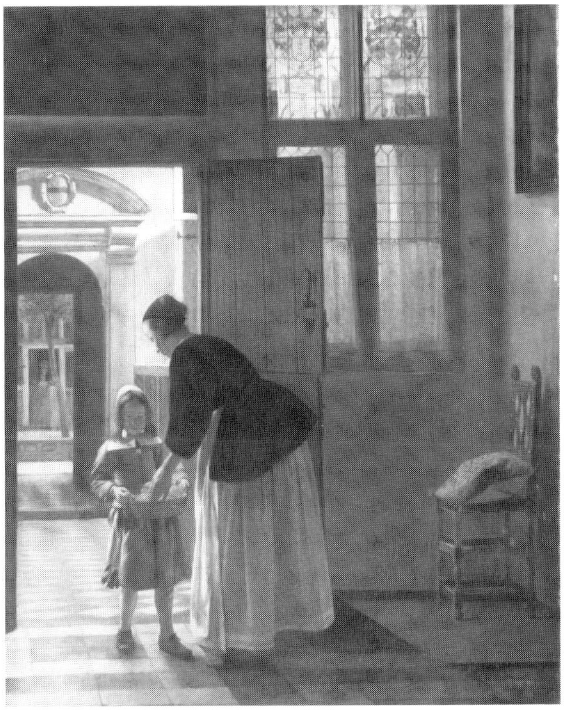

Figure 119. Pieter de Hooch, *A Boy Handing a Woman a Basket* (oil on canvas, 73.5 × 59 cm). London, The Wallace Collection. Photo: The Wallace Collection.

tained in the crowded Dutch cities, where neighbors kept watch over other neighbors, and to maintain one's honor meant to maintain a successful *image* of conformity.[41] In De Hooch's painting, the woman at the doorway is watched by a woman in the house across the way. Each of the women, seeing her neighbor, recognizes and appreciates that the other acts in the way that they both agree is proper, and each takes pleasure in the other's polished domestic display. De Hooch's work in a sense thematizes the female domestic gaze, one that at once judges the conformity of a projected image to an agreed model, tests the beholder's own projected self-image against that which is presented, and finds pleasure in what is seen. To the female eye, domesticity is the imagined space of the self in the realm of representation.[42]

IV. THE DOMESTIC SUBJECT: AT THE BORDERLINE

Women, as both actors and viewers, policed the boundaries of domesticity. Painting itself performed the same function. For it should always be borne in mind that Dutch genre painting does not "depict" daily life; rather, it provides imagined solutions to *problems* of lived existence, and the delimitation of spatial zones and gendered behaviors within them is a crucial problem that it addresses. The very creation of the domestic sphere as that which is female is in part the result of a conspiracy in its representation, as pictorial art constructs the home as the space of the Other, subtly separated from everything defined as public and masculine. Men enter domestic genre scenes only as guests; or they are defined as the "absent presence" through such signs as a male portrait on the wall or a man's cloak thrown over a chair.[43] And a "public" activity like productive labor for profit does not take place within the homes of genre painting – with the significant exception of the labor of painting itself. This is a deceptive, or at least a highly selective, picture: Artisanal craft and paid piecework were certainly carried out in Dutch homes.[44] But as a social fact, home labor produced a blurring of the difference between that which was "public"/male and that which was "domestic"/female, a blurring that painting, as an ideological product, seeks to eradicate.

Thus the space that genre painting defines as "domestic" is more intensely feminine than the home was in reality. That which is masculine does not, physically, belong within its compass. If domestic genre painting provided women with a viewing experience of that which was familiar, it at the same time tantalized men with the sight of that which was not precisely unfamiliar, but which was estranged through painting's fictions. To return here to the bodily metaphors I mentioned earlier, the "home" as pictured in Dutch art is – like the female body – an internal, enclosed entity, possessed by one man, whose precarious entrances must be protected against (other) male invasion, yet which, precisely because of this nature, provokes a desire to penetrate, to know that which is hidden within.[45] Male voyeurism here is not cathected upon the surface of the female body; it involves a deeper ingress into the alluring, erotic privacy of a female space. My metaphors here may seem crude, but so are the desires and anxieties that a society may sublimate through its gendered organization of space.

When Nicolaes Maes's "Eavesdropper" raises her finger to the beholder, the response that she expects is not about listening – as the traditional title implies – but about looking (Fig. 34).[46] Despite the lack of a clear framing device, we understand ourselves to be poised at the threshold of this home, outside, but privy to a quasi-illicit glimpse deep into its interior. At the right, the "world" in the form of a map meets the picture's boundary, emphasizing the nature of the picture plane as a liminal zone between public and private realms. Below this map, a man's red cloak is thrown over a chair, his sword propped up against it. Across the hall, at the left, the plain jacket of a less affluent man hangs over a door. We discover the owners of these coats through a criss-cross movement over the picture's surface and into its space: The hanging jacket belongs to the "downstairs" man at the right, and the elegant cloak to the gentleman in the room at the top of the stairs. Men have thus entered this house, but from the outside – they do not belong there but are merely privileged visitors. One, proposing a toast to an assembled burgher company, is a licit guest, while the other illicitly fondles the household's maid within the home's deepest recesses.

Maes's painting, with its peculiar bifurcated spatial composition, invites the eye to both roam its surface and penetrate its depths, passing through doorways, rising upstairs and descending downward, and finally piercing another doorway back to the outside world again. An entire taxonomy of the home gradually unfolds for the eye, and within that home, social behaviors are carefully organized according to both gender and class. At the very turning point of this scene is, of course, the housewife. Balanced between the world of the banquet and the world of the kitchen, she glances out at us with a smile. But what of her gesture? Is it one of admonition (to our silence, or against lusty downstairs behavior) or one of collusion (we share the maid's naughty secret)?[47] Several readings seem possible, depending on the beholder's interests, concerns, knowledge, and motives in viewing. A woman might be said to view complicitly. Already

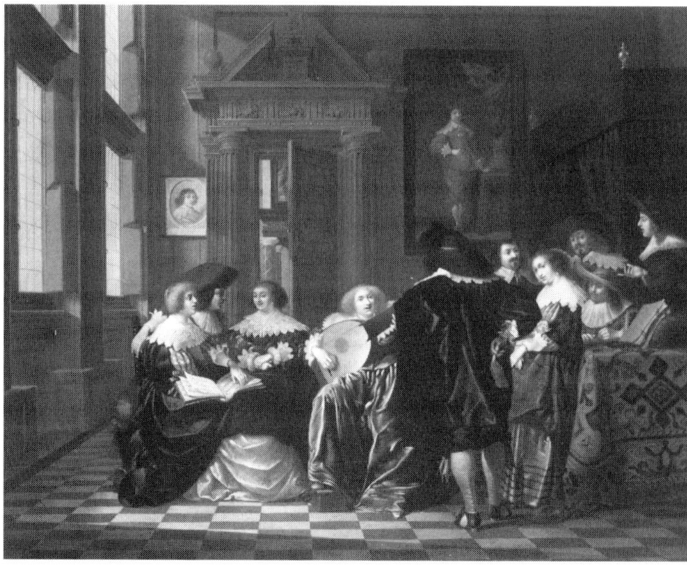

Figure 120. Dirck van Delen, *Merry Company in an Elegant Room,* 1636 (oil on panel, 48.5 × 61.8 cm). Rotterdam, Museum Boymans-Van Beuningen. Photo: copyright Frequin-Photos, The Hague.

cognizant of the nature of the domestic environment, and appreciative of so attractive an example of it, she recognizes a situation and smiles at a class-related problem. The male viewer, a visual visitor to an unfamiliar but highly charged realm, worries about the femininity of both space and inhabitants. The maid is a woman seduced; the housewife (who has emptied the wine glass in her hand) acquiesces to this behavior. Is Juno, goddess of domesticity, asleep at the helm, as her bust above the lintel here suggests? Is the bourgeois woman failing to guard the purity of her sacrosanct world from male penetration as she invites the entrance of his gaze?

I pose these questions because this, I think, is precisely what much Dutch genre painting does. And in so doing, it plays with the anxieties of its male beholders about a space in which purity and femininity have been defined as necessarily interdependent forces in distinguishing it from his, public world. To those who view from that public world, questions of "virtue" are couched as much in terms of the nature of a space as of the behavior of its inhabitants. The hundreds of Dutch paintings showing proper domestic interiors are filled with signals that what *keeps* these spaces virtuous is their exclusion of men, that men are visitors who pose threats to purity, that the beholder's own act of looking is already a transgression that may disturb the morals of space even as it seeks for assurance that they are maintained. I find it significant that in the rare instances when female artists turned their attention to the depiction of female virtue or its potential interruption, they were *not* concerned with the space in which it was located. Judith Leyster's famous *Proposition*, and Geertruydt Roghman's prints of busy housewives, largely isolate their female subjects from any indication of a spatial environment.[48] In images by men, however, tension is created precisely by an interplay between environment and actions. It is the virtue of the *home* that is threatened by the behavior that occurs there.

This tension becomes particularly acute when the behavior at issue generated more widespread social concerns. Pictures of domesticated festivity of men and women together – so-called "merry companies" – are an excellent example. This genre grew out of elegant "garden party" scenes from the early decades of the century, but gradually the site of festivity is moved into the domestic interior, and the companies themselves become more familiarly bourgeois (Fig. 120).[49] The rooms they inhabit are, often, in rich houses; family portraits decorate the walls, tables are neatly carpeted and floors tiled, a bed is in the corner. Here young people, enjoying the leisure excused by youth and permitted as the rites of courtship, chat, play music, eat, drink, and dance. The propriety of their activities is guaranteed by that of the place in which it occurs: the home.

Social permissiveness was also accompanied by social anxiety, however, particularly with regard to the perilous freedom of young women, and it is to this anxiety that painters of "merry companies" address their questions about the virtue of domestic spaces. Often the behavior of these companies is not nearly as virtuous as that shown by Van Delen. In pictures by Dirck Hals, couples kiss and fondle one another, skirts are hitched up, women sit on men's laps and act the part of seductresses, and an excessive amount of drinking has clearly occurred. Yet the participants are still well-dressed, and the rooms they inhabit are still neatly furnished and decorated. To put this another way, in a pictorial taxonomy of feminine festive space, which ranges from the proper home to the improper brothel, there exists a continuum rather than a clear opposition.[50] The gaze into a private, virtuous place finds there apparently public, fallen women, a clash that unsettles any certainty about the true nature of either one. If a brothel can be a home, a home can become a brothel; and the feminine domestic has, almost imperceptibly, become public and available.[51]

Perhaps the most troublingly ambiguous social space of femininity explored in Dutch genre painting is not the home but the marketplace. For the marketplace is, in terms of the social organization of urban space, as "public" as can be; yet by a peculiar twist of Dutch practice and ideology, it was firmly a place of female activity. Unlike housewives in many other European countries, who sent servants to do the shopping, Dutch women considered this task an essential part of their domestic duties.

Men agreed to this, advocated it in didactic treatises, and even boasted of their confidence that *their* women were able to negotiate the hazards of economic life at the market.[52] Furthermore, the sellers and inspectors of market goods in Holland were women, too.[53] Such feminization of a public sphere was only possible, within the framework I have already described, because the space of the market was defined as a kind of extension of the home. It was essentially part of the domestic world, however much this conflicted with basic economic and spatial reality. The market is thus a liminal zone between the public/economic and the private/domestic, a place where domestic economy visibly intersects with the merchants' world of capitalism.[54] Women there are dangerously removed from the confines of the home, and *only* their behavior can guarantee a virtue that spatial coordinates no longer provide.

Dutch market scenes testify at once to the confidence and comfort of female experience there and to the unease of the man confronted with these peculiarly private interactions. Here again the gender of the beholder matters a great deal: she understands; he feels he should understand that which is public but does not. In Emmanuel de Witte's *Poultry Stall* (Fig. 121), three women are doing business in an urban marketplace.[55] We see them from the far side of the stall, with a pile of the goods that are the subject of their conversation mediating our view. The seller's back is turned to us, and the maid's face is hidden by her bonnet, while the broad, red-clad figure of the self-possessed housewife is fully visible; yet her gaze is turned to the seller, her expression opaque. The nature of this economic interaction is made legible only through a language of gesture, six hands that ask and answer, demand and offer, act and rest. Three women from three social classes are bound together through an exchange illegible to those who do not participate in it. They have taken control of this oddly compressed pictorial space and exert in concert a privately feminine power over the public circulation of commodities.

Problems of class and gender, of publicness and privacy, are often worked through to somewhat more comfortable resolutions in "threshold" scenes.[56] These works focus pictorial attention precisely upon the doorway of the burgher home, the area that most unmistakably divides the domestic realm from the outside, those who *belong* within its compass from those who do not. Threshold scenes usually involve a confrontation of persons differentiated in terms of their degree of social fixity to a particular space. Housewives, more ideologically "located" than any other group by their supposed identification with the home, meet at its borderline beggars, street musicians, peddlars, or door-to-door saleswomen.[57] These are all quintessentially unlocated people, people who operate in a world without borders and who, therefore, potentially endanger a society that charts its own stability on a spatial map.[58]

In Jacob Ochtervelt's *Chery Seller at the Door* (Fig. 122), a street peddlar has come to a burgher home with a large basket of cherries, goods that now lie just inside the doorway while she remains just outside of it.[59] The attention of four women is now concentrated on the forthcoming transaction. The housewife looms tallest in the scene, yet she is positioned behind the lower half of a split door, gesturing her instructions. Her daughter kneels in a shaft of sunlight, while the maid stands at the threshold holding out the plate on which the wares will be conveyed into the home. The seller herself, diminished by her placement on the step down to the street, looks deferentially upward to the housewife as she holds in her hand the balance to weigh the cherries. One pan, which extends across the threshold toward the daughter, is full. The other, buoyed up by its emptiness, is observed by another child – a ragged boy in the street. He is excluded from both place and possession as the four women, who all know their "places," map out status at the threshold of domesticity with an almost uncanny precision.

Ochtervelt's painting highlights a point that has been only a subtext in the other works I have discussed: that the boundaries of domesticity are also the boundaries of class. The ideal feminine home is also a wealthy home; the heroines of domesticity are, by implication, the wives of men of substance.

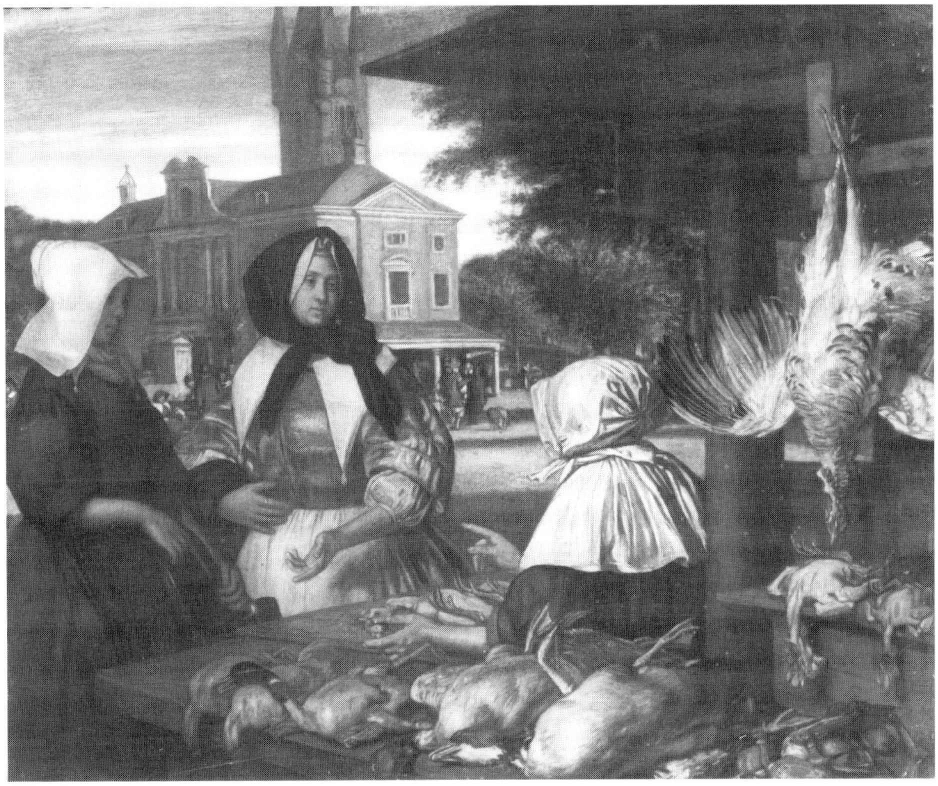

Figure 121. Emmanuel de Witte, *Poultry Stall* (oil on panel, 52 × 63 cm). Stockholm, Nationalmuseum. Photo: The National Swedish Art Museums, Stockholm.

The exclusion of productive work, the leisure of youth, the scrutiny over servants, the endless attention to needlework and cleaning – all those attributes that define virtue in domesticity are options open only to a certain type of woman. Dutch painting makes the connection between propriety and possession seem so tight that we neglect to ask: How many women really experienced this sort of existence? Indeed, it is a question that we are not meant to consider. The ideology of domesticity functions in part as a signifier of the affluence of a whole society; women and their spaces become the ciphers, possessed and possessing, through which a culture expresses its complacent pride in, rather than its embarrassment of, riches. Any class differences are masked by reference to the universality of gender: Women, in guarding their purity, truly guard the wealth of nations.

V. AN ALLEGORY OF PAINTING – II

In 1662 Johannes Vermeer, a young man in the city of Delft, was elected an officer of the painters' Guild of Saint Luke.[60] At that time the guild had just moved to quarters in a building two doors away from the house in which Vermeer himself had been born and raised.[61] Its grand new home was to be decorated inside and out with appropriate figurations of the professions that it housed. A bust of Apelles surmounted the door, and allegories of Painting, Sculpture, and Architecture embellished the interior. At this moment of intense engagement with his profes-

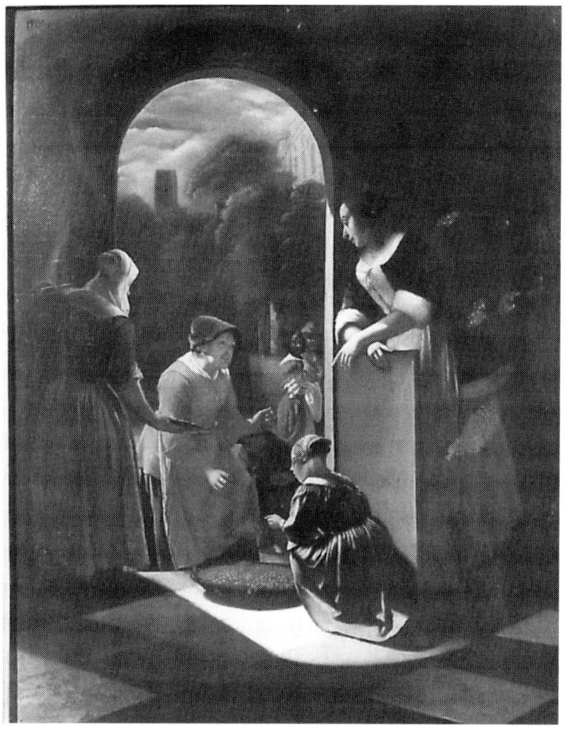

Figure 122. Jacob Ochtervelt, *Cherry-Seller at the Door* (oil on canvas, 78 × 62.9 cm). Antwerp, Museum Mayer van den Bergh. Photo: copyright A.C.L.-Brussels.

sional organization's public face, and of public recognition of his successful career, Vermeer embarked upon a more private project: his own allegory of the art of painting (Fig. 35). The picture remained in Vermeer's home until his death, and when his widow and her mother were selling off his estate, they employed considerable subterfuge to keep this one work in their own hands. These two women were to be its self-appointed primary beholders.[62]

Vermeer, like Gesina ter Borch's friend Jordis, was well acquainted with Ripa's *Iconologia*, for the ostensible subject of his painting is Ripa's figure of History. Standing in the light from an unseen window, her eyes downcast, she clutches a closed book to her enclosed body. In her other hand, she holds the trumpet that announces fame, and her head is crowned with the unfading wreath of laurel. In Vermeer's conception, though, allegorized History is no longer a feminine co-conspirator in the act of pictorial creation. She is a model, at home in the studio. Figuratively, History may "stand behind" the art of painting, but literally, the woman-as-History must always stand before the observant gaze of the male artist.

And yet, in another sense, the woman who is History envelops and encloses the very act of painting itself, for the space both artist and model occupy is a domestic one. Far more clearly than other depictors of studio scenes, Vermeer paints his painter into a proper, private, home. From the beamed ceiling and polished chandelier to the elaborate framed map, brass-studded chairs, and marbled floor, everything in this room speaks of bourgeois domestic comfort.[63] What we see here, then, is not so much a model brought artificially into a painter's studio as a painter who has intruded into the middle of that private, elusive feminine space of the home and who, from within that space, paints the "history" and "fame" of its rightful inhabitant.

The physical entrance into space and direct sight of the woman granted to the pictured painter are not privileges shared by the image's beholder. This home, like so many other painted Dutch homes, bars our presence at the same time as it lures our eye; here, though, both exclusion and access are accomplished by means of feminine representations. At the left, a tapestry that formerly separated our space from the scene before us has been drawn back, and the figure of a woman in blue, woven into its fabric, places imaged woman at the borderline of our domestic vision. Next, on a table within the room itself, lies the bust of Juno, domesticity's ancient goddess.[64] Thus, on the left-hand side of the painting – the traditionally female (sinister) side – represented domesticity is our introduction to the woman's history.[65] On the opposite, right-hand trajectory, the fictive male painter forms the physical barrier between us and the woman, as it is the actual male painter's act of representation that keeps this woman and her world perpetually outside of our reach.

"History," the object of all this visual attention, is intensely aware of her own status as that which is seen. Compare her to Rembrandt's model-in-studio, whose apparent unself-consciousness within that ambiguous environment was so unsettling to behold. Vermeer's woman is highly self-conscious in her occupation of a space that is definitely hers. To us she is on the far side of a room, distanced, inaccessible, mediated. But within her own experience, she is comfortably deep within a place where she belongs. Posed between the window to public space and the intimate gaze of private representation, she presents and permits a view of herself as actress in a domestic costume piece; and the quiet force of her confidence in visibility reverberates throughout her world. Thus, in this private homage to his personal craft, Vermeer at once concedes feminine control over both the understood environment and over visual experience and its representation. In allegorizing the Art of Painting, he acknowledges the fact that within his visual culture, art has been truly domesticated – indeed, that is its very essence, its power, and its history.

Notes

INTRODUCTION

1. This is not to deny however that Dutch artists sometimes painted subjects of the type more frequently encountered in other European countries, namely, history paintings; see Exhib. cat. Washington D.C. 1980–1.
2. For the reception of Dutch painting in the eighteenth and nineteenth centuries, see Grijzenhout and Van Veen 1992.
3. Peter Hecht, one of the contributors to this volume, has recently challenged Emmens's reading of the triptych; see Hecht 1995.
4. See also De Jongh 1995, a volume of De Jongh's collected work which includes revised versions of some of his articles along with one of his lectures that appears in print for the first time.
5. For the following section of this introduction, which discusses and critiques iconological readings of Dutch seventeenth-century paintings, see Franits 1994, pp. 129–34, passim. In De Jongh's recently published collected essays, De Jongh 1995, p. 19, acknowledges Panofsky's influence upon his interpretive method but rightly calls attention to several major conceptual differences between them.
6. Panofsky 1962, pp. 3–17. See also Holly 1984, pp. 158–93; Moxey 1985–6; Falkenburg 1993, pp. 140–7.
7. Panofsky 1953, pp. 140–4. Panofsky argues that disguised symbolism was first developed in Trecento Italy and then perfected in the Netherlands, where it quickly became an intrinsic feature of Netherlandish art.
8. Panofsky 1934, p. 127.
9. For the links between De Jongh's and Panofsky's method, see Falkenburg 1993, pp. 161–2. See also n. 5 above.
10. Cf. De Jongh 1967, pp. 21–2; and especially the essay reprinted in this volume.
11. For emblems, see the essay by Renger reprinted in this volume.
12. See for example, Visscher 1614, pp. iv–v; and De Brune 1624, sig. *1ᵛ. These passages have been cited in several studies by De Jongh; see for example, De Jongh 1967, pp. 8–9; De Jongh 1976, p. 20; De Jongh 1982, pp. 27, 36 n. 4. For Horace's doctrine *ut pictura poesis* and its ramifications for art and literary theory of the sixteenth and seventeenth centuries, see the fundamental study by Lee 1967.
13. Van Mander 1604, *Wtbeeldinge der figuren*, dedication, "Aen Const-rijcken, cloecksinnighen Mr. Cornelis Ketel, Schilder en Dichter," sig. 123ᵛ; Van Hoogstraeten 1678, p. 90. For these passages, see De Jongh 1976, p. 20.
14. It is De Jongh's use of emblems that has proven so influential, particularly among younger art historians. Unfortunately, many historians regarded emblems as magical interpretive keys, which gave rise to the misleading tendency to view Dutch paintings as "painted emblems" and the process of interpreting them as "emblematic interpretation." See Bedaux 1987, pp. 151–4; Idem 1990, 74–6. See also the essay by Renger reprinted in this volume.
15. A fairly comprehensive list of his publications appears in the bibliography of this volume.
16. Here I am thinking of such publications as De Jongh and Vinken 1961 and De Jongh 1967.
17. See Holly 1984, pp. 158–93; Moxey 1985–6; Vanbergen 1986, 39–44, 55–8, 84, 111–12; Idem 1990, pp. 80–4; Falkenburg 1993, pp. 140–7. See also De Jongh 1990, 36–8, which discusses the work of these critics.
18. This point has been made by Sutton 1984, p. xxi; Bedaux 1986, pp. 5–6; Idem 1990, pp. 12–16. For his

defense of the concept of concealed symbols, see De Jongh 1995, pp. 15–18.

19. Panofsky 1962, p. 8. For this problem, see also De Jongh 1992b, pp. 307, 322; Idem 1995, p. 19.
20. See, for example, Bruyn 1988. The scholarly reaction to this essay has been largely negative; see Falkenburg 1993, pp. 162–5. The studies by De Jongh 1990, pp. 43–44, 46–47; and Idem 1992b, pp. 322, 326, both discuss Bruyn's article as well as the problem of applying Panofsky's method to the interpretation of still-life and landscape paintings. See also the contributions by Lawrence Goedde and Celeste Brusati in this volume.
21. Among many others, Sluijter (1990, pp. 6–7; Idem 1992, p. 375; and the essay reprinted in this volume) has frequently called attention to this problem. See also Vanbergen 1986, pp. 104–9, 111–12; Willems 1993, pp. 130–5, passim. De Jongh 1990, p. 37; and Idem 1992b, p. 375, himself notes that a number of scholars are preoccupied with the issue of form and content and their mutual relationship. See also Idem 1995, pp. 13–14.
22. In the essay by Sluijter reprinted in this volume, n. 84; and in Idem 1991, pp. 50, 58, he calls attention to the curious distinction that some scholars make between "meaning" and "meaninglessness" when interpreting art.
23. Alpers 1983. Scholarly reviews of this book varied markedly; among the last, and most illuminating, was Honig 1990.
24. Barthes used the term "reality effect" to describe the formative strategies of French realist authors; see Barthes 1982.
25. See also Sluijter 1990, pp. 22–26. For a critique of Sluijter's article, see Henneke 1994, 415–18.
26. Ample documentation for this – at least for the Leiden *fijnschilders* – is provided by Sluijter 1988c, pp. 15–23. See also Idem 1993.
27. Exhib. cat. Amsterdam 1989–90.
28. For example, Bruyn 1991; Falkenburg 1991, pp. 129–34; Sluijter 1991; De Jongh 1992a, pp. 279–80; De Jongh 1992b, pp. 327–28; Sluijter 1992, p. 383.
29. For Hecht's response to some of these criticisms, see in addition to the essay reprinted here, Raben and Vermeij 1990 (an article based on interviews with Hecht and De Jongh).
30. Goedde 1989c, p. 16, states that "Even when followed thoughtlessly, a convention or formula communicates meaning and can be analyzed for evidence of what contemporaries expected to see – or not to see – and what they found significant and worthy of representation out of all the multiple possibilities of existence." See also Idem 1986, p. 146.
31. Summers 1981–2, pp. 112–14. See also Wolff 1981, pp. 64–5.
32. For historical anthropology and seventeenth-century Dutch art, see Falkenburg 1993. For historical anthropology and seventeenth-century Dutch culture, see Boekhorst, Burke, and Frijhoff 1992.
33. Svetlana Alpers's essay for this volume also discusses the often ambiguous ways in which Dutch paintings articulate emerging concepts of domestic virtue.

CHAPTER ONE. ON THE HISTORY OF RESEARCH CONCERNING THE INTERPRETATION OF DUTCH PAINTING

1. Exhib. cat. Amsterdam 1976. The catalogue was prepared by Jan Baptist Bedaux, Peter Hecht, Eddy de Jongh, Jeroen Stumpel, and Rik Vos.
2. De Jongh 1967.
3. De Jongh's essay has been reprinted in this volume.
4. Warburg 1932.
5. Panofsky 1933.
6. Neumann 1902; Schmidt-Degener 1928.
7. Kauffmann 1920. Schmidt-Degener 1928, p. 23, argues against Rembrandt's connection to the Muiderkring.
8. Kauffmann 1930.
9. See Exhib. cat. Brunswick 1978, cat. no. 10.
10. Kauffmann 1943.
11. Rudolph 1938.
12. Bergström 1947 (an English edition of this book was published in 1956); Bergström 1955. In an essay that appeared in 1938, J. G. van Gelder traced the individual motifs of the flower vase and flower pot from their origins in Christian art to seventeenth-century still lifes. In this study, principally one of the history of motifs, he already suggested interpretations from contemporary sources; see Van Gelder 1938.
13. Exhib. cat. Leiden 1970.
14. Wiegand 1971.
15. Kauffmann 1977.
16. Gudlaugsson 1938.
17. Gudlaugsson 1945.
18. Cats 1618b; De Brune 1624; Spinniker 1714.
19. Green 1872; Idem 1870a; Idem 1870b.
20. De Vries 1899.
21. Praz 1939–47. A second, enlarged edition of Praz's study appeared in 1964.
22. Schöne 1964.
23. Gielow 1915; Volkmann 1923. The latter study was reprinted in 1962.
24. Von Monroy 1942.
25. Evers 1943, c. p. 241 or 160; Kauffmann 1950.
26. De Jongh and Vinken 1961.
27. Slive 1963.
28. Heckscher and Wirth 1959.
29. Henkel and Schöne 1967.
30. Bergström 1966. He treated the same theme in a lec-

ture given to the Art-Historical Society of Berlin on June 14, 1965; see the Society's *Sitzungsberichte*, New Series, 13 (1964–5), p. 15.

31. Emmens 1973.
32. Haverkamp-Begemann 1959; Gudlaugsson 1959–60; Slive 1970–4.
33. See Vischer 1846–57, vol. 3, pp. 662ff.; Riehl 1884, p. iv; Brieger 1922, passim; Böhm 1928. There is a summary of the different definitions of the term in Renger 1970, pp. 9–16.
34. See Stechow and Comer 1975–6.
35. Burckhardt 1919.
36. Slive 1962.
37. Schneede 1968.
38. Reznicek 1963a; Miedema 1975.
39. See the contribution of De Jongh in this volume.
40. See Schöne 1964, p. 26.
41. Alpers 1983.
42. Bedaux 1990.
43. Exhib. cat. Amsterdam 1989–90.
44. Raupp 1983.
45. De Jongh 1992b. See also Hecht 1986 and his contribution to the present volume.

CHAPTER TWO. A SEVENTEENTH-CENTURY THEORY OF ART

1. Horace and Van Mander are cited by Gombrich 1960, p. 191.
2. Angel 1642, p. 56.
3. Vos 1726, vol. 2, p. 515.
4. Van Hoogstraeten 1678, p. 234.
5. De Geest 1702, p. 92.
6. Houbraken 1718–21, vol. 2, p. 1.
7. Vondel is cited by Slive 1953, p. 74, n. 1. For the history of Rembrandt's reputation, see Heiland and Lüdecke 1960; Scheller 1961; and the literature cited there. Within the connections discussed here, it is quite significant that Ploos van Amstel 1785, p. 243, considered Rembrandt's work "less detailed and noble" in comparison with Dou's, although Rembrandt was certainly "a greater poet in coloring."
8. Houbraken 1718–21, pp. 5–6.
9. See, for example, Bauch 1960, p. 219, "Das Thema wird aller äusseren und inneren Bedeutung entkleidet, ebenso wie die rings in den Raum gestellten Gegenstände und dieser selbst." Bauch wrote this about the later development of Dou's work, clearly misled by a modern notion of aesthetic "meaning."
10. De Bie 1661, p. 277.
11. According to Martin 1913, pl. 93, the original triptych must have come into being around 1660. The copy by Laquy – namely, the center painting on canvas and the two wings on panel – were acquired by the Rijksmuseum in 1907–8 from the Six collection. For the history of the original piece, for the description of it in the auction catalogue of 1771, and for a discussion of Laquy's activities, cf. Bille 1961, vol. 1, pp. 39, 40, 46, 47, 56 n. 30; vol. 2, pp. 13–14. See also Martin 1901, pp. 77, 155–6, cat. no. 304.
12. Houbraken 1718–21, vol. 2, p. 5.
13. Ibid., vol. 3, p. 211.
14. This utterance is attributed to Aristotle by Diogenes Laertius, V, 18. For Cicero, Quintillian, and Junius, cf. Ellenius 1960, p. 73, and the literature cited there. For Rodenburgh, see further n. 21, this chapter.
15. Erasmus is cited by Woodward 1904, p. 79, n. 1. For Dutch translations of Plutarch, see Geerebaert 1924, p. 68. The passage quoted here is from T. 1634, p. 4.
16. According to one of the most popular moralists of the Dutch Republic, Jacob Cats, "Een die haer kinders baert, is moeder voor een deel; Maer die haer kinders soocht, is moeder in 'tgheel [Cats 1625, chap. 5, p. 45.]" Amusing, in connection with the view that we "drink in" our character with our mother's milk, is a story in De Brune 1665, p. 120, about an "important official" who was "brought up" on "goat's milk" and consequently had to spend a half-hour everyday "springing and jumping like a goat." In secret, to be sure.
17. Ripa 1644, pp. 349–50.
18. Aristotle, *Physica*, bk. 2, p. 1.
19. Ripa 1644, pp. 286, 287.
20. For example, this representation appears in Pieter Bruegel the Elder's print of *Temperantia;* cf. Bastelaer 1908, pl. 138. In Dou's triptych, human nature is also "tempered" by the arts; see Van Hoogstraeten 1678, pp. 262, 268.
21. For instruction and study, alertness (*Vigilantia*) is naturally demanded, but this can take place in the early morning as well as at night. See Van Veen 1612, pp. 40–1 and the commentary on the emblem *Studio et Vigilantia*, for example, by Rollenhagen 1611–13, vol. 1, no. 67, whose couplet is extensively paraphrased by Rodenburgh 1619, p. 374, no. 67: "wyl de wack're geest Mits als *Aurora* rijst zijn oeffenigh aenvaerden. Iae in de stille nachtens wijsheyts Boeken leest: Waer-uyt hy lieve Vruchten voor zijn Ziel vergaerden; Ver-rykende zyn Gheest / door arbeyd met voor-zicht / Waer d'andren blyven steeds lanternen zonder licht." This poem was again cited in the oft-used grammar by Dafforne 1627, sig. 5 and 6, a little work whose title page is also interesting for its conceit of the theme with which we are concerned here. The "lantern without light" as a man without "reason" is also found in Visscher 1614, pt. 1, no. 23. For the significance of the candle, and, in connection with the meaning of the pen cutter discussed later, also that of the hourglass and book,

cf. Junius 1569, no. 2. This little book was likewise translated by Rollenhagen into Dutch; see, for example, Landwehr 1962, p. 39, no. 118; p. 69, no. 196; and p. 70, no. 197.

22. Ripa 1644, p. 358.
23. For the saying, *Nil penna, sed usus*, see Rollenhagen 1611–13, vol. 1, p. 36. This too was extensively paraphrased by Rodenburgh 1619, p. 358, no. 36: "Wy zien de Voghel-struys zijn wiecken oock gheniet, Maer oeffeninghs gebreck hem drullen op d'Aerde: Dus die een penne heeft, en die staegh oeffend niet, Komt nimmer tot de kunst des schrijvers-lof hooghwaerde . . ." For the saying, *Senza taglio, non vaglio*, see Picinelli 1694, vol. 2, pp. 138–9. It is not the place here to go further into the countless ways in which the "Benefit of Adversity" can be imaged.
24. See Vondel 1927–40, vol. 7, pp. 368–9, and also Van Hoogstraeten 1678, p. 16.
25. Rodenburgh 1619, p. 25. For Van Mander, see Hoecker 1916, esp. p. 20, and the index, for "practice."
26. See Junius 1641, p. 186.
27. Ellenius 1960, p. 73.
28. Van Hoogstraeten 1678, pp. 13–18.
29. The first of these biographers, Von Sandrart 1675, vol. 2, p. 326, names "angeborne Inclination und Neigung," thus natural talent, and "groszen Fleiz." thus practice, as Rembrandt's two most striking qualities. In other words, he lacked a conception of art schooled by theory; Von Sandrart's biography of Rembrandt is reprinted in Slive 1953, pp. 208–9.
30. See Martin 1913, pl. 23.

CHAPTER THREE. REALISM AND SEEMING REALISM IN SEVENTEENTH-CENTURY DUTCH PAINTING

1. Gombrich 1969. The conviction that an artist's environment is reflected in his work is already classic; see Emmens 1968, p. 82.
2. Rosenberg, Slive, and Ter Kuile 1966, p. 114.
3. Mimetic theories will not be further addressed here: Just the terminology itself is problematic. I use the concept of "reality" in its everyday sense, without taking into account perception theory or phenomenology. While not absolutely watertight, the term "seeming realism" is used here for lack of a better one.
4. Bialostocki 1966, pp. 187–230.
5. Knipping 1939–40, vol. 1, pp. 12ff. and passim; Zijderveld 1953, pp. 121–41; Knuvelder 1970–6, vol. 2, pp. 71–6. Literature and the visual arts were closely interconnected in the seventeenth century. For example, many painters belonged to chambers of rhetoric or wrote poetry independently. One spoke of the "gezusters schilderkonst en dichtkonst" (sister arts of painting and poetry). Among the most prevalent clichés in this respect are "stomme poëzie" (dumb poetry) for painting and "sprekend schilderij" (speaking painting) for poetry. See Lee 1967.
6. Grootes 1968, pp. 13–16; Burger 1925, pp. 145–92.
7. Schotel 1874, vol. 2, pp. 171–5. See also Schenck 1968, pp. 44ff.
8. An emblem, or symbol (*zinnebeeld*), usually consists of three parts: a motto, an illustration, and an explanation. Together, these parts ensure a proper understanding of the whole and are meant to be "read" in combination. Usually, the emblem expresses a general idea or moral. There are also device books, whose structure in principle differs little from that of emblem books. However, a device is more closely connected to an intellectual construct, the moral or code of behavior of a particular, usually noble, individual. See Heckscher and Wirth 1959; De Jongh 1967, pp. 8ff.; and Landwehr 1970.
9. On the numerous reprints of Cats's work, see the bibliography in De Jonge van Ellemeet 1887.
10. De Jongh 1967, p. 19.
11. Cats 1622, p. 13: "niet te willen misduyden dat wy deselve beelden ende ghelyckenisse beyde ende tot menschelijcke invallen en tot Goddelijcke bedenckinghen 'tgeheele werck door onverscheydelijcken hebben gebruyckt, en dat oock somwylen met strydige veranderingen, 't welck misschien yemandt mochte oordeelen heet ende kout uyt eenen mont geblasen te zijn." And "niet selden een ende selve sake, nu ten goede, ende dan ten quaden in ghelijckenisse wert getoogen."
12. Gudlaugsson 1959–60, vol. 1, pp. 80ff.; Schneede 1965, pp. 264–5; De Jongh 1968–9, pp. 22–74, esp. 71.
13. For example, *Sanguineus* by Pieter de Jode after Maerten de Vos (Hollstein 1949–, vol. 9, no. 101), *Terra* by Chrispijn de Passe (Hollstein 1949–, vol. 15, no. 524), and *Age XX* also by De Passe (Hollstein 1949–, vol. 15, no. 479).
14. Poirters 1714, pp. 219–20. For the countless reprints of this book that appeared after the first edition of 1646, see Landwehr 1970, nos. 509–37.
15. Cats 1632, sigs. iv–v: "geheel buygsaem ende reckelick [zijn] tot veelderley saecke." And "Datse [that is 'spreucken' and 'spreeckwoorden'] door een aengename duysterheyt sonderlinge bevalligh zijn, en wat anders inden schijn, wat anders nae de waerheyt in sich hebben, waer van de leser naederhant het rechte wit en oogmerck komende te treffen, placht in sijn gemoet een sonderling vernoegen t'ontfan-

gen; niet ongelijck den genen die onder de dichte bladeren eenen schoonen tros druyven, nae lange soecken, eyntelick komt te ontdecken. *De bevindinge leert ons dat veel dingen beter aert hebben alse niet ten volle gesien, maar eenige maten bewimpelt en overschaduwet ons voor-komen. . . .*" The italics in the last sentence of the quote are mine. This translation is taken from Praz 1964, pt. 1, 169–70.

16. Visscher 1614, preface (sig. ii); De Jongh 1967, pp. 21–2.
17. Van Hoogstraeten 1678, pp. 88, 90: "Alhoewel de konst van Schilderen in haer zelve groot is, zegt *Plinius*, zoo behouden nochtans de diepzinnige vonden en heymelijke verstanden, die 'er somtijts in aen te merken zijn, haren byzonderen lof: en zeker hier inne wort het diepzinnich verstand des meesters byzonder gekent: . . . zoo is't . . . den Schilderyen een luister, datze met den eerlijken naem van d'een of d'ander leersame beduidenis bekleet zijn." And "Een eenzaem stuk op 't prijslijkst te versieren, / Geschiet op 't best, uit veelerley manieren, / Met bywerk dat bedektlijk iets verklaert: / Een Zinnebeelt uit beelden dient vergaert. . . ."
18. Würtenberger 1937, pp. 57–8; De Jongh 1967, pp. 6–7, fig. 1; Judson 1970, pp. 97–8, fig. 163.
19. David 1602–3, p. 106: "Het leven vanden mensche opder aerden / is eenen strijdt. Deze weerelt is het veldt / daer den strijdt en slagh ghelevert wordt: ons leven / is den tijdt van vechten / ende de croone te verdienen: ende dan volght den tijdt van ghecroont te werden / veur die wel ghevochten sal hebben."
20. De Brune 1624, p. 163: "Deze aerde is ghelijck een strijd-veld, waer in wy ter preuve ghestelt zijn, teghen onze vyanden. De eeuwighe ruste is de opgehanghen prijs van de gheduerighe on-ruste. Wy en hebben in dit gevecht gheen andere wapenen van doen, als bet gheloove, dat door de liefde krachtigh is."
21. Judson 1970, p. 97, fig. 27; see also Idem 1962, pp. 77–122, esp. pp. 98–100. Dirck Barendsz. also designed a representation for the *Mensheid voor de zondvloed*, that was engraved by Jan Sadeler.
22. MacLaren 1960, pp. 96ff. I intend to discuss this painting and the one mentioned in n. 23 at length elsewhere.
23. Plietzsch 1960, fig. 110.
24. Molenaer's painting with the ball players was with art dealer Enneking in Amsterdam in 1970. Mr. B. Haak kindly drew my attention to it. The other work by Molenaer is in Richmond [Virginia], The Virginia Museum of Fine Arts, and was published by Van Thiel 1967–8, pp. 90–9.
25. De Jongh 1967, p. 21.
26. Kauffmann 1943; Li 1955; Veenstra 1968, pp. 130–67.
27. Van Beverwijck 1651, p. 1: "Daer en is niet in het Verstant, het welck te voren niet van doen gehadt en heeft den dienst van de Sinnen."
28. The traditional view is propagated in an epigram by Jeremias de Decker (1609–66): "Do these five servants of will and lust, / Help or hinder us in their service?" (De dienaren van wil en wellust alle vyf, / Zijn ze ons of hinderlyk of nut in hun bedryf?; De Decker 1726, vol. 2, p. 25). Vondel considered both the positive and negative aspects of the senses in a series of related poems but in his *Altaergeheimenissen* (Altar Mysteries) judged all five of them untrustworthy. Pleading on behalf of faith, Vondel even ousts the sense of Hearing, disregarding the apostolic view that faith arises from the act of hearing (Vondel 1894–9, vol. 1642–5, pp. 167–9; vol. 1657–60, pp. 101–4; and vol. 1645, p. 20: "Op de Tittelprint van d'Altaergeheimenissen"); see also Knipping 1939–40, pp. 51–3.
29. On the hierarchy of Sight and Hearing, see Emmens 1956; Veenstra 1968, pp. 132ff.; and Scheller 1969, pp. 81–147, esp. pp. 109, 112.
30. The special role allotted to the Five Senses in the seventeenth century is clear from the fact that besides being personified by three couples with attributes and by Venus and Amor, they figure on the frontispiece of the enormously popular seventeenth-century songbook, Anon. (c. 1620), with engravings by Chr. de Passe and others. This illustration actually embodies the program of the book, in which the senses are repeatedly alluded to both implicitly and explicitly (pp. 56, 108–9, 110–11).
31. For this painting, see Li 1955, p. 69.
32. See Slive 1970–4, vol. 1, pp. 109–11, for a brief summary of various "drinkers." The *Gula* belongs to a series of *VII Peccatorum Capitalium Imagines* . . . , designed by Philips Galle.
33. *Leerrijke reeksen* was the title of an exhibition of prints held in the Museum Boymans-Van Beuningen in Rotterdam in 1966 (catalogue by B. L. D. Ihle). On the concept of series in the Middle Ages (stimulated primarily by the encyclopedists), see Mâle 1953 (6th edition), pp. 315ff.; and Idem 1923, passim; Frey and Beer 1958. See also Philip 1958, n. 19.
34. Exhib. cat. Rotterdam 1966, pp. 4, 17.
35. Van Veen 1960, under "natuur als openbaring"; Beening 1963, pp. 120ff., 135ff., 143, 145ff., 158ff., 255, and 459–60. See also Panofsky 1962, pp. 64, 150 on the concept of the *paysage moralisé*.
36. Huygens 1892–9, vol. 6, p.36; Cats 1656; Van Veen 1960, pp. 33–4.

37. Stechow 1968, pp. 82–7 (Esaias van de Velde); p. 178, figs. 358–9 (Van der Neer); and p. 182, figs. 367–8 (Verschuier).
38. This method is outlined in Haverkamp-Begemann 1959, p. 37. The painting by Seghers is in Rotterdam, Museum Boymans-van Beuningen. See Rosenberg, Slive, and Ter Kuile 1966, pp. 139–79; Stechow 1968, passim; and Blankert 1965, pp. 13–39.
39. Haverkamp Begemann 1959, p. 216, n. 185.
40. Bergström 1956, pp. 42–97.
41. Van Gelder 1936, pp. 73–82, 155–66.
42. Ibid., p. 81.
43. Bergström 1956, pp. 65–6, fig. 51. In contrast to many other works by Ambrosius Bosschaert which include flowers that would ordinarily bloom at different times of the year, here the bouquet consists solely of four kinds of roses.
44. Bergström 1955, pp. 303–8, 342–9; Idem 1956, p. 43.
45. These words are taken from the last sentence of the six-line inscription under the print by Goltzius of 1582 (Fig. 8). Around the flowers in the man's right hand is written "So passes away the glory of the world" (*Sic transit gloria mundi*) (Hollstein 1949–, vol. 8, no. 250).
46. Van Mander 1616, fol. 118 ("De Slecke"); see also Valerianus 1602, p. 287 ("De Cochlea: Terrenis Addictus"). On the butterfly, see Timmers 1947, p. 783; and Bergström 1955, pp. 307, 342. See also Vignau-Schuurman 1969, under "Schnecke" and "Schmetterling."
47. Bergström 1956, pp. 154–90; Haak 1967; Idem 1968. See also Exhib. cat. Leiden 1970.
48. De Jongh 1967, pp. 58–60. See further n. 51.
49. Ripa 1644, p. 317: "Om de plicht van de Maetigheyt te vertoonen: die daer in bestaet, datmen de tochten van 't gemoed, nae den tijd breydle en betoome."
50. Houbraken 1718–21, vol. 2, pp. 276–7: "Zekere Mevrouw (wier naam ik niet melden wil) die op veere na de schoonste niet was, liet haar pourtret van hem schilderen, 't welk hy zoo even, als het was met al de pokputten en naden had nagebootst. Zy opgestaan zag zoo vies als zy wel mocht, zaggende tegens hem: 'Wat Duivel, Maes, hebje daar voor een monstereuze troony naar my gemaalt! ik begeer 't zoo niet gemaakt te hebben, de honden zouden 't wel nabassen, zoo 't over de straat gedragen wierd.' Maes, die toen haast bemerkte wat 'er voor hem te doen stondt, zeide: 'Mevrouw, 't en is noch niet voltooit,' en verzocht haar andermaal te zitten: nam een Vispenceel en verdreef al die pokputten, zette een blos op de wangen en zeide, 'Mevrouw nu is het gedaan, u believe het nu eens te zien.' Zy het gezien hebbende zeide: 'Ja, zoo moest het wezen.' Zy nam daar genoegen in toen 't er niet geleek."
51. Emmens 1961, esp. pp. 58–9, and figs. 11–12. See also Fischel 1911, figs. 70, 91, 130, 220. For Dutch examples, I cite an engraving by Johannes Bara of 1599, representing Joachim, Count of Ortenburg, and a painted portrait of a magistrate by Eglon van der Neer (with pendant: sale Frederik Muller, Amsterdam, June 4, 1929). Watches served as a *vanitas* attribute, for example, in portraits by Gerard Ter Borch (see Gudlaugsson 1959–60, vol. 1, figs. 101, 102) and Caspar Netscher (portrait of Geertruid Huygens, wife of Ph. Doublet; Hofstede de Groot 1907–28, vol. 5, no. 211).
52. De Jongh and Vinken 1961; De Jongh 1967, pp. 27–34.
53. De Lairesse 1707, vol. 2, p. 5: "door dezen weg [namely, portraits] eerder als door den anderen tot een gouden gedenkpenning, aan een keten van dezelfde stoffe hangende, kan geraaken . . . meenigmaal alleen bevoorrecht om het afbeeldsel van den Oppervorst te schilderen, en door dit middel groote schatten te vergaaderen . . . Wat deze stoffe belangt, het heeft my menigmaal vreemd gedacht, hoe iemand zyne vrijheid kan verlaaten om zich tot een slaaf te maaken, en van de volmaaktheid dezer edele Konst afwyken om zich zelven aan alle de gebreken der Natuur te onderwerpen."
54. Van Mander 1617, fol. 196: "sijd-wegh der Consten." See also Reznicek 1963a.
55. Van Mander 1617, fols. 211 and 207: "Het conterfeyten nae 't leven geeft hy by hem geen plaetse / op dat zijnen gheest daerdoor niet worde verhindert" (Bloemaert). And "beter als gheern doet / dewijl hy zijnen gheest tot soo een besonder dinghen niet can begeven" (Cornelis). [Editor's note: The English translations of these two passages were made by Charles Ford.]
56. Van Hoogstraeten 1678, pp. 75–87, esp. p. 87. See also Emmens 1968, pp. 69, 121.
57. Houbraken 1718–21, vol. 2, p. 276: "*Bruer ik heb deernis met ou, ben dy me van die Martelaren?* ziende op die verdrietige berispingen, en slaafse onderwerpinge van ieders geneigtheit, 't zulke Schilders niet zelden getroost moeten wezen."
58. Wishnevsky 1967.
59. Ibid., pp. 45ff., 155–6 (Moses); pp. 75ff., 181–92 (Diana); pp. 47ff., 158 (David); pp. 91, 196 (Hercules).
60. Ibid., pp. 105–8.
61. Bergström 1966, esp. pp. 164–5.
62. Emmens 1968, p. 144.
63. Floerke 1905; Koch 1967, pp. 62–86; see also Martin 1907.
64. The Catholic churches in the Seven Provinces

became so-called *schuilkerken* ("hidden churches"). As a consequence, the church's role as patron of the arts was reduced to a minimum. While half of the total population of the Northern Netherlands was still Catholic at mid-century, the official repression of Catholicism significantly weakened its impact on seventeenth-century Dutch culture. Nonetheless, there was a "Catholic art," which flourished primarily in the circle of the so-called Haarlem Academists, and in Utrecht, where Catholicism enjoyed greater freedom than elsewhere in the Republic. Many artists were also Catholic, including Goltzius, the Bloemaerts, Terbrugghen, Van Honthorst, Salomon de Bray, Van Goyen, Jan Steen, Adriaen van de Velde, Karel Dujardin, and Johannes Vermeer. Examples of "Catholic art" in this exhibition are Van Baburen's *Crowning of Thorns* (though not entirely certain, Van Baburen was most likely Catholic), and the *Madonna* by Jan van Bijlert (Exhib. cat. Brussels 1971, cat. nos. 5, 18). See Huizinga 1948, pp. 451, 459; Geyl 1961–2, vol. 2, pp. 581ff.; Rogier 1947, vol. 2, pp. 647–91; and Idem 1968, pp. 101–15, 167–77. See also Slive 1956. Noble patrons were few. Frederik Hendrik's court in The Hague did provide some patronage but favored Flemish and Dutch artists influenced by Rubens and a sort of "cool" academicism. See Hudig 1928; Van Gelder 1948–9; and Snoep 1969.

65. Floerke 1905, passim; Koch 1967, pp. 62–86. There are a few representations of the art trade, shop interiors, or how the wares were displayed, including works by David Vinckboons, Job Berckheyde, and Salomon de Bray (Ibid., figs. 34–40).
66. Martin 1907, pp. 17–18; Zumthor 1962, vol. 2, pp. 34ff.
67. *The Travels of Peter Mundy in Europe and Asia 1608–1667*, quoted in Exhib. cat. London 1971–2, p. 35, n. 56. John Evelyn was in Holland in 1641 and was quite impressed by the large number of paintings he saw there; see Floerke 1905, p. 20; and Koch 1967.
68. De Decker 1726, vol. 1, p. 127 ("Lof der Geldzucht"): "Vrouw Schilderkunst . . . meer (zoo 't schynt) op eer dan geldwinst afgerecht, / Geen windei evenwel haer' oeffenaers en legt."
69. Brom 1957, p. 180.
70. Van Hoogstraeten 1678, pp. 353ff. Compare with the remark by Gerard de Lairesse, cited in the section entitled "Portraiture," regarding painters permitted to portray the supreme ruler. On the concepts of "honor" and "profit" (*eer* and *gewin*), see Emmens 1968, pp. 135–137, 159; and Scheller 1969, pp. 132ff.
71. Scheller 1969. See also De Jongh 1969.
72. Gachard 1877, pp. 195–6; Baudouin 1962, esp. p. 38.
73. "die niet zou blozen als ik mijn penselen ter hand nam." The letter, written in Italian, is dated December 18, 1634; the passage in question contains some Latin. See Rooses and Ruelens 1887–1909, vol. 6, p. 82; and Magurn 1955, p. 393.
74. Hirschmann 1916, pp. 53–5, 77–8.
75. Van Mander 1618, sigs. 3–3^v.
76. Van Gelder 1958, p. 15; Taverne 1964, esp. pp. 37–38.
77. Van Mander 1616, sig. 113^v; see also Cartari 1581, p. 274.
78. As far as I know, the combination of Mercury and the old woman is unique. Goltzius here drew a parallel with the traditional antagonists, *Pictura* and *Invidia*. See Pigler 1953–4, pp. 215–35; and Winner 1957, pp. 64–87.
79. The theme was propagated as "exquisite invention" by Leon Battista Alberti in his *Della Pittura* (1435–6); see Alberti 1966, pp. 90–1; Van Mander 1617, sigs. 17^v–18. See Förster 1887, pp. 29–56, 89–113; and Panofsky 1962, pp. 84–5, 158–9.
80. Van Mander 1617, sigs. 17^v–18, "Dus heeft Apelles, zijn avontuere seer gheestich te kennen ghegheven. En dit stuc worde grootlyckx gheacht om der onschult / deucht en const des Meesters / en oock om de wonderlijk fraey Inventie / *die dienstigh magh wesen den ghenen / die des volcks valschen achterclap noch onderworpen is* / tot een hoopigh voorbeelt van vrolycke uytcomst te genieten." The passage by Van Mander (italics mine) is an extension of Alberti's "exquisite invention."
81. Van Hoogstraeten 1678, pp. 91, 314ff: "Schimpschilderyen" and "wraekoeffeningen der Schilders."
82. Hirschmann 1916, p. 78; Pigler 1953–4.
83. Van Mander 1616, sigs. 69, 70^v, "Leerlyck uytlegh op Cacus": "valsche verleydighe wijsmakinghe / oft logen/ die des deuchts ghehoorsame kudde heymelyck en dieflyck ontsteelt"; and "Doch zyn [i.e., Cacus's] ongeherechticheyt openbaer wordende / can tegen de deught niet bestandigh blyven: zyn schande wordt ontdeckt / de duysterlievende valsche meeningen / als nacht-Wlen wijcken."
84. Pigler 1953–4. In 1682, Willem Doudyns made a ceiling painting for the Confrérie Pictura in The Hague, which was admired by Houbraken: "Het middelvak, door Will. Doudyns beschildert, vertoont de Haagse stedemaagt, onder welker bescherming zig de Schilderkonst, Beelthouwery, Glasschildery en Graveerkonst, aanbieden. Hier nevens aan zietmen Pallas verzelt met de Konstliefde, de Grofschilders met ladder en kladpot: De Boekbinders met schroef en pers, en de Stoelmakers met hun gereedschap, in yver ten konsthemel uytbonzen." (The middle area, painted by Will. Doudyns, shows the Hague maiden, offering her

protection to the art of painting, sculpture, glass painting, and engraving. Nearby can be seen Pallas accompanied by the Love of Art assiduously casting out the house painters with ladder and pot of paint, the bookbinders with screw and press, and the furniture makers with their tools from this heaven of the Arts.) Houbraken 1718–21, vol. 1, p. 244; and Hoogewerff 1947, p. 196.

85. Gonnet 1877–8.
86. Hoogewerff 1947, pp. 126–40. See also Reznicek 1963b, pp. 119–23.
87. Reznicek 1961, vol. 1, pp. 28ff.
88. This drawing was published by Taverne 1970.
89. De Bie 1661, p. 12: "Ick wete seer wel Goed-jonstighen LESER, datter veel . . . niet en sullen aenghelockt werden, om den Loff der SCHILDER-CONST met verstand te aenmercken, uyt redenen datter veel Menschen vyandt van deze Const zijn, ende ook niet gheren hooren jemandts lof uyt spreeken, als door een jngheboren belgh-sucht ende hooverdy t' selve benijdende, sal my nochtans troosten met het Latijns spreeckwoordt seggende: Ars nullum habet jnimicum nisi ignorantem, dat den onwetenden alleen vyandt vande Const is."
90. Krul 1634b, pp. 153–4 (Krul used the word *non* instead of *nullum;* the print is by Gerrit Donck). See also Wijngaards 1964, p. 76.
91. Rodenburgh 1619. See also Witstein 1964; Sidney 1965; Clements 1960, pp. 151–71; Weinberg 1961, vol. 1, pp. 250–96.
92. Van Hamel 1918, pp. 56ff.
93. Haak 1967; Idem 1968.
94. De Jongh 1967, pp. 82–5.
95. Knipping 1939–40, vol. 1, pp. 117–20; Vignau-Schuurman 1969, vol. 1, pp. 231ff. The word *Homo* appears in one of the bubbles blown by the boy in an engraving by C. van Sichem, reproduced in Anon. (c. 1620), p. 225.
96. De Jongh 1968–9, esp. pp. 60–2.
97. I will return later to the significance of the lute.
98. Cats 1661, p. 162; Van Beverwijck 1651, p. 141; Ripa 1644, p. 467.
99. Of the remaining details, I single out the tric-trac players in the background. This game was frequently criticized by, among others, Jan van de Velde in a print with an inscription entitled "Verkeerden yver" (Misplaced zeal). See Haverkamp-Begemann 1959, p. 26.
100. A list of paintings of this theme is in Exhib. cat. Paris 1970–1, under nos. 155, 179.
101. De Jongh 1967, p. 86.
102. *Invallende gedachten, op voorvallende gelegentheden* ("Op 't gesichte van een jongen met de blase spelende") in Cats 1656, pp. 16–17; Luiken 1712, pp. 46–7.
103. Anon. 1667. The fact that this almanac appeared simultaneously in Amsterdam and Hoorn is most likely related to the large print run. In the *Groote comptoir almanach* of 1668, published in Amsterdam, the same, though by then very worn, wooden blocks were used as in the previous year. The verses accompanying the months of the year here, however, bear no relationship to the illustrations. The examples I consulted (University Library, Amsterdam, call nos. Z 650 and 641 E 38) contained blank sheets inserted by their owners in order to make notes of accounts and recipes.
104. Ter Gouw 1873, p. 274; Schotel 1873–4, vol. 1, pp. 1–93.
105. "Ghy die naer u welbehagen / Os en Swijn en Kalf doet slaen; / Denckt hoe ghy ten Jongsten Dage / Voor Godts Oordeel sult bestaen." *Slaen*, or strike, here essentially means *slachten*, or slaughter; see the De Vries et al. 1882–, vol. 14, col. 1431, no. 13.
106. See also Emmens 1967, p. 81.
107. Würtenberger 1937, pp. 12–35; Haverkamp-Begemann 1959, pp. 23–4; Judson 1962, p. 105; Goossens 1954, pp. 96ff.
108. Dubiez 1969, fig. 15. Moreover, the combination of the glove and the feather in the painting by Van Mieris is remarkable in itself. The glove could be an allusion to the sense of Touch, as it is in Ripa in the passage mentioned in n. 98. Touch was again connected to libido.
109. Cats 1661, p. 47: "Als geyle vrouwen schoone zijn / Hiet dat juweleelen by een swijn". . ."een sloor, een slons, een rechte slet." In the first edition published in The Hague in 1632, p. 143, the woman is shown without fan or feathers. In Ripa 1644, pp. 469–70, a man representing all the senses "in a single image" sports a forest of feathers on his head, alluding to the fact that "dat de Sinnen sich soo licht bewegen, als de pluymen, door een kleyn windeken" (the senses move as lightly as feathers in a gentle breeze). Feathers also incited Hooft to think of eroticism, although not really of sexuality. In one of his letters to Tesselschade Roemer Visscher, Hooft tells her that a friend of Tesselschade, the singer Francisca Duarte, had left behind her fan (?) during one of her visits to Muiderslot: "Nu bevinden, dat 'er Joffr.e Duarte al meê van haere veêren gelaeten heeft. Die koomen hier nevens overwaeijen. Bruin zijn ze, ende, zoo jk denk, ujt de wieken van dat helsch Engeltjen, de Min, getrokken, ende dat het jonxken in slaep gezongen moest wezen, eer 't zich zoo ontplujmen liet." (Now it seems that Miss Duarte left her feathers. They blow over here somewhere. They are brown and in my opinion must have been plucked from the wings of that infernal little angel called Love, and she must have

lulled him to sleep with her singing before he could be plucked in this manner.) See Worp 1918, pp. 114–15.

110. See n. 5.
111. Gudlaugsson 1945, pp. 14–23; De Groot 1952, pp. 51–6.
112. This drawing by Gesina ter Borch belongs to one of her albums, which are in Amsterdam, Rijksprentenkabinet, inv. no. A 1890–1952 (312-M), p. 24.
113. *The Physician's Visit*, London, Apsley House, The Duke of Wellington Museum.
114. De Jongh 1968–9, pp. 34–5, 54ff.
115. De Vries et al. 1882–, vol. 7, col. 5863.
116. The paintings are in London, Collection of Her Majesty the Queen, Buckingham Palace, and in Amsterdam, Rijksmuseum.
117. P. J. J. van Thiel kindly drew my attention to this painting.
118. De Groot 1952, pp. 62–3. On the flute as a sexual symbol, see also Winternitz 1967, pp. 48ff., 152.
119. De Groot 1952, p. 63. A flutist can be found in a painting rife with erotic allusions entitled *The Courtship*, attributed to Frans van Mieris (Bath, Victoria Gallery).
120. On the lute, see section II.
121. The naked feet of the little girl could be intended as an expression of lust; see Ripa 1644, p. 310: "de voeten . . . zijn een beeldnisse van onse aerdsche begeerlijckheden" (feet . . . are an image of our earthly longings).
122. Judson 1959, p. 236, no. 179.
123. Krul 1634a, p. 4, "de Min (gelijck ghy weet) wert by het vuyr geleecken." See also ibid., p. 8.
124. Praz 1964, pt. 1, pp. 88ff.
125. Cats 1627, pp. 8–9; Krul 1634a, p. 4; Van Veen 1608, pp. 96–7, 138–9, 146–7, 170–1, 188–9, 218–19, and 228–9; Heinsius 1616a, pp. 81–3; De Brune 1624, p. 339.
126. Praz 1964, pt. 1, pp. 88ff.
127. On Dirck Hals, see De Jongh 1967, p. 52. The painting was in the Galerie A. de Ridder in Brussels in 1924.
128. Krul 1634a, pp. 2–3. I use the Amsterdam octavo edition of 1640 because the boat in question is in the same "direction" as that in the painting by Vermeer. See also, Idem 1634b, pp. 48, 145.
129. On the erotic significance of another detail, the slippers in the foreground, see De Jongh 1968–9, pp. 36–7.
130. Snoep 1968–9, esp. p. 96.
131. De Mirimonde 1966; Idem 1967.
132. Westerbaen 1672, vol. 2, p. 721: "Leert op de Luyt, leert op de Clavecijmbel speelen / De snaeren hebben macht om yemands hert te steelen." Compare this adaptation of Ovid to that by Van Heemskerk 1626, p. 122.
133. In this respect, Dirck Hals must be considered a precursor: his *Woman Tearing Up a Letter* (Mainz, Gemäldegalerie) is dated 1631. Gerard ter Borch was actually the first to paint a woman in the act of writing; see Gudlaugsson 1959–60, vol. 1, p. 101.
134. Bray 1967, pp. 10–11.
135. On correspondence manuals, see Schotel 1874, vol. 1, pp. 242–8. Information on Dutch language correspondence manuals was provided by W. Gs. Hellinga.
136. Mostart 1635, pp. 188–97. An adaptation of an English correspondence manual was published in Amsterdam in 1645. Willem Christiaens vander Boxe, the translator, called it *Nederduytsen briefdragher* (Dutch Letter-Carrier) and gave its author as the noble, inventive poet Nicholas Breton (see Breton 1645, pp. 144, 20ff., 85ff., and 98).
137. The popularity of love letter writing emerges also from its criticism. Identical reasoning underlies the fulminations of the Jesuit Adriaan Poirters and that of the Calvinist De Brune against the terminology commonly used by lovers. See De Brune 1624, pp. 19–20; and Poirters 1714, pp. 132–3.
138. Hartlaub 1951; Schwarz 1952; Vignau-Schuurmann 1969, vol. 2, under "Spiegel." See also Van Mander 1616, sig. 119; and David 1610, passim.
139. Cats 1622, pp. 102ff.
140. De Jongh 1970b, p. 7. See also Knipping 1939, vol. 1, pp. 54–5; and Stammler 1959, passim.
141. The last stage is, in fact, when geographical maps are hung as *partes pro toto* instead of world maps. I will address the evolution of "Vrouw Wereld" and the interrelated significance of maps at greater length elsewhere.
142. De Jongh 1970a, p. 1.
143. See Valentiner 1924, figs. 39, 42.
144. De Jongh 1968–9, p. 47.
145. Poirters 1714, p. 320: "is meer als eens gesien dat de sluypende kattekens het vleesch uyt den pot stolen."

CHAPTER FOUR. PICTURING DUTCH CULTURE

1. See De Jongh 1967, and Exhib. cat. Amsterdam 1976.
2. Alpers 1983.
3. See De Jongh 1990–1, and Alpers 1994, p. 18.
4. For an example of the way an economic system can be registered in the making of art, see Alpers 1988.
5. Schama 1987.
6. See Peter Hecht's essay in this volume.
7. For an account of the representation of Dutch women organized by Catsian categories, see Franits 1993.

8. I owe this account of the spatial disposition of women's social roles to the unpublished dissertation of Hollander 1990.
9. Anon. n.d. [1681], pp. 31–2.
10. It is not possible, in my view, to separate out Dutch paintings that represent domestic virtues from those representing wanton women. For a different view of this question, see Franits 1993, passim, and p. 198, n. 6.
11. For a fuller discussion of the artist in the home and to see the images mentioned in the previous paragraphs, see Alpers 1988, pp. 65ff.

CHAPTER FIVE. TOBACCO, SOCIAL DEVIANCE, AND DUTCH ART IN THE SEVENTEENTH CENTURY

1. Knuttel 1908–16, vol. 1, pp. 405–6.
2. Visscher 1614/1949, p. 132: "Veeltijds wat nieuws, selden wat goets."
3. Neander 1622. Subsequent editions of Neander's text appeared in 1623, 1626, 1644, and 1664.
4. Van Beverwijck 1652, p. 150.
5. Van Diemerbroeck 1665, pp. 157, 162–4, 273–4, 294–5.
6. Primrose 1651, pp. 336–9.
7. Chute 1595, pp. 3–21. A Dutch edition of this treatise was published in 1625.
8. Dodoens 1574, pp. 349–51.
9. Van Meteren 1618, fol. 418ᵛ.
10. Davies 1917, p. 40.
11. Ibid.
12. Duco 1978, passim.
13. Primrose 1651, pp. 330–1.
14. Neander 1622, pp. 46, 221–2.
15. Ibid., pp. 47, 223–4.
16. Van de Venne 1634.
17. Idem 1635, p. 70.
18. Schrijver 1630.
19. Le Jolle 1666, p. 1.
20. Van de Venne 1635, pp. 133–6, 145–53.
21. Ibid., title page and p. 158. For the grisaille, see Exhib. cat. Worcester 1979, pp. 113–15.
22. Hofstede de Groot 1907–28, vol. 1, "Jan Steen," nos. 664–848, and Braun 1980, no. 226 (London, The National Gallery); Hofstede de Groot 1907–28, vol 1., no. 712; and Braun 1980, no. 304 (St. Petersburg, Hermitage); Hofstede de Groot 1907–28, vol. 1, nos. 742–Handex ("Handexemplaar": manuscript annotated copy of Hofstede de Groot in The Hague, Rijksbureau voor Kunsthistorisch Documentatie), no. 743a; and Braun 1980, no. 31 (last recorded, London art market); Hofstede de Groot 1907–28, vol. 1, no. 814; and Braun 1980, under no. 285 (last recorded in the Collection of Lord Stonehaven; amended copy of part of the work in Amsterdam, Rijksmuseum: Hofstede de Groot 1907–28, vol. 1, nos. 718–25; and Braun 1980, no. 285); Hofstede de Groot 1907–28, Handexemplaar no. 423b; and Braun 1980, no. 86 (Philadelphia, Philadelphia Museum of Art).
23. Hofstede de Groot 1907–28, vol. 1, no. 829; and Braun 1980, no. 322 (The Hague, Bredius Museum); Hofstede de Groot 1907–28, vol. 1, nos. 795–814i; and Braun 1980, no. 272 (last recorded, London art market, 1977).
24. Hofstede de Groot 1907–28, vol. 1, no. 835; and Braun 1980, no. 262 (Paris, Musée du Louvre); Hofstede de Groot 1907–28, vol. 1, no. 823; and Braun 1980, no. 339 (Amsterdam, Rijksmuseum); Hofstede de Groot 1907, vol. 1, nos. 429a–843; and Braun 1980, no. 340 (The Hague, Mauritshuis); Hofstede de Groot 1907–28, vol. 1, no. 851; and Braun 1980, no. 240 (Oud Beijerland, A. A. Konig Collection).
25. Hofstede de Groot 1907–28, vol. 1, no. 90; and Braun 1980, no. 200 (The Hague, Mauritshuis); Hofstede de Groot 1907–28, vol. 1, no. 111; and Braun 1980, no. 250 (London, National Gallery of Art); Hofstede de Groot 1907–28, vol. 1 nos. 677–80e; and Braun 1980, no. 130 (present location unknown); Hofstede de Groot 1907–28, vol. 1, no. 798; and Braun 1980, no. 112 (present location unknown).
26. Anon. 1681, pp. 259–60.
27. Hofstede de Groot 1907–28, vol. 1, no. 536; and Braun 1980, no. 275. See also Heppner 1939–40, pp. 31–2.
28. Hofstede de Groot 1907–28, vol. 1, no. 694; and Braun 1980, no. 217 (Philadelphia, Philadelphia Museum of Art). Cf. Hofstede de Groot 1907–28, vol. 1, no. 234; and Braun 1980, no. 218 (Munich, Alte Pinakothek): A pipe in a tankard hangs below the window embrasure.
29. Hofstede de Groot 1907–28, vol. 1, no. 90; and Braun 1980, no. 200; Hofstede de Groot 1907–28, vol. 1, no. 529; and Braun 1980, no. 201.
30. Hofstede de Groot 1907–28, vol. 1, no. 88; and Braun 1980, no. 295. Cf. Hofstede de Groot 1907–28, vol. 1, no. 91; and Braun 1980, no. 153 (Allentown, Allentown Art Museum, Kress Foundation); and Hofstede de Groot 1907–28, vol. 1, nos. 95–9; and Braun 1980, no. 334 (present location unknown: for copies, see Braun).
31. Hofstede de Groot 1907–28, vol. 1., no. 102; and Braun 1980, no. 179 (Vienna, Kunsthistorisches Museum).
32. Hofstede de Groot 1907–28, vol. 1, no. 109; and Braun 1980, no. 197.

33. In addition to the Vienna and Apsley House paintings, the basket is to be seen in the following depictions of dissolute households by Steen: Hofstede de Groot 1907–28, vol. 1, no. 111; and Braun 1980, no. 250 (London, National Gallery of Art); Hofstede de Groot 1907–28, vol. 1, no. 112; and Braun 1980, no. 251 (New York, Private Collection). It is to be seen similarly placed in *The Lean Kitchen*, Cheltenham, Cheltenham Art Gallery (Hofstede de Groot 1907–28, vol. 1, no. 118; and Braun 1980, no. 30) and in two scenes of alchemists' dens: Hofstede de Groot 1907–28, vol. 1, no. 230; and Braun 1980, no. 293 (Venice, Accademia); Hofstede de Groot 1907–28, vol. 1, no. 232; and Braun 1980, no. B-53 (Sale, Amsterdam, Christie's, 1982).
34. Van de Venne 1635, p. 161.
35. Neander 1622, p. 62.
36. Herks 1967, passim; Roessingh 1976, passim.
37. Brongers 1964, p. 72.
38. Duco 1978, passim.
39. Brongers 1964, p. 32; Duco 1981, p. 186.
40. Duco 1981, p. 132.
41. Anon. 1681, pp. 182–5.
42. Brooks 1937–52, vol. 2, p. 390, no. 301.

CHAPTER SIX. DIDACTIC AND DISGUISED MEANINGS?

1. For an overview of this literature up to 1984, see Müller-Hofstede 1984. For an overview of the past few years up to 1987, see Haverkamp-Begemann 1987. Additional pertinent articles for this discussion are found in Purtle et al. 1986, and Bock and Gaehtgens 1987. See also the short summary of lectures given at the symposium "Images of the World: Dutch Genre Painting in Its Historical Context" at the Royal Academy of Arts in London, 9–10 November 1984, on the occasion of the exhibition *The Age of Vermeer and De Hooch: Masterpieces of Seventeenth-Century Dutch Genre Painting* (Philadelphia, London, Berlin, 1984) in Ford 1985, pp. 236–9. The aforementioned literature concerns genre and history painting primarily; with regard to landscape painting, various viewpoints have also been presented. In particular, see the introductions to Exhib. cat. Boston 1988; and the outstanding review of this catalogue by Brown 1988, pp. 76–81. Furthermore, a striking insight into the various points of view – one could even speak of a polarization – can be gained from the numerous critiques of Alpers 1983. For example, Gombrich 1983; Gaskell 1984; Glynne 1984; De Jongh 1984; Schama 1984a; Stumpel 1984; Veltman 1984; Bruyn 1985; Grafton and Kaufmann 1985; Bialostocki 1985; and the introduction by Kemp to Alpers 1986 (a German translation of Alpers 1983). The most balanced and thoughtful discussions are the very different commentaries by Grafton and Kaufmann, Gaskell, and Bialostocki.
2. Bialostocki 1985, p. 525. See Idem 1984, p. 429.
3. Alpers 1983, pp. 229–34, "Appendix: On the Emblematic Interpretation of Dutch Art"; and the harsh overview by De Jongh 1984, p. 58, on the use of this terminology, which suggests that this manner of interpretation is entirely based on the use of the emblems. See also Bedaux 1987, pp. 151–7, esp. n. 2, where a good, corrective explanation is given about the methodological use and abuse of emblems. It cannot be denied that the term applies in that many principles that are apropos the function and meaning of emblems were seen as valid for the interpretation of painting.
4. This description is borrowed from Raupp 1983, p. 401; also cited by Bedaux 1987, p. 151.
5. Bruyn 1988, p. 84.
6. For instance, with regard to the interpretation of the works of art, Haak 1984 relies solely on E. de Jongh's iconological approach (see especially the chapter "Realism and Symbolism"). This was also the case earlier, though with varying degrees of insistence, in much more concise surveys by R. H. Fuchs and Madlyn Millner Kahr. A few educational guides from the Rijksmuseum, Amsterdam, may be mentioned as illustrative but are by no means exceptional. With regard to newspaper articles, those by Milder 1984 and Van Gelder 1984 are typical; from this viewpoint, they criticized the large "genre" exhibition in Philadelphia, London, and Berlin of 1984.
7. Bruyn 1981, p. 5: "de meer of minder bloemrijke, op 'Einfühlung' berustende commentaren waarop gidsen hun toeristen, ouders hun kinderen en allerhande scribenten hun lezers en lezeressen tot op de huidige dag vergasten" (the more or less florid commentaries based on "empathy," with which to this day guides regale their tourists, parents their children, and writers their readers.) This "empathy" appears to have vanished in the past few years, at least with regard to Dutch genre pieces.
8. The success may be partially explained by the fact that from the beginning, De Jongh introduced his approach in an appealing form intended for a broader public: see De Jongh 1967; Exhib. cat. Amsterdam 1976; and the essay by De Jongh in this volume. According to an education department employee in a Dutch museum, polls reveal that the public currently prefers information on symbolism and "hidden meanings." Typical of this approach was the slide show based on Bruyn 1988 for the landscape

exhibition at the Rijksmuseum. Bruyn's view was the most theoretical and speculative, and – given the nature of the exhibition – the least appropriate. It was, however, certainly the easiest to put into words, so now moralizing messages and hidden symbolism have also been provided for landscape. It is significant that De Jongh 1984, p. 59, in his criticism of Alpers 1983, expressed fear that her vision would have wide appeal, because it would provide a "unified field theory" wherein diverse phenomena would be seen to express one and the same mentality: something for which we seem to have a deep-seated need. Ironically, De Jongh's approach, which also had Hegelian roots – in this context, see Gombrich 1969, on Panofskian iconology – appears to have had precisely the effect he feared. He used appealing generalizations about the mentality, such as "the tendency to moralize" that is "all encompassing" and "the strong preference for disguising, veiling, for allegorizing and ambiguity" (see the essay by De Jongh in this volume).

9. For the most severe criticism, see the introduction and appendix to Alpers 1983; several points had been formulated earlier in Alpers 1978–9. Kemp's introduction to Alpers 1986 is also very outspoken. Countless critical modes ranging from the temperate to the subtle can be found among the publications mentioned in n. 1.
10. Angel 1642. As the printer notes, it is "een Schets ende voorwerpsel . . . van het aenstaende werck dat by onsen Autheur berust" (a sketch and a draft . . . of the forthcoming work now with the author); unfortunately, no more than this "sketch" was ever published.
11. Virtually no works by Angel (circa 1618 to after 1664) are known, except for an etched *tronie* (head) in the manner of Rembrandt (see Bol 1949). Angel gave his lecture at a time when Leiden painters were busy – and Angel was directly involved – gaining permission to establish a guild to protect them economically and probably also to be recognized as a group with an important socioeconomic status in Leiden society (see Sluijter 1988c, pp. 29–31). Angel's emphasis on the status and dignity of the painter's craft appears to be related to this attempt. The lecture probably appeared at the same time as the city governor's promise to establish several measures for the economic protection of Leiden painters. In the list compiled in 1644 (it was not yet an official guild), Angel figures as *hooftman* (dean). It may be assumed that the painters who signed this list were approximately the same who attended Angel's lecture on Saint Luke's Day (the names of these painters are mentioned later in the text); the complete list of the painters and art dealers was published in Obreen 1879–90, vol. 5, pp. 177–8.
12. Jan A. Emmens, the first to sketch an overview of art theory in the Netherlands in Emmens 1968, quoted Angel only very summarily and lumped him together with Van Mander. On this, see Miedema 1969; and Idem 1973, esp. p. 27. In the latter article, Miedema gives a concise analysis of Angel's pamphlet, primarily contrasting it with Van Mander's *Grondt;* unfortunately, he does not elaborate further. Despite the fact that Angel's treatise is mentioned fairly often, it has not received the place it deserves because it does not fit in with the development of "academic" art theory traceable from Van Mander to Van Hoogstraeten and De Lairesse. This is the case, for instance, in Brenninkmeyer-De Rooij's chapter on art theory in Haak 1984, pp. 60–70. P. Chapman discusses Angel's tract with some thoroughness especially with regard to the title print, in Chapman 1986.
13. Cats 1712, pp. 189–208. On the story itself (partially based on an Aelianus), see Witstein 1980, pp. 61–2.
14. Witstein 1980, p. 65.
15. Ibid., pp. 65–7.
16. Ibid., pp. 70–2.
17. For the plea of the painter, see Cats 1712, p. 196; it is also cited in full in Angel 1642, pp. 27–30. The quotations in my text are taken from Angel.
18. Angel 1642, pp. 27–8: "De waerde Schilder-Kunst verdient al grooter loff, / Want boven haer vermaeck soo komter voordeel off. / Ick winne machtich gelt, ick maecke groote stucken, / Oock weet ick op de Plaet de Vorsten uyt te drucken: / Hier drijf ick handel meed', en vry met groot ghewin, / En dat's een dienstich werck voor huys en huysghesin."
19. Ibid., pp. 28–9: "Maer waerom langh verhaelt? Ick kan te samen voegen / Dat u, dat al het volck, dat Princen kan vernoegen, / En dat oock bovendien mijn voordeel geven kan."
20. Ibid., p. 30.
21. Ibid., pp. 29–30.
22. For the relationship between *eer* (honor) and *gewin* (profit), see Emmens 1968, pp. 170, 174, and 178. In contrast to Italian art theoreticians, who (following contemporary literary theory) ranked honor much higher than profit, Van Mander placed "eere en ghewin" on a par. Moreover, he counseled that one should avoid "Dicht-const Retorica" (rhetorical poetry) because, in contrast to painting, it did not put "meel in de Keucken" (bread on the table). Of course, for Junius, profit as a goal was nothing less than despicable; but Van Hoogstraeten, like Van Mander, equated it with honor (and the love of art).

It is noteworthy that Huygens, after questioning whether painting was still as respected as it had been in Pliny's time and noting that the patronage of distinguished persons, or the practice of painting by distinguished persons, was sufficient to earn respect, wrote in his autobiography: "Altijd heeft ze onmetelijk voordeel opgeleverd (als men tenminste onder dat woord het profit van stoffelijke winst verstaat)" (It has always provided immense advantage [that is, if one takes the word to mean the profit from materialistic gain]). See Huygens 1946, p. 65. See also n. 27, on the financial advantage of painting.

23. It is striking that the only lines by Cats that might suggest a certain didactic purpose (the first sentences spoken by the painter) are the only ones that Angel does not quote: "Wel aen, ick laet het volk haer eygen vuyl ontdecken, /En leggen voor het oog haer onbekende vlecken" (Well now, I will let the people discover their own filth, / And present their unknown stains for all to see). In other words, the painter can present human faults to the observer.

24. See Miedema 1973, pp. 28–33; and Junius 1641. The Dutch translation of Junius appeared in the same year as Angel's lecture; the first Latin edition dates from 1637. For the derivations from Jan de Brune, see n. 28. The learned work of the philologist Junius, in which texts from antiquity were grouped together based on a rhetorical categorization, was influential on art-theoretical writings later in the century but does not clarify the thoughts harbored by Dutch painters at that time (Emmens 1968, pp. 67ff.). On Junius, see also Ellenius 1960, pp. 33–54.

25. See Miedema 1969, p. 28.

26. Angel 1642, pp 12–13. Angel probably derived this story, originating in Pliny, from Van Mander's "Het leven der oude antijcke doorluchtige schilders" in Van Mander 1604, sig. 68r; presumably this anecdote was generally known and would have appealed to Dutch painters (see n. 70). Angel selected several examples of antique artists from Van Mander but arranged them in his own sequence. After the Zeuxis-Parrhasius story, he comments: "Dus is onse Konst van trap tot trap op gheklommen" (Thus our art has risen, step by step).

27. Angel 1642, p. 23. This was Spiering Silvercroon, the emissary of Christina of Sweden; see Sluijter 1988c, pp. 26, 36. For the obsession with prices in the seventeenth century with regard to the work of Dou and Van Mieris, see Ibid, pp. 26–8.

28. Angel 1642, pp. 24–6. This discourse, based on a passage from De Brune's preface to Junius's book, echoes the ongoing (especially in Italy) "*paragone* debate." See Hecht 1984. Following the example of De Brune, Angel turns the traditional accusation that the art of painting is merely "schijn sonder sijn" (semblance without being) into a positive argument: The tangible, three-dimensional character of sculpture is not a merit of the art of imitating nature but a phenomenon of nature itself (cf. also the related line of reasoning in a letter by Galileo cited in Hecht 1984, p. 133). Thereafter follow Angel's most important arguments, namely, a summation of all the things that sculpture cannot represent. The most significant addition he offers in comparison to De Brune are the various metals (gold, silver, copper, tin, and lead); this reflects the increasing emphasis placed during this time on the individual properties of various materials, a point to which Angel returns later.

29. Miedema 1973, pp. 29–30. It is a pity that Miedema treats this so summarily; he primarily mentions the theoretical origins of Angel's categorization without making it clear that Angel's interpretations (in my opinion) have very little to do with them. Angel's requirements are taken as follows: (1) "ghesont Oordeel" (a healthy judgment); (2) "seeckere en ghewisse Teyckenhandt" (a confident and steady drawing hand); (3) "vloeynde Gheest om eyghentlick te Ordineeren" (a fluent mind able to compose naturally); (4) "geestighe Bedencken der aenghename Rijckelijckheyt" (the talent to imagine attractive embellishments); (5) "wel schicken der Daghen en Schaduwen" (the accurate depiction of light and shadow); (6) "goede waerneminghe der eyghen natuerlicke dinghen" (a good observation of actual natural phenomena); (7) "wel-gheoeffent verstant in de Perspectijven" (a well-practiced understanding of perspective); (8) "ervaren in kennisse der Hystorien" (experience in the knowledge of histories); and (9) "begrijp der Matimatische dingen" (an understanding of mathematical matters). Furthermore, a good artist is someone who: (10) "de Anatomy grondich verstaet" (thoroughly understands anatomy); (11) "de Natuyr meer soeckt na te bootsen dan andere Meesters handelinge" (seeks to imitate nature rather than the works of other masters); (12) "de Verwe vleysich onder een weet te smeuren" (has the capacity to combine paint in a succulent manner); (13) "onderscheyt van alle Wolle-Laeckenen, Linde, en Zijde Stoffe weet uyt te drucken" (knows how to represent the difference between all wool, linen, and silk fabrics); and (14) "een wacker, doch soet verliesent Penceel heeft" (has an alert, yet sweetly flowing brush). Angel discusses the knowledge of perspective only summarily and does not discuss the "Matimatische dingen" (mathematical matters) at all.

30. Angel 1642, pp. 35–8.
31. Ibid., pp. 38–9, 31.
32. Ibid., pp. 44–51.
33. Ibid., pp. 39–41.
34. Ibid., pp. 41–3.
35. Ibid., pp. 52–3.
36. Ibid., p. 55.
37. Ibid., pp. 53–4.
38. Ibid., pp. 55–6. For the traditional distinction between *nette* (neat, i.e., precise or detailed) and *losse* (loose) painting, see Emmens 1963, pp. 125–6; and Broos 1978–9, pp. 122–3. With regard to the Leidse *fijnschilders* (fine painters), see Sluijter 1988c, pp. 15–29. For Vasari, painters who painted in the "loose" manner displayed their imagination and virtuosity; also, for Van Mander, the loose manner was more difficult to execute and therefore was reserved for the best painters.
39. Angel 1642, pp. 57–8.
40. Ibid, pp. 39, 55.
41. Ibid., p. 40.
42. Ibid., p. 43, 54–5.
43. Ibid., p. 2.
44. This was already stated by Miedema 1969, p. 31: "een opmerkelijke veronachtzaming van hiërarchie van voorstellingen" (a remarkable disregard of a hierarchy of images).
45. Because the vocabulary previously used for writing about painting applied primarily to narrative, or history painting, it is remarkable that Angel had no problem citing various nonnarrative representations when he wished to clarify matters not solely applicable to history painting. It is noteworthy that Raupp hardly cites Angel in his forced literary-theoretical *Gattungshierarchie* (hierarchy of genres) construed from later art literature that is, according to him, applicable to seventeenth-century painting. When he does briefly refer to Angel, he conveys the latter's point of view incorrectly in order to suit his theory (Raupp 1983, p. 411). Aside from the fact that he makes it seem as though Angel spoke primarily about the problems of history painting, decorum, and *Affektenschilderung* (painting of emotion), it is incorrect to propose that Angel links "realistische Naturwiedergabe" (realistic rendering of nature) to genre pieces in particular (the *corteguarden*, that is, paintings of soldiers). As stated before, Angel cites history painting as well as all other specialties. It is significant that Angel mentions these various specialties in the same breath and that he applies his emphasis on imitating nature to all of them equally.
46. On the basis of this, the recent assumption that history painting was generally considered to be the highest goal of painting during this period seems to rest on somewhat shaky ground (even Van Hoogstraeten remained quite ambivalent about this several decades later). Incidentally, I do not mean to imply that this view was not held by a number of Dutch painters who concentrated intensively on history painting and who were often engaged in a direct dialogue with Italian art; "academic" aspirations can certainly be discerned in this period as well (see Miedema 1987, pp. 13–21). Since the exhibition *Gods, Saints & Heroes* (Exhib. cat. Washington D.C. 1980–1) – in which so many aspects of Dutch history painting were rightly rescued from obscurity – there has been a tendency to exaggerate the proportion of history paintings in Dutch art production (for example, Bialostocki 1984, p. 432). Interest in history painting during this period was quite minimal. In Leiden, for example, there were hardly any history painters active around mid-century, and even in extremely rich Leiden collections of this period, the percentage of history paintings is very small, and these are often sixteenth-century pieces. It is also incorrect to propose, as is done quite often nowadays, that history paintings were generally the most expensive. Among the most expensive paintings of the seventeenth century were depictions of maidservants, fashionably dressed young women, drinkers, etc., by painters such as Dou and Van Mieris.
47. Significantly, in the same year that Angel gave his lecture – the year in which Leiden painters established their own guild (see n. 11) – Jan Orlers published the second edition of his *Beschrijvinge der Stadt Leyden*, to which he added several pages about Leiden painters. In doing so, he appears to have consciously striven to create a respectable Leiden painting tradition. See also Sluijter 1988c, pp. 15, 31.
48. It is probable, for example, that Dou and his equally successful pupil, Frans van Mieris – painters who gained exceptional national and international fame and to whom Angel's ideas would appear to be particularly applicable – considered themselves without reservation as craftsmen (albeit of an extremely high level). Both came from a milieu in which the craft was already carried out on a high socioeconomic level (see Sluijter 1988c, pp. 28–9). For the relationship between craft, guild, and "academic" ambitions, see Miedema 1987, pp. 1–29.
49. Thus, in my view, it is not at all evident that Angel had "een volledige, traditioneel bepaalde waardering voor de literaire, inhoudelijke aspekten van de inventie" (an entirely traditionally determined appreciation for literary aspects of invention), as Miedema wrote in Miedema 1973, p. 31.
50. Chapman 1986, p. 246. In my view, Chapman's opinion that this was the goal of Angel's book is unfound-

ed, as is the idea that "in keeping with humanist art theory he ranks history painting highest" (p. 235). It seems equally incorrect to say that "Angel glorifies the art of painting as an intellectual activity" and that "[he] draws heavily on classical authors and Italian art theory, filtered through Van Mander, and, to a lesser extent, Junius" (p. 234). On the contrary, it seems characteristic that Angel shows little interest in or understanding of all of this. Chapman wrongly perceives Angel as an erudite individual who, to some extent, popularized Van Mander. In addition, the title print (the subject of Chapman's article), though clever, is less erudite than she assumes. Depictions of Athena/Minerva on a pedestal within an enclosed garden were a type of title already used in Leiden (the *Athenae Batavae*); see, for example, Heinsius's edition of Secundus 1618. This type was combined with Minerva as Pictura used in the title page of Marolois (Chapman 1986, Fig. 2).

51. Angel includes a list of names of authors (mostly from antiquity) who wrote about painting in order to demonstrate the dignity of this art. He extracts some names from Junius as well as from Van Mander (Miedema 1973, p. 28). More interesting than the names that he includes are those that he omits: Aside from Junius himself, one searches in vain for important Italian writers such as Leon Battista Alberti and Giorgio Vasari (only Leonardo is mentioned), let alone more recent Italian writers such as Gian Paolo Lomazzo and Giovanni Battista Armenini. Jan Orlers, however, does appear on the list (see n. 47).
52. Nor, for example, does Huygens speak of it in his lengthy account in which he makes no secret of his admiration for many aspects of Dutch painting (Huygens 1946, pp. 64–87). Neither is it mentioned in De Brune's preface to Junius 1641 (see n. 24), where the dignity of painting is emphasized using a variety of arguments. The same can be said of the laudatory poems on painting collected in Asselijn 1654.
53. Camphuysen 1647, pp. 218–19, "Tegen 't geestigdom der schilderkunst," a translation in verse of Johannes Evertsz. Geesteranus's "Idolelenchus" of circa 1620. This is discussed further in n. 75.
54. This is most clearly seen in recent publications by Bruyn. For example, Bruyn 1981 (see n. 7); see also Idem 1986; Idem 1987, pp. 33–59; and Idem 1988 (see n. 5). The quotation cited at the beginning of this article (see n. 5) is quite characteristic.
55. See, for example, De Jongh 1967, pp. 5–22; the essay by De Jongh in this volume; Exhib. cat. Amsterdam 1976, pp. 20, 25, 27–8; Bruyn 1986, p. 11; Idem 1987, pp. 39–42; Raupp 1983, p. 411; Haak 1984, pp. 73–4. In equating the literary theory of comedy with a theoretical framework for genre painting, Raupp even goes so far as to assert that when *vermakelijk* (amusing) is mentioned in art literature, *belerend* (edifying) is really meant (Raupp 1983, p. 407). Again, it seems significant that in seventeenth-century texts on painting, there is frequently mention of the one (*vermakelijk*) and never of the other (*belerend*), while in statements about comical poetry, the authors continually refer to both aspects.
56. Bruyn is the most outspoken in equating the principles of emblem literature with painting, for example: "Wat Cats hier definieert is het embleem of zinnebeeld . . . maar de definitie gaat zonder meer op voor het schijnbaar realistisch bedoelde beeld dat de schilderkunst biedt en datgene wat wij geleerd hebben erachter te zoeken" (What Cats defines here is the emblem; however, the definition certainly applies to the seemingly realistically intended image which painting offers and that which we have learned to seek behind it; Bruyn 1986, p. 11). Differences in form, context, function, and tradition are not considered. Prints with moralizing inscriptions are also, of course, eagerly cited and equated with *the* meaning of the image (and even considered a "guarantee" for it), see Bruyn 1987, p. 35. I shall not elaborate here on the fact that one must be very careful in using prints bearing inscriptions because, after all, they fulfill a very different function than paintings. Moreover, an inscription does not necessarily inform us about the meaning of an image; the inventiveness of the poet, who relies on his own traditions, serves as accompaniment to the "eloquence" of the pictorial image. See, for example, the excellent article by McGrath 1984. A moralization is seldom expressed in poems about paintings; see Porteman 1984, p. 107. In no way do I mean to suggest that emblematic literature and prints with inscriptions cannot be extremely important tools for the interpretation of paintings (see also n. 82).
57. Van Hoogstraeten, 1678, pp. 89–90. See De Jongh 1967, p. 22; the essay by De Jongh in this volume; Exhib. cat. Amsterdam 1976, p. 20; and Haak 1984, p. 75.
58. De Lairesse describes the same idea in greater detail when he says that for clarity it may be necessary to include symbols that represent, for instance, dissimulation, perfidy, or deceit in the form of "beelden, beesjes, of Hiroglifize figuren" (statues, animals, or hieroglyphic figures), "om alle duisterheid en twiffelachtigheden weg te ruimen" (to remove all obscurity and doubts). See De Lairesse 1712, vol. 1, p. 70. The chapter in Van Hoogstraeten 1678 entitled "Van de byvoegsels door zinnebeelden en poëtische uitvindingen" deals entirely with historical representations.

59. Exhib. cat. Amsterdam 1976, p. 14 (citing Van De Venne 1623/1982, p. 63): "Waerom wert Sinne-cunst, sou yder mogen vragen, / Iuyst boven ander cunst soo hooghe voor-gedragen? / Ick seg om dat den geest daer sonderling in speelt; / Men vindt geen dergelijck; soo sin-rijck mee gedeelt" (One might ask, why is it that emblematic art / is held in higher esteem than other arts? / I say, it is because the mind plays a singular role therein; / One finds nothing like it, communicated so ingeniously).
60. See also Porteman 1984, p. 108: "een pleidooi voor het samengaan van de zusterkunsten in de zogenaamde 'Sinne-cunst'" (a plea for the union of the sister arts in the so-called art of emblematic representation). It seems to me characteristic that here, too, whenever Van de Venne speaks about poetry, terms such as an "elevated mind," "learned," "high and deep thoughts," and "edification" appear repeatedly.
61. See n. 23 (the same thought expressed by Cats).
62. Even more remarkable than the words "De seer vermaecklicke en vernuft-barend edel Schilder-const" (the amusing and ingenious noble art of painting) with which Van Mander opens the preface to his *Grondt* – which seem to imply *miscere utile dulci* (the union of the useful with the pleasant) and have been cited as proof that "het lerende en onderhoudende doel van de kunst" (the edifying and entertaining goal of art) was stressed repeatedly (Exhib. cat. Amsterdam 1976, p. 27) – is the fact that he does not discuss this any further. That Van Mander published his artists' biographies "tot nut en vermaeck der Schilders en Const beminders" (for the benefit and amusement of painters and art lovers), a phrase also cited by De Jongh in the aforementioned argument, says nothing about an edifying goal of painting. The fact that only such meager quotations could be brought forward in support of this argument speaks volumes.
63. See Sluijter 1986, pp. 283–6.
64. Miedema 1981, pp. 214–15. See Sluijter 1986, p. 284, esp. n. 2.
65. See Sluijter 1986, pp. 313–21, where it is argued that this must be viewed as an independent commentary on the *Metamorphoses* fitting entirely within a specific literary tradition.
66. Exhib. cat. Amsterdam 1976, p. 27; see n. 62.
67. Raupp 1983, p. 416. Raupp speaks of art literature, but he cites the familiar topos of the bitter pill and the sweet nugget, etc., from works totally unrelated to this literature. (On this repeated topos, but in relation to commentaries on the *Metamorphoses*, see Sluijter 1986, p. 314.)
68. See also, for example, Van de Venne 1623/1982, pp. 59–60. Following De Brune's example, Angel 1642, p. 25, states that everything is transient except God, but "soo konnen de Schilderyen eenige honderde jaren duyren, het welcke ghenoech is" (paintings can last several hundred years, which is enough). The motif of capturing transient matters and vanquishing time occurs very frequently (to name just one example, De Bie says of Van Mieris's art that it "Die soo natuer braveert, en trotst den grijsen tydt" [challenges nature and defies gray time]); see De Bie 1661, p. 404. This motif is common, especially in poems on visual images. The theme of vanquishing time is central to Jan Vos's poem "Strijdt tusschen de doodt en natuur, of zeege der schilderkunst," in Vos 1662/1726, vol. 1, pp. 193–207. It is to be hoped that more literary studies will appear, like those by Porteman, which deal with various poems on visual images; see Porteman 1986. These studies are of great importance for a better understanding of the perception of painting in this period because they can clarify what is traditional and what is special in these poems and in the approach of the poet.
69. On the painting as a "deceit" of the eye, see, for example, Camphuysen 1647, and Van Hoogstraeten 1678. Jan de Brune the Younger elaborates on the subject in De Brune 1665, p. 317: "Doch haer bedroch is een genuchelik en onschadelik bedrogh; want aan dingen, die niet en zijn, zich zo te vergapen, als ofze waren, en daar zoo van geleit te worden, dat wy ons zelven, sonder schade, diets maken datze zijn; hoe kan dat tot de verlusting onzer gemoederen niet dienstigh wezen? Zeker, het vervroolikt yemand buite maat, wanneer hy door een valsche gelikenis der dingen wort bedrogen" (Yet its deceit is enjoyable and harmless, for to gape at things which do not exist as though they actually do exist and to be influenced by them to such an extent that we – of our own accord – without harm make believe they exist; how can that not serve to give us pleasure? Certainly it must give one great joy when one is deceived by a false likeness of things). See also n. 70.
70. Dirck Traudenius's poem on the work of Dou – who was dubbed "de Hollandsche Parrhasius" (the Dutch Parrhasius) – incorporated many of the elements cited: "Zag Zeuxis dit bancket, hy wierd al weer bedrogen: / Hier leit geen verf, maer geest en leven op 't paneel" (If Zeuxis were to see this banquet, he would be deceived once again: / Here it is not paint lying / on the panel but spirit and life). See Traudenius 1662, p. 17. W. van Heemskerck's poem praising Van Mieris advises: "Let hoe Penceel en Verw met 't leven dingt om strijd. / Indien 't Parrhasius, en Zeuxis mogten zien: Zij staakten 't wedspel, / en streên wie de Eerkrans hem zou biên" (Notice how

brush and paint contend with life as in battle. / If Parrhasius and Zeuxis were to see this, they would cease their competition, / and, instead, would vie to offer [Van Mieris] the laurel wreath). This was an inscription that appeared below A. Blooteling's engraving after Van Mieris's self-portrait; it is also cited by Houbraken 1753, vol. 3, p. 5. The painted curtains that appear to hang in front of paintings by, for example, Leiden *fijnschilders* such as Dou, Van Gaesbeeck, De Pape, and Van Mieris undoubtedly allude to this anecdote (see for example Exhib. cat. Leiden 1988, Figs. 11, 37, and cat. nos. 9, 19).

71. Van Hoogstraeten 1678, pp. 24–5.
72. He probably borrowed this from Van Mander 1604, sig. 61ᵛ, who, however, quotes it within a different context.
73. For this, and, in my view, the related fascination with mirrors and reflections in Dutch art of this period, see Sluijter 1988b.
74. This is discussed extensively in Sluijter 1986, pp. 270–7. These thoughts concerning the eye, when linked to paintings, were primarily applied to the much criticized representation of nudes, but in less explicit form this same attitude could be applied to other kinds of paintings and certainly to the scenes of amorous amusement and affluence that dominated genre painting. In several verses devoted to the image of a beloved, Van de Venne employed the idea of the powers of the eye and painting; he ends with the beautiful line: "De oog is noyt vervult, 't gewens is noyt versaet, / soo lang men met de cunst en minsucht omme-gaet" (The eye is never satisfied, desire is never sated, / As long as one remains involved with art and [earthly] love), see ns. 59, 60. Such Petrarchian thoughts seem important for the interpretation of innumerable genre pieces in which a young woman is the center of attention, usually in an amorous situation that implies seduction (a seduction that is often directed at the observer).
75. Camphuysen 1647, p. 224. Furthermore, in an earlier poem included in this collection, Camphuysen speaks about the "verwende Konst, van malle Malery, / Het voedstel van qua'e lust en fieltsche sotterny" (spoiled art of foolish painting, / The food of evil lust and villainous idiocy; Ibid., p. 4).
76. Ibid., p. 223; "'t Geen d' oogen weyt en leyt bevalt den sinnen soet / En d'ydle beeltenis beheerst het swack gemoet. / So komt het dat gy ('t wijl 't gesicht sich laet bedriegen, / En 't hert verwondert staet door 't schoone schilderliegen) / Soo als ghy alles geern in schildery aen-schout, / Alsoo oock in der daet geern doen en hebben sout. / Dus krijght d'onwijse lust door schildery sijn voetsel, / En ondeugt wort geteelt door 't sotte breyns uytbroetsel."
77. See also Goedde 1986, p. 146. He arrives at such a formulation on the basis of his study of seascapes. His working method is based on a thorough investigation of the range of subjects and motifs within a particular theme and the conventions occurring therein. This seems an extremely fruitful point of departure for a more balanced interpretation of meaning. I strove for a similar method with regard to mythological themes in Sluijter 1986, esp. pp. 3, 8.
78. As has already been noted, we are concerned here with art that was sold on a large scale by art dealers and thus had to cater to a broad, primarily anonymous public. The buyer created the context for the work based on his own background. For this reason alone, it is futile to search for *the* meaning of a painting. Rather, a whole range of possible thoughts and associations that relate to a particular theme and manner of representation should be considered (see also Sluijter 1986, pp. 8, 290–2).
79. Camphuysen 1647, p. 224: "Nochtans 't heeft mee (segt gy) sijn nut. Men kan 't uytleggen, / En leven naem en daet al 't saem doen sien, door seggen. / Maer (och!) wat uytleg en wat lof kan veylig staen, / By toonsels die 't gemoet uyt eygen aert beschaen?" Undoubtedly, Camphuysen was referring primarily to biblical and mythological scenes containing erotic allusions, but the manner in which he distinguishes between the effect of the image and the verbal addition seems significant, nevertheless.
80. On the choice and representation of mythological subjects in the Netherlands, see Sluijter 1986, p. 2, passim, esp. chap. 5. In this respect, Schama's interpretations also offer much food for thought; see Schama 1987, especially chaps. 5 and 6. It is noteworthy that when interpreting paintings, Schama uses the traditional iconological method as a point of departure but often arrives at strongly divergent interpretations on the basis of his own approach.
81. For related criticism directed at Panofskian "disguised symbolism" in fifteenth-century Flemish painting, which directly influenced this approach, see Marrow 1986, p. 151; for a critical approach to the term "disguised symbolism," see also Bedaux 1986, pp. 5–26.
82. See Bedaux 1987, pp. 151–4. His theory that there are virtually no genre pieces in which an emblem constitutes a direct source for the representation seems correct. A distorted image has come into being precisely because several examples have been emphatically and successfully brought forward (even in the case of a showpiece such as Dou's *The Quacksalver* [Rotterdam, Museum Boymans-van Beuningen], I do not think that emblems in any way constitute a source for the painting, nor were they of direct

importance to contemporary observers for the interpretation of the work). In this respect, Bedaux's correction of the symbolism of the bunch of grapes is illuminating. See also Sluijter 1986, p. 253 and n. 5, where the overspecific interpretations of the bunch of grapes are also pointed out. This is not intended to deny the importance of emblems as aids to interpretation but to emphasize that they must be used primarily to trace possible associations for specific motifs.

83. On the projection of an undue theoretical load, see Becker 1987, an excellent review of Raupp 1984, a study that bases interpretations almost entirely on art-theoretical concepts.

84. The clearest expression of this is found in the essay by De Jongh from 1971 that is reprinted in this volume; its title "Realism and Seeming Realism" already indicates this schism, and on this basis De Jongh can consider "where symbolism ends and 'empty' form begins" and whether "a painter perhaps meant nothing more than he represented." The same ideas have been expressed more recently in Bruyn 1985; Idem 1986; Idem 1988; Idem 1987. As an alternative to his viewpoint on meaning, Bruyn sees only an implied meaningless "Realität . . . als Selbstzweck" (Realism . . . as goal in itself), "een realistische uitbeelding als zodanig" (a realistic image as such), or "rein aesthetische empfunden Realität" (a purely, aesthetically perceived reality) and interprets the representation of quotidian matters as "een blijkbaar in Holland aanvaarde wetmatigheid" (an evidently accepted standard in Holland) to which conventional symbolism had to be adapted; Idem 1986, p. 7). See also n. 85.

85. Once again, this is expressed most prominently in the aforementioned articles by Bruyn. He even goes so far as to state that the seventeenth century really does not offer anything new, or if it does, "het moet zijn de steeds kunstiger verhulling van deze oude gegevens in de afschildering van de alledaagse omgeving en een steeds subtielere vertakking van de thematiek" (it must be the increasingly clever disguise of the traditional concepts in the representation of quotidian surroundings and the increasingly subtle diversification of the theme; see Bruyn 1981, p. 14). The separation between form and content is complete here. In this view, references to one's own surroundings and the associations that are evoked by them mean nothing; they merely further disguise meanings. Moreover, continually linked to this is the idea that the perceptions of the early eighteenth century can no longer tell us anything about the seventeenth-century approach.

86. Angel 1642, sig. 3ᵛ, "Den Drucker tot den schilders" (The Printer Addressing the Painters).

87. Huygens 1946, p. 66.

88. Van Hoogstraeten 1678, p. 330.

89. Ibid., pp. 11–12. Compare the change with regard to Van Mander, who speaks of the necessary love for Pictura, who is like a beautiful, jealous woman (*Grondt*, sig. 2r, and *Levens*, fol. 143ᵛ); see Van Mander 1604/1973, vol. 2, pp. 365–6.

CHAPTER SEVEN. DUTCH SEVENTEENTH-CENTURY GENRE PAINTING

1. For a list of the most important reviews of Alpers 1983, to which I think should be added Jeroen Stumpel's comments in Stumpel 1984; see the essay by Sluijter in this volume, n. 1. For Bruyn's review of Alpers, see Bruyn 1985. For his review of my exhibition catalogue (Exhib. cat. Amsterdam 1989–90), see Bruyn 1991.

2. For Sluijter's view that the interpretive methods of De Jongh and myself are merely "twee zijden van dezelfde medaille" (two sides of the same coin), see Sluijter 1991, esp. p. 50. For Reindert Falkenburg's attempt to analyze and compare the approaches of Sluijter and myself, see Falkenburg 1991. Jan Baptist Bedaux has entered the debate from a somewhat different angle in the opening pages of Bedaux 1990, pp. 9–19. For Bruyn's comments, see Bruyn 1991. No matter how difficult it is to describe what the different positions are in the so-called debate on meaning in Dutch seventeenth-century art nowadays, I fail to see why somebody would want to add to the confusion by simply misrepresenting what Bedaux and I have said, as was recently done by Schwartz 1991, p. 12. Evidently nobody who has read our books could seriously maintain that whereas: "[Bedaux and Hecht] once exerted their wits to puzzle out subtle meanings lurking between the brushstrokes of everyday scenes, *they now deny flatly that such meanings exist at all*" (my italics).

3. For a full discussion of Dou's 1652 *Kitchen-Maid* and its *paragone* features, see Exhib. cat. Amsterdam 1989–90, pp. 36–9.

4. For the sexualized interpretation of Dou's *Kitchen-Maid* and her attributes, see Sluijter 1991, esp. pp. 52–5; for Dou's *Young Mother*, see Exhib. cat. Amsterdam 1989–90, pp. 52–5.

5. Bruyn's rather drastic statement that we should not be surprised about the evident implausibilities in a picture like Dou's *Young Mother*, because "Dou's interiors never actually have much to do with any reality at all" but rather "raise the problem of their meaning," is to be found in Bruyn 1991, p. 64: "In feite hebben Dou's interieurs nooit veel met enige realiteit te maken; ze zijn klaarblijkelijk helemaal

niet als 'realistisch' bedoeld en stellen, zoals zoveel in zijn werk, het probleem van hun betekenis aan de orde." The pertinent reference to the inventory of King Charles II is taken from Mahon 1949, p. 350; Evelyn's remarks are fully referenced and discussed in Exhib. cat. Amsterdam 1989–90, pp. 54–5. For Traudenius's poem, with its "wildbraet voor 't gezicht," see Ibid, p. 38, and for Houbraken's well-known complaint about the intellectual limitations of Dou's work, see Houbraken 1718–21, vol. 2, pp. 5–6.

6. Again, Bruyn is the most resolute in according no significance whatever to the fact that there is virtually no contemporary evidence to justify an overall symbolic reading of Dutch seventeenth-century genre painting. Of course, Dutch theorists of the time never spoke about such matters, he says, for their texts were essentially modeled on antique rhetoric, and antique rhetoricians instructed people *how* to speak but never told them *what* to say; cf. Bruyn 1991, p. 65. As I see it, the even more alarming problem of that collective loss of memory, which is supposed to have rendered thousands of seventeenth-century paintings as good as meaningless before the century was over, has so far hardly been addressed. I think it is unavoidable, however, to try and imagine what such a hypothesis implies for the practice in the studio, for the situation on the art market, and for the collector's perception of these continuously popular pictures – and I am not sure this is a problem one could easily and convincingly explain away.

7. For a brief discussion of Van Mieris's corrective innovations in relation to the work of his teacher, Dou, see Exhib. cat. Amsterdam 1989–90, pp. 66–73; for a discussion of *The Duet*, see Ibid., pp. 74–7. My suggestion that the subject of a picture like *The Duet* could well have been no more than an attractive motif for the artist to exploit, is contested at length by Bruyn 1991, esp. p. 65, and it is also rejected by De Jongh in Raben and Vermeij 1990, p. 54.

8. The early comments on Van Mieris's *Cloth Shop* are to be found in Von Sandrart 1675, vol. 2, p. 321, and in Houbraken 1718–21, vol. 3, p. 3. For the moralistic interpretation of this painting, see Exhib. cat. Amsterdam 1976, pp. 173–5. The use of a picture within a picture as a so-called *clavis interpretandi* is generally a rather risky business, although obvious allusions were no doubt sometimes made in this particular way; cf. Jan Steen's *Doctor's Visit* (The Hague, Mauritshuis) or Vermeer's *Woman Reading a Letter* (Amsterdam, Rijksmuseum), both discussed in Exhib. cat. Amsterdam 1976, pp. 241–3 and 269–71, respectively. In the case of Van Mieris's *Cloth Shop*, however, the desire for an edifying aspect in an otherwise lighthearted painting seems to have caused a *Mourning of Abel* to be interpreted far too freely as a reference to original sin. If this picture has to allude to anything at all, it might as well refer to the effects of jealousy, the old man in the shop gnashing his teeth while his younger brother, so to speak, is about to steal the show.

9. For a reproduction and discussion of Pot's unmistakable *Vanitas*, see Exhib. cat. Amsterdam 1976, pp. 207–9; for a sampling of the more or less uninterrupted and even international understanding of Jan Steen's painted moralities, see, for example, John Smith's comments on such celebrated pictures as the 1661 *Easy Come, Easy Go* (Rotterdam, Boymans-van Beuningen Museum), the 1663 *Beware of Luxury* (Vienna, Kunsthistorisches Museum), and *Dissolute Household* (London, Apsley House; The Duke of Wellington Museum), all to be found in Smith 1829–42, vol. 4, pp. 49 (no. 148), p. 12 (no. 35), and p. 25 (no. 78), respectively. Charles Blanc, too, was wise enough to remark that Steen seemed "to recommend temperance, glass in hand" (il semblait . . . conseiller la tempérance, le verre à la main), mentioning the former Lonsdale *Effects of Intemperance* as a case in point; cf. his "Jean Steen," in Blanc 1863, vol. 2, p. 4. Finally, mention might for instance be made of Wilhelm Martin, one of the founding fathers of twentieth-century Dutch art history, who also was never in doubt as to the moralizing intent of Jan Steen's "geschilderde bespiegelingen over dronkenschap en ontucht" (painted comments on drunkenness and lechery); cf. Martin 1907, pp. 30–1.

10. The pertinent remarks on Steen's *Large Inn* are to be found in Steengracht van Oostkapelle 1826–30, pt. 3, pp. 10–11. A few decades later, T. van Westrheene was even more explicit about the iconography of this *Tableau de la vie humaine*, as he called it in Van Westrheene 1856, p. 100, no. 10, thus quite surprisingly anticipating the title *Toneel van de wereld* that was given to the picture in 1976; cf. Exhib. cat. Amsterdam 1976, p. 237.

11. For the nineteenth-century awareness of the significance of Cats's emblem for Van Mieris's picture, which is now in Amsterdam, Rijksmuseum, see Cat. Amsterdam 1881, p. 31, no. 95; for the early nineteenth-century comment on the Schalcken pendants in the Mauritshuis, see Steengracht van Oostkapelle 1826–30, pt. 2, pp. 6–8. More information about the history and longstanding recognition of this specific iconography is to be found in Exhib. cat. Amsterdam 1989–90, pp. 208–11, esp. n. 3.

12. For the iconography of Van Mieris's *Inn Scene* and a

referenced discussion of the previous literature on this painting, see Exhib. cat. Amsterdam 1989–90, pp. 78–80.

13. For Van Slingelandt's *Lace-Maker Disturbed*, see Ibid., pp. 226–8; for Blanc's comment on the cock being offered to the young girl, see Blanc 1863, vol. 1, p. 3 ("Pierre van Slingelandt").

14. The near-contemporary description of Vrel's 1654 picture is taken from Berger 1883, p. CL, no. 739 ("ein Stückel . . . warin . . . ein Fraw zum Fenster hinauszschawet"), where the painting is mentioned together with another work by Vrel, showing a "holländischer Camin, darbey ein krancke Fraw sitczt" (Dutch fireplace, with a sick woman sitting by it).

15. For further comments on Schalcken's *Girl Eating an Apple*, see Exhib. cat. Amsterdam 1989–90, pp. 198–200.

16. De Jongh's remarks about "[de] jonge kunsthistorici die . . . kennelijk niets beters weten dan de 17de-eeuwse Hollandse kunst naar de sfeer van het l'art pour l'art toe te schuiven" can be found in De Jongh 1990, p. 48.

17. The documents concerning Schalcken's *Self-Portrait* for Cosimo de Medici were fully published by Prinz 1971, vol. 1, pp. 191–2. The painter's reasons for doing as he did are put into context in Hecht 1980, p. 31. This material was amplified and corrected in Exhib. cat. Amsterdam 1989–90, pp. 212–16, esp. p. 212.

18. Schalcken's somewhat obsessive preference for subjects that might possibly be presented in a nocturnal setting is discussed in Hecht 1980, and again, more extensively and including the comparison with the candlelit scenes by Dou, in Exhib. cat. Amsterdam 1989–90, esp. pp. 212–16, where an illustration of Schalcken's *Denial of St. Peter* is also to be found.

CHAPTER EIGHT. TER BORCH'S LADIES IN SATIN

1. Gudlaugsson 1959–60, the most recent and most reliable monograph on Ter Borch's paintings, refers to these (and other ambitious paintings) as "principal pictures." Gudlaugsson's chronology will generally be followed in this essay. For the version of *The Paternal Admonition* in Amsterdam (Ibid., cat. no. 110, II, c. 1654–55), see Fig. 38. The version of *The Fiancée* in the Petit Palais, Paris (Fig. 61) will be discussed here rather than the nearly identical one in Schwerin (Ibid., cat. no. 112, I, c. 1655). Much additional material on Ter Borch and his family is contained in Kettering 1988.

2. J. G. Wille (1715–1808), engraver to the King of France, made a considerable number of prints after paintings, including Ter Borch's *Seated Girl in Peasant Costume*, Amsterdam, Rijksmuseum, which he titled "Gazettière Hollandaise."

3. Goethe [c. 1910], p. 115. Goethe referred to the painting, which was still in France at the time, as "die sogenannte vaeterliche Ermahnung von Terburg" (As a third [charade] they chose the so-called paternal admonition of Terborch, and who does not know our Wille's admirable engraving of this picture?). Since the French word "*Instruction*" originally signified a lesson, rarely an "*avertissement*" (notice, reprimand), the use of *Ermahnung* indicates a deliberate choice by Germans of Goethe's time to interpret the scene more negatively. (See, for example, Anon. 1694.) A later lithograph by Van Wildt, probably after Wille's engraving, actually prints the title: *Die Väterliche Ermahnung*. My thanks to John Roger Paas and Cathy Yandell for discussion of these terms.

4. For a summary, see Exhib. cat. Philadelphia 1984, cat. no. 9 (by Jan Kelch). In emblem books, candles are used to symbolize easily enflamed love, the transitory, and time in general.

5. Gudlaugsson suggested that a fastidious later collector rubbed out the coin in both versions of the painting (Gudlaugsson 1959–60, vol. 1, p. 97; vol. 2, cat. no. 110, I, and 110, II). In fact, no trace of a coin can be seen in the Amsterdam version (Fig. 38). Ter Borch defined the hand only minimally, along with most other details placed beyond the front spatial plane. Nor does the conservation laboratory of the Rijksmuseum find any evidence of abrasion (personal communication from Martin Bijl). As for the Berlin version (Fig. 60), the present keeper of Dutch pictures in Berlin, Jan Kelch, does indeed consider the canvas rubbed; he notes traces of yellow paint which might originally have described something gold. (Kind communication of Dr. Kelch.) In fact, as early as 1926, W. Drost doubted the appropriateness of Goethe's interpretation of the *Paternal Admonition*, arguing instead that the picture represented a bordello masked as a study of bourgeois manners (Drost 1926, p. 187). The very next Berlin catalogue (1931) stated that a gold coin could actually be seen; the latest catalogue, Cat. Berlin 1978, no. 791, states the same. Nevertheless, arguments against the coin include the fact that the faithful copy that Netscher made of the Berlin version in 1655, immediately after its execution, shows no coin present (for an illustration, see Gudlaugsson 1959–60, vol. 2, pl. XII – the copy is now in Gotha). On positive interpretations of the coin, see n. 64.

6. For a good example, see Dirck van Baburen, *The*

Procuress, Boston, Museum of Fine Arts (Exhib. cat. Philadelphia 1984, color pl. 10). Such works as Ter Borch's *Introduction* and *Suitor's Visit* were similarly understood as close relatives of the *bordeeltje* type. See nn. 66 and 67.

7. Sutton 1984, p. xlv. See also Schama 1984b, an unpublished lecture given in conjunction with the exhibition *Masters of Seventeenth-Century Dutch Genre Painting*, p. 11: When the boundaries between vice and virtue are blurred, the "burden of ethical decisions is thrust back on [the beholder's] own mind." My thanks to Svetlana Alpers for this reference.
8. Guépin 1974, pp. 37, 41, a largely overlooked but highly insightful essay.
9. Stone-Ferrier 1985a, chap. 5.
10. The Ter Borch pictures can be understood as belonging to this tradition. For a good selection of reproductions, see Exhib. cat. Pittsburgh 1986 and Briels 1987.
11. Ter Borch's familiarity with the Amsterdam "high-life interior" as early as his apprentice years is confirmed by his drawing of such a company, dated November 1632, made during or just after a stay in Amsterdam (see Kettering 1988, vol. 2, p. 102). While there he could easily have seen Codde's works. Ter Borch's acquaintance with the work of Delft artists (such as Palamedesz.) is suggested not only by the pictorial evidence that his pictures provide, but by a document of 1653 citing his contact with Vermeer (Montias 1989, pp. 102–3, p. 308 [Document 251]). The pages – attributes of courtliness and supports for the amorous action – in Ter Borch's mature works clearly descend from the serving boys of Codde, Palamedesz., and others.
12. Prints by Hollar, Callot, and Bosse come immediately to mind. For illustrations of Hollar prints, see Bringemeier 1974, pp. 5–13 (my thanks to Jan Kelch for this reference). For a short account of the seventeenth-century costume print, see Exhib. cat. The Hague 1988, pp. 20ff.
13. Ter Borch's stay in London in 1635 with his uncle, the engraver Robert van Voerst, would have allowed him familiarity with Van Dyck's portraiture; this knowledge could have been revived by later visits to The Hague. See Gudlaugsson 1959–60, vol. 1, pp. 33–4, 84; and Kettering 1988, vol. 1, p. 86.
14. The lady in light-colored satin can first be seen in *Girl at Her Toilet* (c. 1648–9, Sale Paris, Drouot, May 31, 1988), then in *The Lady at Her Toilet* (c. 1651, New York, The Metropolitan Museum of Art), and in *Woman at a Mirror* (c. 1651, Amsterdam, Rijksmuseum), each with Gesina serving as model (Gudlaugsson 1959–60, cat. nos. 77, 80, 83, respectively).
15. The slightly later Anholt painting presents a more idealized version of the main figure in *Two Shepherdesses* (Gudlaugsson 1959–60, cat. nos. C299 and 85, respectively). See Kettering 1983a, pp. 79ff. I no longer consider either work a portrait of Gesina (or her sister).
16. Gudlaugsson 1959–60, cat. no. 113.
17. For a full discussion of the colourful dress worn by well-to-do seventeenth-century Dutch women (and men), beginning in the late 1650s, see Groeneweg 1992. See also Idem 1985, p. 421. Groeneweg has commented in conversation with me that elements of the lady's dress in *The Paternal Admonition* (Fig. 60) would have looked quite up-to-date to fashion-conscious viewers of 1654, but the same dress in *The Introduction* (Fig. 65) of c. 1662 would naturally have appeared rather old-fashioned. My warm thanks to Drs. Groeneweg for most generously sharing her ideas and research. My thanks to Karen Schaffer, as well. For earlier commentary on colors in dress, see Der Kinderen-Besier 1950, pp. 184ff., 263–83.
18. Among the many examples of chaste young girls wearing white can be counted Ter Borch's *Portrait of Helena van der Schalcken*, Amsterdam, Rijksmuseum (Gudlaugsson 1959–60, cat. no. 30).
19. A good example of ladies dressed *à la bergère* in white or light-colored satin can be seen in Michel Angelo Immenraedt's *Portrait of Odilia and Philippina van Wassenaer as Shepherdesses*, 1661, The Hague, Gemeentemuseum (Kettering 1983a, pl. 78). Jan Mytens, a resident of The Hague all his life, used light-colored satin for arcadian portraits, as well as for non-arcadian portraits of aristocratic women associated with the court at The Hague (see n. 22).
20. An example of white worn by a deceased wife: Jan Mytens, *Govert van Slingelandt and Christina van Beveren*, Amsterdam, Rijksmuseum (see Exhib. cat. Haarlem 1986, cat. no. 55).
21. An example of a newly married woman in a love garden setting: Bartholomeus van der Helst, *Portrait of Abraham del Court and Maria Keerssegieter*, 1654, Rotterdam, Museum Boymans-van Beuningen (reproduced as Fig. 11 in this volume). One of Vondel's marriage poems refers to the bride in her "witte bruiloftskleed." Vondel uses white in an allegorical sense, however, for in actual practice brides wore black outer garments (for the poem, see Vondel 1937/1986, p. 878). The choice of white may, alternatively, indicate the Amsterdam lady's adoption of the brighter fashions worn in actual life by the elite, as is suggested by Groeneweg 1992.
22. See, for example, Mytens's *Portrait of Jacoba van Orliens*, 1660, Amsterdam, Rijksmuseum. The portraits by Jan Mytens and his colleagues in The Hague are notable for their reflection of the interna-

tional taste at the Dutch court for Van Dyckian falls of light-colored satin.

23. Groeneweg 1992. Which elements of the elite chose to be portrayed in colors and which in black is a complicated subject beyond the scope of the present article. Here I will only note, to oversimplify, that in the first half of the century aristocratic sitters associated with court society at The Hague preferred portrayal in colors, while elsewhere elite sitters preferred the more formal black. The shift by well-to-do Amsterdammers (such as those whom Bartholomeus van der Helst depicted) after 1652 to the "court" style, is discussed by Woodall 1990.
24. Hollander 1970–1, p. 481.
25. This is the argument of Stone-Ferrier 1985a, pp. 164, 172–8, who associates the satin with Dutch pride, "pride" in the best sense of the word: nationalistic pride in Dutch textile production – for the Dutch were important producers of satin fabric – and individual pride in the prosperity that allowed such fine attire (pp. 219–20).
26. The earliest that I have located is a reference to *The Paternal Admonition* (Fig. 38, the Amsterdam version), as "Een staande vrouw in 't wit satyn." See Hoet 1752–70, vol. 2, p. 442. Inventory descriptions often describe the pictures of ladies by Ter Borch's student Caspar Netscher in this same way.
27. For the "Life of Adriaen Van Der Werff," see n. 29. In his 1721 "Life of Ter Borch," Houbraken exclaims – adapting a familiar trope of artistic praise – that the "boven al het wit Satyn zoo natuurlyk, dun en konstig te schilderen, dat het waarlyk Satyn scheen te wezen" (white satin [in Ter Borch's pictures was] so natural . . . that it looked like real satin; Houbraken 1718–21, vol. 3, pp. 33ff.). Reprinted in Gudlaugsson 1959–60, vol. 2, p. 12. For an example of such praise from the nineteenth century, see J. Smith 1829–42, vol. 4, p. 117.
28. See Hal Foster's work on *pronk* still lives (pictures so similar to Ter Borch's in their inclusion of shiny objects, gleaming in the darkness). Foster 1991, p. 4, writes that the very immediacy of the gleaming objects allows them to assume an animating force. Like these objects, I would argue, the satin skirt becomes the "locus of psychic involvement." My thanks to Julie Berger Hochstrasser for this reference.
29. Van de Wetering 1993. Van de Wetering based his remarks partly on a comment about Ter Borch's "*moderne manier*" of rendering satin skirts in the biography of Adriaen van der Werff that the artist seems to have authorized himself (Gaehtgens 1987a, p. 433). See also Gaehtgens 1987b, pp. 92ff. I am grateful to Prof. van de Wetering for discussing this issue of studio practice with me. On cost factors in relation to *fijnschilder* painting, see Montias 1987, p. 462.
30. Gesina was Gerard's half-sister, born in 1631 – thus thirteen years his junior – and raised in their home town of Zwolle. Gesina started serving as Gerard's model around 1648. She began the first album as a *materi-boeck* (a copybook) in 1646, but by page 6 (entered c. 1649), she turned it into a poetry album. Gesina treated the second (1652–c. 1660) as a poetry album from the start. The third album, containing little songbook poetry, began as a "*Kunstboek*" or Art Book. See Kettering 1988, vol. 2, pp. 398ff., and cat. nos. 60–2. In 1654, six years after his return home from his travels, Gerard married Gesina's aunt (whom Gesina seems to have resembled), and moved to nearby Deventer.
31. For example, the Poetry Album, ibid., cat. no. 61, sigs. 4, 8, 9, 12–13, 15, 17–21, 23, 26, 29, 30, 33, 42, 44, 45, 51, 52, 54, 57, 58, 60, 61, 67, 68, 70, 71, 75, 76, 77, 81, 93, 95, 96, 100–4, 106.
32. For the classic account, see Forster 1969, pp. 2ff., 44–5; also Minta 1980 and the various pieces by Nancy Vickers, for example, Vickers 1982. The most significant influence on Dutch Petrarchism came from the French Pléiade poets of whom Ronsard and Du Bellay were the most important. Specifically on Dutch Petrarchism, see Porteman in Hooft 1611/1983, pp. 17ff., 22ff.; and Ypes 1934 (dissertation, out of date by now, though containing helpful references to specific seventeenth-century examples).
33. Porteman in Hooft 1611/1983, p. 17, referring specifically to Hooft's *Emblemata Amatoria*. Although emblems are Porteman's focus, his remarks pertain to much of Dutch love poetry.
34. Kettering 1988, vol. 2, p. 418, and Luijten 1988. It is not certain whether Gesina knew Hooft's *Emblemata Amatoria;* the book was, however, directed to young people like her (Hooft 1611/1983, 1983, pp. 40ff.; and Grootes 1987). Gesina's poetic taste inclined more strongly to popular verse, for example, poems by Jan Harmens Krul, Jacob Cats, and the anonymous contributors to such songbooks as Anon. 1649.
35. Krul 1681, p. 434. On the musical settings of Petrarchan poetry, see Pattison 1948, pp. 92–101.
36. Kettering 1988, vol. 2, p. 417. Gesina's illustrations especially resemble the prints Jan van de Velde made for Starter 1621/1966, for example, Fig. 70 here.
37. Gesina modeled for at least twenty of his paintings. On the other models Gerard used, see nn. 62 and 66.
38. Six drawings from the mid-1650s (Kettering 1988, vol. 1, cat. nos. GJr 82-6) represent subjects far more usual for Gesina than for Gerard: fancy sleighs and a lady equestrian (one dated 165[6], two copied by

Gesina, Ges 29, 30), along with the garden of love scene discussed here.

39. Heinsius 1616b, p. 88. For the hart in Petrarch's poems, see Goodman 1983a, p. 185, and for Shakespeare's use of the hart in *Twelfth Night*, see Vickers, 1982, p. 100.
40. Favis 1974, pp. 89ff., 195ff.
41. Gerard's drawing probably stayed, at least temporarily, in the artist's atelier in Deventer. At some later point, Gesina removed it to Zwolle (annotating it herself with her brother's name).
42. For Ter Borch's paintings in collections in The Hague, see Gudlaugsson 1959–60, cat. nos. 121, 122; in Rotterdam, Ibid., cat. no. 114; in Amsterdam, Ibid., cat. no. 99 or cat. no. 141; and in Delft, Hoet 1752–70, p. 34 (the 1696 Dissius sale). As for sales in The Hague, see Gudlaugsson 1959–60, vol. 1, p. 120 (on Netscher's possible role in this regard) and p. 136, on other artists' familiarity with Ter Borch's art. See also Montias 1987, p. 462, on the riskiness for artists of executing "fine" (labor-intensive) painting "on spec," that is, for the open market, and the need for known patrons. In contrast to Dou, Frans van Mieris the Elder, and Vermeer, Ter Borch seems unlikely to have been favored by a *maecenas*.
43. For the Ter Borch picture in the De la Court collection, see Gudlaugsson 1959–60, cat. no. C 65. On Petronella de la Court, see Van Eeghen 1960, pp. 159ff.; and Veldkamp 1977, pp. 14–15. On Van Ruijven, see Montias 1989, pp. 246ff.
44. Gudlaugsson 1959–60, vol. 1, p. 114, counts Matthys van Gherven and two of Ter Borch's in-laws (in addition to Johannes Renialme) as among those who quite possibly helped to sell his genre pictures and procure portrait commissions in Amsterdam. On Renialme, see Bredius 1915–22, vol. 1, pp. 228ff.; and Montias 1988, pp. 250ff.
45. On the Ter Borch family's position in Zwolle society, see Kettering 1988, vol. 1, pp. xxix and 5. Montias warns against assuming a necessary correspondence between the richness of the milieu depicted in a painting and the wealth of the owner (Montias 1990, pp. 364–5). But in Ter Borch's case, the assumption seems justifiable.
46. Actually, the market for these songbooks was considerably broader than that for fine painting, for by the late seventeenth century, songbooks in relatively cheap octavo editions were available alongside the more luxurious quartos. See Grootes 1987, pp. 72ff. To be sure, Grootes studied the market mainly for early seventeenth-century songbooks. Later in the century, a more diversified market developed, and publishers accordingly produced various "grades" of songbooks. See Kettering 1983a, pp. 23ff.
47. Increasingly, affection was also understood to be advantageous. For a marriage to be successfully "companionate," it should be based on emotional bonds rather than material gain. The result was a degree of choice in mate selection and a later marriage age. See Hajnal 1965, pp. 101ff.; and R. Smith 1979.
48. The summary presented here is based on a selection of writings from what has become a vast literature on marriage and the family. Among the most helpful: Van Deursen 1978–81, vol. 2, pp. 11–31 (translated as Van Deursen 1991); Haks 1985; Exhib. cat. Apeldoorn 1989; *Jeugd en Samenleving*, no. 10–11 (Oct./Nov. 1989) – an issue devoted to studies on Early Modern courtship, marriage, and family, with articles by P. Spierenburg, K. Hazelzet, and others (my thanks to Wayne Franits for the latter two references); Macfarlane 1986; Shorter 1975; Davies 1981; Carter 1974, pp. 94ff.
49. Starter 1966, pp. 54–5.
50. As Gesina wrote herself: "T sij arm of rijck / Elck sijns gelijck" (Whether poor or rich, each with his own kind; Poetry Album sig. 17; Kettering 1988, vol. 1, p. 430). This is typical of the couplets Gesina frequently added to the poems that she inscribed in the Poetry Album.
51. Schama 1987, p. 438. See also Van Deursen 1978–81, vol. 2, pp. 12, 21; Idem 1991, pp. 81ff., 88ff.; Carter 1974, p. 95; Haks 1985, p. 224.
52. Schama 1980, p. 6.
53. Heywood 16??/1902, p. 210, a loose translation of Cats 1618b. In the closely related *Houwelyck* (Cats 1625), Cats repeatedly urges reserved speech. See also Cats's emblem, *Pere é donne senza rumori sono stinate gli meliori* in Cats 1632, pt. 1, pp. 68–70 (my thanks to Wayne Franits for this reference). Cats's *Maechden-plicht* and *Houwelyck* are not technically manuals of behavior (in the mold of Gouge 1627, for example), but the advice he gives certainly accords with the manuals. For commentary on the many Dutch treatises, see Franits 1993.
54. Rosette's comment to Sibille in chap. 2 of Cats 1625, republished many times, as, for example, in Cats 1870, p. 159. Gesina knew Cats's writings well. Among the many verses from Cats that she copied into her albums appear the following: "Al is de vrijster steech noch wort sij wel de bruijt / Maer wil de vrijer niet soo is de vrentschap uijt" (If the lady is stand-offish she'll still become the bride, but if the suitor is hesitant, then the friendship is over), placed beneath the poem on sig. 52 of the Poetry Album (Kettering 1988, vol. 2, p. 446). Restating the verse more positively reinforces, once again, the notion of the entreating suitor and the distanced, passive lady.

Earlier, she copied into the *Materi-boeck* (sig. 20; Kettering 1988, vol. 2, pp. 409–10) an anonymous poem about the strange customs of Parisian *jufferties*, who take the initiative in courtship. But she then added (probably in her own words this time) two couplets warning against this very role reversal. On Cats 1625, see Dresen-Coenders 1989.

55. Roodenburg 1991a, pp. 158–9, a wide-ranging essay.
56. Grootes 1987, p. 84, suggests the likelihood that the self-control advocated in the poetry met with parental approval.
57. A good example from Jacob Cats's writings is *Amor: Formae condimentum*, picturing a monkey with her offspring, followed by a poem on the topus of a lover's propensity to see beauty in the beloved that is invisible to all others (Cats 1627, no. IV). My thanks to Hans Luijten for referring me to this particular emblem, in fact for all the references he provided on the subject of beauty. On Cats, see also Schama 1987, p. 467. For Johan de Brune's thoughts on beauty, see his posthumously published De Brune 1660, pp. 27, 182, 321, for example. For a discussion of the dangers associated with the sense of sight (hence beauty), see the following articles by Eric Jan Sluijter: Sluijter 1988b, p. 163; Idem 1988a, p. 157; and his essay reprinted in this volume.
58. Gudlaugsson 1959–60, cat. no. 84, c. 1650, with the inscription: "Me licet haud vincat Cytherea, senecta colores / Quam cito, me febres et libitina rapit." My thanks to Hans Luijten for discussing this text with me. The viewer of the beautiful woman portrayed in the print was thus given a moral that could be activated when or if necessary. The notion of viewers activating morals is Sluijter's. Although he has written of such viewer response in regard to genre pictures, the notion can more directly be applied to prints with inscriptions such as this (see Sluijter's essay reprinted in this volume).
59. Van Beverwijck 1639, pp. 29–33; another edition in 1643. On the debates about women, see Spies 1986. For a seventeenth-century (tongue in cheek?) response to Van Beverwijck 1639, see the essay by his friend, Jonctijs [1640]. On Italian treatises on beauty, see Rogers 1988; and Cropper 1976. On the extensive English writing for and against women, see Wright 1935, chap. 13, and Henderson and McManus 1985. My thanks to Marieke Spies for discussing the literature on beauty with me.
60. See Kelso 1956, p. 208, on the qualities of the lady in Renaissance writing.
61. See, for example, Hooft's "Voochdesse van mijn siel," 1610, in Hooft 1899, p. 123. See also Starter 1621/1966, p. 29, "Ontelbare schoonheden van mijn Goddin."; and Daniel Jonctijs's many poems associating beauty, love, and virtue, in Jonctijs 1639. It is worth mentioning that Henrik Jordis, Gesina's suitor, praised Gesina's beauty in Neo-Platonic terms (Kettering 1988, vol. 2, pp. 420–1).
62. If a model for the protagonist in *The Lady at Her Toilet* came from the Ter Borch family, it was possibly Jenneken, Ter Borch's youngest sister, but with idealized features. For all (but one) of Ter Borch's earlier toilet scenes, Gesina acted as model, and the individuality of her features was preserved (Gudlaugsson 1959–60, nos. 77, 80, 83, 113).
63. See Vickers 1982, op. cit. (n. 32) p. 105; and Freccero 1975, vol. 5, p. 35. In Dutch poetry such "fetishizing" can be found in Cornelis Ianszoon Schooneman's "Sonnetten van de Schoonheyt," earlier attributed to Bredero; see Bredero 1919.
64. Most recent art historians have ignored the modest black collar worn above the lady's white satin bodice, as well as the multiple possible meanings for the man's upraised hand. See n. 5 on the possibility that it originally held a coin as part of a sexual transaction. An interpretation of a very different sort was offered by C. Boschma, who suggested in 1976 that *The Paternal Admonition* might have represented a marriage proposal. (For a reference to the doctoral *stelling* or position in which Boschma made this suggestion, see Exhib. cat. Philadelphia 1984, cat. no. 9.) In fact, Van Deursen includes goldpieces among the pledges a man might give his betrothed, Van Deursen 1978–81, vol. 2, p. 21. See also Macfarlane 1986, pp. 300ff. If no coin was originally present, viewers might have interpreted the man's gesture as purely rhetorical; see Bulwer 1644, p. 75, gesture IX, *Contraria distinquet* ("to distinguish contraries"). The seventeenth-century Dutch appear not to have known this manual. Nevertheless, it does codify what must have been well-known hand gestures of the time in Europe. On the language of gestures used in late sixteenth- and seventeenth-century acting, with reference to Bulwer's codification, see Joseph 1964, fig. 6.
65. The Petrarchan lady is frequently skilled as a musician. Goodman 1983a, p. 181. Goodman has written about Petrarchism in a number of other contexts as well, including Goodman 1989; Idem 1983b; and Idem 1982.
66. Ter Borch's sister Aeltjen (Aleida), who would have been twenty-four in 1660, may well have served as the model for the principal lady; for comparison, see Kettering 1988, vol. 2, Scrapbook sigs. 71, 153, 154. The suggestion of Sutton – who otherwise writes very sensitively about Ter Borch's paintings – that the woman makes an obscene gesture with her hands, indicates a failure to understand the tone of

the painting (Sutton 1984, p. xlv). He rests his interpretation too exclusively on a single detail. To my mind, the lady by no means shows the *ficus* gesture (thumb between the first two fingers). Rather, this is an ordinary way for a modest lady to hold her hands. See Hollar's 1635 prints depicting a couple greeting; both figures make the same gestures to one another as in Ter Borch's picture (in Exhib. cat. Paris 1979, pl. 15).

67. Gudlauggson and Hoetink both title the painting *Company with a Dancing Pair* (Gudlaugsson 1959–60, p. 330; and Hoetink in Exhib. cat. The Hague 1974, p. 168). Hoetink does indicate that more is at stake here than dancing; he suggests, first, that the gentleman may be placing a ring on the lady's hand and, second, that the older woman in the background may be a procuress (contradictory ideas?). The interpretation, rather, that the action is a courtly greeting is supported by the similar greetings one sees in early seventeenth-century gardens of love (Exhib. cat. Pittsburgh 1986, p. 10); the contemporaneous watercolors of Gesina; and the slightly later engravings of Romein de Hooghe.

68. The chaperone is enclosed within the fur-lined jacket that De Lairesse calls *huis dracht* ("within-door clothing"), De Lairesse 1707, vol. 1, pp. 182–4; translated as *The Art of Painting* (De Lairesse 1738, pp. 138–9). In Gesina's iconographic vocabulary, such jackets signal a woman's domesticity. Gerard, though less consistent, seems to make the same distinction here: the jacket-clad woman, her colors dark, her body bent, her cap that of a married woman, functions as an older sister or aunt.

69. Despite the lack of narrative specificity in the New York *Curiosity*, the pictorial prominence of the standing lady does make her the main love interest, and thus the recipient of the opened love letter on the table. It is appropriate that the standing lady fingers a handkerchief, a luxurious object that the ladies in Gesina's illustrations sometimes carry (Kettering 1988, vol. 2, Poetry Album, sigs. 8, 39, 52, 58, 72). De Jongh considers the handkerchief both a token of love (citing Jacob Cats's advice to young women to give handkerchiefs to their suitors) and a symbol for chastity; Exhib. cat. Haarlem 1986, pp. 111–12. See also Braun-Ronsdorf 1967, p. 22. In the Detroit *Lady at Her Toilet*, the secondary figures are engaged only in serving; the smitten page provides the lady with scented water as a suitor might offer a token of affection.

70. Goedde 1989a, pp. 38ff. ("rhetorically expansive readings" is Goedde's term, p. 40); and Idem 1989c, pp. 18–20 and chap. 5.

71. Ibid., p. 18.

72. De Lairesse 1707, vol. 1, pp. 182–4; Idem 1738, pp. 138–39. De Lairesse begins the section as follows: "Two Virgins are seen at a Table, drinking Tea; the youngest is in her Within-door Dress, and the other, a Friend paying her a visit; each has her cup and saucer; that of the youngest stands filled before her, and she has a teapot in her hand, in order to fill the cup of the other, who, having turned it down, sets it on the Table; she is friendly intreated by the other to drink another Dish; as if she said, –Pray, dear Isabel! one dish more . . ." See Christopher Brown's reference to this passage in Brown 1984, p. 62.

73. See Simons 1988, p. 5 ("performing agent" is Simons's phrase). See also Wolff 1981, p. 95.

74. The section that follows was stimulated by Miles 1985, pp. 82–93; Pointon 1988, p. 154; Culler 1983, pp. 43ff.; and Rogers 1988, p. 56.

75. Showalter 1979, p. 25.

76. On the theory of ego development in women and its redefinitions, see, for example, Miller 1986, chaps. 4, 6 and especially pp. 72ff.; and the various papers by Judith Jordan on empathy, such as Jordan, Surrey, and Kaplan 1982.

77. In Culler's succinct formulation, reading for men is like girl-watching; for women like being watched. Culler 1983, pp. 44ff. (responding to Hartman).

78. Stone-Ferrier 1985a, pp. 213ff. For an illustration, see Exhib. cat. Haarlem 1986, p. 40, fig. 33.

79. Exhib. cat. Haarlem 1986, p. 171. Nevertheless, Van der Helst created similar displays of light-colored satin in a number of his other portraits, where the connection with cloth manufacture would have been more indirect. Perhaps some of the other associations of satin influenced his patrons' choice.

80. Thorstein Veblen's concept of conspicuous consumption is relevant here, that is, the assertion of a man's power by the display of splendid persons and things around him. See Bell 1976, pp. 139ff.

81. Ripa 1644, p. 306: "Praise," for example, is personified by a woman in a white satin garment – white was chosen for "purity and righteousness," and satin chosen probably (though he does not say so specifically) to harmonize with her shining trumpet. The list of color symbols in Gesina's albums offers further indication that colors had iconographical force for the family and likely as well for a broader public: *Wit* (white) for *Suijverheijt* (purity), *bloemerant* (light blue) for *Constant* (constancy), *blaeu* (blue) for *Jalousije* (jealousy), *coulombijn* (pink) for *Liefde* (love). See Kettering 1988, vol. 2, Poetry Album, sigs. 39ᵛ and 111.

82. Kelso 1956, p. 145.

83. E. Jane Burns and Roberta L. Krueger have written perceptively about how male readers responded to

images of the lady in troubadour lyric (Burns and Krueger 1984–5). Although the lady in medieval poetry was more sexually available than her counterpart in Petrarchan poetry, she was still looked upon not as a real woman but as the "other." See also, Miles 1985, pp. 84–6, on the way fourteenth-century male viewers responded to spiritualized, purely visualized images of women; and Maclean 1980, pp. 24–5.

84. Understood in this way, the male viewer's gaze upon her is controlling, the woman turned into an object for his spectatorial possession. For summaries of feminist positions, see Betterton 1988, p. 251; and Gaines 1990, pp. 3–5.
85. For an illustration of the picture by Moreelse and a modern-day version of this response, see Sluijter 1988a, pp. 162–3 and fig. 12.
86. Schama laments this tendency in modern art historians as the "indiscriminate compression of a very finely calibrated range of moral nuance into one erotic portmanteau called 'brothel scene'," Schama 1984b, p. 7.
87. Culler 1983, pp. 43ff., in response to Fetterley 1978, p. xii.
88. Van de Pol 1988, pp. 126ff., makes the point that Vermeer's mother-in-law owned a *koppelaarster* (procuress), probably the one by Van Baburen that Vermeer placed on the wall in two of his pictures. She also calls attention to the placement of representations of nudes in the "Kunstkamer" and bedroom of Petronella de la Court's late seventeenth-century dollhouse, decoration that presumably reflected the owner's own residence. See also n. 43 on the dollhouse itself, and on De la Court's ownership of Ter Borch pictures. For the Vermeer inventory reference, see Montias 1989, p. 308.
89. As a number of writers in the last decade have asserted, women in our culture have learned mobility, that is, they have developed the capacity to adopt different viewpoints – masculine viewpoints and those more favorable to females – often simultaneously. See, for example, Betterton 1988, p. 257, in response to a 1981 essay by Laura Mulvey, reprinted in Mulvey 1989. See Modleski 1982 and Doane 1982, vol. 23, p. 85.
90. As Stone-Ferrier 1985a, p. 213, has observed, their silence may not have expressed acceptance, but at least it implied a new measure of tolerance. The Middelburgh preacher Willem Teellinck did, however, publish *De spiegel der zedigheyt* as late as 1651 (Dordrecht), a book brimming with rules about clothes, for example: "De stoffe moet niet te kostelick zijn" (The fabric mustn't be too expensive). Another seventeenth-century moralist, Johan de Brune, in his posthumously published *Bankket-werk van goede gedagten* (De Brune 1660, vol. 1, pp. 117–18) illustrated *Schijn-deugd* (deceptive virtue) with a costume detail straight out of high society experience: white satin's propensity to soil.
91. Van Boheemen 1989. She discusses not only the more or less faithful translations of Ovid's work, but the free adaptations by Van Heemskerck 1626 (a reworking of his 1622 publication) and Westerbaen 1665.
92. De Lairesse 1707, vol. 1, p. 173, complained about the way unidealized faces, based on humble models (artist's servants and family members) intruded into the fictive world of genre paintings.
93. De Vries considers it unlikely, as a general rule, that many owners and other viewers were intended to recognize the models' identities; see De Vries 1990b, p. 197.
94. Betterton 1988, p. 256.
95. Goedde 1989b uses the notion of the "smart" viewer, borrowed from Umberto Eco. On the relationship between conventions, response, and interpretation, see also the essay by Sluijter reprinted in this volume, and Schama 1984b, p. 3.
96. Both pictures warn against the very behavior they depict. *The Gallant Military Man* (Fig. 71) represents a soldier whose gesture – a palm full of coins – is so obvious that a fastidious later owner would have altered it only with difficulty. *The Glass of Lemonade* (Gudlangsson 1959–60, cat. no. 192, c. 1663–64), iconographically consistent with Van Baburen's *Procuress* in Boston (see n. 6), includes an old lady actively playing the procuress role, encouraging the pair to love. See Schama's sensitive readings of both pictures: Schama 1984b.
97. Laments about such social aping by servant girls and prostitutes can be found in contemporary literature. It is within this context that I understand the description in Anon. [1681] of a prostitute dressed in "an embroidered silk bodice, over a yellow silk skirt." See Böse 1985, pp. 17ff., 148. My thanks to Eric Jan Sluijter for this reference.

CHAPTER NINE. STYLE IN DUTCH ART

1. Haskell 1976, p. 160, for both quotes.
2. There are exceptions, such as Summers 1987, who clarifies the terms "naturalism" and "realism" (p. 3).
3. Taylor 1994, p. 36.
4. Taylor 1994 takes this view and praises the "richness of vocabulary and novelty of perception" in Van de Wetering 1992.
5. The phrase comes from Alpers 1983, in the title of chap. 3. The present article responds frequently to

Alpers's influential book, specifically because of its negative remarks about the study of style in Dutch painting. However, Alpers must be credited for centering discussion on the nature of representation, a question that had previously been addressed with regard to Dutch art only in specialized articles (for example, Liedtke 1976; Wheelock 1977). This aspect of Alpers's approach was applauded in Veltman 1984, which is also of interest for its rebuttal of her dichotomy between Northern and Italian interests in the worlds of art and science.

6. For full citations of these familiar sources, see James 1872 and the bibliography in Exhib. cat. The Hague 1990–1. On Hippolyte Taine as Alpers's predecessor, see De Jongh 1984, p. 53.
7. See Nicolson 1958, pp. 27–8; and Klemm 1986, pp. 15, 336.
8. See Lowenthal 1986, pp. 62 (English translation), 184 (original Latin).
9. Sluijter-Seiffert 1984, no. 21.
10. This is clear from a perusal of Nicolson 1979, who covers everyone but Jacob Backer and Lambert Jacobsz. in Leeuwarden (see Sumowski 1983–94, vol. 1, pp. 133, 145 on Jacobsz, and nos. 2–12 on Backer).
11. See Müllenmeister 1988, whose bibliography lacks Spicer 1983 (on cows).
12. On Bloemaert's style after about 1630, see my entry in Exhib. cat. New York 1985–6, no. 159; and Roethlisberger 1993 on the artist's life and work.
13. On this point, see my entry in Exhib. cat. New York 1992–3, no. 11 (*The Raising of Lazarus* in Lille).
14. See Lowenthal 1986, pp. 63–4, and Lowenthal 1995, pp. 24–5.
15. Sluijter 1986 (see also his contribution to Cavalli-Björkman 1985).
16. Annibale's *Landscape with the Flight to Egypt* of 1604 in the Galleria Doria-Pamphilj, Rome, is more naturalistic than the setting here. Compare Wtewael's *Kitchen Scene* of 1605 in Berlin (Lowenthal 1986, no. A-38, Pl. X) to the market scenes by the Carracci.
17. Alpers 1983. See De Jongh 1984, p. 55, on this point.
18. Gombrich 1961; Crary 1992; Kaufmann 1993; Kemp 1990; and Summers 1987.
19. Manley 1980 and Grafton 1992 place this point in a broader perspective by discussing literary, philosophical, and scientific conventions.
20. Van Hoogstraeten 1678, p. 36; quoted by Alpers 1983, p. 38; and by De Jongh 1984, p. 54, who argues that Alpers's partial quoting of Van Hoogstraeten's sentence misleads the reader.
21. See Exhib. cat. Boston 1982, no. 14, for Ruisdael's *Castle of Bentheim* of 1653 in the Beit Collection, and for a photo of the site.
22. See Kemp 1990, p. 1, on the word empirical.
23. See Wheelock 1981, pp. 43, 160, n. 41; and Wheelock 1987.
24. See Liedtke 1976 and Keith 1994; also Liedtke 1982, pp. 52–4 on Gerard Houckgeest.
25. See Freedberg 1991 and Kaufmann 1993.
26. Compare the comments of Alpers 1983; Veltman 1984; and Kemp 1990 on these international figures.
27. The question is set in a broader context by Grafton 1992. On artistic education, see Exhib. cat. Providence 1984.
28. The basic essay on style as "a vehicle of expression [communicating] the broad outlook of a group" is still Schapiro's of 1953; see the slightly revised version in Schapiro 1994.
29. See the essay by Alpers in this volume.
30. The term "pre-Gombrichian" is borrowed from Potts 1987 (see also Potts 1994, esp. chap. 3 on "Style"). Franits 1994, p. 141, comments on the term "reality effect," which "Keith Moxey and others have adopted [from] Roland Barthes," and offers several valuable reminders on the subject of style (pp. 131–3, 138–42).
31. Slive, Rosenberg, and Ter Kuile 1972, p. 252.
32. Stechow 1968, p. 55.
33. Miedema 1980, p. 159.
34. See Buijsen 1993 and Liedtke 1995.
35. Wölfflin and Riegl serve as straw men in Alpers's assault on "style in art historical discourse [which] has always been perceived and defined on the basis of Italian examples" (Alpers 1987, p. 145).
36. Stechow 1968, p. 72.
37. Ibid., p. 11.
38. Alpers 1983, p. xxv, maintaining, essentially, that stylistic analysis is inappropriate to the field.
39. See, for example, Peter Sutton's essay in Exhib. cat. Boston 1988, and Freedberg 1980 (especially p. 39 on composition in works by Pieter Molijn). Bergström and Jantzen wrote the standard surveys of still life and architectural painting, respectively.
40. Haverkamp-Begemann 1987, p. 519.
41. Sotheby's, London, July 5, 1989, no. 138.
42. See Walford 1991, chap. 4, especially figs. 23, 44.
43. Compare Freedberg 1980, figs. 13, 14.
44. J.-M. Tassel, of Paris. See Freedberg 1980, figs. 37–9, for etchings by Molijn that fall between Goltzius's prints and the painting under discussion.
45. See Beck 1991, pp. 273–91. Eva Allen wrote a dissertation on Molijn (University of Maryland, 1987) and is preparing a monograph in which the painting published here will be included.
46. Alpers 1987, p. 140, maintaining: "For if the question of stylistic persistence is our prime concern, there is no emphasis given to the uniqueness and/or

inventiveness (hence discontinuity versus continuity) that are commonly associated (once again in Renaissance and post-Renaissance art of the West) with the unique individual maker."

47. See Montias 1982; Loughman 1992–3; and De Marchi and Van Miegroet 1994.
48. See the Dutch and English versions of the original Latin text given in Exhib. cat. Leiden 1991–2, pp. 129, 132.
49. Orlers 1641, pp. 376; Exhib. cat. Leiden 1991–2, p. 138.
50. Houbraken 1718–21, vol. 3, pp. 79–80. As noted by J. Bruyn in Exhib. cat. London 1992, p. 87, n. 21, Houbraken tells similar stories about Levecq (vol. 2, p. 153) and De Gelder (vol. 3, p. 206), as did Vasari about the young Raphael.
51. Exhib. cat. Leiden 1991–2, p. 138. See Sluijter 1988c and the comments of Franits 1994, p. 134.
52. Houbraken 1718–21, vol. 2, p. 100, noting, however, that Van den Eeckhout often made the setting "somewhat clearer or brighter."
53. Ibid., vol. 2, pp. 20–1.
54. Ibid., vol. 2, p. 274.
55. See Van Thiel et al. 1976, pp. 675 ff.; and Exhib. cat. Enkhuizen 1990, especially pp. 18–20 on anonymous painters of about 1620.
56. Alpers 1983, pp. 52–3.
57. See Liedtke 1975–6, pp. 155–64, comparing Fig. 4 (composite photograph) and Figs. 5, 11 (Saenredam's sketches of the site).
58. As discussed admirably in Schwartz and Bok 1990, pp. 215–32.
59. James 1872, p. 65, observes that the Dutch artist, "familiar with a meaner and duskier effect" in his environment (compared with that of Guardi's Venice), "must confer a charm as well as borrow one."
60. Alpers 1983, in the title of chap. 4.
61. However, many Dutch topographical drawings (and, it should go without saying, paintings and prints) reveal a keen eye for the picturesque. Those of Willem Schellinks, for example, are consistent with but more poetic than the observations recorded in his diaries, such as "the town of Dover far below, a wonderful view with the setting sun behind it" (Schellinks 1993, pp. 38–9).
62. Considering that the finest maps often served in the same way (see Fig. 41), one might speak of "the artistic impulse in Dutch mapping." See Hedinger 1986.
63. Alpers discusses a painting of an oversized radish, which in her view was "washed" rather than "grown" (*gewassen*) in 1626; see Alpers 1983, p. 183, fig. 128; and De Jongh 1984, p. 54. Kenseth 1991, p. 53, considers the same object a "marvel."
64. See Reznicek 1963a, pp. 251–3, on Van Mander's side road, which was adopted from Vicenzo Danti's idea of *due strade*.
65. As discussed in Gerson 1969 and in most monographs on Rembrandt.
66. Held 1969, p. 5.
67. See the essay by Alpers in this volume; Alpers adds that "they want their findings about Dutch history not to be Dutch specific [meaning?], but to corroborate general truths."
68. See Chapman 1990; Brusati 1990–1; and Chapman 1990–1 on Rembrandt, Van Hoogstraeten, and Jan Steen, respectively.
69. See Crary 1992, p. 32, on misconceptions about the camera obscura, citing Alpers and Wheelock. Wheelock 1977 implausibly associates the development of tonalism in landscape painting with the camera obscura. Compare Montias 1990, p. 371, where tonalism is considered a cost-effective technique that also "had artistic value in and of itself" and "an evocative way of rendering landscape that appealed to a wide public."
70. In contrast, Alpers 1983 discusses Van Goyen's work as a demonstration of the "mapping impulse" (see, for example, p. 132).
71. Van Hoogstraeten 1678, pp. 237–8, as translated by Walsh 1974, pp. 737–8.
72. Walsh 1974, p. 738.
73. See n. 20 above.
74. Van Hoogstraeten 1678, p. 13 (my translation).
75. Von Moltke 1994, pp. 3–4. On Rembrandt's teaching, see Exhib. cat. Amsterdam 1984–5.
76. On the attribution, see Liedtke 1989, pp. 157–60; and Idem 1995–6, p. 4.
77. The expression, of course, is Fromentin's. Alpers 1982, p. 184, evidently refers to American professors of past times when she recalls, "the methodology that I was taught prepared me to deal with Italian art, but not with this."
78. See Stumpel 1984, p. 580, on Alpers's use of the latter distinction.
79. Van Goyen's followers are catalogued in Beck 1991.
80. See Liedtke 1992 and Van de Wetering 1992.
81. See Alpers 1983, p. xxv; and Bruyn 1985, pp. 155, 160, n. 3, on Baxandall's actual usage.
82. This tradition is the subject of Liedtke 1988.
83. On the architectural paintings, see Liedtke 1991a. Gowing 1970, p. 100, and later monographs have drawn attention to Gerard Houckgeest in particular. See also Liedtke 1979.
84. Which is probably why Rembrandt and Vermeer were isolated by Alpers 1983, in her "Epilogue," pp. 222–8.
85. See Liedtke 1991b.

86. See earlier text and n. 53.
87. Exhib. cat. Leiden 1991–2, p. 129.
88. See earlier text and nn. 49, 51.
89. Sluijter 1993, p. 60.
90. Ibid., pp. 15, 62.
91. See Taylor 1992 on Goeree 1668.
92. Taylor 1992, p. 214.
93. Van de Wetering 1992 is comparable to Taylor 1992, which Van de Wetering has recommended in lectures.
94. See Liedtke 1990–1 and especially Grijzenhout and Van Veen 1992.
95. See earlier text and nn. 20, 71.
96. As did Leonardo and artists throughout Europe in the seventeenth century. On Leonardo's *Trattato della Pittura* and Dutch painters, see Liedtke 1976, pp. 72–3. An introduction to the broader subject is provided in Freedberg 1991.
97. See Liedtke 1975–6 and Idem 1976.
98. As discussed in Montias 1990 and in De Marchi and Van Miegroet 1994.

CHAPTER TEN. NATURALISM AS CONVENTION

1. For example, Wiegand 1971 and more recently Bruyn 1987.
2. See, among others, Stone-Ferrier 1985b; Haverkamp-Begemann and Chong 1985; and Chong's entries in Exhib. cat. Boston 1988, esp. cat. nos. 20–2, 83, 88.
3. Alpers 1983, pp. xvii–xxvii, 119–68.
4. Schama 1987, pp. 67–72, insists on the radically novel naturalism of Dutch tonal landscape. See also Freedberg 1980, pp. 9–20; Walford 1991, pp. 15–20; and Brown 1986, pp. 11–13.
5. See the account of the critique of the iconological method in Franits 1994, pp. 129–34. See also Sutton 1988, pp. 12–13; Goedde 1989c, pp. 14–16, 130–47; and the essay by Sluijter in this volume.
6. See Franits 1994 for an overview of the debate with extensive references.
7. On the role of convention in the interpretation of Dutch painting, see the essay by Sluijter in this volume; Franits 1993, pp. 13–16; Goedde 1989c, pp. 1–21, 101–8, 163–206; and Idem 1986, pp. 139–49.
8. See, for example, the comments of Freedberg 1980, pp. 9–18; and Adams 1994, pp. 35–40. Compare the comments on genre painting in Sluijter 1988c, pp. 19–23.
9. Ad van der Woude 1991 estimates a production of between five and ten million pictures in the seventeenth century. While his assumptions may be questioned, his conclusions may be taken as an indication of the enormous numbers of pictures made.
10. Goedde 1986; Idem 1989c.
11. Price 1974, pp. 122–3, 142, 144–5; Montias 1987.
12. Summers 1981–2; Gombrich 1961, pp. 116–78. For the significance of literary conventions in the Renaissance, see also Colie 1973, pp. 1–31.
13. Van de Waal 1952, vol. 1, pp. 1–24.
14. Ibid., pp. 210–38; Schama 1987, pp. 72–81.
15. Franits 1994, pp. 139–40.
16. For surveys of the literature on this picture, see Walford 1991, pp. 149–51; Exhib. cat. Boston 1988, cat. no. 88; and Exhib. cat. Boston 1982, cat. no. 39. Walford 1991, pp. 149–51, emphasizes both the relative rarity of the theme and the degree to which Van Ruisdael gives the mill unprecedented prominence in his composition.
17. For Jan van de Velde's etching of 1617, see De Groot 1979, fig. 72. For other comparable pictures, see Exhib. cat. Boston 1988, p. 460, and cat. 108, fig. 1; these include a number of paintings by Jan Brueghel the Elder (Ertz 1979, pp. 136–142, 164–9); Rembrandt's famous picture in Washington, D.C., National Gallery of Art (for a defense of the traditional attribution, see Schneider 1990, pp. 183–90); and other compositions by Van Ruisdael himself in Cleveland, Cleveland Museum of Art, and in a private collection (Walford 1991, figs. 34, 81).
18. Alice Davies pointed out to me Jan van Kessel's depictions of polder landscapes with pumping mills in a row, which are exceptional instances of this subject in Dutch landscape. See Davies 1992, cat. nos. 50, 51.
19. The text to Van de Velde's *Aestas* reads as follows:
    Aestus adest, gnavisque petunt sub frondibus umbram
    Agricolae: et pingues errant per gramina vaccae
    Rustica mulget oves, spumantiaque ubera mollit,
    Lac premit, imbriferisque apium mel condit in urius
    (Heat reigns all about, and the diligent countryman seeks the shadow of the trees. Fat cows are grazing; the countrywoman milks the sheep, liberating the bursting udders of foaming milk. She will then make cheese; she safely stores the bees' honey in pots.) Translation from De Groot 1979, p. 75.
20. Eco 1985. John Walsh first pointed out the relevance of this article to me.
21. The text accompanying Jan van de Velde's etching does not mention the mill, the most prominent element in the composition.
22. For Renaissance conceptions of weather and cosmology, see Goedde 1989c, pp. 31–5. On the role of light in landscape, see Walford 1991, pp. 25–6, 39–45.
23. Although Chong's view in Exhib. cat. Boston 1988, pp. 461–2, that a seventeenth-century viewer would

have found distinctive features of Van Ruisdael's mill of interest as an object of enterprise and industry is plausible, his assertion that this is the only likely connotation of the mill is at odds with the entire dramatized structure of the picture and the nature of seventeenth-century thought. See Falkenburg 1989, pp. 138–41; Walford 1991, pp. 151, 225, n. 12.

24. Comparison with an eighteenth-century drawing illustrating the mill at Wijk from the other side demonstrates just how significantly Van Ruisdael magnified and dramatized the mill and the entire site. See Exhib. cat. Boston 1982, p. 117, fig. 53.
25. See the essay by De Jongh in this volume.
26. See the studies by Wiegand and Bruyn cited in n. 1. For criticism of their approach to landscape, see Goedde 1989c, pp. 9–15; and Falkenburg 1993, pp. 162–5.
27. See the studies cited in n. 17, and Kauffmann 1977.
28. These motifs are emphasized by Freedberg 1980, pp. 15–16; and Falkenburg 1989, pp. 142–9, among others.
29. Falkenburg 1988; Levesque 1994. See also Goedde 1990, pp. 655–7.
30. Falkenburg 1988, esp. pp. 22–57; Levesque 1994, pp. 5–10.
31. On the role of literary analogues in interpreting Dutch painting, see Goedde 1989c, pp. 15–21, 116–30.
32. Franits 1992.
33. Adams 1994.
34. Ibid., esp. pp. 58, 65–6.
35. Lambert 1985, pp. 186–9; and De Vries 1986, pp. 83–4.
36. On Rembrandt's landscape drawings, see Exhib. cat. Washington D. C. 1990b.
37. Bakker 1990.
38. On this subject matter and the concept of the *schilderachtig*, see Emmens 1968, pp. 124–34. See also the recent essay by Bakker 1995.
39. Van Mander 1604/1973, vol. 1, chap. I.29, sig. 3ᵛ; vol. 2, p. 376; Idem 1603–4/1994, vol. 1, pp. 248–9, sig. 247ᵛ. See Bakker 1995, pp. 148–52.
40. Van Hoogstraeten 1678, p. 176.
41. Huygens 1967, p. 68, vs. 473–80. See Bakker 1995, p. 153.
42. De Bisschop 1671, "Aen den wel-achtbaren Heer Iohan Six," n.p. (For an English translation of De Bisschop, see Van Gelder and Jost 1985, vol. 1, pp. 228–30); De Lairesse 1740, vol. 1, pp. 418–34. See also Bakker 1995, pp. 156–62.
43. Emmens 1968, p. 134. See also Bakker 1995, pp. 156–62.
44. On the role of chance in seventeenth-century Dutch art, see Emmens 1968, pp. 130–4.
45. Huygens 1946, pp. 66–7. Huygens composed his autobiography between 1629 and 1631; see Ibid., p. 124.
46. The word Huygens uses in the original Latin is "*deformitas.*" See Worp 1897, p. 64. On *fantasia*, see Summers 1981, pp. 103–43, esp. pp. 122–43; on the Dutch concepts of *geest, inventie*, and *imaginatie*, see Van Mander 1973, vol. 2, pp. 437–9, 462, 464.
47. Monk 1935, pp. 203–32.
48. Paradoxically, it was the conventionalized vision of nature in both the seventeenth and eighteenth centuries that made a more naturalistic representation of landscape possible and ultimately opened the way to the much more intimately personal relation both to landscape art and to nature itself in Romanticism.
49. Two (one dated 1603) are in Rotterdam, Museum Boymans-van Beuningen; the third, also dated 1603, is in Paris, Fondation Custodia. See Reznicek 1961, vol. 1, cat. nos. 400 (Paris), 404, 405, and pp. 131–3.
50. For example, Lebeer, 1969, p. 38, no. 3. On Bruegel's landscapes, see Gibson 1989, pp. 60–75; and Levesque 1994, pp. 17–33.
51. Exhib. cat. Boston 1988, cat. no. 19.
52. See Reznicek 1961, vol. 1, pp. 130–3; Idem 1986; Stechow 1968, pp. 15–19; Sutton 1988, pp. 23–6.
53. This approach is implicit in the work of Reznicek and Sutton cited in n. 52.
54. For an overview of the landscape types and styles available to Goltzius around 1600, see the essays by Brown and Reznicek, in Exhib. cat. London 1986, pp. 11–21, 57–62, and Parts 1 and 2 of the catalogue. See also Reznicek 1961, vol. 1, pp. 75–6, 107–12, 210–15.
55. London, British Museum. Reznicek 1961, vol. 1, cat. no. 129, and pp. 102–3.
56. Reznicek 1961, vol. 1, pp. 131–2; and Idem 1986, pp. 61–2. For the drawing in Berlin (Fig. 89), see Münz 1961, no. 37. On the problematic nature of the attribution to Bruegel of these village scenes, see Mielke 1985–6; and Boon 1992, vol. 1, pp. xxiv–xxvi, 69–71.
57. See Reznicek 1961, vol. 1, cat. nos. 400, 404, 405, and pp. 131–3. See also Stechow 1968, pp. 15–19. On the Master of the Small Landscapes, see Haverkamp-Begemann 1979; Exhib. cat. London 1986, pp. 18–19, 110–11; Mielke 1985–6, pp. 84–8; and Exhib. cat. Washington D. C. 1986, cat. no. 87.
58. See Exhib. cat. London 1986, pp. 110–11, for a summary of the complex printing history of the series.
59. Reznicek 1961, vol. 1, p. 131. A number of artists imitated the drawing style of Bruegel around 1600. See the work of Mielke and Boon cited in n. 56.
60. For a comparable drawing by De Gheyn, see Van Regteren Altena 1983, vol. 1, p. 95; vol. 2, cat. no. 945; Exhib. cat. Amsterdam 1993–4, cat. no. 315. On

Visscher's work, see Ibid., cat. nos. 323–7; Levesque 1994, pp. 35–54.

61. For example, Goltzius's *Mountain Landscape* in Haarlem, Teylers Museum (Reznicek 1961, vol. 1, cat. no. 396, pp. 107–8, 211), and De Gheyn's mountain panorama in New York, The Pierpont Morgan Library (Van Regteren Altena 1983, vol. 1, pp. 95; vol. 2, cat. no. 1049).
62. For Goltzius's woodcuts and relation to the pastoral landscape, see Exhib. cat. Amsterdam 1992–3, pp. 173–89.
63. Van Mander 1603–4/1994, vol. 1, pp. 396–9. For the engravings in other artists' styles, see Strauss 1977, vol. 2, no. 320. For a concise discussion of Goltzius's works in other artists' styles with references to the literature, see Exhib. cat. Charlottesville 1991, cat. nos. 47–8.
64. Nichols 1992.
65. For the *genera dicendi* and the arts, see among others, Steadman 1990, pp. 34–43; LeCoat 1975, pp. 32–8; and Gombrich 1966, pp. 107–21. On the *genera dicendi*, see also Croll 1966a, pp. 59–61, 77–82; Corbett 1965, pp. 26–7, 541–4; and Colie 1973, pp. 9–12.
66. Croll 1966b.
67. For example, Clark 1949, pp. 29–33. Compare the comments of Fromentin 1882/1963, pp. 130–5. There is a suggestion of this attitude as well in Von Bode 1917, pp. 142, 162. Schama 1988, pp. 69–70, sharply criticizes this view of Dutch naturalism.
68. Gombrich 1961, pp. 139–45.
69. Alpers 1983, pp. xvii–xxvii, 72–118, 119–26.
70. Alpers 1983, p. 84, avoids dealing with the visual character of seventeenth-century scientific illustration. Despite extensive references to this literature, she includes nothing from Van Leeuwenhoek and only one image (her Fig. 45) from Hooke's *Micrographia*, choosing the one illustration that distantly resembles a still life, whereas the vast majority of Hooke's illustrations, like Van Leeuwenhoek's, resemble no category of Dutch painting.
71. What is needed is further work like Bok 1993–4.
72. Walsh 1974, esp. p. 738.
73. See the comments of Schama 1988, p. 68.
74. Walsh 1974, p. 738, commenting on Porcellis's awareness of his artistry and its fictive effects in this picture observes that "the perspective of the window-frame . . . places the spectator directly in front of the boat (his position is emphasized gently but firmly by the thin line of yellow ochre that defines the side of the window frame at left). The window frame is so skillfully painted that for a moment the actual impossibility of our vantage-point does not register (we are not in a ship, and how can we be in a building?). The piece of paper on the sill not only fools the eye but teases the mind, for the date is not drawn on the paper . . . but scratched into the surface of the white paint."
75. For ideas associated with fine (*net*) and painterly (*losse*) painting in the seventeenth-century Netherlands, see Sluijter 1988c, pp. 15 and 46, n. 5, and literature cited there. See also Van de Wetering 1992, pp. 16–22.
76. Filipczak 1987, pp. 85–6.
77. For the relation between Rembrandt's style and technique in painting and Italian art, see Van de Wetering 1992, pp. 16–22. For his drawings, see Sell 1993, chaps. 2 and 4, esp. pp. 123–44.
78. Van Hoogstraeten 1678, pp. 237–8. See Walsh 1974, pp. 737–8, for a discussion of this competition.
79. Montias 1987, pp. 455–64.
80. For discussions of technical analyses of tonal landscapes, see Gifford 1983 and Idem 1995.
81. This is essentially Montias's own conclusion; see Montias 1990, p. 371.

CHAPTER ELEVEN. NATURAL ARTIFICE AND MATERIAL VALUES IN DUTCH STILL LIFE

1. Wheelock 1989, p. 11.
2. See Panofsky 1953, esp. vol. 1, pp. 133ff. and 147ff.
3. See especially Bergström 1955; Idem 1956; and De Jongh 1967; Idem 1982; and the essay by De Jongh reprinted in this volume.
4. De Jongh 1982, pp. 28–9.
5. See for example, Exhib. cat. Leiden 1970; Exhib. cat. Amsterdam 1982; and Exhib. cat. Delft 1988.
6. Particularly important in broadening the interpretive discussion of still life were the catalogue essays in Exhib. cat. Münster 1979–80. See also Schama 1987, pp. 150–88; and Freedberg 1991.
7. See especially Barthes 1972; Bryson 1990; and Idem 1991; and Foster 1992.
8. Barthes 1972.
9. See, in particular, Bryson 1991, pp. 6–8; and Foster 1992, pp. 6–19.
10. Alpers 1983, pp. 72–118.
11. See Taylor 1995, p. 118.
12. See Jones 1993, esp. chap. 2, pp. 64–91.
13. The letter, dated August 25, 1606, is published in Crivelli 1868, p. 75.
14. Borromeo 1625, p. 26; reprinted and translated in Platt 1986, p. 245.
15. On this trope and the identification of still-life painters with their artistry, see Brusati 1990–1.
16. See Van Mander 1604, esp. sigs. 29–34. For the importance of *reflexy-const* in the *Schilder-boeck*, see Melion 1991, esp. pp. 60–77. This discussion owes much to Melion's insightful analysis.

17. Melion 1991, p. 71.
18. Barthes 1972, p. 5.
19. On this painting, see the entry by Bergström in Exhib. cat. Washington 1989, pp. 114–16; Grimm 1988, p. 152; and Brusati 1990–1, pp. 176–8.
20. See the entry on this picture by Bergström in Exhib. cat. Washington 1989, pp. 114–16.
21. It should be noted that in pointing to the representational scope and eye-fooling power of painting, Luttichuys's still life highlights those same defining characteristics of painting articulated somewhat later by his contemporary, Samuel van Hoogstraeten. In his treatise on painting of 1678, Van Hoogstraeten wrote that "Painting is a science for representing all the ideas or concepts that the visible world can produce, and of deceiving the eye with outlines and colors. . . . A perfect painting is like a mirror of nature which makes things that do not exist appear to do so, and deceives in a permissible, pleasurable, and praiseworthy way." [De Schilderkonst is een wetenschap, om alle ideen, ofte denkbeelden, die de gansche zichtbaere Natuer kan geven, te verbeelden: en met omtreck en verwe het oog te bedriegen . . . een volmaekte Schildery is als een spiegel van de Natuer, die de dingen, die niet en zijn, doet schijnen te zijn, en op een geoorloofde, vermakelijke en prijslijke wijze bedriegt.] Van Hoogstraeten 1678, pp. 24–5.
22. Grimm 1988, p. 152, made this same observation but incorporated it into an interpretation of the picture as an "Allegory of Vanity."
23. On the significance of these *trompe-l'oeil* performances, see Brusati 1990–1, pp. 179–82; and Idem 1995, pp. 138–68.
24. For various interpretations of Kalf's *pronk* still lifes, see Exhib. cat. Delft 1988; Alpers 1983, pp. 114–18; Bryson 1990, pp. 124–32.

CHAPTER TWELVE. THE THREE-QUARTER LENGTH LIFE-SIZED PORTRAIT IN SEVENTEENTH-CENTURY HOLLAND

1. Pope-Hennessy 1979, p. 3; Rosenberg 1964, p. 36.
2. Rosenberg 1964, pp. 36, 37.
3. Rosenberg 1964, p. 347, n. 1, citing the *Memoirs of Sophie of Hanover.*
4. Pope-Hennessy 1979, pp. 165, 178, 183.
5. Vinken and De Jongh 1963, pp. 10–14. See also Exhib. cat. London 1989, nos. 85, 86. Campbell 1990, p. x, writes that "many writers on the subject have been content to make subjective and unsupported statements about portraits which relate to their personal reactions to and apprehensions of the sitters and have little to do with the analyses of the paintings themselves." Ibid., p. 9, describes the facial expression of Pontormo's *Portrait of a Halbadier* (Malibu, J. Paul Getty Museum) as an expression of "almost orgasmic vacancy," while Pope-Hennessy 1979, p. 110, wrote that the same youth's features are "ravaged by self-questioning." Schwartz 1992 makes a similar point about two readings of Rembrandt's *Portrait of Johannes Wtenbogaert* (Bruyn et al. 1982–, vol. 2, no. A80). In the nineteenth century, before the sitter was identified, the portrait was described variously as a Dutch regent and a burgomaster. Guiseppe Longhi entitled his engraving after the painting (1811) a "Borgomastro Olandese;" John Smith, in his catalogue of Rembrandt's work of 1836, entitled the portrait a Dutch Regent; and in the 1860 catalogue of the Mentmore collection in which it was located, the portrait was entitled "Burgomaster." The portrait was subsequently identified by Bode and Hofstede de Groot 1897–1906, vol. 8, no. 562, as the Remonstrant minister Wtenbogaert. Tümpel 1986, p. 127, described the face as having "almost meditative, wide eyes wherein the depth and wisdom of age appear to lie," hardly a description of a hardened politician. No doubt changes in taste influenced the authors' initial impressions. But the varying interpretations of the sitter's character results from the authors' a-historical reliance on the effect of the portrait on themselves colored by whom they believe the sitter to be.
6. Van Mander 1604, sig. 281. Van Mander's comments about the financial attraction of portraiture is borne out by the few documents that we have on the subject. In his study of Delft inventories and the records of the Guild of St. Luke, Montias 1982, pp. 142, 146, 193, discovered that portrait painters comprised about fifteen percent of specialists newly inscribed into the Guild of St. Luke between 1613 and 1649, and, among a smaller number of artists, comprised twenty-four percent from 1650 to 1679. Ibid., also points out (p. 244) that the number of actual portraits painted may have been proportionally higher than these percentages indicate, as painters who specialized in other types of paintings also created portraits on occasion.
7. Van Mander 1604, sig. 281. I have quoted from the English translation in Van Mander 1603–4/1994–.
8. Van Hoogstraeten 1678, p. 87. Similarly, Félibien 1725, vol. 5, p. 311, wrote in 1669 that the portrait painter and the painter of a single figure cannot achieve perfection since "one should represent the great actions as the historians do or beautiful subjects like the poets."
9. Wassenbergh 1967. A similar type of survey of the sixteenth-century Dutch portrait as a whole had been published by De Vries 1934.

10. Including Ekkart 1973; Idem 1976–9; Exhib. cat. Enkhuizen 1990; Cat. Rotterdam 1995. See also De Vries 1982 and Idem 1990a.
11. Van Bueren 1991.
12. Blasse-Hegeman et al. 1990; Falkenburg et al. 1995.
13. De Jongh 1991, p. 128.
14. Panofsky 1962; see Holly 1984, esp. chap. 6.
15. Holly 1984, p. 159.
16. De Jongh and Vinken 1961; Vinken and De Jongh 1963. Other early studies include Panofsky 1934 and Van de Waal 1956. The former is perhaps the best-known early employment of this approach. Panofsky uses the symbolism of cultural traditions rather than emblems as his primary source.
17. Including, among others, De Jongh 1974; Van Thiel 1967–8; Bedaux 1987. See especially Ibid., p. 151, n. 2, for a good, corrective explanation of the methodological use and abuse of emblems.
18. Exhib. cat. Haarlem 1986; see also Exhib. cat. Yamaguchi 1994.
19. Chapman 1990.
20. Goffman 1956; Idem 1959; Idem 1974; Idem 1983.
21. Smith 1982 makes the valuable reference to Goffman. Roodenburg 1991a has also fruitfully employed Goffman for the study of gesture in Dutch painting. An essay on melancholy and the English portrait by Strong 1964 is an early exposition of pose as an iconologic code or sign.
22. For a good discussion of the problem in the larger sphere of semiotics, see Bal and Bryson 1991, esp. p. 177.
23. De Jongh 1975–6; Idem 1991.
24. In an article on fruit symbolism in Dutch portraiture, Bedaux 1987, p. 76, challenges the interpretations presented by De Jongh 1974, a landmark article that interpreted grapes as a symbol of chastity. For a broader critique of some of the principles of iconology in a discussion of semiotics, see Bryson and Bal 1991. For a fine articulation of the view that some seventeenth-century Dutch artists may have been more concerned with visual and financial matters than those of symbolism and status, see the essay by Sluijter reprinted in this volume.
25. See, for example, De Jongh 1974.
26. De Jongh 1991, p. 121.
27. De Jongh 1991, p. 122 (see also p. 126); Becker 1991, p. 158.
28. Simmel 1922, pp. 102–3; cited in translation in Simmel 1971, p. xxxiii.
29. See the examples discussed by Freedberg 1989, pp. 213–20; and Van Bueren 1991, pp. 47–9.
30. Discourses are social: They structure the relations of speaker (here artist, patron, and/or sitter) and viewer, usually to influence in some way.
31. See Geertz 1973, p. 360: "thinking is a public activity." This discussion is also indebted to Pocock 1987.
32. Stimulating new approaches have been introduced in the general study of the genre by Brilliant 1991, and by the analytic essays on several works by Albrecht Dürer in Koerner 1993.
33. Jauss 1982, esp. pp. 22–8.
34. The portrait by Pickenoy (Amsterdam, Rijksmuseum) is reproduced in Exhib. cat. Haarlem 1986, no. 23. For those by De Keyser, see Adams 1985, nos. 40, 41.
35. Rosenberg 1964, pp. 59–60.
36. Blankert 1982, p. 57, and cat. nos. 117, 120. For the portrait once attributed to Rembrandt but now to his workshop, see Bruyn et al. 1982–, vol. 2, no. C80.
37. Italian portraits in this mode have not been so harshly judged. Oppé 1909/1970, pp. 110–11, writes of Raphael's *Portrait of Castiglione:* "He portrays his sitter in a moment of complete external repose, when all the moods and characteristics of the sitter are in potentially or subdued activity. All action in art is a limitation of character, because to make a moment permanent is to give it over-emphasis, and no motion of so complex a being as man can be an action of the whole . . . all the qualities which mark off the 'Grand Style' from the haphazard, the affected and the obscure – belong immediately and entirely to this thorough comprehension of the whole character of the sitter and the perception, through him, of all that is enduring and dignified in the creation of which he is a part . . . [The painting has] . . . universal value."
38. Susan Barnes, writing in Exhib. cat. Washington, D.C. 1990a, p. 92, notes that Titian, Giorgione, and Lorenzo Lotto in Italy, or Joos van Cleve, Jan Gossaert, and Jan Cornelisz. Vermeyen in the Netherlands, among others, produced portraits depicting their subjects in implied motion, and that subsequently an "international fashion for formality and immobility typified by the work of Moro in Spain and Bronzino in Italy" arose during the second half of the sixteenth century.
39. See Gerson 1968, p. 286, no. 164.
40. See Slive 1970–4, vol. 3, cat. nos. 32, 33.
41. In 1642, a now unknown portrait by Rembrandt of Andries de Graeff (1611–79) was valued at 500 gulden; Bruyn et al. 1982–, vol. 3, p. 302, no. A 129.
42. As, for example, Bartholomeus van der Helst's *Portrait of a Man* dated 1655 (see De Gelder 1921, no. 251, illus. pl. 24) or Ferdinand Bol's *Portrait of a Man* dated 1662 (see Blankert 1982, no. 107, pl. no. 116).
43. For example, the idea that "primitive" styles such as Romanesque or Gothic were once cited as evidence

of earlier artists' inabilities to master perspective or volume, or "truthful appearance."

44. See Montagu 1994. Social distinction is, of course, only one of many possible functions of comportment. While at least three positions about the relation of the body to the passions were in circulation in the seventeenth century, all agreed that the passions could be read upon the body. One argued that the body was simply transparent to the passions of the soul; another held that the true nature of the individual could be hidden while signs for other passions or psychological states could be performed; a third, and perhaps most widely held, belief was that the individual could only perform, or perfect, passions to which their nature predisposed them.

45. While it is very difficult to read seventeenth-century perceptions through texts, especially those written by foreigners, it is notable that the few comments that survive register the lack of formal distinctions. Roodenburg 1991a, n. 61, relays that Gomes van Trier, the Flemish translator of Guazzo's *De civili conversatione* in 1603, concluded that the Dutch were not interested in civility, one of the obstacles being "that very great misunderstanding of some, who (under the appearance of humble people) want to promote equality here in this world." Fynes Moryson, the English tourist who visited the Netherlands in the 1590s, wrote that "The Nobility or Gentry hath long been rooted out by the people. . . . I could not heare of more then some three Families of Gentlemen in Holland and Zeland (for the Lords of Nassaw are strangers), and these Gentlemen lived after the Plebeian manner of the other inhabitants, so as it were in vaine to seeke for any Order of Knighthood among them," Moryson 1617/1907, vol. 4, p. 470 (III.iv.298). As late as the 1730s, Van Effen 1731–5, vol. 7, p. 10, concluded that the consciousness of rank and station that went along with the rules of civility was more natural with strongly hierarchic states than with a "commonwealth" (such as the Netherlands), "where in a certain way all the inhabitants might be seen as each other's equals"; cited by Roodenburg 1991a, n. 62. See also Van Strien 1993, pp. 213–14.

46. Two fine surveys of the subject are Spierenburg 1981 and Roodenburg 1991a. Roodenburg notes that a revised version of Erasmus, *De civilitate morum puerilium*, was required reading in Dutch Latin schools from 1625, and Stefano Guazzo's *De civili Conversatione* was translated into Dutch as *Van den heuschen burgerlycken ommegangh: een seer sin-rijcke, lieflijcke, ende nuttighe t'samensprekinghe* and published in Alkmaar in 1603. It was only in the second half of the century that additional civility manuals were published in the Northern Netherlands. These include a Latin edition of Guazzo's work published in Leiden in 1650; a Dutch translation of Castiglione's renowned *Libro del Cortegiano*, which appeared in Amsterdam in 1662; [De Courtin] 1672; a Dutch edition of Della Casa 1558/1986 that appeared in 1715; Anon. 1735.

47. For the court or state portrait in general, see Jenkins 1947. Müller-Hofstede 1983 discusses portraits of this type by Rubens.

48. [Van Sommelsdijck] 1667, pp. 31, 34–5, cited by Roodenburg 1991a, p. 184 n. 38. Anon. 1670, a free and abridged English translation of an earlier French travel book, pp. 23–4, describes the immobile comportment of the King: "They which have spoken to me . . . tell me . . . that when they speak to him he changes neither look nor posture but receives, hears, and answers them with the same countenance, nothing in all his body being moveable but his lips and tongue."

49. Anon. 1735. This text is indebted to De Courtin 1672; see Roodenburg 1991a, pp. 156, 184, n. 37.

50. Bredero 1617/1982, and Overbeke 1991, nos. 783, 1726; cited by Roodenburg 1991a, p. 184, n. 39.

51. See further the examples in De Vries 1934 (although attributions for a number of these paintings have changed today).

52. Roodenburg 1991a, pp. 156–7, and n. 22.

53. Oestreich 1982, p. 37, "around 1600, especially in the France of Henry IV and the Netherlands, Stoicism became the ideology, almost the religion, of educated men." On Lipsius's stoicism, see Saunders 1955; for a good corrective, see Den Boer 1979, esp. p. 532, n. 46; see also Forster 1977. For an excellent history of stoic thought and its subsequent reception, see Røstvig 1962. Humanist thought of the Renaissance is an exceedingly complex issue of which Stoicism is only one pole. Bouwsma 1975 lucidly contrasts neo-Stoicism with Augustinianism, which accepted the passions as an important aspect of life. For a brief overview of the neo-Stoic movement in the late sixteenth century in the North, see the afterword to Lipsius 1965, pp. 19–31.

54. Erasmus 1529; Lipsius 1605. For the Stoicism of Erasmus's thought, see Christian 1972.

55. For a list of editions of this important work, see Oestreich 1982, p. 13.

56. Cicero, *Tusculan Disputations* IV.vii.14; Plato had divided the soul itself into three parts (and Aristotle the soul into two), with the lower being the source of the passions, the higher the seat of rationality. Plato, *Timaeus*, 69c–d; *Republic*, IV.xii.436a–b; *Phaedrus*, 246a–b. Aristotle, *Nicomachean Ethics*, I.xiii.9 ("the soul consists of two parts, one irrational and the

other capable of reason"). But Stoics saw passion as error and thus not as a fundamental part of the soul; see Monsarrat 1984, pp. 15–16. Adding a Christian dimension to this philosophy, Renaissance men believed that man's passionate lower nature could at times gain control of his life due to Adam's fall.

57. Desiderius Erasmus in *Parabolae sive similia* (quoted from Erasmus 1974–, vol. 23, p. 153.).
58. Skinner 1978, vol. 2, p. 187; see also p. 279.
59. Latin from Lipsius 1584, quoted by Oestreich 1982, p. 19; I am grateful to David Dodd for the translation.
60. Charron 1606; quoted by Babb 1951, p. 19. Charron's book was published in numerous other editions in the Netherlands, including in Leiden in 1646, 1656, and 1659, and in Amsterdam in 1662. For Charron and his work, see Kogel 1972.
61. Descartes 1637. His friend and correspondent Constantijn Huygens advised, coordinated, and apparently even corrected the proofs of the first edition; see Dibon 1950.
62. Letter of August 4, 1645; see Descartes 1970, pp. 166, 165. Descartes also expresses similar sentiments in his treatise *The Passions of the Soul*, where he writes: "the most feeble souls of all are those whose will . . . allows itself continually to be carried away by present passions" (Descartes 1967, vol. 1, p. 354).
63. Spinoza distinguishes three stages of knowledge. In the first, Opinion, man is in bondage to the passions; in the second, Reason, the passions lose their power when they are understood; in the third and highest, Intuition, man sees all things in God and God in all things, and feels himself part of the eternal order and in a state of peace; see Gilbert and Kuhn 1953.
64. Supplementing if not replacing the older *rederijker* dramas both in style and in subject matter, Seneca's tragedies provided models not only in structure but also in theme for authors from the middle of the sixteenth century onward. These include Dirck Volkertsz. Coornhert, Daniël Heinsius, Gerard Vossius, Hugo Grotius, Jacob Cats, Gerbrand Adriaensz. Bredero, Caspar Barlaeus, Pieter Cornelisz. Hooft, Samuel Coster, Joost van den Vondel, and Henrik L. Spiegel. See Worp 1892, chap. 3, pp. 43–57, which gives a survey of the knowledge and study of Seneca during this period; see also Idem 1904–8, vol. 1, pp. 247 ff. Smits-Veldt 1986, pp. 193–204, treats Bredero, Jacob Cats, Coornhert, and Spiegel. For Heinsius, see Meter 1984, pp. 52–3, 73–5, passim. Most of these authors, however, relied upon Seneca's work and thought selectively; his impact diminished after about 1630; see Parente 1987, pp. 57–8, 132.
65. A well-known classical bust of Seneca appeared in numerous drawings, prints, and paintings. Rubens included Seneca's bust in his portrait of *Justus Lipsius with Peter Paul Rubens, Philip Rubens, and Johannes Woverus, "The Four Philosophers"* (Florence, Palazzo Pitti); see Vlieghe 1987, no. 117; Prinz 1973; Morford 1991, pp. 3–13, and passim. The artist's *Death of Seneca* dating from about 1609 (Munich, Alte Pinakothek) was widely known through an engraving by Cornelis Galle included in Lipsius's edition of the philosopher's works published in 1615. Jacques de Gheyn drew the death of Seneca, and Gerrit van Honthorst (copy, Utrecht, Centraal Museum), Joachim von Sandrart (formerly Berlin, Kaiser Friedrich Museum), and Matthias Stomer (copy, Catania, Museo dei Benedettine) all created paintings of the subject. Pigler 1974, vol. 2, pp. 430–1, lists thirty-nine versions of the death of Seneca from the seventeenth and eighteenth centuries. Stoic ideals have been ascertained in the work of other Northern artists; see Günter 1986.
66. See Denys G. Dyer's introduction to the English translation (Edinburgh University Press, 1975), where he discusses parodies and attacks on neo-Stoicism in deathbed scenes.
67. Hooft 1976–9, vol. 1, pp. 492, 494; cited in translation by Schenkeveld 1991, p. 64.
68. Oestreich 1982, pp. 34, 64, passim.
69. Rabelais 1532–48/1991, book I, chap. 52.
70. Massinger 1624, act I, scene 3.
71. Bouwsma 1975, pp. 31–2.
72. Oestreich 1982, p. 7.
73. Caspar Barlaeus cited in translation by Haak 1969, pp. 76–8. One must take these descriptions with a grain of salt. Moryson 1617/1907, vol. 4, p. 467 (III.iv.287), wrote: "at Leyden, mysselfe have observed the inhabitants of Villages, . . . High injuries and maimes of any member, are punished by the law, which passeth over lighter injuries, not giving such ample satisfactions to the wronged even by word, as the constitutions of the Sweitzers give; so as with them no lesse then in England, quarrels and brawlings are frequent, and often breake out into man-slaughters, wherein those who will revenge themselves by force, first agree between themselves, whether they will strike or stab; and then drawing out long knives, which they ordinarily weare, they wound one another by course, according to their agreement, either by slashes or stabs (which they call schneiden and stecken)." Whether or not either description was historically accurate is unimportant; the point remains that the rhetoric of self-control was in wide circulation.
74. Cited by Moffitt 1990, esp. p. 219, associating the phrase with the court portraiture of Moro and Titian. For a suggestive article by an anthropologist on demeanor in court ritual, see McCracken 1982.

75. Earl of Clarendon 1843, p. 23.
76. Heckscher 1967, p. 130. For this portrait, see Rowlands 1985, no. 13, pl. 26.
77. Horace, *Ars Poetica*, 99–104 (quoted from *Horace, Satires, Epistles and Ars Poetica*, Trans. H. Rushton Fairclough, Cambridge [Mass.], 1966, p. 459).
78. Heinsius terms exposition "implicit" that employs models and examples, or acting out of emotions in particular situations; and exposition "explicit" that describes intentions and feelings. See Daniel Heinsius on the subject with regard to tragedy in Meter 1984, pp. 238–44.
79. Della Casa 1558/1986, p. 48. This work was translated into Dutch in 1715.
80. Meter 1984, p. 156; Kern 1949, pp. 58–9.
81. In discussing the portraits of Michael van Miereveld, Huygens 1946, p. 75, states that "Toch verrichten zij een nobel werk, dat meer dan iets anders voor onze menschelijke behoeften allernoodzakelijkst is, omdat wij door hun toedoen in zekere zin niet sterven en nog als nakomelingen met onze verste voorvaderen vertrouwelijk kunnen spreken. Dit genot is mij zoo lief, dat mij niets aangenamers kan te beurt vallen, dan dat het mij bij het lezen of hooren verhalen over ieders leven en karakter – hij zij een goed of slecht mensch – (en dit soort geschiedenis trekt mij bijzonder aan) mogelijk wordt gemaakt zijn portret te beschouwen."
82. Vossius 1650, published a year after Vossius's death by Franciscus Junius; see Rademaker 1981, p. 324.
83. Personal communication with Pieter Biesboer.
84. Exhib. cat. Haarlem 1986, p. 36; see also Woodall 1990.
85. Elias 1982. Elias's now classic study was first published in 1939.
86. See Groeneweg 1995.
87. Burke 1994, p. xv.
88. In psychoanalytic terms, a process known as condensation.
89. Roodenburg 1991a, pp. 154–6. This does not mean that individuals did not also seek to distinguish themselves socially. For example, there are examples of families creating or inventing forebears for just this purpose; see Dudok van Heel 1990, who has identified a number of spurious genealogies for such well-known families as the De Graeffs. Kretschmar 1977 has discovered that coats of arms were not infrequently fabricated. Van Nierop 1984, p. 228, has identified individuals who adopted noble names. This is symptomatic of a more general cultural practice. The point is that class boundaries were in flux and not at all clear.
90. On civil unrest during this period, from the 1580s through the middle of the seventeenth century, see Duke and Kolff 1969; Knevel 1988; and Dekker 1982, respectively.

CHAPTER THIRTEEN. HOW TO SIT, STAND, AND WALK

1. Throughout the seventeenth century, three generations of bone-setters practiced not in De Rijp but in the neighboring village of Jisp (possibly Huygens or his wife made a mistake). The oldest of them, Willem Taemsz., nicknamed "the iron thumb," was praised by Jacob Cats in his *Trouringh* (Wedding Ring) of 1637. See Van Andel 1941, pp. 172–4.
2. For the full story, see Exhib. cat. The Hague 1987, pp. 96–101.
3. It seems likely that Huygens was all the more concerned about the education of his sons, as the family, because of its Brabant origins, did not have access to political office and thereby to the urban regent class. Such offices remained the perquisite of the "natives of this country." For the difficulties of the Huygens family, see Hofman 1983, pp. 28–9.
4. Elias 1982. Elias's now classic study was first published in 1939.
5. [De Courtin] 1733, p. 223. This text was originally published in French in 1617; Dutch editions were published in 1672, 1675, and 1677.
6. The phrase is, of course, Erving Goffman's; see Goffman 1971.
7. See especially Goffman 1959. On my reservations regarding Elias, see also Roodenburg 1991a, esp. pp. 157–64.
8. Castiglione 1528. It was only in 1662 that his book was translated into Dutch; a second edition was published in 1675; see Idem 1675, p. 51. For a history of the rise, decline, and transformation of this famous text, see Burke 1995.
9. [Erasmus] 1678/1969, pp. 17–18. This book, which originally appeared in Latin in 1530, was written for the eleven-year-old Henry of Burgundy.
10. Anon. 1546. The original manuscript is in the collections of the University Library of Ghent (RES 821). I would like to thank my colleague Theo Meder, who kindly lent me his transcription of the text. For a later edition (Antwerp 1587) and also for some extensive quotations, see Schotel 1873–4, vol. 1, pp. 203–10. On the several editions, see Bijl 1978, pp. 187–96; Jansen-Sieben 1985, pp. 249–60.
11. Van L[aar] n.d., (1735), pp. 68, 169, 171, 179.
12. For this argument and for a general, though incomplete, overview of Dutch manners books, see Spierenburg 1981.
13. Cited after Bijl 1978, p. 250. See also Briels 1985, pp. 1, 14.

14. For a fuller discussion of these problems, see Roodenburg 1991a, pp. 154–7.
15. We even possess a few notes written by Huygens Sr. on the education of his children. See Exhib. cat. The Hague 1987, pp. 79–88.
16. Huygens 1987, p. 32. The original manuscript, written in Latin, is in the collections of the Royal Library in The Hague. It was first published (in Latin) in *Bijdragen en Mededeelingen van het Historisch Genootschap* 18 (1897): 1–122.
17. Ibid., p. 24.
18. Vigarello 1989. For another important and stimulating overview, see Kunzle 1982, pp. 70–104. For the early Dutch Republic, see Roodenburg 1991b.
19. Van Huffel 1923, p. 80: "les epaules basses, et en arriere, tournez les jambes en dehors, serrez les fesses, la tête haute et libre, la poitrine haute et en avant." See also Hasse 1990, p. 50, pp. 119–20.
20. Van Beverwijck 1651, p. 182.
21. Ballexserd 1763, p. 186. This treatise, winning the first prize, was an answer to the question: "Wat het is het beste bestier, 't geen men moet houden omtrent het lighaam der kinderen, zo met opzigt tot hunne kleeding, voedsel, oeffening, als anders, van hunne geboorte af, geduurende hun kindsheid, om ze lang en gezond te doen leeven."
22. Camper 1763, pp. 384, 388. With his answer, Camper won the second prize (see n. 21 above).
23. The corsets probably originated at the Spanish court and reached the French court via Italy; see Kunzle 1982, p. 71. For the upright posture of Spanish courtiers, interpreted by other countries as proud and arrogant, and its relationship with Spanish fashion, see Roodenburg 1991b, pp. 31–2. See also the stimulating essay by Burke 1991, pp. 77–8.
24. Estienne 1578/1883, vol. 1, p. 253. This passage is also quoted by Vigarello 1989, p. 155.
25. Kunzle 1982, p. 75.
26. For Flemish influences on Dutch fashion, see Roodenburg 1991b, pp. 25–9.
27. Vigarello 1989, pp. 179–80.
28. For this friendship, see Huygens 1987, p. 39. Marnix was the first secretary and confidant of William of Orange; Huygens was his fourth secretary.
29. Marnix van St. Aldegonde 1615.
30. We still encounter such notions in the eighteenth century. See Van L[aar] n.d., pp. 171ff.: dancing, riding, fencing, and other physical exercises are favorable to develop a *beeter gesteldheid.*
31. Marnix van St. Aldegonde 1992a, p. 61. This translation is closer to the original than the Latin edition of 1615.
32. See Exhib. cat. The Hague 1987, pp. 79–86. For Marnix's feelings on dancing, see also Marnix van St. Aldegonde 1992b, vol. 2, pp. 82–3. This text is a letter from 1577 and written to the Calvinist minister Caspar van der Heyden. In his letter Marnix defends (civilized) dancing against the negative views of the ministers. Marnix believed that one of the benefits of dancing was physical exercise.
33. Huygens 1987, pp. 23–4.
34. Ibid., pp. 53–4.
35. Exhib. cat. The Hague 1987, p. 140.
36. Voetius 1644, p. 79. The same passage is quoted in Roodenburg 1990, p. 328. For an excellent overview of seventeenth-century dancing and the ideas of the church, see Naerebout 1990.
37. For the strengthening of social hierarchy in the Dutch Republic and its impact on posture and gesture, see Roodenburg 1991a.
38. Van Hoogstraeten 1678, p. 117.
39. Goeree 1682, pp. 297–8, 309. For an even stronger statement, see pp. 149–50: "De oude tronie-bekykers raden ons datmen niet veel by swak-gehalsde moet verkeeren, om datse bedrieglyk vallen aan yder die met haar omgaat. Verminkte of scheef-halsen zijn veelsints verwart in haar reden, ook beschreumd in 't ondernemen van veel dingen."
40. Castiglione 1675, pp. 300ff.
41. According to Theo van der Meer, effeminacy was only associated with homosexuals after several waves of prosecutions that began in 1730. However, during much of the eighteenth century, it was still the contemporary skirt-chaser, the *petit-maître* or *saletjonker*, who was considered the quintessence of effeminacy; see Van der Meer 1995, pp. 396ff.
42. Bolten 1991. For an early and still interesting study on the subject, see Tikkanen 1912.
43. De Lairesse 1707, vol. 1, p. 33.
44. For the exact meaning of the term *welstand*, and for Van Mander's use of *welstand* and *gracelijckheyt in 't buyghen en wenden* interchangeably, see Hessel Miedema's commentary in his edition of Van Mander's *Schilderboek:* Van Mander 1604/973, vol. 2, pp. 448–9.
45. Van Mander 1604/1973, vol. 1, pp. 114–17 (see also Miedema's comments in Ibid., vol. 2, pp. 451–2); Van Hoogstraeten 1678, p. 295; Goeree 1682, pp. 243ff. For the Renaissance background and its roots in classical rhetoric, see also Summers 1981–2; Vickers 1988, pp. 348–51.
46. Van Mander 1604/1973, vol. 1, pp. 125–6.
47. Goeree 1682, pp. 242–3.
48. De Lairesse 1707, vol. 1, p. 52.
49. Ibid., vol. 1, pp. 54–5.
50. Ibid., vol. 1, p. 52.
51. Ibid., vol. 1, pp. 58–9.

52. See my discussion of the *Cortegiano* in section II of this essay.
53. Lomazzo 1584, p. 141.
54. De Lairesse 1707, vol. 1, p. 56.
55. Ibid., vol. 1, pp. 173–4. For a similar verdict on Brouwer, see Van Hoogstraeten 1678, p. 67.
56. For my use of the terms "pictorial tradition" and "iconographic convention" and their importance for studying form as a carrier of meaning, see Sluijter 1992, esp. pp 374–5.
57. Goeree 1682, p. 316.
58. For some examples and commentary (but not on posture or gesture), see Alpers 1972–3 and Idem 1975–6. For Miedema's critical response to Alpers's concept of the "comic mode," see Miedema 1977; see also Alpers 1978–9. For an intelligent discussion of posture and gesture in Jan Steen, see the unpublished lecture by Mariët Westermann, "The Amusements of Jan Steen, Generically Looking," a lecture delivered at the Courtauld Institute of Art (London) on February 26, 1992. She also points to Steen's subversion of proper gesture for comic effect (which was practiced on the stage as well), for example, when he depicts his women of lesser repute with quite graceful gestures.
59. I owe this reference to Elizabeth Wyckoff.
60. For a helpful study of such contrasts, see Exhib. cat. Antwerp 1987, pp. 63–116.
61. For a further exploration of this topic, see Roodenburg 1995.
62. See De Jongh 1992b, pp. 307, 322.
63. See the introduction to Burke 1987. For a recent characterization of *Volkskunde* or "European ethnology" as the study of bagatelles or trifles, see Scharfe 1995.
64. For a related argument, see Falkenburg 1993.
65. For color as a carrier of meaning, see also Franits 1995; for the elbow akimbo, see Spicer 1991.

CHAPTER FOURTEEN. THE SPACE OF GENDER IN SEVENTEENTH-CENTURY DUTCH PAINTING

1. On Gesina ter Borch's album and allegory, see Kettering 1988, vol. 2, pp. 616–21. Kettering feels that Gesina's watercolor is simply an "illustration" of the text provided by Jordis; I have given Gesina slightly more credit for invention because there are many aspects of the image that Jordis's text does not describe adequately if at all. I refer to Gesina ter Borch as "Gesina" not because she is a woman – as art historians often refer to women artists by their first names, and men by their last names – but in order to distinguish her from the many other artistic members of the Ter Borch family.
2. De Jongh 1983, pp. 212–13.
3. See Garrard 1989, pp. 337–70; Idem 1980; Hofrichter 1983.
4. This can be seen in many paintings by Pieter de Hooch.
5. On the cultural definition of "Genius" as male, see Battersby 1989; on this, and on the importance of artistic institutions in women's exclusion from the arts, see also the classic essay by Nochlin 1988.
6. An excellent essay on the historiography of feminist interventions in modernist art history is Tickner 1988. In the field of Dutch art, the classic essay suggesting a potentially feminist view of aesthetics and artistic production is Alpers 1982. Alpers takes up the feminist challenge to rewrite art history by questioning the terms in which it had previously been written. Although in the end her essay is not precisely about gender, it has provided an important stimulus to scholars to consider the perhaps less "masculine" nature of Dutch painting.
7. This is not to say that no Dutch painting engages with the issues of female bodies and male voyeurism. In fact, Dutch "mannerist" art focuses very largely on subjects that thematize precisely this relationship. The themes these artists chose often added an element of implied (narrative) visual threat (Utrecht mannerists) or actual physical cruelty and dismemberment (Haarlem mannerists). Particularly the latter group have received far too little attention with regard to issues of gender. On narrative, the nude, and voyeurism in Dutch history painting, see Sluijter 1985; Idem 1986.
8. See Schama 1987, pp. 375–427; Rybczynski 1986, pp. 51–75.
9. An extremely useful historical and theoretical exploration of the organization of bourgeois public and private "spheres" is Habermas 1989.
10. For a brief discussion of seventeenth-century Dutch amateur women, see Kloek 1993, p. 63. On nineteenth-century women's amateur art – a case study with significant parallels to that of Gesina ter Borch – see Higonnet 1992.
11. Anna Maria van Schurman came from a privileged background (her mother, Eva von Harff de Dreiborn, was of the nobility), and her father encouraged her intellectual and artistic development. She was introduced into the most elite educated circles of her day, where her remarkable learning earned her a high reputation: She was held up as an example of the actual capacity of the female intellect. See Van der Stighelen 1987; De Baar et al. 1992. Van Schurman's remarkable series of self-portrayals are particularly worthy of further study. Other known "artistic women" of this period are the daughters of Roemer

Visscher, Maria Tesselschade Visscher and Anna Visscher; see Smits-Veldt 1994. As testimony of the place of drawing in a girl's education, see for instance Jan Steen's *The Drawing Lesson* (Malibu, J. Paul Getty Museum), in which an artist instructs a girl in his studio.

12. Kettering 1983b.
13. For an interesting discussion of how seventeenth-century visual didactic methods fit into a more general way of thinking about picturing the world, see Svetlana Alpers's comments on Comenius in Alpers 1983, pp. 93–9.
14. On these see Exhib. cat. The Hague 1990; on the example discussed later, see Ibid., p. 69.
15. On women's crafts, see Parker 1984; Parker and Pollock 1981, pp 50–81.
16. On artistic education – academic and artisanal – in early modern Europe, see the essays in Exhib. cat. Providence 1984.
17. On guilds, see still the fundamental study by Hoogewerff 1947; see also Montias 1982. For a more recent study with particular attention to women's opportunities within this economic structure, see Wijsenbeek-Olthuis and Noordegraaf 1993. For a historical study of how women were able to operate as workers within guild trades, see Howell 1986b; a briefer summary of many of her points is given in Howell 1986a.
18. Much useful documentary information about the Leyster/Molenaer business is given in Broersen 1993. It is often implied that upon her marriage Leyster, in a typically female move, sadly gave up her creative outlet in order to support her husband's work. This view is anachronistic. Many *male* painters too gave up painting upon making expedient marriages (Hobbema is the most famous example), for they evidently viewed painting as an unfortunately necessary job rather than as a fulfilling practice; and since Molenaer's career seems always to have been more successful than Leyster's, it was to her financial advantage to manage it. Leyster further expanded their business into an art dealership, and the couple as a team became far wealthier than either could have alone. Women also commonly dealt in very cheap paintings in their role as *uitdraagsters*, dealers in second-hand goods acquired from estate inventories. On these women, see Van Wijngaardens 1995.
19. The most sustained analysis of this is Alpers 1983, esp. pp. 112–18. On the traditional guild framework of painters' struggles for status, see also Miedema 1987 and Sluijter 1988c.
20. A fairly (although not completely) thorough overview of women painters in Holland is provided by Kloek 1993. The breakdown of European women artists according to their family connections is based on the result of my own research. Outside of the Netherlands, most women artists whose fathers were not painters were themselves amateur noblewomen and/or were working in connection with a court as "gentlewoman" artists: Sofonisba Anguissola is an obvious example here. England, where painting was far less publicly exalted and institutionalized than on the Continent, provides a few exceptions to this rule.
21. Rubens, a Northerner with a highly international outlook, is perhaps a borderline case here. While there are no images of his studio as a place of private production, he did receive important visitors at the studio – in a wing of his own home – turning the space into a site of public demonstration of his artistry. Furthermore, the courtyard of his home was itself decorated with allegories of the arts – a quasi-private space marked for quasi-public consumption. Nor was this a unique move on his part; earlier and contemporary Flemish painters (Frans Floris, Jacob Jordaens) decorated their homes with such allegories, as had Cornelis Ketel in Holland and Giorgio Vasari in Italy in the sixteenth century. No seventeenth-century Dutch artist, to my knowledge, decorated a home in such a way; but this is a subject worthy of further research within the present rubric of domestic/public production. On Rubens, see McGrath 1978; Muller 1981–2; Tijs 1984; and, on artists' houses in general, Hüttinger 1985.
22. It is known that the students' "practice cubicles" in Rembrandt's studio were provided with such stoves. See Haverkamp-Begemann 1969.
23. For a useful recent account of the construction of "the Nude," see Nead 1992. The now-classic account of the naked/nude dichotomy is Berger 1972, pp. 45–64.
24. A very stimulating discussion of the kind of viewing that Rembrandt's naked models evoke is that of Bal 1991, esp. 138–48.
25. On Rembrandt's early critics, see Emmens 1968 and Slive 1953. On Rembrandt's nudes, see the more recent and rather telling commentary by Clark 1956, pp. 435–41.
26. Paula Cuneo (unpublished paper) has analyzed these "clues of place" in many etchings, where they are far less obvious than they are in the *Half-Dressed Woman by a Stove.*
27. On Job Berckheyde's painting (St. Petersburg, Hermitage) and several other studio scenes, see Fleischer 1988. I have doubts about his reattribution of the Berckheyde painting to Van Brekelenkam, for it seems highly uncharacteristic of the latter's *oeuvre.* See also Raupp 1984. The Van Ostade *Studio*, not discussed in either of these sources, is in Dresden,

Gemäldegalerie Alte Meister. The studio spaces correspond even more closely to the "craftsman's workshop" scenes as painted by Van Brekelenkam and others; but those very workshops were depicted as integrally part of a home. See n. 44 below.

28. On this painting, see Exhib. cat. Haarlem 1993, pp. 302–7.
29. On this imagery, see Stewart 1977.
30. A few exceptions could be adduced – most notably the Amsterdam Town Hall – but they make up only the tiniest fraction of Dutch artistic output. On public painting, see Brenninkmeyer-De Rooij 1980–1.
31. On the number of artists and the volume of production in Holland, see De Vries 1991 and Van der Woude 1991. I have doubts about the statistics generated in the latter article, which seem to overestimate the bulk and value of artistic production to impossible levels. Two suggestions: Van der Woude perhaps underestimates the "survival rate" of paintings; moreover, he assumes that every artist made a living by producing paintings, which is certainly not true, as many had other jobs as well.
32. The old quip about how every Dutch peasant owned a painting is legendary, but in fact Michael Montias's study of Delft inventories has shown that about two-thirds of the population did live in households possessing paintings: see Montias 1982, p. 220. See also Idem 1991.
33. This is important because in other countries women artists *did* produce histories, as that was by far the privileged genre of painting. Two important examples of contemporary women history painters are Lavinia Fontana (see Cantaro 1989) and Artemisia Gentileschi (see Garrard 1989).
34. No one has ever studied this question, hence my evidence is somewhat circumstantial, but it is an issue that would be well worth pursuing. Women are recorded as buyers in published Antwerp dealers' records, and (again in Antwerp) the inventories of spinsters certainly contain paintings. Perhaps more careful study of dealers' records in the Dutch Republic would tell us more about women as buyers, although since expensive purchases for "collections" were (as I point out later) probably made by men, the documents could be misleading.
35. The two books I am discussing here are Vernoegde 1678 and De Vrye 1678.
36. The major exception to this rule is Alison Kettering's article, "Ter Borch's Ladies in Satin," reprinted in this volume.
37. A good and sensitive example of this sort of art history is the study of domestic genre painting by Franits 1993. In his introduction Franits provides an excellent overview of past ways of interpreting this imagery. His exploration of the notion of domesticity is very different from mine and provides an important counterweight to the present discussion.
38. The one genre of which this question has been asked, although more from the side of production (the gaze of the female artist), is that of still-life painting; see Bryson 1990, esp. p. 164. Bryson's answer, however, seems to call upon an almost biological essentialism, which I have tried to avoid; see Honig 1993. As an alternative way of posing that question in future research, I would suggest the following. Still-life painting originates in the sixteenth-century "Market Scenes" of Pieter Aertsen and Joachim Beuckelaer, works in which an "erotics" of the market object is often developed in tandem with an "erotics" of the market woman, the public woman who appears alongside the goods. In seventeenth-century Dutch painting, a split occurs whereby markets are depicted in terms of *space*, and foodstuffs in terms of a now *domesticated* still life (the banquet or breakfast piece). How, then, is commodity desire reconfigured in the private sphere? Does a possibly female gaze invest objects with a different kind of desirability?
39. Dutch urban domestic architecture is quite different from that of other continental cities in that its rows of small but individual homes strongly demarcated the space of each particular family. In many cities urban housing was arranged around shared courtyards, creating a more communal environment. In Holland, each household was in charge of its own space. On the one hand, this meant greater privacy, but on the other hand, it meant greater moral responsibility. On Dutch urban architecture, see the basic study by Mieschke 1969.
40. On the architectural "boundaries" of domesticity, with an extensive discussion of pictorial representations, see De Mare 1993; see also Idem 1994.
41. On neighborhood life and communal discipline, see Roodenburg 1990.
42. An interesting recent analysis of the vision and visibility of Italian domestic women is Rogers 1993.
43. Paintings by Pieter de Hooch and Quirijn van Brekelenkam provide many examples of the male-as-absence, particularly by using a male portrait (often placed near a window or door to the outside world) decorating a room inhabited entirely by women. See, for instance, Van Brekelenkam's *Woman Giving Market Money to a Maid* (Zürich, Kunsthaus) and De Hooch's *Woman and Child in a Pantry* (Amsterdam, Rijksmuseum).
44. The only painter who did engage significantly with the fact of labor-for-profit within the domestic environment was Quirijn van Brekelenkam, whose work deserves much further study on these grounds. In his

scenes of craftsmen's workshops, the man's wife is often shown nearby, in a space both connected to yet distinct from her husband's, busy with her household work. The spatial and gender dynamics (public/private, business/domestic, male laborer/female client or housewife) of these images are extremely interesting and also remind us of what is conspicuously excluded from other artists' images. See on Van Brekelenkam, Lasius 1992; on the selective treatment of domestic industry in seventeenth-century Dutch painting, with a particular focus on textile work, see Stone-Ferrier 1985a. There are many historical studies of urban women (and men) as paid home laborers. The classic work on women's waged labor is Clark 1919; important material can be found in such recent studies as Berg 1994; Wiesner 1986; Idem 1993 (with good bibliographic essay); Hanawalt 1986; and some of the essays collected in Charles and Duffin 1985.

45. On the link between metaphors of the female body and of physical spaces in early modern Europe, see Vandenbroeck 1991, p. 84.
46. For a recent study of this painting and the implications of its domestic space, see Hollander 1994.
47. See De Jongh 1970a; Exhib. cat. Amsterdam 1976, p. 149; Exhib. cat. Philadelphia 1984, p. 242.
48. On Leyster's painting, see the classic article by Hofrichter 1982. The painting to which Leyster's work is most frequently compared, Gerard ter Borch's so-called *Gallant Officer* (reproduced as Fig. 71 in this volume), is a good example of a work in which the genteel bourgeois environment of threatened virtue is of prime importance. On Roghman's prints, see Peacock 1993–4.
49. Again, this is a genre on which much more work needs to be done. Questions about not only the nature of festive domestic space but also the roles of women within that space have not been addressed sufficiently. Two useful recent discussions, though, are Franits 1993, chap. 1; and Nevitt 1992.
50. Some might argue that the confusion here is our historical one, that we are merely ignorant of certain "clues" that, to the seventeenth-century beholder, would have positively identified certain spaces as brothels and others as homes. Such clues are occasionally provided: For instance, a painting by Dirk Hals clearly shows an inn and not a home (Stockholm, Nationalmuseum); at its left a woman is chalking up the party's reckoning on a board. The architecture of the space is also different from normal domestic interiors: This room is set below street level, as we understand from the man entering via a short flight of steps from the door at the right. These clues, however, are not at all opaque or historically specific (they merely require the beholder to do some close looking), and they are quite unusual. Hals's Stockholm painting actually reveals how lacking his other works are in any indicators that the space of revelry is *not* a home.
51. This is a problem that is also very complexly explored in many works by Jan Steen.
52. A brief discussion of women at the market is given by Franits 1993, pp. 92–5; on the market scene in general, see the present author's entry on "Commerce and Commercial Life" in Muller 1996; Stone-Ferrier 1989; Idem 1992.
53. On women as market sellers, see Merry Wiesner's study of this issue in Germany: Wiesner 1981.
54. On changing notions of the family/economy and domesticity, see Medick 1976.
55. Many of De Witte's paintings show actual marketplaces, and at least one includes the portrait of a specific woman (Adriana van Heusden) doing business there. In the present painting, the marketplace seems to be fictitious (the tower behind the women vaguely resembles that on the Oudekerk in Delft), and Ilse Manke has speculated that the housewife may be a portrait; Manke 1963, cat. no. 232.
56. On threshold scenes, see Schama 1987, pp. 570 ff. Schama is slightly more sanguine than I am about the entirely positive nature of these images, but his emphasis on "residence" as the key issue at stake is, I think, precisely right.
57. The painter may position the beholder either inside or outside the home. Nicolaes Maes and Gabriel Metsu, for instance, usually give us a view *from* the street, whereas Jacob Ochtervelt and Quirijn van Brekelenkam locate us within the house looking out of the door. The ways in which these shifting viewpoints affect our assumptions about both class and gender would merit further study. A rather different but interestingly comparable scenario is portrayed in Jan Steen's *Burgher of Delft*, in which a gentleman meets an impoverished (but not unlocated or dangerous) woman on the front stoop of his home. An excellent discussion of this painting is Muller 1989.
58. On the perception of unlocated people in early modern England, see Beier 1985. For the Netherlands this issue has been studied more thoroughly for the late medieval period, though that is not to say that the issue, much less the anxiety about it, had disappeared in the seventeenth century. See the classic study of Enklaar 1937; and more recently, Pleij 1985.
59. On this painting and other threshold scenes by Ochtervelt, see Kuretsky 1979, pp. 34 ff.
60. Vermeer, when he was elected officer of the guild, was thirty years old; Gesina ter Borch, when she began her album, was twenty-nine.

61. On the location of the new guild hall, see Montias 1989, p. 61; on the hall itself, see Montias 1982, pp. 96–7. In the former study, Montias also speculates that the artist's election to guild officer at such an early age had more to do with the exodus of qualified artists from the city than with any special recognition of his exceptional talent. But whatever the guild's motives, Vermeer was still being granted the highest professional honor he could achieve within his home town.
62. Some writers have speculated that this work was intended for a "public" situation, that Vermeer intended to give it to the guild to adorn their new headquarters. This would indeed have been most appropriate; however, all the evidence suggests that the painting was actually quite a private one to Vermeer. On the story of the efforts of Catherina Bolnes and her mother Maria Thins to keep the *Art of Painting* for themselves, see Montias 1989, pp. 219–20, 228–30.
63. Many of these details have been pointed out by Daniel Arasse as elements that are "wrong" for an artist's studio and which therefore indicate the allegorical nature of the piece; all of them are, however, perfectly "right" for a domestic interior. See Arasse 1994, pp. 42–3.
64. No one to my knowledge has tried to identify this face on the table, more often referred to as a "mask." But it is clearly a plaster cast of an antique bust, a common motif in studio scenes. And in this case, the face is crowned by a band above which the hair is piled. I think, therefore, that this is the bust of Juno. This bust can be seen more clearly in several studio scenes by Michael Sweerts; see Döring 1994, pp. 58–60, figs. 2–3.
65. According to very old conventions of representation, women belong on the left and men on the right, the right being considered the side of greater importance. Hence, in donor portraits, for instance, women appear on *our* right but to the *left* of the represented holy figure, while men appear on the holy figure's right (our left). The continuity of this convention can easily be observed in seventeenth-century Dutch marriage portraiture.

Bibliography

This list consists of primary references (by date or era of author's activity).

Alberti, Leon Battista. *On Painting*. Trans. John Spencer. 2d ed. New Haven, 1966.

Angel, Philips. *Lof der schilder-konst*. Leiden, 1642.

Anon. *Goede manierlijcke seden, hoe de jonghers gaen, staen, eten, drincken, spreken, swijghen, ter tafelen dienen, ende de spijse ontghinnen sullen: met meer schoone onderwijsinghen, wt D. ERASMUS VAN ROTTERDAM ende meer ander gheleerder boecken, doer vraghe ende antwoorde ghestelt*. Antwerp, 1546.

Anon. *Nieuwen ieucht spiegel*. . . . N.p., n.d. (c. 1620).

Anon. *Utrechts zang-prieeltien*. Utrecht, 1649.

Anon. *Groote comptoir almanach*. . . . Amsterdam/Hoorn, 1667.

Anon. *A Journey into Spain*. London, 1670.

Anon. *'t Amsterdamsch hoerdom*. Amsterdam, n.d. (1681).

Anon. *Le dictionnaire de l'académie française*. 2 vols. Paris, 1694.

Anon. *Groot ceremonie-boek der beschaafde zeeden*. Amsterdam, 1735.

Asselijn, Thomas. *Broederschap der schilderkunst*. Amsterdam, 1654.

Ballexserd, Jacques. "Verhandeling over de natuurkundige opvoeding der kinderen. Van de geboorte tot den huwbaren tyd, welke hier bepaald word om 15 of 16 jaaren." In *Verhandelingen uitgegeeven door de Hollandsche Maatschappye der Weetenschappen te Haarlem*, vol. VII, pt. 2. Haarlem, 1763.

Beverwijck, Johan van. *Van de wtnementheyt des vrouwelicken geslachts*. Dordrecht, 1639.

———. *Schat der gesontheydt. Schat der ongesontheydt*. Utrecht, 1651.

———. *Schat der gesondheydt*. In *Alle de Werken*, vol. 1. Amsterdam, 1652.

Bie, Cornelis de. *Het gulden cabinet vande edele vry schilderconst*. Antwerp, 1661.

Bisschop, Jan de. *Paradigmata graphices variorum artificium*. The Hague, 1671.

Borromeo, Federico. *Musaeum Bibliothecae Ambrosianae*. Milan, 1625.

Bredero, G. A. *The Spanish Brabanter* (Amsterdam, 1617). Trans. H. D. Brumble. Binghamton, 1982.

———. *De twaalf sonnetten van de schoonheyt*. Antwerp, 1919.

Breton, Nicholas. *Nederduytsen briefdragher*. Trans. W. C. vander Boxe. Amsterdam, 1645.

Brune, Jan de. *Alle volgeestige werken*. Harlingen, 1665.

Brune, Johan de. *Emblemata of zinne-werck*. Amsterdam, 1624.

———. *Bankket-werk van goede gedagten*. 2d ed. 2 vols. Middelburg, 1660.

Bulwer, John. *Chronomia or The Art of Manuall Rhetorique*. London, 1644.

Camper, Petrus. "Verhandeling over het bestier van kinderen." In *Verhandelingen uitgegeeven door de Hollandsche Maatschappye der Weetenschappen te Haarlem*, vol. VII, pt. 2. Haarlem, 1763.

Camphuysen, Dirk Rafaëlsz. *Stichtelycke rymen*. Amsterdam, 1647.

Cartari, Vincenzo, ed. *Le imagini de i dei de gli antichi*. Lyons, 1581.

Castiglione, Baldassare. *Il cortegiano*. Venice, 1528.

———. *Den volmaakten hoveling, of schat van wetenschap, noodigh tot welleventheyt*. Amsterdam, 1675.

Cats, Jacob. *Maechden-plicht ofte ampt der ionck-vrouwen in eerbaer liefde, aen-ghewesen door sinne-beelden*. Middelburg, 1618a.

———. *Silenus Alcibiadis, sive Proteus*. . . . Middelburg, 1618b.

———. *Silenus Alcibiadis, sive Proteus*. Amsterdam, 1622.

———. *Houwelyck. Dat is de gansche gelegentheyt des echten staets*. Middelburg, 1625.

———. *Proteus ofte minne-beelden verandert in sinnebeelden*. Rotterdam, 1627.

———. *Spiegel vanden ouden ende nieuwen tijdt.* The Hague, 1632.

———. *Ouderdom, buyten-leven, en hof-gedachten op Sorghvliet.* Amsterdam, 1656.

———. "Spiegel vanden ouden ende nieuwen tijdt." In *Alle de Wercken.* Amsterdam, 1661.

———. *Houwelick. Dat is, het gantsche beleyt des echten-staets....* (First published in 1625.) Amsterdam, 1661.

———. "'s Werelts begin, midden, eynde, besloten in den trou-ringh met den proef-steen van den selven (1637)." In *Alle de werken,* vol. 2, pp. 189–208. Amsterdam, 1712.

———. *Al de werken van Jacob Cats.* Schiedam, 1870.

Charron, Pierre. *Of Wisdom Three Books* (1601). Trans. S. Lennard. London, 1606.

Chute, Anthony. *Tobaco. The Distinct and Severall Opinions of the Late and Best Phisitions That Have Written of the Diuers Natures and Qualities Thereof.* London, 1595.

[Courtin, A. de]. *Nieuwe verhandeling van de welgemanierdheidt. welke in Vrankryk onder fraaye leiden gebruikelyk is.* Amsterdam, 1672.

———. *De hoofsche welleventheid, en loffelyke welgemaniertheid, by alle voortreffelyke luiden in Nederland gebruykelyk.* Amsterdam, 1733.

Dafforne, Richard. *Grammatica ofte leez-leerlings steunsel.* Amsterdam, 1627.

David, Jan. *Christeliicken waerseggher....* Antwerp, 1602–3.

———. *Duodecim Specula....* Antwerp, 1610.

Decker, Jeremias de. *Alle de rym-oeffeningen.* 2 vols. Amsterdam, 1726.

Della Casa, Giovanni. *Galateo* (Venice, 1558). Trans. and Intro. K. Eisenbichler and K. Bartlett. Toronto, 1986.

Descartes, René. *Discours de la methode.* Leyden, 1637.

———. *The Philosophical Works of Descartes.* Trans. E. S. Haldane and G. R. T. Ross. 2 vols. Cambridge, 1967.

———. *Descartes: Philosophical Letters.* Trans. A. Kenny. Oxford, 1970.

Diemerbroeck, Ijsbrand van. *Tractatus de peste.* 2d ed. Amsterdam, 1665.

Dodoens, Rembert. *Purgantium aliarumque eo Facientium....* Antwerp, 1574.

Effen, Justus van. *De Hollandsche spectator.* 12 vols. Amsterdam, 1731–5.

Erasmus, Desiderius, ed. *L. Annei Senecae Opera.* 2d ed. Basel, 1529.

———. *Het boeckje van Erasmus aengaende de beleeftheidt der kinderlijcke zeden* (Amsterdam, 1678). Ed. H. de la Fontaine Verwey. Amsterdam, 1969.

———. *Collected Works of Erasmus.* vols. 1–. Toronto, 1974–.

Estienne, Henri. *Deux dialogues du nouveau langage français italianizé* (1578). 2 vols. Ed. P. Ristelhuber. Paris, 1883.

Félibien, Andre. *Entretiens sur les vies et sur les ouvrages des plus excellens peintres anciens et modernes.* Trévoux, 1725.

Geest, Wibrandus de. *Den leermeester der schilderkonst ... eertijds in rijm gestelt door Karel van Mander....* Leeuwarden, 1702.

Goeree, Willem. *Inleyding tot d'algemeene teykenkonst.* Middelburg, 1668.

———. *Natuurlyk en schilderkonstig ontwerp der menschkunde.* Amsterdam, 1682.

Goethe, Wolfgang von. *Die Wahlverwandtschaften.* Leipzig, [c. 1910].

Gouge, William. *Of Domesticall Duties....* London, 1627.

Guazzo, Stefano. *Van den heuschen burgerlycken ommegangh: een seer sin-rijcke, lieflijcke, ende nuttighe t'samensprekinghe.* Trans. G. van Trier. Alkmaar, 1603.

Heemskerk, Johan van. *Minne-kunst, minne-baet. minne-dichten, mengel-dichten.* 2d ed. Amsterdam, 1626.

Heinsius, Daniel. *Emblemata Amatoria.* In *Nederduytsche poemata.* Amsterdam, 1616a.

———. *Nederduytsche poemata.* Amsterdam, 1616b.

Heywood, Thomas. "An Emblematicall Dialogue, Interpreted from the Excellent and Most Learned D. Iac. Catzius, Which Sheweth How Virgins in their Chaste Loves Ought to Beare Themselves (16??)." In W. Band, ed., *Materialien zur Kunde des älteren englischen Dramas,* vol. 3, pp. 203–30. Louvain, 1902.

Hoet, Gerard. *Catalogus of naamlijst van schilderijen ... zoo in Holland als op andere plaatsen in het openbaar verkogt.* 3 vols. The Hague, 1752–70.

Hooft, Pieter Cornelisz. *Gedichten van P.C. Hooft.* 2d ed. Ed. F. A. Stoett and P. Wz. Leendertz. Amsterdam, 1899.

———. *De briefwisseling van Pieter Corneliszoon Hooft.* 3 vols. Ed. H. W. van Tricht et al. Culemborg, 1976–9.

———. *Emblemata Amatoria ...* (1611). Intro. K. Porteman. Leiden, 1983.

Hoogstraeten, Samuel van. *Inleyding tot de hooge schoole der schilderkonst....* Rotterdam, 1678.

Houbraken, Arnold. *De groote schouburgh der Nederlantsche konstschilders en schilderessen.* 3 vols. Amsterdam, 1718–21.

———. *De groote schouburgh der Nederlandtsche konstschilders en schilderessen.* 2d ed. The Hague, 1753.

Huygens, Constantijn. *De gedichten van Constantijn Huygens.* 9 vols. Ed. J. A. Worp. Groningen, 1892–9.

———. *De jeugd van Constantijn Huygens door hemzelf beschreven.* Trans. A. H. Kan. Rotterdam, 1946.

———. *Voorhout, kostelick mal en oogentroost.* Ed. L. Strengholt. Zutphen, 1967.

———. *Mijn jeugd.* Trans. and Ed. C. L. Heesakkers. Amsterdam, 1987.

Jonctijs, Daniel. *Roseliins oochies.* Dordrecht, 1639.

———. *Der mannen opper-waerdigheid beweert, tegens de vrouwelyke lof-redenen van Dr. Johan van Beverwijk.* Rotterdam, 1640.

Junius, Franciscus. *De schilderkonst der oude.* ... (First published in Latin in 1637.) Middelburg, 1641.

Junius, Hadrianus. *Emblemata.* Antwerp, 1569.

Krul, Jan Harmensz. *Minne-beelden: toe-ghepast, de lievende ionckheyt.* Amsterdam, 1634a.

———. *Minnelycke sangh-rympies.* Amsterdam, 1634b.

———. *Pampiere wereld.* 1681.

L[aar], C. van. *Het groot ceremonie-boeck der beschaafde zeeden, welleevendheid, ceremonieel en welvoegende hoffelykheden onderwyzende hoe een ieder (...) zich behoorden te gedraagen, om zich zelven in deeze wereld, bemind en gelukkig te maaken.* Amsterdam, n.d. (1735).

Lairesse, Gerard de. *Het groot schilderboek.* 2 vols. Amsterdam, 1707.

———. *Groot schilderboek.* 2d ed. 2 vols. Amsterdam, 1712.

———. *The Art of Painting.* Trans. J. F. Fritsch. London, 1738.

———. *Groot schilderboeck.* 3rd ed. 2 vols. Amsterdam, 1740.

Le Jolle, Pierre. *Description de la ville d'Amsterdam.* Amsterdam, 1666.

Lipsius, Justus. *De Constantia libri duo.* Antwerp, 1584.

———., ed. *L. Annaei Senecae philosophi opera.* Antwerp, 1605.

———. *De Constantia. Von der Bestendigheit.* Ed. L. Forster. Stuttgart, 1965.

Lomazzo, G. P. *Trattato dell'arte de la pittura.* Milan, 1584.

Luiken, Jan. *Des menschen begin, midden en einde.* Amsterdam, 1712.

Mander, Karel van. *Het schilder-boeck* ... 6 bks. Haarlem, 1604.

———. *Het schilder-boeck, uytbeeldinghe der figueren.* ... Amsterdam, 1616a.

———. *Het schilder-boeck, uytleggingh op den metamorphosis Pub. Ovidii Nasonis.* Amsterdam, 1616b.

———. *Het schilder-boeck, het leven der doorluchtighe Nederlandtsche en Hoogh-Duytsche schilders.* Amsterdam, 1617.

———. *Het schilder-boeck, den grondt der edel vrij schilder-const.* Amsterdam, 1618.

———. *Den grondt der edel vry schilder-const* (1604). Ed. H. Miedema. 2 vols. Utrecht, 1973.

———. *The Lives of the Illustrious Netherlandish and German Painters* (1603–4). vols. 1–. Trans. M. Hoyle, J. Pennial-Boer, and C. Ford. Ed. H. Miedema. Doornspijk, 1994–.

Marnix van St. Aldegonde, Philips. *De Institutione Principuum, ac Nobilium Puerorum Libellus Utilissimus.* Franeker, 1615.

———. *De opvoeding van de jeugd.* Trans. and Ed. H. de Wit-Van Westerhuis. Kampen, 1992a.

———. *Marnixi Epistulae: de briefwisseling van Marnix van St. Aldegonde.* Ed. A. Gerlo and R. de Smet. Brussels, 1992b.

Massinger, Philip. *The Bondman.* London, 1624.

Meteren, Emanuel van. *L'histoire des Pays-Bas.* The Hague, 1618.

Moryson, Fynes. *An Itinerary Containing His Ten Yeeres Travell.* ... (1617). Reprint ed., 4 vols., Glasgow, 1907.

Mostart, D. *Nederduytse secretaris oft zendbrievenschryver, met een tytelboexken.* Amsterdam, 1635.

Neander, Johan. *Tobacologia: hoc est, tabaci seu nicotianae descriptio Medico-Cheirurgico-Pharmaceutica.* Leiden, 1622.

Orlers, Jan Jansz. *Beschrijvinge der stadt Leyden.* 2d ed. Leiden, 1641.

Overbeke, Aernout van. *Anecdota sive Historia Jocosae.* Ed. R. Dekker and H. Roodenburg. Amsterdam, 1991.

Picinelli, Ph. *Mundus symbolicus.* ... 2 vols. Cologne, 1694.

Ploos van Amstel, C. *Redenvoeringen gedaan in de tekenacademie te Amsterdam.* Amsterdam, 1785.

Poirters, Adrianus. *Het masker vande wereldt afgetrocken.* Antwerp, 1714.

Primrose, James. *Popular Errours of the People in the Matter of Physick.* London, 1651.

Rabelais, François. "Gargantua and Pantagruel" (1532–48). In *The Complete Works of François Rabelais,* trans. D. M. Frame, pp. 1–732. Berkeley, 1991.

Rafaëlsz, Dirk. Camphuysen. "Tegen 't geestigdom der schilderkunst" (Trans. of Johannes Evertsz. Geesteranus, "Idolelenchus."). In *Stichtelycke rymen,* pp. 215–32. Amsterdam, 1647.

Ripa, Cesare. *Iconologia of uytbeeldingen des verstands.* ... Trans. D. P. Pers. Amsterdam, 1644.

Rodenburgh, Theodore. *Eglentiers poëtens borst-weringh.* Amsterdam, 1619.

Rollenhagen, Gabriel. *Nucleus emblematum selectissimorum.* 2. vols. Arnhem/Utrecht, 1611–13.

Sandrart, Joachim von. *Teutsche Academie.* 2 vols. Nuremberg, 1675.

Schellinks, William. *The Journal of William Schellinks' Travels in England 1661–1663.* Trans. M. Exwood. Ed. H. L. Lehmann. London, 1993.

Schrijver, Pieter. *Saturnalia, ofte poetische vasten-avondspel, vervattende het gebruik ende misbruik van het tabak.* Trans. S. Ampzing. Haarlem, 1630.

Secundus, Iohannis. *Hagensis Batavi Itineraria.* Leiden, 1618.

Sidney, Sir Philip. *An Apology for Poetry or The Defence of Poesy.* Ed. Geoffrey Sheperd. London, 1965.

[Sommelsdijck, François Aerssen van]. *Voyage d'Espagne, contenant entre plusiers particularitez de ce royaume, trois discours politiques sur les affaires du Protecteur d'Angleterre, de la Reine de Suède, et du Duc de Loraine.* Cologne, 1667.

Spinniker, Adriaan. *Leerzaame zinnebeelden.* Haarlem, 1714.

Starter, Jan Jansz. *Friesche lust-hof* (1621). Intro. J. H. Brouwer. 2 vols. Zwolle, 1966.

T., R. *Eenighe morale of zedige wercken van Plutarchus....* Amsterdam, 1634.

Teellinck, Willem. *De spiegel der zedigheyt.* Dordrecht, 1651.

Traudenius, Dirck. *Tyd-zifter, dat is kort bericht of onderwijs van de onderscheidinge en afbeeldinge de tydts, gevolgd door Rymbundel.* Amsterdam, 1662.

Valerianus, Johannes Pierius. *Hieroglyphica.* Lyons, 1602.

Veen, Octo van. *Amorum emblemata.* Antwerp, 1608.

———. *Quinti Horatii Flacci Emblemata.* 2d ed. Antwerp, 1612.

Venne, Adriaen van de. *Zeevsche nachtegael* (Middelburg, 1623). Intro. P. J. Meertens and P. J. Verkruijsse. Middelburg, 1982.

———. *Sinne-vonck op den Hollandtschen turf....* The Hague, 1634.

———. *Tafereel van de belacchende werelt....* The Hague, 1635.

Vernoegde, Petrus de [pseud.]. *De tien delicatessen des houwelicks.* Amsterdam, 1678.

Visscher, Roemer. *Sinne-poppen.* Amsterdam, 1614.

———. *Sinne-poppen* (Amsterdam, 1614). Ed. L. Brummel. The Hague, 1949.

Voetius, Gisbertus. *Een kort tractaetjen van de danssen, tot dienst van den eenvoudigen.* Utrecht, 1644.

Vondel, Joost van den. *De werken.* 30 vols. Ed. J. van Lennep and J. H. W. Unger. Leiden, 1894–9.

———. *De werken van Vondel.* 11 vols. Ed. J. F. M. Sterck et al. Amsterdam, 1927–40.

———. *Volledige dichtwerken en oorspronkelijk proza verzorgd door Albert Verwey* (1937). Ed. M. B. Smits-Veldt and M. Spies. Amsterdam, 1986.

Vos, Jan. *Alle de gedichten....* 2d ed. 2 vols. (First published in 1662.) Amsterdam, 1726.

Vossius, Joannes. *De quatour artibus popularibus, de philologia, et scientiis mathematicis ... libri tres.* Amsterdam, 1650.

Vrye, H. de [pseud.]. *Den tien vermakelijkheden des houwelyks.* Amsterdam, 1678.

Westerbaen, Jacob. *Den avond-school voor vryers en vrysters, om in de minne-kunst geoeffent en onderwezen te werden....* The Hague, 1665.

———. *Gedichten.* 3 vols. The Hague, 1672.

General Bibliography

Adams, Ann Jensen. *The Paintings of Thomas de Keyser (1596/7–1667): A Study of Portraiture in Seventeenth-Century Amsterdam.* Ph.D. dissertation, Harvard University, Cambridge [Mass.], 1985.

———. "Competing Communities in the 'Great Bog of Europe': Identity and Seventeenth-Century Dutch Landscape Painting." In *Landscape and Power*, ed. W. J. T. Mitchell, pp. 35–76. Chicago, 1994.

Alpers, Svetlana. "Bruegel's Festive Peasants." *Simiolus* 6 (1972–3): 163–76.

———. "Realism as a Comic Mode: Low-Life Painting Seen Through Bredero's Eyes." *Simiolus* 8 (1975–6): 115–44.

———. "Taking Pictures Seriously: A Reply to Hessel Miedema." *Simiolus* 10 (1978–9): 46–50.

———. "Art History and Its Exclusions: The Example of Dutch Art." In *Feminism and Art History: Questioning the Litany*, ed. N. Broude and M. D. Garrard, pp. 182–99. New York, 1982.

———. *The Art of Describing; Dutch Art in the Seventeenth Century.* Chicago, 1983.

———. *Kunst als Beschreibung; holländische Malerei des 17. Jahrhunderts.* Trans. H. U. Davitt, Intro. W. Kemp. Cologne, 1986.

———. "Style Is What You Make It: The Visual Arts Again." In *The Concept of Style*, 2d ed., ed. B. Lang, pp. 137–62. Ithaca, 1987.

———. *Rembrandt's Enterprise: The Studio and the Market.* Chicago, 1988.

———. "Questions of Dutchness." *London Review of Books* 16 (4 August 1994): 18.

Andel, M. A. van. *Chirurgijns, vrije meesters, beunhazen en kwakzalvers. De chirurgijnsgilden en de practijk der heelkunde (1400–1800).* Amsterdam, 1941.

Arasse, Daniel. *Vermeer. Faith in Painting.* Princeton, 1994.

Baar, Mirjam de, et al., eds. *Anna Maria van Schurman (1607–1678). Een uitzonderlijk geleerde vrouw.* Zutphen, 1992.

Babb, Lawrence. *The Elizabethan Malady; A Study of Melancholia in English Literature from 1580 to 1642.* East Lansing, 1951.

Bakker, Boudewijn. "Langhuis and Stolp: Rembrandt's Farm Drawings and Prints," in Exhib. cat. Washington D.C. *Rembrandt's Landscapes: Drawings and Prints*, pp. 33–59. National Gallery of Art, 1990.

———. "'Schilderachtig': Discussions of a Seventeenth-Century Term and Concept." *Simiolus* 23 (1995): 147–62.

Bal, Mieke. *Reading Rembrandt. Beyond the Word–Image Opposition.* Cambridge, 1991.

Bal, Mieke, and Bryson, Norman. "Semiotics and Art History." *The Art Bulletin* 73 (1991): 174–208.

Barthes, Roland. "The World as Object." In *Critical Essays*, trans. R. Howard, pp. 3–12. Evanston, 1972.

———. "The Reality Effect." In *French Literary Theory Today. A Reader*, ed. T. Todorov, trans. R. Carter, pp. 11–17. Cambridge, 1982.

Bastelaer, René van. *Les estampes de Peter Bruegel l'Ancien.* Brussels, 1908.

Battersby, Christine. *Gender and Genius. Towards a Feminist Aesthetics.* London, 1989.

Bauch, Kurt. *Der frühe Rembrandt und seine Zeit.* Berlin, 1960.

Baudouin, Frans. "Rubens' bedrijvigheid als diplomaat." In Exhib. cat. Elewijt, *Rubens diplomaat*, pp. 23–39. Rubenskasteel Elewijt, 1962.

Beck, Hans-Ulrich. *Jan van Goyen.* vol. 4 (*Künstler um Jan van Goyen*). Doornspijk, 1991.

Becker, Jochen. "Review of Hans-Joachim Raupp, *Untersuchungen zu Künstlerbildnis und Künstlerdarstellung in den Niederlanden im 17. Jahrhundert.*" *Oud Holland* 101 (1987): 280–6.

———. "Are These Girls Really So Neat? On Kitchen Scenes and Method." In *Art in History / History in Art: Studies in Seventeenth-Century Dutch Culture*, ed. D. Freedberg and J. de Vries, pp. 139–73. Santa Monica, 1991.

Bedaux, Jan Baptist. "The Reality of Symbols: The Question of Disguised Symbolism in Jan van Eyck's Arnolfini Portrait." *Simiolus* 16 (1986): 5–28.

———. "Fruit and Fertility: Fruit Symbolism in Netherlandish Portraiture of the Sixteenth and Seventeenth Centuries." *Simiolus* 17 (1987): 150–68.

———. *The Reality of Symbols: Studies in the Iconology of Netherlandish Art.* The Hague, 1990.

Beening, Th. J. *Het landschap in de Nederlandse letterkunde van de Renaissance.* Nijmegen, 1963.

Beier, A. L. *Masterless Men. The Vagrancy Problem in England 1560–1640.* London, 1985.

Bell, Quentin. *On Human Finery.* 2d ed. London, 1976.

Berg, Maxine. *The Age of Manufactures, 1700–1820.* London, 1994.

Berger, A. "Inventar der Kunstsammlung des Erzherzogs Leopold WIlhelm von Österreich. . . ." *Jahrbuch der Kunsthistorischen Sammlungen des allerhöchsten Kaiserhauses* 1 (1883): lxxix–clxxvii.

Berger, John. *Ways of Seeing.* Harmondsworth, 1972.

Bergström, Ingvar. *Studier i Holländskt Stillebenmaleri under 1600-talet.* Stockholm, 1947.

———. "Disguised Symbolism in 'Madonna' Pictures and Still Life: I–II." *The Burlington Magazine* 97 (1955): 303–8, 342–9.

———. *Dutch Still-Life Painting in the Seventeenth Century.* London, 1956.

———. "Rembrandt's Double-Portrait of Himself and Saskia at the Dresden Gallery. A Tradition Transformed." *Nederlands Kunsthistorisch Jaarboek* 17 (1966): 143–69.

Betterton, Rosemary. "How Do Women Look? The Female Nude in the Work of Suzanne Valadon." In *Visibly Female: Feminism and Art: An Anthology*, ed. H. Robinson, pp. 250–71. New York, 1988.

Bialostocki, Jan. "Kunst und Vanitas. Pessimismus und Hedonismus der Antike." In *Stil und Ikonographie. Studien zur Kunstwissenschaft*, pp. 187–230. Dresden, 1966.

———. "Einfach Nachahmung der Natur oder symbolische Weltschau; zu den Deutungsproblemen der holländischen Malerei des 17. Jhdt." *Zeitschrift für Kunstgeschichte* 47 (1984): 421–38.

———. "Review of Svetlana Alpers, *The Art of Describing: Dutch Art in the Seventeenth Century.*" *The Art Bulletin* 67 (1985): 520–6.

Bijl, S. W. *Erasmus in het Nederlands tot 1617.* Leiden, 1978.

Bille, Clara de. *De tempel der kunst of het kabinet van den Heer Braamcamp.* 2 vols. Amsterdam, 1961.

Blanc, Charles. *Histoire de peintres de toutes les écoles: École Hollandaise.* 2 vols. Paris, 1863.

Blankert, Albert. "Inleiding." In Exhib. cat. Utrecht, *Nederlandse 17e eeuwse Italianiserende landschapschilders*, pp. 13–39. Centraal Museum, 1965.

———. *Ferdinand Bol (1616–1680). Rembrandt's Pupil.* Trans. I. Rike. Doornspijk, 1982.

Blasse-Hegeman, H., et al., eds. *Nederlandse portretten; bijdragen over de portretkunst in de Nederlanden uit de zestiende, zeventiende en achttiende eeuw (Leidse Kunsthistorisch Jaarboek* 8). The Hague, 1990.

Bock, Henning, and Gaehtgens, Thomas W., eds. *Holländische Genremalerei im 17. Jahrhundert. Symposium Berlin 1984 (Jahrbuch Preussischer Kulturbesitz, Sonderband* 4.) Berlin, 1987.

Bode, Wilhelm von. *Die Meister der holländischen und vlämischen Malerschulen.* Leipzig, 1917.

Bode, Wilhelm von, and Hofstede de Groot, C. *The Complete Works of Rembrandt.* 8 vols. Paris, 1897–1906.

Böhm, F. J. "Begriff und Wesen des Genre." *Zeitschrift für Aesthetik und allgemeine Kunstwissenschaft* 22 (1928): 166–91.

Boekhorst, Peter te, Burke, Peter, and Frijhoff, Willem, eds. *Cultuur en maatschappij in Nederland 1500–1850; een historisch-antropologisch perspectief.* Boom, 1992.

Boer, W. den. "The Dutch Republic and Antiquity." *Bijdragen en Mededelingen Betreffende de Geschiedenis der Nederlanden* 94 (1979): 419–36.

Böse, J. H. *"Had de mensch met één vrou niet connen leven . . ."; prostitutie in de literatuur van de zeventiende eeuw.* Zutphen, 1985.

Boheemen, Petra van. "'Hoe men een lief vinden en krygen zal': Ovidus als leermeester." In Exhib. cat. Apeldoorn, *Kent, en versint, eer datje mint; vrijen en trouwen, 1500–1800*, pp. 53–63. Historisch Museum Marialust, 1989.

Bok, Marten Jan. "Art-Lovers and Their Paintings: Van Mander's Schilder-boeck as a Source for the History of the Art Market in the Northern Netherlands." In Exhib. cat. Amsterdam, *Dawn of the Golden Age Northern Netherlandish Art 1580–1620*, pp. 136–66. Rijksmuseum, 1993–4.

Bol, L. J. "Philips Angel van Middelburg en Philips Angel van Leiden." *Oud Holland* 64 (1949): 3–19.

Bolten, Jaap. *Positur: gaan en staan in de beeldende kunst van de 16de en 17de eeuw.* Leiden, 1991.

Boon, Karel G. *The Netherlandish and German Drawings of the XVth and XVIth Centuries of the Frits Lugt Collection.* 3 vols. Paris, 1992.

Bouwsma, William. "The Two Faces of Humanism, Stoicism and Augustinianism." In *Renaissance*

Thought, Itinerarium Italicum: The Profile of the Italian Renaissance in the Mirror of the European Transformations Dedicated to Paul Oskar Kristeller on . . . His 70th Birthday, ed. H. A. Oberman and T. A. Brady, pp. 3–60. Leiden, 1975.

Braun, Karel. *Alle tot nu toe bekende schilderijen van Jan Steen*. Rotterdam, 1980.

Braun-Ronsdorf, M. *The History of the Handkerchief*. Leigh-on-Sea, 1967.

Bray, Bernard. *L'art de la lettre amoureuse: des manuels aux romans (1550–1700)*. The Hague/Paris, 1967.

Bredius, A. *Künstler-Inventare: Urkunden zur Geschichte der holländischen Kunst des XVIten, XVIIten und XVIIIten Jahrhunderts*. 8 vols. The Hague, 1915–22.

Brenninkmeyer-De Rooij, Beatrijs. "To Behold Is to Be Aware: History Painting in Public Buildings and the Residences of the Stadtholders." In Exhib. cat. Washington D.C., *Gods, Saints and Heroes. Dutch Painting in the Age of Rembrandt*, pp. 65–76. National Gallery of Art, 1980–1.

Brieger, L. *Das Genrebild. Die Entwicklung der bürgerlichen Malerei*. Munich, 1922.

Briels, Jan. "Brabantse blaaskaak en Hollandse botmuil. Cultuurontwikkelingen in het begin van de Gouden Eeuw." *De Zeventiende Eeuw* 1 (1985): 12–36.

———. *Vlaamse schilders in de Noordelijke Nederlanden in het begin van de Gouden Eeuw 1585–1630*. Haarlem, 1987.

Brilliant, Richard. *Portraiture*. Cambridge [Mass.], 1991.

Bringemeier, M. "Volkskundliches zu zwei Gemälden von Gerard Ter Borch." *Rheinisch-Westfälische Zeitschrift für Volkskunde* 21 (1974): 5–13.

Broersen, Ellen. "'Judita Leystar': A Painter of 'Good, Keen Sense'." In Exhib. cat. Haarlem, *Judith Leyster. A Dutch Master and Her World*, pp. 15–38. Frans Halsmuseum, 1993.

Brom, Gerard. *Schilderkunst en litteratuur in de 16e en 17e eeuw*. Utrecht/Antwerp, 1957.

Brongers, George A. *Nicotiana Tabacum. The History of Tobacco and Tobacco Smoking in The Netherlands*. Amsterdam, 1964.

Brooks, Jerome E. *Tobacco. Its History Illustrated by the Books, Manuscripts and Engravings in the Library of George Arents Jr*. 5 vols. New York, 1937–52.

Broos, B. P. J. "Review of Seymour Slive, *Frans Hals*." *Simiolus* 10 (1978–9): 115–23.

Brown, Christopher. *Images of a Golden Past: Dutch Genre Painting of the 17th Century*. London, 1984.

———. "Introduction." In Exhib. cat. London, *Dutch Landscape: The Early Years, Haarlem and Amsterdam 1590–1650*, pp. 11–34. The National Gallery, 1986.

———. "Review of Peter C. Sutton et al., *Masters of 17th-Century Dutch Landscape Painting*." *Simiolus* 18 (1988): 76–81.

Brusati, Celeste. "Stilled Lives: Self-Portraiture and Self-Reflection in Seventeenth-Century Netherlandish Still-Life Painting." *Simiolus* 20 (1990–1): 168–82.

———. *Artifice & Illusion. The Art and Writing of Samuel van Hoogstraeten*. Chicago, 1995.

Bruyn, Josua. *Geschiedschrijving als parabel* (Rede uitgesproken ter gelegenheid van de 349ste dies natalis van de Universiteit van Amsterdam). Amsterdam, 1981.

———. "Review of Svetlana Alpers, *The Art of Describing: Dutch Art in the Seventeenth Century*." *Oud Holland* 99 (1985): 155–60.

———. *Een Gouden Eeuw als erfstuk* (afscheidscollege . . . op 20 September 1985 ter gelegentheid van zijn vertrek als hoogleraar aan de Universiteit van Amsterdam). Amsterdam, 1986.

———. "Mittelalterliche 'doctrina exemplaris' und Allegorie als Komponente des sog. Genrebildes." In *Höllandische Genremalerei im 17. Jahrhundert. Symposium Berlin 1984*, ed. H. Bock and T. W. Gaehtgens, pp. 33–59. Berlin, 1987.

———. "Towards a Scriptural Reading of Seventeenth-Century Dutch Landscape Paintings." In Exhib. cat. Boston, *Masters of 17th-Century Dutch Landscape Painting*, pp. 84–103. Museum of Fine Arts, 1988.

———. "Review of Peter Hecht, *De Hollandse fijnschilders*." *Oud Holland* 105 (1991): 64–9.

Bruyn, Josua, et al. *A Corpus of Rembrandt Paintings*. vols. 1–. Trans. D. Cook-Radmore. The Hague, 1982–.

Bryson, Norman. *Looking at the Overlooked. Four Essays on Still Life Painting*. Cambridge [Mass.], 1990.

———. "In Medusa's Gaze." In Exhib. cat. Rochester, *In Medusa's Gaze. Still-Life Paintings from Upstate New York Museums*, pp. 6–30. Memorial Art Gallery of the University of Rochester, 1991.

Bryson, Norman, and Bal, Mieke. "Semiotics and Art History." *The Art Bulletin* 73 (1991): 174–208.

Bueren, Truus van. *Macht & onderhorigheid binnen de Ridderlijke orde van Sint Jan. De commandeursportretten uit het Sint Jansklooster te Haarlem*. Haarlem, 1991.

Buijsen, Edwin. *The Sketchbook of Jan van Goyen from the Bredius-Kronig Collection*. 2 vols. The Hague, 1993.

Burckhardt, Jacob. "Über die niederländische Genremalerei." In *Vorträge 1844–87*, ed. E. Dürr, pp. 60–102. Basel, 1919.

Burger, C. P. "De rebus van onze oude rederijkers." *Het Boek* 14 (1925): 145–92.

Burke, Peter. *The Historical Anthropology of Early Modern Italy*. Cambridge, 1987.

———. "The Language of Gesture in Early Modern Italy." In *A Cultural History of Gesture from Antiquity till the Present Day*, ed. J. Bremmer and H. Roodenburg, pp. 71–83. Cambridge, 1991.

———. *Venice and Amsterdam. A Study of Seventeenth-Century Elites.* 2d ed. Cambridge, 1994.

———. *The Fortunes of the Courtier. The European Reception of Castiglione's "Courtier."* Cambridge, 1995.

Burns, E. Jane, and Krueger, Roberta L. "Introduction: Courtly Ideology and Woman's Place in Medieval French Literature." *Romance Notes* 25 (1984–5): 205–19.

Campbell, Lorne. *Renaissance Portraits. European Portrait-Painting in the 14th, 15th and 16th Centuries.* New Haven, 1990.

Cantaro, Maria Teresa. *Lavinia Fontana bolognese, "pittora singolare," 1552–1614.* Milan, 1989.

Carter, Alice Clare. "Marriage Counselling in the Early Seventeenth Century: England and The Netherlands Compared." In *Ten Studies in Anglo-Dutch Relations,* ed. J. van Dorsten, pp. 94–127. London, 1974.

Cat. Amsterdam. *Beschrijving der schilderijen in het Museum van der Hoop.* Museum van der Hoop, 1881.

Cat. Berlin *Catalogue of the Paintings, 13th–18th Century,* 2d ed., trans. L. B. Parshall. Staatliche Museen Preussischer Kulturbesitz, 1978.

Cat. Rotterdam. *Nederlandse portretten uit de 17e eeuw: Eigen collectie/Dutch Portraits from the Seventeenth Century: Our Own Collection* (catalogue by R. E. O. Ekkart). Museum Boymans-van Beuningen, 1995.

Cavalli-Björkman, Görel, ed. *Netherlandish Mannerism: Papers Given at a Symposium in Nationalmuseum Stockholm, September 21–22, 1984.* Stockholm, 1985.

Chapman, H. Perry. "A *Hollandse Pictura:* Observations on the Title Page of Philips Angel's *Lof der schilder-konst.*" *Simiolus* 16 (1986): 233–48.

———. *Rembrandt's Self-Portraits: A Study in Seventeenth-Century Identity.* Princeton, 1990.

———. "Jan Steen's Household Revisited." *Simiolus* 20 (1990–1): 183–96.

Charles, Lindsey, and Duffin, Lorna, eds. *Women and Work in Pre-Industrial England.* London, 1985.

Christian, Gregorian. "The Figure of Socrates in Erasmus' Works." *The Sixteenth Century Journal* 3 (1972): 1–10.

Clark, Alice. *The Working Life of Women in the Seventeenth Century.* London, 1919.

Clark, Kenneth. *Landscape into Art.* London, 1949.

———. *The Nude.* Garden City [New York], 1956.

Clements, Robert J. *Picta Poesis. Literary and Humanistic Theory in Renaissance Emblem Books.* Rome, 1960.

Colie, Rosalie L. *The Resources of Kind; Genre Theory in the Renaissance.* Ed. B. K. Lewalski. Berkeley, 1973.

Corbett, Edward P. J. *Classical Rhetoric for the Modern Student.* New York, 1965.

Crary, Jonathan. *Techniques of the Observer: On Vision and Modernity in the Nineteenth Century.* Cambridge [Mass.], 1992.

Crivelli, Giovanni. *Giovanni Brueghel, pittore fiammingo ò sue lettere e quadretti esistenti presso l'Ambrosiana.* Milan, 1868.

Croll, Morris W. "'Attic Prose' in the Seventeenth Century." In *Style, Rhetoric, and Rhythm: Essays by Morris W. Croll,* ed. J. M. Patrick et al., pp. 51–101. Princeton, 1966a.

———. "The Baroque Style in Prose." In *Style, Rhetoric, and Rhythm: Essays by Morris W. Croll,* ed. J. M. Patrick et al., pp. 207–33. Princeton, 1966b.

Cropper, Elizabeth. "On Beautiful Women, Parmigianino, Petrarchismo, and the Vernacular Style." *The Art Bulletin* 58 (1976): 374–94.

Culler, Jonathan. *On Deconstruction: Theory and Criticism after Structuralism.* London, 1983.

Davies, Alice I. *Jan van Kessel (1641–1680).* Doornspijk, 1992.

Davies, G., ed. *Autobiography of Thomas Raymond and Memoirs of the Family of Guise of Elmore, Gloucestershire.* London, 1917.

Davies, Kathleen. "Continuity and Change in Literary Advice on Marriage." In *Marriage and Society: Studies in the Social History of Marriage,* ed. R. B. Outhwaite, pp. 58–80. New York, 1981.

Dekker, Rudolf M. *Holland in beroering. Oproeren in de 17de en 18de eeuw.* Baarn, 1982.

Deursen, A. Th. van. *Het kopergeld van de Gouden Eeuw.* 4 vols. Assen, 1978–81.

———. *Plain Lives in a Golden Age: Popular Culture, Religion and Society in Seventeenth-Century Holland.* Trans. M. Ultee. Cambridge, 1991.

Dibon, P. "Constantijn Huygens et le 'Discours de la Methode'." *Glanes* (1950): 17–26.

Doane, Mary Ann. "Film and the Masquerade – Theorising the Female Spectator." *Screen* 23 (1982): 74–87.

Döring, Thomas. "Belebte Skulpturen bei Michael Sweerts. Zur Rezeptionsgeschichte eines vergessenen Pseudo-Antiken Ausdruckskopfes." In *Festschrift für Prof. Dr. Justus Müller Hofstede (Wallraf-Richartz-Jahrbuch* 45), pp. 55–83. Cologne, 1994.

Dresen-Coenders, L. "'Wegh-wyser ten houwelick'." In Exhib. cat. Apeldoorn, *Kent, en versint, eer datje mint; vrijen en trouwen, 1500–1800,* pp. 20–52. Historisch Museum Marialust, 1989.

Drost, W. *Barockmalerei in den germanischen Ländern.* Potsdam, 1926. Berlin, 1931.

Dubiez, F. J. *Cornelis Anthoniszoon van Amsterdam. Zijn leven en werken ca. 1507–1553.* Amsterdam, 1969.

Duco, Don H. *Goudse pijpen: de geschiedenis van de pijpmakerij te Gouda.* Amsterdam, 1978.

———. "De kleipijp in de zeventiende eeuwse Nederlanden." In *The Archaeology of the Clay Tobacco Pipe, V. Europe,* 2, ed. P. J. Davey, vol. 2, pp. 111–367. Oxford, 1981.

Dudok van Heel, S. A. C. "Amsterdamse burgemeesters zonder stambom. De dichter Vondel en de schilder Colijn vervalsen geschiedenis." *De Zeventiende Eeuw* 5 (1990): 144–51.

Duke, A. C., and Kolff, D. H. A. "The Time of Troubles in the County of Holland, 1566–1567." *Tijdschrift voor Geschiedenis* 82 (1969): 316–37.

Earl of Clarendon, Edward. *The History of the Rebellion and Civil Wars in England.* Oxford, 1843.

Eco, Umberto. "Innovation and Repetition: Between Modern and Post-Modern Aesthetics." *Daedalus* 114 (Summer–Fall 1985): 161–84.

Eeghen, I. H. van. "Het Poppenhuis van Petronella de la Court, Huisvrouw van Adam Oortmans." *Maandblad Amstelodamum* 47 (1960): 159–67.

Ekkart, R. E. O. *Icones Leidenses: De portretverzameling van de Rijksuniversiteit te Leiden.* Leiden, 1973.

———. "De portretten van Pieter Cornelisz. Hooft." In *De briefwisseling van Pieter Corneliszoon Hooft*, 3 vols., ed. H. W. van Tricht et al., vol. 3, pp. 5–21. Culemborg, 1976–9.

Elias, Norbert. *The Civilizing Process.* 2 vols. New York, 1982.

Ellenius, Allan. *De Arte Pingendi. Latin Art Literature in Seventeenth-Century Sweden and Its International Background.* Uppsala, 1960.

Emmens, Jan. "Ay Rembrant, maal *Cornelis* stem." *Nederlands Kunsthistorisch Jaarboek* 7 (1956): 133–65.

———. "Les Ménines de Velasquez Miroir des Princes pour Philippe IV." *Nederlands Kunsthistorisch Jaarboek* 12 (1961): 51–79.

———. "Natuur, onderwijzing en oefening; bij een drieluik van Gerrit Dou." *Album Discipulorum Prof. dr. J. G. van Gelder*, pp. 125–36. Utrecht, 1963.

———. "Reputatie en betekenis van Rembrandt's 'Geslachte os'." *Museumjournaal voor Moderne Kunst* 12 (1967): 81.

———. *Rembrandt en de regels van de kunst.* Utrecht, 1968.

———. "'Eins aber ist nötig'–Zu Inhalt und Bedeutung von Markt- und Küchenstücken des 16. Jahrhunderts." In *Album Amicorum J. G. van Gelder*, ed. J. Bruyn et al., pp. 93–101. The Hague, 1973.

Enklaar, D.Th. *Varende luyden. Studien over middeleeuwsche groepen van onmaatschappelijken in de Nederlanden.* Assen, 1937.

Ertz, Klaus. *Jan Brueghel der Ältere (1568–1625): Die Gemälde.* Cologne, 1979.

Evers, H. G. *Rubens und sein Werk; Neue Forschungen.* Brussels, 1943.

Exhib. cat. Amsterdam. *Tot lering en vermaak; betekenissen van Hollandse genrevoorstellingen uit de zeventiende eeuw.* Rijksmuseum, 1976.

———. *A Flowery Past. A Survey of Dutch and Flemish Flower Painting From 1600 Until the Present* (catalogue by S. Segal). Gallery P. de Boer, 1982.

———. *Bij Rembrandt in de Leer / Rembrandt as Teacher.* Museum het Rembrandthuis, 1984–5.

———. *De Hollandse fijnschilders; van Gerrit Dou tot Adriaen van der Werff* (catalogue by P. Hecht). Rijksmuseum, 1989–90.

———. *Chiaroscuro Woodcuts: Hendrick Goltzius (1558–1617) and His Time* (catalogue by N. Bialler). Rijksmuseum, 1992–3.

———. *Dawn of the Golden Age: Northern Netherlandish Art 1580–1620.* Rijksmuseum, 1993–4.

Exhib. cat. Antwerp. *Over wilden en narren, boeren en bedelaars. Beeld van de andere, vertoog over het zelf* (catalogue by P. Vandenbroeck). Koninklijk Museum voor Schone Kunsten, 1987.

Exhib. cat. Apeldoorn. *Kent, en versint, eer datje mint; vrijen en trouwen, 1500–1800.* Historisch Museum Marialust, 1989.

Exhib. cat. Auckland. *Still-Life in the Age of Rembrandt.* Auckland City Art Gallery, 1982.

Exhib. cat. Boston. *Jacob van Ruisdael.* The Fogg Art Museum, 1982.

———. *Masters of 17th-Century Dutch Landscape Painting.* Museum of Fine Arts, 1988.

Exhib. cat. Brunswick. *Die Sprache der Bilder. Realität und Bedeutung in der niederländischen Malerei des 17. Jahrhunderts.* Herzog Anton Ulrich-Museum, 1978.

Exhib. cat. Charlottesville. *Masterpieces of Renaissance and Baroque Printmaking: A Decade of Collecting.* Bayly Art Museum, 1991.

Exhib. cat. Delft. *A Prosperous Past: The Sumptuous Still Life in the Netherlands 1600–1700* (catalogue by S. Segal). Stedelijk Museum Het Prinsenhof, 1988.

Exhib. cat. Dordrecht. *De zichtbaere werelt: schilderkunst uit de Gouden Eeuw in Hollands oudste stad.* Dordrechts Museum, 1992–3.

Exhib. cat. Enkhuizen. *Portret van Enkhuizen in de Gouden Eeuw* (catalogue by R. E. O. Ekkart). Zuiderzeemuseum, 1990.

Exhib. cat. Haarlem. *Portretten van echt en trouw; huwelijk en gezin in de Nederlandse kunst van de zeventiende eeuw* (catalogue by E. de Jongh). Frans Halsmuseum, 1986.

———. *Judith Leyster. A Dutch Master and Her World.* Frans Halsmuseum, 1993.

Exhib. cat. Leiden. *Ijdelheid der ijdelheden; Hollandse vanitas-voorstellingen uit de zeventiende eeuw.* Stedelijk Museum De Lakenhal, 1970.

———. *Leidse fijnschilders: van Gerrit Dou tot Frans van Mieris de Jonge 1630–1760.* Stedelijk Museum De Lakenhal, 1988.

———. *Rembrandt & Lievens in Leiden.* Stedelijk Museum De Lakenhal, 1991–2.

Exhib. cat. London. *Dutch Pictures from the Royal Collection.* Queen's Gallery at Buckingham Palace, 1971–2.

———. *Dutch Landscape: The Early Years, Haarlem and Amsterdam 1590–1650.* The National Gallery, 1986.

———. *Frans Hals* (catalogue by S. Slive). Royal Academy of Arts, 1989.

———. *Rembrandt: The Master and His Workshop, Paintings.* The National Gallery, 1992.

Exhib. cat. Münster. *Stilleben in Europa.* Westfälisches Landesmuseum für Kunst und Kulturgeschichte, 1979–80.

Exhib. cat. New York. *Liechtenstein: The Princely Collections.* Metropolitan Museum of Art, 1985–6.

———. *Masterworks from the Musée des Beaux-Arts, Lille.* The Metropolitan Museum of Art, 1992–3.

Exhib. cat. Paris. *Le siècle de Rembrandt. Tableaux hollandais des collections publiques françaises.* Musèe du Petit Palais, 1970–1.

———. *Wenzel Hollar, 1607–1677.* Institut Néerlandais, 1979.

Exhib. cat. Philadelphia. *Masters of Seventeenth-Century Dutch Genre Painting.* Philadelphia Museum of Art, 1984.

Exhib. cat. Pittsburgh. *Gardens of Earthly Delight: Sixteenth- and Seventeenth-Century Netherlandish Gardens.* Frick Art Museum, 1986.

Exhib. cat. Providence. *The Children of Mercury. The Education of Artists in the Sixteenth and Seventeenth Centuries.* Bell Gallery, List Art Center (Brown University), 1984.

Exhib. cat. Rotterdam. *Leerrijke reeksen.* Museum Boymans-van Beuningen, 1966.

———. *Perspectives: Saenredam and the Architectural Painters of the 17th century.* Museum Boymans-van Beuningen, 1991.

Exhib. cat. Stockholm. *Rembrandt och hans Tid/Rembrandt and his Age.* Nationalmuseum, 1992.

Exhib. cat. The Hague. *Gerard Ter Borch.* Mauritshuis, 1974.

———. *Huygens herdacht: catalogus bij de tentoonstellinq in de Koninklijke Bibliotheek ter gelegenheid van de 300ste sterfdag van Constantijn Huygens.* Koninklijke Bibliotheek, 1987.

———. *Mode in prent (1550–1914).* Nederlands Kostuum Museum, 1988.

———. *Alba Amicorum. Vijf eeuwen vriendschap op papier gezet.* Rijksmuseum Meermanno-Westreenianum, 1990.

———. *Great Dutch Paintings from America.* Mauritshuis, 1990–1.

Exhib. cat. Washington D.C. *Gods, Saints & Heroes: Dutch Painting in the Age of Rembrandt.* National Gallery of Art, 1980–1.

———. *The Age of Bruegel: Netherlandish Drawings in the Sixteenth Century.* National Gallery of Art, 1986.

———. *Still Lifes of the Golden Age; Northern European Paintings from the Heinz Family Collection.* National Gallery of Art, 1989.

———. *Anthony van Dyck.* National Gallery of Art, 1990a.

———. *Rembrandt's Landscapes: Drawings and Prints.* National Gallery of Art, 1990b.

Exhib. cat. Worcester. *Seventeenth-Century Dutch Painting: Raising the Curtain on New England Private Collections.* Worcester Art Museum, 1979.

Exhib. cat. Yamaguchi. *Faces of the Golden Age: Seventeenth-Century Dutch Portraits* (catalogue by E. de Jongh). The Yamaguchi Prefectural Museum of Art, 1994.

Falkenburg, Reindert L. *Joachim Patinir: Landscape as an Image of the Pilgrimage of Life.* Trans. M. Hoyle. Amsterdam, 1988.

———. "De betekenis van het geschilderde hollandse landschap van de zeventiende eeuw: een beschouwing naar aanleiding van enkele recente interpretaties." *Theoretische Geschiedenis* 16 (1989): 131–53.

———. "Recente visies op de zeventiende-eeuwse Nederlandse genre-schilderkunst." *Theoretische Geschiedenis* 18 (1991): 119–40.

———. "Iconologie en historische antropologie: een toenadering." In *Gezichtspunten: een inleiding in de methoden van de kunstgeschiedenis,* ed. M. Halbertsma and K. Zijlmans, pp. 139–74. Nijmegen, 1993.

Falkenburg, Reindert, et al., eds. *Beeld en zelfbeeld in de Nederlandse kunst, 1550–1750* (*Nederlands Kunsthistorisch Jaarboek* 46). Zwolle, 1995.

Favis, Roberta S. *The Garden of Love in Fifteenth-Century Netherlandish and German Engravings.* Ph.D. dissertation, University of Pennsylvania, Philadelphia, 1974.

Fetterley, J. *The Resisting Reader: A Feminist Approach to American Fiction.* Bloomington, 1978.

Filipczak, Zirka Zaremba. *Picturing Art in Antwerp 1550–1700.* Princeton, 1987.

Fischel, Oskar. *Tizian. Des Meisters Gemälde* (*Klassiker der Kunst.* vol. 3). Stuttgart, 1911.

Fleischer, Roland E. "Quirijn van Brekelenkam and *The Artist's Workshop* in the Hermitage Museum." In *The Age of Rembrandt: Studies in Seventeenth-Century Dutch Painting* (*Papers in Art History from The Pennsylvania State University* 3), ed. R. E. Fleischer and S. S. Munshower, pp. 71–93. University Park [Penn.], 1988.

Floerke, Hanns. *Studien zur niederländischen Kunst- und Kulturgeschichte. Die Formen des Kunsthandels, das*

Atelier und die Sammler in den Niederlanden vom 15.–18. Jahrhundert. Munich, 1905.

Förster, Richard. "Die Verläumdung des Apelles in der Renaissance." *Jahrbuch der Königlich preussischen Kunstsammlungen* 8 (1887), pp. 29–56, 89–113.

Ford, Charles. "Grist to the Mill." *Art History* 8 (1985): 234–42.

Forster, Leonard. *The Icy Fire: Five Studies in European Petrarchism.* Cambridge, 1969.

———. "Lipsius and Renaissance Neostoicism." In *Festschrift for Ralph Farrell*, ed. A. Stephens, H. L. Rogers, and B. Coghlan, pp. 201–20. Bern, 1977.

Foster, Hal. "'A Luminous Shine': The Discourse of Fetishism and 17th-Century Dutch Still Life." Unpublished lecture given at the 79th Annual Conference of the College Art Association of America. Washington D. C., 1991.

———. "The Art of Fetishism." *Princeton Architectural Journal* 4 (1992): 6–19.

Franits, Wayne. "The Pursuit of Love: The Theme of the Hunting Party at Rest in Seventeenth-Century Dutch Art." *Konsthistorisk Tidskrift* 61 (1992): 106–15.

———. *Paragons of Virtue: Women and Domesticity in Seventeenth-Century Dutch Art.* Cambridge, 1993.

———. "Between Positivism and Nihilism: Some Thoughts on the Interpretation of Seventeenth-Century Dutch Paintings." *Theoretische Geschiedenis* 21 (1994): 129–52.

———. "'Young Women Preferred White to Brown': Some Remarks on Nicolaes Maes and the Cultural Context of Late Seventeenth-Century Dutch Portraiture." In *Beeld en zelfbeeld in de Nederlandse kunst, 1550–1750 (Nederlands Kunsthistorisch Jaarboek 46)*, ed. R. Falkenburg et al., pp. 394–415. Zwolle, 1995.

Freccero, J. "The Fig Tree and the Laurel: Petrarch's Poetics." *Diacritics* 5 (1975): 34–70.

Freedberg, David. *Dutch Landscape Prints of the Seventeenth Century.* London, 1980.

———. *The Power of Images.* Chicago, 1989.

———. "Science, Commerce, and Art: Neglected Topics at the Junction of History and Art History." In *Art in History/History in Art: Studies in Seventeenth-Century Dutch Culture*, ed. D. Freedberg and J. de Vries, pp. 377–428. Santa Monica, 1991.

Frey, Gerhard, and Beer, Ellen J. "Elemente." In *Reallexikon zur deutschen Kunstgeschichte*, vol. 4, cols. 1266–88. Stuttgart, 1958.

Fromentin, Eugène. *The Old Masters of Belgium and Holland* (1882). Trans. M. C. Robbins. New York, 1963.

Gachard, P. L. *Histoire politique et diplomatique de Rubens.* Brussels, 1877.

Gaehtgens, Barbara. *Adriaen van der Werff.* Munich, 1987a.

———. "Imitare und Aemulare im Werk Adriaen van der Werffs." In *Holländische, Genremalerei im 17. Jahrhundert. Symposium Berlin, 1984*, ed. H. Bock and T. W. Gaehtgens, pp. 91–116. Berlin, 1987b.

Gaines, Jane. "Introduction: Fabricating the Female Body." In *Fabrications: Costume and the Female Body*, ed. J. Gaines and C. Herzog, pp. 1–27. New York, 1990.

Garrard, Mary D. "Artemisia Gentileschi's *Self-Portrait as the Allegory of Painting.*" *The Art Bulletin* 62 (1980): 97–112.

———. *Artemisia Gentileschi: The Image of the Female Hero in Italian Baroque Art.* Princeton, 1989.

Gaskell, Ivan. "Review of Svetlana Alpers, *The Art of Describing: Dutch Art in the Seventeenth Century.*" *Oxford Art Journal* 7 (1984): 57–60.

Geerebaert, A. *Lijst van de gedrukte Nederlandsche vertalingen der oude Grieksche en Latijnsche schrijvers.* Ghent, 1924.

Geertz, Clifford. *The Interpretation of Cultures.* New York, 1973.

Gelder, J. G. van. "Van blompot en blomglas." *Elseviers Geillustreerd Maandschrift* 91 (1938): 73–82, 155–66.

———. "De schilders van de Oranjezaal." *Nederlands Kunsthistorisch Jaarboek* (1948–9): 118–64.

———. *De schilderkunst van Jan Vermeer* (with commentary by J. A. Emmens). Utrecht, 1958.

Gelder, Jan G. van, and Jost, Ingrid. *Jan de Bisschop and His Icones and Paradigmata.* 2 vols. Ed. Keith Andrews. Doornspijk, 1985.

Gelder, J. J. de. *Bartholomeus van der Helst.* Rotterdam, 1921.

Gelder, Roelof van. "Hoe amusant was Nederland?" *N. R. C. Handelsblad (Cultureel Supplement)*, June 29, 1984, 6.

Gerson, Horst. *Rembrandt Paintings.* Trans. H. Norden. Ed. G. Schwartz. London, 1968.

———. "Rembrandt and the Flemish Baroque: His Dialogue with Rubens." *Delta* 12, no. 2 (Summer 1969): 7–23.

Geyl, P. *Geschiedenis van de Nederlandse stam.* 2d ed. 6 vols. Amsterdam, 1961–2.

Gibson, Walter S. *"Mirror of the Earth:" The World Landscape in Sixteenth-Century Flemish Painting.* Princeton, 1989.

Gielow, Karl. "Die Hieroglyphenkunde des Humanismus in der Allegorie der Renaissance, besonders der Ehrenpforte Kaiser Maximilians I. Ein Versuch." *Jahrbuch der kunsthistorischen Sammlungen des allerhöchsten Kaiserhauses* 32 (1915): 1–232.

Gifford, E. Melanie. "A Technical Investigation of Some Dutch 17th-Century Tonal Landscapes." *AIC*

[American Institute for Conservation of Historic and Artistic Works] Preprints (1983): 39–49.

———. "Style and Technique in Dutch Landscape Painting in the 1620's." In *Historical Painting Techniques, Materials, and Studio Practice: Preprints of Symposium University of Leiden, The Netherlands 26–9 June 1995*, ed. A. Wallert et al., pp. 140–7. Marina del Rey, 1995.

Gilbert, K. E., and Kuhn, H. *A History of Esthetics.* Bloomington, 1953.

Glynne, Jonathan. "So to Speak" (Review of Svetlana Alpers, *The Art of Describing: Dutch Art in the Seventeenth Century*). *Art History* 7 (1984): 247–52.

Goedde, Lawrence O. "Convention, Realism, and the Interpretation of Dutch and Flemish Tempest Painting." *Simiolus* 16 (1986): 139–49.

———. "A Little World Made Cunningly: Dutch Still Life and Ekphrasis." In Exhib. cat. Washington D.C., *Still Lifes of the Golden Age; Northern European Paintings from the Heinz Family Collection*, pp. 35–44. National Gallery of Art, 1989a.

———. "Conventions of Subject and Form in Dutch Landscape and Their Role in Interpretation." Unpublished Lecture given at the Conference of Historians of Netherlandish Art. Cleveland, 1989b.

———. *Tempest and Shipwreck in Dutch and Flemish Art: Convention, Rhetoric, and Interpretation.* University Park [Penn.], 1989c.

———. "Review of Reindert L. Falkenburg, *Joachim Patinir: Landscape as an Image of the Pilgrimage of Life.*" *The Art Bulletin* 72 (1990): 655–7.

Goffman, Erving. "The Nature of Deference and Demeanor." *American Anthropologist* 58 (1956): 473–502.

———. *The Presentation of Self in Everyday Life.* Middelsex, 1959.

———. *Relations in Public: Microstudies of the Public Order.* New York, 1971.

———. *Frame Analysis. An Essay on the Organization of Experience.* New York, 1974.

———. "The Interaction Order." *American Sociological Review* 48 (1983): 1–17.

Gombrich, E. H. *Art and Illusion. A Study in the Psychology of Pictorial Representation.* New York, 1960.

———. *Art and Illusion: A Study in the Psychology of Pictorial Representation.* 2d revised ed. Princeton, 1961.

———. "The Renaissance Theory of Art and the Rise of Landscape." In Idem, *Norm and Form: Studies in the Art of the Renaissance*, pp. 107–21. London, 1966.

———. *In Search of Cultural History.* Oxford, 1969.

———. "Mysteries of Dutch Painting" (Review of Svetlana Alpers, *The Art of Describing: Dutch Art in the Seventeenth Century*). *New York Review of Books*, November 10, 1983, 13–17.

Gonnet, C. J. "Sint Lucas Gilde te Haarlem in 1631." In *Archief voor Nederlandsche Kunstgeschiedenis*, ed. Fr. D. O. Obreen, vol. 1, pp. 228–293. Rotterdam, 1877–8.

Goodman, Elise. "Rubens' *Conversatie a la mode:* Garden of Leisure, Fashion and Gallantry." *The Art Bulletin* 64 (1982): 247–59.

———. "Petrarchism in Titian's *The Lady and the Musician.*" *Storia dell'Arte* (1983a): 179–86.

———. "Poetic Interpretations of the 'Lady at Her Toilette' Theme in Sixteenth-Century Painting." *The Sixteenth Century Journal* 14 (1983b): 426–42.

———. "The Landscape on the Wall in Vermeer." *Konsthistorisk Tidskrift* 58 (1989): 76–88.

Goossens, Korneel. *David Vinckboons.* Antwerp/The Hague, 1954.

Gouw, J. ter. *De oude tijd.* Haarlem, 1873.

Gowing, Lawrence. *Vermeer.* New York, 1970.

Grafton, Anthony. *New Worlds. Ancient Texts: The Power of Tradition and the Shock of Discovery.* Cambridge [Mass.], 1992.

Grafton, Anthony, and Kaufmann, Thomas DaCosta. "Review of Svetlana Alpers, *The Art of Describing: Dutch Art in the Seventeenth Century.*" *Journal of Interdisciplinary History* 16 (1985): 255–65.

Green, Henry, ed. *Andrea Alciati emblematum fontes quatuor.* London, 1870a.

———. *Shakespere and the Emblem Writers.* London, 1870b.

———. *Andrea Alciati and His Books of Emblems.* London, 1872.

Grijzenhout, Frans, and Veen, Henk van, eds. *De Gouden Eeuw in perspectief; Het beeld van de Nederlandse zeventiende-eeuwse schilderkunst in later tijd.* Heerlen, 1992.

Grimm, Claus. *Stilleben. Die niederländischen und deutschen Meister.* Stuttgart 1988.

Groeneweg, Irene. "Kanttekeningen bij een 18de eeuws Nederlands vrouwen-portret in 'antique kleeding'." *Leids Kunsthistorisch Jaarboek* 4 (1985): 415–36.

———. "The Dutch and Their Black Attire in the Seventeenth Century: Devout and Dignified?" Unpublished lecture given at the symposium, *Social Aspects of Clothing.* Tilburg, 1992.

———. "Regenten in het zwart: vroom en deftig?" In *Beeld en zelfbeeld in de Nederlandse kunst, 1550–1750* (*Nederlands Kunsthistorisch Jaarboek* 46), ed. R. Falkenburg et al., pp. 198–251. Zwolle, 1995.

Groot, C. W. de. *Jan Steen. Beeld en woord.* Utrecht/Nijmegen, 1952.

Groot, Irene de. *Landscape: Etchings by the Dutch Masters of the Seventeenth Century.* London, 1979.

Grootes, E. K. "Rederijkers." In Exhib. cat. Amsterdam, *'t Kan verkeeren. Gerbrand Adriaensz Bredero 1585–1618*, pp. 13–16. Amsterdams Historisch Museum, 1968.

———. "Het jeugdig publiek van de 'nieuwe liedboeken' in het eerste kwart van de zeventiende eeuw." In *Het woord aan de lezer; Zeven literatuurhistorische verkenningen*, ed. W. van den and J. Stouten, pp. 72–88. Groningen, 1987.

Gudlaugsson, S. J. *Ikonographische Studien über die holländische Malerei und das Theater des 17. Jahrhunderts* (Ph.D. dissertation, Berlin). Würzburg, 1938.

———. *De Komedianten bij Jan Steen en zijn tijdgenoten*. The Hague, 1945.

———. *Gerard ter Borch*. 2 vols. The Hague, 1959–60.

Günter, Irmscher. "*Ministrae Voluptatum*: Stoicizing Ethics in the Market and Kitchen Scenes of Pieter Aertsen and Joachim Beuckelaer." *Simiolus* 16 (1986): 219–32.

Guépin, J. P. "De rug zonder ommezijde." In Exhib. cat. The Hague, *Gerard Ter Borch*, pp. 31–8. Mauritshuis, 1974.

Haak, Bob. "De vergankelijkheidssymboliek in 16de eeuwse portretten en 17de eeuwse stillevens in Holland I." *Antiek* 2 (1967): 23–30.

———. "De vergankelijkheidssymboliek in 16de eeuwse portretten en 17de eeuwse stillevens in Holland II." *Antiek* 3 (1968): 399–411.

———. *Rembrandt. His Life, His Work, His Time*. New York, 1969.

———. *The Golden Age: Dutch Painters of the Seventeenth Century*. New York, 1984.

Haasse, Hella. *Mevrouw Bentinck: onverenigbaarheid van karakter*. Amsterdam, 1990.

Habermas, Jürgen. *The Structural Transformation of the Public Sphere*. Trans. T. Burger and F. Lawrence. Cambridge, [Mass.], 1989.

Hajnal, J. "European Marriage Patterns in Perspective." In *Population in History*, ed. D. V. Glass and D. E. C. Eversley, pp. 101–43. Chicago, 1965.

Haks, Donald. *Huwelijk en gezin in Holland in de 17de en 18de eeuw*. 2d ed. Utrecht, 1985.

Hamel, A. G. van. *Zeventiende-eeuwsche opvattingen en theorieën over litteratuur in Nederland*. The Hague, 1918.

Hanawalt, Barbara, ed. *Women and Work in Preindustrial Europe*. Bloomington, 1986.

Hartlaub, G. F. *Zauber des Spiegels. Geschichte und Bedeutung des Spiegels in der Kunst*. Munich, 1951.

Haskell, Francis. *Rediscoveries in Art: Some Aspects of Taste, Fashion and Collecting in England and France*. London, 1976.

Haverkamp-Begemann, Egbert. *Willem Buytewech*. Amsterdam, 1959.

———. "Rembrandt as Teacher." In Exhib. cat. Chicago, *Rembrandt After Three Hundred Years*, pp. 21–30. Art Institute of Chicago, 1969.

———. "Joost van Liere." In *Pieter Bruegel und seine Welt*, ed. O. von Simson and M. Winner, pp. 17–28. Berlin, 1979.

———. "The State of Research in Northern Baroque Art." *The Art Bulletin* 69 (1987): 510–19.

Haverkamp-Begemann, Egbert, and Chong, Alan. "Dutch Landscape and Its Associations," In *The Royal Picture Gallery Mauritshuis*, ed. H. R. Hoetink, pp. 56–67. Amsterdam, 1985.

Hecht, Peter. "Candlelight and Dirty Fingers, or Royal Virtue in Disguise: Some Thoughts on Weyerman and Godfried Schalcken." *Simiolus* 11 (1980): 23–38.

———. "The *Paragone* Debate: Ten Illustrations and A Comment." *Simiolus* 14 (1984): 125–36.

———. "The Debate on Symbol and Meaning in Dutch Seventeenth-Century Art: An Appeal to Common Sense." *Simiolus* 16 (1986): 173–87.

———. "Gerrit Dou's Braamcamp Triptych Reconsidered: A Skeptical View of its 'Allegorized' Meaning." In *Shop Talk: Essays in Honor of Seymour Slive*, ed. C. Schneider, W. W. Robinson, and A. I. Davies, pp. 100–2. Cambridge [Mass.], 1995.

Heckscher, William S. "Reflections on Seeing Holbein's Portrait of Erasmus at Longford Castle." In *Essays in the History of Art Presented to Rudolf Wittkower*, ed. D. Fraser, pp. 128–48. London, 1967.

Heckscher, William S., and Wirth, Karl-August. "Emblem, Emblembücher." In *Reallexikon zur deutschen Kunstgeschichte*, vol. 5, cols. 85–228. Stuttgart, 1959.

Hedinger, Bärbel. *Karten in Bilder: zur Ikonographie der Wandkarte in holländischen Interieurgemälden des 17. Jahrhunderts*. Hildesheim, 1986.

Heiland, Susanne, and Lüdecke, Heinz. *Rembrandt und die Nachwelt*. Darmstadt, 1960.

Held, Julius S. *Rembrandt's Aristotle and Other Rembrandt Studies*. Princeton, 1969.

Henderson, Katherine U., and McManus, Barbara F. *Half Humankind: Contexts and Texts of the Controversy about Women in England, 1540–1640*. Urbana, 1985.

Henkel, Arthur, and Schöne, Albrecht. *Emblemata. Handbuch zur Sinnbildkunst des XVI. und XVII. Jahrhunderts*. Stuttgart, 1967.

Henneke, W. M. A. "De Nederlandse zeventiende-eeuwse schilderkunst: *A Piece of History*." *Theoretische Geschiedenis* 21 (1994): 414–26.

Heppner, Albert. "The Popular Theatre of the 'Rederijkers' in the Work of Jan Steen and His Contemporaries." *Journal of the Warburg & Courtauld Institutes* 3 (1939–40): 22–48.

Herks, J. J. *De geschiedenis van de Amersfoortse tabak*. The Hague, 1967.

Higonnet, Anne. "Secluded Vision. Images of Feminine

Experience in Nineteenth-Century Europe." In *The Expanding Discourse. Feminism and Art History*, eds. N. Broude and M. D. Garrard, pp. 168–85. New York, 1992.

Hirschmann, Otto. *Hendrick Goltzius als Maler 1600–1617*. The Hague, 1916.

Hoecker, R. *Das Lehrgedicht des Karel van Mander*. The Hague, 1916.

Hofman, H. A. *Constantijn Huygens (1596–1687): een christelijk bourgeois-gentilhomme in dienst van het Oranjehuis*. Utrecht, 1983.

Hofrichter, Frima Fox. "Judith Leyster's *Proposition* – Between Virtue and Vice (1975)." In *Feminism and Art History. Questioning the Litany*, eds. N. Broude and M. D. Garrard, pp. 173–81. New York, 1982.

———. "Judith Leyster's 'Self-Portrait': Ut Pictura Poesis." In *Essays in Northern European Art. Presented to Egbert Haverkamp-Begemann on his Sixtieth Birthday*, ed. A.-M. Logan, pp. 106–9. Doornspijk, 1983.

Hofstede de Groot, Cornelis. *Beschreibendes und kritisches Verzeichnis der Werke der hervorragendsten holländischen Maler des siebzehnten Jahrhunderts*. 10 vols. Esslingen a. Neckar, 1907–28.

Hollander, Anne. "The Clothed Image: Picture and Performance." *New Literary History* (1970–1): 477–93.

Hollander, Martha. *Structures of Space and Society in the Seventeenth-Century Dutch Interior*. Ph.D. dissertation, University of California at Berkeley, Berkeley, 1990.

———. "The Divided Household of Nicolaes Maes." *Word and Image* 10 (1994): 138–55.

Hollstein, F. W. H. *Dutch and Flemish Etchings, Engravings and Woodcuts ca. 1450–1700*, vols. 1–. Amsterdam, 1949–.

Holly, Michael Ann. *Panofsky and the Foundations of Art History*. Ithaca, 1984.

Honig, Elizabeth Alice. "An Enterprise of Describing. Svetlana Alpers' Art Historical Strategies." *Theoretische Geschiedenis* 17 (1990): 33–9.

———. "Re-viewing Still Life with Norman Bryson." *Theoretische Geschiedenis* 20 (1993): 41–8.

Hoogewerff, G. J. *De geschiedenis van de St. Lucasgilden in Nederland*. Amsterdam, 1947.

Howell, Martha C. "Women, the Family Economy, and the Structures of Market Production in Cities of Northern Europe during the Late Middle Ages." In *Women and Work in Preindustrial Europe*, ed. Barbara A. Hanawalt, pp. 198–222. Bloomington, 1986a.

———. *Women, Production, and Patriarchy in Late Medieval Cities*. Chicago, 1986b.

Hudig, F. W. *Frederik Hendrik en de kunst van zijn tijd*. Amsterdam, 1928.

Hüttinger, Eduard, ed., *Künstler Häuser von der Renaissance bis zur Gegenwart*. Zürich, 1985.

Huffel, W. C. van. *Willem Bentinck van Rhoon. Zijn persoonlijkheid en leven, 1725–1747*. The Hague, 1923.

Huizinga, J. *Nederland's beschaving in de zeventiende eeuw*. In *Verzamelde Werken*, vol. 2, pp. 412–507. Haarlem, 1948.

James, Henry. "The Metropolitan Museum's '1871 Purchase'" (First published in *The Atlantic Monthly*, 1872). In *The Painter's Eye: Notes and Essays on the Pictorial Arts by Henry James*, ed. J. L. Sweeney, pp. 52–66. London, 1956.

Jansen-Sieben, R. "Les 'Contenances de table' d'Érasme en néerlandais." In *Communiquer et traduire. Hommages à Jean Dierickx*, ed. J. P. van Noppen and G. Debusscher, pp. 249–60. Brussels, 1985.

Jauss, Hans Robert. "Literary History as a Challenge to Literary Theory." In *Toward an Aesthetic of Reception*, trans. T. Bahti, Intro. P. de Man, pp. 3–45. Minneapolis, 1982.

Jenkins, Marianna. *The State Portrait; Its Origin and Evolution*. New York, 1947.

Jones, Pamela M. "Federico Borromeo as a Patron of Landscapes and Still Lifes. Christian Optimism in Italy ca. 1600." *The Art Bulletin* 70 (1988): 261–72.

———. *Federico Borromeo and the Ambrosiana. Art Patronage and Reform in Seventeenth-Century Milan*, Cambridge, 1993.

Jongh van Ellemeet, W. C. M. de. *Museum Catsianum*. The Hague, 1887.

Jongh, Eddy de. *Zinne- en minnebeelden in de schilderkunst van de zeventiende eeuw*. N.p. (Amsterdam), 1967.

———. "Erotica in vogelperspectief. De dubbelzinnigheid van een reeks 17de eeuwse genrevoorstellingen." *Simiolus* 3 (1968–9): 22–74.

———. "The Spur of Wit: Rembrandt's Response to an Italian Challenge." *Delta* 12 (Summer 1969): 49–67.

———. "*De luistervink*. Nicolaes Maes (1634–1693)." *Openbaar Kunstbezit* 14 (1970a): 1.

———. "Homo bulla en vrouw wereld: allegorische figuren in geëigende en camouflerende dracht." *Vrij Nederland*, August 1, 1970b, 7.

———. "Grape Symbolism in Paintings of the 16th and 17th Centuries." *Simiolus* 7 (1974): 166–91.

———. "Pearls of Virtue and Pearls of Vice." *Simiolus* 8 (1975–6): 69–97.

———. "Inleiding." In Exhib. cat. Amsterdam, *Tot lering en vermaak; betekenissen van Hollandse genrevoorstellingen uit de zeventiende eeuw*, pp. 14–28. Rijksmuseum, 1976.

———. "The Interpretation of Still-Life Paintings: Possibilities and Limits." In Exhib. cat. Auckland, *Still-Life in the Age of Rembrandt*, pp. 27–37. Auckland City Art Gallery, 1982.

———. "The Artist's Apprentice and Minerva's

Secret: An Allegory of Drawing by Jan de Lairesse." *Simiolus* 13 (1983): 201–17.

———. "Review of Svetlana Alpers, *The Art of Describing: Dutch Art in the Seventeenth Century.*" *Simiolus* 14 (1984): 51–9.

———. "Enige aspecten van de ikonologie, gisteren en vandaag." In *Aspecten van viftig jaar kunsthistorisch onderzoek 1938–1988*, pp. 31–48. Brussels, 1990.

———. "Real Dutch Art and Not-So-Real Dutch Art: Some Nationalistic Views of Seventeenth-Century Netherlandish Painting." *Simiolus* 20 (1990–1): 197–206.

———. "Some Notes on Interpretation." In *Art in History / History in Art: Studies in Seventeenth-Century Dutch Culture*, ed. D. Freedberg and J. de Vries, pp. 119–36. Santa Monica, 1991.

———. "De dissonante veelstemmigheid sinds Haaks *Hollandse schilders in de Gouden Eeuw.*" *Theoretische Geschiedenis* 19 (1992a): 275–91.

———. "De iconologische benadering van de zeventiende-eeuwse Nederlandse schilderkunst." In *De Gouden Eeuw in perspectief; het beeld van de Nederlandse zeventiende-eeuwse schilderkunst in later tijd*, ed. F. Grijzenhout and H. van Veen, pp. 299–329. Heerlen, 1992b.

———. *Kwesties van betekenis. Thema en motief in de Nederlandse schilderkunst van de zeventiende eeuw*. Leiden, 1995.

Jongh, Eddy de, and Vinken, P. J. "Frans Hals als voortzetter van een emblematische traditie. Bij het huwelijksportret van Isaac Massa en Beatrix van der Laen." *Oud Holland* 76 (1961): 117–52.

Jordan, J., Surrey, J., and Kaplan, A. "Women and Empathy." *Work in Progress*. Vol. 2. Stone Center Working Paper Series. Wellesley, 1982.

Joseph, Bertram. L. *Elizabethan Acting*. Oxford, 1964.

Judson, J. Richard. *Gerrit van Honthorst. A Discussion of His Position in Dutch Art*. The Hague, 1959.

———. "Dirck Barentsen 'die . . . des grooten Titiaens boesem heeft ghenoten'." *Bulletin Koninklijke Musea voor Schone Kunsten* (1962): 77–122.

———. *Dirck Barendsz. 1534–1592*. Amsterdam, 1970.

Kauffmann, Hans. "Rembrandt und die Humanisten vom Muiderkring." *Jahrbuch der Preussischen Kunstsammlung* 41 (1920): 46–81.

———. "Review of Wilhelm Valentiner, *Pieter de Hooch. Des Meisters Gemälde.*" *Deutsche Literaturzeitung*, April 17, 1930, 801ff.

———. "Die Fünfsinne in der niederländischen Malerei des 17. Jahrhunderts." In *Kunstgeschichtliche Studien. Dagobert Frey zum 23 April 1943*, ed. H. Tintelnot, pp. 133–57. Breslau, 1943.

———. "Rubens und Isabella Brant in der Geissblattlaube." In *Form und Inhalt. Kunstgeschichteliche Studien Otto Schmitt zum 60. Geburtstag*, ed. H. Wentzel, pp. 257–74. Stuttgart, 1950.

———. "Jacob van Ruisdael, 'Die Mühle von Wijk bij Duurstede'." In *Festschrift für Otto von Simson*, ed. L. Grisebach and K. Renger, pp. 379–97. Frankfurt, 1977.

Kaufmann, Thomas DaCosta. *The Mastery of Nature: Aspects of Art, Science, and Humanism in the Renaissance*. Princeton, 1993.

Keith, Larry. "Carel Fabritius' *A View in Delft*: Some Observations on its Treatment and Display." *National Gallery Technical Bulletin* 15 (1994): 54–63.

Kelso, Ruth. *Doctrine for the Lady of the Renaissance*. Urbana [Ill.], 1956.

Kemp, Martin. *The Science of Art: Optical Themes in Western Art from Brunelleschi to Seurat*. New Haven, 1990.

Kemp, Wolfgang. "Vorwort." In Svetlana Alpers, *Kunst als Beschreibung; Holländische Malerei des 17. Jahrhunderts*, trans. H. U. Davitt, pp. 7–20. Cologne, 1986.

Kenseth, Joy. "The Age of the Marvelous: An Introduction." In Exhib. cat. Hanover, *The Age of the Marvelous*, pp. 25–59. Hood Museum of Art, 1991.

Kern, Edith G. *The Influence of Heinsius and Vossius upon French Dramatic Theory*. Baltimore, 1949.

Kettering, Alison McNeil. *The Dutch Arcadia: Pastoral Art and its Audience in the Golden Age*. Montclair [N.J.], 1983a.

———. "The Ter Borch Studio Estate." *Apollo* 117 (1983b): 443–51.

———. *Drawings from the Ter Borch Studio Estate*. 2 vols. The Hague, 1988.

Kinderen-Besier, J. H. der. *Spelevaart der Mode*. Amsterdam, 1950.

Klemm, Christian. *Joachim von Sandrart; Kunst-Werke u. Lebens-lauf*. Berlin, 1986.

Kloek, Els. "The Case of Judith Leyster: Exception or Paradigm?" In Exhib. cat. Haarlem, *Judith Leyster. A Dutch Master and Her World*, pp. 55–68. Frans Halsmuseum, 1993.

Knevel, Paul. "Onrust onder schutters. De politieke invloed van de Hollandse schutterijen in de eerste helft van de zeventiende eeuw." *Holland* 20 (1988): 158–74.

Knipping, John Baptist. *De Iconographie van de Contra-Reformatie in de Nederlanden*. 2 vols. Hilversum, 1939–40.

Knuttel, Willem P. C., ed. *Acta der particuliere synoden van Zuid-Holland, 1621–1700*. 6 vols. The Hague, 1908–16.

Knuvelder, G. P. M. *Handboek tot de geschiedenis der Nederlandse letterkunde*. 5th ed. 4 vols. 's-Hertogenbosch, 1970–6.

Koch, Georg Friedrich. *Die Kunstausstellung. Ihre Geschichte von den Anfängen bis zum Ausgang des 18. Jahrhunderts.* Berlin, 1967.
Koerner, Joseph Leo. *The Moment of Self-Portraiture in German Renaissance Art.* Chicago, 1993.
Kogel, Renee. *Pierre Charron.* Geneva, 1972.
Kretschmar, F. G. L. O. "Zijn wapens op Nederlandse portretten een betrouwbaar middel tot identificatie?" *Jaarboek van het Centraal Bureau voor Genealogie en het Iconographisch Bureau* 31 (1977): 38–60.
Kunzle, David. *Fashion and Fetishism: A Social History of the Corset, Tight-Lacing and Other Forms of Body-Sculpture in the West.* Totowa [N.J.], 1982.
Kuretsky, Susan Donahue. *The Paintings of Jacob Ochtervelt (1634–1682).* Oxford, 1979.
Lambert, Audrey M. *The Making of the Dutch Landscape: An Historical Geography of the Netherlands.* 2d ed. London, 1985.
Landwehr, John. *Dutch Emblem Books. A Bibliography.* Utrecht, 1962.
———. *Emblem Books in the Low Countries 1554–1949. A Bibliography.* Utrecht, 1970.
Lasius, Angelika. *Quiringh van Brekelenkam.* Doornspijk, 1992.
Lebeer, Louis. *Catalogue raisonné des estampes de Bruegel l'Ancien.* Brussels, 1969.
LeCoat, Gerard. *The Rhetoric of the Arts, 1550–1650.* Frankfurt am Main, 1975.
Lee, Rensselaer W. *Ut Pictura Poesis: The Humanistic Theory of Painting.* New York, 1967.
Levesque, Catherine. *Journey Through Landscape in Seventeenth-Century Holland: The Haarlem Print Series and Dutch Identity.* University Park [Penn.], 1994.
Li, Chu-tsing. *The Five Senses in Art. An Analysis of Its Development in Northern Europe.* Ph.D. dissertation, The University of Iowa, Iowa City, 1955.
Liedtke, Walter. "The New Church in Haarlem Series: Saenredam's Sketching Style in Relation to Perspective." *Simiolus* 8 (1975–6): 145–66.
———. "The *View in Delft* by Carel Fabritius." *The Burlington Magazine* 118 (1976): 61–73.
———. "Hendrick van Vliet and the Delft School." *Museum News* (Fall 1979): 40–52.
———. *Architectural Painting in Delft.* Doornspijk, 1982.
———. "Toward a History of Dutch Genre Painting–II: The South Holland Tradition." In *The Age of Rembrandt: Studies in Seventeenth-Century Dutch Painting (Papers in Art History from The Pennsylvania State University* 3), ed. R. E. Fleischer and S. S. Munshower, pp. 94–131. University Park [Penn.], 1988.
———. "*Dutch and Flemish Paintings from the Hermitage:* Some Notes to an Exhibition Catalogue, with Special Attention to Rembrandt, Van Dyck and Jordaens." *Oud Holland* 103 (1989): 154–68.
———. "Dutch Paintings in America: The Collectors and Their Ideals." In Exhib. Cat. The Hague, *Great Dutch Paintings from America,* pp. 14–59. Mauritshuis, 1990–1.
———. "The Court Style: Architectural Painting in The Hague and London." In Exhib. cat. Rotterdam, *Perspectives: Saenredam and the Architectural Painters of the 17th Century,* pp. 30–42. Museum Boymans-van Beuningen, 1991a.
———. "Pepys and the Pictorial Arts." *Apollo* 133, no. 350 (1991b): 227–37.
———. "Vermeer Teaching Himself." In Exhib. cat. Stockholm, *Rembrandt och hans Tid/Rembrandt and his Age,* pp. 89–105. Nationalmuseum, 1992.
———. "*Pentimenti* in Our Pictures of Salomon van Ruysdael and of Jan van Goyen." In *Shop Talk: Essays in Honor of Seymour Slive,* ed. C. Schneider, W. W. Robinson, and A. I. Davies, pp. 154–7. Cambridge [Mass.], 1995.
———. "Rembrandt and the Rembrandt Style in the Seventeenth Century." In Exhib. cat. New York, *Rembrandt/Not Rembrandt in The Metropolitan Museum of Art,* vol. 2, pp. 3–39. The Metropolitan Museum of Art, 1995–6.
Loughman, John. "Een stad en haar kunstconsumptie: openbare en privé-verzamelingen in Dordrecht, 1620–1719." In Exhib. cat. *De zichtbaere werelt: schilderkunst uit de Gouden Eeuw in Hollands oudste stad,* pp. 34–64. Dordrecht (Dordrechts Museum), 1992–3.
Lowenthal, Anne W. *Joachim Wtewael and Dutch Mannerism.* Doornspijk, 1986.
———. *Joachim Wtewael: Mars and Venus Surprised by Vulcan.* Malibu, 1995.
Luijten, Hans. "'Swiren vol van leer, amblemsche wijs geduijt.' Een opmerkelijk zeventiende-eeuws poëzie-album van Gesina ter Borch." *Bulletin van het Rijksmuseum* 36 (1988): 315–42.
Macfarlane, Alan. *Marriage and Love in England; Modes of Reproduction 1300-1840.* Oxford, 1986.
MacLaren, Neil. *National Gallery Catalogues: The Dutch School.* London, 1960.
Maclean, Ian. *The Renaissance Notion of Women.* Cambridge, 1980.
Magurn, Ruth Saunders. *The Letters of Peter Paul Rubens.* Cambridge [Mass.], 1955.
Mahon, Denis. "Notes on the "Dutch Gift" to Charles II: II." *The Burlington Magazine* 91 (1949): 349–50.
Mâle, Émile. *L'art religieux du XIIIe siècle en France.* 5th ed. Paris, 1923.
———. *L'Art religieux du XIIe siècle en France.* 6th ed. Paris, 1953.

Manke, Ilse. *Emanuel de Witte, 1617–1692.* Amsterdam, 1963.

Manley, Lawrence. *Convention 1500–1750.* Cambridge [Mass.], 1980.

Marchi, Neil de, and Miegroet, Hans J. van. "Art, Value, and Market Practices in the Netherlands in the Seventeenth Century." *The Art Bulletin* 76 (1994): 451–64.

Mare, Heidi de. "The Domestic Boundary as Ritual Area in Seventeenth-Century Holland." In *Urban Rituals in Italy and the Netherlands*, ed. H. de Mare and A. Vos, pp. 109–31. Assen, 1993.

———. "A Rule Worth Following in Architecture? The Significance of Gender Classification in Simon Stevin's Architectural Treatise (1548–1620)." In *Women of the Golden Age. An International Debate on Women in Seventeenth-Century Holland, England and Italy*, ed. E. Kloek, N. Teeuwen, and M. Huisman, pp. 103–20. Hilversum, 1994.

Marrow, James H. "Symbol and Meaning in Northern European Art of the Late Middle Ages and the Early Renaissance." *Simiolus* 16 (1986): 150–72.

Martin, W. *Het leven en de werken van Gerrit Dou.* Leiden, 1901.

———. *Eenige opmerkingen over de waardering onzer schilderkunst in onze gouden eeuw.* The Hague, 1907.

———. *Gerard Dou (Klassiker der Kunst.* vol. 24). Stuttgart, 1913.

McCracken, Grant. "Politics and Ritual Sotto Voce. The Use of Demeanor as an Instrument of Politics in Elizabethan England." *Canadian Journal of Anthropology* 3 (1982): 85–100.

McGrath, Elizabeth. "The Painted Decoration of Rubens's House." *Journal of the Warburg and Courtauld Institutes* 41 (1978): 245–77.

———. "Rubens's *Susanna and the Elders* and Moralizing Inscriptions on Prints." In *Wort und Bild in der niederländischen Kunst und Literatur des 16. and 17. Jahrhunderts*, ed. H. Vekeman and J. Müller-Hofstede, pp. 73–90. Erftstadt, 1984.

Medick, Hans. "The Proto-Industrial Family Economy: The Structural Function of Household and Family During the Transition from Peasant Society to Industrial Capitalism." *Social History* 1 (1976).

Meer, Theo van der. *Sodoms zaad in Nederland. Het ontstaan van homoseksualiteit in de vroegmoderne tijd.* Nijmegen, 1995.

Melion, Walter. *Shaping the Netherlandish Canon. Karel van Mander's Schilder-Boeck.* Chicago, 1991.

Meter, J. H. *The Literary Theories of Daniel Hensius.* Assen, 1984.

Miedema, Hessel. "Review of Jan Emmens, *Rembrandt en de regels van de kunst.*" *Oud Holland* 84 (1969): 249–56.

———. "Philips Angels *Lof der schilder-konst.*" *Proef* (December 1973): 27–33.

———. "Over het realisme in de Nederlandse schilderkunst van de zeventiende eeuw." *Oud Holland* 89 (1975): 2–16.

———. "Realism and Comic Mode: The Peasant." *Simiolus* 9 (1977): 205–19.

———. *De archiefbescheiden van het St. Lukasgilde te Haarlem 1497–1798.* Alphen aan den Rijn, 1980.

———. *Kunst, kunstenaar en kunstwerk bij Karel van Mander; een analyse van zijn levenbeschrijvingen.* Alphen aan den Rijn, 1981.

———. "Kunstschilders, gilde en academie. Over het probleem van de emancipatie van de kunstschilders in de Noordelijke Nederlanden van de 16de en de 17de eeuw." *Oud Holland* 101 (1987): 1–34.

Mielke, Hans. "Review of *L'époque de Lucas de Leyde et Pierre Bruegel.*" *Master Drawings* 23–4 (1985–6): 76–81.

Mieschke, R. *Het Nederlandse woonhuis van 1300–1800.* Haarlem, 1969.

Milder, P. "De kunsthistorische misvattingen over de Gouden Eeuw." *De Volkskrant*, June 22, 1984, 15.

Miles, Margaret R. *Image as Insight; Visual Understanding in Western Christianity and Secular Culture.* Boston, 1985.

Miller, Jean Baker. *Toward a New Psychology of Women.* 2d ed. Boston, 1986.

Minta, Stephen. *Petrarch and Petrarchism; The English and French Traditions.* Manchester, 1980.

Mirimonde, A. P. de. "La musique dan les allégories de l'amour. I. Venus." *Gazette des Beaux-Arts* (1966): 265–90.

———. "La musique dans les allégories de l'amour. II. Eros." *Gazette des Beaux-Arts* (1967): 319–46.

Modleski, Tania. *Loving with a Vengeance: Mass-Produced Fantasies for Women.* New York, 1982.

Moffitt, John F. "The Theoretical Basis of Velazquez's Court Portraiture." *Zeitschrift für Kunstgeschichte* 54 (1990): 216–25.

Moltke, J. W. von. *Arent de Gelder.* Doornspijk, 1994.

Monk, Samuel H. *The Sublime.* New York, 1935.

Monroy, E. F. von. *Embleme und Emblembücher in den Niederlanden 1560–1630* (Ph.D. dissertation, Freiburg im Breisgau, 1942). Utrecht, 1964.

Monsarrat, Gilles D. *Light from the Porch. Stoicism and English Renaissance Literature.* Paris, 1984.

Montagu, Jennifer. *The Expression of the Passions. The Origin and Influence of Charles le Brun's "Conférence sur l'expression générale et particulière."* New Haven, 1994.

Montias, John Michael. *Artists and Artisans in Delft: A Socio-Economic Study of the Seventeenth Century.* Princeton, 1982.

———. "Cost and Value in Seventeenth-Century Dutch Art." *Art History* 10 (1987): 455–66.
———. "Art Dealers in the Seventeenth-Century Netherlands." *Simiolus* 18 (1988): 244–53.
———. *Vermeer and His Milieu; A Web of Social History.* Princeton, 1989.
———. "Socio-Economic Aspects of Netherlandish Art from the Fifteenth to the Seventeenth Century: A Survey." *The Art Bulletin* 72 (1990): 358–73.
———. "Works of Art in Seventeenth-Century Amsterdam: An Analysis of Subjects and Attributions." In *Art in History, History in Art. Studies in Seventeenth-Century Dutch Culture*, ed. D. Freedberg and J. de Vries, pp. 331–72. Santa Monica, 1991.
Morford, Mark. *Stoics and Neostoics; Rubens and the Circle of Lipsius.* Princeton, 1991.
Moxey, Keith. "Panofsky's Concept of 'Iconology' and the Problem of Interpretation in the History of Art." *New Literary History* 17 (1985–6): 265–74.
Müllenmeister, Kurt J. *Roelant Savery: Die Gemälde mit kritischem Oeuvrekatalog.* Freren, 1988.
Müller-Hofstede, Justus. "Höfische und bürgerliche Damenporträts. Anmerkungen zu Rubens' Antwerperner Bildnismalerei 1609–1620." *Pantheon* 41 (1983): 308–21.
———. "'Wort und Bild': Fragen zu Signifikanz und Realität in der holländischen Malerei des 17. Jahrhunderts." In *Wort und Bild in der niederländischen Kunst und Literatur des 16. and 17. Jahrhunderts*, ed. H. Vekeman and J. Müller-Hofstede, pp. ix–xxiii. Erfstadt, 1984.
Münz, Ludwig. *Pieter Bruegel the Elder: The Drawings.* London, 1961.
Muller, Jeffrey M. "The *Perseus and Andromeda* on Rubens's House." *Simiolus* 12 (1981–2): 131–46.
Muller, Sheila, "Jan Steen's *Burgher of Delft and His Daughter:* A Painting and Politics in Seventeenth-Century Holland." *Art History* 12 (1989): 268–97.
———. *Dutch Art: An Encyclopedia.* Hamden [Ct.], 1996.
Mulvey, Laura. "Afterthoughts on 'Visual Pleasure and Narrative Cinema' Inspired by King Vidor's *Duel in the Sun* (1946)." In *Visual and Other Pleasures*, pp. 29–38. Bloomington, 1989.
Naerebout, F. G. "'Snoode exercitien': het zeventiende-eeuwse Nederlandse protestantisme en de dans." *Volkskundig Bulletin* 16 1990: 125–55.
Nead, Lynda. *The Female Nude. Art, Obscenity and Sexuality.* London, 1992.
Neumann, Carl. *Rembrandt.* Berlin, 1902.
Nevitt, Rodney H. *Studies in Dutch Art and Literature of Courtship.* Ph.D. dissertation, Harvard University, Cambridge [Mass.], 1992.
Nichols, Lawrence W. "The 'Pen Works' of Hendrick Goltzius." *Philadelphia Museum of Art Bulletin* 88, nos. 373–4 (Winter 1992): 4–56.
Nicolson, Benedict. *Hendrick Terbrugghen.* London, 1958.
———. *Caravaggism in Europe.* 2d revised ed. Oxford, 1979.
Nierop, H. F. K. van. *Van ridders tot regenten. De Hollandse adel in de zestiende en de eerste helft van de zeventiende eeuw.* The Hague, 1984.
Nochlin, Linda. "Why Have There Been No Great Women Artists? (1971)." In Idem, *Women, Art, and Power and Other Essays*, pp. 145–78. New York, 1988.
Obreen, Frederik D. O. *Archief voor de Nederlandsche kunstgeschiedenis.* 7 vols. Rotterdam, 1879–90.
Oestreich, Gerhard. *Neostoicism and the Early Modern State.* Cambridge, 1982.
Oppé, Adolf Paul. *Raphael.* 1909. Reprint ed., New York, 1970.
Panofsky, Erwin. "Der gefesselte Eros (Zur Genealogie von Rembrandts Danae)." *Oud Holland* 50 (1933): 193–217.
———. "Jan van Eyck's 'Arnolfini' Portrait." *The Burlington Magazine* 64 (1934): 117–27.
———. *Early Netherlandish Painting; Its Origin and Character.* 2 vols. Cambridge [Mass.], 1953.
———. *Studies in Iconology. Humanistic Themes in the Art of the Renaissance.* 2d ed. New York, 1962.
Parente, James A. *Religious Drama and the Humanist Tradition. Christian Theater in Germany and in the Netherlands 1500–1680.* Leiden, 1987.
Parker, Rozsika. *The Subversive Stitch: Embroidery and the Making of the Feminine.* London, 1984.
Parker, Rozsika, and Pollock, Griselda. *Old Mistresses. Women, Art and Ideology.* New York, 1981.
Pattison, Bruce. *Music and Poetry of the English Renaissance.* London, 1948.
Peacock, Martha Moffitt. "Geertruydt Roghman and the Female Perspective in 17th-Century Dutch Genre Imagery." *Woman's Art Journal* 14, no. 2 (1993–4): 3–10.
Philip, L. Brand. "The *Peddler* by Hieronymous Bosch; A Study in Detection." *Nederlands Kunsthistorisch Jaarboek* 19 (1958): 1–81.
Pigler, A. "Neid und Unwissenheit als Widersacher der Kunst." *Acta Historiae Artium*, 1 (1953–4): 215–35.
———. *Barockthemen: eine Auswahl von Verzeichnissen zur Ikonographie des 17. und 18. Jahrhunderts.* 2d enlarged ed. 3 vols. Budapest, 1974.
Platt, Arlene Q. *Cardinal Federico Borromeo as Patron and Critic of the Arts and His 'MUSAEUM' of 1625.* New York, 1986.
Pleij, Herman, ed. *Van schelmen en schavuiten. Laatmiddeleeuwse vagebondteksten.* Amsterdam, 1985.
Plietzsch, Eduard. *Holländische und flämische Maler des XVII Jahrh.* Leipzig, 1960.

Pocock, J. G. A. "Texts as Events: Reflections on the History of Political Thought." In *Politics of Discourse. The Literature and History of Seventeenth-Century England*, ed. K. Sharpe and S. N. Zwicker, pp. 21–34. Berkeley, 1987.

Pointon, Marcia. "History of Art and the Undergraduate Syllabus." In *The New Art History*, ed. A. L. Rees and F. Borzello, pp. 146–56. Atlantic Highlands [N.J.], 1988.

Pol, Lotte van de. "Beeld en werkelijkheid van de prostitutie in de zeventiende eeuw." In *Soete minne en helsche boosheit; seksuele voorstellingen in Nederland, 1300–1800*, ed. G. Hekma and H. Roodenburg, pp. 109–44. The Hague, 1988.

Pope-Hennessy, John. *The Portrait in the Renaissance*. 2d ed. New York, 1979.

Porteman, Karel. "Geschreven met de linkerhand? Letteren tegenover schilderkunst in de Gouden Eeuw." In *Historische letterkunde*, ed. M. Spies, pp. 93–113. Groningen, 1984.

———. "Vondels gedicht 'Op een Italiaensche schildery van Suzanne'." In *'T ondersoeck leert: studies over middeleeuwse en 17de-eeuwse literatuur ter nagedachtenis van Prof. dr. I. Rens*, ed. G. van Eemeren and F. Willaert, pp. 301–18. Amersfoort, 1986.

Potts, Alex. "Review of Norman Bryson, *Vision and Painting: The Logic of the Gaze*." *The Burlington Magazine* 129 (1987): 29–32.

———. *Flesh and the Ideal: Winckelmann and the Origins of Art History*. New Haven, 1994.

Praz, Mario. *Studies in Seventeenth-Century Imagery*. 2 pts. London, 1939–47.

———. *Studies in Seventeenth-Century Imagery*. 2d ed. 2 pts. Rome, 1964.

Price, J. L. *Culture and Society in the Dutch Republic During the 17th Century*. London, 1974.

Prinz, Wolfgang. *Die Sammlung der Selbstbildnisse in den Uffizien*. 3 vols. Berlin, 1971.

Prinz, Wolfram. "The 'Four Philosophers' by Rubens and the Pseudo-Seneca in Seventeenth-Century Painting." *The Art Bulletin* 55 (1973): 410–28.

Purtle, Carol J., et al., eds. "Tradition and Innovation: A Selection of Papers Read at the First International Research Conference of the Historians of Netherlandish Art in Pittsburgh, 9–12 October 1985." *Simiolus* 16 (1986): 91–190.

Raben, Remco, and Vermeij, Roos. "Wortelloof en cultuurhistorie; kunstopvattingen van Peter Hecht en Eddy de Jongh." *Leidschrift* 6, no. 3 (1990): 41–58.

Rademaker, C. S. M. *Life and Work of Joannes Vossius (1577–1649)*. Assen, 1981.

Raupp, Hans-Joachim. "Ansätze zu einer Theorie der Genremalerei in den Niederlanden im 17. Jahrhundert." *Zeitschrift für Kunstgeschichte* 46 (1983): 401–18.

———. *Untersuchungen zu Künstlerbildnis und Künstlerdarstellung in den Niederlanden im 17. Jahrhundert*. Hildesheim, 1984.

Regteren Altena, I. Q. van. *Jacques de Gheyn: Three Generations*. 3 vols. The Hague, 1983.

Renger, Konrad. *Lockere Gesellschaft. Zur Ikonographie des Verlorenen Sohnes und von Wirtshausszenen in der niederländischen Malerei*. Berlin, 1970.

Reznicek, E. K. J. *Die Zeichnungen von Hendrick Goltzius*. 2 vols. Utrecht, 1961.

———. "Realism as a 'Side Road or Byway' in Dutch Art." In *The Renaissance and Mannerism. Studies in Western Art. Acts of the Twentieth International Congress of the History of Art*, ed. I. E. Rubin, vol. 2, pp. 247–53. Princeton, 1963a.

———. "Twee 'grootsmoediche' Haagse schilders." In *Album Discipulorum J. G. van Gelder*, ed. J. Bruyn et al., pp. 119–23. Utrecht, 1963b.

———. "Hendrick Goltzius and His Conception of Landscape." In Exhib. cat. London, *Dutch Landscape: The Early Years, Haarlem and Amsterdam 1590–1650*, pp. 57–62. The National Gallery, 1986.

Riehl, B. *Geschichte des Sittenbildes in der deutschen Kunst bis zum Tode Pieter Brueghel des Älteren*. Berlin, 1884.

Roessingh, H. K. *Inlandse tabak. Expansie en contractie van een handelsgewas in de 17e en 18e eeuw in Nederland*. Wageningen, 1976.

Roethlisberger, Marcel G. *Abraham Bloemaert and His Sons: Paintings and Prints*. 2 vols. Doornspijk, 1993.

Rogers, Mary. "The Decorum of Women's Beauty: Trissino, Firenzuola, Luigini and the Representation of Women in Sixteenth-Century Painting." *Renaissance Studies* 2 (1988): 47–88.

———. "An Ideal Wife at the Villa Maser: Veronese, the Barbaros and Renaissance Theorists of Marriage." *Renaissance Studies* 7 (1993): 379–97.

Rogier, L. J. *Geschiedenis van het katholicisme in Noord-Nederland in de 16e and 17e eeuw*. 2d ed. 2 vols. Amsterdam, 1947.

———. *Eenheid en scheiding. Geschiedenis der Nederlanden 1477–1813*. 2d ed. Utrecht/Antwerp, 1968.

Roodenburg, Herman. *Onder censuur. De kerkelijke tucht in de gereformeerde gemeente van Amsterdam, 1578–1700* (proefschrift, Vrije Universiteit te Amsterdam). Hilversum, 1990.

———. "The 'Hand of Friendship': Shaking Hands and Other Gestures in the Dutch Republic." In *A Cultural History of Gesture from Antiquity till the Present Day*, ed. J. Bremmer and H. Roodenburg, pp. 152–89. Cambridge, 1991a.

———. "Over korsetten, lichaamshouding en gebaren. Een cultuurhistorische verkenning van de 'nieuwe fatsoenen' tussen ruwweg 1580 en 1630." *Textielhistorische Bijdragen* 31 (1991b): 20–39.

———. "'Welstand' en 'wellevendheid.' Over houdingen en gebaren en gelaatsuitdrukking in de schilderkunst, de toneelkunst en de rhetorica: de inbreng van het classicisme." In *Beeld en zelfbeeld in de Nederlandse kunst, 1550–1750* (*Nederlands Kunsthistorisch Jaarboek* 46), ed. R. Falkenburg et al., pp. 416–39. Zwolle, 1995.

Rooses, Max, and Ruelens, Charles, eds. *Peter Paul Rubens; correspondance et documents épistolaires concernant sa vie et ses oeuvres....* 6 vols. Antwerp, 1887–1909.

Rosenberg, Jakob. *Rembrandt, Life and Work.* 2d ed. Cambridge [Mass.], 1964.

Rosenberg, Jakob, Slive, Seymour, and Ter Kuile, E. H. *Dutch Art and Architecture 1600 to 1800.* Harmondsworth, 1966.

Røstvig, Maren-Sofie. *The Happy Man: Studies in the Metamorphoses of a Classical Ideal.* 2 vols. Oslo, 1962.

Rowlands, John. *Holbein. The Paintings of Hans Holbein the Younger. Complete Edition.* Boston, 1985.

Rudolph, Hermann. "Vanitas. Die Bedeutung mittelalterlicher und humanistischer Bildinhalte in der niederländischen Malerei des 17. Jahrhunderts." In *Festschrift Wilhelm Pinder zum sechzigsten Geburtstage,* pp. 405–33. Leipzig, 1938.

Rybczynski, Witold. *Home. A Short History of an Idea.* New York, 1986.

Saunders, Jason L. *Justus Lipsius: The Philosophy of Renaissance Stoicism.* New York, 1955.

Schama, Simon. "Wives and Wantons: Versions of Womanhood in 17th-Century Dutch Art." *Oxford Art Journal* 3 (1980): 5–13.

———. "The Dutch Master's Revenge" (Review of Svetlana Alpers, *The Art of Describing: Dutch Art in the Seventeenth Century*). *New Republic* (May 14, 1984a): 25–31.

———. "The Sexual Economy of Genre Painting." Unpublished lecture given at the symposium, *Images of the World: Dutch Genre Painting in Its Historical Context.* London, Royal Academy, 1984b.

———. *The Embarrassment of Riches: An Interpretation of Dutch Culture in the Golden Age.* New York, 1987.

———. "Dutch Landscapes: Culture as Foreground." In Exhib. cat. Boston, *Masters of 17th-Century Dutch Landscape Painting,* pp. 64–83. Museum of Fine Arts, 1988.

Schapiro, Meyer. *Theory and Philosophy of Art: Style, Artist and Society.* New York, 1994.

Scharfe, Martin. "Bagatellen. Zu einer Pathognomik der Kultur." *Zeitschrift für Volkskunde* 91 (1995): 1–26.

Scheller, R. W. "Rembrandt's reputatie van Houbraken tot Scheltema." *Nederlands Kunsthistorisch Jaarboek* 12 (1961): 81–118.

———. "Rembrandt en de encyclopedische kunstkamer." *Oud Holland* 84 (1969): 81–147.

Schenck, Eva-Maria. *Das Bilderrätsel* (Ph.D. dissertation, Cologne). Cologne, 1968.

Schenkeveld, Maria A. *Dutch Literature in the Age of Rembrandt.* Amsterdam, 1991.

Schmidt-Degener, F. *Rembrandt und die holländische Barock.* (First published in Dutch in 1919.) Berlin, 1928.

Schneede, Uwe M. *Das repräsentative Gesellschaftsbild in der niederländischen Malerei des 17. Jahrhunderts und seine Grundlagen bei Hans Vredeman de Vries* (Ph.D. dissertation, Kiel). Kiel, 1965.

———. "Gabriel Metsu und der holländische Realismus." *Oud Holland* 83 (1968): 45–61.

Schneider, Cynthia P. *Rembrandt's Landscapes.* New Haven, 1990.

Schneider, Norbert. *The Art of the Still Life: Still Life Painting in the Early Modern Period.* Trans. H. Beyer. Cologne, 1990.

Schöne, Albrecht. *Emblematik und Drama im Zeitalter des Barock.* Munich, 1964.

Schotel, G. D. J. *Vaderlandsche volksboeken en volkssprookjes van de vroegste tijden tot het einde der 18e eeuw.* 2 vols. Haarlem, 1873–4.

Schwartz, Gary. "Art in History." In *Art in History, History in Art: Studies in Seventeenth-Century Dutch Culture,* ed. D. Freedberg and J. de Vries, pp 7–16. Santa Monica, 1991.

———. "Zwaar door de tijd beproefd." *N. R. C. Handelsblad (Cultureel Supplement),* July 3, 1992, 2.

Schwartz, Gary, and Bok, Marten Jan. *Pieter Saenredam: The Painter and His Time.* Maarssen, 1990.

Schwarz, Heinrich. "The Mirror in Art." *The Art Quarterly* 15 (1952): 97–118.

Shorter, Edward. *The Making of the Modern Family.* New York, 1975.

Showalter, Elaine. "Towards a Feminist Poetics." In *Women Writing and Writing about Women,* ed. M. Jacobus, pp. 22–41. London, 1979.

Sell, Stacey L. "Rembrandt's Draftsmanship and the Traditions of Renaissance Art." Ph.D. dissertation, University of Virginia, Charlottesville, 1993.

Simmel, Georg. *Das Problem des Porträts; zur Philosophie der Kunst.* Potsdam, 1922.

———. *On Individuality and Social Forms. Selected Writings.* Ed. and Intro. D. N. Levine. Chicago, 1971.

Simons, Patricia. "Women in Frames: The Eye, the Gaze, the Profile in Renaissance Portraiture." *History Workshop* 25 (1988): 4–30.

Skinner, Quentin. *The Foundations of Modern Political Thought.* 2 vols. Cambridge, 1978.

Slive, Seymour. *Rembrandt and His Critics 1630–1730.* The Hague, 1953.

———. "Notes on the Relationship of Protestantism to Seventeenth-Century Dutch Painting." *The Art Quarterly* 19 (1956): 3–15.

———. "Realism and Symbolism in Seventeenth-Century Dutch Painting." *Daedalus* 91 (1962): 469–500.

———. "On the Meaning of Frans Hals' '*Malle Babbe*'." *The Burlington Magazine* 105 (1963): 432–6.

———. *Frans Hals.* 3 vols. London, 1970–4.

Slive, Seymour, Rosenberg, Jakob, and Kuile, E. H. ter *Dutch Art and Architecture: 1600 to 1800.* Harmondsworth, 1972.

Sluijter, Eric Jan. "Some Observations on the Choice of Narrative Mythological Subjects in Late Mannerist Painting in the Northern Netherlands." In *Netherlandish Mannerism: Papers Given at a Symposium in Nationalmuseum Stockholm, September 21–22, 1984,* ed. G. Cavalli-Björkman, pp. 61–72. Stockholm, 1985.

———. *De 'heydensche fabulen' in de Noordnederlandse schilderkunst circa 1590–1670* (proefschrift, Rijksuniversiteit te Leiden). Enschede, 1986.

———. "Een stuck waerin een jufr. voor de spiegel van Gerrit Douw." *Antiek* 23 (1988a): 150–61.

———. "'Een volmaekte schilderij is als een spiegel van de natuer': spiegel en spiegelbeeld in de Nederlandse schilderkunst van de zeventiende eeuw." In *Oog in oog met de spiegel,* ed. N. Brederoo et al., pp. 146–63. Amsterdam, 1988b.

———. "Schilders van 'cleyne, subtile end curieuse dingen': Leidse 'fijnschilders' in contemporaine bronnen." In Exhib. cat. Leiden, *Leidse fijnschilders; van Gerrit Dou tot Frans van Mieris de Jonge, 1630–1760,* pp. 15–55. Stedelijk Museum De Lakenhal, 1988c.

———. "Hoe realistisch is de Noordnederlandse schilderkunst van de zeventiende eeuw? De problemen van een vraagstelling." *Leidschrift* 6, no. 3 (1990): 5–39.

———. "Over fijnschilders en 'betekenis'; naar aanleiding van Peter Hecht, *De Hollandse fijnschilders.*" *Oud Holland* 105 (1991): 50–63.

———. "Nieuwe kunsthistorische benaderingen en het veranderende beeld van de zeventiende-eeuwse Nederlandse schilderkunst." In *De Gouden Eeuw in perspectief: het beeld van de Nederlandse zeventiende-eeuwse schilderkunst in later tijd,* ed. F. Grijzenhout and H. van Veen, pp. 360–98. Heerlen, 1992.

———. *De lof der schilderkunst: over schilderijen van Gerrit Dou (1613–1675) en een traktaat van Philips Angel uit 1642.* Hilversum, 1993.

Sluijter-Seiffert, Nicolette. *Cornelis van Poelenburch (ca. 1593–1667)* (proefschrift, Rijksuniversiteit te Leiden). Enschede, 1984.

Smith, David R. *Masks of Wedlock: Seventeenth-Century Dutch Marriage Portraiture.* Ann Arbor, 1982.

Smith, John. *Catalogue Raisonné of the Works of the Most Eminent Dutch . . . Painters.* 8 vols. and supplement. London, 1829–42.

Smith, R. M. "Reflections." In *The Sociology of the Family: New Directions for Britain,* ed. C. Harris, pp. 74–112. Keele, 1979.

Smits-Veldt, Mieke B. *Samuel Coster, ethicus-didacticus. Een onderzoek naar dramatische opzet en morele instructie van Ithys, Polyxena en Iphigenia.* Groningen, 1986.

———. *Maria Tesselschade. Leven met talent en vriendschap.* Zutphen, 1994.

Snoep, D. P. "Een 17de eeuws liedboek met tekeningen van Gerard ter Borch de Oude en Pieter en Roeland van Laer." *Simiolus* 3 (1968–9): 77–134.

———. "Honselaersdijk: restauraties op papier." *Oud Holland* 84 (1969): 270–94.

Spicer, Joanneath. "'De Koe voor d'aerde statt': The Origins of the Dutch Cattle Piece." In *Essays in Northern European Art Presented to Egbert Haverkamp-Begemann on his Sixtieth Birthday,* ed. A.-M. Logan, pp. 251–6. Doornspijk, 1983.

———. "The Renaissance Elbow." In *A Cultural History of Gesture from Antiquity till the Present Day,* ed. J. Bremmer and H. Roodenburg, pp. 84–128. Cambridge, 1991.

Spierenburg, Petrus Cornelis. *Elites and Etiquette: Mentality and Social Structure in the Early Modern Northern Netherlands.* Rotterdam, 1981.

Spies, Marijke. "Charlotte de Huybert en het gelijk; de geleerde en de werkende vrouw in de zeventiende eeuw." *Literatuur: Tijdschrift over Nederlandse Letterkunde* 3 (1986): 339–50.

Stammler, Wolfgang. *Frau Welt. Eine mittelalterliche Allegorie.* Freiburg [Switzerland], 1959.

Steadman, John M. *Redefining a Period Style: "Renaissance," "Mannerist," and "Baroque" in Literature.* Pittsburgh, 1990.

Stechow, Wolfgang. *Dutch Landscape Painting of the Seventeenth Century.* 2d ed. London, 1968.

Stechow, Wolfgang, and Comer, Christopher. "The History of the Term *Genre.*" *Allen Memorial Art Museum Bulletin* 33 (1975–6): 89–94.

Steengracht van Oostkapelle, J. *De voornaamste schilderijen van het koninklijk kabinet te 's Gravenhage.* 4 pts. The Hague, 1826–30.

Stewart, Alison G. *Unequal Lovers. A Study of Unequal Couples in Northern Art.* New York, 1977.

Stighelen, Katlijne van der. *Anna Maria van Schurman (1607–1678).* Leuven, 1987.

Stone-Ferrier, Linda. *Images of Textiles: The Weave of Seventeenth-Century Dutch Art and Society.* Ann Arbor, 1985a.

———. "Views of Haarlem: A Reconsideration of Ruisdael and Rembrandt." *The Art Bulletin* 67 (1985b): 417–36.

———. "Gabriel Metsu's Vegetable Market at Amsterdam: Seventeenth-Century Dutch Market Paintings and Horticulture." *The Art Bulletin* 71 (1989): 428–52.

———. "Gabriel Metsu's *Vegetable Market at Amsterdam* and Its Relationship to a Bredero Farce." *Artibus et Historiae* 25 (1992): 163–80.

Strauss, Walter. *Hendrick Goltzius 1558–1617: The Complete Woodcuts and Engravings.* 2 vols. New York, 1977.

Strien, C. D. van. *British Travellers in Holland During the Stuart Period: Edward Browne and John Locke as Tourists in the United Provinces.* Leiden, 1993.

Strong, Roy. "The Elizabethan Malady; Melancholy in Elizabethan and Jacobean Portraiture." *Apollo* 79 (1964): 264–9.

Stumpel, Jeroen. "Review of Svetlana Alpers, *The Art of Describing: Dutch Art in the Seventeenth Century.*" *The Burlington Magazine* 126 (1984): 580–1.

Summers, David. "Conventions in the History of Art." *New Literary History* 13 (1981–2): 103–25.

———. *Michelangelo and the Language of Art.* Princeton, 1981.

———. *The Judgment of Sense: Renaissance Naturalism and the Rise of Aesthetics.* Cambridge, 1987.

Sumowski, Werner. *Gemälde der Rembrandt-Schüler.* 6 vols. Landau, 1983–94.

Sutton, Peter. "Masters of Dutch Genre Painting." In Exhib. cat. Philadelphia, *Masters of Seventeenth-Century Dutch Genre Painting*, pp. xiii–lxvi. Philadelphia Museum of Art, 1984.

———. "Introduction." In Exhib. cat. Boston, *Masters of 17th-Century Dutch Landscape Painting*, pp. 1–63. Museum of Fine Arts, 1988.

Taverne, E. R. M. "Pictura. Enkele allegorieën op de schilderkunst." In Exhib. cat. Nijmegen, *Het Schildersatelier in de Nederlanden 1500–1800*, pp. 31–46. De Waag, 1964.

———. "Een Amsterdams Lucasfeest in 1618." *Simiolus* 4 (1970): 19–27.

Taylor, Paul. "The Concept of *Houding* in Dutch Art Theory." *Journal of the Warburg and Courtauld Institutes* 55 (1992): 210–32.

———. "Review of David Freedberg and Jan de Vries, eds., *Art in History/History in Art: Studies in Seventeenth-Century Dutch Culture.*" *The Burlington Magazine* 136 (1994): 36.

———. *Dutch Flower Painting, 1600–1720.* New Haven, 1995.

Thiel, P. J. J. van. "Marriage Symbolism in a Musical Party by Jan Miense Molenaar." *Simiolus* 2 (1967–8): 90–9.

Thiel, Pieter J. J., et al. *All the Paintings of the Rijksmuseum in Amsterdam: A Completely Illustrated Catalogue.* Amsterdam, 1976.

Tickner, Lisa. "Feminism, Art History, and Sexual Difference." *Genders* 3 (Fall 1988): 93–128.

Tijs, Rutger J. *P. P. Rubens en J. Jordaens. Barok in eigen huis.* Antwerp, 1984.

Tikkanen, J. J. *Die Beinstellungen in der Kunstgeschichte. Ein Beitrag zur Geschichte der künstlerischen Motive.* Helsingfors, 1912.

Timmers, J. J. M. *Symboliek en iconographie der Christelijke kunst.* Roermond, 1947.

Tümpel, Christian. *Rembrandt: Mythos und Methode.* Konigstein im Taunus, 1986.

Valentiner, Wilhelm. *Nicolaes Maes.* Stuttgart, 1924.

Vanbergen, J. F. H. H. *Voorstelling en betekenis. Theorie van de kunsthistorische interpretatie.* Assen, 1986.

———. "Nieuwe tendensen in de kunsthistorische interpretatie." In *Aspecten van viftig jaar kunsthistorisch onderzoek 1938–1988*, pp. 67–87. Brussels, 1990.

Vandenbroeck, Paul. "Stadscultuur: tussen bovengrondse eenheid en onderhuidse strijd." In Exhib. cat. Brussels, *Stad in Vlaanderen. Cultuur en maatschappij 1477–1787*, pp. 77–92. Galerij van het Gemeentekrediet, 1991.

Veen, P. A. F. van. *De soeticheydt des buyten-levens, verghe-selschapt met de boucken.* The Hague, 1960.

Veenstra, Fokke. *Ethiek en moraal bij P. C. Hooft.* Zwolle, 1968.

Veldkamp, M. *Het zeventiende-eeuwse poppenhuis in het Centraal Museum.* Utrecht, 1977.

Veltman, Kim H. "Review of Svetlana Alpers, *The Art of Describing: Dutch Art in the Seventeenth Century.*" *Kunstchronik* 37 (1984): 262–7.

Vickers, Brian. *In Defence of Rhetoric.* Oxford, 1988.

Vickers, Nancy. "Diana Described: Scattered Woman and Scattered Rhyme." In *Writing and Sexual Difference*, ed. E. Abel, pp. 95–109. Chicago, 1982.

Vigarello, Georges. "The Upward Training of the Body from the Age of Chivalry to Courtly Civility." In *Fragments for a History of the Human Body*, pt. 2, ed. M. Feher, pp. 149–99. New York, 1989.

Vignau-Schuurman, Th. A. G. Wilberg, *Die emblematischen Elemente im Werke Joris Hoefnagels.* 2 vols. Leiden, 1969.

Vinken, P. J., and De Jongh, E. "De boosaardigheid van Hals' regenten en regentessen." *Oud Holland* 78 (1963):1–26.

Vischer, F. Th. *Aesthetik oder Wissenschaft des Schönen.* 3 vols. Leipzig, 1846–57.

Vlieghe, Hans. *Rubens Portraits of Identified Sitters Painted in Antwerp* (*Corpus Rubenianum Ludwig Burchard* 19, no. 2). London, 1987.

Volkmann, Ludwig. *Bilderschriften der Renaissance. Hieroglyphik und Emblematik in ihren Beziehungen und Fortwirkungen.* Leipzig, 1923.

Vries, A. B. de. *Het noord-nederlandsch portret in de tweede helft van de 16de eeuw.* Amsterdam, 1934.

Vries, A. G. C. de. *De Nederlandsche emblemata. Geschiedenis en bibliographie tot de 18e eeuw.* Amsterdam, 1899.

Vries, Jan de. "The Dutch Rural Economy and the Landscape: 1590–1650." In Exhib. cat. London, *Dutch Landscape: The Early Years, Haarlem and Amsterdam 1590–1650*, pp. 79–86. The National Gallery, 1986.

———. "Art History." In *Art in History, History in Art. Studies in Seventeenth-Century Dutch Culture*, ed. D. Freedberg and J. de Vries, pp. 249–82. Santa Monica, 1991.

Vries, Lyckle de. *Wybrand de Geest. 'De Friessche adelaar.' Portretschilder in Leeuwarden 1592–c. 1661.* Leeuwarden, 1982.

———. "Portraits of People at Work." In *Werk. Opstellen voor Hans Locher*, ed. J. de Jong, V. Schmidt, and R. Vos, pp. 52–9. Groningen, 1990a.

———. "Tronies and Other Single Figured Netherlandish Paintings." *Nederlandse portretten; bijdragen over de portretkunst in de Nederlanden uit de zestiende. zeventiende en achttiende eeuw* (*Leids Kunsthistorisch Jaarboek* 8, 1989), ed. E. J. Sluijter et al., pp. 185–202. The Hague, 1990b.

Vries, M. de, et al., eds. *Woordenboek der Nederlandsche taal.* vols. 1–. Leiden 1882–.

Waal, H. van de. *Drie eeuwen vaderlandsche geschied-uitbeelding, 1500–1800.* 2 vols. The Hague, 1952.

———. "De Staalmeesters en hun legende." *Oud Holland* 71 (1956): 61–107.

Walford, E. John. *Jacob van Ruisdael and the Perception of Landscape.* New Haven, 1991.

Walsh, John. "The Dutch Marine Painters Jan and Julius Porcellis – II: Jan's Maturity and 'de jonge Porcellis'." *The Burlington Magazine* 116 (1974): 734–45.

Warburg, Aby. "Sandro Botticelli's 'Geburt der Venus' und 'Frühling.' Eine Untersuchung über die Vorstellungen von der Antike in der italienischen Frührenaissance (1893)." In *Gesammelte Schriften. Die Erneuerung der heidnischen Antike*, vol. 1, pp. 1–59. Berlin, 1932.

Wassenbergh, A. *De portretkunst in Friesland in de zeventiende eeuw.* Lochem, 1967.

Weinberg, Bernard. *A History of Literary Criticism in the Italian Renaissance.* 2 vols. Chicago, 1961.

Westrheene, T. van. *Jan Steen.* The Hague, 1856.

Wetering, Ernst van de. Unpublished lecture given at the symposium held in conjunction with the exhibition *De Hollandse fijnschilders.* Amsterdam, Rijksmuseum, 1990.

———. "Rembrandt's Manner: Technique in the Service of Illusion." In Exhib. cat. London, *Rembrandt: The Master and His Workshop, Paintings*, pp. 12–39. The National Gallery, 1992.

———. "Het satijn van Gerard ter Borch." *Kunstschrift* 6 (1993): 28–37.

Wheelock, Arthur K. "Constantijn Huygens and Early Attitudes towards the Camera Obscura." *History of Photography* 1 (1977): 93–103.

———. *Jan Vermeer.* New York, 1981.

———. "Pentimenti in Vermeer's Paintings: Changes in Style and Meaning." In *Holländische Genremalerei im 17. Jahrhundert: Symposium Berlin 1984*, ed. H. Bock and T. B. Gaehtgens, pp. 385–412. Berlin, 1987.

———. "Still Life: Its Visual Appeal and Theoretical Status in the Seventeenth Century." In Exhib. cat. Washington D.C., *Still Lifes of the Golden Age; Northern European Paintings from the Heinz Family Collection*, pp. 11–25. National Gallery of Art, 1989.

Wiegand, W. *Ruisdael-Studien: ein Versuch zur Ikonologie der Landschaftsmalerei* (Ph.D. dissertation, Hamburg). Hamburg, 1971.

Wiesner, Merry E. "Paltry Peddlers or Essential Merchants? Women in the Distributive Trades in Early Modern Nuremberg." *The Sixteenth Century Journal* 12, no. 2 (1981): 3–13.

———. *Working Women in Renaissance Germany.* New Brunswick, 1986.

———. *Women and Gender in Early Modern Europe.* Cambridge, 1993.

Wijngaardens, Hilde van. "Barber Jacobs en andere uitdraagsters." *Ons Amsterdam* 47, no. 3 (1995): 58–61.

Wijngaards, N. *Jan Harmens Krul. Zijn leven, zijn werk en zijn betekenis.* Zwolle, 1964.

Wijsenbeek-Olthuis, Thera, and Noordegraaf, Leo. "Painting for a Living: The Economic Context of Judith Leyster's Career." In Exhib. cat. Haarlem, *Judith Leyster. A Dutch Master and Her World*, pp. 39–54. Frans Halsmuseum, 1993.

Willems, G. "Verklaren en ordenen. Over stijlanalytische benaderingen." In *Gezichtspunten: een inleiding in de methoden van de kunstgeschiedenis*, ed. M. Halbertsma and K. Zijlmans, pp. 103–38. Nijmegen, 1993.

Winner, Matthias. *Die Quellen der Pictura-Allegorien in gemalten Bildergalerien des 17. Jahrhunderts zu Antwerpen* (Ph.D. dissertation, Cologne). Cologne, 1957.

Winternitz, Emanuel. *Musical Instruments and Their Symbolism in Western Art.* London, 1967.

Wishnevsky, Rose. *Studien zum "portrait historié" in den*

Niëderlanden (Ph.D. dissertation, Munich). Munich, 1967.

Witstein, S. F. *Bronnen en bewerkingswijze van de ontleende gedeelten in Rodenburghs Eglentiers poëtens borst-weringh (1619).* Amsterdam, 1964.

———. "Portret van een dichter bij Cats." In *Een wett-steen vande ieught: Verzamelde artikelen van Prof. dr. S.F. Witstein*, ed. T. Harmsen et al., pp. 61–75. Groningen, 1980.

Wolff, Janet. *The Social Production of Art.* New York, 1981.

Woodall, Joanna. "Status Symbols: Role and Rank in Seventeenth-Century Netherlandish Portraiture." *Dutch Crossing, A Journal of Low Countries Studies* 42 (1990): 34–68.

Woodward, W. H. *Desiderius Erasmus Concerning the Aim and Method of Education.* Cambridge, 1904.

Worp, Jacob Adolf. *De invloed van Seneca's treurspelen op ons tooneel.* Amsterdam, 1892.

———. "Fragment eener autobiographie van Constantijn Huygens." *Bijdragen en Mededeelingen van het Historisch Genootschap* 18 (1897): 1–121.

———. *Geschiedenis van het drama en van het toneel in Nederland.* 2 vols., Groningen, 1904–8.

———. *Een onwaerdeerlycke vrouw. Brieven en verzen van en aan Maria Tesselschade.* The Hague, 1918.

Woude, Ad van der. "The Volume and Value of Paintings in Holland at the Time of the Dutch Republic." In *Art in History, History in Art: Studies in Seventeenth-Century Dutch Culture*, ed. D. Freedberg and J. de Vries, pp. 285–329. Santa Monica, 1991.

Wright, L. *Middle-Class Culture in Elizabethan England.* Chapel Hill, 1935.

Würtenberger, Franzsepp. *Das holländische Gesellschaftsbild.* Schramberg, 1937.

Ypes, C. *Petrarca in de Nederlandse letterkunde.* Amsterdam, 1934.

Zijderveld, A. "Cesare Ripa's *Iconologia* in ons land." In Idem, *Keur uit het werk van Dr. A. Zijderveld*, pp. 121–41. Amsterdam, 1953.

Zumthor, Paul. *Het dagelijks leven in de gouden eeuw.* 2 vols. Utrecht-Antwerp, 1962.

Index

Numbers in *italics* indicate illustrations.